Penguin Books
The Anatomy of Human Destructiveness

Dr Erich Fromm, the psychologist, social philosopher and author, was born in Frankfurt-am-Main in 1900. He studied sociology and psychology at the Universities of Heidelberg, Frankfurt and Munich, receiving his Ph.D. from the University of Heidelberg in 1922. After additional studies in psychiatry and psychology in Munich, he trained at the Berlin Psychoanalytic Institute, graduating in 1931.

Dr Fromm went to the United States in 1933 at the invitation of the Chicago Psychoanalytic Institute. In 1934 he moved to New York together with the Frankfurt Institute of Social Research, of which he was a staff member until 1938. He continued in private practice and taught at Columbia University. In 1946 he became one of the founders of the William Alonson White Institute of Psychiatry, Psychoanalysis and Psychology. He has also taught at Yale, New York University, Bennington College, and Michigan State University. In 1949 he accepted a professorship at the National Autonomous University of Mexico, and started the Department of Psychoanalysis at the Graduate Department of the University Medical School, where he was made an Honorary Professor on his retirement in 1965. He now lives in Switzerland.

Dr Fromm's books have been translated into many languages and among the most well-known are *Escape from Freedom*, *Man for Himself*, *The Forgotten Language*, *The Sane Society*, *The Art of Loving*, *You Shall Be As Gods*, *The Crisis of Psychoanalysis* and *To Have or To Be?*

Acknowledgement

Grateful acknowledgement is made to the following for permission to quote from the publications listed:

Daedalus, Journal of the American Academy of Arts and Sciences, from 'The Design of Cultures', by B. F. Skinner, Summer 1961, issue on 'Evolution and Man's Progress'. Copyright © 1961 by Journal of the American Academy of Arts and Sciences. Farrar, Straus and Giroux, Inc., from *Marinetti: Selected Writings*, edited and with an Introduction by R. W. Flint. Copyright © 1971 by Farrar, Straus, and Giroux, Inc. Harcourt Brace Jovanovich, Inc., from *On Aggression*, by Konrad Lorenz, © 1963 by G. Borotha-Schoeler Verlag; © 1966 by Konrad Lorenz; and *Myth of the Machine*, by Lewis Mumford, © 1967 by Harcourt Brace Jovanovich. Hoover Institution Press, from *Heinrich Himmler: A Nazi in the Making, 1900–1926*, by Bradley F. Smith. Copyright © 1971 by the Board of Trustees of the Leland Stanford Junior University; and *Adolf Hitler: His Family, Childhood and Youth*, by Bradley F. Smith. Copyright © 1967 by the Board of Trustees of the Leland Stanford Junior University. Houghton Mifflin Co., from *In the Shadow of Man*, by J. Van Lawick-Goodall. Copyright © 1970 by Houghton Mifflin Co. *Journal of Abnormal Psychology*, from 'Behavioral Study of Obedience', LXVII (1963), pp. 371–8, by S. Milgram. Copyright © 1963 by the American Psychological Association. McGraw-Hill Book Co., Inc., from *Catal Huyuk: A Neolithic Town in Anatolia*, by James Mellaart. Copyright © 1967 by Thames and Hudson, Ltd. Macmillan Publishing Co., Inc., from *The Informed Heart*, by Bruno Bettelheim. Copyright © 1960

Contents

Preface

This study is the first volume of a comprehensive work on psychoanalytic theory. I started with the study of aggression and destructiveness because, aside from being one of the fundamental theoretical problems in psychoanalysis, the wave of destructiveness engulfing the world makes it also one of the most practically relevant ones.

When I started this book over six years ago I greatly underestimated the difficulties I would encounter. It soon became apparent that I could not write adequately about human destructiveness if I remained within the limits of my main field of competence, that of psychoanalysis. While this investigation is primarily meant to be a psychoanalytic one, I also needed a modicum of knowledge in other fields, particularly neurophysiology, animal psychology, palaeontology, and anthropology, in order to avoid working in too narrow and, hence, a distorting frame of reference. At least I had to be able to check my conclusions with the main data from other fields to make certain that my hypotheses did not contradict them and to determine whether, as was my hope, they confirmed my hypothesis.

Since no work existed that reports and integrates the findings on aggression in all these fields, or even summarizes them in any one specific field, I had to make such an attempt myself. This attempt, I thought, would also serve my readers by offering them the possibility of sharing with me the global view of the problem of destructiveness rather than a view taken from the standpoint of a single discipline. There are, it is clear, many pitfalls in such an attempt. Obviously, I could not acquire competence in all these fields – least of all, the

one in which I started out with little knowledge: the neurosciences. I was able to gain a modicum of knowledge in this
field not only by studying it myself but also through the
kindness of neuroscientists, a number of whom gave me
guidance and answered my many questions and some of
whom read the relevant part of the manuscript. Although
specialists will realize that I have nothing new to offer them
in their particular fields, they may also welcome the
opportunity of a better acquaintance with data from other
areas on a subject of such central importance.

An insoluble problem is that of repetitions and overlap-
ping from my previous work. I have been working on the
problems of man for more than thirty years and, in the
process, focusing on new areas while deepening and widening my insights in older ones. I cannot possibly write about
human destructiveness without presenting ideas that I have
of the new concepts with which this book deals. I have tried
to hold down repetition as much as possible – referring to the
more extensive discussion in previous publications; but
repetitions were nevertheless unavoidable. A special
problem in this respect is *The Heart of Man*, which contains
some of my new findings on necrophilia–biophilia in a nuclear form. My presentation of these findings is greatly
expanded in the present book, both theoretically and with
regard to clinical illustration. I did not discuss certain
differences between the views expressed here and in
previous writings, since such a discussion would have taken
a great deal of space and is not of sufficient interest for
most readers.

There remains only the pleasant task of expressing my
thanks to those who helped me in the writing of this book.

I want to thank Dr Jerome Brams, to whom I am much
indebted for his helpfulness in the theoretical clarification
of problems of behaviourism and for his never tiring assistance in the search for relevant literature.

I am gratefully indebted to Dr Juan de Dios Hernández
for his help in facilitating my study of neurophysiology. He

clarified many problems through hours of discussion, oriented me in the vast literature, and commented on those parts of the manuscript dealing with the problems of neurophysiology.

I am thankful to the following neuroscientists who helped me by sometimes extended personal conversations and letters: the late Dr Raul Hernández Peón, Drs Robert B. Livingston, Robert G. Heath, Heinz von Foerster, and Theodore Melnechuk who also read the neurophysiological sections of the manuscript. I am also indebted to Dr Francis O. Schmitt for arranging a meeting for me with members of the Neurosciences Research Program, Massachusetts Institute of Technology, at which members discussed questions that I addressed to them. I thank Albert Speer, who in conversation and correspondence, was most helpful in enriching my picture of Hitler. I am indebted also to Robert M. W. Kempner for information he had collected as one of the American prosecutors in the Nürnberg trials.

I am also thankful to Dr David Schecter, Dr Michael Maccoby, and Gertrud Hunziker-Fromm for their reading of the manuscript and for their valuable critical and constructive suggestions; to Dr Ivan Illich and Dr Ramon Xirau for their helpful suggestions in philosophical matters; to Dr W. A. Mason for his comments in the field of animal psychology; to Dr Helmuth de Terra for his helpful comments on problems of palaeontology; to Max Hunziker for his helpful suggestions in reference to surrealism, and to Heinz Brandt for his clarifying information and suggestions on the practices of Nazi terror. I am thankful to Dr Kalinkowitz for the active and encouraging interest he showed in this work. I also thank Dr Illich and Miss Valentina Boresman for their assistance in the use of the bibliographic facilities of the Center for Intercultural Documentation in Cuernavaca, Mexico.

I want to use this occasion to express my warm gratitude to Mrs Beatrice H. Mayer, who over the last twenty years has not only typed and retyped the many versions of each manuscript I have written, including the present one, but has also edited them with great sensitivity, understanding, and conscientiousness with respect to language and by making many valuable suggestions.

In the months I was abroad, Mrs Joan Hughes took care of the manuscript very competently and constructively, which I thankfully acknowledge.

I express my thanks, also, to Mr Joseph Cunneen, senior editor, Holt, Rinehart and Winston, for his very able and conscientious editorial work and his constructive suggestions. I want to thank, furthermore, Mrs Lorraine Hill, managing editor, and Mr Wilson R. Gathings and Miss Cathie Fallin, production editors, Holt, Rinehart and Winston, for their skill and care in coordinating the work on the manuscript in its various stages of production. Finally, I thank Marion Odomirok for the excellence of her conscientious and penetrating editing.

This investigation was supported in part by Public Health Service Grant No. MH 13144-01, MH 13144-02, National Institute of Mental Health. I acknowledge a contribution by the Albert and Mary Lasker Foundation that enabled me to obtain additional help by an assistant.

E. F.

New York
May 1973

Terminology

The equivocal use of the word 'aggression' has created great confusion in the rich literature on this topic. The term has been applied to the behaviour of a man defending his life against attack, to a robber killing his victim in order to obtain money, to a sadist torturing a prisoner. The confusion goes even further: the term has been used for the sexual approach of the male to the female, to the forward-driving impulses of a mountain climber or a salesman, and to the peasant ploughing the earth. This confusion is perhaps due to the influence of behaviourist thinking in psychology and psychiatry. If one calls aggression all 'noxious' acts – that is, those that have the effect of damaging or destroying a non-living thing, a plant, an animal, or a man – then, of course, the quality of the impulse behind the noxious act is entirely irrelevant. If acts that are meant to destroy, acts that are meant to protect, and acts that are meant to construct are all denoted by one and the same word, then indeed there is no hope of understanding their 'cause'; they have no common cause because they are entirely different phenomena, and one is in a theoretically hopeless position if one tries to find the cause of 'aggression'.[1]

Let us take Lorenz as an example; his concept of aggression is originally that of a biologically adaptive, evolutionarily developed impulse that serves the survival of the

1. It should be noted, though, that Freud was not unaware of the distinctions of aggression (cf. the Appendix). Furthermore, in Freud's case the underlying motive is hardly to be found in a behaviouristic orientation; more likely he just followed the customary usage and, in addition, chose the most general terms, in order to accommodate his own broad categories such as death instinct.

individual and the species. But, since he applied 'aggression' also to blood-lust and cruelty, the conclusion is that these irrational passions are *also* innate, and since wars are understood as being caused by pleasure in killing, the further conclusion is that wars are caused by an innate destructive trend in human nature. The word 'aggression' serves conveniently as a bridge to connect biologically adaptive aggression (which is not evil) with human destructiveness which indeed is evil. The core of this kind of 'reasoning' is:

> Biologically adaptive aggression = innate
> Destructiveness and cruelty = aggression
> Ergo: Destructiveness and cruelty = innate. Q E D.

In this book I have used the term 'aggression' for defensive, reactive aggression that I have subsumed under 'benign aggression', but call 'destructiveness' and 'cruelty' the specifically human propensity to destroy and to crave for absolute control ('malignant aggression'). Whenever I have used 'aggression' because it seemed useful in a certain context other than in the sense of defensive aggression, I have qualified it, to avoid misunderstanding.

Another semantic problem is offered by the use of 'man' as a word to denote mankind, or humankind. The usage of the word 'man' for both man and woman is not surprising in a language that has developed in patriarchal society, but I believe it would be somewhat pedantic to avoid the word in order to make the point that the author does not use it in the spirit of patriarchalism. In effect, the contents of the book should make that clear beyond any doubt.

I have also, in general, used the word 'he' when I referred to human beings, because to say 'he or she' each time would be awkward; I believe words are very important, but also that one should not make a fetish of them and become more interested in the words than in the thought they express.

In the interest of careful documentation, quotations within this book are accompanied by citations of author and year of publication. This is to enable the reader to find the fuller reference in the Bibliography. The dates are not, therefore, always related to the time of writing, as in the citation Spinoza (1927).

As the generations pass they grow worse. A time will come when they have grown so wicked that they will worship power; might will be right to them and reverence for the good will cease to be. At last, when no man is angry any more at wrongdoings or feels shame in the presence of the miserable, Zeus will destroy them too. And yet even then something might be done, if only the common people would rise and put down rulers that oppress them.

Greek myth on the Iron Age

> When I look at history, I am
> a pessimist ... but when I look
> at prehistory, I am an optimist.
> J. C. Smuts

On the one hand, man is akin to many species of animals in that he fights his own species. But on the other hand, he is, among the thousands of species that fight, the only one in which fighting is disruptive ... Man is the only species that is a mass murderer, the only misfit in his own society.

N. Tinbergen

Introduction:
Instincts and Human Passions

The increase in violence and destructiveness on a national and world scale has turned the attention of professionals and the general public alike to the theoretical inquiry into the nature and causes of aggression. Such a concern is not surprising; what is surprising is the fact that this preoccupation is so recent, especially since an investigator of the towering stature of Freud, revising his earlier theory centred around the sexual drive, had already in the 1920s formulated a new theory in which the passion to destroy ('death instinct') was considered equal in strength to the passion to love ('life instinct', 'sexuality'). The public, however, continued to think of Freudianism chiefly in terms of presenting the libido as man's central passion, checked only by the instinct for self-preservation.

This situation changed only in the middle of the sixties. One probable reason for this change was the fact that the level of violence and the fear of war had passed a certain threshold throughout the world. But a contributing factor was the publication of several books dealing with human aggression, particularly *On Aggression* by Konrad Lorenz (1966). Lorenz, a prominent scholar in the field of animal behaviour[1] and particularly that of fishes and birds, decided

1. Lorenz gave the name 'ethology' to the study of animal behaviour, which is peculiar terminology since ethology means literally 'the science of behaviour' (from the Greek *ethos* 'conduct', 'norm'). To denote the study of animal behaviour Lorenz should have called it 'animal ethology'. That he did not choose to qualify ethology implies, of course, his idea that human behaviour is to be subsumed under animal behaviour.

to venture out into a field in which he had little experience or competence, that of *human* behaviour. Although rejected by most psychologists and neuroscientists, *On Aggression* became a best-seller and made a deep impression on the minds of a vast sector of the educated community, many of whom accepted Lorenz's view as the final answer to the problem.

The popular success of Lorenz's ideas was greatly enhanced by the earlier work of an author of a very different type, Robert Ardrey (*African Genesis*, 1961, and *The Territorial Imperative*, 1967). Not a scientist but a gifted playwright, Ardrey wove together many data about man's beginnings into an eloquent though very biased brief that was to prove man's innate aggressiveness. These books were followed by those of other students of animal behaviour, such as *The Naked Ape* (1967) by Desmond Morris and *On Love and Hate* (1972) by Lorenz's disciple, I. Eibl-Eibesfeldt.

All these works contain basically the same thesis: man's aggressive behaviour as manifested in war, crime, personal quarrels, and all kinds of destructive and sadistic behaviour is due to a phylogenetically programmed, innate instinct which seeks for discharge and waits for the proper occasion to be expressed.

Perhaps Lorenz's neo-instinctivism was so successful not because his arguments are so strong, but because people are so susceptible to them. What could be more welcome to people who are frightened and feel impotent to change the course leading to destruction than a theory that assures us that violence stems from our animal nature, from an ungovernable drive for aggression, and that the best we can do, as Lorenz asserts, is to understand the law of evolution that accounts for the power of this drive? This *theory* of an innate aggressiveness easily becomes an *ideology* that helps to

---

It is an interesting fact that John Stuart Mill, long before Lorenz, had coined the term 'ethology' as denoting the science of *character*. If I wanted to put the main point of this book in a nutshell I would say that it deals with 'ethology' in Mill's and not in Lorenz's sense.

soothe the fear of what is to happen and to rationalize the sense of impotence.

There are other reasons to prefer this simplistic answer of an instinctivist theory to the serious study of the causes of destructiveness. The latter calls for the questioning of the basic premises of current ideology; we are led to analyse the irrationality of our social system and to violate taboos hiding behind dignified words, such as 'defence', 'honour', and, 'patriotism'. Nothing short of an analysis in depth of our social system can disclose the reasons for the increase in destructiveness, or suggest ways and means of reducing it. The instinctivistic theory offers to relieve us of the hard task of making such an analysis. It implies that, even if we all must perish, we can at least do so with the conviction that our 'nature' forced this fate upon us, and that we understand why everything had to happen as it did.

Given the present alignment in psychological thought, criticism of Lorenz's theory of human aggression is expected to fit into the other and dominant theory in psychology, that of *behaviourism*. In contrast to instinctivism, behaviourist theory does not interest itself in the subjective forces which drive man to behave in a certain way; it is not concerned with what he feels, but only in the way he behaves and in the social conditioning that shapes his behaviour.

It was only in the twenties that the focus in psychology shifted radically from *feeling* to *behaviour*, with emotions and passions thereafter removed from many psychologists' field of vision as irrelevant data, at least from a scientific standpoint. The subject matter of the dominant school in psychology became *behaviour*, not *the behaving man*: the 'science of the psyche' was transformed into the science of the engineering of animal and human conduct. This development has reached its peak in Skinner's neo-behaviourism, which is today the most widely accepted psychological theory in the universities of the United States.

The reason for this transformation of psychology is easy to find. The student of man is, more than any other scientist, influenced by the atmosphere of his society. This is so because not only are his ways of thinking, his interests, the questions he raises, all partly socially determined as in the natural sciences, but in his case the subject matter itself, man, is thus determined. Whenever a psychologist speaks of man, his model is that of the men around him – and most of all himself. In contemporary industrial society, men are cerebrally oriented, feel little, and consider emotions a useless ballast – those of the psychologists as well as those of their subjects. The behaviouristic theory seems to fit them well.

The present alternative between instinctivism and behaviourism is not favourable to theoretical progress. Both positions are 'mono-explanatory', depending on dogmatic preconceptions, and investigators are required to fit data in one or the other explanation. But are we really confronted with the alternative of accepting either the instinctivist or the behaviourist theory? Are we forced to choose between Lorenz and Skinner; are there no other options? This book affirms that there is another option, and examines the question of what it is.

We must distinguish in man *two entirely different kinds of aggression*. The first, which he shares with all animals, is a phylogenetically programmed impulse to attack (or to flee) when vital interests are threatened. This *defensive*, 'benign' aggression is in the service of the survival of the individual and the species, is biologically adaptive, and ceases when the threat has ceased to exist. The other type, 'malignant' aggression, i.e., *cruelty and destructiveness*, is specific to the human species and virtually absent in most mammals; it is not phylogenetically programmed and not biologically adaptive; it has no purpose, and its satisfaction is lustful. Most previous discussion of the subject has been vitiated by the failure to distinguish between these two kinds of aggression, each of which has different sources and different qualities.

Defensive aggression is, indeed, part of human nature,

even though not an 'innate'[2] instinct, as it used to be classified. In so far as Lorenz speaks of aggression as defence, he is right in his assumptions about the aggressive instinct (even though the theory regarding its spontaneity and self-renewing quality is scientifically untenable). But Lorenz goes further. By a number of ingenious constructions he considers *all* human aggression, including the passion to kill and to torture, as being an outcome of biologically given aggression, transformed from a beneficial to destructive force because of a number of factors. However, so many empirical data speak against this hypothesis as to make it virtually untenable. The study of animals shows that mammals – and especially the primates – although possessing a good deal of defensive aggression, are not killers and torturers. Palaeontology, anthropology, and history offer ample evidence against the instinctivistic thesis: (1) human groups differ so fundamentally in the respective degree of destructiveness that the facts could hardly be explained by the assumption that destructiveness and cruelty are innate; (2) various degrees of destructiveness can be correlated to other psychical factors and to differences in respective social structures, and (3) the degree of destructiveness increases with the increased development of civilization, rather than the opposite. Indeed, the picture of innate destructiveness fits history much better than prehistory. If man were endowed only with the biologically adaptive aggression that he shares with his animal ancestors he would be a relatively peaceful being; if chimpanzees had psychologists, the latter would hardly consider aggression a disturbing problem about which they should write books.

However, man differs from the animal by the fact that he is a killer; he is the only primate that kills and tortures members of his own species without any reason, either biological or economic, and who feels satisfaction in doing so. It

2. Recently Lorenz has qualified the concept of 'innate' by acknowledging the simultaneous presence of the factor of learning (K. Lorenz, 1965).

is this biologically non-adaptive and non-phylogenetically programmed, 'malignant' aggression that constitutes the real problem and the danger to man's existence as a species, and it is the main aim of this book to analyse the nature and the conditions of this destructive aggression.

The distinction between benign-defensive and malignant-destructive aggression calls for a further and more fundamental distinction, that between *instinct*[3] and *character*, or more precisely, between drives rooted in man's physiological needs (organic drives) and those specifically human passions rooted in his character ('character-rooted, or human passions'). The distinction between instinct and character will be further discussed at great length in the text. I shall try to show that character is man's 'second nature', the substitute for his poorly developed instincts; furthermore that the human passions (such as the striving for love, tenderness, freedom as well as the lust for destruction, sadism, masochism, the craving for power and property) are answers to 'existential needs', which in turn are rooted in the very conditions of human existence. To put it briefly, *instincts* are answers to man's *physiological* needs, man's character-conditioned *passions* are answers to his *existential* needs and they are specifically human. While these existential needs are the same for all men, men differ among themselves with regard to their dominant passions. To give an example: man can be driven by love or by the passion to destroy; in each case he satisfies one of his existential needs: the need to 'effect', or to move something, to 'make a dent'. Whether man's dominant passion is love or whether it is destructiveness depends largely on social circumstances; these circumstances, however, operate in reference to man's biologically given existential situation and the needs springing from it and not to an infinitely malleable, undifferentiated psyche, as environmentalist theory assumes.

When we want to know, however, what the conditions of

3. The term 'instinct' is used here provisionally, although it is somewhat dated. Later on I shall use the term 'organic drives'.

human existence are, we are led to further questions: what is man's nature? What is it by virtue of which he is man? Needless to say, the present climate in the social sciences is not very hospitable to the discussion of such problems. They are generally considered the subject matter of philosophy and religion; in terms of positivistic thinking, they are treated as purely subjective speculations without any claim to objective validity. Since it would be inopportune to anticipate at this point the complex argument on the data offered later, I shall content myself now with only a few remarks. In our attempt to define the essence of man, we are not referring to an abstraction arrived at by the way of metaphysical speculations like those of Heidegger and Sartre. We refer to the real conditions of existence common to man *qua* man, so that the essence of each individual is identical with the existence of the species. We arrive at this concept by empirical analysis of the anatomical and neurophysiological structure and its psychical correlations which characterize the species *homo*. We thus shift the principle of explanation of human passions from Freud's *physiological* to a *sociobiological* and historical principle. Since the species *Homo sapiens* can be defined in anatomical, neurological and physiological terms, we should also be able to define him as a species in psychical terms. The point of view from which these problems will be treated here may be called existentialist, albeit not in the sense of existentialist philosophy.

This theoretical basis opens up the possibility for a detailed discussion of the various forms of character-rooted, malignant aggression, especially of *sadism* – the passion for unrestricted power over another sentient being – and of *necrophilia* – the passion to destroy life and the attraction to all that is dead, decaying, and purely mechanical. The understanding of these character structures will, I hope, be facilitated by the analysis of the character of a number of well-known sadists and destroyers of the recent past: Stalin, Himmler, Hitler.

Having traced the steps this study will follow, it may be

useful to indicate, if only briefly, some of the general premises and conclusions the reader will find in the following chapters: (1) We will not be concerned with behaviour separated from the behaving man; we shall deal with the human drives, regardless of whether or not they are expressed in immediately observable behaviour. This means, with regard to the phenomenon of aggression, we will study the origin and intensity of aggressive impulses and not aggressive behaviour independent from its motivation. (2) These impulses can be conscious, but more often they are unconscious. (3) They are, most of the time, integrated in a relatively stable character structure. (4) In a more general formulation, this study is based on the theory of psychoanalysis. From this follows that the method we will use is the psychoanalytic method of discovering the unconscious inner reality through interpretation of the observable and often seemingly insignificant data. The term 'psychoanalysis', however, is not used in reference to the classic theory, but to a certain revision of it. Key aspects of this revision will be discussed later; at this point I should like to say only that it is not a psychoanalysis based on the libido theory, thereby avoiding the instinctivistic concepts that are generally assumed to be the very essence of Freud's theory.

This identification of Freudian theory with instinctivism, however, is very much open to doubt. Freud was actually the first modern psychologist who, in contrast to the dominant trend, investigated the realm of human passions – love, hate, ambition, greed, jealousy, envy; passions which had previously been dealt with only by dramatists and novelists became, through Freud, the subject matter of scientific exploration.[4] This may explain why his work found a much warmer and more understanding reception among artists

4. Most older psychologies, such as that in the Buddhist writings, the Greeks, and the medieval and modern psychology up to Spinoza, dealt with the human passions as their main subject matter by a method combining careful observation (although without experimentation) and critical thinking.

than among psychiatrists and psychologists – at least up to the time when his method became the instrument to satisfy an increasing demand for psychotherapy. Here, the artists felt, was the first scientist who dealt with their own subject matter, man's 'soul', in its most secret and subtle manifestations. Surrealism showed this impact of Freud on artistic thinking most clearly. In contrast to older art forms, it dismissed 'reality' as irrelevant, and was not concerned with behaviour – all that mattered was the subjective experience; it was only logical that Freud's interpretation of dreams should become one of the most important influences for its development.

Freud could not but conceive his new findings in the concepts and terminology of his own time. Never having freed himself from the materialism of his teachers, he had, as it were, to find a way to disguise human passions, presenting them as outcomes of an instinct. He did this brilliantly by a theoretical *tour de force*; he enlarged the concept of sexuality (libido) to such an extent that all human passions (aside from self-preservation) could be understood as the outcome of one instinct. Love, hate, greed, vanity, ambition, avarice, jealousy, cruelty, tenderness – all were forced into the straitjacket of this scheme and dealt with theoretically as sublimations of, or reaction formations against, the various manifestations of narcissistic, oral, anal, and genital libido.

In the second period of his work, however, Freud tried to break out of this scheme by presenting a new theory, which was a decisive step forward in the understanding of destructiveness. He recognized that life is not ruled by two egoistic drives, one for food, the other for sex, but by two passions – love and destruction – that do not serve physiological survival in the same sense that hunger and sexuality do. Still bound by his theoretical premises, however, he called them 'life instinct' and 'death instinct', and thereby gave human destructiveness its importance as one of two fundamental passions in man.

This study frees such passions as the strivings to love, to be free, as well as the drive to destroy, to torture, to control, and to submit, from their forced marriage to instincts. Instincts are a purely natural category, while the character-rooted passions are a sociobiological, historical category.[5] Although not directly serving physical survival they are as strong – and often even stronger – than instincts. They form the basis for man's interest in life, his enthusiasm, his excitement; they are the stuff from which not only his dreams are made but art, religion, myth, drama – all that makes life worth living. Man cannot live as nothing but an object, as dice thrown out of a cup; he suffers severely when he is reduced to the level of a feeding or propagating machine, even if he has all the security he wants. Man seeks for drama and excitement; when he cannot get satisfaction on a higher level, he creates for himself the drama of destruction.

The contemporary climate of thought encourages the axiom that a motive can be intense only when it serves an organic need – i.e., that only instincts have intense motivating power. If one discards this mechanistic, reductionist viewpoint and starts from a holistic premise, one begins to realize that man's passions must be seen in terms of their function for the life process of the whole organism. Their intensity is not due to specific physiological needs, but to the need of the whole organism to survive – to grow both physically and mentally.

These passions do not become powerful only *after* the physiological needs have been satisfied. They are at the very root of human existence, and not a kind of luxury which we can afford after the normal, 'lower' needs have been satisfied. People have committed suicide because of their failure to realize their passions for love, power, fame, revenge. Cases of suicide because of a lack of sexual satisfaction are virtually non-existent. These non-instinctual passions excite man, fire him on, make life worth living; as von Holbach, the philosopher of the French Enlightenment, once said:

5. cf. R. B. Livingston (1967) on the question of the extent some of them are built into the brain; discussed in Chapter 10.

'*Un homme sans passions et désires cesserait d'être un homme*' ('A man without passions or desires would cease to be a man' P. H. D. d'Holbach, 1822). They are so intense precisely because man would not be man without them.[6]

The human passions transform man from a mere thing into a hero, into a being that in spite of tremendous handicaps tries to make sense of life. He wants to be his own creator, to transform his state of being unfinished into one with some goal and some purpose, allowing him to achieve some degree of integration. Man's passions are not banal psychological complexes that can be adequately explained as caused by childhood traumata. They can be understood only if one goes beyond the realm of reductionist psychology and recognizes them for what they are: *man's attempt to make sense out of life and to experience the optimum of intensity and strength he can (or believes he can) achieve under the given circumstances*. They are his religion, his cult, his ritual, which he has to hide (even from himself) in so far as they are disapproved of by his group. To be sure, by bribery and blackmail, i.e., by skilful conditioning, he can be persuaded to relinquish his 'religion' and to be converted to the general cult of the no-self, the automaton. But this psychic cure deprives him of the best he has, of being a man and not a thing.

The truth is that all human passions, both the 'good' and the 'evil', can be understood only as a person's attempt to make sense of his life and transcend banal, merely life-sustaining existence. Change of personality is possible only

6. This statement by Holbach is of course to be understood in the context of the philosophical thinking of his time. Buddhist or Spinozist philosophy have an entirely different concept of passions; from their standpoint Holbach's description would be empirically true for the majority of people, but Holbach's position is exactly the opposite of what they consider to be the goal of human development. In order to appreciate the difference I refer to the distinction between 'irrational passions', such as ambition and greed, and 'rational passions', such as love and care for all sentient beings (which will be discussed later on). What is relevant in the text, however, is not this difference, but the idea that life concerned mainly with its own maintenance is inhuman.

if he is able to 'convert himself' to a new way of making sense of life by mobilizing his life-furthering passions and thus experiencing a superior sense of vitality and integration to the one he had before. Unless this happens he can be domesticated, but he cannot be cured. But even though the life-furthering passions are conducive to a greater sense of strength, joy, integration, and vitality than destructiveness and cruelty, the latter are as much an answer to the problem of human existence as the former. Even the most sadistic and destructive man is human, as human as the saint. He can be called a warped and sick man who has failed to achieve a better answer to the challenge of having been born human, and this is true; he can also be called a man who took the wrong way in search of his salvation.[7]

These considerations by no means imply, however, that destructiveness and cruelty are not vicious; they only imply that vice is human. They are indeed destructive of life, of body and spirit, destructive not only of the victim but of the destroyer himself. They constitute a paradox: they express *life turning against itself in the striving to make sense of it.* They are the only true perversion. Understanding them does not mean condoning them. But unless we understand them, we have no way to recognize how they may be reduced, and what factors tend to increase them.

Such understanding is of particular importance today, when sensitivity towards destructiveness-cruelty is rapidly diminishing, and necrophilia, the attraction to what is dead, decaying, lifeless, and purely mechanical, is increasing throughout our cybernetic industrial society. The spirit of necrophilia was expressed first in literary form by F. T. Marinetti in his *Futurist Manifesto* of 1909. The same tendency can be seen in much of the art and literature of the last decades that exhibits a particular fascination with all that is decayed, unalive, destructive, and mechanical. The

7. *Salvus* (connected with *salus*) =healthy, safe, unhurt, well, sound. In this sense each man needs salvation (in a non-theological sense), that is to say, to be made well and safe.

Falangist motto, 'Long live death', threatens to become the secret principle of a society in which the conquest of nature by the machine constitutes the very meaning of progress, and where the living person becomes an appendix to the machine.

This study tries to clarify the nature of this necrophilous passion and the social conditions that tend to foster it. The conclusion will be that help in any broad sense can come only through radical changes in our social and political structure that would reinstate man to his supreme role in society. The call for 'law and order' (rather than for life and structure) and for stricter punishment of criminals, as well as the obsession with violence and destruction among some 'revolutionaries', are only further instances of the powerful attraction of necrophilia in the contemporary world. We need to create the conditions that would make the growth of man, this unfinished and uncompleted being – unique in nature – the supreme goal of all social arrangements. Genuine freedom and independence and the end of all forms of exploitative control are the conditions for mobilizing the love of life, which is the only force that can defeat the love for the dead.

Part One
Instinctivism, Behaviourism,
Psychoanalysis

I
The Instinctivists

The Older Instinctivists

I will forgo presenting here a history of instinct theory as the reader can find it in many textbooks.[1] This history began far back in philosophical thought, but as far as modern thought is concerned, it dates from the work of Charles Darwin. All post-Darwinian research on instincts has been based on Darwin's theory of evolution.

William James (1890), William McDougall (1913, 1932) and others have drawn up long lists in which each individual instinct was supposed to motivate corresponding kinds of behaviour, such as James's instincts of imitation, rivalry, pugnacity, sympathy, hunting, fear, acquisitiveness, kleptomania, constructiveness, play, curiosity, sociability, secretiveness, cleanliness, modesty, love, and jealousy – a strange mixture of universal human qualities and specific socially conditioned character traits (J. J. McDermott, ed., 1967). Although these lists of instincts appear today somewhat naïve, the work of these instinctivists is highly sophisticated, rich in theoretical constructions, and still impressive by its level of theoretical thought; it is by no means dated. Thus, for instance, James simply was quite aware that there might be an element of learning even in the first performance of an instinct, and McDougall was not unaware of the moulding influence of different experiences and cultural back-

1. I recommend especially R. Fletcher (1968) for its penetrating history of the instinct theory.

grounds. The instinctivism of the latter forms a bridge to Freud's theory. As Fletcher has emphasized, McDougall did not identify instinct with a 'motor mechanism' and a rigidly fixed motor response. For him the core of an instinct was a '*propensity*', a 'craving', and this affective-connative core of each instinct 'seems capable of functioning in relative independence of both the cognitive and the motor part of the total instinctive disposition' (W. McDougall, 1932).

Before discussing the two best-known modern representatives of the instinctivistic theory, the 'neo-instinctivists' Sigmund Freud and Konrad Lorenz, let us look at a feature common to both them and the older instinctivists: the conception of the instinctivistic model in mechanistic-hydraulic terms. McDougall envisaged energy held back by 'sluice gates' and 'bubbling over' (W. McDougall, 1913) under certain conditions. Later he used an analogy in which each instinct was pictured as a 'chamber in which gas is constantly liberated' (W. McDougall, 1923). Freud, in his concept of the libido theory, also followed a hydraulic scheme. The libido increases——> tension rises ——> unpleasure increases; the sexual act decreases tension and unpleasure until the tension begins to rise again. Similarly, Lorenz thought of reaction specific energy like 'a gas constantly being pumped into a container' or as a liquid in a reservoir that can discharge through a spring-loaded valve at the bottom (K. Lorenz, 1950). R. A. Hinde has pointed out that in spite of various differences, these and other instinct models 'share the idea of a substance capable of energizing behaviours, held back in a container and subsequently released in action' (R. A. Hinde, 1960).

The Neo-instinctivists:
Sigmund Freud and Konrad Lorenz

Freud's Concept of Aggression[2]

The great step forward made by Freud beyond the older instinctivists, and particularly McDougall, was that he unified all 'instincts' under two categories – the sexual instincts and the instinct for self-preservation. Thus Freud's theory can be considered the last step in the development of the history of the instinct theory; as I shall show later, this very unification of the instincts under one (with the exception of the ego instinct) was also the first step in overcoming the whole instinctivistic concept, even though Freud was not aware of this. In the following I shall deal only with Freud's concept of aggression, since his libido theory is well known to many readers and can be read in other works, best of all in Freud's *Introductory Lectures on Psychoanalysis* (1915–16, 1916–17, and 1933).

Freud had paid relatively little attention to the phenomenon of aggression as long as he considered sexuality (libido) and self-preservation the two forces dominating man. From the 1920s on, this picture changed completely. In *The Ego and the Id* (1923) and in his later writings, he postulated a new dichotomy: that of life instinct(s) (Eros) and death instinct(s). Freud described the new theoretical phase in the following terms: 'Starting from speculations on the beginning of life and from biological parallels I drew the conclusion that, besides the instinct to preserve living substance, there must exist another, contrary instinct seeking to dissolve those units and to bring them back to their primaeval, inorganic state. That is to say, as well as Eros there was an instinct of death' (S. Freud, 1930).

The death instinct is directed against the organism itself

2. A detailed history and analysis of Freud's concept of aggression will be found in the Appendix.

and thus is a self-destructive drive, or it is directed outward, and in this case tends to destroy others rather than oneself. When blended with sexuality, the death instinct is transformed into more harmless impulses expressed in sadism or masochism. Even though Freud suggested at various times that the power of the death instinct can be reduced (S. Freud, 1927), the basic assumption remained: man was under the sway of an impulse to destroy either himself or others, and he could do little to escape this tragic alternative. It follows that, from the position of the death instinct, aggression was not essentially a reaction to stimuli but a constantly flowing impulse rooted in the constitution of the human organism.

The majority of psychoanalysts, while following Freud in every other way, refused to accept the theory of the death instinct; perhaps this was because this theory transcended the old mechanistic frame of reference and required biological thinking that was unacceptable to most, for whom 'biological' was identical with the physiology of the instincts. Nevertheless, they did not altogether reject Freud's new position. They made a compromise by acknowledging a 'destructive instinct' as the other pole of the sexual instinct, and thus they could accept Freud's new emphasis on aggression without submitting to an entirely new kind of thinking.

Freud has taken an important step forward, passing from a purely physiological-mechanistic to a biological approach that considers the organism as a whole and analyses the biological sources of love and hate. His theory, however, suffers from severe defects. It is based on rather abstract speculations and offers hardly any convincing *empirical evidence*. Furthermore, while Freud brilliantly tried to interpret *human* impulses in terms of the new theory, his hypothesis is inconsistent with animal behaviour. For him, the death instinct is a biological force in all living organisms: this should mean that animals, too, express their death instinct either against themselves or against others. Hence one should find more illness or early death in less outwardly aggressive animals, and vice versa; but, of course, there are no data supporting this idea.

That aggression and destructiveness are not biologically given and spontaneously flowing impulses will be demonstrated in the next chapter. At this point I only want to add that Freud has greatly obscured the analysis of the phenomenon of aggression by following the custom of using the term for the most different kinds of aggression, thus facilitating his attempt to explain them all by *one* instinct. Since he was certainly not behaviouristically inclined, we may assume that the reason was his general tendency to arrive at a dualistic concept in which two basic forces are opposed to each other. This dichotomy was at first that between self-preservation and libido, and later that between life and death instincts. For the elegance of these concepts, Freud had to pay the price of subsuming every passion under one of the two poles, and hence of putting together trends which in reality do not belong together.

Lorenz's Theory of Aggression

While Freud's theory of aggression was and still is very influential, it was complex and difficult and has never been popular in the sense that it was read by and impressed a popular audience. On the contrary, Konrad Lorenz's *On Aggression* (K. Lorenz, 1966) became within a short time of its publication one of the most widely read books in the field of social psychology.

The reasons for this popularity are not difficult to discern. First of all, *On Aggression* is an immensely readable book, much like Lorenz's earlier charming *King Solomon's Ring* (1952), and quite different in this respect from Freud's heavy treatises on the death instinct or, for that matter, Lorenz's own papers and books written for the specialist. Furthermore, as was pointed out earlier in the Introduction, it appeals to the thinking of many people today who prefer to believe that our drift towards violence and nuclear war is due to biological factors beyond our control, rather than to open their eyes and see that it is due to social, political, and economic circumstances of our own making.

For Lorenz,[3] as for Freud, human aggressiveness is an instinct fed by an ever-flowing fountain of energy, and not necessarily the result of a *reaction* to outer stimuli. Lorenz holds that energy specific for an instinctive act accumulates continuously in the neural centres related to that behaviour pattern, and if enough energy has been accumulated an *explosion* is likely to occur even without the presence of a stimulus. However, the animal and man usually find stimuli which release the dammed-up energy of the drive; they do not have to wait passively until the proper stimulus appears. They search for and even produce stimuli. Following W. Craig, Lorenz called his behaviour 'appetite behaviour'. Man, he says, creates political parties in order to find stimuli for the release of dammed-up energy, rather than political parties being the cause of aggression. But in cases where no outside stimulus can be found or produced, the energy of the dammed-up aggressive drive is so great that it will explode, as it were, and be acted out *in vacuo*, i.e., 'without demonstrable external stimulation . . . the vacuum activity performed without an object – exhibits truly photographic similarity to normal performance of the motor actions involved . . . This demonstrates that the motor coordination patterns of the instinctive behaviour pattern are hereditarily determined down to the finest detail' (K. Lorenz, 1970; originally in German, 1931–42).[4]

3. cf. for a detailed and by now classic review of Lorenz's (and N. Tinbergen's) concepts of instinct, and for an overall critique of Lorenz's position, D. S. Lehrman (1953). Furthermore, for a critique of *On Aggression*, see the review by L. Berkowitz (1967) and K. E. Boulding's review (1967). See also N. Tinbergen's critical evaluation of Lorenz's theory (1968), and L. Eisenberg's short and penetrating critique (1972).

4. Later, under the influence of the critique by a number of American psychologists and by N. Tinbergen, Lorenz modified this statement to allow for the influence of learning (K. Lorenz, 1965).

For Lorenz, then, aggression is primarily *not* a reaction to outside stimuli, but a 'built-in' inner excitation that seeks for release and will find expression regardless of how adequate the outer stimulus is: '*It is the spontaneity of the instinct that makes it so dangerous*' (K. Lorenz, 1966; italics added). Lorenz's model of aggression, like Freud's model of the libido, has been rightly called a *hydraulic* model, in analogy to the pressure exercised by dammed-up water or steam in a closed container.

This hydraulic concept of aggression is, as it were, one pillar on which Lorenz's theory rests; it refers to the *mechanism* through which aggression is produced. The other pillar is the idea that aggression is in the service of life, that it serves the survival of the individual and of the species. Broadly speaking, Lorenz assumes that intraspecific aggression (aggression among members of the same species) has the function of furthering the survival of the species. Lorenz proposes that aggression fulfills this function by the spacing out of individuals of one species over the available habitat; by selection of the 'better man', relevant in conjunction with the defence of the female, and by establishing a social rank order (K. Lorenz, 1964). Aggression can have this preservative function all the more effectively because in the process of evolution deadly aggression has been transformed into behaviour consisting of symbolic and ritual threats which fulfil the same function without harming the species.

But, Lorenz argues, the instinct that served the animal's survival has become 'grotesquely exaggerated', and has 'gone wild' in man. Aggression has been transformed into a threat rather than a help to survival.

It seems as if Lorenz himself had not been satisfied with these explanations of human aggression and felt a need to add another that leads, however, outside the field of ethology. He writes:

Above all, it is more than probable that the destructive intensity of the aggressive drive, still a *hereditary* evil of mankind, is the consequence of a process of intra-specific selection which worked on our forefathers for roughly forty thousand years, that is, throughout the Early Stone Age. [Lorenz probably means the Late Stone Age.] When man had reached the stage of having weapons, clothing, and social organization, so overcoming the dangers of starving, freezing, and being eaten by wild animals, and these dangers ceased to be the essential factors influencing selection, an evil intra-specific selection must have set in. The factor influencing selection was now the wars waged between hostile neighbouring tribes. These must have evolved in an extreme form of all those so-called 'warrior virtues' which unfortunately many people still regard as desirable ideals. (K. Lorenz, 1966)

This picture of the constant war among the 'savage' hunters-food-gatherers since the full emergence of *Homo sapiens* around 40,000 or 50,000 BC is a widely accepted cliché adopted by Lorenz without reference to the investigations which tend to show that there is no evidence for it.[5] Lorenz's assumption of forty thousand years of organized warfare is nothing but the old Hobbesian cliché of war as the natural state of man, presented as an argument to prove the innateness of human aggressiveness. The logic of Lorenz's assumption is that man *is* aggressive because he *was* aggressive; and he *was* aggressive because he *is* aggressive.

Even if Lorenz were right in his thesis of continuous warfare in the Late Palaeolithic, his genetic reasoning is open to question. If a certain trait is to have a selective advantage this must be based on the increased production of fertile offspring of the carriers of the trait. But in view of the likelihood of a higher loss of the aggressive individuals in wars, it is doubtful whether selection could account for the maintenance of a high incidence of this trait. In fact, if one considers such a loss as negative selection, the gene frequency should diminish.[6] Actually, the population density

5. The question of the aggression among the food gatherers and hunters is discussed at length in Chapter 8.

6. I am indebted to Professor Kurt Hirschhorn for a personal communication in which he outlines the genetic problem involved in the above-mentioned view.

in that age was extremely low, and for many of the human tribes after the full emergence of *Homo sapiens* there was little need to compete and to fight each other for food or space.

Lorenz has combined two elements in his theory. The first is that animals as well as men are innately endowed with aggression, serving the survival of the individual and the species. As I shall show later, the neurophysiological findings show that this defensive aggression is a reaction to threats to the animal's vital interests, and does not flow spontaneously and continually. The other element, the hydraulic character of dammed-up aggression, is used to explain the murderous and cruel impulses of man, but little supporting evidence is presented. Both a life-serving and a destructive aggression are subsumed under one category, and what connects them is mainly a word: 'aggression'. In contrast to Lorenz, Tinbergen has expressed the problem in full clarity:

On the one hand, man is akin to many species of animals in that he fights his own species. But on the other hand, he is, among the thousands of species that fight, the only one in which fighting is disruptive . . . Man is the only species that is a mass murderer, the only misfit in his own society. Why should this be so? (N. Tinbergen, 1968).

Freud and Lorenz: Their Similarities and Differences

The relationship between Lorenz's and Freud's theories is a complicated one. They have in common the hydraulic concept of aggression, even though they explain the origin of the drive differently. But they seem to be diametrically opposed to each other in another aspect. Freud hypothesized a destructive instinct, an assumption which Lorenz declares to be untenable on biological grounds. His aggressive drive serves life, and Freud's death instinct is the servant of death.

But this difference loses most of its significance in the light of Lorenz's account of the vicissitudes of the originally defensive and life-serving aggression. By a number of complicated and often questionable constructions, defensive aggression is supposed to be transformed in man into a spontaneously flowing and self-increasing drive that seeks to create circumstances which facilitate the expression of aggression, or that even explodes when no stimuli can be found or created. Hence even in a society that is organized from a socioeconomic viewpoint in such a way that major aggression could find no proper stimuli, the very demand of the aggressive instinct would force its members to change it or, if they would not, aggression would explode even without any stimulus. Thus the conclusion at which Lorenz arrives, that man is driven by an innate force to destroy, is, for all practical purposes, the same as Freud's. Freud, however, sees the destructive drive opposed by the equally strong force of Eros (life, sex), while for Lorenz love itself is a product of the aggressive instinct.

Both Freud and Lorenz agree that the failure to express aggression in action is unhealthy. Freud has postulated in the earlier period of his work that repression of sexuality can lead to mental illness; later on he applied the same principle to the death instinct and taught that the repression of outward-directed aggression is unhealthy. Lorenz states that 'present-day civilized man suffers from insufficient discharge of his aggressive drive'. Both, by different routes, arrive at a picture of man in which aggressive-destructive energy is continuously produced, and very difficult, if not impossible in the long run, to control. The so-called evil in animals becomes a real evil in man, even though according to Lorenz its roots are not evil.

'Proof' by Analogy These similarities between Freud's and Lorenz's respective theories about aggression must not, however, becloud their main difference. Freud was a student of men, a keen observer of their manifest behaviour and of the various manifestations of their unconscious. His theory of the death instinct may be wrong, or incomplete, or it may rest on insufficient evidence, yet it was gained in

the process of constant observation of man. Lorenz, on the other hand, is an observer of animals, especially of the lower animals, and doubtless a very competent one. But his knowledge about man does not go beyond that of an average person; he has not refined it either by systematic observation or by sufficient acquaintance with the literature.[7] He naïvely assumes that observations about himself and acquaintances are applicable to all men. His main method, however, is not even self-observation, but analogies drawn from the behaviour of certain animals to that of man. Scientifically speaking, such analogies prove nothing; they are suggestive and pleasing to the lover of animals. They go together with a high degree of anthropomorphizing that Lorenz indulges in. Precisely because they give the pleasant illusion to a person that he 'understands' what the animal is 'feeling' they become very popular. Who would not like to possess King Solomon's ring?

Lorenz bases his theories of the hydraulic nature of aggression on experiments with animals – mainly fish and birds under conditions of captivity. The question at issue is: Does the same aggressive drive that leads to killing unless it is redirected – which Lorenz observed in certain fish and birds – also operate in man?

Since there is no direct proof for this hypothesis with regard to man and the non-human primates, Lorenz presents a number of arguments to prove his point. His main approach is by way of *analogy*; he discovers similarities between human behaviour and the behaviour of the animals studied by him, and concludes that both kinds of behaviour have the same cause. This method has been criticized by many psychologists; already in 1948, Lorenz's eminent colleague, N. Tinbergen, was aware of the dangers '*inherent in the*

7. Lorenz, at least when writing *On Aggression*, seems not to have had any first-hand knowledge of Freud's work. There is not a single direct reference to his writings, and what references there are refer to what psychoanalytic friends told him about Freud's position; regrettably they are not always right, or they have not been accurately understood.

*procedure of using physiological evidence from lower evolutionary
levels, lower levels of neural organizations, and simpler forms of
behaviour as analogies for the support of physiological theories of
behaviour mechanisms at higher and more complex levels*' (N.
Tinbergen, 1948; italics added).

A few examples will illustrate Lorenz's 'proof by analogy'.[8] Speaking about cichlids and Brazilian mother-of-
pearl fish, Lorenz reports the observation that if each fish
can discharge its healthy anger on a neighbour of the same
sex it does not attack its own mate ('redirected aggression').[9]
He then comments:

Analogous behaviour can be observed in human beings. In the
good old days when there was still a Hapsburg monarchy and
there were still domestic servants, I used to observe the following,
regularly predictable behaviour in my widowed aunt. She never
kept a maid longer than eight to ten months. She was always
delighted with a new servant, praised her to the skies, and swore
that she had at last found the right one. In the course of the next
few months her judgement cooled, she found small faults, then
bigger ones, and towards the end of the stated period she discovered
hateful qualities in the poor girl, who was finally discharged without a reference after a violent quarrel. After this explosion the old
lady was once more prepared to find a perfect angel in her next
employee.

It is not my intention to poke fun at my long-deceased and
devoted aunt. I was able, or rather obliged, to observe exactly the
same phenomenon in serious, self-controlled men, myself included,
once when I was a prisoner-of-war. So-called polar disease, also
known as expedition choler, attacks small groups of men who are
completely dependent on one another and are thus prevented from
quarrelling with strangers or people outside their own circle of
friends. From this it will be clear that the damming up of aggression will be more dangerous, the better the members of the group

8. The tendency to make quite illegitimate analogies from biological
to social phenomena had already been demonstrated by Lorenz in 1940
in an unfortunate paper (K. Lorenz, 1940) arguing that state laws must
substitute for principles of natural selection when the latter fail to properly take care of the biological needs of the race.

9. N. Tinbergen's term.

know, understand, and like each other. In such a situation, as I know from personal experience, all aggression and intra-specific fight behaviour undergo an extreme lowering of their threshold values. Subjectively this is expressed by the fact that one reacts to small mannerisms of one's best friends – such as the way in which they clear their throats or sneeze – in a way that would normally be adequate only if one had been hit by a drunkard. (K. Lorenz, 1966)

It does not seem to occur to Lorenz that the personal experiences with his aunt, his fellow prisoners-of-war, and himself do not necessarily say anything about the universality of such reactions. He also seems to be quite unaware of a more complex psychological interpretation one might give his aunt's behaviour, instead of the hydraulic one which claims that her aggressive potential rose every eight to ten months to such a degree that it had to explode.

From a psychoanalystic standpoint, one would assume that his aunt was a very narcissistic, exploitative woman; she demanded that a servant should be completely 'devoted' to her, have no interests of her own, and gladly accept the role of a creature who is happy to serve her. She approaches each new servant with the fantasy that she is the one who will fulfill her expectations. After a short 'honeymoon' during which the aunt's fantasy is still sufficiently effective to blind her to the fact that the servant is not 'right' – and perhaps also helped by the fact that the servant in the beginning makes every effort to please her new employer – the aunt wakes up to the recognition that the servant is not willing to live up to the role for which she has been cast. Such a process of awakening lasts, of course, some time until it is final. At this point the aunt experiences intense disappointment and rage, as any narcissistic-exploitative person does when frustrated. Not being aware that the cause for this rage lies in her impossible demands, she rationalizes her disappointment by accusing the servant. Since she cannot give up her desires, she fires the servant and hopes that a new one will be 'right'. The same mechanism repeats itself until she dies or cannot get any more servants. Such a development is by no means found only in the relations of employers and servants. Often the history of marriage conflicts is identical; however, since it is easier to fire a servant than to divorce, the outcome is often that of a lifelong battle in which each partner tries to punish the other for ever-accumulating wrongs. The problem that confronts us here is that of a specific human character, namely the narcissistic-exploitative character, and not that of an accumulated instinctive energy.

In a chapter on 'Behavioural Analogies to Morality', Lorenz makes the following statement:

> However, nobody with a real appreciation of the phenomena under discussion can fail to have an ever-recurring sense of admiration for those physiological mechanisms which enforce, in animals, selfless behaviour aimed towards the good of the community, and which work in the same way as the moral law in human beings. (K. Lorenz, 1966)

How does one recognize 'selfless' behaviour in animals? What Lorenz describes is an instinctively determined action pattern. The term 'selfless' is taken from human psychology and refers to the fact that a human being can forget his self (one should say, more correctly, his ego) in his wish to help others. But has a goose, or a fish, or a dog a self (or an ego) which it can forget? Is selflessness not dependent on the fact of human self-awareness and the neurophysiological structure on which it rests? This question arises with regard to many other words Lorenz uses in describing animal behaviour, such as 'cruelty', 'sadness', 'embarrassment'.

One of the most important and interesting parts of Lorenz's ethological data is the 'bond' which forms between animals (his main example are geese) as a reaction to threats from without against the group. But the analogies he draws to explain human behaviour are sometimes astounding:

> Discriminative aggression towards strangers and the bond between the members of a group enhance each other. The opposition

of 'we' and 'they' can unite some wildly contrasting units. Confronted with present-day China, the United States and the Soviet Union occasionally seem to feel as 'we'. The same phenomenon, which incidentally has some of the earmarks of war, can be studied in the roll-cackle ceremony of greylag geese. (K. Lorenz, 1966)

Is the American–Soviet attitude determined by instinctive patterns which we have inherited from the greylag goose? Is the author trying to be more or less amusing, or does he actually intend to tell us something about the connection between geese and the American and Soviet political leaders?

Lorenz goes even further in making analogies between animal behaviour (or interpretations thereof) and his naïve notions about human behaviour, as in his statement about human love and hate: 'A personal bond, an individual friendship, is found only in animals with highly developed intra-specific aggression; in fact, this bond is the firmer, the more aggressive the particular animal and species is' (K. Lorenz, 1966). So far, so good; let us assume the correctness of Lorenz's observations. But at this point he jumps into the realm of human psychology; after stating that intra-specific aggression is millions of years older than personal friendship and love, he concludes that '*there is no love without aggression*' (K. Lorenz, 1966; italics added). This sweeping declaration, unsupported by any evidence as far as human love is concerned, but contradicted by most observable facts, is supplemented by another statement which does not deal with intraspecific aggression but with the 'ugly little brother of love', hate. 'As opposed to ordinary aggression, it is directed towards one individual, just as love is, and probably *hate presupposes the presence of love*: one can really hate only where one has loved and, even if one denies it, still does' (K. Lorenz, 1966; italics added). That love is sometimes transformed into hate has often been said, even though it is more correct to say that it is not love which suffers this transformation, but the wounded narcissism of the loving person, that is to say, the non-love which causes hate. To claim one hates only where one has loved, however, turns the element of truth in the statement into plain absurdity. Does the oppressed hate the oppressor, does the mother of the child hate its murderer, does the tortured hate the torturer because they once loved him or still do?

Another analogy is drawn from the phenomenon of '*militant enthusiasm*'. This is 'a specialized form of communal aggression, clearly distinct from and yet functionally related to the more primitive forms of petty individual aggression' (K. Lorenz, 1966). It is a 'sacred custom' which owes its motivating force to phylogenetically evolved behaviour patterns. Lorenz asserts there 'cannot be the slightest doubt that human militant enthusiasm evolved out of a communal defence response of our prehuman ancestors' (K. Lorenz, 1966). It is the enthusiasm shared by the group in defence against a common enemy.

Every man of normally strong emotions knows, from his own experience, the subjective phenomena that go hand in hand with the response of militant enthusiasm. A shiver runs down the back and, as more exact observation shows, along the outside of both arms. One soars elated, above all the ties of everyday life, one is ready to abandon all for the call of what, in the moment of this specific emotion, seems to be a sacred duty. All obstacles in its path become unimportant; the instinctive inhibitions against hurting or killing one's fellows lose, unfortunately, much of their power. Rational considerations, criticism, and all reasonable arguments against the behaviour, dictated by militant enthusiasm are silenced by an amazing reversal of all values, making them appear not only untenable but base and dishonourable. Men may enjoy the feeling of absolute righteousness even while they commit atrocities. Conceptual thought and moral responsibility are at their lowest ebb. As a Ukranian proverb says: 'When the banner is unfurled, all reason is in the trumpet.' (K. Lorenz, 1966)

Lorenz expresses

a reasonable hope that our moral responsibility may gain control over the primeval drive, but our only hope of its ever doing so rests on the humble recognition of the fact that militant enthusiasm is an instinctive response with a phylogenetically determined releasing mechanism and that the only point at which intelligent and responsible supervision can get control is in the conditioning of the response to an object which proves to be a genuine value under the scrutiny of the categorical question. (K. Lorenz, 1966)

Lorenz's description of normal human behaviour is rather astounding. No doubt many men do 'enjoy the feeling of absolute righteousness even while they commit atrocities' – or rather, to put it in more adequate psychological terms, many enjoy committing atrocities without any moral inhibitions and without experiencing a sense of guilt. But it is an untenable scientific procedure to claim, without even trying to muster evidence for it, that this is a universal human reaction, or that it is 'human nature' to commit atrocities during war, and to base this claim on an alleged instinct based on the questionable analogy with fishes and birds.

The fact is that individuals and groups differ tremendously in their tendency to commit atrocities when hate is aroused against another group. In the First World War British propaganda had to invent the stories of German soldiers bayoneting Belgian babies, because there were too few real atrocities to feed the hatred against the enemy. Similarly, the Germans reported few atrocities committed by their enemies, for the simple reason that there were so few. Even during the Second World War, in spite of the increasing brutalization of mankind, atrocities were generally restricted to special formations of the Nazis. In general, regular troops on both sides did not commit war crimes on the scale which would be expected to follow from Lorenz's description. What he describes, as far as atrocities are concerned, is the behaviour of sadistic or blood-thirsty character types; his 'militant enthusiasm' is simply a nationalistic and emotionally somewhat primitive reaction. To assert that a readiness to commit atrocities once the flag has been unfurled is an instinctively given part of human nature would be the classic defence against the accusation of violating the principles of the Geneva Convention. Although I am sure Lorenz does not mean to defend atrocities, his argument amounts, in fact, to such a defence. His approach blocks the understanding of the character systems in which they are rooted, and the individual and social conditions that cause their development.

Lorenz goes even further, arguing that without military enthusiasm (this 'true autonomous instinct') 'neither art, nor science, nor indeed any of the great endeavours of humanity would have come into being' (K. Lorenz, 1966). How can this be when the first condition for the manifestation of this instinct is that 'a social unit with which the subject identifies must appear to be threatened by some danger from outside' (K. Lorenz, 1966)? Is there any evidence that art and science flower only when there is an outside threat?

Lorenz explains the love of neighbour, expressed in the willingness to risk one's life for him, as 'a matter of course if he is your best friend and has saved yours a number of times: you do it without even thinking' (K. Lorenz, 1966). Instances of such 'decent behaviour' in tight spots easily occur, 'provided they are of a kind that occurred often enough in the Palaeolithic period to produce phylo-genetically adapted social norms to deal with the situation' (K. Lorenz, 1966).

Such a view of love of neighbour is a mixture of instinc-tivism and utilitarianism. You save your friend because he has saved your life a number of times; what if he did it only once, or not at all? Besides, you only do it because it happened often enough in the Palaeolithic period!

Conclusions about War At the conclusion of his analysis of the instinctive aggression in man, Lorenz finds himself in a position similar to that of Freud in his letter to Einstein about *Why War?* (1933). Neither man is happy to have arrived at conclusions that would seem to indicate that war is ineradicable because it is the result of an instinct. However, while Freud could call himself, in a very broad sense, a 'pacifist', Lorenz would hardly fit into this category, although he is quite aware that nuclear war would be a catastrophe without precedent. He tries to find ways that would help society avoid the tragic effects of the aggressive instinct; indeed, in the nuclear age he is almost forced to look for possibilities for peace in order to make his theory of the innate destructiveness of man acceptable. Some of his proposals are similar to those made by Freud, but there is a considerable difference between them. Freud's suggestions are made with scepticism and modesty, whereas Lorenz declares, 'I do not mind admitting that . . . I think I have something to teach mankind that may help it to change for the better. This conviction is not as presumptuous as it might seem . . .' (K. Lorenz, 1966).

Indeed, it would not be presumptuous if Lorenz had something of importance to teach. Unfortunately, his suggestions hardly go beyond worn-out clichés, 'simple precepts' against the danger of 'society's becoming completely disintegrated by the misfunctioning of social behaviour patterns':

1. 'The most important precept is . . . "Know thyself",' by which he means that 'we must deepen our insight into the causal concatenations governing our own behaviour' (K. Lorenz, 1966) – that is, the laws of evolution. As one element in this knowledge to which he gives special emphasis, Lorenz mentions 'the objective, ethological investigation of all the possibilities of discharging aggression in its primal form on substitute objects' (K. Lorenz, 1966).

2. 'The psychoanalytic study of so-called sublimation.'

3. 'The promotion of personal acquaintance and, if possible, friendship between individual members of different ideologies or nations.'

4. 'The fourth and perhaps the most important measure to be taken immediately is the intelligent and responsible channelling of militant enthusiasm' – that is, to help the

'younger generation ... to find genuine causes that are worth serving in the modern world'.

Let us look at this programme point by point.

Lorenz makes a distorted use of the notion of the classic 'know thyself' – not only of the Greek notion, but also that of Freud, whose whole science and therapy of psychoanalysis are built on self-knowledge. For Freud self-knowledge means that man becomes conscious of what is unconscious; this is a most difficult process, because it encounters the energy of resistance by which the unconscious is defended against the attempt to make it conscious. Self-knowledge in Freud's sense is not an intellectual process alone, but simultaneously an affective process, as it was already for Spinoza. It is not only knowledge by the brain, but also knowledge by the heart. Knowing oneself means gaining increasing insight, intellectually *and* affectively, in heretofore secret parts of one's psyche. It is a process which may take years for a sick person who wants to be cured of his symptoms and a lifetime for a person who seriously wants to be himself. Its effect is one of increased energy because energy is freed from the task of upholding repressions; thus the more man is in touch with his inner reality, the more he is awake and free. On the other hand, what Lorenz means by 'know thyself' is something quite different; it is the *theoretical* knowledge of the facts of evolution, and specifically of the instinctive nature of aggression. An analogy to Lorenz's concept of self-knowledge would be the theoretical knowledge of Freud's theory of the death instinct. In fact, following the reasoning of Lorenz, psychoanalysis as a therapy would not have to consist of anything but reading the collected works of Freud. One is reminded of a statement by Marx, that if somebody who knows the laws of gravity finds himself in deep water and cannot swim, his knowledge will not prevent him from drowning; as a Chinese sage said, 'Reading prescriptions does not make one well.'

Lorenz does not elaborate the second of his precepts, sublimation; the third, 'the promotion of personal acquaintance and, if possible, friendship between individual members of different ideologies and nations', Lorenz himself concedes is an 'obvious' plan – even airlines advertise international travel as serving the cause of peace; unfortunately this concept of the aggression-lowering function of personal acquaintance does not happen to be true. There is ample evidence for this. The British and the Germans were very well acquainted with each other before 1914, yet their mutual hatred when the war broke out was ferocious. There is even more telling proof. It is notorious that no war between countries elicits as much hate and cruelty as civil war, in which there is no lack of acquaintance between the two warring sides. Does the fact of mutual intimate knowledge diminish the intensity of hate among members of a family?

'Acquaintance' and 'friendship' cannot be expected to lower aggression because they represent a superficial knowledge *about* another person, a knowledge of an 'object' which I look at from the outside. This is quite different from the penetrating, emphatic knowledge in which I understand the other's experiences by mobilizing those within myself which, if not the same, are similar to his. Knowledge of this kind requires that most repressions within oneself are lowered in intensity to a point where there is little resistance to becoming aware of new aspects of one's unconscious. The attainment of a non-judgemental understanding can lower aggressiveness or do away with it altogether; it depends on the degree to which a person has overcome his own insecurity, greed, and narcissism, and not on the amount of information he has about others.[10]

10. It is an interesting question why civil wars are in fact much fiercer and why they elicit much more destructive impulses than international wars. It seems plausible that the reason lies in that usually, at least as far as modern international wars are concerned, they do not aim at the destruction or extinction of the enemy. Their aim is a limited one: to force the opponent to accept conditions for peace which are damaging, but by no means a threat to the existence of the population of the defeated country. (Nothing could illustrate this better than that Germany, the loser in two world wars, became more prosperous after each

The last of Lorenz's four precepts is the 'channelling of militant enthusiasm'; one of his special recommendations is athletics. But the fact is that competitive sports stimulate a great deal of aggression. How intense this is was highlighted recently when the deep feeling aroused by an international soccer match led to a small war in Latin America.

If there is no evidence that sport lowers aggression, at the same time it should be said that there is also no evidence that sport is motivated by aggression. What often produces aggression in sports is the competitive character of the event, cultivated in a social climate of competition and increased by an overall commercialization, in which not pride of achievement but money and publicity have become the most attractive goals. Many thoughtful observers of the unfortunate Olympic games in Munich, 1972, have recognized that instead of furthering goodwill and peace, they furthered competitive aggressiveness and nationalistic pride.[11]

A few other statements of Lorenz on war and peace are worth quoting because they are good examples of his ambiguity in this area. 'Supposing,' he says,

that, being a patriot of my home country (which I am), I felt an unmitigated hostility against another country (which I emphatically do not), I still could not wish *whole-heartedly* for its destruction *if* I realized that there were people living in it who, like myself, were enthusiastic workers in the field of inductive natural science, or revered Charles Darwin and were enthusiastically propagating the truth of his discoveries, or still others who shared my apprecia-

---

defeat than before). Exceptions to this rule are wars which aim at the physical extinction or enslavement of the total enemy population, like some of the wars – although by no means all – which the Romans conducted. In civil war the two opponents have the aim, if not to destroy each other physically, to destroy each other economically, socially, and politically. If this hypothesis is correct, it would mean that the degree of destructiveness is by large dependent on the severity of the threat.

11. The poverty of what Lorenz has to say about channelling militant enthusiasm becomes particularly clear if one reads William James's classic paper 'The Moral Equivalents of War' (1911).

tion of Michelangelo's art, or my enthusiasm for Goethe's *Faust*, or for the beauty of a coral reef, or for wildlife preservation or a number of minor enthusiasms I could name. I should find it quite impossible to hate, *unreservedly*, any enemy, if he shared only one of my identifications with cultural and ethical values. (K. Lorenz, 1966; italics added)

Lorenz hedges the denial of the wish for destruction of a whole country by the word 'wholeheartedly', and by qualifying hate by 'unreservedly'. But what is a 'half-hearted' wish for destruction, or a 'reserved' hate? More important, his condition for not wanting the destruction of another country is that there are people who share his particular tastes and enthusiasms (those who revere Darwin seem to qualify only if they also enthusiastically propagate his discoveries): it is not enough that they are human beings. In other words, the total destruction of an enemy is undesirable only if and because he is similar to Lorenz's own culture, and even more specifically, to his own interests and values.

The character of these statements is not changed by Lorenz's demand for a 'humanistic education' – i.e., an education offering an optimum of common ideals with which an individual can identify. This was the kind of education current in German high schools before the First World War, but the majority of the teachers of this humanism were probably more war-minded than the average German. Only a very different and radical humanism, one in which the primary identification is with life and with mankind, can have an influence against war.

Idolatry of Evolution Lorenz's position cannot be fully understood unless one is aware of his quasi-religious attitude towards Darwinism. His attitude in this respect is not rare, and deserves further study as an important sociopsychological phenomenon of contemporary culture. The deep need of man not to feel lost and lonely in the world had, of course, been previously satisfied by the concept of a God who had created this world and was concerned with each and every creature. When the theory of evolution destroyed the picture of God as the supreme Creator, confidence in God as the all-powerful Father of man fell with it, although many were able to combine a belief in God with the acceptance of the Darwinian theory. But for many of those for whom God was dethroned, the need for a godlike figure did not disappear. Some proclaimed a new god, Evolution, and worshipped Darwin as his prophet. For Lorenz and many others the idea of evolution became the core of a whole system of orientation and devotion. Darwin had revealed the ultimate truth regarding the origin of man; all human phenomena which might be approached and explained by economic, religious, ethical, or political consideration were to be understood from the point of view of evolution. This quasi-religious attitude towards Darwinism becomes apparent in Lorenz's use of the term 'the great constructors', referring to selection and mutation. He speaks of the methods and aims of the 'great constructors' very much in the way a Christian might speak of God's acts. He even uses the singular, the 'great constructor', thus coming even closer to the analogy with God. Nothing, perhaps, expresses the idolatrous quality of Lorenz's thinking more clearly than the concluding paragraph of *On Aggression*:

We know that in the evolution of vertebrates, the bond of personal love and friendship was the epoch-making invention created by the great constructors when it became necessary for two or more individuals of an aggressive species to live peacefully together and to work for a common end. We know that human society is built on the foundation of this bond, but we have to recognize the fact that the bond has become too limited to encompass all that it should: it prevents aggression only between those who know each other and are friends, while obviously it is all active hostility between all men of all nations or ideologies that must be stopped. The obvious conclusion is that love and friendship should embrace all humanity, that we should love all our human brothers indiscriminately. This commandment is not new. Our reason is quite able to understand its necessity as our feeling is able to appreciate its beauty, but nevertheless, *made as we are, we are unable to obey it*. We can feel the full, warm emotion of friendship and love only for individuals, and the utmost exertion of will-power cannot alter this fact. *But the great constructors can*, and *I believe* they will. *I believe* in the power of human reason, as *I believe* in the power of natural selection. *I believe* that reason can and will exert a selection pressure in the right direction. *I believe* that this, in the not too distant future, will endow our descendants with the faculty of fulfilling the greatest and most beautiful of all commandments. (K. Lorenz, 1966; italics added)

The great constructors will win out, where God and man have failed. The commandment of brotherly love has to remain ineffective, but the great constructors will give it life. The last part of the statement ends in a true confession of faith: I believe, I believe, I believe . . .

The social and moral Darwinism preached by Lorenz is a romantic, nationalistic paganism that tends to obscure the true understanding of the biological, psychological, and social factors responsible for human aggression. Here lies Lorenz's fundamental difference from Freud, in spite of the similarities in their views on aggression. Freud was one of the last representatives of Enlightenment philosophy. He genuinely believed in reason as the one strength man has and which alone could save him from confusion and decay. He genuinely postulated the need for self-knowledge by the uncovering of man's unconscious strivings. He overcame the loss of God by turning to reason – and felt painfully weak. But he did not turn to new idols.

2
Environmentalists and Behaviourists

Enlightenment Environmentalism

The diametrically opposite position to that of the instinctivists would seem to be that held by the environmentalists. According to their thinking, man's behaviour is exclusively moulded by the influence of the environment, i.e., by social and cultural, as opposed to 'innate' factors. This is particularly true with regard to aggression, one of the main obstacles to human progress.

In its most radical form this view was already presented by the philosophers of the Enlightenment. Man was supposed to be born 'good' and rational, and it was due to bad institutions, bad education, and bad example that he developed evil strivings. Some denied that there were any physical differences between the sexes (*l' âme n'a pas de sexe*) and proposed that whatever differences existed, aside from the anatomical ones, were exclusively due to education and social arrangements. In contrast to behaviourism, however, these philosophers were not concerned with methods of human engineering and manipulation but with social and political change. They believed that the 'good society' would create the good man, or rather, allow the natural goodness of man to manifest itself.

Behaviourism

Behaviourism was founded by J. B. Watson (1914); it was based on the premise that 'the subject matter of human psycology is *the behaviour or activities of the human being*'. Like logical positivism, it ruled out all 'subjective' concepts which could not be directly observed, such as 'sensation, perception, image, desire, and even thinking and emotion, as they are subjectively defined' (J. B. Watson, 1958).

Behaviourism underwent a remarkable development from the less sophisticated formulations of Watson to the brilliant neo-behaviourism of Skinner. But this mainly represents a refinement of the original thesis, rather than a greater depth or originality.

B. F. Skinner's Neo-behaviourism

Skinnerian neo-behaviourism[1] is based on the same principle as Watson's concepts: psychology as a science need not and must not be concerned with feelings or impulses or any other subjective events;[2] it disdains any attempt to speak of a 'nature' of man or construct a model of man, or to analyse

1. Since a full consideration of the merits of Skinnerian theory would lead too far away from our main problem, I shall restrict myself in the following to the presentation of the general principles of neo-behaviourism and to the more detailed discussion of some points which seem to be relevant for our discussion. For the study of Skinner's system one should read B. F. Skinner (1953). For a brief version cf. B. F. Skinner (1963). In his latest book (1971) he discusses the general principles of his system, especially their relevance for culture. See also the brief discussion between Carl R. Rogers and B. F. Skinner (1956) and B. F. Skinner (1961). For a critique of Skinner's position, cf. Noam Chomsky (1959). See also the counterargument of K. MacCorquodale (1970) and N. Chomsky (1971). Chomsky's reviews are thorough and far-reaching and make their points so brilliantly that there is no need to repeat them. Nevertheless Chomsky's and my own psychological positions are so far apart that I have to present some of my critique in this chapter.

2. Skinner, in contrast to many behaviourists, even concedes that 'private events' need not be entirely ruled out of scientific considerations and adds that 'a behavioural theory of knowledge suggests that the private world which, if not entirely unknowable, is at least not likely to be known well' (B. F. Skinner, 1963). This qualification makes Skinner's concession little more than a polite bow to the soul-psyche, the subject matter of psychology.

various human passions which motivate human behaviour. To consider human behaviour as impelled by intentions, purposes, aims or goals, would be a pre-scientific and useless way of looking at it. Psychology has to study *what* reinforcements tend to shape human behaviour and *how* to apply the reinforcements most effectively. Skinner's 'psychology' is the science of the engineering of behaviour; its aim is to find the right reinforcements in order to produce a desired behaviour.

Instead of the simple conditioning in the Pavlovian model, Skinner speaks of 'operant' conditioning. Briefly, this means that unconditioned behaviour, provided it is desirable from the experimenter's standpoint, is rewarded, i.e., followed by pleasure. (Skinner believes the rewarding reinforcement to be much more effective than the punishing.) As a result, the subject will eventually continue to behave in the desired fashion. For example, Johnny does not like spinach particularly; he eats it, mother rewards him with a praising remark, an affectionate glance, or an extra piece of cake, whichever is most reinforcing for Johnny as measured by what works best – i.e., she administers 'positive reinforcements'. Johnny will eventually love to eat spinach, particularly if the reinforcements are effectively administered in terms of their schedules. In hundreds of experiments Skinner and others have developed the techniques for this operant conditioning. Skinner has shown that by the proper use of positive reinforcement, the behaviour of animals and humans can be altered to an amazing degree, even in opposition to what some would loosely call 'innate' tendencies.

To have shown this is undoubtedly the great merit of Skinner's experimental work; it also supports the views of those who believe that the social structure (or 'culture' in the parlance of most American anthropologists) can shape man, even though not necessarily through operant conditioning. It is important to add that Skinner does not neglect genetic endowment. In order to render his position correctly, one should say that apart from genetic endowment, behaviour is determined entirely by reinforcement.

Reinforcement can occur in two ways: it happens in the normal cultural process, or it can be planned, according to Skinnerian teaching, and thus lead to a 'design for culture' (B. F. Skinner, 1961, 1971).

Goals and Values

Skinner's experiments are not concerned with the *goals* of the conditioning. The animal or the human subject is conditioned to behave in a certain way. What it (he) is conditioned to is determined by the decision of the experimenter who sets the goals for the conditioning. Usually the experimenter in these laboratory situations is not interested in *what* he is conditioning an animal or human subject for, but rather in the fact that he can condition them to the goal of his choice, and in how he can do it best. However, serious problems arise when we turn from the laboratory to realistic living, to individual or social life. In this case the paramount questions are: to *what* are people being conditioned, and who determines these goals?

It seems that when Skinner speaks of culture, he still has his laboratory in mind, where the psychologist who proceeds without value judgements can easily do so because the goal of the conditioning hardly matters. At least, that is perhaps one explanation why Skinner does not come to grips with the issue of goals and values. For example, he writes, 'We admire people who behave in original or exceptional ways, not because such behaviour is itself admirable, but because we do not know how to encourage original or exceptional behaviour in any other way' (C. R. Rogers and B. F. Skinner, 1956). This is nothing but circuitous reasoning: we admire originality because we can condition it only by admiring it.

But why do we want to condition it if it is not a desirable goal in itself?

Skinner does not face this question, although even with a modicum of sociological analysis an answer could be given. The degree of originality and creativity that is desirable in various classes and occupational groups in a given society varies. Scientists and top managers, for instance, need to have a great deal of these qualities in a technological-bureaucratic society like ours. For blue-collar workers to have the same degree of creativity would be a luxury – or a threat to the smooth functioning of the whole system.

I do not believe that this analysis is a sufficient answer to the problem of the value of originality and creativity. There is a great deal of psychological evidence that striving for creativeness and originality are deeply rooted impulses in man, and there is some neurophysiological evidence for the assumption that the striving for creativity and originality is 'built in' in the system of the brain (R. B. Livingston, 1967). I only want to stress that the impasse of Skinner's position is due to the fact that he pays no attention to such speculations or to those of psychoanalytic sociology and hence believes that questions are not answerable if they are not answerable by behaviourism.

Here is another example of Skinner's fuzzy thinking on the subject of values:

Most people would subscribe to the proposition that there is no value judgement involved in deciding how to build an atomic bomb, but would reject the proposition that there is none involved in deciding to build one. The most significant difference here may be that the scientific practices which guide the designer of the bomb are clear, while those which guide the designer of the culture which builds the bomb are not. We cannot predict the success or failure of a cultural invention with the same accuracy as we do that of a physical invention. It is for this reason that we are said to resort to value judgements in the second case. What we resort to is guessing. It is only in this sense that value judgements take up where science leaves off. When we can design small social inter-actions and, possibly, whole cultures with the confidence we bring to physical technology, the question of value will not be raised. (B. F. Skinner, 1961)

Skinner's main point is that there is really no essential difference between the lack of value judgement in the technical problem of designing the bomb and the decision to build one. The only difference is that the motives for building the bomb are not 'clear'. Maybe they are not clear to Professor Skinner, but they are clear to many students of history. In fact there was more than one reason for the decision to build the atomic bomb (and similarly for the hydrogen bomb): the fear of Hitler's building the bomb; perhaps the wish to have a superior weapon against the Soviet Union for possible later conflicts (this holds true especially for the hydrogen bomb); the logic of a system that is forced to increase its armaments to support its struggle with competing systems.

Quite aside from these military, strategic, and political reasons, there is, I believe, another one which is equally important. I refer to the maxim that is one of the axiomatic norms of cybernetic society: 'something *ought* to be done because it is technically *possible* to do it'. If it is possible to build nuclear weapons, they must be built even if they might destroy us all. If it is possible to travel to the moon or to the planets, it must be done, even if at the expense of many unfulfilled needs here on earth. This principle means the negation of all humanistic values, but it nevertheless represents a value, maybe the supreme norm of 'technotronic' society.[3]

3. I have discussed this idea in *The Revolution of Hope* (E. Fromm, 1968). Independently, H. Ozbekhan has formulated the same principle in his paper, 'The Triumph of Technology: "Can" Implies "Ought"' (H. Ozbekhan, 1966).
Dr Michael Maccoby has drawn my attention to some results of his study of the management of highly developed industries, which indicate that the principle 'can implies ought' is more valid in industries which produce for the military establishment than for the remaining, more competitive industry. But even if this argument is correct, two factors must be considered: first, the size of the industry which works directly or indirectly for the armed forces; second, that the principle has taken hold of the minds of many people who are not directly related to industrial production. A good example was the initial enthusiasm for space

Skinner does not care to examine the reasons for building the bomb, and he asks us to wait for further development of behaviourism to solve the mystery. In his views on social processes he shows the same inability to understand hidden, non-verbalized motives as he does in his treatment of psychical processes. Since most of what people say about their motivation in political as well as in personal life is notoriously fictitious, the reliance on what is *verbalized* blocks the understanding of social and psychical processes.

In other instances Skinner smuggles in values without, apparently, being aware of it. In the same paper, for instance, he writes: 'None, I am sure, wishes to develop new master–slave relationships or bend the will of the people to despotic rulers in new ways. These are patterns of control appropriate to a world without science' (B. F. Skinner, 1961). In which decade is Professor Skinner living? Are there no systems that do indeed want to bend the will of the people to dictators? And are these systems only to be found in cultures 'without science'? Skinner seems still to believe in an old-fashioned ideology of 'progress': the Middle Ages were 'dark' because they had no science and science necessarily leads to the freedom of man. The fact is that no leader or government explicitly states his intention of bending the will of the people any more; they are apt to use new words which sound like the opposite of the old ones. No dictator calls himself a dictator, and every system claims that it expresses the will of the people. In the countries of the 'free world', on the other hand, 'anonymous authority' and manipulation have replaced overt authority in education, work and politics.

Skinner's values also emerge in the following statement:

If we are *worthy* of our democratic heritage we shall, of course, be ready to resist any tyrannical use of science for immediate or selfish purposes. But if we *value* the achievements and goal of

---

flights; another example is the tendency in medicine to construct and use gadgets regardless of their real importance for a specific case.

democracy we must not refuse to apply science to the design and construction of cultural patterns, even though we may then find ourselves in some sense in the position of controllers. (B. F. Skinner, 1961; italics added)

What is the basis of this value in neo-behaviouristic theory?
    What about the controllers?

Skinner's answer is that 'all men control and all men are controlled' (C. R. Rogers and B. F. Skinner, 1956). This sounds reassuring for a democratically minded person, but is a vague and rather meaningless formula, as soon becomes clear:

In noticing how the master controls the slave or the employer the worker, we commonly overlook reciprocal effects and, by considering action in one direction only, are led to regard control as exploitation, or at least the gaining of a one-sided advantage, but the control is actually mutual. *The slave controls the master as completely as the master the slave* [italics added], in the sense that the techniques of punishment employed by the master have been selected by the slave's behaviour in submitting to them. This does not mean that the notion of exploitation is meaningless or that we may not appropriately ask, *cui bono?* In doing so, however, we go beyond the account of the *social episode itself* [italics added] and consider certain long-term effects which are clearly related to the question of value judgements. A comparable consideration arises in the analysis of any behaviour which alters a cultural practice. (B. F. Skinner, 1961)

I find this statement shocking; we are asked to believe that the relationship between master and slave is a reciprocal one, although the notion of exploitation is not 'meaningless'. For Skinner the exploitation is *not* part of the social episode itself; only the techniques of control are. This is the view of a man who looks at social life as if it were an episode in his laboratory, where all that matters to the experimenter is his technique – and not the 'episodes' themselves, since whether the rat is peaceful or aggressive is entirely irrelevant in this artificial world. And as if that were not enough, Skinner states that the exploitation by the master is 'clearly related' to the question of value judgements. Does Skinner believe that exploitation or, for that matter, robbery, torture, and murder are not 'facts' because they are clearly related to value judgements? This would indeed mean that all social and psychological phenomena, if they can also be judged as to their value, cease to be facts which can be examined scientifically.[4]

One can explain Skinner's saying that slave and slaveowner are in a reciprocal relationship only by the ambiguous use he makes of the word 'control'. In the sense in which the word is used in real life, there can be no question that the slave-owner controls the slave, and that there is nothing 'reciprocal' about the control except that the slave may have a minimum of counter-control – for instance, by the threat of rebellion. But this is not what Skinner is talking about. He speaks of control in the very abstract sense of the laboratory experiment, into which real life does not intrude. He actually repeats in all seriousness what has often been told as a joke, the story about a rat that tells another rat how well it has conditioned its experimenter: whenever the rat pushes a certain lever, the experimenter has to feed it.

Because neo-behaviourism has no theory of man, it can only see behaviour and not the behaving person. Whether somebody smiles at me because he wants to hide his hostility, or a salesgirl smiles because she has been instructed to smile (in the better stores), or whether a friend smiles at me because he is glad to see me, all this makes no difference to neo-behaviourism, for 'a smile is a smile'. That it should make no difference to Professor Skinner as a person is hard to believe, unless he were so alienated that the reality of persons no longer matters to him. But if the difference does matter, how could a theory that ignores it be valid?

Nor can neo-behaviourism explain why quite a few persons conditioned to be persecutors and torturers fall mentally

4. By the same logic the relation between torturer and the tortured is 'reciprocal', because the tortured, by his manifestation of pain, conditions the torturer to use the most effective instruments of torture.

sick in spite of the continuation of 'positive reinforcements'. Why does positive reinforcement not prevent many others from rebelling, out of the strength of their reason, their conscience, or their love, when all conditioning works in the opposite direction? And why are many of the most adapted people, who should be star witnesses to the success of conditioning, often deeply unhappy and disturbed or suffer from neurosis? There must be impulses inherent in man which set limits to the power of conditioning; to study the failure of conditioning seems just as important, scientifically, as its success. Indeed, man can be conditioned to behave in almost every desired way; but only 'almost'. He reacts to those conditions that conflict with basic human requirements in different and ascertainable ways. He can be conditioned to be a slave, but he will react with aggression or decline in vitality; or he can be conditioned to feel like part of a machine and react with boredom, aggression, and unhappiness.

Basically, Skinner is a naïve rationalist who ignores man's passions. In contrast to Freud, he is not impressed by the power of passions, but believes that man always behaves as his self-interest requires. Indeed, the whole principle of neo-behaviourism is that self-interest is so powerful that by appealing to it – mainly in the form of the environment's rewarding the individual for acting in the desired sense – man's behaviour can be completely determined. In the last analysis, *neo-behaviourism is based on the quintessence of bourgeois experience: the primacy of egotism and self-interest over all other human passions.*

The Reasons for Skinnerism's Popularity

Skinner's extraordinary popularity can be explained by the fact that he has succeeded in blending elements of traditional, optimistic, liberal thought with the social and mental reality of cybernetic society.

Skinner believes that man is malleable, subject to social

influences, and that nothing in his 'nature' can be considered to be a final obstacle to development towards a peaceful and just society. Thus his system attracts those psychologists who are liberals and who find in Skinner's system an argument to defend their political optimism. He appeals to those who believe that desirable social goals like peace and equality are not just rootless ideals, but can be established in reality. The whole idea that one can 'design' a better society on a scientific basis appeals to many who earlier might have been socialists. Did not Marx, too, want to design a better society? Did he not call his brand of socialism 'scientific' in contrast to 'Utopian' socialism? Is not Skinner's way particularly attractive at a point in history when the political solution seems to have failed and revolutionary hopes are at their lowest?

But Skinner's implied optimism alone would not have made his ideas so attractive were it not for his combining of traditional liberal views with their very negation.

In the cybernetic age, the individual becomes increasingly subject to manipulation. His work, his consumption, and his leisure are manipulated by advertising, by ideologies, by what Skinner calls 'positive reinforcements'. The individual loses his active, responsible role in the social process; he becomes completely 'adjusted' and learns that any behaviour, act, thought, or feeling which does not fit into the general scheme puts him at a severe disadvantage; in fact he *is* what he is *supposed to be*. If he insists on being himself, he risks, in police states, his freedom or even his life; in some democracies, he risks not being promoted, or more rarely, he risks even his job, and perhaps most importantly, he risks feeling isolated, without communication with anybody.

While most people are not clearly aware of their discomfort, they dimly sense their fear of life, of the future, of the boredom caused by the monotony and the meaninglessness of what they are doing. They sense that the very ideals in which they want to believe have lost their moorings in social reality. What relief it is for them to learn that conditioning is the best, the most progressive, and the most effective solution. Skinner recommends the hell of the isolated, manipulated man of the cybernetic age as the heaven of progress. He dulls our fears of where we are going by telling us that we need not be afraid; that the direction our industrial system has taken is the same as that which the great humanists had dreamt of, except that it is scientifically grounded. Moreover, Skinner's theory rings true, because it is (almost) true for the alienated man of the cybernetic society. In summary, Skinnerism is the psychology of opportunism dressed up as a new scientific humanism.

I am not saying that Skinner *wants* to play this role of apologist for the 'technotronic' age. On the contrary, his political and social naïveté can make him write sometimes more convincingly (and confusedly) than he could if he were aware of what he is trying to condition us to.

Behaviourism and Aggression

The behaviouristic method is so important for the problem of aggression because most investigators of aggression in the United States have written with a behaviouristic orientation. Their reasoning is, briefly stated: if Johnny discovers that by being aggressive his younger brother (or mother, and so on) will give him what he wants, he will become a person who tends to behave aggressively; the same would hold true for submissive, courageous, or affectionate behaviour. The formula is that one does, feels, and thinks in the way that has proved to be a successful method of obtaining what one wants. Aggression, like all other behaviour, is purely learned on the basis of seeking one's optimal advantage.

The behaviouristic view on aggression has been succinctly expressed by A. H. Buss, who defines aggression as 'a response that delivers noxious stimuli to another organism'. He writes:

There are two reasons for excluding the concept of intent from the definition of aggression. First, it implies teleology, a purposive act directed towards a future goal, and this view is inconsistent with the behavioural approach adopted in this book. Second, and more important, is the difficulty of applying this term to behavioural events. Intent is a private event that may or may not be capable of verbalization, may or may not be accurately reflected in a verbal statement. One might be led to accept intent as an inference from the reinforcement history of the organism. If an aggressive response has been systematically reinforced by a specific consequence, such as flight of the victim, the recurrence of the aggressive response might be said to involve an 'intent to cause flight'. However, this kind of interference is superfluous in the analysis of behaviour; it is more fruitful to examine directly the relation between reinforcement history of an aggressive response and the immediate situation eliciting the response.

In summary, *intent* is both awkward and unnecessary in the analysis of aggressive behaviour; rather, the crucial issue is the nature of the reinforcing consequences that affect the occurrence and the strength of aggressive responses. In other words, what are the classes of reinforcers that affect aggressive behaviour? (A. H. Buss, 1961)

By 'intent' Buss understands conscious intent. But Buss is not totally unreceptive to the psychoanalytic approach: 'If anger is not *the* drive for aggression, is it fruitful to regard it as a drive? The position adopted here is that it is not fruitful' (A. H. Buss, 1961).[5]

Such outstanding behaviourist psychologists as A. H. Buss and L. Berkowitz are much more sensitive to the phenomenon of man's feelings than Skinner is, but Skinner's basic principle that the deed, not the doer, is an object for scientific observation, holds true for their position too. They thereby do not give proper weight to the fundamental findings of Freud: that of psychical forces determining behaviour, the

5. L. Berkowitz has taken a stand in many ways similar to that of A. H. Buss; he too is not unreceptive to the idea of motivating emotions, but essentially stays within the framework of behaviouristic theory; he modifies the frustration–aggression theory but does not reject it (L. Berkowitz, 1962 and 1969).

largely unconscious character of these forces, and 'awareness' ('insight') as a factor which can bring about changes in the energy charge and direction of these forces.

Behaviourists claim that their method is 'scientific' because they deal with what is visible, i.e., with overt behaviour. But they do not recognize that 'behaviour' itself, separated from the behaving person, cannot be adequately described. A man fires a gun and kills another person; the behavioural act in itself – firing the shot that kills the person – if isolated from the 'aggressor', means little, psychologically. In fact, a behaviouristic statement would be adequate only about the gun; with regard to *it* the motivation of the man who pulls the trigger is irrelevant. But *his* behaviour can be fully understood only if we know the conscious *and* unconscious motivation moving him to pull the trigger. We do not find a *single* cause for his behaviour, but we can discover the psychical structure inside this man – his character – and the many conscious and unconscious factors which at a certain point led to his firing the gun. We find that we can explain the *impulse* to fire the gun as being determined by many factors in his character system, but that his *act* of firing the gun is the most contingent among all factors, and the least predictable one. It depends on many accidental elements in the situation, such as easy access to a gun, absence of other people, the degree of stress, and the conditions of his whole psychophysiological system at the moment.

The behaviourist maxim that observable behaviour is a scientifically reliable datum is simply not true. The fact is that the behaviour itself is different depending on the motivating impulse, even though on superficial inspection this difference may not be visible.

A simple example demonstrates this: each of two fathers, with different character structures, spanks his son because he believes that the child needs this kind of punishment for the sake of his healthy development. The fathers behave in what seems to be an identical manner. They slap the children with their hands. Yet, if we compare the behaviour of a loving and concerned father with that of a sadistic father, we find that the behaviour is in reality not the same. Their way of holding the child and of talking to the child before and after the punishment, their facial expression, make the behaviour of one quite different from that of the other. Correspondingly, the children's reactions to the respective behaviours differ. The one child senses the destructive, or sadistic quality of the punishment; the other has no reason to doubt his father's love. All the more so because this single instance of the father's behaviour is only one among innumerable behaviours the child has experienced before and which have formed his picture of his father and his reaction to him. The fact that both fathers have the conviction that they are punishing the child for his own good makes hardly any difference, except that this moralistic conviction may obliterate such inhibitions as the sadistic father may otherwise have. On the other hand, if the sadistic father never beats his child, perhaps because he is afraid of his wife, or because it is against his progressive ideas of education, his 'non-violent' behaviour will produce the same reaction because his eyes convey to the child the same sadistic impulse that his hands would do in beating him. Because children are generally more sensitive than adults, they respond to the father's impulse and not to an isolated bit of behaviour.

Or let us take another example: we see a man who shouts and has a red face. We describe his behaviour as 'being angry'. If we ask why he is angry, the answer may be 'because he is frightened'. 'Why is he frightened?' 'Because he suffers from a deep sense of impotence.' 'Why is this so?' 'Because he has never dissolved the ties to mother and is emotionally still a little child.' (This sequence is, of course, not the only possible one.) Each of these answers is 'true'. The difference between them lies in that they refer to ever deeper (and usually less conscious) levels of experience. The deeper the level to which the answer refers, the more relevant it is for the understanding of his behaviour. Not just for the understanding of his motivations, but for recognizing the behaviour in every detail. In a case like this, for instance, a sensitive observer will *see* the expression of frightened help-lessness in his face, rather than only the rage. In another case a man's obvious behaviour may be the same, but a sensitive awareness of his face will show hardness and intense destruc-tiveness. His angry behaviour is only the controlled expres-sion of destructive impulses. The two similar behaviours are in fact quite dissimilar, and aside from intuitive sensitivity, the scientific way of understanding the differences requires the understanding of motivation – i.e., of the two respective character structures.

I have not given the customary answer: 'he is angry be-cause he has been – or feels – insulted'. Such an explanation puts all the emphasis on the triggering stimulus, but ignores that the stimulus' power to stimulate depends also on the character structure of the stimulated person. A group of people confronted with the same stimulus will react dif-ferently to it according to their characters. A may be attrac-ted to the stimulus; B repulsed; C frightened; D will ignore it.

Buss is, of course, perfectly right in stating that intent is a private event that may or may not be capable of verbaliza-tion. But this is precisely the dilemma of behaviourism: be-cause it has no method for examining unverbalized data, it has to restrict its investigation to those data that it can handle, which are usually too crude to lend themselves to subtle theoretical analysis.

On Psychological Experiments

If a psychologist sets himself the task of understanding human behaviour he must devise methods of investigation which are adequate to the study of human beings *in vivo*, while practically all behaviouristic studies are done *in vitro*. (Not in the meaning of this word in the physiological labora-tory, but in the equivalent sense, namely that the subject is observed under controlled, artificially arranged conditions, not in the 'real' process of living.) Psychology seems to have wanted to attain respectability by imitating the method of the natural sciences, albeit those of fifty years ago, and not in terms of 'scientific' method current in the most advanced natural sciences.[6] Furthermore, the lack of theoretical significance is often covered up by impressive-looking mathematical formulations which are not germane to the data and do not add anything to their value.

To devise a method for the observation and analysis of human behaviour outside the laboratory is a difficult undertaking, but it is a necessary condition for the understanding of man. There are, in principle, two fields of observation for the study of man:

1. The direct and detailed observation of another person is one method. The most elaborate and fruitful situation of this kind is the psychoanalytic situation, the 'psychoanalytic laboratory' as Freud devised it; it permits the expression of the patient's unconscious impulses, and the examination of their connection with his overt 'normal' and 'neurotic' behaviour.[7] Less intensive, yet also quite fruitful, is an interview – or better, a series of interviews – which, if possible, should also include the study of some dreams and certain projective tests. But one should not underestimate the knowledge in depth which a skilled observer can obtain simply by observing a person minutely for a while (including of course his gestures, voice, posture, facial expression, hands, etc.). Even without personal knowledge, diaries, letters, and a detailed history of a person, this kind of observation can be an important source for the understanding in depth of his character.

2. Another method for the study of man *in vivo* is to trans-

6. cf. J. Robert Oppenheimer's address (1955) and many similar statements by outstanding natural scientists.

7. I put the two terms in quotation marks because they are often loosely used and sometimes have become identical with socially adapted and non-adapted, respectively.

form given situations in life into a 'natural laboratory', rather than to bring life into the psychological laboratory. Instead of constructing an artificial social situation, as the experimenter does in his psychological laboratory, one studies the experiments life itself offers; one chooses *given social situations* which are comparable and transforms them into the equivalent of experiments by the *method* of studying them. By keeping some factors constant, others variable, this natural laboratory also permits the testing of various hypotheses. There are many comparable situations, and one can test whether one hypothesis stands up in all situations, and if not, whether the exceptions can be sufficiently explained without changing the hypothesis. One of the simplest forms of such 'natural experiments' are *enquêtes* (using long and open-ended questionnaires and/or personal interviews) with selected representatives from certain groups, such as age or occupational groups, prisoners, hospital inmates, and so forth. (The use of the conventional battery of psychological tests is, in my opinion, not sufficient for the understanding of the deeper layers of the character.)

To be sure, the use of 'natural experiments' does not permit us to arrive at the 'accuracy' of laboratory experiments, because no two social constellations are identical; but by observing not 'subjects' but people, not artifacts but life, one does not have to pay as the price of an alleged (and often doubtful) accuracy the triviality of the experiment's results. I believe that the exploration of aggression either in the laboratory of the psychoanalytic interview or in a socially given 'laboratory' is, from a scientific standpoint, much preferable to the methods of the psychological laboratory, as far as analysis of behaviour is concerned; however, it requires a much higher level of complex theoretical thinking than do even very clever laboratory experiments.[8]

8. I have found 'interpretative questionnaires' to be a valuable tool in the study of underlying and largely unconscious motivations of groups. An interpretative questionnaire analyses the not-intended meaning of an answer (to an open question) and interprets the answers in a char-

To illustrate what I have just said, let us look at a very interesting – and one of the most highly regarded experiments in the field of aggression, the 'Behavioral Study of Obedience' by Stanley Milgram, conducted at Yale University in its 'interaction laboratory' (S. Milgram, 1963).[9]

The subjects were forty males between the ages of twenty and fifty, drawn from New Haven and the surrounding communities. Subjects were obtained by a newspaper advertisement and direct mail solicitation. Those who responded to the appeal believed they were to participate in a study of memory and learning at Yale University. A wide range of occupations is represented in the sample. Typical subjects were postal clerks, high school teachers, salesmen, engineers and labourers. Subjects ranged in educational level from one who had not finished elementary school, to those who had doctorate and other professional degrees. They were paid $4.50 for their participation in the experiment. However, subjects were told that payment was simply for coming to the laboratory, and that the money was theirs no matter what happened after they arrived.

One naïve subject and one victim (an accomplice of the experimenter) performed in each experiment. A pretext had to be devised that would justify the administration of electric shock by the naïve subject.[10] This was effectively accomplished by the cover story. After a general introduction on the presumed relation between punishment and learning, subjects were told:

---

acteristic sense rather than takes them at their face value. I had first applied this method in 1932 in a study at the Institute of Social Research, University of Frankfurt, and used it again in the 1960s in a study of the social character of a small Mexican village. Among the main collaborators in the first study were Ernest Schachtel, the late Anna Hartoch-Schachtel, and Paul Lazarsfeld (as statistical consultant). This study was finished in the mid thirties, but only the questionnaire and sample answers were published (M. Horkheimer, ed., 1936). The second study has been published (E. Fromm and M. Maccoby, 1970). Maccoby and I have also devised a questionnaire to determine the factors that indicate the necrophilic character, and Maccoby has applied this questionnaire to various groups with satisfactory results (M. Maccoby, 1972a).

9. All following quotations are from S. Milgram (1963).

10. No actual electric shocks were administered, but this was not known to the teacher-subjects.

'But actually, we know *very little* about the effects of punishment on learning, because almost no truly scientific studies have been made of it in human beings.

'For instance, we don't know how much punishment is best for learning – and we don't know how much difference it makes as to who is giving the punishment, whether an adult learns best from a younger or an older person than himself – or many things of that sort.

'So in this study we are bringing together a number of adults of different occupations and ages. And we're asking some of them to be teachers and some of them to be learners.

'We want to find out just what effect different people have on each other as teachers and learners and also what effect punishment will have on learning in this situation.

'Therefore, I'm going to ask one of you to be the teacher here tonight and the other one to be the learner.

'Does either of you have a preference?'

Subjects then drew slips of paper from a hat to determine who would be the teacher and who would be the learner in the experiment. The drawing was rigged so that the naïve subject was always the teacher and the accomplice always the learner. (Both slips contained the word 'teacher'.) Immediately after the drawing, the teacher and learner were taken to an adjacent room and the learner was strapped into an 'electric chair' apparatus.

The experiment explained that the straps were to prevent excessive movement while the learner was being shocked. The effect was to make it impossible for him to escape from the situation. An electrode was attached to the learner's wrist, and electrode paste was applied 'to avoid blisters and burns'. Subjects were told that the electrode was attached to the shock generator in the adjoining room.

... The subject is told to administer a shock to the learner each time he gives a wrong response. Moreover – and this is the key command – the subject is instructed to 'move one level higher on the shock generator each time the learner flashes a wrong answer'. He is also instructed to announce the voltage level before administering a shock. This serves to continually remind subjects of the increasing intensity of shocks administered to the learner ... In all conditions the learner gives a predetermined set of responses to the word pair test based on a schedule of approximately three wrong answers to one correct answer. In the present experimental condition no vocal response or other sign of protest is heard from the learner until Shock Level 300 is reached. When the 300 volt shock is administered, the learner pounds on the wall of the room in which he is bound to the electric chair. The pounding can be heard by the subject. From this point on, the learner's answers no longer appear on the four-way panel ... If the subject indicated his unwillingness to go on, the experimenter responded with a sequence of 'prods', using as many as necessary to bring the subject into line.

Prod 1: Please continue, *or* Please go on.

Prod 2: The experiment requires that you continue.

Prod 3: It is absolutely essential that you continue.

Prod 4: You have no other choice, you *must* go on.

The prods were always made in sequence: Only if Prod 1 had been unsuccessful, could Prod 2 be used. If the subject refused to obey the experimenter after Prod 4, the experiment *was* terminated. The experimenter's tone of voice was at all times firm, but not impolite. The sequence was begun anew on each occasion that the subject balked or showed reluctance to follow orders.

Special prods. If the subject asked if the learner was liable to suffer permanent physical injury, the experimenter said:

'Although the shocks may be painful, there is no permanent tissue damage, so please go on.' (Followed by Prods 2, 3, and 4 if necessary.)

If the subject said that the learner did not want to go on, the experimenter replied:

'Whether the learner likes it or not, you must go on until he has learned all the word pairs correctly. So please go on.' (Followed by Prods 2, 3, and 4 if necessary.)

What were the results of this experiment? 'Many subjects showed signs of nervousness in the experimental situation, and especially upon administering the more powerful shocks. In a large number of cases *the degree of tension reached extremes that are rarely seen in socio-psychological laboratory studies.*' (Italics added.) Subjects were observed to sweat, tremble, stutter, bite their lips, groan, and dig their finger-nails into their flesh. These were characteristic rather than exceptional responses to the experiment.

One sign of tension was the regular occurrence of nervous

laughing fits. Fourteen of the forty subjects showed definite signs
of nervous laughter and smiling. The laughter seemed entirely
out of place, even bizarre. Fullblown, uncontrollable seizures were
observed for three subjects. On one occasion we observed a
seizure so violently convulsive that it was necessary to call a halt
to the experiment. The subject, a forty-six-year-old encyclopedia
salesman, was seriously embarrassed by his untoward and uncontrollable behaviour. In the post-experimental interviews subjects took pains to point out that they were not sadistic types
and that the laughter did not mean they enjoyed shocking the
victim.

Somewhat in contrast to the experimenter's original expectation, none of the forty subjects stopped prior to Shock
Level 300 at which the victim began kicking on the wall and
no longer providing answers to the teacher's multiple-choice
questions. Only five out of the forty subjects refused to obey
the experimenter's commands beyond the 300-volt level;
four more administered one further shock, two broke off at
the 330-volt level and one each at 345, 360, and 375 volts.
Thus a total of fourteen subjects (=35 per cent) defied the
experimenter. The 'obedient' subjects

often did so under extreme stress ... and displayed fear similar to
those who defied the experimenter; yet they obeyed.
  After the maximum shocks had been delivered, and the experimenter called a halt to the proceedings, many obedient subjects heaved sighs of relief, mopped their brows, rubbed their
fingers over their eyes, or nervously fumbled cigarettes. Some shook
their heads, apparently in regret. Some subjects had remained
calm throughout the experiment, and displayed only minimal
signs of tension from beginning to end.

In the discussion of the experiment the author states that it
yielded two findings that were surprising:

The first finding concerns the sheer strength of obedient tendencies manifested in this situation. Subjects have learned from
childhood that it is a fundamental breach of moral conduct to
hurt another person against his will. Yet, twenty-six students
abandon this tenet in following the instructions of an authority

who has no special powers to enforce his commands . . . The second unanticipated effect was the extraordinary tension generated by the procedures. One might suppose that a subject would simply break off or continue as his conscience dictated. Yet this is very far from what happened. There were striking reactions of tension and emotional strain. One observer related:

'I observed a mature and initially poised businessman enter the laboratory smiling and confident. Within twenty minutes he was reduced to a twitching, stuttering wreck, who was rapidly approaching a point of nervous collapse. He constantly pulled on his earlobe, and twisted his hands. At one point he pushed his fist into his forehead and muttered: "*Oh God, let's stop it.*" And yet he continued to respond to every word of the experimenter, and obeyed to the end.'

The experiment is indeed very interesting – as an examination not only of obedience and conformity but of cruelty and destructiveness as well. It seems almost to simulate a situation that has happened in real life, that of the culpability of soldiers who behaved in an extremely cruel and destructive manner under orders from their superiors (or what they believed to be orders) which they executed without question. Is this also the story of the German generals who were sentenced in Nürnberg as war criminals; or the story of Lieutenant Calley and some of his subordinates in Vietnam?

I do not think that this experiment permits any conclusion with regard to most situations in real life. The psychologist was not only an authority to whom one owes obedience, but a representative of *Science* and of one of the most prestigious institutions of higher education in the United States. Considering that science is widely regarded as the highest value in contemporary industrial society, it is very difficult for the average person to believe that what science commands could be wrong or immoral. If the Lord had not told Abraham not to kill his son, Abraham would have done it, like millions of parents who practised child sacrifice in history. For the believer neither God nor his modern equivalent, Science, can command anything that is wrong. For this reason, plus others mentioned by Milgram, the high degree of obedience is not more surprising than that 35 per cent of the group refused at some point to obey; in fact this disobedience of more than a third might well be considered more surprising – and encouraging.

Another surprise seems to be equally unjustified: that there was so much tension. The experimenter expected that 'a subject would simply break off or continue as his conscience dictated'. Is that really the manner in which people solve conflicts in real life? Is it not precisely the peculiarity of human functioning – and its tragedy – that man tries *not* to face his conflicts; that is, that he does *not* choose consciously between what he craves to do – out of greed or fear – and what his conscience forbids him to do? The fact is that he removes the awareness of the conflict by rationalization, and the conflict manifests itself only unconsciously in increased stress, neurotic symptoms, or feeling guilty for the wrong reasons. Milgram's subjects behave very normally in this regard.

Some further interesting questions suggest themselves at this point. Milgram assumes that his subjects are in a conflict situation because they are caught between obedience to authority and behaviour patterns learned from childhood on: not to harm other people.

But is this really so? Have we learned 'not to harm other people'? That may be what children are told in Sunday school. In the realistic school of life, however, they learn that they must seek their own advantage even if other people are harmed. It seems that on this score the conflict is not as sharp as Milgram assumes.

I believe that the most important finding of Milgram's study is the strength of the reactions *against* the cruel behaviour. To be sure, 65 per cent of the subjects could be 'conditioned' to *behave* cruelly, but a reaction of indignation or horror against this sadistic behaviour was clearly present in most of them. Unfortunately the author does not give accurate data on the number of 'subjects' who remained calm throughout the experiment. For the understanding of human behaviour, it would be most interesting to know more about them. Apparently they had little or no feeling of opposition to the cruel acts they were performing. The next question is why this was so. One possible answer is that they enjoyed the suffering of others and felt no remorse when their behaviour was sanctioned by authority. Another possibility is that they were such highly alienated or narcissistic people that they were insulated against what went on in other people; or they might be 'psychopaths', lacking in any kind of moral reaction. As for those in whom the conflict manifested itself in various symptoms of stress and anxiety, it should be assumed that they are people who do not have a sadistic or destructive character. (If one had undertaken an interview in depth, one would have seen the differences in character and even could have made an educated guess as to how people would behave.)

The main result of Milgram's study seems to be one he does not stress: the presence of conscience in most subjects, and their pain when obedience made them act against their conscience. Thus, while the experiment can be interpreted as another proof of the easy dehumanization of man, the subjects' reactions show rather the contrary – the presence of intense forces within them that find cruel behaviour intolerable. This suggests an important approach to the study of cruelty in real life: to consider not only cruel *behaviour* but the – often unconscious – guilty conscience of those who obey authority. (The Nazis had to use an elaborate system of camouflage of atrocities in order to cope with the conscience of the average man.) Milgram's experiment is a good illustration of the difference between conscious and unconscious aspects of behaviour, even though no use has been made of it to explore this difference.

Another experiment is particularly relevant here because it deals directly with the problem of the causes of cruelty.

The first report of this experiment was published in a short paper (P. G. Zimbardo, 1972) which is, as the author wrote me, an excerpt from an oral report presented before a Congressional Subcommittee on Prison Reform. Because of that paper's brevity, Dr Zimbardo does not consider it a fair basis for a critique of his work; I follow his wish, although regretfully, because there are certain discrepancies between it and the later paper (C. Haney, C. Banks, and P. Zimbardo, in press)[11], which I would have liked to point out. I shall only briefly refer to his first paper in reference to two crucial points: (a) the attitude of the guards, and (b) the central thesis of the authors.

The purpose of the experiment was to study the behaviour of normal people under a particular situation, that of playing the roles of prisoners and guards respectively, in a 'mock prison'. The general thesis that the authors believe is proved by the experiment is that many, perhaps the majority of people, can be made to do almost anything by the strength of the situation they are put in, regardless of their morals, personal convictions, and values (P. H. G. Zimbardo, 1972); more specifically, that in this experiment the prison situation transformed most of the subjects who played the role of 'guards' into brutal sadists and most of those who played the role of prisoners into abject, frightened, and submissive men, some having such severe mental symptoms that they had to be released after a few days. In fact, the reactions of both groups were so intense that the experiment which was to have lasted for two weeks was broken off after six days.

I doubt that the experiment proved this behaviourist thesis and shall set forth the reasons for my doubts. But first I must acquaint the reader with the details of the experiment as described in the second report. Students applied in answer to a newspaper advertisement asking for male volunteers to participate in a psychological study on prison life in return for payment of $15.00 per day. The students who responded

11. Except as otherwise noted, the following quotations are from the joint paper, the manuscript of which Dr Zimbardo kindly sent me.

completed an extensive questionnaire concerning their family background, physical and mental health history, prior experience and attitudinal propensities with respect to sources of psyco-pathology (including their involvement in crime). Each respondent who completed the background questionnaire was interviewed by one of the two experimenters. Finally, the twenty-four subjects who were judged to be most stable (physically and mentally), most mature, and least involved in anti-social behaviours were selected to participate in the study. On a random basis, half the Ss were assigned the role of 'guard', half were assigned to the role of 'prisoner.'

The final sample of subjects chosen 'was administered a battery of psychological tests on the day prior to the start of the simulation, but to avoid any selective bias on the part of the experimenter-observers, scores were not tabulated until the study was completed'. According to the authors, they had selected a sample of individuals who did not deviate from the normal range of the population, and who showed no sadistic or masochistic predisposition.

The 'prison' was constructed in a thirty-five-foot section of a basement corridor in the psychology building at Stanford University. All the subjects were told that

they would be assigned either the guard or the prisoner role on a completely random basis and all had voluntarily agreed to play either role for $15.00 per day for up to two weeks. They signed a contract guaranteeing a minimally adequate diet, clothing, housing and medical care as well as the financial remuneration in return for their stated 'intention' of serving in the assigned role for the duration of the study.

It was made explicit in the contract that those assigned to be prisoners should expect to be under surveillance (had little or no privacy) and to have some of their basic civil rights suspended during their imprisonment, excluding physical abuse. They were given no other information about what to expect nor instructions about behaviour appropriate for a prisoner role. Those actually assigned to this treatment were informed by phone to be available at their place of residence on a given Sunday when we would start the experiment.

The subjects assigned to be guards attended a meeting with the 'Warden' (an undergraduate research assistant) and the 'Superintendent' of the prison (the principal investigator). They were told that their task was to 'maintain the reasonable degree of order in the prison necessary for its effective functioning'.

It is important to mention what the authors understand by 'prison'. They do not use the word in its generic sense as a place of internment for law offenders, but in a specific sense portraying the conditions existing in certain American prisons.

Our intention was not to create a *literal* simulation of an American prison, but rather a functional representation of one. For ethical, moral and pragmatic reasons we could not detain our subjects for extended or indefinite periods of time, we could not exercise the threat and promise of severe physical punishment, we could not allow homosexual or racist practices to flourish, nor could we duplicate certain other specific aspects of prison life. Nevertheless, we believed that we could create a situation with sufficient mundane realism to allow the role-playing participation to go beyond the superficial demands of their assignment into the deep structure of the characters they represented. To do so, we established functional equivalents for the activities and experiences of actual prison life which were expected to produce qualitatively similar psychological reactions in our subjects – feelings of power and powerlessness, of control and oppression, of satisfaction and frustration, of arbitrary rule and resistance to authority, of status and anonymity, of machismo and emasculation.

As the reader will see presently from the description of the methods used in the prison, this description is a considerable understatement of the treatment employed in the experiment, which is only vaguely hinted at in the last words. The actual methods were those of severe and systematic humiliation and degradation, not only because of the behaviour of the guards, but through the prison rules arranged by the experimenters.

By the use of the term 'prison' it is implied that at least all prisons in the United States – and in fact in any other country – are of this type. This implication ignores the fact that there are others, such as some Federal prisons in the United States and their equivalent abroad, which are not evil to the degree the authors introduced into their mock prison.

How were the 'prisoners' treated? They had been told to keep themselves ready for the beginning of the experiment.

With the cooperation of the Palo Alto City Police Department all of the subjects assigned to the prisoner treatment were unexpectedly 'arrested' at their residences. A police officer charged them with suspicion of burglary or armed robbery, advised them of their legal rights, handcuffed them, thoroughly searched them (often as curious neighbours looked on) and carried them off to the police station in the rear of a police car. At the station they went through the standard routines of being fingerprinted, having an identification file prepared and then being placed in a detention cell. Each prisoner was blindfolded and subsequently driven by one of the experimenters and a subject-guard to our mock prison. Throughout the entire arrest procedure, the police officers involved maintained a formal, serious attitude, avoiding answering any questions of clarification as to the relation of this 'arrest' to the mock prison study.

Upon arrival at our experimental prison, each prisoner was stripped, sprayed with a delousing preparation (a deodorant spray) and made to stand alone naked for a while in the cell yard. After being given the uniform described previously and having an ID picture taken ('mug shot'), the prisoner was put in his cell and ordered to remain silent.

Since 'arrests' were carried out by the *real* police (one wonders about the legality of their participation in this procedure), as far as the subjects knew these were real charges, especially since the officers did not answer questions about the connection between the arrest and the experiment. What were the subjects to think? How were they to know that the 'arrest' was no arrest; that the police had lent themselves to making these false accusations and to use force just to give more colour to the experiment?

The uniforms of the 'prisoners' were peculiar. They con-sisted of

loosely fitting muslin smocks with an identification number in front and back. No underclothes were worn beneath these 'dresses'. A light chain and lock were placed around one ankle. On their feet they wore rubber sandals and their hair was covered with a nylon stocking made into a cap . . . The prisoners' uniforms were designed not only to de-individuate the prisoners but to be humiliating and serve as symbols of their dependence and sub-servience. The ankle chain was a constant reminder (even during their sleep when it hit the other ankle) of the oppressiveness of the environment. The stocking cap removed any distinctiveness associated with hair length, colour or style (as does shaving of heads in some 'real' prisons and the military). The ill-fitting uni-forms made the prisoners feel awkward in their movements; since these dresses were worn without undergarments, the uniform forced them to assume unfamiliar postures, more like those of a woman than a man – another part of the emasculating process of becoming a prisoner.

What were the reactions of the prisoners and the guards to this situation during the six days of the experiment?

The most dramatic evidence of the impact of this situation upon the participants was seen in the gross reactions of five prisoners who had to be released because of extreme emotional depression, crying, rage and acute anxiety. The pattern of symptoms was quite similar in four of the subjects and began as early as the second day of imprisonment. The fifth subject was released after being treated for a psychosomatic rash which covered portions of his body. Of the remaining prisoners, only two said they were not willing to forfeit the money they had earned in return for being 'parolled'. When the experiment was terminated prematurely after only six days, all the remaining prisoners were delighted by their unexpected good fortune . . .

While the response of the prisoners is rather uniform and only different in degree, the response of the guards offers a more complex picture:

In contrast, most of the guards seemed to be distressed by the decision to stop the experiment and it appeared to us that they had become sufficiently involved in their roles so that they now enjoyed the extreme control and power which they exercised and were reluctant to give it up.

The authors describe the attitude of the 'guards':

None of the guards ever failed to come to work on time for their shift, and indeed, on several occasions guards remained on duty voluntarily and uncomplainingly for extra hours – without additional pay.

The extremely pathological reactions which emerged in both groups of subjects testify to the power of the social forces operating, but still there were individual differences seen in styles of coping with this novel experience and in degrees of successful adaptation to it. Half the prisoners did endure the oppressive atmosphere, and not all the guards resorted to hostility. Some guards were tough but fair ('played by the rules'), some went far beyond their roles to engage in creative cruelty and harassment, while a few were passive and rarely instigated any coercive control over the prisoners.

Regrettably we are not given any more precise information than 'some', 'some', 'a few'. This seems to be an unnecessary lack of precision when it should have been very easy to mention the exact numbers. This is all the more surprising since in the earlier communication in *Trans-Action* somewhat more precise and substantially different statements were made. The percentage of actively sadistic guards, 'quite inventive in their techniques of breaking the spirit of the prisoners', is estimated there as being about *one third*. The rest are divided among the two other categories which are described, respectively, as (1) being 'tough but fair' or (2) 'good guards from the prisoner's point of view since they did them small favours and were friendly'; this is a very different characterization from that of 'being passive and rarely instigating coercive control', as expressed in the later report.

Such descriptions indicate a certain lack of precision in the formulation of the data, which is all the more regrettable when it occurs in connection with the crucial thesis of the experiment. The authors believe it proves that the situation alone can within a few days transform normal people into abject, submissive individuals or into ruthless sadists. It seems to me that the experiment proves, if anything, rather the contrary. If in spite of the whole spirit of this mock prison which, according to the concept of the experiment was meant to be degrading and humiliating (obviously the guards must have caught on to this immediately), two thirds of the guards did not commit sadistic acts for personal 'kicks', the experiment seems rather to prove that one can *not* transform people so easily into sadists by providing them with the proper situation.

The difference between behaviour and character matters very much in this context. It is one thing to *behave* according to sadistic rules and another thing to want to be and to *enjoy* being cruel to people. The failure to make this distinction deprives this experiment of much of its value, as it also marred Milgram's experiment.

This distinction is also relevant for the other side of the thesis, namely that the battery of tests had shown that there was no predisposition among the subjects for sadistic or masochistic behaviour, that is to say, that the tests showed no sadistic or masochistic character traits. As far as psychologists are concerned, to whom manifest behaviour is the main datum, this conclusion may be quite correct. However, on the basis of psychoanalytic experience it is not very convincing. Character traits are often entirely unconscious and, furthermore, cannot be discovered by conventional psychological tests; as far as projective tests are concerned, such as the TAT or the Rorschach, only investigators with considerable experience in the study of unconscious processes will discover much unconscious material.

The data on the 'guards' are open to question for still another reason. These subjects were selected precisely because they represented more or less average, normal men, and they were found to be without sadistic predispositions. This result contradicts empirical evidence which shows that the percentage of unconscious sadists in an average population is not zero. Some studies (E. Fromm, 1936; E. Fromm and M. Maccoby, 1970) have shown this, and a skilled observer can detect it without the use of questionnaires or tests. But whatever the percentage of sadistic characters in a normal population may be, the complete absence of this category does not speak well for the aptness of the tests used with regard to this problem.

Some of the puzzling results of the experiment are probably to be explained by another factor. The authors state that the subjects had difficulty in distinguishing reality from the role they were playing, and assume this to be a result of the situation; this is indeed true, but the experimenters built this result into the experiment. In the first place the 'prisoners' were confused by several circumstances. The conditions they were told and under which they entered into the contract were drastically different from those they found. They could not possibly have expected to find themselves in a degrading and humiliating atmosphere. More important for the creation of the confusion is the cooperation of the police. Since it is most unusual for police authorities to lend themselves to such an experimental game, it was very difficult for the prisoners to appreciate the difference between reality and role-playing. The report shows that they did not even know whether their arrest had anything to do with the experiment, and the officers refused to answer their questions about this connection. Would not any average person be confused and enter the experiment with a sense of puzzlement, of having been tricked, and of helplessness?

Why did they not quit immediately, or after one or two days? The authors fail to give us a clear picture of what the 'prisoners' were told about the conditions for being released from the mock prison. At least I did not find any mention of their having ever been told that they had the right to quit if they found a continued stay intolerable. In fact, when some tried to break out the guards prevented them by force. It seems that they were given the impression that only the parole board could give them permission to leave. Yet the authors say:

One of the most remarkable incidents of the study occurred during a parole board hearing when each of five prisoners eligible for parole was asked by the senior author whether he would be willing to forfeit all the money earned as a prisoner if he were to be paroled (released from the study). Three of the five prisoners said, 'yes', they would be willing to do this. Notice that the original incentive for participating in the study had been the promise of money, and they were, after only four days, prepared to give this up completely. And, more surprisingly, when told that this possibility would have to be discussed with the members of the staff before a decision could be made, each prisoner got up quietly and was escorted by a guard back to his cell. If they regarded themselves simply as 'subjects' participating in an experiment for money, there was no longer any incentive to remain in the study and they could have easily escaped this situation which had so clearly become aversive for them by quitting. Yet, so powerful was the control which the situation had come to have over them, so much a reality had this simulated environment become, that they were unable to see that their original and singular motive for remaining no longer obtained, and they returned to their cells to await a 'parole' decision by their captors.

Could they have escaped the situation so easily? Why were they not told in this meeting: 'Those of you who want to quit are free to leave immediately, they will only forfeit the money.' If they had still stayed on after this announcement, indeed the authors' statement about their docility would have been justified. But by saying the 'possibility would have to be discussed with the members of the staff before a decision could be made' they were given the typical bureaucratic buck-passing answer; it implied that the prisoners had no *right* to leave.

Did the prisoners really 'know' that all this was an experiment? It depends on what 'knowing' means here and what the effects are on the prisoners' thinking processes if they are intentionally confused from the very beginning and do not know any longer what is what and who is who.

Aside from its lack of precision and the lack of a self-critical evaluation of the results, the experiment suffers from another failure: that of checking its results with real prison situations of the same type. Are most prisoners in the worst type of American prison slavishly docile, and are most guards brutal sadists? The authors cite only one ex-convict and a prison priest as evidence for the thesis that the results of the mock prison correspond to those found in real prisons. Since it is a crucial question for the main thesis of the experiments, they should have gone much further in establishing comparisons – for instance, by systematic interviews with many ex-prisoners. Also, instead of simply speaking of 'prisons', they should have presented more precise data on the percentage of prisons in the United States that correspond to the degrading type of prison they tried to duplicate.

The failure of the authors to check their conclusions with a realistic situation is particularly regrettable since there is ample material at hand dealing with a prison situation far more brutal than that of the worst American prisons – Hitler's concentration camps.

As far as the spontaneous cruelty of SS guards is concerned, the question has not been systematically studied. In my own limited efforts to secure data on the incidence of spontaneous sadism of the guards – i.e., sadistic behaviour going beyond the prescribed routine and motivated by individual sadistic lust – I have received estimates from former prisoners ranging from 10 to 90 per cent, the lower estimates more often coming from former political prisoners.[12] To establish the facts it would be necessary to undertake a thorough study of the sadism of guards in the Nazi concen-

12. Personal communications from H. Brandt and Professor H. Simonson – both of whom spent many years in concentration camps as political prisoners – and others who preferred not to be mentioned by name. cf. also H. Brandt (1970).

tration camp system; such a study might use several approaches. For example:

1. Systematic interviews with former concentration camp inmates – relating their statement to their age, reason for arrest, duration of imprisonment, and other relevant data – and similar interviews with former concentration camp guards.[13]

2. 'Indirect' data, such as the following: the system used, at least in 1939, to 'break' new prisoners during the long train trip to the concentration camp, such as inflicting severe physical pain (beatings, bayonet wounds), hunger, extreme humiliations. The SS guards executed these sadistic orders, showing no mercy whatsoever. Later, however, when the prisoners were transported by train from one camp to another nobody touched these by now 'old prisoners' (B. Bettelheim, 1960). If the guards had wanted to amuse themselves by sadistic behaviour, they certainly could have done so without fearing any punishment.[14] That this did not occur frequently might lead to certain conclusions about the individual sadism of the guards. As far as the attitude of the prisoners is concerned, the data from concentration camps tend to disprove Haney, Banks, and Zimbardo's main thesis, which postulates that individual values, ethics, convictions do not make any difference as far as the compelling influence of the environment is concerned. On the contrary, differences in the attitude, respectively, of apolitical, middle-class prisoners (mostly Jews) and prisoners with a genuine political conviction or religious conviction or both demonstrate that the values and convictions of prisoners do make a critical difference in the reaction to conditions of the concentration camp that are common to all of them.

13. I know from Dr J. M. Steiner that he is preparing a study based on such interviews for the press; this promises to be an important contribution.

14. At that time a guard had to submit a written report only when he had killed a prisoner.

Bruno Bettelheim has given a most vivid and profound analysis of this difference:

Non-political middle class prisoners (a minority group in the concentration camps) were those least able to withstand the initial shock. They were utterly unable to understand what had happened to them and why. More than ever they clung to what had given them self respect up to that moment. Even while being abused, they would assure the SS they had never opposed Nazism. They could not understand why they, who had always obeyed the law without question, were being persecuted. Even now, although unjustly imprisoned, they dared not oppose their oppressors even in thought, though it would have given them a self respect they were badly in need of. All they could do was plead, and many grovelled. Since law and police had to remain beyond reproach, they accepted as just whatever the Gestapo did. Their only objection was that *they* had become objects of a persecution which in itself must be just, since the authorities imposed it. They rationalized their difficulty by insisting it was all a 'mistake'. The SS made fun of them, mistreating them badly, while at the same time enjoying scenes that emphasized the position of superiority. The prisoner group as a whole was especially anxious that their middle class status should be respected in some way. What upset them most was being treated 'like ordinary criminals'.

Their behaviour showed how little the apolitical German middle class was able to hold its own against National Socialism. No consistent philosophy, either moral, political, or social, protected their integrity or gave them strength for an inner stand against Nazism. They had little or no resources to fall back on when subject to the shock of imprisonment. Their self esteem had rested on a status and respect that came with their positions, depended on their jobs, on being head of a family, or similar external factors . . .

Nearly all of them lost their desirable middle class characteristics, such as their sense of propriety and self respect. They became shiftless, and developed to an exaggerated extent the undesirable characteristics of their group: pettiness, quarrelsomeness, self pity. Many became chisellers and stole from other prisoners. (Stealing from, or cheating the SS was often considered as honourable as stealing from prisoners was thought despicable.) They seemed incapable of following a life pattern of their own any more, but copied those developed by other groups of prisoners. Some followed the behaviour pattern set by the criminals. Only very few adopted the ways of political prisoners, usually the most desirable of all patterns, questionable as it was. Others tried to do in prison what they preferred to do outside of it, namely to submit without question to the ruling group. A few tried to attach themselves to the upper class prisoners and emulate their behaviour. Many more tried to submit slavishly to the SS, some even turning spy in their service (which, apart from these few, only some criminals did). This was no help to them either, because the Gestapo liked the betrayal but despised the traitor. (B. Bettelheim, 1960)

Bettelheim has given here a penetrating analysis of the sense of identity and self-esteem of the average member of the middle class: his social position, his prestige, his power to command are the props on which his self-esteem rests. If these props are taken away, he collapses morally like a deflated balloon. Bettelheim shows *why* these people were demoralized and why many of them became abject slaves and even spies for the SS. One important element among the causes for this transformation must be stressed; these non-political prisoners could not grasp the situation; they could not understand why they were in the concentration camp, because they were caught in their conventional belief that only 'criminals' are punished – and *they* were not criminals. This lack of understanding and the resulting confusion contributed considerably to their collapse.

The *political* and *religious* prisoners reacted entirely differently to the same conditions.

For those *political* prisoners who had expected persecution by the SS, imprisonment was less of a shock because they were physically prepared for it. They resented their fate, but somehow accepted it as something that fit their understanding of the course of events. While understandably and correctly anxious about their future and what might happen to their families and friends, they certainly saw no reason to feel degraded by the fact of imprisonment, though they suffered under camp conditions as much as other prisoners.

As conscientious objectors, all *Jehovah's Witnesses* were sent to the camps. They were even less affected by imprisonment and kept their integrity thanks to rigid religious beliefs. Since their only crime in the eyes of the S S was a refusal to bear arms, they were frequently offered freedom in return for military service. They steadfastly refused.

Members of this group were generally narrow in outlook and experience, wanting to make converts, but on the other hand exemplary comrades, helpful, correct, dependable. They were argumentative, even quarrelsome only when someone questioned their religious beliefs. Because of their conscientious work habits, they were often selected as foremen. But once a foreman, and having accepted an order from the S S, they insisted that prisoners do the work well and in the time allotted. Even though they were the only group of prisoners who never abused or mistreated other prisoners (on the contrary, they were usually quite courteous to fellow prisoners), S S officers preferred them as orderlies because of their work habits, skills, and unassuming attitudes. Quite in contrast to the continuous internecine warfare among the other prisoner groups, the Jehovah's Witnesses never misused their closeness to S S officers to gain positions of privilege in the camp. (B. Bettelheim, 1960)

Even if Bettelheim's description of the political prisoners is very sketchy[15] he makes it quite clear nevertheless that those concentration camp inmates who had a conviction and believed in it reacted to the same circumstances in an entirely different way from the prisoners who had no such convictions. This fact contradicts the behaviourist thesis Haney *et al.* tried to prove with their experiment.

One cannot help raising the question about the value of such 'artificial' experiments, when there is so much material available for 'natural' experiments. This question suggests itself all the more because experiments of this type not only lack the alleged accuracy which is supposed to make them preferable to natural experiments, but also because the artificial set-up tends to distort the whole experimental situation as compared with one in 'real life'.

What is meant here by 'real life'?

It would perhaps be better to explain the term by a few

15. For a much fuller description see H. Brandt (1970).

examples than by a formal definition that would raise philosophical and epistemological questions whose discussion would take us far away from the main line of our thought.

In 'war games' a certain number of soldiers are declared to have been 'killed' and guns 'destroyed'. They are, according to the rules of the game, but this has no consequences for them as persons, or as things; the 'dead' soldier enjoys his short rest, the 'destroyed' cannon will go on serving its purpose. The worst fate for the losing side would be that its commanding general might be handicapped in his further career. In other words, what happens in the war game does not affect anything in the realistic situation of most of those involved.

Games played for money are another case in point. Most people who bet on cards, roulette, or the horses are very aware of the borderline between 'game' and 'reality'; they play only for amounts whose loss does not seriously affect their economic situation, i.e., has no serious consequences.

A minority, the real 'gamblers', will risk amounts whose loss would, indeed, affect their economic situation up to the point of ruin. But the 'gambler' does not really 'play a game'; he is involved in a very realistic, often dramatic form of living. The same 'game-reality' concept holds true for a sport like fencing; neither of the two persons involved risks his life. If the situation is constructed in such a way that he does, we speak of a duel, not of a game.[16]

If in psychological experiments the 'subjects' were clearly aware that the whole situation is only a game, everything would be simple. But in many experiments, as in that of Milgram, they are misinformed and lied to; as for the prison experiment it was set up in such a way that the awareness that everything was only an experiment would be mini-

16. M. Maccoby's studies on the significance of the game attitude in the social character of Americans has sharpened my awareness of the dynamics of the 'game' attitude. (M. Maccoby, to be published soon. See also M. Maccoby, 1972.)

mized or lost. The very fact that many of these experiments, in order to be undertaken at all, must operate with fakery demonstrates this peculiar unreality; the participants' sense of reality is confused and their critical judgement greatly reduced.[17]

In 'real life' the person knows that his behaviour will have consequences. A person may have a fantasy of wanting to kill somebody, but only rarely does the fantasy lead to deeds. Many express these fantasies in dreams because in the state of sleep fantasies have no consequences. Experiments in which the subjects lack a complete feeling of reality may cause reactions that represent unconscious tendencies, rather than show how the subject would behave in reality.[18] Whether an event is real or a game is of decisive importance for still another reason. It is well known that a *real* danger tends to mobilize 'emergency energy' to deal with it, often to an extent that the person involved would never have thought of himself as having the required physical strength, skill, or endurance. But this emergency energy is mobilized only when the whole organism is confronted with a real danger, and for good neurophysiological reasons; dangers the person daydreams about do not stimulate the organism in this way, but only lead to fear and worry. The same principle holds true not only for emergency reactions in face of danger, but for the difference between fantasy and reality in many other respects, as for instance the mobilization of moral inhibitions and reactions of conscience which

17. They remind one of an essential feature of TV commercials, in which an atmosphere is created that confuses the difference between fantasy and reality, and which lends itself to the suggestive influence of the 'message'. The viewer 'knows' that the use of a certain soap will not bring about a miraculous change in his life, yet simultaneously another part of him does believe this. Instead of deciding what is real and what is fiction, he continues to think in the twilight of non-differentiation between reality and illusion.

18. For this reason an occasional murderous dream only permits the qualitative statement that such impulses exist, but no quantitative statement about their intensity. Only their frequent recurrence would permit also quantitative analysis.

fail to be aroused when the whole situation is not felt to be real.

In addition, the role of the experimenter must be considered in laboratory experiments of this type. He presides over a fictitious reality constructed and controlled by him. In a certain sense *he* represents reality for the subject and for this reason his influence is a hypnoid one akin to that of a hypnotist towards his subject. The experimenter relieves the subject, to some extent, of his responsibility and of his own will, and hence makes him much more prone to obey the rules than the subject would be in a non-hypnoid situation.

Finally, the difference between the mock prisoners and real prisoners is so great that it is virtually impossible to draw valid analogies from observation of the former. For a prisoner who has been sent to prison for a certain action, the situation is very real; he knows the reasons (whether his punishment is just or not is another problem); he knows his helplessness and the few rights he has, he knows his chances for an earlier release. Whether a man knows that he is to stay in prison (even under the worst conditions) for two weeks or two months or two years or twenty years obviously is a decisive factor that influences his attitude. This factor alone is critical for his hopelessness, demoralization, and sometimes (although exceptionally) for the mobilization of new energies – with benign or malignant aims. Furthermore, a prisoner is not 'a prisoner'. Prisoners are individuals and they react individually according to the differences in their respective character structures. But this does not imply that their reaction is *only* a function of their character and not one of their environment. It is merely naïve to assume that it must be either this or that. The complex and challenging problem in each individual – and group – is to find out what the specific interaction is between a given character structure and a given social structure. It is at this point that real investigation begins, and it is only stifled by the assumption that the situation is the one factor which explains human behaviour.

The Frustration-Aggression Theory

There are many other behaviouristically oriented studies of aggression;[19] none, however, develops a general theory of the origins of aggression and violence, with the exception of the frustration-aggression theory developed by J. Dollard *et al.* (1939), which claims to have found the cause of all aggression. More specifically, that 'the occurrence of aggressive behaviour always presupposes the existence of frustration and contrariwise, the existence of frustration always leads to some form of aggression' (J. Dollard *et al.*, 1939). Two years later one of the authors, N. E. Miller, dropped the second part of the hypothesis, allowing that frustration could instigate a number of different types of responses, only one of them being aggression (N. E. Miller, 1941).

This theory was, according to Buss, accepted by practically all psychologists, with very few exceptions. Buss himself comes to the critical conclusion that 'the emphasis on frustration has led to an unfortunate neglect of the other large class of antecedents (noxious stimuli) as well as the neglect of aggression as an instrumental response. Frustration is only one antecedent of aggression and it is not the most potent one' (A. H. Buss, 1961).

A thorough discussion of the frustration-aggression theory is impossible within the framework of this book because of the extent of the literature which would have to be dealt with.[20] I shall restrict myself in the following to a few basic points.

The simplicity of the original formulation of the theory is greatly marred by the ambiguity of what is understood by

19. cf. an excellent survey of psychological studies on violence (E. I. Megargee, 1969).

20. Among the most significant discussions of the frustration-aggression theory to be mentioned, aside from A. H. Buss's work, is L. Berkowitz's 'Frustration-Aggression Hypothesis Revisited' (1969). Berkowitz is critical, yet on the whole, positive; and he cites a number of the more recent experiments.

frustration. Basically there are two meanings in which the term has been understood: (a) The interruption of an on-going, goal-directed activity. (Examples would be a boy with his hand in the cooky jar, when mother enters and makes him stop; or a sexually aroused person, interrupted in the act of coitus.) (b) Frustration as the negation of a desire or wish – 'deprivation', according to Buss. (Examples, the boy who asks mother to give him a cooky and she refuses; or a man propositions a woman and is rejected.)

One reason for the ambiguity of the term 'frustration' lies in that Dollard *et al.* have not expressed themselves with the necessary clarity. Another reason lies probably in that the word 'frustration' is popularly used in the second sense, and that psychoanalytic thinking has also contributed to this usage. (For instance, a child's wish for love is 'frustrated' by his mother.)

Depending on the meaning of frustration, we deal with two entirely different theories. Frustration in the first sense would be relatively rare because it requires that the intended activity has already begun. It would not be frequent enough to explain all or even a considerable part of aggression. At the same time the explanation of aggression as the result of the interruption of an activity may be the only sound part of the theory. To prove or disprove it, new neuro-physiological data may be of decisive value.

On the other hand, the theory which is based on the second meaning of frustration does not seem to stand up against the weight of the empirical evidence. First of all, we might consider a basic fact of life: that nothing important is achieved without accepting frustration. The idea that one can learn without effort, i.e., without frustration, may be good as an advertising slogan, but is certainly not true in the acquisition of major skills. Without the capacity to accept frustration man would hardly have developed at all. And does not everyday observation show that many times people suffer frustrations without having an aggressive response? What can, and often does, produce aggression is what the frustration *means* to the person, and the psychological meaning of frustration differs according to the total constellation in which the frustration occurs.

If a child, for instance, is forbidden to eat candy, this frustration, provided the parent's attitude is genuinely loving and free from pleasure in controlling, will not mobilize aggression; but if this prohibition is only one of many manifestations of the parent's desire for control, or if, for instance, a sibling is permitted to eat it, considerable anger is likely to be the result. What produces the aggression is not the frustration as such, but the injustice or rejection involved in the situation.

The most important factor in determining the occurrence and intensity of frustration is the *character* of a person. A very greedy person, for instance, will react angrily when he does not get all the food he wants, and a miserly person, when his wish to buy something cheap is frustrated; the narcissistic person feels frustrated when he does not get the praise and recognition he expects. The character of the person determines in the first place *what* frustrates him, and in the second place the *intensity* of his reaction to frustration.

Valuable as many of the behaviouristically oriented psychological studies on aggression are in terms of their own goals, they have not resulted in the formulation of a global hypothesis on the causes of violent aggression. 'Few of the studies that we examined', concludes Megargee in his excellent survey of the psychological literature, 'attempted to test theories of human violence. Those empirical studies which did focus on violence *were generally not designed to test theories*. Investigations that did focus on important theoretical issues generally investigated milder aggressive behaviour or used infra-human subjects' (E. I. Megargee, 1969; italics added). Considering the brilliance of the investigators, the means for research at their disposal, and the number of students eager to excel in scientific work, these meagre results seem to confirm the assumption that behaviouristic psychology does not lend itself to the development of a systematic theory concerning the sources of violent aggression.

3
Instinctivism and Behaviourism: Their Differences and Similarities

A Common Ground

The man of the instinctivists lives the past of the species, as the man of the behaviourists lives the present of his social system. The former is a machine that can only produce inherited patterns of the past; the latter is a machine[1] that can only produce social patterns of the present. Instinctivism and behaviourism have one basic premise in common: that man has no psyche with its own structure and its own laws.

For instinctivism in Lorenz's sense the same holds true; this has been formulated most radically by one of Lorenz's former students, Paul Leyhausen. He criticizes those psychologists dealing with humans (*Humanpsychologen*) who claim that anything psychic can only be explained psychologically, i.e., on the basis of psychological premises. (The 'only' is a slight distortion of their position for the sake of a better argument.) Leyhausen claims that, on the contrary,

If there is an area where we certainly can *not* find the explanation for psychic events and experiences, it is the area of the psyche itself; this is so for the same reason that we cannot find an explanation for digestion in the digestive processes, but in those special ecological conditions that existed about a billion years ago. These conditions exposed a number of organisms to selective pressures which made them assimilate not only inorganic food-

1. In H. von Foerster's (1970) sense of a 'trivial machine'.

stuffs, but also those of an organic nature. In the same way psychical processes are also achievements which have come about as a result of selective pressures of life – and species – preserving value. Their explanation is in every sense pre-psychological ... (K. Lorenz, P. Leyhausen, 1968; my translation)

Put in simpler language, Leyhausen maintains that one can explain psychological data by the evolutionary process alone. The crucial point here is what is meant by 'explain'. If, for instance, one wants to know how the effect of fear is *possible* as the result of the evolution of the brain from the lowest to the highest animals, then this is a task for those scientists who investigate the evolution of the brain. However, if one wants to explain *why* a person is frightened, the data on evolution will not contribute much to the answer: the explanation must be essentially a psychological one. Perhaps the person is threatened by a stronger enemy, or is coping with his own repressed aggression, or suffers from a sense of powerlessness, or a paranoid element in him makes him feel persecuted, or – many other factors that alone or in combination may explain his fright. To want to explain the fright of a particular person by an evolutionary process is plainly futile.

Leyhausen's premise, that the only approach to the study of human phenomena is the evolutionary one, means that we understand the psychical process in man exclusively by knowing how, in the process of evolution, he became what he is. Similarly, he suggests that digestive processes are to be explained in terms of conditions as they existed millions of years ago. Could a physician dealing with disturbances of the digestive tract help his patient if he were concerned with the evolution of digestion, rather than with the causes of the particular symptom in this particular patient? For Leyhausen evolution becomes the only science, and absorbs all other sciences dealing with man. Lorenz, as far as I know, never formulated this principle so drastically, but his theory is built on the same premise. He claims that man understands himself only and *sufficiently* if he understands the evolutionary process which made him become what he is now.[2]

In spite of the great differences between instinctivistic and behaviouristic theory, they have a common basic orientation. They both exclude the *person*, the behaving man, from their field of vision. Whether man is the product of conditioning, or the product of animal evolution, he is exclusively determined by conditions outside himself; he has no part in his own life, no responsibility, and not even a trace of freedom. Man is a puppet, controlled by strings – instinct or conditioning.

More Recent Views

In spite of – or perhaps because of – the facts that instinctivists and behaviourists share certain similarities in their respective pictures of man and in their philosophical orientation, they have fought each other with a remarkable fanaticism. 'Nature *or* nurture', 'instinct *or* environment' became flags around which each side rallied, refusing to see any common ground.

In recent years there has been a growing tendency to overcome the sharp alternatives of the instinctivist-behaviourist war. One solution was to change the terminology; some tended to reserve the term 'instinct' for the lower animals and to speak instead of 'organic drives' when discussing human motivations. In this way some developed such formulations as 'most of man's behaviour is learned, whereas most of a bird's behaviour is not learned' (W. C. Alee, H. W. Nissen, M. F. Nimkoff, 1953). This latter formulation is characteristic of the new trend to replace the

2. The Lorenz–Leyhausen position has its parallel in a distorted form of psychoanalysis which assumes that psychoanalysis is identical with the understanding of the patient's history without the necessity of understanding the dynamics of the psychic process as it is at present.

old 'either-or' by a 'more-or-less' formulation, thus taking account of gradual change in the weight of the respective factors. The model for this view is a continuum, on the one end of which is (almost) complete innate determination, on the other end (almost) complete learning.

F. A. Beach, an outstanding opponent of instinctivistic theory, writes:

Perhaps a more serious weakness in the present psychological handling of instinct lies in the assumption that a two-class system is adequate for the classification of complex behaviour. The implication that all behaviour must be determined by learning or by heredity, neither of which is more than partially understood, is entirely unjustified. The final form of any response is affected by a multiplicity of variables, only two of which are genetical and experiential factors. It is to the identification and analysis of all these factors that psychology should address itself. When this task is properly conceived and executed there will be no need nor reason for ambiguous concepts of instinctive behaviour. (F. A. Beach, 1955)

In a similar vein, N. R. F. Maier and T. C. Schneirla write:

Because learning plays a more important role in the behaviour of higher than in the behaviour of lower forms, the natively determined behaviour patterns of higher forms become much more extensively modified by experience than those of lower forms. It is through such modification that the animal may become adjusted to different environments and escape from the narrow bounds the optimum condition imposes. Higher forms are therefore less dependent upon specific external environmental conditions for survival than are lower forms.

Because of the interaction of acquired and innate factors in behaviour it is impossible to classify many behaviour patterns. Each type of behaviour must be separately investigated. (N. R. F. Maier and T. C. Schneirla, 1964)

The position taken in this book is in some respects close to that of the authors just mentioned and others who refuse to continue fighting under the flags of 'instincts' versus 'learning'. However, as I shall show in Part Three, the more important problem from the standpoint of this study is the difference between 'organic drives' (food, fight, flight, sexuality – formerly called 'instincts'), whose function it is to guarantee the survival of the individual and the species, and 'non-organic drives' (character-rooted passions),[3] which are not phylogenetically programmed and are not common to all men: the desire for love and freedom; destructiveness, narcissism, sadism, masochism.

Often these non-organic drives that form man's second nature are confused with organic drives. A case in point is the sexual drive. It is a psychoanalytically well-established observation that often the intensity of what is subjectively felt as sexual desire (including its corresponding physiological manifestations) is due to non-sexual passions such as narcissism, sadism, masochism, the wish for power, and even anxiety, loneliness, and boredom.

For a narcissistic male, for instance, the sight of a woman may be sexually exciting because he is excited by the possibility of proving to himself how attractive he is. Or a sadistic person may be sexually excited by the chance to conquer a woman (or, as the case may be, a man) and to control her or him. Many people are bound for years to each other emotionally just by this motive, especially when the sadism of one fits the masochism of the other. It is rather well known that fame, power, and wealth makes its possessor sexually attractive if certain physical conditions are present. In all these instances the physical desire is mobilized by non-sexual passions which thus find their satisfaction. Indeed, it is anybody's guess how many children owe their existence to vanity, sadism, and masochism, rather than to genuine physical attraction, not to speak of love. But people, especially men, prefer to think

3. 'Non-organic' does not mean, of course, that they have no neuro-physiological substrate, but that they are not initiated by, nor do they serve organic needs.

that they are 'over-sexed' rather than that they are 'over vain'.[4]

The same phenomenon has been clinically studied minutely in cases of compulsive eating. This symptom is not motivated by 'physiological' but by 'psychic' hunger, engendered by the feeling of being depressed, anxious, 'empty'.

My thesis – to be demonstrated in the following chapters – is that destructiveness and cruelty are not instinctual drives, but passions rooted in the total existence of man. They are one of the ways to make sense of life; they are not and could not be present in the animal, because they are by their very nature rooted in the 'human condition'. The main error of Lorenz and other instinctivists is to have confused the two kinds of drives, those rooted in *instinct*, and those rooted in *character*. A sadistic person who waits for the occasion, as it were, to express his sadism, looks as if he fitted the hydraulic model of a dammed-up instinct. But only people with a sadistic character wait for the opportunity to behave sadistically, just as people with a loving character wait for the opportunity to express their love.

The Political and Social Background of Both Theories

It is instructive to examine in some detail the social and political background of the war between the environmentalists and the instinctivists.

The environmental theory is characterized by the spirit of the political revolution of the middle classes in the eighteenth century against feudal privileges. Feudalism had rested on the assumption that its order was a *natural* one; in the battle against this 'natural' order, which the middle classes wanted to overthrow, one was prone to arrive at the

4. This is particularly clear in the phenomenon of 'machismo', the virtue of maleness (A. Aramoni, 1965; cf. also, E. Fromm and M. Maccoby, 1970).

theory that the status of a person was not at all dependent on any innate or natural factors, but that it depended entirely on social arrangements, the improvement of which was the task of the revolution. No vice or stupidity was to be explained as being due to human nature as such, but to the bad and vicious arrangements of society: hence there was no obstacle to an absolute optimism in the future of man.

While environmentalist theory was thus closely related to the revolutionary hopes of the rising middle classes in the eighteenth century, the instinctivist movement based on Darwin's teaching reflects the basic assumption of nineteenth-century capitalism. Capitalism as a system in which harmony is created by ruthless competition between all individuals would appear to be a *natural* order if one could prove that the most complex and remarkable phenomenon, man, is a product of the ruthless competition among all living beings since the emergence of life. The development of life from monocellular organisms to man would seem to be the most splendid example of free enterprise, in which the best win through competition and those who are not fit to survive in the progressing economic system are eliminated.[5]

The reasons for the victorious anti-instinctivistic revolution, led by K. Dunlap, Zing Yang Kuo, and L. Bernard in the 1920s, may be seen in the difference between the capitalism of the twentieth century and that of the nineteenth. I shall mention only a few points of difference which are relevant here. Nineteenth-century capitalism was one of fierce competition among capitalists which led to the elimination of the weaker and less efficient among them. In twentieth-century capitalism, the element of competition has to some extent given way to cooperation among the big enterprises. Hence the proof that fierce competition cor-

5. This historical interpretation has nothing to do with the validity of Darwinian theory, although perhaps it has to do with the neglect of some facts like the role of cooperation and with the popularity of the theory.

responded to a law of nature was no longer needed. Another important point of difference lies in the change of the method of control. In nineteenth-century capitalism, control was largely based on the exercise of strict patriarchal principles, morally supported by the authority of God and king. Cybernetic capitalism, with its gigantic centralized enterprises and its capacity to provide the workers with amusements *and* bread, is able to maintain control by psychological manipulation and human engineering. It needs a man who is very malleable and easily influenced, rather than one whose 'instincts' are controlled by fear of authority. Finally, contemporary industrial society has a different vision of the aim of life than that of the last century. At that time the ideal – at least for the middle classes – was independence, private initiative, to be 'the captain of my ship'. The contemporary vision, however, is that of un-limited consumption and unlimited control over nature. Men are fired by the dream that one day they will completely control nature and thus be like God; why should there be anything in *human* nature that cannot be controlled?

But if behaviourism expresses the mood of the twentieth-century industrialism, how can we explain the revival of instinctivism in the writings of Lorenz and its popularity among the broad public? As I have pointed out, one reason for this is the sense of fear and hopelessness that pervades many people because of the ever-increasing dangers and that nothing is done to avert them. Many who had faith in pro-gress and had hoped for basic changes in man's fate, instead of carefully analysing the social process which led to their disillusionment, are taking refuge in the explanation that man's nature must be responsible for this failure. Finally, there are the personal and political biases of the authors who become spokesmen for the new instinctivism.

Some writers in this field are only dimly aware of the political and philosophical implications of their respective theories. Nor have the connections found much attention among the commentators on these theories. But there are exceptions. N. Pastore (1949) compared the sociopolitical views of twenty-four psychologists, biologists, and sociologists concerning the nature–nurture problem. Among the twelve 'liberals', or radicals, eleven were environmentalists and one a hereditarian; among the twelve 'conservatives', eleven were hereditarians and one an environmentalist. Even considering the small number of persons involved, this result is quite telling.

Other authors are aware of the emotional implications, but usually only of those in the hypotheses of their opponents. A good example of this one-sided awareness is a statement by one of the most distinguished representatives of orthodox psychoanalysis, R. Waelder:

> I am referring to a group of critics who either were outright Marxists or at least belonged to that branch of Western liberal tradition of which Marxism itself was an offshoot, i.e., the school of thought which passionately believed that man is 'good' by nature and whatever ills and evils there are in human affairs are due to rotten institutions – perhaps to the institution of private property or, in a more recent and more moderate version, to a so-called 'neurotic culture' . . .
>
> But whether evolutionist or revolutionary, whether moderate or radical or of one-track mind, no believer in the fundamental goodness of man and in the exclusive responsibility of external causes for human suffering could help being disturbed by a theory of an instinct of destruction or a death instinct. For if this theory is true, potentialities for conflict and for suffering are inherent in human affairs, and attempts to abolish or mitigate suffering appear to be, if not hopeless undertakings, at least far more complicated ones than the social revolutionaries had fancied them to be. (R. Waelder, 1956)

Penetrating as Waelder's remarks are, it is nevertheless noteworthy that he only sees the bias of the anti-instinctivists and not of those who share his own position.

4

The Psychoanalytic Approach to the Understanding of Aggression

Does the *psychoanalytic approach* offer a method for understanding aggression that avoids the shortcomings both of the behaviouristic and the instinctivistic approaches? At first glance, it seems as if psychoanalysis not only has avoided their shortcomings, but that it is afflicted, in fact, by a combination of them. Psychoanalytic theory is at the same time instinctivistic[1] in its general theoretical concepts and environmentalistic in its therapeutic orientation.

That Freud's theory[2] is instinctivistic, explaining human behaviour as the result of the struggle between the instinct for self-preservation and the sexual instinct (and in his later theory between the life and death instincts) is too well known to require any documentation. The environmentalist framework can also be easily recognized when one considers that analytic therapy attempts to explain the development of a person by the specific environmental constellation of infancy, i.e., the impact of the family. This aspect, however, is reconciled with instinctivism by the assumption that the modifying influence of the environment occurs via the influence of the libidinous structure.

In practice, however, patients, the public, and frequently analysts themselves pay only lip service to the specific vicissitudes of the sexual instincts (very often these vicissitudes are reconstructed on the basis of 'evidence' which in itself is

1. Freud's use of the term *Trieb*, which is usually translated 'instinct', refers to instinct in a wider sense, as a somatically rooted drive, impelling but not strictly determining consummatory behaviour.

2. A detailed analysis of the development of Freud's theory of aggression is to be found in the Appendix.

often a construction based on the system of theoretical expectations) and take a totally environmentalistic position. Their axiom is that every negative development in the patient is to be understood as the result of damaging influences in early childhood. This has led sometimes to irrational self-accusation on the part of parents who feel guilty for every undesirable or pathological trait that appears in a child after birth, and to a tendency of people in analysis to put the blame for all their troubles on their parents, and to avoid confronting themselves with the problem of their own responsibility.

In the light of all this, it would seem legitimate for psychologists to classify psychoanalysis as *theory* under the category of instinctivistic theories, and thus their argument against Lorenz is *eo ipso* an argument against psychoanalysis. But caution is necessary here; the question is: How should one define psychoanalysis? Is it the sum total of Freud's theories, or can we distinguish between the original and creative and the accidental, time-conditioned parts of the system, a distinction that can be made in the work of all great pioneers of thought? If such a distinction is legitimate, we must ask whether the libido theory belongs to the core of Freud's work or whether it is simply the form in which he organized his new insights because there was no other way to think of and to express his basic findings, given his philosophical and scientific environment (E. Fromm, 1970a).

Freud himself never claimed that the libido theory was a scientific certainty. He called it 'our mythology', and replaced it with the theory of the Eros and death 'instincts'. It is equally significant that he defined psychoanalysis as a theory based on resistance and transference – and by omission, not on the libido theory.

But perhaps more important than Freud's own statements is to keep in mind what gave his discoveries their unique historical significance. Surely it could not have been the instinctivistic theory as such; instinct theories had been quite popular since the nineteenth century. That he singled out the *sexual* instinct as the source of all passions (aside from the instinct for self-preservation) was, of course, new and revolutionary at a time still ruled by Victorian middle-class morality. But even this special version of the instinct theory would probably not have made such a powerful and lasting impact. It seems to me that what gave Freud his historical significance was the discovery of unconscious processes, not philosophically or speculatively, but empirically, as he demonstrated in some of his case histories, and most of all in his fundamental opus, *The Interpretation of Dreams* (1900). If it can be shown, for instance, that consciously peaceful and conscientious man has powerful impulses to kill, it is a secondary question whether one explains these impulses as being derived from his 'Oedipal' hate against his father, as a manifestation of his death instinct, as a result of his wounded narcissism, or as due to other reasons. Freud's revolution was to make us recognize the unconscious aspect of man's mind and the energy which he uses to repress the awareness of undesirable desires. Freud showed that good intentions mean nothing if they cover up the unconscious desires; he unmasked 'honest' dishonesty by demonstrating that it is not enough to have 'meant' well *consciously*. He was the first scientist to explore the depth, the underworld in man, and that is why his ideas had such an impact on artists and writers at a time when most psychiatrists still refused to take his theories seriously.

But Freud went further. He not only showed that forces operate in man of which he is not aware and that rationalizations protect him from awareness; he also explained that these unconscious forces are integrated in a system to which he gave the name 'character' in a new, dynamic sense.[3]

3. Freud's theory of character can be understood more easily on the basis of 'system theory' which began to develop in the 1920s and has greatly furthered the thinking in some natural sciences, such as biology and neurophysiology and some aspects of sociology. The failure to com-

Freud began to develop this concept in his first paper on the 'anal character' (S. Freud, 1908). Certain behaviour traits, such as stubbornness, orderliness, and parsimony, he pointed out, were more often than not to be found together as a syndrome of traits. Furthermore, wherever that syndrome existed, one could find peculiarities in the sphere of toilet training and in the vicissitudes of sphincter control and in certain behavioural traits related to bowel movements and faeces. Thus Freud's first step was to discover a syndrome of behavioural traits and to relate them to the way the child acted (in part as a response to certain demands by those who trained him) in the sphere of bowel movements. His brilliant and creative next step was to relate these two sets of behavioural patterns by a theoretical consideration based on a previous assumption about the evolution of the libido. This assumption was that during an early phase of childhood development, after the mouth has ceased to be the main organ of lust and satisfaction, the anus becomes an important erogenous zone, and most libidinal wishes are centred around the process of the retention and evacuation of the excrements. His conclusion was to explain the syndrome of behavioural traits as sublimation of, or reaction formation against, the libidinous satisfaction or frustration of anality. Stubbornness and parsimony were supposed to be the sublimation of the original refusal to give up the pleasure of retaining the stool; orderliness, the reaction formation against the original desire of the infant to evacuate whenever he pleased. Freud showed that the three original traits of the syndrome, which until then had appeared to be quite unrelated to each other, formed part of a

---

prehend systemic thinking may very well be responsible for the lack of understanding of Freud's characterology as well as of Marx's sociology, which is based on viewing society as a system. P. Weiss presented a general system of theory of animal behaviour (P. Weiss, 1925). In two recent papers he has given a brief and succinct picture of his views on the nature of the system which is the best introduction to the subject I know (P. Weiss, 1967, 1970). cf. also L. von Bertalanffy (1968) and C. W. Churchman (1968).

structure, or system, because they were all rooted in the same source of anal libido which manifests itself in these traits, either directly or by reaction formation or by sublimation. In this way Freud was able to explain why these traits are charged with energy and, in fact, very resistant to change.[4]

One of the most important additions was the concept of the 'oral-sadistic' character (the exploitative character, in my terms). There are other concepts of character formation, depending on what aspects one wants to stress: such as the authoritarian[5] (sado-masochistic) character, the rebellious and the revolutionary character, the narcissistic and the incestuous character. These latter concepts, most of which do not form part of classic psychoanalytic thinking, are related to each other and overlap; by combining them one can get a still fuller description of a certain character.

Freud's theoretical explanation for character structure was the notion that the libido (oral, anal, genital) was the source that gave energy to the various character traits. But even if one discounts the libido theory, his discovery loses none of its importance for the clinical observation of the syndromes, and the fact that a common source of energy feeds them remains equally true. I have attempted to demonstrate that the character syndromes are rooted and nourished in the particular forms of relatedness of the individual to the outside world and himself; furthermore, that inasmuch as the social group shares a common character structure ('social character') the socio-economic

4. Traits which were added later to the original syndrome are: exaggerated cleanliness and punctuality; they are also to be understood as reaction formations to the original anal impulses.

5. I developed this concept in a study of German workers and employees (E. Fromm, 1936), see footnote on p. 79, see also E. Fromm (1932, 1941, 1970). T. W. Adorno *et al.* (1950) dealt with the topic in some respects of the earlier study of the authoritarian character of workers and employees, but without its psychoanalytic approach and the dynamic concept of character.

conditions shared by all members of a group mould the social character (E. Fromm, 1932, 1936, 1941, 1947, 1970; E. Fromm and M. Maccoby, 1970).[6]

The extraordinary importance of the concept of character is that it transcends the old dichotomy: instinct–environment. The sexual instinct in Freud's system was supposed to be very malleable, and to a large extent moulded by environmental influences. Thus character was understood as being the outcome of the interaction between instinct and environment. This new position was possible only because Freud had subsumed all instincts under one, i.e., sexuality (aside from the instinct for self-preservation). The many instincts we find in the lists of the older instinctivists were relatively fixed, because each motive of behaviour was attributed to a special kind of innate drive. But in Freud's scheme the differences between the various motivating forces were explained as the result of environmental influence in the libido. Paradoxically, then, Freud's enlargement of the concept of sexuality enabled him to open the door to the acceptance of environmental influences far beyond what was possible for the pre-Freudian instinct theory. Love, tenderness, sadism, masochism, ambition, curiosity, anxiety, rivalry – these and many other drives were no longer each attributed to a special instinct, but to the influence of the environment (essentially the significant persons in early childhood), via the libido. Freud consciously remained loyal to the philosophy of his teachers, but by the assumption of a super-instinct he transcended his own instinctivistic viewpoint. It is true he still hobbled his thought by the predominance of the libido theory, and it is time to leave this instinctive baggage behind altogether. What I want to stress at this point is that Freud's 'in-

6. Erik H. Erikson (1964) in the late development of his theory arrived at a similar point of view in terms of 'modes' without emphasizing so clearly the difference from Freud. He demonstrated in regard to the Yurok Indians that character is not determined by libidinal fixations, and he rejects an essential part of the libido theory for the sake of social factors.

stinctivism' was very different from traditional instinctivism, and in fact was the beginning of overcoming it.

The description given thus far suggests that 'character determines behaviour', that the character trait, whether loving or destroying, drives man to behave in a certain way, and that man in acting according to his character feels satisfied. Indeed, the character trait tells us how a person would *like* to behave. But we must add an important qualification: *if he could*.

What does this 'if he could' mean?

We must return here to one of the most fundamental of Freud's notions, the concept of the 'reality principle', based on the instinct for self-preservation, versus the 'pleasure principle', based on the sexual instinct. Whether we are driven by the sexual instinct or by a non-sexual passion in which a character trait is rooted, the conflict between what we would like to do and the demands of self-interest remains crucial. We cannot always behave as we are driven to by our passions, because we have to modify our behaviour to some extent in order to remain alive. The average person tries to find a compromise between what his character would make him want to do and what he must do in order not to suffer more or less harmful consequences. The degree to which a person follows the dictates of self-preservation (ego interest) varies, of course. At the one extreme the weight of ego interests is zero; this holds true for the martyr and a certain type of fanatical killer. At the other extreme is the 'opportunist' for whom self-interest includes everything that could make him more successful, popular, or comfortable. Between these two extremes all people can be arranged, characterized by a specific blend of self-interest and character-rooted passions.

How much a person represses his passionate desires depends not only on factors within himself but on the situation; if the situation changes, repressed desires become conscious and are acted out. This holds true, for instance, for the person with a sadistic-masochistic character. Everybody knows the type of person who is submissive to his boss and sadistically domineering to his wife and children. Another case in point is the change that occurs in character when the total social situation changes. The sadistic character who may have posed as a meek or even friendly individual may become a fiend in a terroristic society in which sadism is valued rather than deplored. Another may suppress sadistic behaviour in all visible actions, while showing it in a subtle expression of the face or in seemingly harmless and marginal remarks.

Repression of character traits also occurs with regard to the most noble impulses. In spite of the fact that the teachings of Jesus are still part of our moral ideology, a man acting in accordance with them is generally considered a fool or a 'neurotic'; hence many people still rationalize their generous impulses as being motivated by self-interest.

These considerations show that the motivating power of character traits is influenced by self-interest in varying degrees. They imply that character constitutes the main motivation of human behaviour, but restricted and modified by the demands of self-interest under varying conditions. It is the great achievement of Freud not only to have discovered the character traits which underlie behaviour, but also to have devised means to study them, such as the interpretation of dreams, free association, and slips of the tongue.

Here lies the fundamental difference between behaviourism and psychoanalytic characterology. Conditioning works through its appeal to self-interest, such as the desire for food, security, praise, avoidance of pain. In animals, self-interest proves to be so strong that by repeated and optimally spaced reinforcements self-interest proves to be stronger than other instincts like sex or aggression. Man of course also behaves in accordance with his self-interest; but not always, and not necessarily so. He often acts according to his passions, his meanest and his noblest, and is often willing – and able – to risk his self-interest, his fortune, his freedom and his life in the pursuit of love, truth, and integrity – or for hate, greed, sadism, and destructiveness. In this very difference lies the reason conditioning cannot be a sufficient explanation for human behaviour.

To sum up What was epoch-making in Freud's findings was that he found the key to the understanding of the system of forces which make up man's character system and to the contradictions within the system. The discovery of unconscious processes of the dynamic concept of character was radical because it went to the roots of human behaviour; it was disquieting because nobody can hide any longer behind his good intentions; they were dangerous, because if everybody *were* to know what he *could* know about himself and others, society would be shaken to its very foundations.

As psychoanalysis became successful and respectable it shed its radical core and emphasized that which is generally acceptable. It kept that part of the unconscious which Freud had emphasized, the sexual strivings. The consumer society did away with many of the Victorian taboos (not because of the influence of psychoanalysis but for a number of reasons inherent in its structure). To discover one's incestuous wishes, 'castration fear', 'penis envy', was no longer upsetting. But to discover repressed character traits such as narcissism, sadism, omnipotence, submission, alienation, indifference, the unconscious betrayal of one's integrity, the illusory nature of one's concept of reality, to discover all this in oneself, in the social fabric, in the leaders one follows – this indeed is 'social dynamite'. Freud only dealt with an instinctual id; that was quite satisfactory at a time when he did not see any other way to explain human passion except in terms of instincts. But what was revolutionary then is conventional today. The instinct theory instead of being considered a hypothesis, needed at a certain period, became the strait-jacket of orthodox psychoanalytic theory and slowed down the further development of the understanding of man's passions, which had been Freud's central interest.

It is for these reasons that I propose that the classification of psychoanalysis as 'instinctivistic' theory, which is correct in a formal sense, does not really refer to the substance of psychoanalysis. Psychoanalysis is essentially a theory of unconscious strivings, of resistance, of falsification of reality according to one's subjective needs and expectations ('transference'), of character, and of conflicts between passionate strivings embodied in character traits and the demands for self-preservation. In this revised sense (although based on the core of Freud's discoveries) the approach of this book to the problem of human aggression and destructiveness is psychoanalytic – and neither instinctivistic nor behaviouristic.

An increasing number of psychoanalysts have given up Freud's libido theory, but frequently they have not replaced it by an equally precise and systematic theoretical system; the 'drives' they employ are not sufficiently grounded, either in physiology or in the conditions of human existence or in an adequate concept of society. They often use somewhat superficial categories – for instance Karen Horney's 'competition' – which are not too different from the 'cultural patterns' of American anthropology. In contrast, a number of psychoanalysts – most of them influenced by Adolf Meyer – have given up Freud's libido theory and have constructed what seems to me one of the most promising and creative developments in psychoanalytic theory. Mainly on the basis of their study of schizophrenic patients, they arrived at an ever deepening understanding of the unconscious processes going on in interpersonal relations. By being free from the restrictive influence of the libido theory, and particularly the concepts of *id*, *ego*, and *superego*, they can describe fully what goes on in the relationship between two people and within each one of them in his role as a participant. Among the most outstanding representatives of this school – aside from Adolf Meyer – are Harry Stack Sullivan, Frieda Fromm-Reichmann, and Theodore Lidz. In my opinion R. D. Laing has succeeded in giving the most penetrating analyses, not only because he has probed radically into the personal and subjective factors but because his analysis of the social situation is equally radical and free from the uncritical acceptance of present-day society as being sane. Aside from those mentioned so far, the names of Winnicot, Fairbairn, Balint, and Guntrip, among others, represent the development of psychoanalysis from a theory and therapy of instinctual frustration and control into a 'theory and therapy that encourages the rebirth and growth of an authentic self within an authentic relationship' (H. Guntrip, 1971). The work of some 'existentialists', such as L. Binswanger, is by comparison lacking in precise descriptions of the interpersonal processes, substituting somewhat vague philosophical notions for precise clinical data.

Part Two
The Evidence Against the
Thesis Instinctivist

5
Neurophysiology

It is the aim of the chapters in this section to show that the relevant data in the fields of neurophysiology, animal psychology, palaeontology, and anthropology do not support the hypothesis that man is innately endowed with a spontaneous and self-propelling aggressive drive.

The Relationship of Psychology to Neurophysiology

Before entering into the discussion of the neurophysiological data, a few words need to be said about the relationship of psychology, the science of the mind, to the neurosciences, the sciences of the brain.

Each science has its own subject matter, its own methods, and the direction it takes is determined by the applicability of its methods to its data. One cannot expect the neurophysiologist to proceed in the way that would be most desirable from the standpoint of the psychologist, or vice versa. But one can expect both sciences to remain in close contact and to assist each other; this is possible only if both sides have some elementary knowledge that at least permits each to understand the language of the other and to appreciate its most basic findings. If the students of both sciences were in such close contact, they would find that there are certain areas in which the findings of one can be related to those of the other; this is the case, for instance, with regard to the problem of defensive aggression.

However, in most instances psychological and neurophysiological investigations and their respective frames of reference are far apart, and the neuroscientist cannot at present satisfy the psychologist's desire for information about problems such as the neurophysiological equivalent of passions like destructiveness, sadism, masochism, or narcissism,[1] nor can the psychologist be of much help to the neurophysiologist. It would seem that each science should proceed in its own way and solve its own problems, until one day, one must assume, they both have developed to the point where they can approach the same problems with their different methods and can interrelate their findings. It surely would be absurd for either science to wait until the other has brought forth positive or negative evidence for its hypotheses. As long as a psychological theory is not contradicted by clear neurophysiological evidence, the psychologist must have only the normal scientific distrust of his findings, provided they are based on adequate observation and interpretation of data.

R. B. Livingston makes these observations on the relationship between the two sciences:

A real union will be established between psychology and neurophysiology when a large number of scientists are well grounded in both disciplines. How secure and useful a junction will be achieved remains to be seen: nonetheless, new areas for research have appeared, wherein students of behaviour can manipulate the brain in addition to the environment and wherein students of the brain can make use of behavioural concepts and techniques. Many of the traditional identifications of the two fields are being lost. We should actively discard any remaining provincialism and sense of jurisdiction and rivalry between these disciplines. Whom are we against? Only ignorance in ourselves.

1. This general statement needs to be qualified by pointing to the attempts of the late Raúl Hernández Peón to discover the neurophysiological equivalent of dream activity; to R. G. Heath's neurophysiological studies on schizophrenia and boredom, and to P. D. MacLean's attempts to find neurophysiological explanations for paranoia. Freud's own contribution to neurophysiology has been discussed by K. Pribram (1962). See P. Ammacher (1962) on the significance of Freud's neurological background; cf. also R. R. Holt (1965).

Despite recent progress, there are as yet relatively few resources around the world for basic research in psychology and neurophysiology. Problems that need solution are staggering. Understanding can be advanced only through our modification of present concepts. These in turn are subject to change only through resourceful experimental and theoretical pursuits. (R. B. Livingston, 1962)

Many people are misled into thinking, as popular reports sometimes suggest, that neurophysiologists have found many answers to the problem of human behaviour. Most scholars in the field of the neurosciences, on the contrary, have a very different attitude. T. H. Bullock, who is an expert on the nervous systems of invertebrates, electric fish, and marine mammals, in his paper, 'Evolution of Neurophysiological Mechanism', begins 'with a disclaimer of our ability to contribute fundamentally at present to the real question', and goes on to state that 'at bottom we do not have a decent inkling of the neuronal mechanism of learning or the physiological substratum of instinctive patterns or virtually any complex behavioural manifestation' (T. H. Bullock, 1961).[2] Similarly, Birger Kaada states:

Our knowledge and concepts of the central neural organization of aggressive behaviour are constricted by the fact that most of the information has been derived from animal experiments, hence almost nothing is known about the relation of the central nervous system to the 'feeling' or 'affective' aspects of emotions. We are entirely confined to observation and experimental analysis of the expressive or behavioural phenomena and the objectively recorded peripheral bodily changes. Obviously, even these procedures are

2. More recently, however, while still standing by this statement, Bullock has qualified it by a more optimistic note: 'Since 1958, neuroscience has gone a long way toward understanding some higher functions, such as recognition, and control of emotions, and has made significant advances toward understanding the mechanism of association, if not yet of learning. We are well on the way to providing relevant insights, e.g., to saying what may be the biological basis of aggression, and whether there is a hydraulic mechanism and whether it is inherent' (personal communication to Dr T. Melnechuk who wrote me about it).

not entirely reliable and despite extensive research efforts it is difficult to interpret behaviour on the basis of these clues alone. (B. Kaada, 1967)

One of the most outstanding neuroscientists, W. Penfield, comes to the same conclusion:

> Those who hope to solve the problem of the neurophysiology of the mind are like men at the foot of a mountain. They stand in the clearings they have made on the foothills, looking up at the mountain they hope to scale. But the pinnacle is hidden in eternal clouds and many believe it can never be conquered. Surely if the day does dawn when man has reached complete understanding of his own brain and mind, it may be his greatest conquest, his final achievement.
>
> There is only one method that a scientist may use in his scientific work. This is the method of observation of the phenomena of nature followed by comparative analysis and supplemented by experimentation in the light of reasoned hypothesis. Neurophysiologists who follow the rules of the scientific method in all honesty will hardly pretend that their own scientific work entitles them to answer these questions. (W. Penfield, 1960)[3]

More or less radical pessimism has been expressed by a number of neuroscientists with regard to the rapprochement between neuroscience and psychology in general, and particularly with regard to the value of present-day neurophysiology in contributing to the explanation of human behaviour. This pessimism has been expressed by H. von Foerster and

3. Not only the neurosciences and psychology but many other fields need to be integrated to create a *science of man* – fields such as palaeontology, anthropology, history, the history of religions (myths and rituals), biology, physiology, genetics. The subject matter of the 'science of man' is *man*: man as a total biologically and historically evolving human being who can be understood only if we see the interconnectedness between all his aspects, if we look at him as a process occurring within a complex system with many subsystems. The 'behavioural sciences' (psychology and sociology), a term made popular by the Rockefeller Foundation's programme, are interested mainly in *what* man *does* and how he can be *made to do* what he does, not *why* he does and in *who* he *is*. They have to a considerable extent become an obstacle to and a substitute for the development of an integrated science of man.

T. Melnechuk,[4] and by H. R. Maturana and F. C. Varela (forthcoming).[5] F. G. Worden, also in a critical vein, writes: 'Examples from neuroscience research are given to illustrate how, as investigators become more directly concerned with conscious phenomena, the inadequacies of the materialistic doctrine are increasingly troublesome, giving rise to the search for better conceptual systems' (F. G. Worden, forthcoming).[5]

From a number of oral and written communications from neuroscientists I have the impression that this sober view is shared by an increasing number of investigators. The brain is more and more understood as a *whole*, as one system, so that behaviour cannot be explained by referring to some of its parts. Impressive data supporting this view have been presented by E. Valenstein (1968), who has shown that the supposed hypothalamic 'centres' for hunger, thirst, sex, etc., are not, if they really exist, as pure as previously thought – that stimulation of a 'centre' for one behaviour can elicit behaviour appropriate to another if the environment provides stimuli consistent with the second. D. Ploog (1970) has shown that the 'aggression' (actually, non-verbal communication of threat) elicited in a squirrel monkey will not be believed by another monkey if the threat is made by the second monkey's social inferior. These data are consistent with the holistic view that the brain takes account, in its reckoning of what behaviour to command, of more than one strand of incoming stimulation – that the total state of the physical and social environment at the time modifies the meaning of a specific stimulus.

However, the scepticism regarding the capacity of neurophysiology to explain human behaviour adequately does not mean a denial of the *relative* validity of the many experimental findings, especially in the last decades. These find-

4. Personal communications from H. von Foerster and from T. Melnechuk.

5. I appreciate the authors' having allowed me to read their manuscripts before publication.

ings, while they might be reformulated and integrated in a more global view, are valid enough to give us important clues for the understanding of one kind of aggression, that of *defensive aggression*.

The Brain as a Basis for Aggressive Behaviour[6]

The study of the relationship between brain functioning and behaviour was largely governed by Darwin's proposition that the structure and functioning of the brain are governed by the principle of the survival of the individual and the species.

Neurophysiologists since then have concentrated their efforts on finding the brain areas which are the substrates of the most elementary impulses and behaviours needed for survival. There is general agreement with MacLean's conclusion, who called these basic brain mechanisms the four Fs: 'feeding, fighting, fleeing and . . . the performance of sexual activities' (P. D. MacLean, 1958). As can easily be recognized, these activities are vitally necessary for the physical survival of the individual and the species. (That man has basic needs beyond physical survival whose realization is necessary for his functioning as a total being will be discussed later.)

As far as aggression and flight are concerned, the work of a number of investigators – W. R. Hess, J. Olds, R. G. Heath, J. M. R. Delgado, and others – has suggested that they are 'controlled'[7] by different neural areas in the brain. It has

6. In this discussion I shall only present the most important and generally accepted data. The work done in this field in the last twenty years is so enormous that it would be beyond my competence to enter into the hundreds of detailed problems that arise, nor would it be useful to quote the correspondingly large literature which can be found in a number of works mentioned in the text.

7. According to some authors quoted above, the term 'controlled' is quite inadequate. They see the response as one to processes going on in other parts of the brain, interacting with the specific area which is stimulated.

been shown that, for example, the effective reaction of rage and its corresponding aggressive behaviour pattern can be *activated* by direct electrical stimulation of various areas, such as the amygdala, the lateral hypothalamus, some parts of the mesencephalon, and the central grey matter; and it can be *inhibited* by stimulating other structures, such as the septum, the circumvolution of the cingulum, and the caudal nucleus.[8] With great surgical ingenuity some investigators[9] were able to implant electrodes in a number of specific areas of the brain. They established a two-way connection for observation. By low-voltage electrical stimulation of an area they were able to study changes of behaviour in animals, and later in man. They could demonstrate, for instance, the arousal of intensely aggressive behaviour by the direct electric stimulation of certain areas, and the inhibition of aggression by stimulating certain others. On the other hand, they could measure the electrical activity of these various areas of the brain when emotions like rage, fear, pleasure, etc., were aroused by environmental stimuli. They could also observe the permanent effects produced by the destruction of certain areas of the brain.

It is indeed quite impressive to witness how a relatively small increase in the electric charge in an electrode implanted in one of the neural substrates of aggression can produce a sudden outburst of uncontrolled, murderous rage and how the reduction of electric stimulation or the stimulation of an aggression-inhibitory centre can equally suddenly stop this aggression. Delgado's spectacular experiment of stopping a charging bull by the stimulation

8. The neocortex also exerts a predominantly exitatory effect on rage behaviour. See K. Ackert's experiments with the ablation of the neocortex of the temporal pole (K. Ackert, 1967).

9. cf. W. R. Hess (1954), J. Olds and P. Milner (1954), R. G. Heath, ed. (1962), J. M. R. Delgado (1967, 1969 with extensive bibliography). See, furthermore, the volume by V. H. Mark and F. R. Ervin (1970), which contains a clear and concise presentation, easily understood also by the layman in this field, of the essential data on neurophysiology as they refer to violent behaviour.

of an inhibitory area (by remote control) has aroused considerable popular interest in this procedure (J. M. R. Delgado, 1969).

That a response is activated in some brain areas and inhibited in others is by no means only characteristic of aggression; the same duality exists with regard to other impulses. The brain is, in fact, organized as a *dual system*. Unless there are specific stimuli (external or internal), aggression is in a state of fluid equilibrium, because activating and inhibiting areas keep each other in a relatively stable balance. This can be recognized particularly clearly when either an activating or an inhibiting area is destroyed. Starting with the classic experiment by Heinrich Klüver and P. C. Bucy (1934) it has been demonstrated, for instance, that destruction of the amygdala transformed animals (rhesus monkeys, wolverines, wildcats, rats, and others) in such a way that they lost – at least temporarily – their capacity for aggressive, violent reactions, even under strong provocation.[10] On the other hand, the destruction of aggression-inhibiting areas, such as small areas of the ventromedial nucleus of the hypothalamus, produces permanently aggressive cats and rats.

Given the dual organization of the brain, the crucial question arises: What are the factors that disturb the balance and produce manifest rage and corresponding violent behaviour?

We have already seen that one way in which such disturbance of the balance can be produced is by electric stimulation or destruction of any of the inhibitory areas (aside from hormonal and metabolic changes). Mark and Ervin emphasize that such disturbance of the equilibrium can also occur due to various forms of brain disease that alter the normal circuitry of the brain.

But what are the conditions that change the equilibrium and mobilize aggression, aside from these two instances, one of which is experimentally introduced and the other

10. cf. V. H. Mark and F. R. Ervin (1970).

pathological? What are the causes of 'innate' aggression in animals and humans?

The Defensive Function of Aggression

In reviewing both the neurophysiological and the psychological literature on animal and human aggression, the conclusion seems unavoidable that aggressive behaviour of animals is a response to *any kind of threat to the survival* or, as I would prefer to say more generally, *to the vital interests of the animal* – whether as an individual or as a member of its species. This general definition comprises many different situations. The most obvious are a direct threat to the life of the individual or a threat to his requirements for sex and food; a more complex form is that of 'crowding', which is a threat to the need for physical space and/or to the social structure of the group. But what is common to all conditions for the arousal of aggressive behaviour is that they constitute a threat to vital interests. Mobilization of aggression in the corresponding brain areas occurs in the service of life, in response to threats to the survival of the individual or of the species; that is to say, *phylogenetically programmed aggression, as it exists in animals and man, is a biologically adaptive, defensive reaction.* That this should be so is not surprising if we remember the Darwinian principle in regard to the evolution of the brain. Since it is the function of the brain to take care of survival, it would provide for immediate reactions to any threat to survival.

Aggression is by no means the only form of reaction to threats. The animal reacts to threats to his existence either with rage and attack or with fear and flight. In fact, flight seems to be the more frequent form of reaction, except when the animal has no chance to flee and therefore fights – as the *ultima ratio*.

Hess was the first to discover that by the electrical stimulation of certain regions of the hypothalamus of a cat, the

animal would react either by attack or by flight. As a consequence he subsumed these two kinds of behaviour under the
category of '*defence reaction*', indicating that both reactions
are in defence of the animal's life.

The neuronal areas which are the substrate for attack and
flight are close together, yet distinct. A great deal of work on
this question has followed the pioneer studies by W. R. Hess,
H. W. Magoun, and others, especially by Hunsperger and
his group in Hess's laboratory and by Romaniuk, Levinson,
and Flynn.[11] In spite of certain differences in the results to
which these various investigators have arrived, they confirm
the basic findings of Hess.

Mark and Ervin summarize the present state of knowledge in the following paragraph:

> Any animal, regardless of its species, reacts to a life-threatening
> attack with one of two patterns of behaviour: either with flight,
> or with aggression and violence – that is, fight. The brain always
> acts as a unit in directing any behaviour; consequently, the
> mechanisms in the brain that initiate and limit these two dissimilar
> patterns of self-preservation are closely linked to one another, as
> well as to all other parts of the brain; and their proper functioning
> depends on the synchronization of many complex and delicately
> balanced subsystems. (V. H. Mark and F. R. Ervin, 1970)

The 'Flight' Instinct

The data on fight and flight as defence reactions make the
instinctivistic theory of aggression appear in a peculiar light.
The impulse to flee plays – neurophysiologically and be-
haviourally – the same if not a larger role in animal behaviour than the impulse to fight. Neurophysiologically, both
impulses are integrated in the same way; there is no basis
for saying that aggression is more 'natural' than flight.
Why then, do instinctivists talk about the intensity of the
innate impulses of aggression, rather than about the innate
impulse for flight?

11. cf. the detailed review of these studies in B. Kaada (1967).

If one were to translate the reasoning of the instinctivists regarding the impulse for fight to that of flight one would arrive at this kind of statement: 'Man is driven by an innate impulse to flee; he may try to control this impulse by his reason, yet this control will prove to be relatively inefficient, even though some means can be found that may serve to curb the power of the "flight instinct".'

Considering the emphasis that has been given to innate human aggression as one of the gravest problems of social life, from religious positions down to the scientific work of Lorenz, a theory centred around man's 'uncontrollable flight instinct' may sound funny, but it is neurophysiologically as sound as that of 'uncontrollable aggression'. In fact, from a biological standpoint it would seem that flight serves self-preservation better than fight. To political or military leaders it may, in fact, not sound so funny, but rather sensible. They know from experience that man's nature does not seem to incline towards heroism and that many measures have to be taken to motivate man to fight and to prevent him from running away in order to save his life.

The student of history may raise the question whether the instinct for flight has not proved to be at least as powerful a factor as that for fight. He may come to the conclusion that history has been determined not so much by instinctive aggression as by the attempt to suppress man's 'flight instinct'. He may speculate that a large part of man's social arrangements and ideological efforts have been devoted to this aim. Man had to be threatened with death to instill in him a feeling of awe for the superior wisdom of his leaders, to make him believe in the value of 'honour'. One tried to terrorize him with the fear of being called a coward or a traitor, or one simply got him drunk with liquor or with the hope of booty and women. Historical analysis might show that the repression of the flight impulse and the apparent dominance of the fight impulse is largely due to cultural rather than to biological factors.

These speculations are only intended to point to the

ethological bias in favour of the concept of *Homo aggressivus*; the fundamental fact remains, that the brain of animals and humans has built-in neuronal mechanisms which mobilize aggressive behaviour (or flight) in response to threats to the survival of the individual or the species, and that this type of aggression is biologically adaptive and serves life.

Predation and Aggression

There is still another kind of aggression that has caused a great deal of confusion: that of *predatory* land animals. Zoologically they are clearly defined; they comprise the families of cats, hyenas, wolves and bears.[12]

Experimental evidence is rapidly accumulating to indicate that the neurological basis for predatory aggression is distinct from that of defensive aggression.[13] Lorenz has made the same point from the ethological standpoint:

> The motivation of the hunter is basically different from that of the fighter. The buffalo which the lion fells provokes his aggression as little as the appetizing turkey which I have just seen hanging in the larder provokes mine. The differences in these inner drives can clearly be seen in the expressive movements of the animal: a dog about to catch a hunted rabbit has the same kind of excitedly happy expression as he has when he greets his master or awaits some longed-for treat. From many excellent photographs it can be seen that the lion, in the dramatic movement before he springs, is in no way angry. Growling, laying the ears back, and other well-known expression movements of fighting behaviour are seen

12. Bears are difficult to categorize in this respect. Some bears are omnivorous; they kill and eat the meat of smaller or wounded animals, but do not stalk them as, for instance, lions do. On the other hand, the polar bear, living under extreme climatic conditions, stalks seals in order to kill and eat them and thus can be considered a true predator.

13. This point has been emphasized by Mark and Ervin (1970) and demonstrated by the studies of Egger and Flynn who stimulated the specific area in the lateral part of the hypothalamus and obtained behaviour that reminded the observers of an animal stalking or hunting a prey (M. D. Egger and J. P. Flynn, 1963).

in predatory animals only when they are very afraid of a wildly
resisting prey, and even then the expressions are only suggested.
(K. Lorenz, 1966)

K. E. Moyer, on the basis of the available data concerning
the neurophysiological bases of various kinds of aggression,
distinguished predatory from other types of aggression and
comes to the conclusion that 'experimental evidence is
rapidly accumulating to indicate that the neurological basis
for this (predatory) aggression is distinct from that of other
kinds' (K. E. Moyer, 1968).

Not only does predatory behaviour have its own neurophysiological substrate, distinct from that for defensive
aggression, but the behaviour itself is different. It does not
show rage and is not interchangeable with flight behaviour,
but it is purpose-determined, accurately aimed, and the
tension ends with the accomplishment of the goal – the
attainment of food. The predatory instinct is not one of
defence, common to all animals, but of food-finding,
common to certain animal species that are morphologically
equipped for this task. Of course, predatory behaviour is
aggressive,[14] but it must be added that this aggression is
different from the rage-connected aggression provoked by a
threat. It is close to what is sometimes called 'instrumental'
aggression, i.e. aggression in the service of attaining a desired goal. Non-predatory animals lack this kind of aggression.

The difference between defensive and predatory aggression is important for the problem of human aggression
because man is phylogenetically a non-predatory animal,
and hence his aggression, as far as its neurophysiological

14. An important fact is that many predatory animals – wolves, for
instance – are unaggressive towards their own species. Not only in the
sense that they do not kill each other – which may be sufficiently explained, as Lorenz does, as being due to the necessity to restrict the
use of their ferocious weapons for the sake of the survival of the species –
but also in the sense that they are quite friendly and amiable in their
social contact with each other.

roots are concerned, is not of the predatory type. It should be remembered that human dentition 'is poorly adapted for the flesh-eating habits of man, who still retains the tooth form of his fruit- and vegetable-eating ancestors. It is interesting to note, too, that man's digestive system has all the physiological hallmarks of a vegetarian, not a carnivore' (J. Napier, 1970). The diet even of primitive hunters and food gatherers was 75 per cent vegetarian and only 25 per cent or less carnivorous.[15] According to I. DeVore: 'All of the Old World primates have essentially a vegetarian diet. So do all of the extant men with the most primitive human economic organization, the remaining hunter-gatherers of the world, except for the arctic Eskimo ... Although future archaeologists studying contemporary bushmen might conclude that the cracking stones found with bushmen arrowheads were used for pounding bones to get marrow, they were actually used by women to crack open the nuts that happened to provide 80 per cent of the bushman economy' (I. DeVore, 1970).

Nevertheless, perhaps nothing has contributed more to the picture of the intensity of the innate aggressiveness of animals, and indirectly of man, than the image of the predatory animal. We do not have far to go to find the reasons for this bias.

Man has surrounded himself for many thousands of years with domesticated animals – such as the dog and the cat – which are predatory. In fact, this is one of the reasons man tamed them: he uses the dog to hunt other animals and to attack threatening humans; he uses the cat to chase mice and rats. On the other hand, man was impressed by the aggressiveness of the wolf, the main enemy of his herds of sheep, or of the fox, which devoured his chickens.[16] Thus

15. The whole question of the alleged predatory characteristics of man will be discussed in Chapter 7.

16. It may not be accidental that Hobbes, who portrayed man as a 'wolf' to his fellowmen, lived in a sheep-raising country. It would be interesting to examine the origin and popularity of fairy tales dealing with the dangerous wolf, like *Little Red Riding Hood*, in this light.

the animals man has chosen to have nearest in his field of vision have been predatory, and he could hardly have distinguished between predatory and defensive aggressiveness since in their effect both types of aggression result in killing; nor was he able to observe these animals in their own habitat and to appreciate their social and friendly attitude among themselves.

The conclusion which we have arrived at on the basis of the examination of the neurophysiological evidence is essentially the same as the one which two of the most outstanding investigators of aggression, J. P. Scott and Leonard Berkowitz, have suggested, even though their respective theoretical frames of reference differ from mine. Scott writes: 'A person who is fortunate enough to exist in an environment which is without stimulation to fight will not suffer physiological or nervous damage because he never fights. This is a quite different situation from the physiology of eating, where the internal processes of metabolism lead to definite physiological changes which eventually produce hunger and stimulation to eat, without any change in the external environment' (J. P. Scott, 1958). Berkowitz speaks of a 'wiring diagram', a '*readiness*' to react aggressively to certain stimuli, rather than of 'aggressive energy' which may be transmitted genetically (L. Berkowitz, 1967).

The data of the neurosciences which I have discussed have helped to establish the concept of one kind of aggression – life preserving, biologically adaptive, defensive aggression. They have been useful for the purpose of showing that man is endowed with a potential aggression which is mobilized by threats to his vital interests. None of these neurophysiological data, however, deal with that form of aggression which is characteristic of man and which he does not share with other mammals: his propensity to kill and to torture without any 'reason', but as a goal in itself, a goal not pursued for the sake of defending life, but desirable and pleasureful in itself.

The neurosciences have not taken up the study of these

passions (with the exception of those caused by brain damage), but it can be safely stated that Lorenz's instinctivistic-hydraulic interpretation does not fit well with the model of brain functioning as most neuroscientists see it and is not supported by neurophysiological evidence.

6

Animal Behaviour

The second critical field in which empirical data could contribute to establishing the validity of the instinctivistic theory of aggression is that of *animal behaviour*. Animal aggression needs to be separated into three different types: (1) predatory aggression, (2) intra-specific aggression (aggression against animals of the same species), (3) inter-specific aggression (aggression against animals of different species).

As indicated before, there is agreement among students of animal behaviour (including Lorenz) that the behavioural patterns and neurological processes in *predatory* aggression are not analogous to the other types of animal aggression and hence should be treated separately.

As far as *intra-specific* aggression is concerned, most observers agree that animals rarely destroy members of other species, except when in defence, i.e., when they feel threatened and cannot flee. This limits the phenomenon of animal aggression mainly to intra-specific aggression, i.e., aggression between animals of the same species, the phenomenon which Lorenz deals with exclusively.

Intra-specific aggression has the following characteristics: (a) In most mammals it is not 'bloody', it does not aim at killing, destruction or torture, but is essentially a threatening posture which serves as a warning. On the whole we find among most mammals a great deal of bickering, quarrelling, or threatening behaviour, but very little bloody fighting and destruction, as we find it in human behaviour. (b) Only in certain insects, fish, birds, and, among mammals, rats, is destructive behaviour customary. (c) The threatening behaviour is a reaction to what the animal experiences as a threat to its vital interests and hence is defensive, in the sense of the neurophysiological concept of 'defensive aggression'. (d) There is no evidence that there is a spontaneous aggressive impulse in most mammals which is dammed up until it finds a more or less adequate occasion to be discharged. As far as animal aggression is defensive, it is based on certain phylogenetically patterned neuronal structures, and there would be no quarrel with Lorenz's position were it not for his hydraulic model and his explanation of human destructiveness and cruelty as innate and rooted in defensive aggression.

Man is the only mammal who is a large-scale killer and sadist. To answer the question why this is so is the purpose of the next chapters. In this discussion on animal behaviour I want to show in detail that many animals fight their own species, but that they fight in a 'non-disruptive', non-destructive way and that the data on the life of mammals in general and the prehuman primates in particular do not suggest the presence of an innate 'destructiveness' which man is supposed to have inherited from them. Indeed, that if the human species had approximately the same degree of 'innate' aggressiveness as that of chimpanzees living in their natural habitat, we would live in a rather peaceful world.

Aggression in Captivity

In studying aggression among animals and especially among the primates, it is important to begin with a distinction between their behaviour while living in their own habitat and their behaviour in captivity, that is, essentially, in zoos. Observations show that primates in the wild show little aggression, while primates in the zoo can show an excessive amount of destructiveness.

This distinction is of fundamental importance for the understanding of human aggression because man thus far in his history has hardly ever lived in his 'natural habitat', with the exception of the hunters and food gatherers and the first agriculturalists down to the fifth millennium B C. 'Civilized' man has always lived in the 'Zoo' – i.e., in various degrees of captivity and unfreedom – and this is still true, even in the most advanced societies.

I shall begin with a few examples of primates in the zoo, which have been well studied. The best known perhaps are the *hamadryas* baboons, which Solly Zuckerman studied at the London Zoo in Regents Park ('Monkey Hill') in 1929–30. Their area, 100 feet long and sixty feet wide, was large by zoo standards, but extremely small compared with the natural range of their habitat. Zuckerman observed a great deal of tension and aggression among these animals. The stronger ones brutally and ruthlessly kept the weaker ones down, and even mothers would take food away from the hands of their babies. The principal victims were females and the young, who sometimes were injured or killed accidentally during the battles. Zuckerman saw one male bully deliberately attack a baby monkey twice, and this little monkey was found dead in the evening. Eight out of sixty-one males died by violence, while many others died from disease (S. Zuckerman, 1932).

Other observations of primate behaviour in zoos were made in Zürich by Hans Kummer (1951)[1] and in Whipsnade, England, by Vernon Reynolds (1961)[1]. Kummer kept the baboons in an enclosure fifteen by twenty-seven yards in area. In Zürich, serious bites which caused nasty wounds were commonplace. Kummer made a detailed comparison of aggression among the animals in the Zürich Zoo and among those living in the wild, which he studied in Ethiopia, and found that the incidence of aggressive acts in the zoo was nine times as frequent in females and seventeen and a half times as frequent in adult males as it was in wild bands. Vernon Reynolds studied twenty-four rhesus mon-

1. Quoted by C. and W. M. S. Russell (1968).

keys in an enclosure which was octagonal, with each side only ten yards long. Although the space to which the animals were confined was smaller than that of Monkey Hill, the degree of aggression was less extreme. Nevertheless, there was more violence than in the wild; many animals were wounded and one female was hurt so badly that she had to be shot.

Of particular interest with regard to the influence of ecological conditions on aggression are various studies on rhesus monkeys (*Macaca mulata*), especially those by C. H. Southwick (1964), also C. H. Southwick, M. Beg, M. Siddiqi (1965). Southwick has found that environmental and social conditions invariably exert a major influence on the form and frequency of 'agonistic' behaviour (i.e., of behaviour in response to conflict) in captive rhesus monkeys. His study permits distinguishing between environmental changes, i.e., number of animals in a given space, and social changes, i.e., the introduction of new animals into an existing group. He comes to the conclusion that decreasing space results in increasing aggression, but that changes in the social structure by the introduction of new animals 'produced far more dramatic increases in aggressive interaction than did environmental changes' (C. H. Southwick, 1964).

Increased aggression by narrowing of space has resulted in more aggressive behaviour among many other mammal species. L. H. Matthews, from the study of the literature and his own observations in the London Zoo, states that he could not find any cases among mammals of fighting to the death, except under crowded conditions (L. H. Matthews, 1963). An outstanding investigator of animal behaviour, Paul Leyhausen, has emphasized the role of the disturbance of relative hierarchy among cats when they were caged together in a small space. 'The more crowded the cages, the less relative hierarchy there is. Finally a despot emerges, "pariahs" appear, and they are driven to frenzy and all sorts of unnatural behaviour by continuous and brutal attacks by all the others. The community turns into a spiteful mob. They all seldom relax, they never look at ease, and there is continuous hissing, growling and even fighting' (P. Leyhausen, 1956).[2]

Even the transitory crowding by fixed feeding stations resulted in increased aggression. In the winter of 1952, three American scientists, C. Cabot, N. Collias, and R. C. Guttinger (quoted by C. and W. M. S. Russell, 1968), observed deer near the Flag River, Wisconsin, and found that the amount of quarrelling depended on the number of deer in the fixed area of the station, that is, on their density. When only from five to seven deer were present only one quarrel was seen per deer per hour. When from twenty-three to thirty deer were present the rate was 4.4 quarrels per deer per hour. Similar observations have been made with wild rats by the American biologist, J. B. Calhoun (1948).

It is important to note that the evidence shows that the presence of an ample *food supply* does *not* prevent increasing aggressiveness under conditions of crowding. The animals in the London Zoo were well fed, and yet crowding resulted in increased aggressiveness. It is also interesting that among rhesus monkeys even a 25 per cent reduction in food resulted in no change in agonistic interactions, according to Southwick's observations, and that a 50 per cent reduction actually resulted in a significant decrease in agonistic behaviour.[3]

From the studies of increased aggressiveness of primates in captivity – and studies of other mammals have shown the same result – it seems to follow that crowding is the main condition for increased violence. But 'crowding' is only a label, and a rather deceptive one, because it does not tell us which factors in crowding are responsible for this increased aggression.

2. cf., also, P. Leyhausen's discussion on crowding (1965), particularly his discussion of the influence of crowding on man.

3. Similar phenomena can be found among humans where starvation conditions decrease rather than increase aggressiveness.

Is there a 'natural' need for a minimum of private space?[4] Does crowding prevent the animal from exercising its innate need for exploration and free movement? Is crowding felt as a threat to the animal's body to which it reacts with aggression?

While these questions can be fully answered only on the basis of further studies, Southwick's findings suggest that there are at least two different elements in crowding which must be kept apart. One is the *reduction of space*; the other is the *destruction of the social structure*. The importance of the second factor is clearly borne out by Southwick's observation, mentioned earlier, that the introduction of a strange animal usually creates even more aggression than crowding. Of course, often both factors are present, and it is difficult to determine which of the two is responsible for the aggressive behaviour.

Whatever the specific blend of these factors is in animal crowding, each of them can generate aggression. The narrowing down of space deprives the animal of important vital functions of movement, play, and the exercise of its faculties which can develop only when it has to search for its own food. Hence the 'space-deprived' animal may feel threatened by this reduction of its vital functions and react with aggression. The breakdown of the social structure of an animal group is, according to Southwick, even more of a threat. Every animal species lives within a social structure characteristic for this species. Whether hierarchical or not, it is the frame of reference to which the animal's behaviour is adapted. A tolerable social equilibrium is a necessary condition for its existence. Its destruction through crowding constitutes a massive threat to the animal's existence, and intense aggression is the result one would expect, given the defensive role of aggression, especially when flight is impossible.

Crowding can occur under the conditions of existence in a

4. cf. T. E. Hall's interesting studies on human spatial requirements (1963, 1966).

zoo as was seen among Zuckerman's baboons. But more often the animals in a zoo are not crowded but suffer from restriction of space. Captive animals, although they are well fed and protected, have 'nothing to do'. If one believes that satisfaction of all physiological needs is enough to provide for a feeling of well-being in an animal (and in man), their zoo existence should make them very content. But this parasitic existence deprives them of stimuli that would permit an active expression of their physical and mental faculties; hence they often become bored, dull, and apathetic. A. Kortlandt reports that 'unlike *zoo* chimpanzees, which generally look increasingly dull and vacant with the years, the older chimpanzees among those living in the wild seemed to be more lively, more interested in everything, and more human' (A. Kortlandt, 1962).[5] S. E. Glickman and R. W. Sroges (1966) make a similar point speaking of the constant 'dull stimulus world' provided by zoo cages and the resulting 'boredom'.

Human Aggression and Crowding

If crowding is an important condition for animal aggression, the question suggests itself whether it is also an important source of human aggression. This idea is widely held and has been expressed by P. Leyhausen, who argues that there is no other remedy for 'rebellion', 'violence', and 'neuroses' than 'to establish the balance of numbers in human societies and quickly to find effective means of controlling them at the optimum level' (P. Leyhausen, 1965).[6]

This popular identification of '*crowding*' with *population*

5. An example is a silver-haired old chimpanzee who remained the leader of the group even though he was physically far inferior to younger apes; apparently life in freedom, with all its many stimulations, had developed a kind of wisdom in him which qualified him as a leader.

6. The same thesis has been expressed by C. and W. M. S. Russell (1968, 1968a).

density has created much confusion. Leyhausen, in his over-simplifying and conservative approach, ignores the fact that the problem of contemporary crowding has two aspects: the destruction of a viable social structure (particularly in the industrialized parts of the world), and the disproportion between the size of population and the economic and social basis for its existence, mainly in the non-industrialized parts of the world.

Man needs a social system in which he has his place and in which his relations to others are relatively stable and supported by generally accepted values and ideas. What has happened in modern industrial society is that traditions, and common values, and genuine social personal ties with others have largely disappeared. The modern mass man is isolated and lonely, even though he is part of a crowd; he has no convictions which he could share with others, only slogans and ideologies he gets from the communications media. He has become an atom (the Greek equivalent of 'individual'=indivisible), held together only by common, though often simultaneously antagonistic interests, and by the cash nexus. Emile Durkheim (1897) called this phenomenon '*anomie*' and found that it was the main cause of suicide which had been increasing with the growth of industrialization. He referred by anomie to the destruction of all traditional social bonds, due to the fact that all truly collective organization had become secondary to the state and that all genuine social life had been annihilated. He believed that people living in the modern political state are 'a disorganized dust of individuals'.[7] Another master of sociology, F. Tönnies (1926), undertook a similar analysis of modern societies and made the distinction between the traditional 'community' (*Gemeinschaft*) and modern society (*Gesellschaft*) in which all genuine social bonds have disappeared.

That not population density as such, but lack of social structure, genuine common bonds and interest in life are the

7. A similar view was expressed by E. Mayo (1933).

causes of human aggression can be shown by many examples. One of the most striking are the kibbutzim in Israel, which are very crowded, with little space for the individual and little privacy (this was even more the case years ago when the kibbutzim were poor). Yet there was an extraordinary lack of aggressiveness among their members. The same holds true for other 'intentional communities' all over the world. Another example are countries like Belgium and Holland, two of the most densely populated parts of the world, whose population is nevertheless not characterized by special aggressiveness. There could hardly be more crowding than there was at the Woodstock or the Isle of Wight youth festivals, and yet both were remarkably free from aggressiveness. To take another example, Manhattan Island was one of the most densely populated places in the world thirty years ago, but it was not then, as it is today, characterized by excessive violence.

Anyone who has lived in a big apartment building where several hundred families live together knows that there are few places where a person has as much privacy and is as little intruded upon by the presence of next-door neighbours as in such a densely populated building. By comparison there is much less privacy in a small village where the houses are much more dispersed and population density is much smaller. Here the people are more aware of each other, watch and gossip about each other's private lives, and are constantly in each other's field of vision; the same holds true, although to a much lesser degree, for suburban society.

These examples tend to show that it is not crowding as such, but the social, psychological, cultural, and economic conditions under which it occurs that are responsible for aggression. It is obvious that overpopulation, i.e., population density *under conditions of poverty*, causes stress and aggression; the big cities of India, as well as the slums in American cities, are an example of this. Overpopulation and the resulting population density are malignant, when, due to the lack of decent housing, people lack the most elementary conditions for protection from immediate and constant intrusion by others. Overpopulation means that the number of people in a given society surpasses the economic basis for providing them with adequate food, housing and meaningful leisure. There is no doubt that overpopulation has evil consequences and that the numbers must be reduced to a level which is commensurate with the economic basis. But, in a society which has the economic basis to support a dense population, the density itself does not deprive the citizen of his privacy, and it does not expose him to constant intrusion of others.

An adequate standard of living, however, takes care only of the lack of privacy and constant exposure to others. It does not solve the problem of *anomie*, of the lack of *Gemeinschaft*, of the individual's need to live in a world that has human proportions, whose members know each other as persons. The *anomie* of industrial society can only be removed if the whole social and spiritual structure is changed radically: if the individual is not only adequately fed and housed, but the interests of society become identical with the interests of each individual; when the relationship to one's fellowman and the expression of one's powers, rather than the consumption of things and antagonisms to one's fellowman, become the principles which govern social and individual life. This is possible under the condition of high population density, but it requires radical rethinking of all our premises and radical social change.

It follows from these considerations that all analogies from animal to human crowding are of limited value. The animal has an instinctive 'knowledge' of the space and the social organization it needs. It reacts instinctively with aggression in order to remedy a disturbance of its space and social structure. It has no other way to respond to threats to its vital interests in these respects. But man has many other ways. He can change the social structure, he can develop bonds of solidarity and of common values beyond what is instinctually given. The animal's solution to crowding is a biological instinctive one; man's solution is social and political.

Aggression in the Wild

Fortunately, there are a number of recent studies of animals living in the wild which clearly show that the aggressiveness to be observed under conditions of captivity is not present when the same animals live in their natural habitat.[8]

Among the monkeys, baboons have the reputation of a certain violence, and they have been carefully studied by S. L. Washburn and I. DeVore (1971). For reasons of space, I shall only mention Washburn and DeVore's conclusion, namely that if the general social structure is not disturbed, there is little aggressive behaviour; whatever aggressive behaviour there is, is essentially one of gestures or threat

8. Field studies of nonhuman primates were first undertaken by H. W. Nissen (1931) with the study of the chimpanzee; by H. C. Bingham (1932), with the study of the gorilla, and by C. R. Carpenter (1934), with the study of the howler monkey. For almost twenty years after these studies, the entire subject of primate field studies lay dormant. Although a number of brief field studies were made in the intervening years, a new series of long-term careful observations did not begin until the middle of the fifties with the establishment of the Japan Monkey Center of Kyoto University and S. A. Altman's study of the rhesus monkey colony on Cayo Santiago. Today there are well over fifty individuals engaged in such studies. The best collection of papers on primate behaviour is to be found in I. DeVore, ed. (1965) with a very comprehensive bibliography. Among the papers in this volume I want to mention here are the one by K. R. L. Hall and I. DeVore (1965); the one on 'Rhesus Monkeys in North India' by C. H. Southwick, M. Beg, and M. R. Siddiqi (1965); 'The Behaviour of the Mountain Gorilla' by G. B. Schaller (1965); 'The Chimpanzees of the Bodongo Forest' by V. and F. Reynolds (1965); and 'Chimpanzees of the Gombe Stream Reserve' by Jane Goodall (1965). Goodall continued with the same research until 1965 and published her further findings combined with the earlier ones under her married name, Jane van Lawick-Goodall (1968). In the following I have also used A. Kortlandt (1962) and K. R. L. Hall (1964).

postures. It is worthwhile to note, considering the previous discussion on crowding, they report observing no fighting between baboon troops that met at the waterhole. They counted more than four hundred baboons around a single waterhole at one time, and yet they did not observe any aggressive behaviour among them. They also observed the baboons to be very unaggressive towards members of other animal species. This picture is confirmed and complemented by the study on the Chacma baboon (*Papio ursinus*) by K. R. L. Hall (1960).

The study of aggressive behaviour among *chimpanzees*, the primates that most resemble man, is of particular interest. Until recent years almost nothing was known of their way of life in Equatorial Africa. However, three separate observations of chimpanzees in their natural habitat have by now been carried out and offer very interesting material with regard to aggressive behaviour.

V. and F. Reynolds, who studied the chimpanzees of the Bodongo Forest, report an exceedingly low incidence of aggression. 'During 300 observation hours, seventeen quarrels involving actual fighting or displays of threat or anger were seen and none of these lasted more than a few seconds' (V. and F. Reynolds, 1965). Only four of these seventeen quarrels involved two adult males. The observations of chimpanzees of the Gombe Stream Reserve by Jane Goodall are essentially the same: 'Threatening behaviour was seen on four occasions when a subordinate male tried to take food before a dominant one ... Instances of attack were seldom observed and mature males were seen fighting only on one occasion' (J. Goodall, 1965). On the other hand, there are 'a number of activities and gestures like grooming and courting behaviour' whose main function is apparently to establish and maintain good relations between the individual chimpanzees of the community. Their groups are largely temporary, and no stable relationships other than mother–infant could be found (J. Goodall, 1965). A dominance hierarchy proper was not observed among these chimpanzees, although there were seventy-two clear-cut dominance interactions observed.

A. Kortlandt mentions an observation concerning the uncertainty of chimpanzees which, as we shall see later, is very important for the understanding of the evolution of man's 'second nature', his character. He writes:

All the chimpanzees I observed were cautious, hesitant creatures. This is one of the major impressions one carries away from studying chimpanzees at close range in the wild. Behind their lively, searching eyes one senses a doubting, contemplative personality, always trying to make sense out of a puzzling world. It is as if the certainty of instinct has been replaced in chimpanzees by the uncertainty of intellect – but without the determination and decisiveness that characterize man. (A. Kortlandt, 1962)

Kortlandt notes that, as experiments with captive animals have shown, the behaviour patterns of chimpanzees are much less innate than those of monkeys.[9]

From the van Lawick-Goodall observations I want to quote here a specific one because it offers a good example for Kortlandt's important statement about the hesitancy and lack of decisiveness in the behaviour of the chimpanzee. This is the report:

One day Goliath appeared some distance up the slope with an unknown pink female (in heat) close behind him. Hugo and I quickly put out a pile of bananas where both chimps could see the fruit and hid in the tent to watch. When the female saw our camp she shot up a tree and stared down. Goliath instantly stopped also, and looked up at her. Then he glanced at the bananas. He moved a short way down the slope, stopped, and looked back at his female. She had not moved. Slowly Goliath continued down, and this time the female climbed silently from the tree and we lost sight of her in the undergrowth. When Goliath looked around

9. K. J. and C. Hayes of the Yerkes Laboratories of Primate Biology in Orange Park, Florida, who raised a chimpanzee in their home and systematically submitted it to a 'forced' humanizing education, measured its IQ as 125 at the age of two years and eight months (C. Hayes, 1951; and K. J. Hayes and C. Hayes, 1951).

and saw that she had gone, he simply raced back. A moment later the female again climbed into a tree, followed by Goliath, who had every hair on end. He groomed her a while but every so often glanced towards camp. Although he could no longer see the bananas he knew that they were there, and since he had been away for about ten days his mouth was probably watering.

In time he climbed down and once more walked towards us, stopping every few steps to stare back at the female. She sat motionless, but Hugo and I both had the distinct impression that she wanted to escape from Goliath's company. When Goliath had come a bit farther down the slope the vegetation obviously hid the female from his view because he looked back and then quickly climbed a tree. She was still sitting there. He climbed down, walked another few yards, and then shot up another tree. Still there. This went on for a further five minutes as Goliath proceeded towards the bananas.

When he reached the camp clearing Goliath faced an added problem – there were no trees to climb and he couldn't see the female from the ground. Three times he stepped into the open, then turned and rushed back up the last tree. The female did not move. Suddenly Goliath seemed to make up his mind and, at a fast canter, raced over to the bananas. Seizing only one he turned back and raced to climb his tree again. Still the female sat on the same branch. Goliath finished his banana and, as though slightly reassured, hastened back to the pile of fruit, gathered up a whole armful, and rushed back to the tree. This time the female had gone; while Goliath gathered the bananas she had climbed down from her branch, repeatedly glancing towards him over her shoulder, and vanished silently.

Goliath's consternation was amusing to watch. Dropping his bananas he raced up to the tree where he had left her, peered all around, and then he too vanished into the undergrowth. For the next twenty minutes he searched for that female. Every few minutes we saw him climbing up yet another tree, staring in every direction: but he never found her and finally gave up, returned to camp, and looking quite exhausted, sat slowly eating bananas. Even so, he kept turning his head to gaze back up the slope. (J. van Lawick-Goodall, 1971)

The incapacity of the male chimpanzee to come to a decision whether first to eat the bananas or mount the female is quite striking. If we observed this same behaviour in a man, we would say that he was suffering from obsessional doubt, because the normal human would have no difficulty in acting according to the dominant impulse in his character structure; the oral receptive character would first eat the banana and postpone the satisfaction of his sexual impulse; the 'genital character' would let the food wait until he was sexually gratified. In either case he would act without doubt or hesitancy. Since we can hardly assume that the male in this example is suffering from an obsessional neurosis, the question why he behaves in this way seems to find its answer in Kortlandt's statement to which van Lawick-Goodall regrettably makes no reference.

Kortlandt describes the chimpanzee's remarkable tolerance towards the young as well as their deference towards the old, even when they no longer had physical power. Van Lawick-Goodall stresses the same characteristic:

Chimpanzees normally show a good deal of tolerance in their behaviour towards each other. This is especially true of males, less so with females. A typical instance of tolerance of a dominant to a subordinate animal occurred when an adolescent male was feeding from the only ripe cluster of fruits in a palm tree. A mature male climbed up but did not try to force the other away; he merely moved up beside the younger and the two fed side by side. Under similar circumstances a subordinate chimpanzee may move up to a dominant one, but before attempting to feed, it normally reaches out to touch the other on the lips, thigh, or genital area. Tolerance between males is particularly noticeable during the mating season, as for example on the occasion described above when seven males were observed copulating with one female with no signs of aggression between them; one of these males was an adolescent. (J. van Lawick-Goodall, 1971)

On *gorillas* observed in the wild, G. B. Schaller reports that on the whole 'interaction' between groups was peaceful. Aggressive bluff charges were made by one male as noted above, and 'I once observed weak aggressiveness in the form of incipient charges towards intruders from another group by a female, a juvenile and an infant. Most intergroup aggressiveness was confined to staring and snapping.' Serious aggressive attacks among gorillas were not witnessed by Schaller. This is all the more remarkable because the gorilla group home ranges not only overlapped, but seem to have been commonly shared amongst the gorilla population. Hence there would be ample occasion for friction (G. B. Schaller, 1963, 1965).

Special attention should be paid to van Lawick-Goodall's reports on feeding behaviour because her observations have been used by a number of authors as an argument for the carnivorous or 'predatory' character of chimpanzees. She states that 'the chimpanzees of the Gombe Stream Reserve (and probably in most places throughout the range of the species as a whole) are omnivorous ... The chimpanzee is primarily vegetarian; that is, by far the greatest proportion of foods constituting his diet as a whole is vegetable' (J. van Lawick-Goodall, 1968). There were certain exceptions to this rule. During the course of her field study she or her assistant observed chimpanzees feeding on the flesh of other mammals in twenty-eight instances. In addition, examining occasional samples of faeces during the first two and a half years and regular samples in the last two and a half years, altogether the remnants of thirty-six different mammals were found in dung, over and above those the chimpanzees were observed eating. In addition she reports four instances during these years in which in three cases a male chimpanzee caught and killed an infant baboon, and in one the killing involved a, probably female, red colobus monkey. Furthermore, she observed sixty-eight mammals eaten (mostly primates) within forty-five months, or roughly one and a half per month, by a group of fifty chimpanzees. These figures confirmed the author's previous statement that the chimpanzees' 'diet on the whole is vegetable' and hence that meat eating is exceptional. Yet, in her popular book *In the*

Shadow of Man, the author states flatly that she and her husband 'saw chimpanzees eating meat fairly frequently' (J. van Lawick-Goodall, 1971), but without quoting the qualifying data in her previous work that show the relative infrequency of meat eating. I stress this point because in publications after this study, comments abound emphasizing the 'predatory' character of chimpanzees, based on van Lawick-Goodall's 1971 version of the data. But chimpanzees are, as many authors had stated, omnivorous; they live mainly on a vegetable diet. That they eat meat occasionally (in fact rarely), does not make them carnivorous and surely not predatory animals. But the use of the words 'predatory' and 'carnivorous' insinuate that man is born with an innate destructiveness.

Territorialism and Dominance

The popular picture of animal aggressiveness has been largely influenced by the concept of *territorialism*. Robert Ardrey's *Territorial Imperative* (1967) has left the general public with the implication that man is dominated by an instinct for defence of his territory, inherited from his animal ancestors. This instinct is supposed to be one of the main sources of animal and human aggressiveness. Analogies are easily drawn, and the facile idea appeals to many that war is caused by the power of this same instinct.

The idea, however, is quite erroneous for a number of reasons. In the first place there are many animal species for whom the concept of territoriality does not apply. 'Territoriality occurs only in higher animals such as the vertebrates and arthropods and even there in a very spotty fashion' (J. P. Scott, 1968a). Other students of behaviour, like Zing Yang Kuo, are 'rather inclined to think that the so-called "territorial defence" is, after all, merely a fancy name for the reaction patterns to strangers, flavoured with anthropomorphism and nineteenth-century Darwinism. Further and more systematic experimental explorations are necessary to decide this issue' (Zing Yang Kuo, 1960).

N. Tinbergen distinguishes between the territorialism of the species and that of the individual: 'It seems certain that territories are selected mainly on the basis of properties to which the animals react innately. This makes all animals of the same species, or at least of the same population, select the same general type of habitat. However, the personal binding of a male to its own territory – a particular representative of the species' breeding habitat – is the result of a learning process' (N. Tinbergen, 1953).

In the description of primates we have seen how often there is an overlap of territory. If the observation of apes teaches us anything, it is that various groups of primates are quite tolerant and flexible with regard to their territory and simply do not offer a picture that would permit the analogy to a society, jealously guarding its frontiers and forcibly preventing the entry of any 'foreigner'.

The assumption that territorialism is the basis for human aggressiveness is erroneous for still another reason. Defence of territory has the function *of avoiding* the serious fighting that would become necessary if the territory were invaded to such an extent as to generate crowding. Actually the threat behaviour in which territorial aggression manifests itself is the instinctively patterned way of upholding spatial equilibrium and peace. The instinctive equipment of the animal has the function that legal arrangements have in man. Hence the instinct becomes obsolete when other symbolic ways are available to mark a territory and to warn: no trespassing. It is also worth keeping in mind that, as we shall see later, most wars start for the purposes of gaining advantages of various kinds and not in defence against a threat to one's territory – except in the ideology of the war makers.

Equally wrong impressions exist popularly about the concept of *dominance*. In many species, but by no means in all, one finds that the group is organized hierarchically. The strongest male takes precedence in food, sex, and grooming over other males on lower orders of the hierarchy.[10] But dominance, like territorialism, by no means exists in all animals and, again, not regularly in the vertebrates and mammals.

With regard to dominance among the nonhuman primates we find a great difference between some of the monkey species like the baboons and macaques, in whom one finds rather well-developed and strict hierarchical systems, and the apes with whom dominance patterns are much less strong. Of the mountain gorillas, Schaller reports:

Definite dominance interactions were observed 110 times. Dominance was most frequently asserted along narrow trails, when one animal claimed the right of way, or in the choice of sitting place, when the dominant animal supplanted the subordinate one. Gorillas showed their dominance with a minimum of actions. Usually an animal low in the rank order simply moved out of the way at the mere approach or brief stare of a high-ranking one. The most frequently noted gesture involving bodily contact was a light tap with the back of the hand of a dominant individual against the body of a subordinate one. (G. B. Schaller, 1965)

In their report on the chimpanzees of the Bodongo Forest, V. and F. Reynolds state:

Although there was some evidence of differences in status between individuals, dominance interactions formed a minute fraction of the observed chimpanzee behaviour. There was no evidence of a linear hierarchy of dominance among males or females; and there were no permanent leaders of groups. (V. and F. Reynolds, 1965)

T. E. Rowell, in his study of baboons, argues against the whole concept of dominance and states that

10. One has more rarely drawn a parallel from this hierarchy to the 'instinctive' roots for dictatorship than one has from territorialism to patriotism, although the logic would be the same. The reason for this different treatment lies probably in that it is less popular to construct an instinctive basis for dictatorship than for 'patriotism'.

circumstantial evidence suggests that hierarchical behaviour is associated with environmental stress of various kinds and under stress it is the lower-ranking animal which first shows physiological symptoms (lower disease resistance, for example). If it is sub-ordinate behaviour that determines rank (rather than dominant behaviour as usually assumed), the stress factor can be seen as directly affecting all animals to different degrees dependent on their construction, producing physiological and behavioural (sub-mitting behaviour) changes at the same time, the latter in turn giving rise to a hierarchical social organization. (T. E. Rowell, 1966)

He comes to the conclusion 'that the hierarchy appears to be maintained chiefly by subordinates' behaviour patterns, and by the low – rather than the high-ranking animals' (T. E. Rowell, 1966).

W. A. Mason also expresses strong reservations based on his studies of chimpanzees:

The view taken here is that 'dominance' and 'subordination' are simply conventional designations for the fact that chimpanzees often stand in the relationship to each other of intimidator and intimidated. Naturally, we would expect the larger, stronger, more boisterous, and more aggressive animals in any group (being intimidating to almost everyone else) to display a kind of generalized dominance status. Presumably this accounts for the fact that in the wild, mature males are generally dominant over adult females, and they, in turn, are dominant over adolescents and juveniles. Apart from this observation, however, there is no indication that chimpanzee groups as a whole are organized hierarchically; nor is there any convincing evidence of an autono-mous drive for social supremacy. Chimpanzees are wilful, im-pulsive, and greedy, certainly a sufficient basis for the development of dominance and subordination, without the participation of specialized social motives and needs.

Dominance and subordination can thus be regarded as the natural by-product of social intercourse, and but one facet of the relationship between two individuals ... (W. A. Mason, 1970)

For dominance, as far as it exists, the same comment applies which I have made with regard to territorialism. It functions to give peace and coherence to the group and to prevent friction that could lead to serious fighting. Man substitutes agreements, etiquette, and laws for the missing instinct.

Animal dominance has been widely interpreted as a fierce 'bossiness' of the leader who enjoys having power over the rest of the group. It is true that among monkeys, for instance, the authority of the leader is often based on the fear he engenders in the others. But among the apes, as for instance the chimpanzee, it is often not fear of the retaliatory power of the strongest animal, but his competence in leading the group which establishes his authority. As an example of this, mentioned earlier, Kortlandt (1962) reports about an old chimpanzee who retained his leadership because of his experience and wisdom, in spite of the fact that he was physically weak.

Whatever the role of dominance in animals is, it seems to be pretty clear that the dominant animal must constantly merit his role – that is to say, show his greater physical strength, wisdom, energy, or whatever it is that makes him accepted as a leader. A very ingenious experiment with monkeys, reported by J. M. R. Delgado (1967), suggests that if the dominant animal loses his distinguishing qualities even momentarily, his commanding role ends. In human history, when dominance becomes institutionalized and no longer a function of personal competence as is still the case in many primitive societies, it is not necessary for the leader to be in constant possession of his outstanding qualities, in fact it is not even necessary that he has them. The social system conditions people to see in the title, the uniform, or whatever else it may be, the proof that the leader is competent, and as long as these symbols, supported by the whole system, are present, the average man does not even dare to ask himself whether the emperor wears clothes.

Aggressiveness Among Other Mammals

Not only do primates show little destructiveness but all other mammals, predatory and non-predatory, fail to exhibit aggressive behaviour such as would correspond to what it might be if Lorenz's hydraulic theory were correct.

Even among the most aggressive mammals, rats, the intensity of aggressiveness is not as great as Lorenz's examples indicate. Sally Carrighar has called attention to the difference between an experiment with rats which Lorenz quotes in favour of his hypothesis and another experiment which clearly shows that the critical point was not an innate aggressiveness of the rat but certain conditions that were responsible for greater or lesser aggressiveness:

According to Lorenz, Steiniger put brown rats from different localities into a large enclosure which provided them with completely natural living conditions. At first the individual animals seemed afraid of each other; they were not in an aggressive mood, but bit each other if they met by chance, particularly if two were driven towards each other along one side of the enclosure, so that they collided at speed.[11]

Steiniger's rats soon began to attack one another and fought until all but one pair were killed. The descendants of that pair formed a clan, which subsequently slaughtered every strange rat introduced into the habitat.

During the same years that this study was being conducted, John B. Calhoun in Baltimore was also investigating the behaviour of rats. There were fifteen rats in F. Steiniger's original population; fourteen in Calhoun's – also strangers to one another. But Calhoun's enclosure was sixteen times larger than Steiniger's and more favourable in other ways: 'harbourages' were provided for rats pursued by hostile associates (such refuges would probably

11. Most animal psychologists, incidentally, would not call 'completely natural' the conditions provided by any enclosure – especially if the enclosure were so small that individuals collided when racing along the fence.

exist in the wild), and all Calhoun's rats were identified by markings.

For twenty-seven months, from a tower in the centre of the large area, the movements of all the individual rats were recorded. After a few fights while getting acquainted, they separated into two clans, neither of which tried to eliminate the other. There was a good deal of crossing back and forth unchallenged – so often by some individuals that they were dubbed messengers.[11] (S. Carrighar, 1968)

In contrast to the vertebrates and lower invertebrates, as J. P. Scott, one of the most outstanding students of animal aggression, has .pointed out, aggression is very common among the arthropods, as the fierce fighting of lobsters indicates, and among social insects like wasps and certain spiders, in which the female attacks the male and eats him. A great deal of aggression can also be found among fish and reptiles. He writes:

The comparative physiology of fighting behaviour in animals yields the extremely important conclusion that the primary stimulation for fighting behaviour is external; that is, there is no spontaneous internal stimulation which makes it necessary to an individual to fight irrespective of the outside environment. The physiological and emotional factors involved in the agonistic behavioural system are thus quite different from those involved in sexual and ingestive behaviour.

And further on Scott states:

Under natural conditions hostility and aggression in the sense of *destructive and maladaptive* [italics added] agonistic behaviour are hard to find in animal societies.

Addressing himself to the specific problem of the spontaneous internal stimulation which Lorenz postulates, Scott writes:

All of our present data indicate that fighting behaviour among the higher mammals, including man, originates in external stim-

12. cf. S. A. Barnett and M. M. Spencer (1951) and S. A. Barnett (1958, 1958a).

ulation and that there is no evidence of spontaneous internal stimulation. Emotional and physiological processes prolong and magnify the effects of stimulation, but do not originate it.[13] (J. P. Scott, 1968a)

Has Man an Inhibition Against Killing?

One of the most important points in the chain of Lorenz's explanations for human aggression is the hypothesis that man, in contrast to predatory animals, has not developed instinctive inhibitions against killing co-specifics; he explains this point by the assumption that man, like all non-predatory animals, has not dangerous natural weapons like claws, etc., and hence does not need such inhibitions; it is only because he has weapons that his lack of instinctive inhibitions becomes so dangerous.

But is it really true that man has no inhibitions against killing?

Man's historical record is so frequently characterized by killing that at first it would seem unlikely that he has any inhibitions. However, this answer becomes questionable if we reformulate our question to read: Has man any inhibitions against killing living beings, humans, and animals with whom he identifies to a greater or lesser degree, i.e., who are not complete 'strangers' to him and to whom he is related by affective bonds?

There is some evidence that such inhibitions might exist and that a sense of guilt may follow the act of killing.

That the element of familiarity and empathy plays a role in the generation of inhibitions against killing animals can easily be detected from reactions to be observed in everyday life. Many people show a definite aversion to killing and eating an animal with which they are familiar or one they have kept as a pet, like a rabbit or a goat. There are a large number of people who would not kill such an animal and to

13. Zing Yang Kuo, in his experimental studies of animal fighting in mammals, has come to similar conclusions (1960).

whom the idea of eating it is plainly repulsive. The same people usually have no hesitation in eating a similar animal where this element of empathy is lacking. But there is not only an inhibition against killing with regard to animals that are individually known, but also inasmuch as a sense of identity is felt with the animal as another living being. There might be a conscious or unconscious feeling of guilt related to the destruction of life, especially when there is a certain empathy. This sense of closeness to the animal and need to reconcile oneself to killing it is quite dramatically manifested in the rituals of the bear cult of Palaeolithic hunters (J. Mahringer, 1952).[14]

The sense of identity with all living beings that share with man the quality of *life* has been made explicit as an important moral tenet in Indian thinking and has led to the prohibition against killing any animal in Hinduism.

It is not unlikely that inhibitions against killing also exist with regard to other humans, provided there is a sense of identity and empathy. We have to begin with the consideration that for primitive man the 'stranger', the person who does not belong to the same group, is often not felt as a fellow man, but as 'something' with which one does not identify. There is generally greater reluctance to kill a member of the same group, and the most severe punishment for misdeeds in primitive society often was ostracism, rather than death. (This is still apparent in the punishment of Cain in the Bible.) But we are not restricted to these examples of primitive society. Even in a highly civilized culture like the Greek, the slaves were experienced as not being entirely human.

We find the same phenomenon in modern society. All governments try, in the case of war, to awaken among their

14. I believe a similar reason underlies the Jewish ritual of not eating meat with milk. Milk and its products are symbols of life; they symbolize the living animal. The prohibition to eat meat and milk products together seems to indicate the same tendency to make a sharp distinction between the live animal and the dead animal used as food.

own people the feeling that the enemy is not human. One does not call him by his proper name, but by a different one, as in the First World War when the Germans were called 'Huns' by the British or 'Boches' by the French. This destruction of the humanness of the enemy came to its peak with enemies of a different colour. The war in Vietnam provided enough examples to indicate that many American soldiers had little sense of empathy with their Vietnamese opponents, calling them 'gooks'. Even the word 'killing' is eliminated by using the word 'wasting'. Lieutenant Calley, accused and convicted for murdering a number of Vietnamese civilians, men, women, and children, in My Lai, used as an argument for his defence the consideration that he was not taught to look at the soldiers of the NLF ('Viet Cong') as human beings but only as 'the enemy'. Whether that is sufficient defence or not is not the question here. It is certainly a strong argument, because it is true and puts into words the underlying attitude towards the Vietnamese peasants. Hitler did the same by calling 'political enemies' he wanted to destroy *Untermenschen* ('subhumans'). It seems almost a rule, when one wants to make it easier for one's own side to destroy living beings of the other, to indoctrinate one's own soldiers with a feeling that those to be slaughtered are non-persons.[15]

15. Tom Wicker in reflections on the wholesale slaughter of hostages and inmates by the forces that stormed the prison in Attica, New York, wrote a very thoughtful column making the same point. He refers to a statement issued by New York State Governor Nelson A. Rockefeller after the massacre at Attica which begins with the sentence: 'Our hearts go out to the families of the hostages who died at Attica', then Wicker writes: 'Much of what went wrong at Attica – and of what is wrong at most other American prisons and "corrections facilities" – can be found in the simple fact that neither in that sentence nor in any other did the governor or any official extend a word of sympathy to the families of the dead prisoners.

'True, at that time, it was thought that the deaths of the hostages had been caused by the prisoners, rather than – as is now known – by the bullets and buckshot of those ordered by the state authorities to go over the walls shooting. But even had the prisoners, instead of the police, been

Another way of making the other a 'non-person' is cutting all affective bonds with him. This occurs as a permanent state of mind in certain severe pathological cases, but it can also occur transitorily in one who is not sick. It does not make any difference whether the object of one's aggression is a stranger or a close relative or a friend; what happens is that the aggressor cuts the other person off emotionally and 'freezes' him. The other ceases to be experienced as human and becomes a 'thing – over there'. Under these circumstances there are no inhibitions against even the most severe forms of destructiveness. There is good clinical evidence for the assumption that destructive aggression occurs, at least to a large degree, in conjunction with momentary or chronic emotional withdrawal.

Whenever another being is not experienced as human, the act of destructiveness and cruelty assumes a different quality. A simple example will show this. If a Hindu or a Buddhist, for instance, provided he has a genuine and deep feeling of empathy with all living beings, were to see the average modern person kill a fly without the slightest hesitation, he might judge this act as an expression of considerable callousness and destructiveness; but he would

---

the killers of hostages, they still would have been human beings, certainly their mothers and wives and children still would have been human beings. But the official heart of the state of New York and its officials did not go out to any of them.

'That is the root of the matter; prisoners, particularly black prisoners, in all too many cases are neither considered nor treated as human beings. And since they are not, neither are their families.'

Wicker continues: 'Time and again, members of the special observers' group that tried to negotiate a settlement at Attica heard the prisoners plead that they, too, were human beings and wanted above all to be treated as such. Once, in a negotiating session through a steel-barred gate that divided prisoner-held and state-held territory, Assistant Corrections Commissioner Walter Dunbar told the prisoner leader, Richard Clark: "In thirty years, I've never lied to an inmate."

'"But how about to a man?" Clark said quietly' (*The New York Times*, 18 September 1971).

be wrong in this judgement. The point is that for many people the fly is simply not experienced as a sentient being and hence is treated as any disturbing 'thing' would be; it is not that such people are especially cruel, even though their experience of 'living beings' is restricted.

7
Palaeontology

Is Man One Species?

It should be recalled that Lorenz's use of animal data referred to intra-specific aggression and not to aggression between different animal species. The question is: Can we be really sure that humans in their relationship to other humans experience each other as co-specifics and hence react with genetically prepared behaviour patterns towards co-specifics? Do we not see, on the contrary, that among many primitive peoples even a man of another tribe or living in a neighbouring village some miles away is looked upon as a complete stranger or even not human, and hence there is no empathy with him? Only in the process of social and cultural evolution has the number of people who are accepted as being human increased. It seems that there are good reasons to assume that man does not experience his fellow man as a member of the same species, because his recognition of another man is not facilitated by those instinctive or reflex-like reactions by which either smell, form, certain colours, etc., give immediate evidence of species identity among animals. In fact, in many animal experiments, it has been demonstrated that even the animal can be deceived or made to feel uncertain about who are his co-specifics.

Precisely because man has less instinctive equipment than any other animal, he does not recognize or identify co-specifics as easily as animals. For him different language, customs, dress, and other criteria perceived by the mind rather than by instincts determine who is a co-specific and who is not, and any group which is slightly different is not supposed to share in the same humanity. From this follows the paradox that man, precisely because he lacks instinctive equipment, also lacks the experience of the identity of his species and experiences the stranger as if he belonged to another species; in other words, *it is man's humanity that makes him so inhuman.*

If these considerations are correct, Lorenz's case would collapse, because all his ingenious constructions and the conclusions he draws are based on aggression among members of the same species. In this case an entirely different problem would arise, namely that of the innate aggressiveness of animals towards members of *other* species. As far as this interspecific aggression is concerned, the data on animals show, if anything, less evidence that such interspecific aggression is genetically programmed except in cases where the animal is threatened or among predatory animals. Could a case be made for the hypothesis that man is the descendant of a predatory animal? Could we assume that man, although not another man's wolf, is another man's sheep?

Is Man a Predatory Animal?

Is there any evidence to suggest that man's ancestors were predatory?

The earliest hominid who may have been one of man's ancestors is the *Ramapithecus* who lived in India about fourteen million years ago.[1] The form of his dental arcade was

1. Whether or not *Ramapithecus* was a hominid and a direct ancestor of man is still controversial. (See the detailed presentation of the argument in D. Pilbeam, 1970.) Almost all palaeontological data are based on a good deal of speculation and, hence, are highly controversial. By following one author one may come to a different picture than by following another. However, for our purpose the many disputed details of human evolution are not essential, and as far as the major points of development are concerned, I have tried to present what seems to be the consensus of

similar to those of other hominids and much more manlike than that of present-day apes; even though he may have eaten meat in addition to his mainly vegetable diet, it would be absurd to think of him as a predatory animal.

The earliest hominid fossils we know after *Ramapithecus* are those of *Australopithecus robustus* and the more advanced *Australopithecus africanus*, found by Raymond Dart in South Africa in 1924 and believed to date from almost two million years ago. *Australopithecus* has been the subject of a great deal of controversy. The great majority of palaeoanthropologists today accept the thesis that the australopithecines were hominids, while a few investigators, such as D. R. Pilbeam and E. L. Simons (1965), assume that *A. africanus* is to be considered as the first appearance of *Homo*.

In the discussion of the australopithecines, much has been made of their use of tools, in order to prove that they were human or at least man's ancestors. Lewis Mumford, however, has convincingly pointed out that the importance of tool-making as sufficient identification of man is misleading and rooted in the bias inherent in the current concept of technics (L. Mumford, 1967). Since 1924 new fossils have been discovered, but their classification is controversial, as well as the question whether *Australopithecus* was to any considerable extent a meat eater, hunter, or tool-maker.[2]

---

most students in this field. But even with regard to major stages of human evolution I omit some controversy from the context in order not to make it too burdensome. For the following analysis I have used mainly these works: D. Pilbeam (1970), J. Napier (1970), J. Young (1971), I. Schwidetzki (1971), S. Tax, ed. (1960), B. Rensch, ed. (1965), A. Roe and G. C. Simpson (1958, 1967), A. Portman (1965), S. L. Washburn and P. Jay, eds. (1968), B. G. Campbell (1966), and a number of papers, some of which are indicated in the text.

2. S. L. Washburn and F. C. Howell (1960) write that it is very unlikely that the early and small-bodied australopithecines, who augmented their basically vegetable diet with meat, did much killing, 'whereas the later and larger forms which probably replaced them could cope with small and/or immature animals. There is no evidence to suggest that such creatures were capable of preying on the large herbivorous mammals so characteristic of the African Pleistocene.' The same point

Nevertheless, most investigators agree that *A. africanus* was an omnivorous animal, characterized by the flexibility of his diet. B. G. Campbell (1966) comes to the conclusion that *Australopithecus* ate small reptiles; birds; small mammals, such as rodents; roots, and fruits. He ate such small animals as he could capture without weapons or setting traps. Hunting, on the contrary, presupposes cooperation and an adequate technique which came into existence only much later and coincides with the emergence of man in Asia around 500,000 B C.

Whether *Australopithecus* was a hunter or not, it is beyond any doubt that the hominids like their pongid ancestors were not predatory animals with the instinctual and morphological equipment which characterizes carnivorous predators such as lions and wolves.

In spite of this unequivocal evidence, not only the dramatizing Ardrey, but even a serious scholar like D. Freeman has attempted to identify *Australopithecus* as the palaeontological 'Adam' who brought the original sin of destructiveness into the human race. Freeman speaks of the australopithecines as a 'carnivorous adaptation', having 'predatory, murderous and cannibalistic predilections. Thus palaeonanthropology has, during the last decade, revealed a phylogenetic basis for the conclusions about human aggression which have been reached by psychoanalytic research into man's nature.' He summarizes: 'In broad anthropological perspective then, it may be argued that man's nature and skills and, ultimately, human civilization, owe their existence to the kind of predatory adaptation first achieved by the carnivorous *Australopithecinae* on the grasslands of southern Africa in the Lower Pleistocene' (D. Freeman, 1964).

---

of view was expressed by Washburn in an earlier paper (1957) where he wrote that 'it is probable that the australopithecines were themselves the game rather than the hunters'. Later on, however, he suggested that the hominids, including the australopithecines, 'might possibly' have been hunters (S. L. Washburn and C. S. Lancaster, 1968).

In the discussion following the presentation of his paper, Freeman does not seem to be so convinced: 'So, in the light of recent palaeoanthropological discoveries the hypothesis has now been advanced that certain aspects of human nature (including *possibly* aggressivity and cruelty) may well be connected with the special predatory and carnivorous adaptations which were so basic to hominid evolution during the Pleistocene period. This, in my view, is a *hypothesis that deserves to be investigated* scientifically and dispassionately, for it concerns matters about which we are at present most ignorant' (D. Freeman, 1964; italics added). What, in the paper, was the *fact* that palaeoanthropology revealed conclusions about human aggression has become, in the discussion, a *hypothesis* that 'deserved to be investigated'.

Such investigation is obscured by a confusion to be found in Freeman – as well as the works of a number of other authors – among 'predatory', 'carnivorous', and 'hunting'. Zoologically, predatory animals are clearly defined. They are the families of cats, hyenas, dogs, and bears, and they are characterized as having toes with claws, and sharp canines. The predatory animal finds his food by attacking and killing other animals. This behaviour is genetically programmed, with only a marginal element of learning, and furthermore, as has been mentioned before, predatory aggression has a neurologically different basis from aggression as a defence reaction. One cannot even call the predatory animal a particularly aggressive animal, for in its relations with its co-species it is sociable and even amiable, as for instance, we have seen the behaviour of wolves. Predatory animals (with the exception of bears that are mainly vegetable feeders and quite unfitted for the chase) are exclusively meat eaters. But not all meat-eating animals are predatory. The omnivorous animals that eat vegetables *and* meat do not for this reason belong to the order of the Carnivora. Freeman is aware that 'the term "carnivorous" when it is used to refer to the behaviour of the hominidae has to have a meaning *quite distinct* from that which it has when applied to species within the order Carnivora' (J. D. Carthy, F. J. Ebling, 1964; italics added). But why then call hominids carnivorous, instead of omnivorous? The resulting confusion only helps establish the following equation in the mind of the reader: meat eater = carnivorous = predatory, ergo, man's hominid ancestor was a predatory animal equipped with the instinct to attack other animals, including other men; ergo, man's destructiveness is innate, and Freud is right. *Quod erat demonstrandum!*

All we may conclude about *A. africanus* is that he was an omnivorous animal in whose diet meat played a more or less important role and that he killed animals as a source of food if they were small enough. A diet of meat does not transform the hominid into a predatory animal. Furthermore, it is by now a widely accepted fact, expressed by Sir Julian Huxley and others, that diet – vegetable or meat – has nothing to do with generating aggressiveness.

Nothing justifies the assumption that *Australopithecus* had the instincts of a predatory animal which, provided 'he' was man's ancestor, could be made responsible for 'predatory' genes in man.

8
Anthropology

In this chapter I shall present detailed data on primitive hunters and food gatherers, the Neolithic agriculturists, and the new urban societies. In this way the reader is put in a position to judge for him or herself whether the data support the conventional thesis that the more primitive the man, the more aggressive he is. In many cases they are the findings of a younger generation of anthropologists in the last ten years, and contrasting older views are not yet corrected in the minds of most non-specialists.

'Man the Hunter' – The Anthropological Adam?

If the *predatory* quality of man's hominid ancestors cannot be made responsible for his innate aggressiveness, can there be a human ancestor, a *prehistorical Adam* who is responsible for man's 'fall'? This is what S. L. Washburn, one of the greatest authorities in this field, and his co-authors believe, and they identify this 'Adam' as man, *the hunter*.

Washburn starts from the premise that in view of the fact that man has lived during 99 per cent of his history as a hunter, we owe our biology, psychology, and customs to the hunters of the time past:

In a very real sense our intellect, interests, emotions and basic social life – all are evolutionary products of the success of the hunting adaptation. When anthropologists speak of the unity of mankind, they are stating that the selection pressures of the hunting and gathering way of life were so similar and the result so successful that populations of *Homo sapiens* are still fundamentally the same everywhere.[1] (S. L. Washburn and C. S. Lancaster, 1968)

The crucial question, then, is: What is this 'psychology of the hunter'?

Washburn calls it a 'carnivorous psychology' fully developed by the Middle Pleistocene, around 500,000 years ago or even earlier:

> The world view of the early human carnivore must have been very different from that of his vegetarian cousins. The interests of the latter could be satisfied in a small area, and other animals were of little moment, except for the few which threatened attack. But desire for meat leads animals to know a wider range and to learn the habits of many animals. Human territorial habits and psychology are fundamentally different from those of apes and monkeys. For at least 300,000 years (perhaps twice that) carnivorous curiosity and aggression have been added to the inquisitiveness and dominance striving of the ape. This carnivorous psychology was fully formed by the middle Pleistocene and it may have had its beginnings in the depredations of the australopithecines. (S. L. Washburn and V. Avis, 1958)

Washburn identifies the 'carnivorous psychology' with a drive for and pleasure in killing. He writes: 'Man takes pleasure in hunting other animals. Unless careful training has hidden the natural drives, men enjoy the chase and the kill. In most cultures *torture and suffering are made public spectacles for the enjoyment of all*' (S. L. Washburn and V. Avis, 1958; italics added).

Washburn insists: 'Man has a carnivorous psychology. It is easy to teach people to kill, and it is hard to develop customs which avoid killing. Many human beings enjoy seeing other human beings suffer or enjoy the killing of animals ... public beatings and torture are common in many cultures' (S. L. Washburn, 1959). In the last two statements Washburn implies that not only killing, but cruelty as well, are part of hunting psychology.

1. Washburn and Lancaster (1968) contains rich material on all aspects of hunting life. See also S. L. Washburn and V. Avis (1958).

What are Washburn's arguments in favour of this alleged innate joy in killing and cruelty?

One argument is 'killing as a sport' (he speaks of 'killing' as a sport, rather than of 'hunting', which would be more correct). He writes: 'Perhaps this is most easily shown by the extent of the efforts devoted to maintain killing as a sport. In former times royalty and nobility maintained parks where they could enjoy the sport of killing, and today the United States government spends many millions of dollars to supply game for hunters' (S. L. Washburn and C. S. Lancaster, 1968). A related example is: 'people who use the lightest fishing tackle to prolong the fish's futile struggle, in order to maximize the personal sense of mastery and skill' (S. L. Washburn and C. S. Lancaster, 1968).

Washburn points to the popularity of war:

And until recently war was viewed in much the same way as hunting. Other human beings were simply the most dangerous game. War has been far too important in human history for it to be other than pleasurable for the males involved. It is only recently with the entire change in the nature and conditions of war, that this institution has been challenged, that the wisdom of war as a normal part of national policy or as an approved road to personal social glory has been questioned. (S. L. Washburn and C. S. Lancaster, 1968)

In connection with this, Washburn states:

The extent to which the biological bases for killing have been incorporated into human psychology may be measured by the ease with which boys can be interested in hunting, fishing, fighting, and games of war. It is not that these behaviours are inevitable, but they are easily learned, satisfying, and have been socially rewarded in most cultures. The skills for killing and the pleasures of killing are normally developed in play, and the patterns of play prepare the children for their adult roles. (S. L. Washburn and C. S. Lancaster, 1968)

Washburn's claim that many people enjoy killing and cruelty is true as far as it goes, but all it means is that there are sadistic individuals and sadistic cultures; but there are others that are not sadistic. One will find, for instance, that sadism is much more frequently to be found among frustrated individuals and social classes who feel powerless and have little pleasure in life, for example the lower class in Rome who were compensated for their material poverty and social impotence by sadistic spectacles, or the lower middle class in Germany from whose ranks Hitler recruited his most fanatical following; it is also to be found in ruling classes that feel threatened in their dominant position and their property[2] or in suppressed groups that thirst for revenge.

The idea that hunting produces pleasure in torture is an unsubstantiated and most implausible statement. Hunters as a rule do not enjoy the suffering of the animal, and in fact a sadist who enjoys torture would make a poor hunter; nor do fishermen as a rule use the procedure mentioned by Washburn. There is also no evidence for the assumption that primitive hunters were motivated by sadistic or destructive impulses. On the contrary, there is some evidence to show that they had an affectionate feeling for the killed animals and possibly a feeling of guilt for the kill. Among Palaeolithic hunters, the bear was often addressed as 'grandfather' or was looked upon as the mythical ancestor of man. When the bear was killed, apologies were offered; before he was eaten, a sacred meal took place with the bear as an 'honoured guest', before whom were placed the best dishes; finally the bear was ceremoniously buried (J. Mahringer, 1952).[3]

The psychology of hunting, including that of the contemporary hunter, calls for extensive study, but a few observations can be made even in this context. First of all,

2. The mass slaughter of the French Communards, 1871, by the victorious army of Thiers is a drastic example.

3. cf. the authors quoted by Mahringer. A similar attitude can be found among the hunting rituals of the Navajo Indians; cf. R. Underhill (1953).

one must distinguish between hunting as a sport of ruling
élites (for instance, the nobility in a feudal system) and all
other forms of hunting, such as that of primitive hunters,
farmers protecting their crops or chickens, and individuals
who love to hunt.

'Élite hunting' seems to satisfy the wish for power and
control, including a certain amount of sadism, characteristic
of power élites. It tells us more about feudal psychology than
about the psychology of hunting.

Among the motivations of the primitive professional and
the modern passionate hunter, at least two kinds must be
distinguished. The first have their roots in the depth of
human experience. In the act of hunting, a man becomes,
however briefly, part of nature again. He returns to the
natural state, becomes one with the animal, and is freed
from the burden of the existential split: to be part of nature
and to transcend it by virtue of his consciousness. In stalking
the animal he *and* the animal become equals, even though
man eventually shows his superiority by the use of his
weapons. In primitive man this experience is quite conscious. Through disguising himself as an animal, and
considering an animal as his ancestor, he makes this
identification explicit. For modern man, with his cerebral
orientation, this experience of oneness with nature is difficult
to verbalize and to be aware of, but it is still alive in many
human beings.

Of at least equal importance for the passionate hunter is
an entirely different motivation, that of enjoyment in his
skill. It is amazing how many modern authors neglect this
element of skill in hunting, and focus their attention on the
act of killing. After all, hunting requires a combination of
many skills and wide knowledge beyond that of handling a
weapon.

This point has been discussed in detail by William S.
Laughlin, who also starts out with the thesis that 'hunting is
the master behaviour pattern of the human species' (W. S.
Laughlin, 1968). Laughlin, however, does not even mention

pleasure in killing or cruelty as part of the hunting behaviour pattern, but describes it in these general terms:
'Hunting has placed a premium upon inventiveness, upon
problem solving, and has imposed a real penalty for failure
to solve the problem. Therefore it has contributed as much
to advancing the human species as to holding it together
within the confines of a single variable species' (W. S.
Laughlin, 1968).

Laughlin points out, and this is a very important point to
be kept in mind in view of the conventional over-emphasis
on tools and weapons:

> Hunting is obviously an instrumental system in the real sense
> that something gets done, several ordered behaviours are per-
> formed with a crucial result. The technological aspects, the spears,
> clubs, hand-axes, and all the other objects suitable for museum
> display, are essentially meaningless apart from the context in
> which they are used. They do not represent a suitable place to
> begin analysis because their position in the sequence is remote
> from the several preceding complexes.[4] (W. S. Laughlin, 1968)

The efficiency of hunting is to be understood not on the
basis of the advancement of its technical bases, but by the
increasing skill of the hunter:

> There is ample documentation, though surprisingly few system-
> atic studies, for the postulate that primitive man is sophisticated
> in his knowledge of the natural world. This sophistication encom-
> passes the entire macroscopic zoological world of mammals,
> marsupials, reptiles, birds, fish, insects, and plants. Knowledge of
> tides, meteorological phenomena generally, astronomy and other
> aspects of the natural world are also well developed among some
> variations between groups with reference to the sophistication and
> extent of their knowledge, and to the areas in which they have
> concentrated ... I will here only cite the relevance of this sophis-
> tication to the hunting behaviour system and to its significance
> for the evolution of man ... man, the hunter, was learning animal
> behaviour and anatomy, including his own. He domesticated

4. Laughlin's observation gives full support to one of Lewis Mumford's main theses concerning the role of tools in the evolution of man.

himself first and then turned to other animals and to plants. In this sense, hunting was the school of learning that made the human species self-taught. (W. S. Laughlin, 1968)

In short, the motivation of the primitive hunter was not pleasure in killing, but the learning and optimal performance of various skills, i.e., the development of man himself.[5]

Washburn's argument regarding the ease with which boys can be interested in hunting, fighting, and games of war ignores the fact that boys can be easily induced to any kind of pattern that is culturally accepted. To conclude that this interest of boys in popularly accepted behaviour patterns proves the innate character of the pleasure in killing testifies to a remarkable naïve attitude in matters of social behaviour. Furthermore it should be noted that there are a number of sports – from Zen sword fighting to fencing, judo, and karate – in which it is quite obvious that their fascination does not lie in the pleasure to kill, but in the skill they allow to be displayed.

Equally untenable is Washburn and Lancaster's statement that 'almost every human society has regarded killing members of certain other human societies as desirable' (Washburn and Lancaster, 1968). This is a repetition of a popular cliché, and the only source offered for it is the paper by D. Freeman (1964), discussed above, which is biased by the Freudian view. The facts are that, as we shall see further on, wars among primitive hunters are characteristically un-

5. Today, when almost everything is made by machines, we notice little pleasure in skill except perhaps the pleasure people experience with hobbies like carpentry or the fascination of the average person when he can watch a goldsmith or weaver at his work; perhaps the fascination with a performing violinist is not only caused by the beauty of the music he produces but by the display of his skill. In cultures where most of the production is by hand and rests on skill, it is unmistakably clear that work is enjoyable because of the skill involved in it, and to the degree to which this skill is involved. The interpretation of the pleasure in hunting as pleasure in killing, rather than in skill, is indicative of the person of our time for whom the only thing that counts is the *result* of an effort, in this case killing, rather than the process itself.

bloody, and mostly not aimed at killing. To claim that the institution of war has only recently been challenged is, of course, to ignore the history of a wide range of philosophical and religious teaching, especially that of the Hebrew prophets.

If we do not follow Washburn's reasoning, the question remains whether there are other patterns which hunting behaviour has engendered. It seems, indeed, that there are two behaviour patterns that might have been genetically programmed through hunting behaviour: cooperation and sharing. Cooperation between members of the same band was a practical necessity for most hunting societies; so was the sharing of food. Since meat is perishable in most climates except that of the Arctic, it could not be preserved. Luck in hunting was not equally divided among all hunters; hence the practical outcome was that those who had luck today would share their food with those who would be lucky tomorrow. Assuming hunting behaviour led to genetic changes, the conclusion would be that modern man has an innate impulse for cooperation and sharing, rather than for killing and cruelty.

Unfortunately, man's record of cooperation and sharing is rather spotty, as the history of civilization shows. One might explain this by the fact that hunting life did not produce genetic changes, or that the impulses for sharing and cooperation have become deeply repressed in cultures whose organization discouraged these virtues and instead encourages ruthless egotism. Nevertheless, one might still speculate whether the tendency to cooperate and to share which we find in many societies today outside of the modern industrialized world do not point to the innate character of these impulses. In fact, even in modern warfare, in which the soldier by and large does not feel much hate against his enemy, and only exceptionally indulges in cruelty,[6] we find

6. This is to some extent different in wars like that in Vietnam, in which the 'native' enemy is not experienced as being human. See also p. 142-3.

a remarkable degree of cooperation and sharing. While in civilian life most people do not risk their lives to save another man's life or share their food with others, in war this is a daily occurrence. Perhaps one might even go further and suggest that one of the factors which make war attractive is precisely the possibility of practising deeply buried human impulses which our society, when at peace, considers – in fact, although not ideologically – to be foolish.

Washburn's idea on hunting psychology is only one example of the bias in favour of the theory of man's innate destructiveness and cruelty. In the whole field of the social sciences one can observe a high degree of partisanship when it comes to questions immediately related to actual emotional and political problems. Where the ideology and interest of a society are concerned, objectivity usually yields to bias. Modern society, with its almost limitless readiness for destruction of human lives for political and economic ends, can best defend itself against the elementary human question of its right to do so by the assumption that destructiveness and cruelty are not engendered by our social system, but are innate qualities in man.

Aggression and Primitive Hunters

Fortunately, our knowledge of hunting behaviour is not restricted to speculations; there is a considerable body of information about still existing primitive hunters and food gatherers to demonstrate that hunting is not conducive to destructiveness and cruelty, and that primitive hunters are relatively unaggressive when compared to their civilized brothers.

The question arises whether we can apply our knowledge of these primitive hunters to prehistoric hunters, at least to those living since the emergence of modern man, '*Homo sapiens sapiens*', about forty thousand to fifty thousand years ago.

The fact is that very little is known about man since his

emergence, and not too much even about *H. sapiens sapiens* in his hunting-gathering stage. Thus a number of authors quite correctly have cautioned against drawing conclusions from modern primitives as to their prehistorical ancestors (J. Deetz, 1968).[7] Nevertheless, as G. P. Murdock says, interest in contemporary hunters exists 'because of the light they may shed on the behaviour of Pleistocene man'; and most of the other participants in the symposium on *Man the Hunter* (R. B. Lee and I. DeVore, eds., 1968) would seem to be in accord with this formulation. Even though we cannot expect prehistoric hunter-gatherers to have been identical to the most primitive contemporary hunters and food gatherers, it must be considered that (1) *H. sapiens sapiens* was anatomically and neurophysiologically not different from man today, and (2) the knowledge of still existing primitive hunters is bound to contribute to the understanding of at least one crucial problem in regard to prehistoric hunters: the influence of hunting behaviour on personality and on social organization. Aside from this, the data on primitive hunters demonstrates that qualities often attributed to human nature, such as destructiveness, cruelty, asociability – in short, those of Hobbes's 'natural man' – are remarkably missing in the least 'civilized' men!

Before discussing still existing primitive hunters, a few remarks need to be made about the Palaeolithic hunter. M. D. Sahlins writes:

In selective adaptation to the perils of the Stone Age, human society overcame or subordinated such primate propensities as selfishness, indiscriminate sexuality, dominance and brute competition. It substituted kinship and cooperation for conflict, placed solidarity over sex, morality over might. In its earliest days it accomplished the greatest reform in history, the overthrow of human primate nature, and thereby secured the evolutionary future of the species. (M. D. Sahlins, 1960)

There are certain direct data on the life of the prehistoric hunter to be found in animal cults which point to the fact

7. cf. also, G. P. Murdock (1968).

that he lacked the alleged innate destructiveness. As Mumford has pointed out, the cave paintings associated with the life of prehistoric hunters did not exhibit any fighting between men.[8]

Despite the caution required in making analogies, however, the most impressive data are certainly those of still existing hunters/food-gatherers. Colin Turnbull, a specialist in this study, has reported:

> In the two groups known to me, there is an almost total lack of aggression, emotional or physical, and this is borne out by the lack of warfare, feuding, witchcraft, and sorcery.
>
> I am also not convinced that hunting is itself an aggressive activity. This is something that one must see in order to realize; the act of hunting is not carried out in an aggressive spirit at all. Due to the consciousness of depleting natural resources, there is actually a regret at killing life. In some cases, this killing may even bear an element of compassion. My experience with hunters has shown them to be very gentle people, and while it is certainly true that they lead extremely hard lives, this is not the same thing as being aggressive.[9] (C. M. Turnbull, 1965)

None of the other participants in the discussion with Turnbull contradicted him.

The most comprehensive description of the anthropological findings of primitive hunters and food gatherers is offered by E. R. Service in *The Hunters* (E. R. Service, 1966). His monograph includes all such societies, with the exception of those sedentary groups along the north-west coast of North America which exist in a particularly bountiful environment, and those other hunting-gathering societies that become extinct so soon after contact with civilization that our knowledge of them is too fragmentary.[10]

8. The same view has been expressed by the palaeoanthropologist Helmuth de Terra (personal communication).

9. cf., for a vivid description of this general statement, Turnbull's presentation on the social life of a primitive African hunter society, the Mbutu Pygmies (C. M. Turnbull, 1965).

10. The societies with which Service deals are the following: the Eskimos, the Algonkian and Athabascan hunters of Canada, the Shoshone

The most obvious and probably most crucial characteristic of the hunting-gathering societies is their nomadism, required by the foraging economy which leads to loose integration of families into a 'band' society. As for their needs – in contrast to modern man who requires a house, an automobile, clothing, electricity, and so on – for the primitive hunter 'food, and the few devices employed in obtaining it, is the focus of economic life . . . in a more fundamental sense than it is in more complicated economies' (E. R. Service, 1966).

There is no full-time specialization of labour other than the age and sex divisions that are found in any family. Food consists to a smaller extent of meat (perhaps about 25 per cent), while the gathering of seeds, roots, fruits, nuts, and berries constitute the main diet, furnished by the work of women. As M. J. Meggitt says: 'A vegetarian stress seems to be one of the prime distinguishing features of hunting and fishing, and gathering economies' (M. J. Meggitt, 1964). Only the Eskimos live by hunting and fishing alone, and Eskimo women do most of the fishing.

There is broad cooperation of men in the hunt, which is a normal concomitant of the low state of technological development in band society. 'For several reasons having to do with the very simplicity of the technology and the lack of control over the environment, many hunting-gathering peoples are quite literally the most leisured peoples in the world' (E. R. Service, 1966).

Economic relations are especially instructive. Service writes:

We are accustomed, because of the nature of our own economy, to think that human beings have a 'natural propensity to truck and barter', and that economic relations among individuals or groups are characterized by 'economizing', by 'maximizing' the result of effort, by 'selling dear and buying cheap'. Primitive peoples do none of these things, however; in fact, most of the time

of the Great Basin, the Indians of Tierra del Fuego, the Australians, the Semang of the Malay Peninsula, the Andaman Islanders.

it would seem that they do the opposite. They 'give things away', they admire generosity, they expect hospitality, they punish thrift as selfishness.

And strangest of all, the more dire the circumstances, the more scarce (or valuable) the goods, the less 'economically' will they behave and the more generous do they seem to be. We are considering, of course, the form of exchange among persons *within* a society and these persons are, in band society, all kinsmen of some sort. There are many more kinsmen in a band than there are people in our own society who actually maintain close social relations; but an analogy can be drawn with the economy of a modern family, for it, too, contrasts directly with the principles ascribed to the formal economy. We 'give' food, do we not, to our children? We 'help' our brothers and 'provide for' aged parents. Others do, or have done, or will do, the same for us.

At the generalized pole, because close social relations prevail, the emotions of love, the etiquette of family life, the morality of generosity all together condition the way goods are handled, and in such a way that the economic attitude towards the goods is diminished. Anthropologists have sometimes attempted to characterize the actual transaction with words like 'pure gift' or 'free gift' in order to point up the fact that this is not trade, but barter, and that the sentiment involved in the transaction is not one of a balanced exchange. But these words are not quite evocative of the actual nature of the act; they are even somewhat misleading.

Once Peter Freuchen was handed some meat by an Eskimo hunter and responded by gratefully thanking him. The hunter was cast down, and Freuchen was quickly corrected by an old man: 'You must not thank for your meat: it is your right to get parts. In this country, nobody wishes to be dependent on others. Therefore, there is nobody who gives or gets gifts, for thereby you become dependent. With gifts you make slaves just as with whips you make dogs.'[11]

The word 'gift' has overtones of charity, not of reciprocity. In no hunting-gathering society is gratitude expressed, and, as a matter of fact, it would be wrong even to praise a man as 'generous' when he shares his game with his campmates. On another occasion he could be said to be generous, but not in response to

11. Peter Freuchen (1961).

a particular incident of sharing, for then the statement would have the same implication as an expression of gratitude: that the sharing was unexpected, that the giver was not generous simply as a matter of course. It would be right to praise a man for his hunting prowess on such an occasion, but not for his generosity. (E. R. Service, 1966)

Of particular importance, both economically and psychologically, is the question of poverty. One of the most widespread clichés today is that the love for property is an innate trait in man. Usually the confusion is made between property in instruments one needs for one's work and in certain private items like ornaments, etc. and property in the sense of owning the means of production, that is to say, things through whose exclusive possession other people can be made to work for oneself. Such means of production in the industrial society are essentially machines or capital to be invested in machine production. In primitive society the means of production are land and hunting areas.

In no primitive band is anyone denied access to the resources of nature – no individual owns these resources ...

The natural resources on which the bands depend are collective, or communal, property, in the sense that the territory might be defended by the whole band against encroachment by strangers. Within the band, all families have equal rights to acquire these resources. Moreover, kinsmen in neighbouring bands are allowed to hunt and gather at will, at least on request. The most common instance of apparent restriction in rights to resources occurs with respect to nut- or fruit-bearing trees. In some instances, particular trees or clumps of trees are allocated to individual families of the band. This practice is more a division of labour, however, than a division of property, for its purpose seems to be to prevent the waste of time and effort that would occur if several scattered families headed for the same area. It is simply to conventionalize the allotted use of the several groves, inasmuch as trees are much more permanently located than game or even wild vegetables and grasses. At any rate, even if one family acquired many nuts or fruits and another failed, the rules of sharing would apply so that no one would go hungry.

The things that seem most like private property are those that are made and used by individual persons. Weapons, knives and scrapers, clothing, ornaments, amulets, and the like, are frequently regarded as private property among hunters and gatherers . . . But it could be argued that in primitive society even these personal items are not private property in the true sense. Inasmuch as the possession of such things is dictated by their use, they are functions of the division of labour rather than an ownership of the 'means of production'. Private ownership of such things is meaningful only if some people possess them and others do not – when, so to speak, an exploitative situation becomes possible. But it is hard to imagine (and impossible to find in ethnographic accounts) a case of some person or persons who, through some accident, owned no weapons or clothing and could not borrow or receive such things from more fortunate kinsmen. (E. R. Service, 1966)

Social relations among the members of hunting-gathering society are characterized by the absence of what is called 'dominance' among animals. Service states:

Hunting-gathering bands differ more completely from the apes in this matter of dominance than do any other kinds of human society. There is no peck-order based on physical dominance at all, nor is there any superior-inferior ordering based on other sources of power such as wealth, hereditary classes, military or political office. The only consistent supremacy of any kind is that of a person of greater age and wisdom who might lead a ceremony.

Even when individuals possess greater status or prestige than others, the manifestation of the high status and the prerogatives are the opposite of ape-like dominance. Generosity and modesty are required of persons of high status in primitive society, and the rewards they receive are merely the love or attentiveness of others. A man, for example, might be stronger, faster, braver, and more intelligent than any other member of the band. Will he have higher status than the others? Not necessarily. Prestige will be accorded him only if these qualities are put to work in the service of the group – in hunting, let us say – and if he therefore produces more game to give away, and if he does it properly, modestly. Thus, to simplify a bit, greater strength in ape society results in greater dominance, which results in more food and mates and any other things desired by the dominant one; in primitive human society greater strength must be used in the service of the community, and the person, to earn prestige, must literally sacrifice to do so, working harder for less food. As for the mates, he ordinarily has but one wife just the other men.

It seems that the most primitive human societies are at the same time the most egalitarian. This must be related to the fact that because of rudimentary technology this kind of society depends on cooperation more fully more of the time than any other. Apes do not regularly cooperate and share, human beings do – that is the essential difference. (E. R. Service, 1966)

Service gives a picture of the kind of authority we find among the hunter-gatherer peoples. In these societies there is of course a need for administration of group action:

Administration is the role authority assumes with respect to problems of concerted group action. It is what we ordinarily mean by the word 'leadership'. The necessities for administration of group action and close coordination are varied and numerous in hunting-gathering societies. They would include such usual things as camp movements, a collaborative hunting drive, and particularly any kind of skirmishing with enemies. But despite the obvious significance of leadership in such activities, a hunting-gathering society is, as in other matters, distinctive in that it has no formal leadership of the sort that we see in later stages of cultural development. There is no permanent office of headman; leadership moves from one person to another depending on the type of activity that is being planned. For example, one very old man might be the favourite for planning a ceremony because of his great ritual knowledge, but another person, younger and more skilled at hunting, might be the normal leader of the hunting party.

Above all, there is no leader or headman in the sense usually associated with the word *chief*.[12] (E. R. Service, 1966)

This lack of hierarchy and chiefs is all the more noteworthy because it is a widely accepted cliché that such

12. M. J. Meggitt (1960; quoted by E. R. Service, 1966), has arrived at almost identical conclusions with regard to Australian elders. See also the distinction made in E. Fromm (1941), between rational and irrational authority.

control institutions as are to be found in virtually all civilized societies are based on a genetic inheritance from the animal kingdom. We have seen that among chimpanzees the dominance relationships are rather mild, but they are nevertheless there. The social relationships of primitive people show that man is not genetically prepared for this kind of dominance-submission psychology. An analysis of historical society, with five or six thousand years of exploitation of the majority by a ruling minority, shows very clearly that the dominance-submission psychology is an adaptation to the social order, and not its cause. For the apologists of a social order based on control by an élite, it is of course very convenient to believe that the social structure is the outcome of an innate need of man and, hence, natural and unavoidable. The egalitarian society of the primitive shows that this is just not so.

The question must arise how primitive man protects himself against asocial and dangerous members, in the absence of an authoritarian or bureaucratic authoritarian régime. There are several answers to this question. First of all, much of the control of behaviour is achieved merely in terms of custom and etiquette. But assuming that custom and etiquette did not prevent individuals from asocial behaviour, what are the sanctions against them? The usual sanction is a general withdrawal from the culprit and a diminished degree of courtesy towards him; there is gossip and ridicule; in extreme cases, ostracism. If a person constantly misbehaves, and his behaviour harms groups other than his own, his own group may even decide to kill him. However, these cases are extremely rare, and most problems are solved by the authority of the older and wiser males in the group.

These data clearly contradict the Hobbesian picture of man's innate aggression which would lead to the war of every man against every man, unless the state monopolized violence and punishment, thus satisfying indirectly the thirst for revenge against the wrongdoers. As Service points out,

The fact of the matter, of course, is that band societies are not riven into pieces, even though there are no formal adjudicative bodies to hold them together ...

But although feuds and warfare are relatively rare in band societies, they do consistently *threaten* and there must be some way of stopping them or of preventing their spread. Often they begin as mere quarrels between individuals, and for this reason it is important to stop them early. Within a given community the adjudication of a quarrel between two persons will ordinarily be handled by an elder who is a common relative of them both. It would be ideal if this person were in the same relationship to each one of the quarrelling men, for then it would be evident that he would not be so likely to take sides. But of course this is not always the case, nor is it always possible that the person in this kinship status position might want to adjudicate. Sometimes one person is clearly enough in the right and the other in the wrong, or one person popular and the other unpopular, that the public becomes the adjudicator and the case is settled as soon as this common opinion becomes well-known.

When quarrels are not settled in any of the above ways, then some form of contest is held, preferably a game, that takes the place of an outright battle. Wrestling or head-butting contests are typical forms of quasi-duelling in Eskimo society. It is done in public and the winner is considered by the public to have won his case. Particularly interesting is the famous Eskimo song duel: the weapons used are words, 'little, sharp words, like the wooden splinters which I hack off with my axe'.

Song duels are used to work off grudges and disputes of all orders, save murder. An East Greenlander, however, may seek his satisfaction for the murder of a relative through a song contest if he is physically too weak to gain his end, or if he is so skilled in singing as to feel certain of victory. Inasmuch as East Greenlanders get so engrossed in the mere artistry of singing as to forget the cause of the grudge, this is understandable. Singing skill among these Eskimos equals or outranks gross physical prowess.

The singing style is highly conventionalized. The successful singer uses the traditional patterns of composition which he attempts to deliver with such finesse as to delight the audience to enthusiastic applause. He who is most heartily applauded is 'winner'. To win a song contest brings no restitution in its train. The sole advantage is in prestige (E. A. Hoebel, 1954).

One of the advantages of the song duel carried on at length is that it gives the public time to come to a consensus about who is correct or who should admit guilt in the dispute. Ordinarily, people have some idea of whose side they are on, but as in most primitive communities the unanimity of the community as a whole is felt to be so desirable that it takes a while before the people can find out where the majority opinion lies. Gradually more people are laughing a little harder at one of the duellist's verses than at the other's until it becomes apparent where the sympathy of the community lies, and then opinion quickly becomes unanimous and the loser retires in discomfiture. (E. R. Service, 1966)

Among other hunting societies private quarrels are not solved as charmingly as by the Eskimos, but by a spear-throwing duel:

When a dispute is between an accuser and a defendant, which is commonly the case, the accuser ritually hurls the spears from a prescribed distance, while the defendant dodges them. The public can applaud the speed, force, and accuracy of the accuser as he hurls his spears, or then can applaud the adroitness with which the defendant dodges them. After a time unanimity is achieved as the approval for one or the other's skill gradually becomes overwhelming. When the defendant realizes that the community is finally considering him guilty, he is supposed to fail to dodge a spear and allow himself to be wounded in some fleshy part of his body. Conversely, the accuser simply stops throwing the spears when he becomes aware that public opinion is going against him. (C. W. M. Hart and A. R. Pilling, 1960)

Primitive Hunters – The Affluent Society?

A very relevant point – and one even interesting for the analysis of contemporary industrial society – is made by M. D. Sahlins with regard to the whole question of economic scarcity among primitive hunters and the modern attitude towards the problem of what constitutes poverty. He argues against the premise that led to the idea of the

aggressiveness of primitive hunters, namely that life in the
Palaeolithic period was one of extreme scarcity and constant
confrontation with starvation. In contrast, Sahlins emphasizes that the society of primitive hunters was the
'original affluent society'.

> By common understanding, an affluent society is one in which all
> the people's wants are easily satisfied; and though we are pleased
> to consider this happy condition the unique achievement of
> industrial civilization, a better case can be made for hunters and
> gatherers, even many of the marginal ones spared to ethnography.
> For wants are 'easily satisfied' either by producing much or
> desiring little and there are, accordingly, two possible roads to
> affluence ... Adopting a Zen strategy a people can enjoy an
> unparalleled material plenty, although perhaps only a low stand-
> ard of living. That I think describes the hunters.[13] (M. D. Sahlins,
> 1968)

Sahlins makes some further very pertinent statements:

> Scarcity is the peculiar obsession of a business economy, the
> calculable condition of all who participate in it. The market makes
> freely available a dazzling array of products – all these 'good
> things' are within a man's reach – but never his grasp, for one
> never has enough to buy everything. To exist in a market economy
> is to live out a double tragedy, beginning in inadequacy and
> ending in deprivation ... We stand sentenced to life at hard
> labour. It is from this anxious vantage that we look back on the
> hunter. But if modern man, with all his technical advantages, still
> hasn't got the wherewithal, what chance has this naked savage
> with his puny bow and arrow? Having equipped the hunter with
> bourgeois impulses and Palaeolithic tools, we judge his situation
> hopeless in advance.[14]

13. R. B. Lee ('What Hunters Do for a Living: Or How to Make Out
on Scarce Resources') also questions the assumption that a hunter-
gatherer life is generally a precarious one of struggle for existence:
'Recent data on hunter-gatherers show a radically different picture'
(R. B. Lee and I. DeVore, 1968).

14. A similar point has been made by S. Piggott who writes: 'Repu-
table archaeologists have sometimes failed to appreciate the fallacy inherent in rating prehistoric communities in terms of their surviving
material culture. Words such as "degenerate" are taken from their usage

Scarcity is not an intrinsic property of technical means. It is a relation between means and ends. We might entertain the empirical possibility that hunters are in business for their health, a finite objective, and bow and arrow are adequate to that end. A fair case can be made that hunters often work much less than we do, and rather than a grind the food quest is intermittent, leisure is abundant, and there is more sleep in the daytime *per capita* than in any other conditions of society . . . Rather than anxiety, it would seem, the hunters have a confidence born of affluence, of a condition in which all the people's wants (such as they are) are generally easily satisfied. This confidence does not desert them during hardship. [This attitude has been expressed by the Philosophy of the Penan of Borneo: 'If there is no food today, there will be tomorrow.'] (M. D. Sahlins, 1968)

Sahlins's remarks are important because he is one of the few anthropologists who do not accept the frame of reference and value judgements of present-day society as necessarily valid. He shows to what degree social scientists distort the picture of societies under their observation by judging them from what seems to be the 'nature' of economics, just as they come to conclusions about the nature of man from the data, if not of modern man, at least of man as we know him through most of his civilized history.

Primitive Warfare

Although defensive aggression, destructiveness, and cruelty are not ordinarily the cause of war, these impulses manifest themselves in warfare. Hence some data on primitive warfare will help to complete the picture of primitive aggression.

---

to denote an assumed place in a typological series of pots, for instance, and transferred with an emotive and even moral connotation to the makers of the vessels; people with poor and scanty pottery become stigmatized as "poverty-stricken", though their poverty may well have been only in their failure to provide the archaeologist with his favourite product' (S. Piggott, 1960).

Meggitt gives a summation of the nature of warfare among the Walbiri of Australia, which Service states may be accepted as an apt characterization of warfare in hunting-gathering societies generally:

Walbiri society did not emphasize militarism – there was no class of permanent or professional warriors; there was no hierarchy of military command; and groups rarely engaged in wars of conquest. Every man was (and is still) a potential warrior, always armed and ready to defend his rights; but he was also an individualist, who preferred to fight independently. In some disputes kinship ties aligned men into opposed camps, and such a group may occasionally have comprised all the men of a community. But there were no military leaders, elected or hereditary, to plan tactics and ensure that others adopted the plans. Although some men were respected as capable and courageous fighters and their advice was valued, other men did not necessarily follow them. Moreover, the range of circumstances in which fights occurred was in effect so limited that men knew and could employ the most effective techniques without hesitation. This is still true today even of young bachelors.

There was in any case little reason for all-out warfare between communities. Slavery was unknown; portable goods were few; and the territory seized in a battle was virtually an embarrassment to the victors, whose spiritual ties were with other localities. Small-scale wars of conquest against other tribes occurred occasionally, but I am sure that they differed only in degree from intra-tribal and even intra-community fights. Thus the attack on the Waringari that led to the occupation of the water holes in the Tanami area involved only Waneiga men – a few score at most; and I have no evidence that communities ever entered into a military alliances, either to oppose other Walbiri communities or other tribes. (M. J. Meggitt, 1960)

Technically speaking, this kind of conflict among primitive hunters can be described as war; in this sense one may conclude that 'war' has always existed within the human species, and hence, that it is the manifestation of an innate drive to kill. This reasoning, however, ignores the profound differences in the warfare of lower and of higher primitive cultures[15] as well as the warfare of civilized cultures. Primitive warfare, particularly that of the lower primitives, was neither centrally organized nor led by permanent chieftains; it was relatively infrequent; it was not war of conquest nor was it bloody war aimed at killing as many of the enemy as possible. Most civilized war, in contrast, is institutionalized, organized by permanent chieftains, and aims at conquest of territory and/or acquisition of slaves and/or booty.

In addition, and perhaps most important of all, is the frequently overlooked fact that there is no important economic stimulus among primitive hunter-gatherers to full-scale war.

The birth–death ratio in hunting-gathering societies is such that it would be rare for population pressure to cause some part of the population to fight others for territorial acquisition. Even if such a circumstance occurred it would not lead to much of a battle. The stronger, more numerous, group would simply prevail, probably even without a battle, if hunting rights or rights to some gathering spot were demanded. In the second place there is not much to gain by plunder in hunting-gathering society. All bands are poor in material goods and there are no standard items of exchange that serve as capital or as valuables. Finally, at the hunting-gathering level the acquisition of captives to serve as slaves for economic exploitation – a common cause of warfare in more modern times – would be useless, given the low productivity of the economy. Captives and slaves would have a difficult time producing more than enough food to sustain themselves. (E. R. Service, 1966)

The overall picture of warfare among primitive hunter-gatherers given by Service is supported and supplemented by a number of other investigators, some of whom are quoted in the following paragraphs.[16] D. Pilbeam stresses

15. cf. Q. Wright (1965).
16. I shall not discuss such older authors as W. J. Perry (1917, 1923, 1923a) and G. E. Smith (1924, 1924a) because they have been generally discarded by modern investigators, and it would take too much space to defend the value of their contributions.

the absence of war, in contrast to occasional feuds, together with the role of example rather than power among the leaders in a hunting society, and the principle of reciprocity and generosity, and the central role of cooperation (D. Pilbeam, 1970).

U. H. Stewart comes to the following conclusion concerning territoriality and warfare:

There have been many contentions that primitive bands own territories or resources and fight to protect them. Although I cannot assert that this is never the case, it is probably very uncommon. First, the primary groups that comprise the larger maximum bands intermarry, amalgamate if they are too small or split off if too large. Second, in the cases reported here, there is no more than a tendency for primary groups to utilize special areas. Third, most so-called 'warfare' among such societies is no more than revenge for alleged witchcraft or continued inter-family feuds. Fourth, collecting is the main resource in most areas, but I know of no reported defence of seed areas. Primary bands did not fight one another, and it is difficult to see how a maximum band could assemble its manpower to defend its territory against another band or why it should do so. It is true that durian trees, eagle nests, and a few other specific resources were sometimes individually claimed, but how they were defended by a person miles away has not been made clear. (U. H. Stewart, 1968)

H. H. Turney-High (1971) comes to similar conclusions. He stressed that while the experiences of fear, rage and frustration are universal, the art of war develops only late in human evolution. Most primitive societies were not capable of war because war requires a sophisticated level of conceptualization. Most primitive societies could not imagine an organization necessary to conquer or defeat a neighbour. Most primitive wars are nothing but armed mêlées, not wars at all. According to Rapaport, Turney-High's work did not find a very friendly reception among anthropologists because he stressed that secondary accounts of battles written by professional anthropologists were hopelessly inadequate and sometimes downright misleading; he believed that primary sources were more reliable, even when they were by amateur ethnologists generations ago.[17]

Quincy Wright's monumental work (1,637 pages including an extensive bibliography) presents a thorough analysis of warfare among primitive people based on the statistical comparison of the main data to be found among six hundred and fifty-three primitive peoples. The shortcoming of his analysis lies in the fact that he is more descriptive than analytical in the classification of primitive societies as well as of different kinds of warfare. Nevertheless, his conclusions are of considerable interest because they show a statistical trend that corresponds to the results of many other authors: 'The collectors, lower hunters and lower agriculturalists are the least warlike. The higher hunters and higher agriculturalists are more warlike, while the highest agriculturalists and the pastors are the most warlike of all' (Q. Wright, 1965). This statement confirms the idea that warlikeness is not a function of man's natural drives that manifest themselves in the most primitive form of society, but of his development in civilization. Wright's data show that the more division of labour there is in a society, the more warlike it is, and that societies with class-systems are the most warlike of all peoples. Eventually his data show that the greater the equilibrium among groups and between the group and its physical environment, the less warlikeness one finds, while frequent disturbances of the equilibrium result in an increase in warlikeness.

Wright differentiates among four kinds of war – defensive, social, economic, and political. By defensive war, he refers to the practice of people who have no war in their mores and who fight only if actually attacked, 'in which case they make spontaneous use of available tools and hunting weapons to

17. D. C. Rapaport, in his Foreword to Turney-High's book (H. H. Turney-High, 1971), quotes the most eminent historian of war, Hans Delbrück, who found 'that the only detail Herodotus got right in his reconstruction of the battle of Marathon was the identities of the victors and vanquished'.

defend themselves, but regard this necessity as a misfortune'. By social war he refers to people with whom war 'is usually not very destructive of life'. (This warfare corresponds to Service's description of war among hunters.) Economic and political wars refer to people who make war in order to acquire women, slaves, raw materials, and land and/or, in addition, for the maintenance of a ruling dynasty or class.

Almost everybody reasons: if civilized man is so warlike, how much more warlike must primitive man have been![18] But Wright's results confirm the thesis that the most primitive men are the least warlike and that warlikeness grows in proportion to civilization. If destructiveness were innate in man, the trend would have to be the opposite.

A view similar to Wright's has also been expressed by M. Ginsberg, who writes:

It would seem that war in this sense grows with the consolidation of groups and economic development. Among the simplest peoples we ought to speak rather of feuds, and these unquestionably occur on grounds of abduction of women, or resentments of trespass or personal injury. It must be conceded that these societies are peaceful by comparison with the more advanced of the primitive peoples. But violence and fear of violence are there and fighting

18. cf. also S. Andreski (1964), who takes a position similar to the one of this book and the other writers mentioned in the text. He cites a very interesting statement by a Chinese philosopher, Han Fei-tzu, *c.* fifth century BC: 'The men of old did not till the field, but the fruits of plants and trees were sufficient for food. Nor did the women weave, for the furs of birds and animals were enough for clothing. Without working there was enough to live, there were few people and plenty of supplies, and therefore the people did not quarrel. So neither large rewards nor heavy punishments were used, but the people governed themselves. But nowadays people do not consider a family of five children as large, and each child having again five children, before the death of the grandfather, there may be twenty-five grandchildren. The result is that there are many people and few supplies, that one has to work hard for a meagre return. So the people fall to quarrelling and though rewards may be doubled and punishments heaped up, one does not get away from disorder' (quoted from J. J. L. Duyvendak, 1928).

occurs, though that is obviously and necessarily on a small scale. The facts are not adequately known, and if they do not support the view of a primitive idyllic peace, they are perhaps compatible with the view of those who think that primary or unprovoked aggressiveness is not an inherent element of human nature. (E. Glover and M. Ginsberg, 1934)

Ruth Benedict (1959) makes the distinction between 'socially lethal' and 'non-lethal' wars. In the latter, the aim is not that of subjugating other tribes to the victor as masters and profiteers; although there was much warfare among North American Indians,

The idea of conquest never arose in aboriginal North America, and this made it possible for almost all these Indian tribes to do a very extreme thing: to separate war from the state. The state was personified in the Peace Chief, who was a leader of public opinion in all that concerned the in-group and in his council. The Peace Chief was permanent, and though no autocratic ruler he was often a very important personage. But he had nothing to do with war. He did not even appoint the war chiefs or concern himself with the conduct of war parties. Any man who could attract a following led a war party when and where he would, and in some tribes he was in complete control for the duration of the expedition. But this lasted only till the return of the war party. The state, according to this interpretation of war, had no conceivable interest in these ventures, which were only highly desirable demonstrations of rugged individualism turned against an out-group where such demonstrations did not harm the body politic. (R. Benedict, 1959)

Benedict's point is important because it touches upon the connection of war, state, and private property. Socially non-lethal war is to a large extent an expression of adventurousness and the wish to have trophies and be admired, but it was not invoked by the impulse to conquer people or territory, to subjugate human beings, or to destroy the basis for their livelihood. Benedict comes to the conclusion that 'elimination of war is not so uncommon as one would think from the writings of political theorists of the prehistory of war . . . It is a complete misunderstanding to lay this havoc [war] to any biological need of man to go to war. The havoc is man-made' (R. Benedict, 1959). Another outstanding anthropologist, E. A. Hoebel (1958), characterizes warfare among early North American Indians in these terms: 'They come closer to William James's Moral Equivalents of War. They release aggressions harmlessly: they provide exercise, sport and amusement without destruction; and only mildly is there any imposition of desires by one party on the other' (E. A. Hoebel, 1958). He comes to the general conclusion that man's propensity to war is obviously not an instinct, because it is an elaborate cultural complex. He gives as an interesting example the pacifistic Shoshones and the violent Comanches who in 1600 were still culturally and racially one.

The Neolithic Revolution[19]

The detailed description of the life of primitive hunters and food gatherers has shown that man – at least since he fully emerged fifty thousand years ago – was most likely not the brutal, destructive, cruel being and hence not the prototype of 'man the killer' that we find in more-developed stages of his evolution. However, we cannot stop there. In order to understand the gradual development of man the exploiter and the destroyer, it is necessary to deal with the development of man during the period of early agriculture and, eventually, with his transformation into a builder of cities, a warrior, and a trader.

From the emergence of man, approximately half a million years ago to about 9000 B C, man did not change in one res-

19. In the following analysis I follow mainly V. G. Childe (1936), G. Clarke (1969), S. Cole (1967), J. Mellaart (1967), and the discussion of Childe's viewpoint by G. Smolla (1967). A different hypothesis is suggested by C. O. Sauer (1952). I have also greatly benefited from Mumford's treatment of the topic (1961, 1967).

pect: he lived from what he gathered or hunted, but did not produce anything new. He was completely dependent on nature and did not himself influence or transform it. This relationship to nature changed radically with the invention of agriculture (and animal husbandry) which occurred roughly with the beginning of the Neolithic period, more precisely, the 'Proto-Neolithic' period as archaeologists call it today – from 9000 to 7000 BC – in an area stretching over one thousand miles from western Iran to Greece, including parts of Iraq, Syria, Lebanon, Jordan, Israel, and the Anatolian Plateau in Turkey. (It started later in Central and Northern Europe.) For the first time man made himself, within certain limits, independent of nature by using his inventiveness and skill to produce something beyond that which nature had thus far yielded to him. It was now possible to plant more seed, to till more land, and to breed more animals, as the population increased. Surplus food could be slowly accumulated to support craftsmen who devoted most of their time to the manufacture of tools, pottery, and clothing.

The first great discovery made in this period was the cultivation of wheat and barley, which had been growing wild in this area. It was discovered that by putting seed of these grasses into the earth, new plants would grow; that one could select the best seed for sowing, and eventually the accidental crossing of varieties was observed, which produced grains very much larger than the seeds of the wild grasses. The process of development from wild grasses to high-yielding modern wheat is not yet fully known. It involved gene mutations, hybridization, and chromosome doubling, and it has taken thousands of years to achieve the artificial selection by man on the level of present-day agriculture. For man in the industrial age, accustomed to looking down on non-industrialized agriculture as a primitive and rather obvious form of production, the Neolithic discoveries may not seem comparable to the great technical discoveries of our day, of which he is so proud. Yet the fact that the expectation that seed would grow was proved correct by results gave rise to an entirely new concept: man recognized that he could use his will and intention to *make* this happen, instead of things just 'happening'. It would not be exaggerated to say that the discovery of agriculture was the foundation for all scientific thinking and later technological development.

The second discovery was that of animal breeding which was made in the same period. Sheep were already domesticated in the ninth millennium in northern Iraq, and cattle and pigs around 6000 BC. Sheep and cattle-raising resulted in additional food supply: milk and a greater abundance of meat. The increased and more stable food supply permitted a sedentary, instead of a nomadic form of life, and led to the construction of permanent villages and towns.[20]

In the Proto-Neolithic period tribes of hunters invented and developed a new settled economy based on the domestication of plants and animals. Although the earliest remains of domesticated plants do not yet much antedate 7000 BC, 'the standard of domestication reached and the variety of crops grown presupposes a long prehistory of earlier agriculture which may well go back to the beginning of the Proto-Neolithic, about 9000 BC'[21] (J. Mellaart, 1967).

It took about 2000 to 3000 years before a new discovery was made, necessitated by the need to store foodstuff: the

20. This does not imply that *all* hunters were nomadic and *all* agriculturists sedentary. Childe mentions a number of exceptions to this rule.

21. Childe has been criticized for not having done justice to the complexity of the Neolithic development by speaking of 'the Neolithic Revolution'. While this criticism has merit, it must on the other hand not be forgotten that the change in man's mode of production is so fundamental that the word 'revolution' seems to have its place. See also Mumford's remarks pointing out that the dating of the great agricultural advance between 9000 and 7000 BC does not do justice to the fact that we are dealing with a gradual process that took place over a much longer period in four, possibly five stages (L. Mumford, 1967). He quotes especially O. Ames (1939) and E. Anderson (1952). I recommend Mumford's analysis of the Neolithic culture to anyone interested in a more detailed and very penetrating picture.

art of pottery (baskets were made earlier). With the invention of pottery, the first technical invention had been made, which led to the insight into chemical processes. Indeed, 'building a pot was a supreme instance of creation by man' (V. G. Childe, 1936).[22] Thus one can distinguish within the Neolithic period itself one 'a-ceramic' stage, i.e., a period in which pottery had not been invented, and the ceramic stage. Some older villages in Anatolia, such as the older levels of Hacilar, were a-ceramic while Çatal Hüyük was a town that had rich pottery.

Çatal Hüyük was one of the most highly developed Neolithic towns in Anatolia. Although only a relatively small part has been excavated since 1961, it has already yielded the most important data for the understanding of Neolithic society in its economic, social, and religious aspects.[23]

Since the beginning of the excavations, ten levels have been dug out, the oldest dated *c.* 6500 B C.

After 5600 B C the old mound of Çatal Hüyük was abandoned, for what reasons is not known, and a new site was founded across the river, Çatal Hüyük West. This appears to have been occupied for at least another 700 years until it also was deserted, without, however, any obvious signs of violence or deliberate destruction. (J. Mellaart, 1967)

One of the most surprising features of Çatal Hüyük is the degree of its civilization:

22. Childe elaborates on this theme in an interesting statement: 'The lump of clay was perfectly plastic; man could mould it as he would. In making a tool of stone or bone he was always limited by the shape and size of the original material; he could only take bits away from it. No such limitations restrict the activity of the potter. She can form her lump as she wishes; she can go on adding to it without any doubts as to the solidity of the joints. In thinking of "creating", the free activity of the potter in "making form where there was no form" constantly recurs to man's mind; the similes in the Bible taken from the potter's craft illustrate the point' (V. G. Childe, 1936).

23. The most detailed picture of Çatal Hüyük is given by the archaeologist who directed the excavations, J. Mellaart (1967).

Çatal Hüyük could afford luxuries such as obsidian mirrors, ceremonial daggers, and trinkets of metal beyond the reach of most of its known contemporaries. Copper and lead were smelted and worked into beads, tubes and possibly small tools, thus taking the beginnings of metallurgy back into the seventh millennium. Its stone industry in local obsidian and imported flint is the most elegant of the period; its wooden vessels are varied and sophisticated, its woollen textile industry fully developed. (J. Mellaart, 1967)

Make-up sets for women and very attractive bracelets for men and women were found in the burial sites. They knew the art of smelting copper and lead. The use of a great variety of rocks and minerals shows, according to Mellaart, that prospecting and trade formed a most important item of the city's economy.

In spite of this developed civilization, the social structure seems to have lacked certain elements characteristic of much later stages of evolution. Apparently there was little class distinction between rich and poor. While, according to Mellaart, social inequality is suggested by the sizes of buildings, equipment, and burial gifts, 'this is never a glaring one'. Indeed, looking at the plans of the excavated section of the city one finds that the difference in size of the buildings is very small, and negligible when compared with the difference in later urban societies. Childe notes that there is no definitive evidence of chieftainship in early Neolithic villages, and Mellaart does not mention any evidence of it from Çatal Hüyük. There were apparently many priestesses (perhaps also priests), but there is no evidence of a hierarchical organization. While in Çatal Hüyük the surplus produced by new methods of agriculture must have been large enough to support the manufacture of luxuries and trade, the earlier and less-developed of the Neolithic villages produced, according to Childe, only a small surplus and hence had an even greater degree of economic equality than that of Çatal Hüyük. He points out that the Neolithic crafts must have been household industries and that craft traditions are not individual but collective. The experience and wisdom of all the community's members are constantly being pooled; the occupation is public, its rules are the result of communal experience. The pots from a given Neolithic village bear the stamp of a strong collective tradition, rather than of individuality. Besides there was as yet no shortage of land; when the population grew, young men could go off and start a village of their own. Under these economic circumstances the conditions were not given for the differentiation of society into different classes, or for the formation of a permanent leadership whose function it would be to organize the whole economy and who would exact their price for this skill. This could happen only later when many more discoveries and inventions had been made, when the surplus was much greater and could be transformed into 'capital' and those owning it could make profits by making others work for them.

Two observations are of special importance from the point of view of aggression: there is no evidence of any sack or massacre during the eight hundred years of the existence of Çatal Hüyük so far explored in the excavations. Furthermore, and even more impressive evidence for the absence of violence, among the many hundreds of skeletons unearthed, not a single one has been found that showed signs of violent death (J. Mellaart, 1967).

One of the most characteristic features of Neolithic villages, including Çatal Hüyük, is *the central role of the mother* in their social structure and their religion.

Following the older division of labour, where men hunted and women gathered roots and fruits, agriculture was most likely the discovery of women, while animal husbandry was that of men. (Considering the fundamental role of agriculture in the development of civilization, it is perhaps no exaggeration to state that modern civilization was founded by women.) The earth's and woman's capacity to give birth – a capacity that men lack – quite naturally gave the

mother a supreme place in the world of the early agriculturalists. (Only when men could create material things by
intellect, i.e., magically and technically – could they claim
superiority.) The mother, as Goddess (often identified with
mother earth), became the supreme goddess of the religious
world, while the earthly mother became the centre of family
and social life.

The most impressive direct evidence for the central role
of mothers in Çatal Hüyük lies in the fact that children were
always buried with their mother, and never with their father.
The skeletons were buried underneath the mother's divan (a
kind of platform in the main room), which was larger than
that of the father and always had the same location in the
house. The burial of children exclusively with their mother
is a characteristically matriarchal trait: the children's
essential relationship is considered to be to the mother and
not to the father, as in the case in patriarchal societies.

Although this burial system is an impressive datum in
favour of the assumption of the matriarchal structure of
Neolithic society, this thesis finds its full confirmation with
the data we have on the religion of Çatal Hüyük and other
excavated Neolithic villages in Anatolia.[24]

These excavations have revolutionized our concepts of
early religious development. The most outstanding feature
is the fact that this religion was centred around the figure of
the mother-goddess. Mellaart concludes: ' Çatal Hüyük and
Hacilar have established a link . . . [whereby] a continuity
in religion can be demonstrated from Çatal Hüyük to
Hacilar and so on till the great "Mother-Goddesses" of
archaic and classical times, the shadowy figures known as
Cybele, Artemis and Aphrodite' (J. Mellaart, 1967).

The central role of mother-goddess can be clearly seen in

24. In the following I shall sometimes use the term 'matricentric'
rather than matriarchal, because the latter implies that women ruled
over men, which seems to be true in some cases – for instance, according
to Mellaart, in Hacilar – but probably not in Çatal Hüyük, where the
woman (mother) apparently played a dominant role, but not one of
domination.

the figures, wall paintings, and reliefs in the numerous shrines that have been excavated. In contrast to findings in other Neolithic sites, those of Çatal Hüyük do not entirely consist of mother-goddesses, but also show a male deity symbolized by a bull or, more frequently, by a bull's head or horns. But this fact does not substantially alter the predominance of the 'great mother' as the central deity. Among forty-one sculptures excavated, thirty-three were exclusively of goddesses. The eight sculptures in which a male god is symbolized are virtually all to be understood in reference to the goddess, partly as her sons and partly as her consorts. (On one of the older levels figurines of the goddess were found exclusively.) The central role of the mother-goddess is further demonstrated by the fact that she is shown alone, together with a male, pregnant, giving birth, but never subordinate to a male. There are some shrines in which the goddess is giving birth to a bull's or a ram's head. (Compare this with the typically patriarchal story of the female being given birth by the male: Eve and Athene.)

The mother-goddess is often found accompanied by a leopard, clothed with a leopard skin, or symbolically represented by leopards, at the time the most ferocious and deadly animal of that region. This would make her the mistress of wild animals, and it also indicates her double role as the goddess of life and of death, like so many other goddesses. 'Mother earth', who gives birth to her children and receives them again after their individual life cycle has ended, is not necessarily a destroying mother. Yet she sometimes is (like the Hindu goddess Kali); to find the reasons why this development should have taken place requires a lengthy speculation which I must forgo.

The mother-goddess of the Neolithic religion is not only the mistress of wild animals. She is also the patroness of the hunt, the patroness of agriculture, and the mistress of plant life.

Mellaart makes these summarizing remarks on the role of women in the Neolithic society, including Çatal Hüyük:

What is particularly noteworthy in the Neolithic religion of Anatolia, and this applies to Çatal Hüyük as much as to Hacilar, is the complete absence of sex in any of the figurines, statuettes, plastic reliefs, or wall-paintings. The reproductive organs are never shown, representations of phallus and vulva are unknown, and this is the more remarkable as they were frequently portrayed both in the Upper Palaeolithic and in the Neolithic and post-Neolithic cultures outside Anatolia.[25] It seems that there is a very simple answer to this seemingly puzzling question, for emphasis on sex in art is invariably connected with male impulse and desire. If Neolithic woman was the creator of Neolithic religion, its absence is easily explained and a different symbolism was created in which breast, navel and pregnancy stand for the female principle, horns and horned animal heads for the male. In an early Neolithic society like that of Çatal Hüyük one might biologically expect a greater proportion of women than men and this is indeed reflected in the burials. Moreover, in the new economy a great number of tasks were undertaken by the women, a pattern that has not changed in Anatolian villages to this day, and this probably accounts for her social pre-eminence. As the only source of life she became associated with the processes of agriculture, with the taming and nourishing of domesticated animals, with the ideas of increase, abundance and fertility. Hence a religion which aimed at exactly the same conservation of life in all its forms, its propagation and the mysteries of its rites connected with life and death, birth and resurrection, were evidently part of her sphere rather than that of man. It seems extremely likely that the cult of the goddess was administered mainly by women, even if the presence of male priests is by no means excluded . . .[26] (J. Mellaart, 1967)

25. cf. L. Mumford's (1967) stress on the importance of the sexual element in many of the female figurines; he is certainly right in this emphasis. It seems that it was only in the Anatolian Neolithic culture that this sexual element was absent. It remains a question for further investigation whether this sexual emphasis in other Neolithic cultures makes it necessary to qualify the idea that all Neolithic cultures were matriarchal.

26. Matriarchal societies have been studied by Soviet scholars more than by their Western colleagues. This is due, one must assume, to the fact that Engels (1891) was greatly impressed by Bachofen's (originally published 1861) and Morgan's (1870) findings. See also Z. A. Abra-

The data that speak in favour of the view that Neolithic society was relatively egalitarian, without hierarchy, exploitation, or marked aggression, are suggestive. The fact, however, that these Neolithic villages in Anatolia had a matriarchal (matricentric) structure, adds a great deal more evidence to the hypothesis that Neolithic society, at least in Anatolia, was an essentially unaggressive and peaceful society. The reason for this lies in the spirit of affirmation of life and lack of destructiveness which J. J. Bachofen believed was an essential trait of all matriarchal societies.

Indeed, the findings brought to light by the excavation of Neolithic villages in Anatolia offer the most complete material evidence for the existence of matriarchal cultures and religions postulated by J. J. Bachofen in his work *Das Mutterrecht*, first published in 1861. By the analysis of Greek and Roman myths, rituals, symbols, and dreams he had achieved something that only a genius could do: with his penetrating analytic power he reconstructed a phase of social organization and religion for which hardly any material evidence was available to him. (An American ethnologist, L. H. Morgan, (1870, 1877) arrived independently at very similar conclusions on the basis of his study of North American Indians.) Almost all anthropologists – with a few notable exceptions – declared Bachofen's findings to be without any scientific merit; in fact, it was not until 1967 that an English translation of a selection of Bachofen's writings was published (J. J. Bachofen, 1967).

There were probably two reasons for the rejection of Bachofen's theory: first, that it was almost impossible for anthropologists living in a patriarchal society to transcend

---

mova (1967), who discusses the mother-goddess in her double role of mistress of home and hearth and of sovereign mistress of animals, especially game animals. See also A. P. Okladnikov (1972), the Soviet anthropologist who points to the connection between matriarchy and the cult of death. See, furthermore, the interesting discussion of Palaeolithic goddesses by A. Marshack (1972) who links the goddesses with the moon and the lunar calendar.

their social and mental frames of reference and to imagine that male rule was not 'natural'. (Freud, for the same reason, arrived at his view of women as castrated men.) Second, the anthropologists were so accustomed to believing only in material evidence like skeletons, tools, weapons, etc., that they found it difficult to believe that myths or drama are not less real than artifacts; this whole attitude resulted also in a lack of appreciation for the potency and subtlety of penetrating, theoretical thinking.

The following paragraphs from Bachofen's *Mutterrecht* give an idea of this concept of the matriarchal spirit:

The relationship which stands at the origin of all culture, of every virtue, of every nobler aspect of existence, is that between mother and child; it operates in a world of violence as the divine principle of love, of union, of peace. Raising her young, the woman learns earlier than the man to extend her loving care beyond the limits of the ego to another creature, and to direct whatever gift of invention she possesses to the preservation and improvement of the other's existence. Woman at this stage is the repository of all culture, of all benevolence, of all devotion, of all concern for the living and grief for the dead. Yet the love that arises from motherhood is not only more intense, but also more universal ... Whereas the paternal principle is inherently restrictive, the maternal principle is universal; the paternal principle implies limitation to definite groups, but the maternal principle, like the life of nature, knows no barriers. The idea of motherhood produces a sense of universal fraternity among all men, which dies with the development of paternity. The family based on father right is a closed individual organism, whereas the matriarchal family bears the typically universal character that stands at the beginning of all development and distinguishes material life from higher spiritual life. Every woman's womb, the mortal image of the earth mother Demeter, will give brothers and sisters to the children of every other woman; the homeland will know only brothers and sisters until the day when the development of the paternal system dissolves the undifferentiated unity of the mass and introduces a principle of articulation.

The matriarchal cultures present many expressions and even juridical formulations of this aspect of the maternal principle. It is the basis of the universal freedom and equality so frequent among matriarchal peoples, of their hospitality, and of their aversion to restriction of all sorts ... And in it is rooted the admirable sense of kinship and fellow feeling which knows no barriers or dividing lines and embraces all members of a nation alike. Matriarchal states were particularly famed for their freedom from internecine strife and conflict ... The matriarchal peoples – and this is no less characteristic – assigned special culpability to the physical injury of one's fellow men or even of animals ... An air of tender humanity, discernible even in the facial expression of Egyptian statuary, permeates the culture of the matriarchal world.[27] (J. J. Bachofen, 1967)

Prehistoric Societies and 'Human Nature'

This picture of the mode of production and social organization of hunters and Neolithic agriculturalists is quite suggestive in regard to certain psychical traits that are generally supposed to be an intrinsic part of human nature. Prehistoric hunters and agriculturalists had no opportunity to develop a passionate striving for property or envy of the 'haves', because there was no private property to hold on to and no important economic differences to cause envy. On the contrary, their way of life was conducive to the development of cooperation and peaceful living. There was no basis for the formation of the desire to exploit other human beings. The idea of exploiting another person's physical or psychical energy for one's own purposes is absurd in a society where economically and socially there is no basis for exploitation.

The impulse to control others also had little chance to develop. The primitive band society and probably prehistoric hunters since about fifty thousand years ago were fundamentally different from civilized society precisely because human relations were not governed by the principles of control and power; their functioning depended on mutual-

27. cf., also, E. Fromm (1934, 1970e).

ity. An individual endowed with the passion for control would have been a social failure and without influence. Finally, there was little incentive for the development of greed, since production and consumption were stabilized at a certain level.[28]

Do the data on hunter-gatherers and early agriculturalists suggest that the passion of possessiveness, exploitation, greed, envy did not yet exist and are exclusively products of civilization? It does not seem to me that such a sweeping statement can be made. We do not have enough data to substantiate it, nor is it likely to be correct on theoretical grounds, since individual factors will engender these vices in some individuals even under the most favourable social circumstances. But there is a great difference between cultures which foster and encourage greed, envy, and exploitativeness by their social structure, and cultures which do the opposite. In the former, these vices will form part of the 'social character' – i.e., of a syndrome to be found in the majority of people; in the latter, they will be individual aberrations from the norm which have little chance to influence the whole society. This hypothesis gains further strength if we now consider the next historical stage, urban development, which seems to have introduced not only new kinds of civilization but also those passions which are generally attributed to man's natural endowment.

28. It should be noted in passing that in many highly developed societies, such as the feudal society in the Middle Ages, the members of one occupational group – such as the guilds – did not strive for increasing material profit, but for enough to satisfy the traditional standard of living. Even the knowledge that the members of social classes above them had more luxuries to consume did not generate greed for this surplus consumption. The process of living was satisfying, and hence, no greater consumption appeared desirable. The same holds true for the peasants. Their rebellions in the sixteenth century were not because they wanted to consume as much as the class above them, but they wanted the basis for a dignified human existence and fulfilment of the traditional obligations the land owners had towards them.

The Urban Revolution[29]

A new kind of society developed in the fourth and third millennia BC which can best be characterized in Mumford's brilliant formulation:

Out of the early neolithic complex a different kind of social organization arose: no longer dispersed in small units, but unified in a large one: no longer 'democratic', that is, based on neighbourly intimacy, customary usage, and consent, but authoritarian, centrally directed, under the control of a dominant minority: no longer confined to a limited territory, but deliberately 'going out of bounds' to seize raw materials and enslave helpless men, to exercise control, to exact tribute. This new culture was dedicated, not just to the enhancement of life, but to the expansion of collective power. By perfecting new instruments of coercion, the rulers of this society had, by the Third Millennium BC, organized industrial and military power on a scale that was never to be surpassed until our own time. (L. Mumford, 1967)

How had it happened?

Within a short period, historically speaking, man learned to harness the physical energy of oxen and the energy of the winds. He invented the plough, the wheeled cart, the sailing boat, and he discovered the chemical processes involved in the smelting of copper ores (to some extent known earlier), and the physical properties of metals, and he began to work out a solar calendar. As a consequence, the way was prepared for the art of writing and standards and measures. 'In no period of history till the days of Galileo', writes Childe, 'was progress in knowledge so rapid or far-reaching discoveries so frequent' (V. G. Childe, 1936).

But social change was not less revolutionary. The small villages of self-sufficient farmers were transformed into populous cities nourished by secondary industries and foreign trade, and these new cities were organized as city

29. The term was coined by Childe (1936), and its use is criticized by Mumford (1967).

states. Man literally created new land. The great cities of Bablylonia rose on a sort of platform of reeds, laid criss-cross upon the alluvial mud. They dug channels to water the fields and drain the marshes, they built dykes and mounds to protect men and cattle from the waters and raise them above the flood. This creation of tillable land required a great deal of labour and this 'capital in the form of human labour was being sunk in the land' (V. G. Childe, 1936).

Another result of this process was that a specialized labour force had to be used for this kind of work, and for cultivating the land necessary to grow food for those others who were specialized in crafts, public works, and trade. They had to be organized by the community and directed by an élite which did the planning, protecting, and controlling. This means that a much greater accumulation of surplus was needed than in the earlier Neolithic villages, and that this surplus was not just used as food reserve for times of need or growing population, but as capital to be used for an expanding production. Childe has pointed to another factor inherent in these conditions of life in the river valleys – the exceptional power of the society to coerce its members. The community could refuse a recalcitrant member access to water by closing the channels leading it to his field. This possibility of coercion was one of the foundations upon which the power of kings, priests, and the dominant élite rested once they had succeeded in replacing or, ideologically speaking, 'representing' – the social will.

With the new forms of production, one of the most decisive changes in the history of man took place. His product was no longer limited to what he could produce by his own work, as had been the case in hunting societies and early agriculture. It is true that with the beginning of Neolithic agriculture man had already been able to produce a small surplus, but this surplus only helped to stabilize his life. When, however, it grew, it could be used for an entirely new purpose; it became possible to feed people who did not directly produce food, but cleared the marshes, built houses and cities and pyramids, or served as soldiers. Of course, such use could only take place when technique and division of labour had reached a degree which made it possible for human labour to be so employed. At this point surplus grew immensely. The more fields were ploughed, the more marshes were drained, the more surplus could be produced. This new possibility led to one of the most fundamental changes in human history. *It was discovered that man could be used as an economic instrument, that he could be exploited, that he could be made a slave.*

Let us follow this process in more detail in its economic, social, religious, and psychological consequences. The basic economic facts of the new society were, as indicated above, greater specialization of work, the transformation of surplus into capital, and the need for a centralized mode of production. The first consequence of this was the rise of different classes. The privileged classes did the directing and organizing, claiming and obtaining for themselves a disproportionately large part of the product, that is to say, a standard of living which the majority of the population could not obtain. Below them were the lower classes, peasants and artisans. Below those were the slaves, prisoners taken as a result of wars. The privileged classes organized their own hierarchy headed originally by permanent chiefs – eventually by kings, as representatives of the gods – who were the nominal heads of the whole system.

Another consequence of the new mode of production is assumed to have been *conquest* as an essential requisite to the accumulation of communal capital needed for the accomplishment of the urban revolution. But there was a still more basic reason for the invention of war as an institution: the contradiction between an economic system that needed unification in order to be optimally effective, and political and dynastic separation that conflicted with this economic need. War as an institution was a new invention, like kingdom or bureaucracy, made around 3000 BC. Then as now, it was not caused by psychological factors, such as human aggression, but, aside from the wishes for power and glory of the kings and their bureaucracy, was the result of objective conditions that made war useful and which, as a consequence, tended to generate and increase human destructiveness and cruelty.[30]

These social and political changes were accompanied by a profound change in the role of women in society and of the mother figure in religion. No longer was the fertility of the soil the source of all life and creativity, but the intellect which produced new inventions, techniques, abstract thinking, and the state with its laws. No longer the womb, but the mind became the creative power, and simultaneously, not women, but men dominated society.

This change is poetically expressed in the Babylonian hymn of creation, Enuma Elish. This myth tells us of a victorious rebellion of the male gods against Tiamat, the 'Great Mother' who ruled the universe. They form an alliance against her and choose Marduk to be their leader. After a bitter war Tiamat is slain, from her body heaven and earth are formed, and Marduk rules as supreme God.

However, before he is chosen to be the leader, Marduk has to pass a test, which may seem insignificant – or puzzling – to modern man, but it is the key to the understanding of the myth:

> Then they placed a garment in their midst;
> To Marduk, their first-born, they said:
> 'Verily, O lord, thy destiny is supreme among the gods,
> Command "to destroy and to create," (and) it shall be!

30. Childe suggests that when the need for more land arose, older settlers had either to be taken away, to be replaced, or to be dominated by a conquering group, and hence that some sort of warfare must have been waged before the urban revolution had been consummated. But he admits that this cannot be demonstrated by archaeological evidence. He therefore takes the position that in the prelude to the urban revolution, after 6000 BC 'warfare has to be admitted, though only on a small scale and of a spasmodic kind' (V. G. Childe, 1936). However this may be, not before the city-state with its kings and its hierarchy had developed did bloody wars of conquest become a permanent institution.

By the word of thy mouth let the garment be destroyed;
Command again, and let the garment be whole!'
He commanded with his mouth,
  and the garment was destroyed.
Again he commanded, and the garment was restored.
When the gods, his fathers, beheld the efficiency of his word
They rejoiced (and) did homage, (saying)
  'Marduk is king!'

A. Heidel, 1942

The meaning of this test is to show that man has overcome his inability for natural creation – a quality which only the soil and the female had – by a new form of creation, that by the word (thought). Marduk, who can create in this way, has overcome the natural superiority of the mother and hence can replace her. The biblical story begins where the Babylonian myth ends: the male god creates the world by the *word* (E. Fromm, 1951).

One of the most significant features of the new urban society was that it was based on the principle of patriarchal rule, in which the principle of control is inherent: control of nature, control of slaves, women and children. The new patriarchal man literally 'makes' the earth. His technique is not simply modification of the natural processes, but their domination and control by man, resulting in new products which are not found in nature. Men themselves came under the control of those who organized the work of the community, and hence the leaders had to have power over those they controlled.

In order to achieve the aims of this new society, everything, nature *and* man, had to be controlled and had to either exercise – or fear – power. In order to become controllable, men had to learn to obey and to submit, and in order to submit they had to believe in the superior power – physical and/or magic – of their rulers. While in the Neolithic village, as well as among primitive hunters, leaders guided and counselled the people and did not exploit them, and while their leadership was accepted voluntarily or, to use another term, while prehistoric authority was 'rational' authority resting on competence, the authority of the new patriarchal system was one based on force and power; it was exploitative and mediated by the psychical mechanism of fear, 'awe', and submission. It was 'irrational authority'.

Lewis Mumford has expressed the new principle governing the life of the city very succinctly: 'To exert power in every form was the essence of civilization; the city found a score of ways of expressing struggle, aggression, domination, conquest – and servitude.' He points out that the new ways of the cities were 'rigorous, efficient, often harsh, even sadistic', and that the Egyptian monarchs and their Mesopotamian counterparts 'boasted on their monuments and tablets of their personal feats in mutilating, torturing, and killing with their own hands their chief captives' (L. Mumford, 1961).

As a result of my clinical experience in psychoanalytic therapy I had long come to the conviction (E. Fromm, 1941) that the essence of sadism is the passion for unlimited, godlike control over men and things.[31] Mumford's view of the sadistic character of these societies is an important confirmation of my own.[32]

In addition to sadism, the passion to destroy life and the attraction to all that is dead (necrophilia) seem to develop in the new urban civilization. Mumford also speaks of the destructive, death-oriented myth to be found in the new social order, and quotes Patrick Geddes as saying that each historic civilization begins with a living, urban core, the polis, and ends in a common graveyard of dust and bones, a Necropolis, or city of the dead: fire-scorched ruins, shattered buildings, empty workshops, heaps of meaningless refuse, the population massacred or driven into slavery (L.

31. This view will be discussed in detail in Chapter 11.

32. This is more than a coincidence; it follows from our fundamental common position, the stress on the fundamental distinction between what serves life and what strangles it.

Mumford, 1961). Whether we read the story of the Hebrews' conquest of Canaan or the story of the Babylonians'
wars, the same spirit of unlimited and inhuman destructiveness is shown. A good example is Sennacherib's stone
inscription on the total annihilation of Bablylon:

The city and (its) houses from its foundation to its top, I destroyed, I devastated, I burned with fire. The wall and the outer
wall, temples and gods, temple towers of brick and earth, as many
as they were, I razed and dumped them into the Arakhtu Canal.
Through the midst of that city I dug canals, I flooded its site with
water, and the very foundation thereof I destroyed. I made its
destruction more complete than that by a flood. (Quoted by
L. Mumford, 1961)

The history of civilization, from the destruction of Carthage
and Jerusalem to the destruction of Dresden, Hiroshima,
and the people, soil, and trees of Vietnam, is a tragic record
of sadism and destructiveness.

Aggressiveness in Primitive Cultures

Thus far we have dealt only with the aggression to be found
among prehistorical societies and among still existing primitive hunter-gatherers. What can we learn from other, more
advanced yet still primitive cultures?

It should be easy to examine this question by consulting a
work dealing with aggression on the basis of the vast amount
of anthropological data collected. But it is surprising – and a
somewhat shocking fact – that no such work exists; evidently the phenomenon of aggression has not, so far, been
considered of sufficient importance by anthropologists to
lead them to summarize and interpret their data from this
point of view. There is only the brief paper by Derek Freeman, in which he attempts to give a summary of the anthropological data on aggression in order to support the
Freudian thesis (D. Freeman, 1964). Equally short is a

summarizing paper by another anthropologist, H. Helmuth (1967). Helmuth presents anthropological data and emphasizes the opposite point of view, the relative absence of aggression among primitive societies.

In the following pages I shall offer a number of other studies on aggression in primitive societies, beginning with the analysis of data I undertook from the most accessible anthropological publications. Since the studies in these publications were not made with a selective bias for the viewpoint for or against aggression, respectively, they can be considered a kind of 'random' sample in a very loose sense of the word. Nevertheless, I do not imply that the results of this analysis are in any way statistically valid in terms of the distribution of aggressiveness among primitive cultures in general. My main purpose is clearly not a statistical one, but to demonstrate that non-aggressive societies are not as rare or 'puny' as Freeman and other exponents of the Freudian theory indicate. I also wanted to show that aggressiveness is not just *one trait*, but part of a *syndrome*; that we find aggression regularly together with other traits in the system, such as strict hierarchy, dominance, class division, etc. In other words, aggression is to be understood as part of the *social character*, not as an isolated behaviour trait.[33]

Analysis of Thirty Primitive Tribes

I analysed thirty primitive cultures from the standpoint of aggressiveness versus peacefulness. Three of them were described by Ruth Benedict (1934);[34] thirteen by Margaret

33. I want to express my indebtedness to the late Ralph Linton, with whom I gave a seminar at Yale University in 1948 and 1949 on the character structure of primitive societies, for what I learned from him in these seminars and in many private conversations. I also want to express my appreciation for the stimulation I received from George P. Murdock who participated in these seminars, even though our views remained very different.

34. The Zuñi, Dobu, Kwakiutl.

Mead (1961);[35] fifteen by G. P. Murdock (1934),[36] and one by C. M. Turnbull (1965).[37] The analysis of these thirty societies permits us to distinguish three different and clearly delineated systems (A, B, C). These societies are not simply differentiated in terms of 'more or less' aggression, or 'more or less' non-aggression, but in terms of different character systems distinguished from each other by a number of traits that form the system, some of which do not have any obvious connection with aggression.[38]

System A: Life-Affirmative Societies

In this system the main emphasis of ideals, customs and institutions is that they serve the preservation and growth of life in all its forms. There is a minimum of hostility, violence, or cruelty among people, no harsh punishment, hardly any crime, and the institution of war is absent or plays an exceedingly small role. Children are treated with kindness, there is no severe corporal punishment; women are in general considered equal to men, or at least not

35. The Arapesh, Greenland Eskimos, Bachiga, Ifugao, Kwakiutl, Manus, Iroquois, Ojibwa, Samoans, Zuñi, Bathonga, Dakota, Maori.
36. The Tasmanians, Aranda, Samoans, Semang, Todas, Kazaks, Ainus, Polar Eskimos, Haidas, Crows, Iroquois, Hopi, Aztecs, Incas, Witotos, Nama Hotentots, and the Ganda. (I have not, however, considered in this context his description of the Aztecs and the Incas since they were highly developed and complex societies and therefore not suitable for this brief analysis.)
37. The Mbutu.
38. The Zuñi and the Kwakiutl are described both by R. Benedict and by M. Mead; the Iroquois and the Samoans are described both by M. Mead and G. P. Murdock; they are, of course, analysed only once. Among the primitive hunters described by E. R. Service (1966), the Semangs, the Eskimos, and the Australians are among this sample. The Semangs and the Eskimos fall under system A, the Australians under system B. I have not classified the Hopi because the structure of their society seems to be too contradictory to permit classification. They have many traits which would put them in system A, but their aggressiveness suggests some doubt whether they do not belong in system B (cf. D. Eggan, 1943).

exploited or humiliated; there is a generally permissive and affirmative attitude towards sex. There is little envy, covetousness, greed and exploitativeness. There is also little competition and individualism and a great deal of cooperation; personal property is only in things that are used. There is a general attitude of trust and confidence, not only in others but particularly in nature; a general prevalence of good humour, and a relative absence of depressive moods.

Among the societies falling under this life-affirmative category, I have placed the Zuñi Pueblo Indians, the Mountain Arapesh and the Bathonga, the Aranda, the Semangs, the Todas, the Polar Eskimos, and the Mbutus.

One finds in the system A group both hunters (for instance, the Mbutus) and agriculturists/sheep-owners (like the Zuñis). In it are societies with relatively abundant food supply and others characterized by a good deal of scarcity. This statement by no means implies, however, that the characterological differences are not dependent on and largely influenced by the differences of the socio-economic structure of these respective societies. It only indicates that the obvious economic factors, such as poverty or wealth, hunting or agriculture, etc., are not the only critical factors for the development of character. In order to understand the connection between economy and social character one would have to study the total socio-economic structure of each society.

System B : Nondestructive-Aggressive Societies

This system shares with the first the basic element of not being destructive, but differs in that aggressiveness and war, although not central, are normal occurrences, and in that competition, hierarchy and individualism are present. These societies are by no means permeated by destructiveness or cruelty or by exaggerated suspiciousness, but they do not have the kind of gentleness and trust which is characteristic of the system A societies. System B could perhaps be best characterized by stating that it is imbued with a spirit of male aggressiveness, individualism, the desire to get things and to accomplish tasks. In my analysis the following fourteen tribes fall under this category: the Greenland Eskimos, the Bachigas, the Ojibwas, the Ifugaos, the Manus, the Samoans, the Dakotas, the Maoris, the Tasmanians, the Kazaks, the Ainus, the Crows, the Incas, and the Hottentots.

System C: Destructive Societies

The structure of the system C societies is very distinct. It is characterized by much interpersonal violence, destructiveness, aggression, and cruelty, both within the tribe and against others, a pleasure in war, maliciousness, and treachery. The whole atmosphere of life is one of hostility, tension, and fear. Usually there is a great deal of competition, great emphasis on private property (if not in material things then in symbols), strict hierarchies, and a considerable amount of war-making. Examples for this system are: the Dobus, and the Kwakiutl; the Haidas, the Aztecs, the Witotos, and the Ganda.

I do not claim that my classification of each society under these categories is not open to controversy. But whether one agrees or disagrees with the classification of a few societies does not make too much difference, because my main point is not statistical, but qualitative. The main contrast lies between systems A and B on the one hand, which are both life affirming, and system C, which is basically cruel or destructive, i.e., sadistic or necrophilous.

Examples of the Three Systems

In order to help the reader to get a better picture of the nature of the three systems, I shall give in the following a more detailed example of a characteristic society for each system.

The Zuñi Indians (System A) The Zuñi Indians have been thoroughly studied by Ruth Benedict (1934) as well as by Margaret Mead, Irving Goldman, Ruth Bunzel, and others. They live by agriculture and sheep herding in the south-western United States. Like other Pueblo Indian societies they inhabited numerous cities in the twelfth and thirteenth centuries, but their history can be followed much further back to its simple beginnings in one-room stone houses, to each of which was attached an underground ceremonial chamber. Economically, they can be said to live in a state of abundance, although their appreciation for material goods is not very high. In their social attitude there is little compe-tition even though there is a limitation of irrigable land. They are organized along matricentric lines, although priests and civil officials are men. Individuals who are aggressive, competitive, and non-cooperative are regarded as aberrant types. Work is done essentially in cooperation, with the exception of sheep raising which is exclusively a man's occupation. In economic activities rivalry is excluded, again with the exception of sheep raising, where one finds some squabbles, but no deep rivalries. On the whole, little attention is paid to individual achievement. Inasmuch as there is some quarrelling, it is mainly caused by sexual jealousy and not in relation to economic activities or posses-sions.

Hoarding is practically unknown; while there are richer and poorer individuals, wealth remains highly fluid, and it is characteristic of the Zuñi attitude towards material goods that a man would lend his jewellery willingly, not only to friends but to any member of the society who asks for it. In spite of a certain amount of sexual jealousy, marriages on the whole are lasting, although there is easy divorce. Women are, as one would expect in a matricentric society, in no way subordinate to men. There is a great deal of gift giving, but in contrast to a number of competitive societies, this does not have the function of emphasizing one's own wealth or of humiliating the one to whom the gift is given, and no attempt is made to maintain reciprocity. Wealth does not remain long in one family, as it is acquired by individual work and industriousness, and exploitation of others is unknown. While there is private ownership of land, litigations are rare and quickly settled.

The Zuñi system can only be understood by the fact that material things are relatively little valued and the fact that the major interest in life is religious. To put it in another way, the dominant value is life and living itself, not things and their possessions. Songs, prayers, rituals, and dances are the major and most important elements in this system. They are directed by priests who are highly respected, although they do not exercise any censures or jurisdiction. The value of religious life as against ownership and economic success is seen in that officials who have the function of judges in cases of material litigation are not held in great respect, quite in contrast to the priests.

Personal authority is perhaps the most rigorously disparaged trait among the Zuñi. The definition of a good man is one who has 'a pleasing address, a yielding disposition and a generous heart'. Men never act violently and do not contemplate violence even when the wife is unfaithful. During the initiation period boys are whipped and frightened by *kachinas*, but in contrast to many other cultures even this initiation is never in any way an ordeal. Murder hardly exists; as Benedict reports from her own observation, there is no memory of homicide. Suicide is outlawed. Themes of terror and danger are not cultivated in their myths or tales. There is no sense of sin, especially in connection with sex, and sexual chastity is generally regarded with disfavour. Sex is considered to be an incident in a happy life, but by no means, as in some other rather aggressive societies, the only source of pleasure. There seems to be some fear connected with sex, but in so far as there is fear, men are afraid of women and of sexual intercourse with them. Goldman mentions the prevalence of the theme of castration fear in a matriarchal society. This indicates man's fear of women rather than, as in Freud's concept, the fear of a punishing father.

Is this picture of a system characterized by unaggressiveness, non-violence, cooperation, and enjoyment of life changed by the fact that one finds also jealousies and quarrels? No society could be characterized as non-violent and peaceful if it has to live up to an absolute ideal of complete absence of hostility or of any quarrels. But such a point of view is rather naïve. Even basically unaggressive and non-violent people will occasionally react with annoyance under certain conditions, especially those with a choleric temperament. This does not mean, however, that their *character* structure is aggressive, violent, or destructive. One might even go further and say that in a culture where expressions of anger are as much tabooed as they are in the Zuñi culture, sometimes a relatively mild quantity of anger will pile up and be expressed in a quarrel; but only if one is dogmatically attached to the view of man's innate aggression will one interpret these occasional quarrels as indicating the depth and intensity of the repressed aggression.

Such an interpretation is based on a misuse of the Freudian discovery of unconscious motivation. The logic of this reasoning is: if a suspected trait is manifest, its existence is obvious and undeniable; but if it is completely absent, this very absence proves its presence; it must be repressed, and the less it shows manifestly, the more intense it must be in order to require such thorough repression. With this method one can prove anything, and Freud's discovery is transformed into a means for empty dogmatism. Every psychoanalyst agrees, in principle, that the assumption that a certain drive is repressed requires that we have empirical evidence for the repression in dreams, fantasies, unintended behaviour, and so on. However, this theoretical principle is often neglected in the analysis of persons and of cultures. One is so convinced of the validity of the premise required by the theory that a certain drive exists, that one does not bother to discover its empirical manifestation. The analyst who proceeds this way acts in good faith because he is unaware of the fact that he expects to find what the theory claims – and nothing else. In the weighing of the anthropological evidence, care must be taken to avoid this error, without losing sight of the principle of psychoanalytic dialectics that a trend can exist without being consciously perceived.

In the case of the Zuñi there is no evidence that the absence of manifest hostility is due to an intense repression of aggression and hence there is no valid reason to question the picture of an unaggressive, life-loving, cooperative system.

Another method of ignoring the data offered by a non-aggressive society is either to ignore them altogether or to maintain that they are of no importance. Thus Freud, for instance in the famous letter to Einstein, dealt with the problem of peaceful primitive societies in the following way: 'We are told that in certain happy regions of the earth, where nature provides in abundance everything that man requires, there are races whose life is passed in tranquillity, and who know neither coercion nor aggression. I can scarcely believe it and I should be glad to hear more of these fortunate beings' (S. Freud, 1933). I do not know what Freud's attitude would have been if he had known more about these 'fortunate beings'. It seems he never made a serious attempt to inform himself about them.

The Manus (System B) The Manus (M. Mead, 1961) are an illustration for a system which is clearly distinguished from system A because the main aim of life is not living and enjoyment, art and ritual, but the attainment of personal success through economic activities. On the other hand, the system of the Manus is very different from system C, of which the Dobus will be shown as an example. The Manus are not essentially violent, destructive or sadistic, nor are they malicious or treacherous.

The Manus are sea-dwelling, fishing people living in villages built on piles in the lagoons along the south coast of the Great Admiralty Island. They trade their surplus catch with nearby agricultural land dwellers and obtain from them manufactured articles from more distant sections of the Archipelago. All their energy is completely dedicated to material success, and they drive themselves so hard that many men die in their early middle age; in fact it is rare for a man to live to see his first grandchild. This obsession for relentless work is upheld not only because of the fact that success is the main value, but because of the shame related to failure. Not to be able to pay back one's debts is a matter which leads to humiliation of the afflicted individual; not to have any economic success which promotes a certain amount of capital accumulation puts one in the category of a man without any social prestige. But whatever social prestige a man has won by hard work is lost when he is no longer economically active.

The main emphasis in the training of the young is laid upon the respect for property, shame, and physical efficiency. Individualism is enhanced by the fact that relatives compete with each other for the child's allegiance, and the child learns to consider itself valuable. Their marriage code is a strict one, resembling nineteenth-century middle-class morality. The main vices are sex offences, scandalmongering, obscenity, failure to pay debts, failure to help relatives, and failure to keep one's house in repair. The training for hard work and competition seems to be contradicted by one phase in the life of the young men before their marriage. The young unmarried men form a kind of community, living in a common clubhouse, sharing a common mistress (usually a war prisoner) and their tobacco and betel nut. They live a rather merry, roistering life on the borders of society. Perhaps this interval is necessary to produce a modicum of pleasure and contentment during one period of a male's life. But this idyllic life is interrupted for good by the act of marriage. In order to marry, the young man has to borrow money, and for the first few years of his marriage there is only one goal for him, to repay the debt incurred to his financial backer. He must not even enjoy his wife too much as long as he owes part of her to his sponsor. When this first obligation is met, those who want to avoid failure devote their life to amassing property themselves, which makes them backers of other marriages; this is one condition of their becoming leaders in the community. Marriage itself is largely an economic affair in which personal affection and sexual interests play a small role. The relationship between man and wife remains, as is not surprising under these circumstances, antagonistic, at least for approximately the first fifteen years of marriage. Only when they begin to arrange marriages for their children and their dependants does the relationship of couples assume a certain character of cooperation. Energy is so completely devoted to the overriding aim of success that personal motives of affection, loyalty, preference, dislike, and hatred are all barred. It is of crucial importance for the understanding of this system that while there is little love and affection, there is also little destructiveness or cruelty. Even within the fierce competition which dominates the whole picture, the interest is not to humiliate others but only to maintain one's own position. Cruelty is relatively absent. In fact, those who do not succeed at all, who are failures, are left alone, not made the butt of aggression. War is not excluded, but in general it is disapproved of except as a way of keeping young men out of mischief. While war served sometimes for the capture of women for use as prostitutes, on the whole it was considered disruptive of trade and was not a way for success. Their ideal personality was not at all that of a hero but of a highly competitive, successful, industrious and non-passionate man.

Their religious ideas clearly reflect this system. Their religion is not based on the attempt to attain ecstasy or oneness with nature but has purely practical purposes: placating ghosts with slight formal offerings; instituting methods for discovering causes of illness and misfortune and remedying these causes.

The centre of life in this system is property and success, the main obsession is work, and the greatest fear is failure. It is almost necessary that in such a system, a great deal of anxiety is engendered. But it is important that in spite of this anxiety, no major degree of destructiveness and hostility is part of their social character.

There are a number of other societies in the system B group which are less competitive and possessive than the Manus, but I preferred to choose the Manus because this example permits one to delineate more clearly the difference between an individualistic-aggressive character structure and the cruel and sadistic character structure in system C.

The Dobu (System C) The inhabitants of the Dobu Islands (R. Benedict, 1934) are a good example for system C. While in close vicinity of the Trobriand Islanders, so well known by the publications of Malinowski, their environment and character are entirely different. While the Trobriands live on fertile islands that provide easy and plentiful living, the Dobuan islands, on the other hand, are of volcanic nature with small pockets of soil and poor fishing opportunities.

The Dobuans are not known among their neighbours for their poverty, however, but for their dangerousness. While they have no chiefs, they are a well-organized group arranged in concentric circles, within each of which specified traditional forms of hostility are allowed. Aside from a matrilineal grouping, the *susu* ('mother's milk'), where one finds a certain amount of cooperation and trust, the Dobuans' interpersonal relations have the principle of distrusting everybody as a possible enemy. Even marriage does not lessen the hostility between the two families. A certain degree of peace is established by the fact that the couple live during alternate years in the village of the husband and in the village of the wife. The relationship between husband and wife is full of suspiciousness and hostility. Faithfulness is not expected, and no Dobuan will admit that a man and woman are ever together even for the shortest period except for sexual purposes.

Two features are the main characteristics of this system; the importance of private ownership and of malignant sorcery. The exclusiveness of ownership among them is characterized by its fierceness and ruthlessness, for which Benedict gives many examples. Ownership of a garden and its privacy is respected to such a degree that by custom, man and wife have intercourse within it. Nobody must know the amount of property anyone has. It is as secret as if it had been stolen. The same sense of ownership exists with regard to ownership of incantations and charms. The Dobus have 'disease charms' which produce and cure illnesses and each illness has a special charm. Illness is explained exclusively as a result of malevolent use of a charm. Some individuals own a charm which completely controls the production and cure of a certain illness. This disease-and-cure monopoly for one illness naturally gives them considerable power. Their whole life is governed by magic since no result in any field is possible without it, and magical formulae quite aside from those connected with illness are among the most important items of private property.

All existence is cut-throat competition and every advantage is gained at the expense of the defeated rival. But competition is not as in other systems, open and frank, but secret and treacherous. The ideal of a good and successful man is one who has cheated another of his place.

The most admired virtue and the greatest achievement is *wabuwabu*, a system of sharp practices which stresses one's own gains at the expense of another's loss. The art is to reap personal advantage in a situation in which others are victims. (This is a system quite different from that of the market which, in principle at least, is based on a fair exchange by which both sides are supposed to profit.) Even more characteristic of the spirit in this system is their treachery. In ordinary relations the Dobuan is sauve and unctuously polite. As one man puts it: 'If we wish to kill a man we approach him, we eat, drink, sleep, work and rest with him, it may be for several moons. We bide our time. We call him friend' (R. Benedict, 1934). As a result, in the not infrequent case of murder, suspicion falls on those who have tried to be friends with the victim.

Aside from material possessions, the most passionate desires are in the field of sex. The problem of sex is complicated, if we think of their general joylessness. Their conventions exclude laughter, and make dourness a virtue. As one of them says, 'In the gardens we do not play, we do not sing, we do not yodel, we do not relate legends' (R. Benedict, 1934). In fact, Benedict reports of one man crouching on the outskirts of a village of another tribe where the people were dancing, and he indignantly repudiated the suggestion that he might join: 'My wife would say I had been happy' (R. Benedict, 1934). Happiness for them is a paramount taboo. Nevertheless, this dourness and taboo on happiness or pleasurable activities goes together with promiscuity and with a high estimation of sexual passion and sexual techniques. In fact the basic sexual teaching by which girls are prepared for marriage is that the way to hold their husband is to keep him sexually exhausted.

It seems, in contrast to the Zuñi, sexual satisfaction is almost the only pleasureful and exhilarating experience the Dobuans permit themselves. Nevertheless, as we would expect, their sexual life is coloured by their character structure, and it would seem that their sexual satisfaction carries with it only a modicum of joy and in no way is a basis for warm and friendly relations between man and woman. Paradoxically, they are very prudish and in this respect, as Benedict mentions, as extreme as the Puritans. It seems that, precisely because happiness and enjoyment are tabooed, sex must assume the quality of something bad though very desirable. Indeed, sexual passion can serve as a compensation for joylessness just as much as it can be an expression of joy. With the Dobuans it clearly seems to be the former.[39]

Summarizing, Benedict states:

Life in Dobu fosters extreme forms of animosity and malignancy which most societies have minimized by their institutions. Dobuan institutions, on the other hand, exalt them to the highest degree. The Dobuan lives out without repression man's worst nightmares of the ill-will of the universe, and according to his view of life virtue consists in selecting a victim upon whom he can vent the malignancy he attributes alike to human society and to the powers of nature. All existence appears to him as a cut-throat struggle in which deadly antagonists are pitted against one another in a contest for each one of the goods of life. Suspicion and cruelty are his trusted weapons in the strife and he gives no mercy, as he asks none. (R. Benedict, 1934)

The Evidence for Destructiveness and Cruelty

The anthropological data have demonstrated that the instinctivistic interpretation of human destructiveness is not tenable.[40] While we find in all cultures that men defend

39. The obsessional emphasis on sex by otherwise joyless people can be observed in present-day Western society among the 'swingers' who practise group sex and are extremely bored, unhappy, and conventional people clinging to sexual satisfaction as the only relief from continuous boredom and loneliness. It may not be too different from those sectors of the consumer society, including also many members of the younger generation, for whom sexual consumption has been freed from restrictions, and for whom sex (like drugs) is the only relief in an otherwise bored and depressed mental state.

40. A study that deals with aggressiveness among primitive peoples by studying the rate of homicide and suicide among forty non-literate societies was undertaken by S. Palmer (1955). He combined homicidal and suicidal acts as destructive acts and compared their incidence in these forty societies. Among those he studied, there is one group with a low index of destructiveness (0-5); in this group we find eight cultures. One group with a medium degree of destructiveness (6-15); in this group

themselves against vital threats by fighting (or by fleeing), destructiveness and cruelty are minimal in so many societies that these great differences could not be explained if we were dealing with an 'innate' passion. Furthermore, the fact that the least-civilized societies like the hunter-gatherers and early agriculturalists show less destructiveness than the more-developed ones speaks against the idea that destructiveness is part of human 'nature'. Finally, the fact that destructiveness is not an isolated factor, but as we have seen, part of a syndrome, speaks against the instinctivisitic thesis.

But the fact that destructiveness and cruelty are not part of human nature does not imply that they are not widespread and intense. This fact does not have to be proved. It has been shown by many students of primitive society,[41] although it is important to keep in mind that these data refer to more developed – or deteriorated – primitive societies and not to the most primitive ones, the hunter-gatherers. Unfortunately, we ourselves have been and still are witnesses of such extraordinary acts of destruction and cruelty that we need not even look at the historical record.

In view of this I shall not cite the ample material on human destructiveness which is familiar, while the newer findings about hunter-gatherers and early Neolithic agriculturalists needed to be quoted extensively because they are relatively little known except among specialists.

---

are fourteen societies. One group with a very high degree of destructiveness (16-42); in this group there are eighteen cultures. If one combines low and medium aggressiveness, we find twenty-two with low and medium aggressiveness versus eighteen with high aggressiveness. Although this is a higher percentage of very aggressive societies than I found in my analysis of the thirty primitive cultures, nevertheless, Palmer's analysis does not confirm the thesis of the extreme aggressiveness of primitive peoples.

41. M. R. Davie (1929), for instance, brings ample material on primitive destructiveness and torture. See also Q. Wright (1965) on warfare in civilization.

I want to caution the reader in two respects. First, much confusion arises because of the use of the word 'primitive' for pre-civilized cultures of very different kinds. What they have in common is the lack of a written language, of an elaborate technique, of the use of money, but with regard to their economic, social, and political structure primitive societies differ radically from each other. In fact there is no such thing as 'primitive societies' – except as an abstraction – but only various types of primitive societies. Lack of destructiveness is characteristic for hunter-gatherers and is to be found in some more highly developed primitive societies, while in many others and in civilized societies destructiveness dominates the picture, and not peacefulness.

Another error against which I want to caution is to ignore the spiritual and religious meaning and motivation of actually destructive and cruel acts. Let us consider one drastic example, the sacrifice of children, as it was practised in Canaan at the time of the Hebrew conquest and in Carthage down to its destruction by the Romans, in the third century B C. Were these parents motivated by the destructive and cruel passion to kill their own children? Surely this is very unlikely. The story of Abraham's attempt to sacrifice Isaac, a story meant to speak against sacrifice of children, movingly emphasizes Abraham's love for Isaac; nevertheless Abraham does not waver in his decision to kill his son. Quite obviously we deal here with a religious motivation which is stronger than even the love for the child. The man in such a culture is completely devoted to his religious system, and he is not cruel, even though he appears so to a person outside this system.

It may help to see this point if we think of a modern phenomenon which can be compared with child sacrifice, that of war. Take the First World War. A mixture of economic interests, ambition, and vanity on the part of the leaders, and a good deal of stupid blundering on all sides brought about the war. But once it had broken out (or even a little bit earlier), it became a 'religious' phenomenon. The state, the nation, national honour, became the idols, and both sides voluntarily sacrificed their children to these idols. A large percentage of the young men of the British and of the German upper classes which are responsible for the war were wiped out in the early days of the fighting. Surely they were loved by their parents. Yet, especially for those who were most deeply imbued with the traditional concepts, their love did not make them hesitate in sending their children to death, nor did the young ones who were going to die have any hesitation. The fact that, in the case of child sacrifice, the father kills the child directly while, in the case of war, both sides have an arrangement to kill each other's children makes little difference. In the case of war, those who are responsible for it know what is going to happen, yet the power of the idols is greater than the power of love for their children.

One phenomenon that has often been quoted as a proof of man's innate destructiveness is that of cannibalism. Much has been made by the defenders of the thesis of man's innate destructiveness of findings which seem to indicate that even the most primitive form of man, Peking Man (around 500,000 BC), was a cannibal.

What are the facts?

The fragments of forty skulls were found in Choukoutien, assumed to have belonged to the most primitive *Homo* known, Peking Man. Hardly any other bones were found. The skulls were mutilated at the base, which suggests that the brain had been extracted. The further conclusion was made that the brain was eaten and hence that the Choukoutien findings prove that the earliest man known of was a cannibal.

However, none of these conclusions have been proved. We do not even know who killed the men whose skulls were found, for what purpose, and whether this was the exception or a typical case. Mumford (1967) has stressed the point convincingly, as has also K. J. Narr (1961), that these conjectures are nothing but speculations. Whatever the facts about Peking Man are, the widespread later cannibalism, as L. Mumford states, especially in Africa and New Guinea, cannot be taken as proof for cannibalism among man at a lower stage. (This is the same problem we have found in the phenomenon that the most primitive men are less destructive than the more developed and, incidentally, also have a more advanced form of religion than many more developed primitives (K. J. Narr, 1961).)

Among the many speculations about the meaning of the possible extraction of the brain in Peking Man, one deserves special attention, i.e., the assumption that we deal here with a ritualistic act in which the brain was not eaten for nourishment but as sacred food. A. C. Blanc in his study of ideologies in early man has pointed out, like the previously mentioned authors, that we know almost nothing of the religious ideas of Peking Man, but that it is possible to think of him as the first one to practise ritualistic cannibalism (A. C. Blanc, 1961).[42] Blanc suggests a possible connection between the findings in Choukoutien and findings in Monte Circeo of Neanderthal skulls that showed a mutilation of the base of the skull in order to extract the brain. He believes that there is enough evidence available now to permit the conclusion that we deal here with a ritualistic act. Blanc points out that these mutilations are identical with those produced by head-hunters in Borneo and Melanesia, where head-hunting clearly has a ritualistic meaning. It is interesting that these tribes, as Blanc states, are 'not particularly bloodthirsty or aggressive and have rather high morals' (A. C. Blanc, 1961).

42. Blanc points to the Dionysiac mysteries of ancient Greece and writes: 'Finally, it may not be insignificant to note that St Paul, in his Letter to the Corinthians, stresses with particular strength the motive of the real presence of Christ's blood and flesh in the eucharistic ritual: a powerful means of promoting the penetration and acceptance of Christianity and its major ritual in Greece, where the tradition of the Dionysiac symbolic ritual meal was particularly strong and deeply felt' (A. C. Blanc, 1961).

All these data lead to the conclusion that our knowledge of Peking Man's cannibalism is nothing more than a plausible construction, and if true, we deal most likely with a ritualistic phenomenon, entirely different from most of the destructive and non-ritualistic cannibalism in Africa, South America, and New Guinea (M. R. Davie, 1929). The rarity of *prehistorical* cannibalism is clearly indicated by the fact that E. Vollhard, in his monograph *Kannibalismus*, had stated that no valid evidence for the existence of early cannibalism had yet been observed and that he changed his mind only in 1942 when Blanc showed him the evidence of the Monte Circeo skull (reported by A. C. Blanc, 1961).

In head-hunting we also find ritualistic motives, like those in ritualistic cannibalism. To what extent head-hunting changes from a religiously meaningful ritual to behaviour generated by sadism and destructiveness deserves much more examination than has been devoted to this problem so far. Torture is perhaps much more rarely a ritualistic performance than an expression of sadistic impulses, whether it occurs in a primitive tribe or in a lynch mob today.

All these phenomena of destructiveness and cruelty require for their understanding an appreciation of the religious motivation that may be present rather than a destructive or cruel one. But this distinction finds little understanding in a culture in which there is little awareness of the intensity of strivings for non-practical, non-material goals, and of the power of spiritual and moral motivation.

However, even if a better understanding of many instances of destructive and cruel *behaviour* will reduce the incidence of destructiveness and cruelty as psychical *motivations*, the fact remains that enough instances remain to suggest that man, in contrast to virtually all mammals, is the only primate who can feel intense pleasure in killing and torturing. I believe I have demonstrated in this chapter that this destructiveness is neither innate, nor part of 'human nature', and that it is not common to all men. The question of what other and specifically human conditions are responsible for this potential viciousness of man will be discussed and I hope – at least to some extent – answered in the following chapters.

Part Three
The Varieties of Aggression and
Destructiveness and Their
Respective Conditions

9
Benign Aggression

Preliminary Remarks

The evidence presented in the previous chapter has led to the conclusion that defensive aggressiveness is 'built in' in the animal and human brain and serves the function of defence against threats to vital interests.

If human aggression were more or less at the same level as that of other mammals – particularly that of our nearest relative, the chimpanzee – human society would be rather peaceful and non-violent. But this is not so. Man's history is a record of extraordinary destructiveness and cruelty, and human aggression, it seems, far surpasses that of man's animal ancestors, and man is, in contrast to most animals, a real 'killer'.

How are we to explain this 'hyper-aggression' in man? Does it have the same source as animal aggression, or is man endowed with some other specifically human potential for destructiveness?

An argument can be made for the first assumption by pointing out that animals, too, exhibit extreme and vicious destructiveness when the environmental and social balance is disturbed, although this occurs only as an exception – for instance, under conditions of crowding. It could be concluded that man is so much more destructive because he has created conditions like crowding or other aggression-producing constellations that have become normal rather than exceptional in his history. Hence, man's hyper-aggression is not due to a greater aggressive *potential* but to the fact that aggression-producing *conditions* are much more frequent for humans than for animals living in their natural habitat.[1]

This argument is valid – as far as it goes. It is also important, because it leads to a critical analysis of man's condition in history. It suggests that man, during most of his history, has lived in a zoo and not 'in the wild' – i.e., under the condition of liberty conducive to human growth and well-being. Indeed, most data about man's 'nature' are basically of the same order as Zuckerman's original data on the Monkey Hill baboons in the London Zoo (S. Zuckerman, 1932).

But the fact remains that man often acts cruelly and destructively even in situations that do not include crowding. Destructiveness and cruelty can cause him to feel intense satisfaction; masses of men can suddenly be seized by lust for blood. Individuals and groups may have a character structure that makes them eagerly wait for – or create – situations that permit the expression of destructiveness.

Animals, on the other hand, do not enjoy inflicting pain and suffering on other animals, nor do they kill 'for nothing'. Sometimes an animal seems to exhibit sadistic behaviour – for instance, a cat playing with a mouse; but it is an anthropomorphic interpretation to assume that the cat enjoys the suffering of the mouse; any fast-moving object can serve as a plaything, whether it is a mouse or a ball of wool. Or, to take another example: Lorenz reports an incident of two doves caged together in too-close confinement. The stronger one flayed the other alive, feather by feather, until Lorenz came and separated them. But here again, what might seem a manifestation of unrestricted cruelty is really a reaction to the deprivation of space and falls under the category of defensive aggression.

The wish to destroy for the sake of destruction is different. Only man seems to take pleasure in destroying life without any reason or purpose other than that of destroying. To put it more generally, only man appears to be des-

1. This view has been expressed by C. and W. M. S. Russell (1968a).

tructive beyond the aim of defence or of attaining what he needs.

The thesis to be developed in this chapter is that man's destructiveness and cruelty cannot be explained in terms of animal heredity or in terms of a destructive instinct, but must be understood on the basis of those factors by which man *differs* from his animal ancestors. The problem is to examine *in what manner and to what degree the specific conditions of human existence are responsible for the quality and intensity of man's lust for killing and torturing.*[2]

Even to the degree that man's aggressiveness has the same defensive character as the animal's, it is much more frequent, for reasons that lie in the human condition. This chapter will deal first with man's defensive aggression and then with what is unique in man.

If we agree to call 'aggression' all acts that cause, and are intended to cause, damage to another person, animal, or inanimate object, the most fundamental distinction among all kinds of impulses subsumed under the category of aggression is that between *biologically adaptive, life-serving, benign aggression and biologically non-adaptive, malignant aggression.*

This distinction has already been mentioned in the discussion of the neurophysiological aspects of aggression. To sum up briefly: biologically adaptive aggression is a response to threats to vital interests; it is phylogenetically programmed; it is common to animals and men; it is not spontaneous or self-increasing, but reactive and defensive; it aims at the removal of the threat, either by destroying or by removing its source.

Biologically non-adaptive, malignant aggression, i.e.,

2. L. von Bertalanffy has taken a position similar in principle to that presented here. He writes: 'There is no doubt about the presence of aggressive and destructive tendencies in the human psyche which are of the nature of biological drives. However, the most pernicious phenomena of aggression, transcending self-preservation and self-destruction, are based upon a characteristic feature of man above the biological level, namely his capability of creating symbolic universes in thought, language and behaviour' (L. von Bertalanffy, 1956).

destructiveness and cruelty, is not a defence against a threat; it is not phylogenetically programmed; it is characteristic only of man, it is biologically harmful because it is socially disruptive; its main manifestations – killing and cruelty – are pleasureful without needing any other purpose; it is harmful not only to the person who is attacked but also to the attacker. Malignant aggression, though not an instinct, is a human potential rooted in the very conditions of human existence.

The distinction between biologically adaptive aggression and biologically non-adaptive aggression ought to help to clarify a confusion in the whole discussion of human aggression. Those who explain the frequency and intensity of human aggression as being due to an innate trait of human nature often force their opponents, who have refused to relinquish the hope for a peaceful world, to minimize the degree of man's destructiveness and cruelty. Thus the defenders of hope have often been driven into taking a defensive and over-optimistic view of man. The distinction between defensive and malignant aggression makes this unnecessary. It only implies that the malignant part of man's aggression is not innate, and hence not ineradicable, but it admits that malignant aggression is a human potential and more than a learned pattern of behaviour that readily disappears when new patterns are introduced.

Part Three will examine the nature of and conditions for both benign and malignant aggression, while dealing at much greater length with the latter. Before starting, I want to remind the reader that in contrast to behaviourist theory, the following analysis of all types of aggression has as its subject matter aggressive *impulses*, regardless of whether or not they are expressed in aggressive *behaviour*.

Pseudo-aggression

By pseudo-aggression I refer to those aggressive acts that may cause harm, but are not intended to do so.

Accidental Aggression

The most obvious example of pseudo-aggression is accidental, unintended aggression, i.e., an aggressive act that hurts another person, but was not intended to do any harm. The classical example for this type of aggression is the firing of a gun which accidentally hurts or kills a bystander. Psychoanalysis has somewhat reduced the simplicity of the legal definition of accidental acts by introducing the concept of unconscious motivation, so that one can raise the question of whether what appears to be accidental was not unconsciously intended by the aggressor. This consideration would decrease the number of cases that fall under the category of unintended aggression, but it would be a purely dogmatic over-simplification to assume that every accidental aggression is due to unconscious motives.

Playful Aggression

Playful aggression has as its aim the exercise of skill. It does not aim at destruction or harm, and it is not motivated by hate. While fencing, sword fighting, and archery developed from the need to kill an enemy in defence or attack, their original function has been almost completely lost, and they have become an art. This art is practised, for instance, in Zen Buddhist sword fighting, which requires great skill, complete control of the whole body, complete concentration – qualities it shares with an art apparently as completely different as that of the tea ceremony. A Zen master of sword fighting does not harbour the wish to kill or destroy, nor has he any hate. He makes the proper movement, and if the opponent is killed, it is because the latter 'stood in the wrong place'.[3] A classic psychoanalyst may argue that unconsciously the sword fighter is motivated by hate and the wish to destroy his opponent; this is his privilege, but he would show little grasp of the spirit of Zen Buddhism.

The bow and arrow were also once weapons of attack and defence with an aim to destroy, but today the art of archery is a pure exercise in skill, as is shown so instructively in E. Herrigel's little book *Zen in the Art of Archery* (1953). In Western culture we find the same phenomenon, that fencing and sword fighting have become a sport. Though these may not involve the spiritual aspects of Zen art, they also represent a kind of fighting without the intention to harm. Similarly, among primitive tribes we also frequently find fighting that seems to be largely a display of skill and only in a minor way an expression of destructiveness.

Self-Assertive Aggression

By far the most important case of pseudo-aggression is that which is more or less equivalent to self-assertion. It is aggression in the literal sense of its root – *aggredi*, from *ad gradi* (*gradus* means 'step' and *ad*, 'towards'), which means 'to move (go, step) forward' – just as regression, from *regredi*, means 'to move backwards'. *Aggredi*, or in the now obsolete English form 'to aggress', is an intransitive verb. One can aggress, i.e., move forward, but one cannot 'aggress' *somebody*, in the sense that one can attack somebody. The word 'aggress' must early have assumed the meaning of attack, since, in war, moving forward was usually the beginning of an attack.

To be aggressive, in its original meaning of 'aggressing', can be defined as *moving forward towards a goal without undue hesitation, doubt, or fear*.

The concept of assertive aggression seems to find some confirmation in observations made of the link between the

3. Personal communication from the late Dr D. T. Suzuki.

male hormone and aggression. A number of experiments have shown that male hormones tend to generate aggressive behaviour. For an answer to the question why this should be so, we must consider that one of the most basic differences between male and female is the difference in function during the sexual act. The anatomic and physiological conditions of male sexual functioning require that the male be capable of piercing the hymen of the virgin, that he should not be deterred by the fear, hesitation, or even resistance she might manifest; in animals, the male must hold the female in position during the act of mounting. Since the male capacity to function sexually is a basic requirement for the survival of the species, one might expect that nature has endowed the male with some special aggressive potential. This expectation appears to be borne out by a number of data.

Many experiments have been made to study the connection between aggression and either the castration of the male or the effects of injecting male hormones into a castrated male. The basic studies in this field were done in the forties.[4] One of the classic experiments is that described by Beeman. He showed that when adult male mice (twenty-five days old) were castrated, sometime after the operation they no longer fought as they did before castration, but instead behaved peacefully. However, if the same animal were then administered male hormones, they began fighting again, stopping once more when the male hormone was withdrawn. Beeman could also demonstrate, however, that the mice did not stop fighting if they were not given a rest after the operation, but were conditioned to a continued daily routine of fighting (E. A. Beeman, 1947). This indicates that the male hormone was a *stimulation* for fighting behaviour, but not a condition without which it could not occur.

Similar experiments have also been done with chimpanzees by G. Clark and H. G. Bird (1946). The result was that

4. cf. F. A. Beach (1945).

the male hormone raised the level of aggressiveness (dominance) and the female hormone lowered it. Later experiments – for instance, those reported by E. B. Sigg – confirm the older work of Beeman and others. Sigg comes to the conclusion:

It may be stated that the precipitation of aggressive behaviour in isolated mice is probably based on multihormonal imbalance lowering the threshold to the aggression-eliciting trigger stimulus. The male gonadal hormones are critically involved in this response whereas other endocrine changes (adreno-cortical, adreno-medullary and thyroid) may be contributory and consequential. (S. Garattini and E. B. Sigg, ed., 1969)

Of the other papers in the same volume dealing with the problem of the relationship of sex hormones and aggression, I want to mention only one more study, that by K. M. J. Lagerspetz. He reports on experiments that tend to demonstrate that in mice conditioned to be highly aggressive, both mounting and copulation were totally inhibited, while in mice conditioned to be non-aggressive, sexual behaviour was not inhibited. The author concludes that 'these results suggest that these two types of behaviour are alternatives which can be selectively inhibited and reinforced [and they] do not substantiate the belief that aggressive and sexual behaviour are due to a common arousal which is further channelled by environmental stimuli' (K. M. J. Lagerspetz, 1969). Such a conclusion contradicts the assumption that aggressive impulses contribute to male sexual impulses. It is outside my competence to evaluate this apparent contradiction. I shall, however, offer a hypothetical suggestion a little further on in the text.

Another possible basis for the assumption of a connection between maleness and aggression are the findings and speculations on the nature of the Y chromosome. The female carries two sex chromosomes (XX); the male pair of sex chromosomes consists of one X and one Y (XY). However, in the process of cell division abnormal developments can occur, the most important one from the standpoint of aggression being a male who has one X and two Y chromosomes (XYY). (There are other constellations having an extra sex chromosome which do not interest us here.) XYY individuals seem to show certain physical abnormalities. They are usually above average in height, rather dull, and with a relatively high incidence of epileptic and epileptoform conditions. The feature that interests us here is that they may also show an extraordinary amount of aggressiveness. This assumption was first made on the basis of a study of mentally abnormal (violent and dangerous) inmates in a special security institution in Edinburgh (P. A. Jacobs *et al.*, 1965). Seven of the one hundred ninety-seven males were of an XYY constitution (3.5 per 100), which is probably a significantly higher percentage than that found in the general population.[5] After the publication of this work about a dozen other studies have been made whose results tend to confirm and enlarge upon those of the first one.[6] These studies, however, do not permit any definite conclusions, and assumptions based on them must await confirmation by research done on larger samples and using more refined methods.[7]

5. These figures are debatable, however, since estimates of the percentage of XYY among the general population vary between 0·5–3·5 per 1,000.

6. cf. M. F. A. Montagu (1968) and J. Nielsen (1968), especially the literature quoted there.

7. The latest survey on this question arrives at the conclusion that the link between aggression and XYY chromosomes is as yet unproven. The author writes: 'The preponderant opinion among the Conference participants was that the behavioural aberrations implied or documented thus far do not indicate a direct cause and effect relationship with the XYY chromosome constitution. Thus, it would not be possible to say at the present time that the XYY complement is definitely or invariably associated with behavioural abnormalities . . . Moreover, the widespread publicity notwithstanding, individuals with the XYY anomaly have *not* been found to be more aggressive than matched offenders with normal chromosome constitutions. In this respect, it appears that premature and incautious speculations may have led to XYY persons being falsely stigmatized as unusually aggressive and violent compared to other offenders' (S. A. Shah, 1970).

Male aggression has usually been understood in the literature as not different from what is generally called aggression – that is, attacking behaviour aimed at doing damage to another person. But if this were the nature of male aggression, it would be very puzzling from a biological standpoint. What could be the biological function of a hostile, damaging male attitude towards the female? It would be disruptive to the elementary bond of male–female relationship, and still more importantly from a biological standpoint, it would tend to damage the female, on whom rests the responsibility of bearing and rearing children. [8] While it is true that under certain constellations, especially those of patriarchal dominance and exploitation of women, a deep antagonism develops between the sexes, it would be inexplicable why such antagonism should be desirable from a biological standpoint and that it should have developed as a result of the evolutionary process. On the other hand, as I remarked before, it is biologically necessary for the male to have a capacity for moving forward and of overcoming obstacles. This, however, is not in itself a hostile or attacking behaviour; it is self-assertive aggression. That male aggression is basically different from destructiveness or cruelty is confirmed by the fact that there is no evidence whatsoever that would lead to the assumption that women are less destructive or cruel than men.

This view would seem also to explain some of the difficulties implied in the previously cited experiment by Lagerspetz, who found that mice showing a high degree of fighting behaviour had no interest in copulation (K. M. J. Lagerspetz, 1969). If aggression in the sense in which it is generally used were part of male sexuality, or even stimulated it, we should expect the opposite result. The apparent contradiction between Lagerspetz's experiments and those

8. Copulation between animals sometimes gives the impression of fierce aggression on the part of the male; observations by trained observers indicate that reality does not correspond to the appearances, and that at least among mammals, the male does not cause the female any harm.

of other authors seems to find a simple solution if we differentiate between hostile aggression and aggression in the sense of moving forward. The fighting mice, we can assume, are in a hostile, attacking mood that excludes sexual stimulation. On the other hand, the administration of male hormones in the other experiments does not generate hostility but the tendency to move forward and hence to reduce inhibitions of normal fighting behaviour.

Lagerspetz's thesis is borne out by observation of normal human behaviour. People in a state of anger and hostility have little sexual appetite and sexual stimuli do not greatly affect them. I am speaking here of hostile angry, attacking tendencies, and not of sadism, which is, indeed, compatible and often blended with sexual impulses. In brief, anger, i.e., basically defensive aggression, weakens sexual interest; *sadistic* and *masochistic* impulses, while not generated by sexual behaviour, are compatible with it, or stimulating.

Self-assertive aggression is not restricted to sexual behaviour. It is a basic quality required in many life situations, such as in the behaviour of a surgeon and of a mountain climber and in most sports; it is also a quality necessary for the hunter. A successful salesman also needs this type of aggression, and this is expressed when one speaks of an 'aggressive salesman'. In all these situations, successful performance is possible only when the person involved is endowed with unimpeded self-assertion – that is, if he can pursue his aim with determination and without being deterred by obstacles. Of course, this quality is also necessary in a person who attacks an enemy. A general lacking in aggressiveness in this sense will be a hesitant and poor officer; an attacking soldier who lacks it will easily retreat. But one must differentiate between aggression with the aim to damage and the self-assertive aggression that only facilitates the pursuit of a goal, whether it is to damage or to create.

In animal experiments where the injection of male hormones renews or increases the fighting capacity of the animal, one has to distinguish carefully between two possible interpretations: (1) that the hormones generate rage and aggression, and (2) that they increase the self-assertion of the animal in pursuing its already existing hostile aims that were integrated by other sources. In reviewing the experiments on the influence of male hormones on aggression, my impression is that both interpretations are possible, but for biological reasons the second seems more likely. Further experiments focused on this difference will probably offer convincing evidence for the one or the other hypothesis.

The connection between self-assertion, aggression, male hormones, and – possibly – Y chromosomes suggests the possibility that men may be equipped with more self-assertive aggression than women and make better generals, surgeons, or hunters, while women may be more protective and caring and make better physicians and teachers. No conclusion can be drawn, of course, from the behaviour of women today, since it is largely the result of the existing patriarchal order. Furthermore, the whole question would have a purely statistical and not an individual significance. Many men lack self-assertive aggressiveness, and many women perform excellently those tasks that require it. Obviously, there is not a simple relationship between maleness and the self-assertive aggressiveness, but a highly complex one about whose details we know almost nothing. This is no surprise to the geneticist who knows that a genetic disposition can be translated into a certain type of behaviour, but can be understood only in terms of its interconnection with other genetic dispositions and with the total life situation into which a person is born and has to live. It must furthermore be considered that self-assertive aggression is a necessary quality for survival and not only for the performance of the particular activities mentioned above; hence it is a biologically reasonable assumption that all human beings are endowed with it, and not only men. Whether the specific male aggression affects only sexual behaviour or, on the other hand, whether the phenomenon of the inherent bisexuality of men and women takes sufficient care of female assertive aggression must remain idle speculation until a great many more empirical data on the influence of male hormones and chromosomes are available.

There is, however, one important fact that has been pretty well established clinically. The person with an unimpeded self-assertive aggression tends, in general, to be less hostile in a defensive sense than the person whose self-assertion is defective. This holds true both for defensive aggression and for malignant aggression like sadism. The reasons for this are easy to see. As to the first, defensive aggression is a response to a threat. The person with un-impeded self-assertive aggression feels less easily threatened and, hence, is less readily in a position of having to react with aggression. The sadistic person is sadistic because he is suffering from an impotence of the heart, from the in-capacity to move the other, to make him respond, to make oneself a loved person. He compensates for that impotence with the passion to have power *over* others. Since self-assertive aggression enhances the person's capacity for achieving his aims, its possession greatly diminishes the need for sadistic control.[9]

As a final observation on self-assertive aggression, I would indicate that the degree to which it is developed in a given person is of great significance for his whole character structure and for certain forms of neurotic symptoms. The shy or inhibited person, as well as the one with compulsive obsessional tendencies, suffers from an impediment of this type of aggression. The therapeutic task is, first, to help the person to become aware of this impediment, then, to understand how it developed, and most importantly, to understand by what other factors in his character system and in his environment it is supported and supplied with energy.

Perhaps the most important factor that leads to the weakening of self-assertive aggression is an authoritarian

9. cf. the discussion of sadism in Chapter 11.

atmosphere in family and society, where self-assertion is equated with disobedience, attack, sin. For all irrational and exploitative forms of authority, self-assertion – the pursuit by another of his real goals – is the arch sin because it is a threat to the power of the authority; the person subject to it is indoctrinated to believe that the aims of the authority are also his, and that obedience offers the optimal chance for fulfilling oneself.

Defensive Aggression

Difference Between Animals and Man

Defensive aggression is biologically adaptive, for reasons already mentioned in the discussions of the neurophysiological basis of aggression. To repeat them briefly: the brain of animals is phylogenetically programmed to mobilize attack or flight impulses when vital interests of the animal are threatened, such as food, space, the young, access to females. Basically, the aim is to remove the danger; this can be done, and more often than not is done, by flight, or if flight is not possible, by fighting or assuming effective threatening postures. The aim of defensive aggression is not lust for destruction, but the preservation of life. Once the aim has been attained, the aggression and its emotional equivalents disappear.

Man, too, is phylogenetically programmed to react with attack or flight if his vital interests are threatened. Even though this innate tendency operates less rigidly in man than in lower mammals, there is no lack of evidence that man tends to be motivated by his phylogenetically prepared tendency for defensive aggression when his life, health, freedom, or property (in those societies where private property exists and is highly valued) are threatened. To be sure, this reaction can be overcome by moral or religious convictions and training, but it is in practice the reaction of most individuals and groups. In fact, defensive aggression accounts perhaps for most of man's aggressive impulses.

It could be said that the neural equipment for defensive aggression is identical in animals and man; this statement is correct, however, only in a limited sense. This is mainly because these aggression-integrating areas are part of the *whole* brain, and because the human brain with its large neo-cortex and its vastly greater number of neural connections is different from the animal brain.

But even though the neurophysiological basis for defensive aggression is not identical with that of the animal, it is similar enough to permit the statement that *this same neurophysiological equipment leads to an incidence of defensive aggression many times greater in man than in the animal*. The reason for this phenomenon lies in specific conditions of *human* existence. They are, mainly, the following:

1. The animal perceives as a threat only 'clear and present danger'. To be sure, its instinctive equipment and its individually acquired and genetically inherited memories induce the awareness of dangers and threats often more accurately than they are perceived by man.

But man, being endowed with a capacity for foresight and imagination, reacts not only to present dangers and threats or to memories of dangers and threats but to the dangers and threats he can imagine as possibly happening in the future. He may conclude, for instance, that because his tribe is richer than a neighbouring tribe that is well trained in warfare, the other will attack his own some time from now. Or he may reason that a neighbour whom he has harmed will take revenge when the time is favourable. In the political field the calculation of future threats is one of the central preoccupations of politicians and generals. If an individual or a group feels threatened, the mechanism of defensive aggression is mobilized even though the threat is not immediate; hence man's capacity to foresee future threats enhances the frequency of his aggressive reactions.

2. Man is capable not only of foreseeing *real* dangers in the

future; he is also capable of being persuaded and brain-washed by his leaders to see dangers when in reality they do not exist. Most modern wars, for instance, have been prepared by systematic propaganda of this type; the population was persuaded by its leaders that it was in danger of being attacked and destroyed, and thus reactions of hate against the threatening nations have been provoked. Often no threat existed. Especially since the French Revolution, with the appearance of large citizens' armies rather than relatively small armies consisting of professional soldiers, it is not easy for a nation's leader to tell the people to kill and be killed because industry wants cheaper raw materials, cheaper labour, or new markets. Only a minority would be willing to participate in the war if it were justified by declaring such aims. If, on the other hand, a government can make the population believe that it is being threatened, the normal biological reaction against threat is mobilized. In addition, these predictions of threat from the outside are often self-fulfilling: the aggressor state, by preparing for war, forces the state that is about to be attacked to prepare also, thereby providing the 'proof' of the alleged threat.

The arousal of defensive aggression by means of brain-washing can occur only in humans. In order to persuade people that they are threatened, one needs, above all, the medium of language; without this, most suggestion would be impossible. In addition, one needs a social structure that provides a sufficient basis for brain-washing. It is hard to imagine, for example, that this kind of suggestion would work among the Mbutu, the African pygmy hunters living contentedly in the forest and having no permanent authorities. In their society there is no man with sufficient power to make the incredible credible. On the other hand, in a society that has figures carrying great authority – such as sorcerers or political and religious leaders – the basis for such suggestion is present. By and large, the power of suggestion exercised by a ruling group is in proportion to the group's power over the ruled and/or the capacity of the rulers to use an elaborate ideological system to reduce the faculty of critical and independent thinking.

3. A third specifically human condition of existence contributes to a further increase of human defensive aggressiveness compared with animal aggressiveness. Man, like the animal, defends himself against threat to his vital interests. *But the range of man's vital interests is much wider than that of the animal.* Man must survive not only physically but also psychically. He needs to maintain a certain psychic equilibrium lest he lose the capacity to function; for man everything necessary for the maintenance of his psychic equilibrium is of the same vital interest as that which serves his physical equilibrium. First of all, man has a vital interest in retaining his frame of orientation. His capacity to act depends on it, and in the last analysis, his sense of identity. If others threaten him with ideas that question his own frame of orientation, he will react to these ideas as to a vital threat. He may rationalize this reaction in many ways. He will say that the new ideas are inherently 'immoral', 'uncivilized', 'crazy', or whatever else he can think of to express his repugnance, but this antagonism is in fact aroused because 'he' feels threatened.

Man needs not only a frame of orientation but also objects of devotion, which become a vital necessity for his emotional equilibrium. Whatever they are – values, ideals, ancestors, father, mother, the soil, country, class, religion, and hundreds of other phenomena – they are perceived as sacred. Even customs can become sacred because they symbolize the existing values.[10] The individual – or the group – reacts to an attack against the 'sacred' with the same rage and aggressiveness as to an attack against life.

What has been said about reactions to threats to vital interests can be expressed also in a different and more

10. It is characteristic for this phenomenon that the Greek word *ethos* – meaning, literally, behaviour – has assumed the meaning of the 'ethical', just as 'norm' (originally the word for a carpenter's tool) was used in the double sense of what is 'normal' and what is 'normative'.

generalized way by stating that fright tends to mobilize either aggression or the tendency to flight. The latter is often the case when a person still has a way out that saves a modicum of 'face', but if he is driven into a corner and no possibility of evasion is left, the aggressive reaction is more likely to occur. One factor, however, must not be overlooked: the flight reaction depends on the interaction of two factors: the first is the magnitude of the realistic threat, the second is the degree of physical and psychical strength and self-confidence of the threatened person. On the one end of the continuum will be events which will frighten virtually everybody; on the other, there will be such a sense of helplessness and impotence that almost everything will frighten the anxious person. Hence fright is as much conditioned by real threats as it is by an inner environment that generates it even with little outside stimulation.

Fright, like pain, is a most uncomfortable feeling, and man will do almost anything to get rid of it. There are many ways to get rid of fright and anxiety, such as the use of drugs, sexual arousal, sleep, and the company of others. One of the most effective ways of getting rid of anxiety is to become aggressive. When a person can get out of the passive state of fright and begin to attack, the painful nature of fright disappears.[11]

Aggression and Freedom

Among all the threats to man's vital interests, the threat to his freedom is of extraordinary importance, individually and socially. In contrast to the widely held opinion that this desire for freedom is a product of culture and more specifically of learning-conditioning, there is ample evidence to suggest that the desire for freedom is a biological reaction of the human organism.

11. I am indebted to Dr Juan de Dios Hernández for his stimulating suggestions on the neurophysiological level, which I omit here as they would require a lengthy technical discussion.

One phenomenon that supports this view is that through-out history nations and classes have fought their oppressors if there was any possibility of victory, and often even if there was none. The history of mankind is, indeed, a history of the fight for freedom, a history of revolutions, from the war of liberation of the Hebrews against the Egyptians, the national uprisings against the Roman Empire, the German peasant rebellions in the sixteenth century, to the American, French, German, Russian, Chinese, Algerian, and Viet-namese revolutions.[12] Leaders have all too frequently used the slogan that they are leading their people in a battle for freedom, when in reality their aim has been to enslave them. That no promise appeals more powerfully to the heart of man is evidenced by the phenomenon that even those leaders who want to suppress freedom find it necessary to promise it.

Another reason for assuming there is an inherent impulse in man to fight for freedom lies in the fact that freedom is the condition for the full growth of a person, for his mental health and his well-being; its absence cripples man and is unhealthy. Freedom does not imply lack of constraint, since any growth occurs only within a structure, and any structure

12. The revolutions that have occurred in history must not obscure the fact that infants and children also make revolutions, but since they are powerless, they have to use their own methods, those of guerrilla war-fare, as it were. They fight against suppression of their freedom by various individual methods, such as stubborn negativism, refusal to eat, refusal to be toilet trained, bed-wetting, up and on to·the more drastic methods of autistic withdrawal and pseudo mental debility. The adults behave like any élite whose power is challenged. They use physical force, often blended with bribery, to protect their position. As a result, most children surrender and prefer submission to constant torment. No mercy is shown in this war until victory is achieved, and our hospitals are filled with its casualties. Nevertheless, it is a remarkable fact that all human beings – the children of the powerful as well as those of the powerless – share the common experience of once having been powerless and of hav-ing fought for their freedom. That is why one may assume that every human being – aside from his biological equipment – has acquired in his childhood a revolutionary potential that, though dormant for a long time, might be mobilized under special circumstances.

requires constraint (H. von Foerster, 1970). What matters is whether the constraint functions primarily for the sake of another person or institution, or whether it is autonomous – i.e., that it results from the necessities of growth inherent in the structure of the person.

As a condition for the unstunted development of the human organism, freedom is a vital biological interest of man,[13] and threats to his freedom arouse defensive aggression as do all other threats to vital interests. Is it surprising then that aggression and violence continue to be generated in a world in which the majority are deprived of freedom, especially the people in the so-called underdeveloped countries? Those in power – i.e., the whites – would perhaps be less surprised and indignant if they were not accustomed to considering the yellows, the browns and the blacks as non-persons and, hence, not expected to react humanly.[14]

But there is an additional reason for this blindness. Even the whites, powerful as they are, have surrendered their freedom because their own system has forced them to do so, although in a less drastic and overt way. Perhaps they hate those who fight for it today all the more because they are reminded of their own surrender.

The fact that genuine revolutionary aggression, like all aggression generated by the impulse to defend one's life, freedom or dignity, is biologically rational and part of normal human functioning must not deceive one into forgetting that destruction of life always remains destruction, even when it is biologically justified; it is a matter of one's religious, moral, or political principles whether one believes that it is humanly justified or not. But whatever

13. Not only of man. The deteriorating effect on the animal of life in the zoo has been mentioned before and seems to outweigh the contrary views of even as great an authority as Hediger (H. Hediger, 1942).

14. Skin colour has this effect only if it is combined with powerlessness. The Japanese have become persons since they acquired power at the beginning of this century; the image of the Chinese changed for the same reason only a·few years ago. The possession of advanced technology has become the criterion of being human.

one's principles in this respect are, it is important to be aware how easily purely defensive aggression is blended with (non-defensive) destructiveness and with the sadistic wish to reverse the situation by controlling others instead of being controlled. If and when this happens, revolutionary aggression is vitiated and tends to renew the conditions it was seeking to abolish.

Aggression and Narcissism[15]

In addition to the factors already discussed, one of the most important sources of defensive aggression is the wounding of *narcissism*.

The concept of narcissism was formulated by Freud in terms of his libido theory. Since the schizophrenic patient does not seem to have any 'libidinous' relationship to objects (either in reality or in fantasy), Freud was led to the question: 'What has happened to the libido which has been withdrawn from external objects in schizophrenia?' His answer was: 'The libido that has been withdrawn from the external world has been directed to the ego and thus gives rise to an attitude which may be called narcissism.' In addition, Freud assumed that the original state of man in early infancy was narcissism ('primary narcissism'), in which there were not yet any relationships to the outside world; in the course of normal development the child increased his libidinal relationships to the outside world in scope and intensity, but under special circumstances (the most drastic one being insanity) the libido is withdrawn from objects and directed back to the ego ('secondary narcissism'); even in the case of normal development, however, a human being remains to some extent narcissistic throughout his life (S. Freud, 1914).

In spite of this statement, the concept of narcissism has not played the important role it deserves in the clinical investigations of psychoanalysts. It has been mainly applied

15. For a more detailed discussion of narcissism, see E. Fromm (1964).

to early infancy and to psychoses,[16] but its far-reaching importance lies precisely in its role for the normal, or the so-called neurotic personality. This role can be fully understood only if narcissism is freed from the restricting frame of reference of the libido theory. Narcissism can then be described as a state of experience in which only the person himself, *his* body, *his* needs, *his* feelings, *his* thoughts, *his* property, everything and everybody pertaining to *him* are experienced as fully real, while everybody and everything that does not form part of the person or is not an object of his needs is not interesting, is not fully real, is perceived only by intellectual recognition, while *affectively* without weight and colour. A person, to the extent to which he is narcissistic, has a double standard of perception. Only he himself and what pertains to him has significance, while the rest of the world is more or less weightless or colourless, and because of this double standard the narcissistic person shows severe defects in judgement and lacks the capacity for objectivity.[17]

Often the narcissistic person achieves a sense of security in his own entirely subjective conviction of his perfection, his superiority over others, his extraordinary qualities, and not through being related to others or through any real work or achievement of his own. He needs to hold on to his narcissistic self-image, since his sense of worth as well as his sense of identity are based on it. If his narcissism is threat-

16. In recent years many analysts have questioned the concept of primary narcissism in infancy and assume the existence of object relations at a much earlier period than Freud did. Freud's idea of the totally narcissistic nature of psychoses has also been abandoned by most psychoanalysts.

17. In the following I deal only with narcissism that manifests itself in the sense of grandiosity. There is another form of narcissism that, although it seems to be the opposite, is only another manifestation of the same thing; I refer to negative narcissism, in which a person is constantly and anxiously concerned with his health to the point of hypochondria. This manifestation is of no importance in this context. It should be noted, however, that·the two manifestations are often blended; we need only think of Himmler's hypochondriacal preoccupation with his health.

ened, *he* is threatened in a vitally important area. When others wound his narcissism by slighting him, criticizing him, showing him up when he has said something wrong, defeating him in a game or on numerous other occasions, a narcissistic person usually reacts with intense anger or rage, whether or not he shows it or is even aware of it. The intensity of this aggressive reaction can often be seen in the fact that such a person will never forgive someone who has wounded his narcissism and often feels a desire for vengeance which would be less intense if his body or his property had been attacked.

Most persons are not aware of their own narcissism, but only of those of its manifestations which do not overtly reveal it. Thus, for instance, they will feel an inordinate admiration for their parents or for their children, and they have no difficulty in expressing these feelings because such behaviour is usually judged positively as filial piety, parental affection, or loyalty; but if they were to express their feelings about their own person, such as 'I am the most wonderful person in the world', 'I am better than anyone else', etc., they would be suspected not only of being extraordinarily vain, but perhaps even of not being quite sane. On the other hand, if a person has achieved something that finds recognition in the field of art, science, sports, business, or politics, his narcissistic attitude appears not only to be realistic and rational, but is also constantly fed by the admiration of others. In these cases he can give full rein to his narcissism because it has been socially sanctioned and confirmed.[18] In present-day Western society there is a peculiar interconnection between the narcissism of the celebrity and the needs of the public. The latter wants to be in touch with famous people because the life of the average person is empty and boring. The mass media live from selling fame, and thus everybody is satisfied; the narcissistic performer, the public, and the fame merchants.

18. The problem of narcissism and creativity is a very complex one and would need a much longer discussion than is possible here.

Among political leaders a high degree of narcissism is very frequent; it may be considered an occupational illness – or asset – especially among those who owe their power to their influence over mass audiences. If the leader is convinced of his extraordinary gifts and of his mission, it will be easier to convince the large audiences who are attracted by men who appear to be so absolutely certain. But the narcissistic leader does not use his narcissistic charisma only as a means for political success; he needs success and applause for the sake of his own mental equilibrium. The idea of his greatness and infallibility is essentially based on his narcissistic grandiosity, not on his real achievements as a human being.[19] And yet he cannot do without the narcissistic inflation because his human core – conviction, conscience, love, and faith – is not very developed. Extremely narcissistic persons are often almost forced to become famous, since otherwise they might become depressed and insane. But it takes much talent – and appropriate opportunities – to influence others to such a degree that their applause validates these narcissistic

19. That does not mean that he is nothing but bluff; this is true frequently enough, but not always. Woodrow Wilson, Franklin D. Roosevelt, and Winston Churchill, for instance, were very narcissistic persons, yet they did not lack in important political achievements. But these achievements were not such as to justify their feeling of self-assurance and unquestionable rightness often manifested in arrogance; at the same time, their narcissism was limited in comparison with that of a man like Hitler. That explains why Churchill did not suffer from severe mental consequences when he lost the 1948 election, and I assume the same would have been the case with Roosevelt if he had experienced defeat, although the fact must not be ignored that even after political defeat they would have retained a great number of admirers. Wilson's case may be somewhat different; it would be a subject for study whether his political defeat did not create serious psychic problems that interacted with his physical illness. With Hitler and Stalin the case seems to be clear. Hitler preferred to die rather than to face defeat. Stalin showed signs of psychic crisis during the first weeks after the German attack in 1941, and it seems likely that he suffered from paranoid tendencies in the last years of his life after he had created so many enemies that he may have sensed he was no longer the beloved father of his subjects.

dreams. Even when such people succeed, they are driven to seek further success, since for them failure carries the danger of collapse. Popular success is, as it were, their self-therapy against depression and madness. In fighting for their aims, they are really fighting for their sanity.

When, in group narcissism, the object is not the individual but the group to which he belongs, the individual can be fully aware of it, and express it without any restrictions. The assertion that 'my country' (or nation, or religion) is the most wonderful, the most cultured, the most powerful, the most peace-loving, etc., does not sound crazy at all; on the contrary, it sounds like the expression of patriotism, faith, and loyalty. It also appears to be a realistic and rational value judgement because it is shared by many members of the same group. This consensus succeeds in transforming the fantasy into reality, since for most people reality is constituted by general consensus and not based on reason or critical examination.[20]

Group narcissism has important functions. In the first place, it furthers the solidarity and cohesion of the group, and makes manipulation easier by appealing to narcissistic prejudices. Secondly, it is extremely important as an element giving satisfaction to the members of the group and particularly to those who have few other reasons to feel proud and worthwhile. Even if one is the most miserable, the poorest, the least respected member of a group, there is compensation for one's miserable condition in feeling 'I am a part of the most wonderful group in the world. I, who in reality am a worm, become a giant through belonging to the group.' Consequently, the degree of group narcissism is commensurate with the lack of real satisfaction in life. Those social classes which enjoy life more are less fanatical (fanaticism is a characteristic quality of group narcissism) than those which, like the lower middle classes, suffer from

20. Sometimes the consensus even of a small group suffices to create reality – in the most extreme cases even the consensus of two (*folie à deux*).

scarcity in all material and cultural areas and lead a life of unmitigated boredom.

At the same time, fostering group narcissism is very inexpensive from the standpoint of the social budget; in fact, it costs practically nothing compared with the social expense required to raise the standard of living. Society has only to pay ideologists who formulate the slogans that generate social narcissism; indeed, many social functionaries, like school teachers, journalists, ministers, and professors, participate even without being paid, at least with money. They receive their reward from feeling proud and satisfied to be serving such a worthy cause – and through enhanced prestige and promotion.

Those whose narcissism refers to their group rather than to themselves as individuals are as sensitive as the individual narcissist, and they react with rage to any wound, real or imaginary, inflicted upon their group. If anything, they react more intensely and certainly more consciously. An individual, unless he is mentally very sick, may have at least some doubts about his personal narcissistic image. The member of the group has none, since his narcissism is shared by the majority. In case of conflict between groups that challenge each other's collective narcissism, this very challenge arouses intense hostility in each of them. The narcissistic image of one's own group is raised to its highest point, while the devaluation of the opposing group sinks to the lowest. One's own group becomes a defender of human dignity, decency, morality, and right. Devilish qualities are ascribed to the other group; it is treacherous, ruthless, cruel, and basically inhuman. The violation of one of the symbols of group narcissism – such as the flag, or the person of the emperor, the president, or an ambassador – is reacted to with such intense fury and aggression by the people that they are even willing to support their leaders in a policy of war.

Group narcissism is one of the most important sources of human aggression, and yet this, like all other forms of defensive aggression, is a reaction to an attack on vital interests. It differs from other forms of defensive aggression in that intense narcissism in itself is a semi-pathological phenomenon. In considering the causes and the function of bloody and cruel mass massacres as they occurred between Hindus and Moslems at the time of the partition of India or recently between Bengali Moslems and their Pakistani rulers, group narcissism certainly plays a considerable role; this is not surprising if we appreciate the fact that we are dealing here with virtually the poorest and most miserable populations anywhere in the world. But certainly narcissism is not the only cause of these phenomena, whose other aspects will be discussed later.

Aggression and Resistance

Another important source of defensive aggression is aggression as a reaction to any attempt to bring repressed strivings and fantasies into awareness. This type of reaction is one of the aspects of what Freud called 'resistance', and it has been explored systematically by the psychoanalytic method. Freud found that if the analyst touched on repressed material the patient would 'resist' his therapeutic approach. This is not a matter of conscious unwillingness on the part of the patient or of dishonesty or of secretiveness; he is defending himself against the discovery of the unconscious material without being aware either of the material or of his resistance. There are many reasons why a person may repress certain strivings, often throughout his life. He might be afraid of being punished, of not being loved, or of being humiliated if his repressed impulses were known to others (or to himself, in so far as self-respect and self-love are concerned).

Psychoanalytic therapy has shown the many different reactions resistance can generate. The patient can turn away from the sensitive topic and talk about something else; he can feel sleepy and tired; he can find a reason not to come to the interview – or he can become very angry against the analyst and find some reason to quit the analysis. Here is a brief example: a writer I was analysing, who was proud of his lack of opportunism, told me during a session that he had changed a manuscript because he thought by this change he would make a better case for his message. He thought he had made the right decision and was surprised that afterwards he felt somewhat depressed and had a headache. I suggested that his real motive probably was that he expected the changed version to be more popular and to result in more fame and money for him than the original one; furthermore, that his depressed mood and his headache probably had something to do with this act of self-betrayal. I had hardly finished saying this when he jumped up shouting at me with intense rage that I was a sadist, that I enjoyed spoiling his anticipated pleasure, an envious man begrudging his future success, an ignorant man who knew nothing about his field of writing, and many more invectives. (It must be noted that the patient was normally a very courteous man who, both before and after this outburst, treated me with respect.) He could hardly have done more to confirm my interpretation. The mention of his unconscious motivation was to him a threat to his self-image and to his sense of identity. He reacted to this threat with intense aggression, as if it were a threat to his body or his property. The aggression in such cases has one aim: to destroy the witness who has the evidence.

In psychoanalytic therapy one can observe with great regularity that resistance is being built up when repressed material is touched. But we are by no means restricted to the psychoanalytic situation in order to observe this phenomenon. Examples from daily life abound. Who has not seen the mother who reacts with fury when someone tells her that she wants to keep her children close to her because she wants to possess and control them – and not because she loves them so much? Or the father who is told that his concern for his daughter's virginity is motivated by his own sexual interest in her? Or a certain type of patriot who is reminded of the profit interest behind his political convictions? Or a certain type of revolutionary who is reminded of the personal destructive impulses behind his ideology? In fact, questioning another's motive violates one of the most respected taboos of courtesy – and a very necessary one, inasmuch as courtesy has the function of minimizing the arousal of aggression.

Historically, the same thing happens. Those who told the truth about a particular régime have been exiled, jailed, or killed by those in power whose fury had been aroused. To be sure, the obvious explanation is that they were dangerous to their respective establishments, and that killing them seemed the best way to protect the *status quo*. This is true enough, but it does not explain the fact that the truth-sayers are so deeply hated even when they do not constitute a real threat to the established order. The reason lies, I believe, in that by speaking the truth they mobilize the resistance of those who repress it. To the latter, the truth is dangerous not only because it can threaten their power but because it shakes their whole conscious system of orientation, deprives them of their rationalizations, and might even force them to act differently. Only those who have experienced the process of becoming aware of important impulses that were repressed know the earthquake-like sense of bewilderment and confusion that occurs as a result. Not all people are willing to risk this adventure, least of all those who profit, at least for the moment, from being blind.

Conformist Aggression

Conformist aggression comprises various acts of aggression that are performed not because the aggressor is driven by the desire to destroy, but because he is told to do so and considers it his duty to obey orders. In all hierarchically structured societies obedience is perhaps the most deeply ingrained trait. Obedience is equated with virtue, disobedience with sin. To be disobedient is the arch crime from which all other crimes follow. Abraham was willing to kill his son out of obedience. Antigone is killed by Creon for her disobedience to the laws of the state. Armies, especially, cultivate obedience, since their very essence is built on an absolute reflex-like acceptance of commands that precludes any questioning. The soldier who kills and maims, the bomber pilot who destroys thousands of lives in one moment, are not necessarily driven by a destructive or cruel impulse, but by the principle of unquestioning obedience.

Conformist aggression is sufficiently widespread to deserve serious attention. From the behaviour of boys in a juvenile gang to that of soldiers in an army, many destructive acts are committed in order not to appear 'yellow', and out of obedience to orders. It is these motivations, and not human destructiveness, that are the root of this type of aggressive behaviour, which is often wrongly interpreted as indicating the power of innate aggressive impulses. Conformist aggression might as well have been classified as pseudo-aggression; the reason for not doing so is that obedience as a consequence of the need to conform will in many cases mobilize aggressive impulses that otherwise might not have become manifest. Furthermore, the impulse not to obey or not to conform constitutes for many an inner threat, against which they defend themselves by performing the required aggressive act.

Instrumental Aggression

Another biologically adaptive type of aggression is instrumental aggression, which has the aim of obtaining that which is *necessary* or *desirable*. The aim is not *destruction as such*; this serves only as an instrument for attaining the real aim. In this respect it is similar to defensive aggression, but in other important aspects it is different. It does not seem to have a phylogenetically programmed neuronal basis such as that which programmes defensive aggression; among mammals, only animals of prey, whose aggression is instrumental to obtaining food, are endowed with an innate neuronal pattern that impels them to attack their prey. The hunting behaviour of hominids and *Homo* is based on learning and experience, and does not seem to be phylogenetically programmed.

The difficulty with instrumental aggression lies in the ambiguity of the terms 'necessary' and 'desirable'.

It is easy to define necessary in terms of an unquestionable physiological need, as, for instance, warding off starvation. If a man steals or robs because he and his family do not have even the minimal amount of food they need, the aggression is clearly an act motivated by physiological necessity. The same would hold true for a primitive tribe on the verge of starvation which attacks another tribe that is better off. But these clear-cut examples of necessity are relatively rare today. Other, more complicated cases are much more frequent. The leaders of a nation realize that their economic situation will be seriously endangered in the long run unless they can conquer territory having the raw materials they need, or unless they defeat a competing nation. Although frequently such reasons are merely an ideological cover for the desire for increasing power or the personal ambition of the leaders, there are wars which do respond to a historical necessity, at least in a broad, relative sense.

But what is desirable? In a narrow sense of the word one could answer: *The desirable is what is necessary.* In this instance 'desirable' is based on the objective situation. More frequently, however, desirable is defined as *that which is desired*. If we use the term in this sense, the problem of instrumental aggression assumes another aspect, and in fact the most important one in the motivation of aggression. The truth is that people desire not only what is necessary in order to survive, not only that which provides the material basis for a good life; most people in our culture – and in similar periods of history – are *greedy*: greedy for more food, drink, sex, possessions, power, and fame. Their greed may refer more to one than to another of these objects; what all people have in common is that they are insatiable and hence never satisfied. Greed is one of the strongest non-instinctive passions in man, and it is clearly a symptom of physical dysfunctioning, of inner emptiness and a lack of a centre within oneself. It is a pathological manifestation of the failure to develop fully, as well as one of the fundamental sins in Buddhist, Jewish, and Christian ethics.

A few examples will illustrate the pathological character of greed: it is well-known that overeating, which is one form of greed, is frequently caused by states of depression; or that compulsive buying is one attempt to escape from a depressed mood. The act of eating or buying is a symbolic act of filling the inner void and, thus, overcoming the depressed feeling for the moment. Greed is a passion – that is to say, it is charged with energy and relentlessly drives a person towards the attainment of his goals.

In our culture greed is greatly reinforced by all those measures that tend to transform everybody into a consumer. Of course the greedy person does not need to be aggressive, provided he has enough money to buy what he desires. But the greedy person who does not have the necessary means must attack if he wants to satisfy his desires. The most drastic example of this is the drug addict who is possessed by his greed for the drug (although in his case increasingly reinforced by physiological sources). The many who do not have the money to buy drugs, rob, assault, or even kill in order to get the necessary means. Destructive as their behaviour is, their aggression is instrumental and not their goal. On a historical scale greed is one of the most frequent causes of aggression and is probably as strong a motive for instrumental aggression as the desire for what is objectively necessary.

The understanding of greed is obscured by its identification with self-interest. The latter is a normal expression of a biologically given drive, that for self-preservation, the aim of which is to obtain what is necessary for the preservation of life or of a customary, traditional standard of living. As Max Weber, Tawney, von Brentano, Sombart, and others have shown, man in the Middle Ages was motivated by the desire to preserve his traditional standard of living, whether as a peasant or as an artisan. The demands of the revolutionary peasants in the sixteenth century were not to have what the artisans in the cities had, nor did the artisans strive for the wealth of a feudal baron or a rich merchant. Even as late as the eighteenth century we find laws that forbid a merchant to try to take customers away from a competitor by making his own store look more attractive or by praising his wares to the disadvantage of those of another merchant. Only with the full development of capitalism – as earlier, in comparable societies like that of the Roman Empire – did greed become a key motive for an ever-increasing number of citizens. However, greed, perhaps because of a still-lingering religious tradition, is a motive to which hardly anyone dares to confess. The dilemma was solved by rationalizing greed as self-interest. The logic went: self-interest is a biologically given striving anchored in human nature; self-interest equals greed; ergo: greed is rooted in human nature – and not a character-conditioned human passion. QED.

On the Causes of War

The most important case of instrumental aggression is *war*. It has become fashionable to consider war as caused by the power of man's destructive instinct. Instinctivists and psychoanalysts[21] have given this explanation of war. Thus, for instance, an important representative of psychoanalytic orthodoxy, E. Glover, argues against M. Ginsberg that 'the

21. See A. Strachey (1957); see also E. F. M. Durbin and J. Bowlby (1939) who, in contrast, reason with great skill that peaceful cooperation is as natural and fundamental a tendency in human relations as fighting, yet consider war essentially a psychological problem.

riddle of war lies ... deep in the unconscious', and he compares war with an 'inexpedient form of instinct adaptation' (E. Glover and M. Ginsberg, 1934).[22]

Freud himself took a much more realistic view than his followers. In his famous letter to Albert Einstein, *Why War?* (S. Freud, 1933), he did not take the position that war was *caused* by human destructiveness, but saw its cause in realistic conflicts between groups which always have been solved by violence, since there was no international enforceable law according to which – as in civil law – the conflicts could have been solved peacefully. He attributed only an auxiliary role to the factor of human destructiveness, as facilitating the readiness of people to go to war once the government has decided to wage war.

The thesis that war is caused by innate human destructiveness is plainly absurd for anyone who has even the slightest knowledge of history. The Babylonians, the Greeks,[23] up to the statesmen of our time, have planned war for what they thought were very realistic reasons and weighed the pros and cons very thoroughly, even though,

22. At the time of revising this part of the manuscript reports from the 27th Congress of the International Psychoanalytic Association, 1971, held in Vienna, seem to indicate a change in attitude in the matter of war. Dr A Mitscherlich said that 'all of our theories are going to be carried away by history' unless psychoanalysis is applied to social problems, and furthermore, 'I fear that nobody is going to take us very seriously if we continue to suggest that war comes about because fathers hate their sons and want to kill them, that war is filicide. We must, instead, aim at finding a theory that explains group behaviour, a theory that traces this behaviour to the conflicts in society that actuate the individual drives.' Such attempts have indeed been made by psychoanalysts since the early thirties, but have led to their expulsion from the International Psychoanalytic Association under one pretext or another. Official permission for this new 'endeavour' was given by Anna Freud at the end of the Congress, adding cautiously, 'We should let a formulation of a theory of aggression wait until we know much more from our clinical studies about what really constitutes aggressivity.' (Both quotations are from the Paris edition of the *Herald Tribune*, 29 and 31 July 1971.)

23. For a very telling example see Thucydides' description of the Peloponnesian War.

naturally, their calculations were often erroneous. Their motives were manifold: land for cultivation, riches, slaves, raw materials, markets, expansion – and defence. Under special circumstances, a wish for revenge or in a small tribe the passion for destruction has been among the factors that motivated wars, but such cases are atypical. This view that war is caused by man's aggression is not only unrealistic but harmful. It detracts attention from the real causes and thus weakens the opposition to them.

The thesis about the innate tendency for war is not only repudiated by the historical record but also, and very importantly, by the history of primitive warfare. We have shown earlier in the context of aggression among primitive peoples that they – particularly the hunters and food gatherers – are the least warlike, and that their fighting is characterized by its relative lack of destructiveness and bloodthirstiness. We have furthermore seen that with the growth of civilization the frequency and bloodiness of wars have increased. If war were caused by innate destructive impulses, the reverse would have to be true. The humanitarian tendencies in the eighteenth, nineteenth, and twentieth centuries brought about reductions of destructiveness and cruelty in war which were codified – and respected, up to and including the First World War – in various international treaties. From this progressive perspective it seemed that civilized man is less aggressive than primitive man, and the still-existing occurrence of war was explained as caused by stubbornness of the aggressive instincts, which refuse to give in to the beneficial influence of civilization. But, in fact, the destructiveness of civilized man was projected into man's nature, and thus history was confused with biology.

It would far exceed the frame of this volume if I tried to present even a brief analysis of the causes of war, and I have to limit myself to giving only one example, that of the First World War.[24]

24. The literature on the military, political, and economic aspect of the 1914–1918 war is so large that even an abbreviated bibliography would

The First World War was motivated by the economic interests and ambitions of the political, military, and industrial leaders on both sides, and not by a need of the various nations involved to give vent to their dammed-up aggression. These motivations are well known, and need not be described here in detail. By and large, it can be said that the German aims in the 1914–1918 war were also its main motivations: economic hegemony in Western and Central Europe and territory in the east. (These were, in fact, also the aims of Hitler, whose foreign policy was essentially the continuation of that of the imperial government.) The aims and motivations of the Western Allies were similar. France wanted Alsace-Lorraine; Russia, the Dardanelles; England, parts of the German colonies, and Italy, at least a small part of the booty. Had it not been for these aims, some of which were stipulated in secret treaties, peace would have been concluded years earlier and the lives of many millions of people of both sides would have been spared.

Both sides in the First World War had to appeal to the sense of self-defence and freedom. The Germans claimed they were encircled and threatened, and furthermore, that they were fighting for freedom by fighting the Czar; their enemies claimed that they were threatened by the aggressive militarism of the German Junkers, and they were fighting for freedom by fighting the Kaiser. To think that this war owed its origin to the wish of the French, the German, the British, and the Russian populations to discharge their aggressiveness is untrue and serves only one function, that of detracting attention from those persons and social conditions responsible for one of the great slaughters in history.

As far as enthusiasm for this war was concerned, one must distinguish between the initial enthusiasm and the motiva-

fill many pages. I find that the two most profound and enlightening works on the causes of the First World War are those by two outstanding historians: G. W. F. Hallgarten (1963) and F. Fischer (1967).

tions of the respective populations to continue fighting. As far as the German side is concerned, one must differentiate two groups in the population. The small group of nationalists – a small minority of the people as a whole – were clamouring for a war of conquest many years before 1914. They consisted mainly of high school teachers, a few university professors, journalists, and politicians, supported by some leaders of the German Navy and by some sectors of heavy industry. Their psychical motivation might be described as a mixture of group narcissism, instrumental aggression, and the wish to make a career and to gain power within and through this nationalistic movement. The vast majority of the population showed a good deal of enthusiasm only shortly before and after the outbreak of the war. Here, too, one finds significant differences and reactions among the various social classes; for instance, the intellectuals and the students behaved with more enthusiasm than the working class. (An interesting datum which throws some light on this question is that the leader of the German government, the Reichschancellor von Bethman-Hollweg, as the German Foreign Office documents published after the war show, was aware that it would be impossible to win the consent of the Social Democratic Party, the strongest party in the Reichstag, unless he could first declare war on Russia and therefore make the workers feel that they were fighting against autocracy and for freedom.) The whole population was under the systematic suggestive influence of the government and the press in the few days before the outbreak and after the beginning of the war, to convince them that Germany was to be humiliated and attacked, thus in this way impulses of defensive aggression were mobilized. The population as a whole, however, was not motivated by strong impulses of instrumental aggression, i.e., the wish to conquer foreign territory. This is borne out by the fact that government propaganda even at the beginning of the war either denied any aims of conquest, or later on, when the generals were dictating foreign policy, aims of conquest were described as necessary for the future safety of the German Reich; however, the initial enthusiasm disappeared after a few months, never to return.

It is most remarkable that when Hitler started his attack against Poland and, thus, as a consequence triggered the Second World War, popular enthusiasm for the war was practically nil. The population, in spite of years of heavy militaristic indoctrination, showed very clearly that they were not eager to fight this war. (Hitler even had to stage a phony attack on a Silesian radio station by alleged Polish soldiers – in reality, disguised Nazis – in order to awaken the sense of defence against an attack.)

But although the German population definitely did not want this war (the generals were also reluctant), they went into the war without resistance and fought bravely until the end.

The psychological problem lies here, not in the *causation* of the war but in the question: What psychological factors make war *possible* even though they do not cause it?

There are a number of relevant factors to consider in answering this question. In the First World War (also, with some modifications, in the Second World War) once it had started, the German (or French, Russian, British) soldiers went on fighting because they felt that losing the war would mean disaster for the whole nation. The individual soldiers were motivated by the feeling that they were fighting for their lives, and that it was a matter of killing or being killed. But even these feelings would not have been sufficient to sustain the willingness to go on. They also knew that they would be shot if they ran away, although even these motivations did not prevent large-scale mutinies from occurring in all armies; in Russia and Germany they led eventually to revolutions in 1917 and 1918. In France there was almost no army corps in 1917 in which the soldiers did not mutiny, and it was only due to the skill of the French generals in preventing one military unit from knowing what went on in other units that these mutinies were suppressed by a mixture of wholesale executions and some improvements in the conditions in the daily life of the soldiers.

Another important factor for the possibility of war is the deeply ingrained feeling of respect for and awe of authority. The soldier had traditionally been made to feel that to obey his leaders was a moral and religious obligation for the ful- filment of which he should be ready to pay with his life. It took about three to four years of the horror of life in the trenches and growing insight into the fact that they were being used by their leaders for aims of war that had nothing to do with defence, to break down this attitude of obedience, at least in a considerable part of the army and the popula- tions at home.

There are other, more subtle emotional motivations that make war possible and that have nothing to do with aggression. War is exciting, even if it entails risks for one's life and much physical suffering. Considering that the life of the average person is boring, routinized, and lacking in adventure, the readiness to go to war must be understood as a desire to put an end to the boring routine of daily life – and to throw oneself into an adventure, the only adven- ture, in fact, the average person may expect to have in his life.[25]

War, to some extent, reverses all values. War encourages deep-seated human impulses, such as altruism and solidarity to be expressed – impulses that are stunted by the principles of egotism and competition that peacetime life engenders in modern man. Class differences, if not absent, disappear to a considerable extent. In war, man is man again, and has a chance to distinguish himself, regardless of privileges that his social status confers upon him as a citizen. To put it in a very accentuated form: war is an indirect rebellion against

25. But one must not overestimate this factor. The example of countries like Switzerland, the Scandinavian nations, Belgium, and the Nether- lands demonstrates that the factor of adventurousness cannot cause a population to want war if the country is not attacked and if there is no reason for the governments to start war.

the injustice, inequality and boredom governing social life in peacetime, and the fact must not be underestimated that while a soldier fights the enemy for his life, he does not have to fight the members of his own group for food, medical care, shelter, clothing; these are all provided in a kind of perversely socialized system. The fact that war has these positive features is a sad comment on our civilization. If civilian life provided the elements of adventurousness, solidarity, equality, and idealism that can be found in war, it may be very difficult, we may conclude, to get people to fight a war. The problem for governments in war is to make use of this rebellion by harnessing it for the purpose of war; simultaneously it must be prevented from becoming a threat to the government by enforcing strict discipline and the spirit of obedience to the leaders who are depicted as the unselfish, wise, courageous men protecting their people from destruction.[26]

To conclude, major wars in modern times and most wars between the states of antiquity were not caused by dammed-up aggression, but by instrumental aggression of the military and political élites. This has been shown in the data about the difference in the incidence of war from the most primitive to the higher developed cultures. The more primitive a civilization, the less wars do we find (Q. Wright, 1965).[27] The same trend can be seen in the fact that the number and intensity of wars has risen with the development of technical civilization; it is highest among the powerful states with a strong government and lowest among primitive man without permanent chieftainship. As shown in the following table, the number of battles engaged in by the principal European powers in modern times shows the same

26. It is characteristic for this dilemma that in the international treaties governing the treatment of war prisoners, all powers agreed on the stipulation that forbids a government to propagandize 'their' prisoners of war against their respective governments. In short, one has agreed that each government has a right to kill the soldiers of the enemy, but it must not make them disloyal.

27. cf. 'Primitive Warfare' in Chapter 8.

trend. The table reports the number of battles in each century since 1480 (Q. Wright, 1965):

YEARS	NUMBER OF BATTLES
1480–99	9
1500–99	87
1600–99	239
1700–99	781
1800–99	651
1900–40	892

What those authors who explain that war is caused by man's innate aggression have done is to consider modern war as normal, assuming that it must be caused by man's 'destructive' nature. They have tried to find the confirmation for this assumption in the data on animals and on our prehistoric ancestors, which have had to be distorted in order to serve this purpose. This position resulted from the unshakeable conviction of the superiority of present-day civilization over pre-technical cultures. The logic was: if civilized man is plagued by so many wars and so much destructiveness, how much worse must primitive man have been, who is far behind in the development towards 'progress'. Since destructiveness must not be blamed on our civilization, it must be explained as the result of our instincts. But the facts speak otherwise.

The Conditions for the Reduction of Defensive Aggression

Since defensive aggression is a phylogenetically prepared reaction to threats to vital interests, it is not possible to change its biological basis, although it can be controlled and modified like impulses rooted in other instinctive dispositions. However, the main condition for the reduction of defensive aggression is the decrease of those realistic factors that mobilize it. To outline a programme of social changes that would accomplish this is a task that could obviously not be undertaken within the framework of this book.[28] I will restrict myself only to a few remarks.

The main condition is, of course, that neither individuals nor groups are threatened by others. This depends on the existence of material bases that can provide a dignified life for all men and make the domination of one group by another neither possible nor attractive. Such a condition could be realized in the foreseeable future by means of a different system of production, ownership, and consumption than the present one; but to say that this state could be achieved does not, of course, mean that it will be achieved or that it would be easy to achieve. It is, in fact, a task of such staggering difficulty that for this reason alone many people with good intentions prefer not to do anything; they hope to avert a catastrophe by ritualistically singing the praises of progress.

The establishment of a system that guarantees the provision of basic necessities for all means the disappearance of dominant classes. Man will have to cease to live under 'zoo' conditions – i.e., his full freedom will have to be restored and all forms of exploitative control will have to disappear. That man is incapable of dispensing with controlling leaders is a myth disproved by all those societies that function well without hierarchies. Such a change would, of course, involve radical political and social changes that would alter all human relations, including the family structure, the structure of education, of religion, and relations between individuals in work and leisure.

As far as defensive aggression is a reaction not to real threats, but to alleged threats produced by mass suggestion and brainwashing, the same fundamental social changes would abolish the basis for the use of this kind of psychic force. Since suggestibility is based on the powerlessness of the individual and on his awe of leaders, the social and

28. I have discussed some of these problems in *The Sane Society* (1955) and in *The Revolution of Hope* (1968a).

political changes just mentioned would lead to its disappearance and, correspondingly, to the development of independent critical thinking.

Finally, in order to reduce group narcissism, the misery, monotony, dullness, and powerlessness that exist in large sectors of the population would have to be eliminated. This cannot be accomplished simply by bettering material conditions. It can only be the result of drastic changes in the social organization to convert it from a control-property-power orientation to a life orientation; from *having* and *hoarding* to *being* and *sharing*. It will require the highest degree of active participation and responsibility on the part of each person in his role as a worker or employee in any kind of enterprise, as well as in his role as a citizen. Entirely new forms of decentralization must be devised, as well as new social and political structures that will put an end to the society of anomie, the mass society consisting of millions of atoms.

None of these conditions are independent from each other. They are part of a system, and hence, reactive aggression can be reduced to a minimum only if the whole system as it has existed during the last six thousand years of history can be replaced by a fundamentally different one. If this occurs, the visions that were utopian with the Buddha, the Prophets, Jesus, and the humanist utopians of the Renaissance will be recognized as rational and realistic solutions serving the basic biological programme of man: the preservation and growth of both the individual and the human species.

10

Malignant Aggression: Premises

Preliminary Remarks

Biologically adaptive aggression serves life. This is understood in principle, biologically and neurophysiologically, even though much more information is still needed. It is a drive man shares with all other animals, although with certain differences that have been discussed above.

What is unique in man is that he can be driven by impulses to kill and to torture, and that he feels lust in doing so; he is the only animal that can be a killer and destroyer of his own species without any rational gain, either biological or economic. To explore the nature of this biologically nonadaptive, malignant destructiveness is the object of the following pages.

Malignant aggression, let us remember, is specifically human and not derived from animal instinct. It does not serve the physiological survival of man, yet it is an important part of his mental functioning. It is one of the passions that are dominant and powerful in some individuals and cultures, although not in others. I shall try to show that destructiveness is one of the possible answers to psychic needs that are rooted in the existence of man, and that its generation results, as was stated earlier, from *the interaction of various social conditions with man's existential needs*. This hypothesis makes it necessary to build a theoretical basis upon which we can attempt to examine the following questions: What are the specific conditions of human existence? What is man's nature or essence?

Although present-day thought, especially in psychology,

is not very hospitable to such questions, which are usually considered as belonging to the realm of philosophy and other purely 'subjective speculations', I hope to demonstrate in the following discussion that there are indeed areas for empirical examination.

Man's Nature

For most thinkers since the Greek philosophers, it was self-evident that there is something called human nature, something that constitutes the essence of man. There were various views about what constitutes it, but there was agreement that such an essence exists – that is to say, that there is something by virtue of which man is man. Thus man was defined as a rational being, as a social animal, an animal that can make tools (*Homo faber*), or a symbol-making animal.

More recently, this traditional view has begun to be questioned. One reason for this change was the increasing emphasis given to the historical approach to man. An examination of the history of humanity suggested that man in our epoch is so different from man in previous times that it seemed unrealistic to assume that men in every age have had in common something that can be called 'human nature'. The historical approach was reinforced, particularly in the United States, by studies in the field of cultural anthropology. The study of primitive peoples has discovered such a diversity of customs, values, feelings, and thoughts that many anthropologists arrived at the concept that man is born as a blank sheet of paper on which each culture writes its text. Another factor contributing to the tendency to deny the assumption of a fixed human nature was that the concept has so often been abused as a shield behind which the most inhuman acts are committed. In the name of human nature, for example, Aristotle and most thinkers up to the eighteenth century defended slavery.[1] Or in order to prove the rationality and necessity of the capitalist form of society, scholars have tried to make a case for acquisitiveness, competitiveness, and selfishness as innate human traits. Popularly, one refers cynically to 'human nature' in accepting the inevitability of such undesirable human behaviour as greed, murder, cheating, and lying.

Another reason for scepticism about the concept of human nature probably lies in the influence of evolutionary thinking. Once man came to be seen as developing in the process of evolution, the idea of a substance which is contained in his essence seemed untenable. Yet I believe it is precisely from an evolutionary standpoint that we can expect new insight into the problem of the nature of man. New contributions have been made in this direction by such authors as Karl Marx, R. M. Bucke,[2] Teilhard de Chardin, T. Dobzhansky: a similar approach is proposed also in this chapter.

The main argument in favour of the assumption of the existence of a human nature is that we can define the essence of *Homo sapiens* in morphological, anatomical, physiological, and neurological terms. In fact we give an exact and generally accepted definition of the species man by data referring to posture, formation of the brain, the teeth, diet, and many other factors by which we clearly differentiate him from the most developed non-human primates. Surely we must assume, unless we regress to a view that considers body and mind as separate realms, that the species man must be definable mentally as well as physically.

1. Exceptions among the Greeks would be the Stoics, defenders of the equality of all men, and in the Renaissance, such humanists as Erasmus, Thomas More, and Juan Luis Vives.

2. Richard M. Bucke was a Canadian psychiatrist, a friend of Emerson, a bold and imaginative mind, and in his time one of the leading figures in North American psychiatry. Although he is completely forgotten by psychiatrists, his book *Cosmic Consciousness* (rev. ed. 1946) has been read for almost a hundred years by non-professionals.

Darwin himself was very aware of the fact that man *qua* man was characterized not only by specific physical but also by specific psychical attributes. The most important ones he mentions in *The Descent of Man* are as follows (abbreviated and paraphrased by G. G. Simpson):

In proportion with his higher intelligence, man's behaviour is more flexible, less reflex or instinctive.

Man shares such complex factors as curiosity, imitation, attention, memory, and imagination with other relatively advanced animals, but has them in higher degree and applies them in more intricate ways.

More, at least, than other animals, man reasons and improves the adaptive nature of his behaviour in rational ways.

Man regularly both uses and makes tools in great variety.

Man is self-conscious; he reflects on his past, future, life, death, and so forth.

Man makes mental abstractions and develops a related symbolism; the most essential and complexly developed outcome of these capacities is language.

Some men have a sense of beauty.

Most men have a religious sense, taking that term broadly to include awe, superstition, belief in the animistic, supernatural, or spiritual.

Normal men have a moral sense; in later terms, man ethicizes.

Man is a cultural and social animal and has developed cultures and societies unique in kind and in complexity. (G. G. Simpson, 1949)

If one examines Darwin's list of psychic traits, several elements stand out. He mentions a number of disparate single items, some uniquely human, such as self-consciousness, symbol and culture making, an aesthetic, moral, and religious sense. This list of specific human characteristics suffers from the fact that it is purely descriptive and enumerative, is unsystematic, and makes no attempt to analyse their common conditions.

He does not mention in his list specifically human passions and emotions like tenderness, love, hate, cruelty, narcissism, sadism, masochism, and so on. Others he treats as instincts. For him, all men and animals,

> especially the primates, have some few instincts in common. All have the same senses, intuitions, and sensations, similar passions, affections, and emotions, even the more complex ones, such as jealousy, suspicion, emulation, gratitude, and magnanimity: they practise deceit and are revengeful; they are sometimes susceptible to ridicule, and even have a sense of humour; they feel wonder and curiosity; they possess the same faculties of imitation, the association of ideas, and reason though in very different degrees. (C. Darwin, 1946)

Clearly, our attempt to consider the most important human passions as specifically human, and not as inherited from our animal ancestors, can find no support in Darwin's view.

The advance of thought among students of evolution since Darwin is manifest in the views of one of the most eminent contemporary investigators, G. G. Simpson. He insists that man has essential attributes other than those of animals. 'It is important to realize', he writes, 'that man is an animal but it is even more important to realize that the essence of his unique nature lies precisely in those characteristics that are not shared with any other animal. His place in nature and its supreme significance are not defined by his animality but by his humanity' (G. G. Simpson, 1949).

Simpson suggests as the basic definition of *Homo sapiens* the interrelated factors of intelligence, flexibility, individualization, and socialization. Even if his answer is not entirely satisfactory, his attempt to understand man's essential traits as being interrelated and rooted in one basic factor and his recognition of the transformation of quantitative into qualitative change constitute a significant step beyond Darwin (G. G. Simpson, 1944; 1953).

From the side of psychology, one of the best-known attempts to describe man's specific needs is that made by Abraham Maslow, who drew up a list of man's 'basic needs' – physiological and aesthetic needs, needs for safety, belongingness, love, esteem, self-actualization, knowledge and understanding (A. Maslow, 1954). This list is a somewhat unsystematic enumeration, and regrettably, Maslow did not try to analyse the common origin of such needs in the nature of man.

The attempt to define the nature of man in terms of the specific conditions – biological and mental – of the species man leads us first to some considerations concerning the birth of man.

It seems simple to know when a human individual comes into existence, but in fact it is not quite as simple as it seems. The answer might be: at the time of conception, when the foetus has assumed definite human form, in the act of birth, at the end of weaning; or one might even claim that most men have not yet been fully born by the time they die. We would best decline to fix a day or an hour for 'the birth' of an individual, and speak rather of a *process* in the course of which a person comes into existence.

If we ask when man *as a species* was born, the answer is much more difficult. We know much less about the evolutionary process. Here we are dealing with millions of years; our knowledge is based on accidental findings of skeletons and tools whose significance is still much disputed.

Yet in spite of the insufficiency of our knowledge, there are a few data which, even though in need of modification in detail, give us a general picture of the process we may call the birth of man. We could date the *conception* of man back at the beginning of unicellular life, about one and a half billion years ago, or to the beginning of the existence of primitive mammals, about two hundred million years ago; we might say that human development begins with man's hominid ancestors who may have lived about fourteen million years ago or possibly earlier. We could date his *birth* from the appearance of the first man, *Homo erectus*, of whom the various specimens found in Asia cover a time from about one million to about five hundred thousand years ago

(Peking Man); or from only about forty thousand years ago when modern man (*Homo sapiens sapiens*) emerged, who was in all essential biological aspects identical to man today.[3] Indeed, if we look at man's development in terms of historical time, we might say that man proper was born only a few minutes ago. Or we might even think that he is still in the process of birth, that the umbilical cord has not yet been severed, and that complications have arisen that make it appear doubtful whether man will ever be born or whether he is to be stillborn.

Most students of human evolution date the birth of man to one particular event: *the making of tools*, following Benjamin Franklin's definition of man as *Homo faber*, man the tool-maker. This definition has been sharply criticized by Marx who considered it 'characteristic of Yankeedom'.[4] Among modern writers, Mumford has most convincingly criticized this orientation based on tool-making (L. Mumford, 1967).

One must look for a concept of man's nature in the process of human evolution rather than in isolated aspects like tool-making, which bears so clearly the stamp of the contemporary obsession with production. We have to arrive at *an understanding of man's nature on the basis of the blend of the two fundamental biological conditions that mark the emergence of man*. One was *the ever-decreasing determination of behaviour by instincts*.[5] Even taking into account the many controversial views about the nature of instincts, it is generally accepted that the higher an animal has risen in the stages of evolution, the less is the weight of stereotyped behaviour patterns that are strictly determined and phylogenetically programmed in the brain.

3. cf. the discussion in D. Pilbeam (1970); also M. F. A. Montagu (1967) and G. Smolla (1967).

4. cf., for an understanding of Marx's concept of human nature, E. Fromm (1961, 1968).

5. The term 'instincts' is used here in a loose fashion in order to simplify the discussion. It is not used in the dated sense of 'instinct' as excluding learning, but in the sense of 'organic drives'.

The process of ever-decreasing determination of behaviour by instincts can be plotted as a continuum, at the zero end of which we will find the lowest forms of animal evolution with the highest degree of instinctive determination; this decreases along with animal evolution and reaches a certain level with the mammals; it decreases further in the development going up to the primates, and even here we find a great gulf between monkeys and apes, as Yerkes and Yerkes have shown in their classic investigation. (R. M. and A. V. Yerkes 1929.) In the species *Homo* instinctive determination has reached its maximum decrease.

The other trend to be found in animal evolution is *the growth of the brain, and particularly of the neocortex*. Here, too, we can plot the evolution as a continuum – at one end, the lowest animals, with the most primitive nervous structure and a relatively small number of neurons; at the other, man, with a larger and more complex brain structure, especially a neocortex three times as large as that of even his hominid ancestors, and a truly fantastic number of inter-neuronal connections.[6]

6. C. Judson Herrick has tried to give an approximate idea of the potentialities of neuronal circuits: 'Every neuron of the cerebral cortex is enmeshed in a tangle of very fine fibres of great complexity, some of which come from very remote parts. It is probably safe to say that the majority of cortical neurons are directly or indirectly connected with every cortical field. This is the anatomical basis of cortical associational processes. The interconnections of these associational fibres form an anatomical mechanism which permits, during a train of cortical associations, numbers of different functional combinations of cortical neurons that far surpass any figures ever suggested by the astronomers in measuring the distances of stars ... It is the capacity for making this sort of combination and re-combination of the nervous elements that determines the practical value of the system ... If a million cortical nerve cells were connected one with another in groups of only two neurons each in all possible combinations, the number of different patterns of interneuronic connection thus provided would be expressed by $10^{2,783,000}$ ... On the basis of the known structure of the cortex ... the number of intercellular connections that are anatomically present and available for use in a short series of cortical neurons of the visual area simultaneously excited by the retinal image ... would far exceed the

Considering these data, man can be defined as the primate that emerged at the point of evolution where instinctive determination had reached a minimum and the development of the brain a maximum. This combination of minimal instinctive determination and maximum brain development had never occurred before in animal evolution and constitutes, biologically speaking, a completely new phenomenon.

When man emerged, his behaviour was little guided by his instinctive equipment. Aside from some elementary re-actions, such as those to danger or to sexual stimuli, there is no inherited programme that tells him how to decide in most instances in which his life may depend on a correct decision. It would thus seem that, biologically, man is the most helpless and frail of all animals.

Does the extraordinary development of his brain make up for his instinctive deficit?

To some extent it does. Man is guided by his intellect to make right choices. But we know also how weak and un-reliable this instrument is. It is easily influenced by man's desires and passions and surrenders to their influence. Man's brain is insufficient not only as a substitute for the weakened instincts, but it complicates the task of living tremendously. By this I do not refer to *instrumental intelligence*, the use of thought as an instrument for the manipulation of objects in order to satisfy one's needs; after all, man shares this with animals, especially with the primates. I refer to that aspect in which man's thinking has acquired an entirely new quality, that of *self-awareness*. Man is the only animal who not only knows objects but who knows that he knows. Man is the only animal who has not only instrumental intelli-gence, but reason, the capacity to use his thinking to *under-stand* objectively – i.e., to know the nature of things as they are in themselves, and not only as means for his satisfaction.

102,783,000 already mentioned as the theoretically possible combinations in groups of two only' (C. J. Herrick, 1928). For comparative purposes Livingston adds: 'Recall that the number of atoms in the universe is estimated to be about 10^{66}.'

Gifted with self-awareness and reason, man is aware of himself as a being separate from nature and from others; he is aware of his powerlessness, of his ignorance; he is aware of his end: death.

Self-awareness, reason, and imagination have disrupted the 'harmony' that characterizes animal existence. Their emergence has made man into an anomaly, the freak of the universe. He is part of nature, subject to her physical laws and unable to change them, yet he transcends nature. He is set apart while being a part; he is homeless, yet chained to the home he shares with all creatures. Cast into this world at an accidental place and time, he is forced out of it accidentally and against his will. Being aware of himself, he realizes his powerlessness and the limitations of his existence. He is never free from the dichotomy of his existence: he cannot rid himself of his mind, even if he would want to; he cannot rid himself of his body as long as he is alive – and his body makes him want to be alive.

Man's life cannot be lived by repeating the pattern of his species; *he* must live. Man is the only animal who does not feel at home in nature, who can feel evicted from paradise, the only animal for whom his own existence is a problem that he has to solve and from which he cannot escape. He cannot go back to the pre-human state of harmony with nature, and he does not know where he will arrive if he goes forward. Man's existential contradiction results in a state of constant disequilibrium. This disequilibrium distinguishes him from the animal, which lives, as it were, in harmony with nature. This does not mean, of course, that the animal necessarily lives a peaceful and happy life, but that it has its specific ecological niche to which its physical and mental qualities have been adapted by the process of evolution. Man's existential, and hence unavoidable disequilibrium can be relatively stable when he has found, with the support of his culture, a more or less adequate way of coping with his existential problems. But this relative stability does not imply that the dichotomy has disappeared; it is merely dormant and becomes manifest as soon as the conditions for this relative stability change.

Indeed, in the process of man's self-creation this relative stability is upset again and again. Man, in his history, changes his environment, and in this process he changes himself. His knowledge increases, but so does his awareness of his ignorance; he experiences himself as an individual, and not only as a member of his tribe, and with this his sense of separateness and isolation grows. He creates larger and more efficient social units, led by powerful leaders – and he becomes frightened and submissive. He attains a certain amount of freedom – and becomes afraid of this very freedom. His capacity for material production grows, but in the process he becomes greedy and egotistical, a slave of the things he has created.

Every new state of disequilibrium forces man to seek for new equilibrium. Indeed, what has often been considered man's innate drive for progress is his attempt to find a new and if possible better equilibrium.

The new forms of equilibrium by no means constitute a straight line of human improvement. Frequently in history new achievements have led to regressive developments. Many times, when forced to find a new solution, man runs into a blind alley from which he has to extricate himself; and it is indeed remarkable that thus far in history he has been able to do so.

These considerations suggest a hypothesis as to how to define the essence or nature of man. I propose that man's nature cannot be defined in terms of a specific quality, such as love, hate, reason, good or evil, but only in terms of fundamental *contradictions* that characterize human existence and have their root in the biological dichotomy between missing instincts and self-awareness. Man's existential conflict produces certain psychic needs common to all men. He is forced to overcome the horror of separateness, of powerlessness, and of lostness, and find new forms of relating himself to the world to enable him to feel at home. I have called these psychic needs existential because they are rooted in the very conditions of human existence. They are shared by all men, and their fulfilment is as necessary for man's remaining sane as the fulfilment of organic drives is necessary for his remaining alive. But each of these needs can be satisfied in different ways, which vary according to the differences of his social condition. These different ways of satisfying the existential needs manifest themselves in passions, such as love, tenderness, striving for justice, independence, truth, hate, sadism, masochism, destructiveness, narcissism. I call them character-rooted passions – or simply human passions – because they are integrated in man's *character*.

While the concept of character will be discussed at length further on, it will suffice here to say that *character is the relatively permanent system of all non-instinctual strivings through which man relates himself to the human and natural world*. One may understand character as the human substitute for the missing animal instincts; it is man's *second nature*. What all men have in common are their organic drives (even though highly modifiable by experience) and their existential needs. What they do not have in common are the kinds of passions that are dominant in their respective characters – character-rooted passions. The difference in character is largely due to the difference in social conditions (although genetically given dispositions also influence the formation of the character); for this reason one can call character-rooted passions a historical category and instincts a natural category. Yet the former are not a purely historical category either, inasmuch as the social influence can only work through the biologically given conditions of human existence.[7]

7. This distinction between the two kinds of drives corresponds essentially to the one made by Marx. He spoke of two kinds of human drives and appetites: the '*constant*', or fixed ones – such as hunger or sexual drive – which are an integral part of human nature and can be changed only in their form and in the direction they take in various cultures, and the '*relative appetites*', which 'owe their origin to certain social structures and certain conditions of production and communica-

We are now ready to discuss man's existential needs and the variety of character-rooted passions that in turn constitute different answers to these existential needs. Before starting this discussion let us look back and raise a question of method. I have suggested a 'reconstruction' of man's mind as it may have been at the beginning of prehistory. The obvious objection to this method is that it is a theoretical reconstruction for which there is no evidence whatsoever – or so it would appear. However, evidence is not completely lacking for the formulation of some tentative hypothesis that may be disproven or confirmed by further findings.

This evidence lies essentially in those findings which indicate that man, perhaps as early as half a million years ago (Peking Man) had cults and rituals, manifesting that his concerns went beyond satisfying his material needs. The history of prehistoric religion and art (not separable in those times) is the main source for the study of primitive man's mind. Obviously, I cannot set forth into this vast and as yet controversial territory within the context of this study. What I want to stress is that the presently available data, as well as those still to be found in regard to primitive religions and rituals, will not reveal the nature of prehistoric man's minds unless we have a key with which we can decipher it. This key, I believe, is our own mind. Not our conscious thoughts, but those categories of thought and feeling that are buried in our unconscious and yet are an experiential core present in all men of all cultures; briefly, it is what I would like to call man's 'primary human experience'. This primary human experience is in itself rooted in man's existential situation. For this reason it is common to all men and does not need to be explained as being racially inherited.

The first question, of course, is whether we can find this key; whether we can transcend our normal frame of mind

tion' (K. Marx and F. Engels, MEGA, vol. 5; my translation). He spoke of some of these appetites as 'inhuman', 'depraved', 'unnatural', and 'imaginary'.

and transpose ourselves into the mind of the 'original man'. Drama, poetry, art, myth have done this, but not psychology, with the exception of psychoanalysis. The various psychoanalytic schools have done it in different ways; Freud's original man was a historical construct of the member of a patriarchally organized male band, ruled and exploited by a father-tyrant against whom the sons rebel, and whose internalization is the basis for the formation of the super-ego and a new social organization. Freud's aim was to help the contemporary patient to discover his own unconscious by letting him share the experience of what Freud believed to be his earliest ancestors.

Even though this model of original man was fictitious and the corresponding 'Oedipus complex' was not the deepest level of human experience, Freud's hypothesis opened up an entirely new possibility: that all men of every period and culture had shared a basic experience with their common ancestors. Thus Freud added another historical argument to the humanist belief that all men share the common core of humanity.

C. G. Jung made the same attempt in a different and in many respects more sophisticated way than Freud's. He was particularly interested in the variety of myths, rituals, and religions. He used myth ingeniously and brilliantly as a key for the understanding of the unconscious, and thus built a bridge between mythology and psychology more systematically and extensively than any of his predecessors.

What I am suggesting here is not only to use the past for the understanding of the present, of our unconscious, but also to use our unconscious as a key to the understanding of prehistory. This requires the practice of self-knowledge in the psychoanalytical sense: the removal of a major part of our resistance against the awareness of our unconscious, thus reducing the difficulty of penetrating from our conscious mind to the depth of our core.

Provided we are able to do this, we can understand our fellowmen who live in the same culture as we do, also men of an entirely different culture, and even a mad man. We can also sense what original man must have experienced, what existential needs he had, and in what ways men (including ourselves) can respond to these needs.

When we see primitive art, down to the cave paintings of thirty thousand years ago, or the art of radically different cultures like the African or Greek or that of the Middle Ages, we take it for granted that we understand them, in spite of the fact that these cultures were radically different from ours. We dream symbols and myths that are like those men thousands of years ago conceived when they were awake. Are they not a common language of all humanity, regardless of vast differences in conscious perception? (E. Fromm, 1951).

Considering that contemporary thinking in the field of human evolution is so one-sidedly oriented along the lines of man's bodily development and his material culture, of which skeletons and tools are the main witnesses, it is not surprising that few investigators are interested in the mind of early man. Yet the view I have presented here is shared by a number of outstanding scholars, whose whole philosophical outlook differs from that of the majority; I am referring especially to the views, particularly close to my own, of the palaeontologist F. M. Bergounioux and the zoologist and geneticist T. Dobzhansky.

Bergounioux writes:

Even though he [man] can legitimately be considered a primate, of which he possesses all the anatomical and physiological characteristics, he alone forms a biological group whose originality none will dispute ... Man felt himself brutally torn from his environment and isolated in the middle of a world whose measure and laws he did not know; he therefore felt obliged to learn, by constant bitter effort and his own mistakes, everything he had to know to survive. The animals surrounding him came gathering, searching for water, doubling or fleeing to defend themselves against innumerable enemies; for them, periods of rest and activity succeed each other in an unchanging rhythm fixed by the needs for food or sleep, reproduction or protection. Man detaches himself from his surroundings; he feels alone, abandoned, ignorant of everything except that he knows nothing ... His first feeling thus was existential anxiety, which may even have taken him to the limits of despair. (F. M. Bergounioux, 1964)

A very similar view was expressed by Dobzhansky:

Self-awareness and foresight brought, however, the awesome gifts of freedom and responsibility. Man feels free to execute some of his plans and to leave others in abeyance. He feels the joy of being the master, rather than a slave, of the world and of himself. But the joy is tempered by a feeling of responsibility. Man knows that he is accountable for his acts: he has acquired the knowledge of good and evil. This is a dreadfully heavy load to carry. No other animal has to withstand anything like it. There is a tragic discord in the soul of man. Among the flaws in human nature, this one is far more serious than the pain of childbirth. (T. Dobzhansky, 1962)

The Existential Needs of Man and the Various Character-Rooted Passions [8]

A Frame of Orientation and Devotion

Man's capacity for self-awareness, reason, and imagination – new qualities that go beyond the capacity for instrumental thinking of even the cleverest animals – requires a picture of the world and of his place in it that is structured and has inner cohesion. Man needs a map of his natural and social world, without which he would be confused and unable to act purposefully and consistently. He would have no way of orienting himself and of finding for himself a fixed point that permits him to organize all the impressions that impinge upon him. Whether he believed in sorcery and magic

8. The material in the following pages is an expansion of the discussion of the same subject (E. Fromm, 1947 and 1955); to avoid repetition as much as possible, I have given only a shortened version of the older material.

as final explanations of all events, or in the spirit of his ancestors as guiding his life and fate, or in an omnipotent god who will reward or punish him, or in the power of science to give answers to all human problems – from the standpoint of his need for a frame of orientation, it does not make any difference. His world makes sense to him, and he feels certain about his ideas through the consensus with those around him. Even if the map is wrong, it fulfils its psychological function. But the map was never entirely wrong – nor has it ever been entirely right, either. It has always been enough of an approximation to the explanation of phenomena to serve the purpose of living. Only to the degree to which the *practice* of life is freed from its contradictions and its irrationality can the theoretical picture correspond to the truth.

The impressive fact is that we do not find any culture in which there does not exist such a frame of orientation. Or any individual either. Often an individual may disclaim having any such overall picture and believe that he responds to the various phenomena and incidents of life from case to case, as his judgement guides him. But it can be easily demonstrated that he takes his own philosophy for granted, because to him it is only common sense, and he is unaware that all his concepts rest upon a commonly accepted frame of reference. When such a person is confronted with a fundamentally different total view of life he judges it as 'crazy' or 'irrational' or 'childish', while he considers himself as being only logical. The need for the formation of a frame of reference is particularly clear in the case of children. They show, at a certain age, a deep need for a frame of orientation and often make it up themselves in an ingenious way, using the few data available to them.

The intensity of the need for a frame of orientation explains a fact that has puzzled many students of man, namely the ease with which people fall under the spell of irrational doctrines, either political or religious or of any other nature, when to the one who is not under their influence it seems obvious that they are worthless constructs. Part of the answer lies in the suggestive influence of leaders and in the suggestibility of man. But this does not seem to be the whole story. Man would probably not be so suggestive were it not that his need for a cohesive frame of orientation is so vital. The more an ideology pretends to give answers to all questions, the more attractive it is; here may lie the reason why irrational or even plainly insane thought systems can so easily attract the minds of men.

But a map is not enough as a guide for action; man also needs a goal that tells him where to go. The animal has no such problems. Its instincts provide it with a map as well as with goals. But man, lacking instinctive determination and having a brain that permits him to think of many directions in which he could go, needs an object of total devotion; he needs an object of devotion to be the focal point of all his strivings and the basis for all his effective – and not only proclaimed – values. He needs such an object of devotion for a number of reasons. The object integrates his energies in one direction. It elevates him beyond his isolated existence, with all its doubts and insecurity, and gives meaning to life. In being devoted to a goal beyond his isolated ego, he transcends himself and leaves the prison of absolute egocentricity.[9]

The objects of man's devotion vary. He can be devoted to an idol which requires him to kill his children or to an ideal that makes him protect children; he can be devoted to the

9. The term 'transcendence' is traditionally used in a theological frame of reference. Christian thinking takes for granted that man's transcendence implies transcendence beyond himself to God; thus theology tries to prove the need for belief in God by pointing to man's need for transcendence. This logic, however, is faulty unless the concept of God is used in a purely symbolic sense standing for 'not-self'. There is a need to transcend one's self-centred, narcissistic, isolated position to one of being related to others, of openness to the world, escaping the hell of self-centredness and hence self-imprisonment. Religious systems like Buddhism have postulated this kind of transcendence without any reference to a god or superhuman power; so did Meister Eckhart, in his boldest formulations.

growth of life or to its destruction. He can be devoted to the goal of amassing a fortune, of acquiring power, of destruction, or to that of loving and of being productive and courageous. He can be devoted to the most diverse goals and idols; yet while the difference in the objects of devotion are of immense importance, the need for devotion itself is a primary, existential need demanding fulfilment regardless of *how* this need is fulfilled.

Rootedness

When the infant is born he leaves the security of the womb, the situation in which he was still part of nature – where he lived through his mother's body. At the moment of birth he is still symbiotically attached to mother, and even after birth he remains so longer than most other animals. But even when the umbilical cord is cut there remains a deep crazing to undo the separation, to return to the womb or to find a new situation of absolute protection and security.[10]

But the way to paradise is blocked by man's biological,

10. It is one of Freud's achievements to have discovered the depth of the fixation to mother as the central problem of normal and pathological development (the 'Oedipus complex'). But he was forced by his own philosophical premises to interpret this fixation as a sexual one, and he thus narrowed the importance of his discovery. Only towards the end of his life did he begin to see that there was also a pre-Oedipal attachment to mother. But he could not go beyond these more marginal remarks and did not revise the old concept of 'incest'. A few analysts, especially S. Ferenczi and his students, and more recently J. Bowlby (1958 and 1969), have seen the real nature of the fixation to mother. Recent experiments with primates (H. R. Harlow, J. L. McGaugh, and R. F. Thompson, 1971) and with infants (R. Spitz and G. Cobliner, 1965) have clearly demonstrated the supreme importance of the tie to mother. The analytic data unearthed show what role the non-sexual incestuous strivings play in the life of both the normal and the neurotic person. Since I have stressed this point in my work for many years, I shall quote here only the last treatment of it in *The Sane Society* (1955) and in *The Heart of Man* (1964). cf. on symbiosis E. Fromm (1941, 1955, 1964); also M. S. Mahler (1968), based on her earlier papers since 1951.

and particularly by his neurophysiological constitution. He has only one alternative: either to persist in his craving to regress, and to pay for it by symbolic dependence on mother (and on symbolic substitutes, such as soil, nature, god, the nation, a bureaucracy), or to progress and find new roots in the world by his own efforts, by experiencing the brotherhood of man, and by freeing himself from the power of the past.

Man, aware of his separateness, needs to find new ties with his fellowman; his very sanity depends on it. Without strong affective ties to the world, he would suffer from utter isolation and lostness. But he can relate himself to others in different and ascertainable ways. He can love others, which requires the presence of independence and productiveness, or if his sense of freedom is not developed, he can relate to others symbiotically – i.e., by becoming part of them or by making them part of himself. In this symbiotic relationship he strives either to control others (sadism), or to be controlled by them (masochism). If he cannot choose either the way of love or that of symbiosis, he can solve the problem by relating exclusively to himself (narcissism); then he becomes the world, and loves the world by 'loving' himself. This is a frequent form of dealing with the need for relatedness (usually blended with sadism), but it is a dangerous one; in its extreme form it leads to some forms of madness. A last and malignant form of solving the problem (usually blended with extreme narcissism) is the craving to destroy all others. If no one exists outside of me, I need not fear others, nor need I relate myself to them. By destroying the world I am saved from being crushed by it.

Unity

The existential split in man would be unbearable could he not establish a sense of unity within himself and with the natural and human world outside. But there are many ways of re-establishing unity.

Man can anaesthetize his consciousness by inducing states of trance or ecstasy, mediated by such means as drugs, sexual orgies, fasting, dancing, and other rituals that abound in various cults. He can also try to identify himself with the animal in order to regain the lost harmony; this form of seeking unity is the essence of the many primitive religions in which the ancestor of the tribe is a totem animal, or in which man identifies with the animal by acting like one (for instance the Teutonic *berserkers* who identified themselves with a bear) or by wearing an animal mask. Unity can also be established by subordinating all energies to one all-consuming passion, such as the passion for destruction, power, fame, or property.

'To forget oneself', in the sense of anaesthetizing one's reason, is the aim of all these attempts to restore unity within oneself. It is a tragic attempt, in the sense that either it succeeds only momentarily (as in a trance or in drunkenness) or even if it is permanent (as in the passion for hate or power), it cripples man, estranges him from others, twists his judgement, and makes him as dependent on this particular passion as another is on hard drugs.

There is only one approach to unity that can be successful without crippling man. Such an attempt was made in the first millennium BC in all parts of the world where man had developed a civilization – in China, in India, in Egypt, in Palestine, in Greece. The great religions springing from the soil of these cultures taught that man can achieve unity not by a tragic effort to undo the fact of the split, by eliminating reason, but by fully developing human reason and love. Great as are the differences between Taoism, Buddhism, prophetic Judaism, and the Christianity of the Gospels, these religions had one common goal: to arrive at the experience of oneness, not by regressing to animal existence but by becoming fully human – oneness within man, oneness between man and nature, and oneness between man and other men. In the short historical time of twenty-five hundred years man does not seem to have made much progress in achieving the goal that was postulated by these religions. The inevitable slowness of man's economic and social development plus the fact that the religions were co-opted by those whose social function it was to rule and manipulate men seem to account for this. Yet the new concept of unity was as revolutionary an event in man's psychical development as the invention of agriculture and industry was for his economic development. Nor was this concept ever totally lost; it was brought to life in the Christian sects, among the mystics of all religions, in the ideas of Joachim de Fiore, among the Renaissance humanists, and in a secular form in the philosophy of Marx.

The alternative between regressive and progressive ways of achieving salvation is not only a social-historical one. Each individual is confronted with the same alternative; his margin of freedom not to choose the regressive solution in a society that has chosen it is indeed small – yet it exists. But great effort, clear thinking, and guidance by the teachings of the great humanists is necessary. (Neurosis can be understood best as the battle between two tendencies within an individual; deep character analysis leads, if successful, to the progressive solution.)

Another solution to man's existential split problem is quite characteristic of contemporary cybernetic society: to be identified with one's social role; to feel little, to lose oneself by reducing oneself to a thing; the existential split is camouflaged because man becomes identified with his social organization and forgets that he is a person; he becomes, to use Heidegger's term, a 'one', a non-person. He is, we might say, in a 'negative ecstasis'; he forgets himself by ceasing to be 'he', by ceasing to be a person and becoming a thing.

Effectiveness

Man's awareness of himself as being in a strange and overpowering world, and his consequent sense of impotence could easily overwhelm him. If he experienced himself as entirely passive, a mere object, he would lack a sense of his own will, of his identity. To compensate for this he must acquire a sense of being able to do something, to move somebody, to 'make a dent', or, to use the most adequate English word, to be 'effective'. We use the word today in referring to an 'effective' speaker or salesman, meaning one who succeeds in getting results. But this is a deterioration of the original meaning of 'to effect' (from the Latin *ex-facere*, to do). To effect is the equivalent of: to bring to pass, to accomplish, to realize, to carry out, to fulfil; an effective person is one who has the capacity to do, to effect, to accomplish something. To be able to effect something is the assertion that one is not impotent, but that one is an alive, functioning, human being. To be able to effect means to be active and not only *to be affected*; to be active and not only passive. It is, in the last analysis, *the proof that one is*. The principle can be formulated thus: *I am, because I effect*.

A number of investigations have stressed this point. At the beginning of this century K. Groos, the classic interpreter of play, wrote that an essential motive in the child's play was the 'joy in being a cause'; this was his explanation of the child's pleasure in making a clatter, moving things around, playing in puddles, and similar activities. His conclusion was: 'We demand a knowledge of the effects and to be ourselves the producers of these effects' (K. Groos, 1901). A similar idea was expressed fifty years later by J. Piaget who observed the child's special interest in objects that he effects by his own movements (J. Piaget, 1952). R. W. White used a similar concept in describing one of the basic motivations in man as 'competence motivation', and proposed the word 'effectance' for the motivational aspect of competence (R. W. White, 1959).

The same need is manifested in the fact that the first real sentence of some children from about the age of fifteen to eighteen months is some version of 'I do – I do,' repeated, and that also for the first time 'me' is often used before 'mine' (D. E. Schecter, 1968).[11] Due to his biological situation the child is necessarily in a state of extraordinary helplessness up to the age of eighteen months, and even later he is largely dependent on the favours and goodwill of others. The degree of the child's natural powerlessness changes every day, while in general adults are much slower in changing their attitude towards the child. The child's tantrums, his crying, his stubbornness, the different ways in which he tries to battle adults, are among the most visible manifestations of his attempt to have an effect, to move, to change, to express his will. The child is usually defeated by the superior strength of the adult, but the defeat does not remain without consequences; it would seem to activate a tendency to overcome the defeat by doing actively what one was forced to endure passively: to rule when one had to obey; to beat when one was beaten; in short, to *do* what one was *forced* to *suffer*, or to do what one was forbidden to do. Psychoanalytic data show amply that neurotic tendencies and sexual peculiarities, like voyeurism, compulsive masturbation, or a compulsive need for sexual intercourse, often are the outcome of such early prohibitions. It seems almost as if this compulsive transformation from the passive to the active role were an attempt, even though an unsuccessful one, to heal still open wounds. Perhaps the general attraction of 'sin', of doing the forbidden, also finds its explanation here.[12] Not only does that which was not permissible attract, but also that which is not possible. It seems that man is profoundly attracted to move to the personal, social, and natural borders of his existence, as if driven to look beyond the narrow frame in which he is forced to exist. This impulse may be an important conducive factor in great discoveries, as well as in great crimes.

11. Also, D. E. Schecter, personal communication.

12. In order to avoid misunderstanding, I should like to emphasize that one cannot isolate a single factor (a prohibition) from the total interpersonal situation of which it is a part. If the prohibition occurs in a non-oppressive situation, it will not have the the consequences it has in a constellation in which it serves to break the child's will.

The adult, too, feels the need to reassure himself that he *is* *by being able to effect.* The ways to achieve a sense of effecting are manifold: by eliciting an expression of satisfaction in the baby being nursed, a smile from the loved person, sexual response from the lover, interest from the partner in conversation; by work – material, intellectual, artistic. But the same need can also be satisfied by having power *over* others, by experiencing their fear, by the murderer's watching the anguish in the face of his victim, by conquering a country, by torturing people, by sheer destruction of what has been constructed. The need to 'effect' expresses itself in interpersonal relations as well as in the relationship to animals, to inanimate nature, and to ideas. In the relationship to others the fundamental alternative is to feel either the potency to effect love or to effect fear and suffering. In the relationship to things, the alternative is between constructing and destroying. Opposite as these alternatives are, they are responses to the same existential need: to effect.

In studying depressions and boredom one can find rich material to show that the sense of being condemned to ineffectiveness – i.e., to complete vital impotence (of which sexual impotence is only a small part) – is one of the most painful and almost intolerable experiences, and man will do almost anything to overcome it, from drug and work addiction to cruelty and murder.

Excitation and Stimulation

The Russian neurologist Ivan Sechenov was the first to establish, in *Reflexes of the Brain,* that the nervous system has the need to be 'exercised' – i.e., to experience a certain minimum of excitation (Sechenov, 1863).

R. B. Livingston states the same principle:

> The nervous system is a source for activity as well as integration. The brain is not merely *reactive* to outside stimuli; it is itself spontaneously active ... Brain cell activity begins in embryonic life and probably contributes to organizational development.

Brain development occurs most rapidly prior to birth and for a few months thereafter. Following this period of exuberant growth, the rate of development decreases markedly; yet, even in the adult, there is no point beyond which development ceases, beyond which the capacities for reorganization following disease or injury disappear.

And further on:

The brain consumes oxygen at a rate comparable to that of active muscle. Active muscle can sustain such a rate of oxygen consumption for only a short period, but the nervous system continues its high rate for a lifetime, awake or asleep, from birth until death. (R. B. Livingston, 1967)

Even in tissue culture, nerve cells continue to be biologically and electrically active.

One area in which the need for constant excitation of the brain can be recognized is the phenomenon of dreaming. It has been well established that a considerable proportion of our sleeping time (about 25 per cent) is spent in dreaming (the difference between individuals is not whether or not they dream, but whether or not they remember their dreams), and that individuals appear to show semi-pathological reactions if they are prevented from dreaming (W. Dement, 1960). It is a relevant question why the brain, comprising only 2 per cent of the body weight, is the only organ (aside from the heart and lungs) that remains active during sleep, while the rest of the body is in a state of rest; or to put it in neurophysiological terms, why the brain uses 20 per cent of the body's total intake of oxygen day *and* night. It would seem that this means that the neurons 'ought' to be in a state of greater activity than the cells in other parts of the body. As to the reasons for this, one could speculate that sufficient oxygen supply to the brain is of such vital importance for living that the brain is provided with an extra margin of activity and excitation.

The infant's need for stimulation has been demonstrated by many investigators. R. Spitz has shown the pathological effects of lack of stimulation on infants; the Harlows and others have demonstrated that early deprivation of contact with mother results in severe psychic damage to monkeys.[13] The same problem has been studied by D. E. Schecter in pursuit of his thesis that social stimulation constitutes a basis for the child's development. He arrives at the conclusion that 'without adequate social (including perceptual) stimulation, as for instance in blind and institutionalized infants, deficits develop in emotional and social relationships, in language, abstract thinking, and inner control' (D. E. Schecter, 1973).

Experimental studies have also demonstrated the need for stimulation and excitation. E. Tauber and F. Koffler (1966) demonstrated the optokinetic nystagmus reaction to movement in newborns. 'Wolff and White (1965) observed visual pursuit of objects with conjugate eye movements in three- to four-day-olds; Fantz (1958) described more prolonged visual fixation on more complex visual patterns as against simpler ones during the early weeks of infancy' (D. E. Schecter, 1973).[14] Schecter adds: 'Of course, we cannot know the quality of the infant's subjective perceptual experience but only the fact of a discriminating visual motor response. Only in a loose manner of speaking may we conclude that infants "prefer" complex stimulus patterns' (D. E. Schecter, 1973). The experiments on sensory deprivation at McGill University[15] have shown that the elimination of most outside stimuli, even when accompanied by the satisfaction of all physiological needs (with the exception of sex) and rewarded by better-than-average pay, resulted in certain disturbances in perception; the subjects showed irritability, restlessness, and emotional instability to such a

13. I am indebted to Dr R. G. Heath for having shown me some of these 'catatonic' monkeys in the Department of Psychiatry, Tulane University, New Orleans, Lousiana.

14. I am indebted to Dr D. E. Schecter for allowing me to read his paper in manuscript.

15. cf. the series of papers by W. H. Bexton *et al.* (1954), W. Heron *et al.* (1956), T. H. Scott *et al.* (1959), and B. K. Doane *et al.* (1959).

degree that a number of them stopped participating in the experiment after only a few hours, in spite of the financial loss.[16]

Observations of daily life indicate that the human organism as well as the animal organism are in need of a certain minimum of excitation and stimulation, as they are of a certain minimum of rest. We see that men eagerly respond to and seek excitation. The list of excitation-generating stimuli is endless. The difference between people – and cultures – lies only in the form taken by the main stimuli for excitation. Accidents, a murder, a fire, a war, sex are sources of excitation; so are love and creative work; Greek drama was certainly as exciting for the spectators as were the sadistic spectacles in the Roman Colosseum, but exciting in a different way. The difference is very important, yet little attention has been given to it. Although this means making a short detour, it seems worthwhile to discuss this difference, if only briefly.

In psychological and neurophysiological literature the term 'stimulus' has been used almost exclusively to denote what I call here a 'simple' stimulus. If a man is threatened with danger to his life, his response is simple and immediate, almost reflex-like, because it is rooted in his neurophysiological organization. The same holds true for the other physiological needs like hunger and, to a certain extent, sex. The responding person 'reacts', but *he* does not act – by which I mean to say he does not actively integrate any response beyond the minimum activity necessary to run away, attack, or become sexually excited. One might also say that in this kind of response the brain and the whole physiological apparatus act *for* man.

What is usually overlooked is the fact that there is a different kind of stimulus, one that *stimulates the person to be active*. Such an activating stimulus could be a novel, a poem, an idea, a landscape, music, or a loved person. None of

16. The idea that they showed quasi-psychotic reactions rests, in my opinion, on an erroneous interpretation of the data.

these stimuli produce a simple response; they invite you, as it were, to respond by actively and sympathetically relating yourself to them; by becoming actively *interested*, seeing and discovering ever-new aspects in your 'object' (which ceases to be a mere 'object'), by becoming more awake and more aware. You do not remain the passive object upon which the stimulus acts, to whose melody your body has to dance, as it were; instead you express your own faculties by being related to the world; you become active and productive. The simple stimulus produces a *drive* – i.e., the person is driven by it; the activating stimulus results in a *striving* – i.e., the person is actively striving for a goal.

The difference between these two kinds of stimuli and responses has very important consequences. Stimuli of the first, simple kind, if repeated beyond a certain threshold, are no longer registered and lose their stimulating effect. (This is due to a neurophysiological principle of economy that eliminates the awareness of stimuli that indicate by their repetitiveness that they are not important.) Continued stimulation requires that the stimulus should either increase in intensity or change in content; a certain element of novelty is required.

Activating stimuli have a different effect. They do not remain 'the same'; because of the productive response to them, they are always new, always changing: the stimulated person (the 'stimulee') brings the stimuli to life and changes them by always discovering new aspects in them. Between the stimulus and the 'stimulee' exists a mutual relationship, not the mechanical one-way relations S →R.

This difference is easily confirmed by anybody's experience. One can read a Greek drama, or a poem by Goethe, or a novel by Kafka, or a sermon by Meister Eckhart, or a treatise by Paracelsus, or fragments by the pre-Socratic philosophers, or the writings of Spinoza or Marx without ever getting bored – obviously, these examples are personal, and everyone should replace them by others closer to him; these stimuli are always alive; they wake up the reader and increase his awareness. On the other hand, a cheap novel is boring on a second reading, and conducive to sleep.

The significance of activating and simple stimuli is crucial for the problem of learning. If learning means to penetrate from the surface of phenomena to their roots – i.e., to their causes, from deceptive ideologies to the naked facts, thus approximating the truth – it is an exhilarating, active process and a condition for human growth. (I do not refer here only to book learning, but to the discoveries a child or an illiterate member of a primitive tribe makes of natural or personal events.) If, on the other hand, learning is merely the acquisition of information mediated by conditioning, we are dealing with a simple stimulus in which the person is acted upon by the stimulation of his need for praise, security, success, and so forth.

Contemporary life in industrial societies operates almost entirely with such simple stimuli. What is stimulated are such drives as sexual desire, greed, sadism, destructiveness, narcissism; these stimuli are mediated through movies, television, radio, newspapers, magazines, and the commodity market. On the whole, advertising rests upon the stimulation of socially produced desires. The mechanism is always the same: simple stimulation →immediate and passive response. Here lies the reason why the stimuli have to be changed constantly, lest they become ineffective. A car that is exciting today will be boring in a year or two – so it must be changed in the search for excitation. A place one knows well automatically becomes boring, so that excitement can be had only by visiting different places, as many as possible in one trip. In such a framework, sexual partners also need to be changed in order to produce excitation.

The description given so far needs to be qualified by stressing that it is not only the stimulus that counts. The most stimulating poem or person will fail completely with someone who is incapable of responding because of his own fear, inhibition, laziness, passivity. The activating stimulus requires a 'touchable' stimulee in order to have an effect –

touchable not in the sense of being educated, but of being humanly responsive. On the other hand, the person who is fully alive does not necessarily need any particular outside stimulus to be activated; in fact, he creates his own stimuli. The difference can be clearly seen in children. Up to a certain age (around five years) they are so active and productive that they 'make' their own stimuli. They create a whole world out of scraps of paper, wood, stones, chairs, practically anything they find available. But when after the age of six they become docile, unspontaneous, and passive, they want to be stimulated in such a way that they can remain passive and only 're-act'. They want elaborate toys and get bored with them after a short while; in brief, they already behave as their elders do with cars, clothes, places to travel, and lovers.

There is another important difference between simple and activating stimuli. The person who is driven by the simple stimulus experiences a mixture of release, thrill satisfaction; when he is 'satisfied' (from the Latin *satis-facere*, 'to make enough'), he 'has enough'. The activating stimulation, on the contrary, has no satisfaction point – i.e., it never makes the person feel he 'has enough', except, of course, when normal physical tiredness sets in.

I believe that one can formulate a law based on neurophysiological and psychological data in reference to the difference between the two kinds of stimuli: the more 'passivating' a stimulus is, the more frequently it must be changed in intensity and/or in kind; the more activating it is, the longer it retains its stimulating quality and the less necessary is change in intensity and content.

I have dealt at such length with the organism's need for stimulation and excitation because it is one of the many factors generating destructiveness and cruelty. It is much easier to get excited by anger, rage, cruelty, or the passion to destroy than by love and productive and active interest; that first kind of excitation does not require the individual to make an effort – one does not need to have patience and discipline, to learn, to concentrate, to endure frustration, to practise critical thinking, to overcome one's narcissism and greed. If the person has failed to grow, simple stimuli are always at hand or can be read about in the newspapers, heard about in the radio news reports, or watched on television and in movies. People can also produce them in their own minds by finding reasons to hate, to destroy, and to control others. (The strength of this craving is indicated by the millions of dollars the mass media make by selling this kind of excitation.) In fact, many married couples stay together for this reason: the marriage gives them the opportunity to experience hate, quarrels, sadism, and submission. They stay together not *in spite* of their fights, but *because of* them. Masochistic behaviour, the pleasure in suffering or submitting, has one of its roots in this need for excitement. Masochistic persons suffer from the difficulty of being able to *initiate* excitation and of reacting readily to normal stimuli; but they can react when the stimulus overpowers them, as it were, when they can give themselves up to the excitement forced upon them.

Boredom–Chronic Depression

The problem of stimulation is closely linked to a phenomenon that has no small part in generating aggression and destructiveness: *boredom*. From a logical standpoint it would have been more adequate to have discussed boredom in the previous chapter, together with other causes of aggression, but this would have been impractical because the discussion on stimulation is a necessary premise for the understanding of boredom.

With regard to stimulation and boredom we can distinguish between three types of persons: (1) The person who is capable of responding productively to activating stimuli is not bored. (2) The person who is in constant need of ever changing, 'flat' stimuli is chronically bored, but since he compensates for his boredom, he is not aware of it. (3) The person who fails in the attempt to obtain excitation by any kind of normal stimulation is a very sick individual; sometimes he is acutely aware of his state of mind; sometimes he is not conscious of the fact that he suffers. This type of boredom is fundamentally different from the second type in which boredom is used in a *behavioural* sense, i.e., the person is bored when there is an insufficient stimulation, but he is *capable* of responding when his boredom is compensated. In the third instance it cannot be compensated. We speak here of boredom in a dynamic, characterological sense, and it could be described as a state of chronic depression. But the difference between compensated and uncompensated chronic boredom is only quantitative. In both types of boredom the person lacks in productivity; in the first type he can cure the symptom – although not its cause – by proper stimuli; in the second even the symptom is incurable.

The difference is also visible in the use of the term 'bored'. If someone says 'I am depressed', he usually refers to a state of mind. If somebody says 'I am bored', he usually means to say something about the world outside, indicating that it does not provide him with interesting or amusing stimuli. But when we speak of a 'boring person' we refer to the person himself, to his character. We do not mean that he is boring today because he has not told us an interesting story; when we say he is a boring person we mean he is boring *as a person*. There is something dead, unalive, uninteresting in him. Many people would readily admit they are *bored*; very few would admit that they are *boring*.

Chronic boredom – compensated or uncompensated – constitutes one of the major psychopathological phenomena in contemporary technotronic society, although it is only recently that it has found some recognition.[17]

17. cf. A. Burton (1967), who calls depression the 'illness of our society', and W. Heron (1957). I have pointed to the significance of boredom as pervading our society and to its aggression-producing

Before entering into the discussion of depressive boredom (in the dynamic sense), some remarks on boredom in a behavioural sense seem to be in order. The persons who are capable of responding productively to 'activating stimuli' are virtually never bored – but they are the exception in cybernetic society. The vast majority, while not suffering from a grave illness, can be nevertheless considered suffering from a milder form of pathology: insufficient inner productivity. They are bored unless they can provide themselves with ever-changing, simple – not activating – stimuli.

There are several probable reasons that chronic, compensated boredom is generally not considered pathological. Perhaps the main reason is that in contemporary industrial society most people are bored, and a shared pathology – the 'pathology or normalcy' – is not experienced as pathology. Furthermore, 'normal' boredom is usually not conscious. Most people succeed in compensating for it by participating in a great number of 'activities' that prevent them from consciously feeling bored. Eight hours of the day they are busy making a living; when the boredom would threaten to become conscious, after business hours, they avoid this danger by the numerous means that prevent manifest boredom: drinking, watching television, taking a ride, going to parties, engaging in sexual activities, and, the more recent fashion, taking drugs. Eventually their natural need for sleep takes over, and the day is ended successfully if boredom has not been experienced consciously at any point. One may state that one of the main goals of man today is 'escape from boredom'. Only if one appreciates the intensity of reactions caused by unrelieved boredom can one have any idea of the power of the impulses engendered by it.

Among the working class boredom is much more conscious than among the middle and upper classes, as amply evidenced in workers' demands in contract negotiations.

---

function in *The Revolution of Hope* (1968a) as well as in my earlier writings.

They lack the genuine satisfaction experienced by many persons on a higher social level whose work allows them, at least to some extent, to be involved in creative planning, exercising their imaginative, intellectual, and organizational facilities. That this is so is clearly borne out by the fact, amply demonstrated in recent years, that the growing complaint of blue-collar workers today is the painful boredom they experience in their working hours, besides their more traditional complaint about insufficient wages. Industry tries to remedy this in some cases by what is often called 'job enrichment', which consists of having the worker do more than one operation, planning and laying out his own job as he likes, and generally assuming more responsibility. This seems to be an answer in the right direction, but it is a very limited one considering the whole spirit of our culture. It has also often been suggested that the problem does not lie in making the work more interesting but in shortening it to such an extent that man can develop his faculties and interests in his leisure time. But the proponents of this idea seem to forget that leisure time itself is manipulated by the consumption of industry and is fundamentally as boring as work, only less consciously so. Work, man's exchange with nature, is such a fundamental part of human existence that only when it ceases to be alienated can leisure time become productive. This, however, is not only a question of changing the nature of work, but of a total social and political change in the direction of subordinating the economy to the real needs of man.

In the picture of the two kinds of non-depressive boredom given so far it would appear that the difference is only between the different kinds of stimuli; whether they are activating or not, they both relieve boredom. This picture, however, is an oversimplification; the difference goes much deeper and complicates considerably what seemed to be a neat formulation. The boredom that is overcome by activating stimuli is really ended, or rather it never existed, because the productive person, ideally speaking, is never bored and has no difficulty in finding the proper stimuli. On the other hand, the unproductive, inwardly passive person remains bored even when his manifest, conscious boredom is relieved for the moment.

Why should this be so? The reason seems to lie in that in the superficial relief from boredom, the whole person, and particularly his deeper feeling, his imagination, his reason, in short all his essential facilities and psychic potentialities remain untouched; they are not brought to life; the boredom-compensating means are like a bulky food without any nutritional value. The person continues to feel 'empty' and unmoved on a deeper level. He 'anaesthetizes' this uncomfortable feeling by momentary excitation, 'thrill', 'fun', liquor, or sex – but *unconsciously* he remains bored.

A very busy lawyer who often worked twelve hours a day or more and said that he was absorbed by his job and never felt bored, had the following dream:

I see myself as a member of a chain gang in Georgia where I was extradited from my hometown in the East for some unknown crime. To my surprise I can easily take off the chains, but I must go on doing the prescribed work, which consists of carrying bags of sand from one truck to another away in the distance and then taking the same bags back to the first truck. I experience a sense of intense mental pain and depression during the dream and wake up in a frightened mood as from a nightmare, relieved that it was only a dream.

Whereas during the first weeks of analytic work he had been quite cheerful, saying how satisfied he felt in life, he was quite shaken by this dream and began to bring up many different ideas about his work. Without going into details, I only want to state that he began to speak about the fact that what he was doing really did not make sense, that it was essentially always the same, and that it served no purpose except that of making money, which he felt was not enough as something to live for. He spoke about the fact that in spite of a good deal of variety in the problems he had to solve, they were basically all the same, or could be solved by a few, ever-repeated methods.

Two weeks later he had the following dream: 'I saw myself sitting at the desk in my office, but I felt like a zombie. I hear what goes on and see what people do, but I feel that I am dead and that nothing concerns me.'

The associations for this dream brought forward more material about a sense of feeling unalive and depressed. In a third dream he reported: 'The building in which my office is located is going up in flames, but nobody knows how it happened. I feel powerless to help.'

It hardly needs to be said that this last dream expressed his deep hatred of the law firm of which he is the head; he had been completely unconscious of this because it did not 'make sense'.[18]

Another example of unconscious boredom is given by H. D. Esler. He reports of a patient, a good-looking student who carried on with many girl friends and was very successful in this sector of his life; although he insisted that 'life is great', sometimes he felt somewhat depressed. When he was hypnotized during the treatment, he saw 'a black barren place with many masks'. When asked where the black barren place was, he said it was inside him. That everything was dull, dull, dull; that the masks represent the different roles he takes to fool people into thinking he is feeling well. He began to express his feelings about life: 'It is a feeling of nothingness.' When the therapist asked him if sex was also dull, he said, 'Yes, but not as dull as other things.' He stated that 'his three children by a previous marriage bored him, although he felt closer to them than he did to most people; that in his nine years of marriage he went through the motions of living and was occasionally relieved by drinking'. He talked about his father as 'an ambitious, dull, lonely man who never had a friend in his life'. The therapist asked him if he was lonely with his son; the answer was, 'I tried very

18. This dream and the comments were reported to me by a student whose work I supervised years ago.

hard to relate to him but was unable to.' When asked if he wanted to die, the patient said, 'Yes, why not?' but he also answered yes when asked whether he wanted to live. Eventually he had a dream in which 'there was sunlight and it was warm and there was grass'. When asked whether there were people there he said, 'No, there were no people but there was a potential for them coming.' When awakened from the hypnotic trance, he was surprised at the things he had said.[19]

While the depressed and bored feeling was occasionally conscious, it became fully conscious only in the hypnotic state. The patient succeeded by his active and ever-new sexual exploits to compensate for his bored state, just as the lawyer did by work, but the compensation occurred mainly in consciousness. It permitted the patient to repress his boredom, and he could go on with this repression as long as the compensation worked properly. But compensations do not alter the fact that on a deeper level of inner reality the boredom is not removed or even lessened.

It seems that the boredom-compensating consumption offered by the normal channels of our culture does not fulfil its function properly; hence, other means of boredom relief are sought. Alcohol consumption is one of the means man employs to help him forget his boredom. In the past few years a new phenomenon has demonstrated the intensity of the boredom among members of the middle class. I am referring to the practice of group sex among 'swingers'. It is estimated that there are in the United States one or two million people, chiefly middle class and mostly conservative in their political and religious views, whose main interest in life is sexual activity shared among several couples, provided that they are not husband and wife. The main condition is that no emotional tie is to develop and that the partners are constantly changed. According to the description by investigators who have studied these people (G. T. Bartell, 1971), they explain that before they started

19. Dr H. D. Esler, personal communication.

swinging they were so bored that even many hours of television viewing did not help them. The personal relationship
between husband and wife was such that there was nothing
left to communicate about. This boredom is relieved by the
constantly changing sexual stimuli, and even their marriages
have, as they say, 'improved', because they now at least
have something to talk about – i.e., the sexual experiences of
each of them with other men and women. 'Swinging' is a
somewhat more complex version of what used to be simple
marital promiscuity, which is hardly a new phenomenon;
what is perhaps new is the systematic exclusion of affects,
and that group sex is now proposed as a means 'to save a
tired marriage'.

Another more drastic means for the relief of boredom is
the use of psychodrugs, starting in the teens and spreading
to older age groups, particularly among those who are not
socially settled and have no interesting work to do. Many
users of drugs, especially among young people who have a
genuine longing for a deeper and more genuine experience
of life – indeed, many of them are distinguished by their life
affirmation, honesty, adventurousness, and independence –
claim that the use of drugs 'turns them on' and widens their
horizon of experience. I do not question this claim. But the
taking of drugs does not change their character and, hence,
does not eliminate the permanent roots of their boredom. It
does not promote a higher state of development; this can be
achieved only by taking the path of patient, effortful work
within oneself, by acquiring insight and learning how to be
concentrated and disciplined. Drugs are in no way conducive to 'instant enlightenment'.

Not the least dangerous result of insufficiently compensated boredom is violence and destructiveness. This outcome
most frequently takes the passive form of being attracted to
reports of crimes, fatal accidents, and other scenes of bloodshed and cruelty that are the staple diet fed to the public by
press, radio, and television. People eagerly respond to such
reports because they are the quickest way to produce excite-

ment, and thus alleviate boredom without any inner activity. Usually overlooked in the discussion of the effect of the portrayal of violence is that inasmuch as portrayal of violence has an effect, boredom is a necessary condition. Yet there is only a short step from passive enjoyment of violence and cruelty to the many ways of actively producing excitement by sadistic or destructive behaviour; the difference between the 'innocent' pleasure of embarrassing or 'teasing' someone and participating in a lynch mob is only quantitative. In either instance the bored person himself produces the source of excitation if it does not offer itself ready-made. The bored person often is the organizer of a 'mini-Colosseum' in which he produces his small-scale equivalents of the large-scale cruelty staged in the Colosseum. Such persons have no interest in anything, nor do they have any contact with anybody except of the most superficial kind. Everybody and everything leaves them cold. They are affectively frozen, feel no joy – but also no sorrow or pain. They feel nothing. The world is grey, the sky is not blue; they have no appetite for life and often would rather be dead than alive. Sometimes they are acutely and painfully aware of this state of mind, often they are not.

This type of pathology offers problems of diagnosis. The most severe cases might be diagnosed by many psychiatrists as a psychotic endogenous depression. Yet the diagnosis seems questionable because some characteristic features of endogenous depression are lacking. These persons do not tend to accuse themselves, to feel guilty, to be preoccupied with their failure, nor do they have the typical facial expression of melancholic patients.[20]

Aside from this most severe type of depression-boredom, there is a much more frequent clinical picture for which the most obvious diagnosis would be chronic 'neurotic

20. I am indebted to Dr R. G. Heath for very stimulating personal communications concerning patients suffering from extreme forms of boredom as well as for giving me the opportunity to interview two of these patients. See also R. G. Heath (1964).

depression' (E. Bleuler, 1969). In the clinical picture so frequent today not only causes for but also the fact of being depressed is unconscious; such persons are often not aware of feeling depressed, yet it can be easily demonstrated that they are. The terms more recently used, 'masked depression' or 'smiling depressions', seem to characterize the picture quite well. The diagnostic problem is still more complicated by the features in the clinical picture that lend themselves to a diagnosis of a 'schizoid' character.

I shall not pursue this diagnostic problem any further because it does not seem to contribute much to a better understanding of such persons. The difficulties of a correct diagnosis will be treated later on. Perhaps we deal, in the persons suffering from chronic, uncompensated boredom, with a peculiar blend of depressed and schizophrenic elements in varying degrees of malignancy. What matters for our purpose is not the diagnostic label, but the fact that among such persons we find extreme forms of destructiveness. They frequently do not seem to be bored or depressed at all. They can adapt themselves to their environment and often seem to be happy; *some are* apparently so well adapted that parents, teachers, ministers praise them as models. Others come to the attention of the authorities due to a variety of criminal acts and are considered 'asocial' or 'criminal', although not bored or depressed. Usually they tend to repress the awareness of being bored; most of all they want to appear perfectly normal to everyone else. When they come to a psychotherapist they will report that they find it difficult to choose a career, or to study, but generally they tend to present as normal a picture as they can. It takes a concerned and skilled observer to discover the sickness hidden behind the smooth, cynical surface.

H. D. Esler has done just that and has found among many adolescents in a boys' training school the condition of what he calls 'unconscious depression'.[21] I shall give in the

21. Much of the following is based on personal communications with Dr H. D. Esler, who will publish his material in a forthcoming book.

following some examples that also demonstrate that this condition is one of the sources of acts and destructiveness that seem in many instances to be the only form of relief.

One girl, hospitalized in a state mental hospital, had slashed her wrists and explained her act by saying that she wanted to see if she had any blood. This was a girl who felt non-human, without any response to anyone; she did not believe she could express or, for that matter, feel any affect. (Schizophrenia was excluded by a thorough clinical examination.) Her lack of interest and incapacity to respond was so great that to see her own blood was the only way in which she could convince herself that she was alive and human.

One of the boys in the training school, for instance, threw rocks up on top of his garage and let them roll down, and would try to catch each rock with his head. His explanation was that this was the only way in which he could *feel something*. He made five suicidal attempts. He cut himself in areas that would be painful and always made it known to the guards that he had done so, in order that he could be saved. He reported that feeling the pain made him feel at least something.

Another adolescent spoke of walking city streets 'with a knife up my sleeve, and I would stick it into people as they walked by'. He experienced pleasure in watching the agony on the victim's face. He also took dogs into the alley and killed them with his knife 'just for fun'. One time he said with emphasis, 'Now I think those dogs felt it when I stuck the knife into them.' The same boy confessed that while he was chopping wood during an outing in the woods with a schoolteacher and his wife, he saw the schoolteacher's wife standing there alone and had a tremendous urge to plant the axe in her head. Fortunately, she reacted on seeing a strange look on his face and asked for the axe. This seventeen-year-old boy had a baby face; an intern who saw him for vocational counselling thought he was charming and could not understand why he was in the institution. The truth was that the charm he portrayed was manipulative and very shallow.

Similar cases are to be found today all over the Western world and are occasionally reported in the papers. The following U P I and A P dispatch from Bisbee, Arizona, 1972, is a typical example:

A sixteen-year-old high school honour student and choir boy was in custody at a juvenile home today after allegedly telling police he shot his parents to death because he wanted to see how it would feel to kill somebody.

The bodies of Joseph Roth, sixty, and his wife, Gertrude, fifty-seven, were found at their home in nearby Douglas on Thanksgiving Day by Sheriff's deputies. Authorities said both had been shot once in the chest with a hunting rifle Wednesday night. Roth was a high school audio-visual instructor and Mrs Roth was a junior high teacher.

Cochise County attorney Richard Riley said the boy, Bernard J. Roth – 'the nicest boy you want to meet' – turned himself in to police Thursday and was composed and polite while being questioned.

'"The people [his parents] are getting old,"' Riley quoted the boy as saying. '"I'm not mad at them. I have no hostilities."'

'The boy said he had been having thoughts about killing his parents for a long time,' Riley said. 'He wanted to know what it felt like to kill somebody.'[22]

The motive for these killings does not seem to be hate, but as in the cases mentioned before, an unbearable sense of boredom and impotence and the need to experience that there is someone who will react, someone on whom one can make a dent, some deed that will make an end of the monotony of daily experience. Killing is one way of experiencing that one *is* and that one can produce an effect on another being.

This discussion of depression-boredom has dealt only with the psychological aspects of boredom. This does not

22. Sudden outbursts of violence may be caused by brain disease, such as tumours, and such cases have, of course, nothing to do with depressive-bored states.

imply that neurophysiological abnormalities may not also be involved, but as Bleuler has already emphasized, they could only play a secondary role, while the decisive conditions are to be found in the overall environmental situation. I think it is highly probable that even cases of severe depression-boredom would be less frequent and less intense, even given the same family constellation, in a society where a mood of hope and love of life predominated. But in recent decades the opposite is increasingly the case, and thus a fertile soil for the development of individual depressive states is provided.

Character Structure

There is a need of a different kind, rooted exclusively in the human situation – the need for development of a *character structure*. This need has to do with the phenomenon that was dealt with before, the decreasing significance of instinctive equipment in man. Effective behaviour presupposes that one can act immediately – that is, without being delayed by too much doubt and in a relatively integrated manner. This is precisely the dilemma of which Kortlandt has spoken (see Chapter 6) with regard to chimpanzees when he mentions their lack of decisiveness and their hesitant and somewhat ineffective behaviour (A. Kortlandt, 1962).

It seems plausible to speculate that man, being still less determined by instinct than the chimpanzee, would have been a biological failure if he had not developed a substitute for the instincts he lacked. This substitute also had to have the *function* of instincts: enabling man to act *as if* he were motivated by instincts. This substitute is the human character. Character is the specific structure in which human energy is organized in the pursuit of man's goals; it motivates behaviour according to its dominant goals: a person acts 'instinctively', we say, in accordance with his character. To use Heraclitus's phrase, character is man's fate. The miser does not ponder whether he should save or spend; he is driven to save and to hoard; the exploitative-sadistic character is driven by the passion to exploit; the sadistic character, by the passion to control; the loving-productive character cannot help striving for love and sharing. These character-conditioned drives and strivings are so strong and unquestionable for the respective persons that they feel that theirs is simply a 'natural' reaction, and find it difficult to really believe that there are other people whose nature is quite different. When they cannot help becoming aware of it, they prefer to think that these others suffer from some kind of deformation and are deviants from human nature. Anybody who has some sensitivity in judging other people (it is of course much more difficult with regard to oneself) senses whether a person has a sadistic or a destructive or a loving character; he sees enduring traits behind the overt behaviour and will be capable of sensing the insincerity of a destructive character who *behaves* as if he were a loving person.[23]

The question is: Why was the species man, in contrast to the chimpanzee, able to develop a character? The answer may lie in certain biological considerations.

Human groups from the very beginning have lived under very diverse environmental circumstances, both as regards different areas in the world and as regards fundamental changes of climate and vegetation within the same area. Since the emergence of *Homo* there has been relatively little adaptation to differences transmitted by genetic change, although there has been some. But the more *Homo* developed the less was adaptation a result of genetic changes, and in

23. I do not mean to imply that animals have *no* character. Undoubtedly they have their individuality, which is familiar to anyone who knows a species of animals well. But it must be considered that this individuality is to some extent one of temperament, a genetically given disposition, and not an acquired trait. Furthermore, the question, Have animals character or not? is as little fruitful as the old question, Have animals intelligence or not? It is to be assumed that the more an animal is instinctively determined, the less can we find elements of character and vice versa.

the last forty thousand years such changes are virtually nil. Yet these different environmental situations made it necessary for each group to adapt its behaviour to these respective situations, not only by learning but also by developing a 'social character'. The concept of social character is based on the consideration that each form of society (or social class) needs to use human energy in the specific manner necessary for the functioning of that particular society. Its members must *want* to do what they *have* to do if the society is to function properly. *This process of transforming general psychic energy into specific psycho-social energy is mediated by the social character* (E. Fromm, 1932, 1941, 1947, 1970). The means by which social character is formed are essentially cultural. Through the agency of the parents, society transmits to the young its values, prescriptions, commands, etc. But since chimpanzees have no language they cannot transmit symbols, values, and ideas; in other words, they lack the conditions for the formation of character. In more than a rudimentary sense, *character* is a *human phenomenon*; only man was able to create a substitute for his lost instinctive adaptation.

The acquisition of character was a very important and necessary element in the process of human survival, but it had also many disadvantages and even dangers. Inasmuch as character is formed by traditions and motivates man without appealing to his reason, it is often not adapted to or is sometimes even in direct contradiction to new conditions. For example, concepts like the absolute sovereignty of the state are rooted in an older type of social character and are dangerous for the survival of man in the atomic age.

The concept of character is crucial for the understanding of the manifestations of malignant aggression. The destructive and sadistic passions in a person are usually organized in his character system. In a sadistic person, for instance, the sadistic drive is a dominant part of his character structure and motivates him to behave sadistically, limited only by his concern for self-preservation. In a person with a sadistic character, a sadistic impulse is constantly active, waiting only for a proper situation and a fitting rationalization to be acted out. Such a person corresponds almost completely to Lorenz's hydraulic model (see Chapter 1) inasmuch as character-rooted sadism is a spontaneously flowing impulse, seeking for occasions to be expressed and creating such occasions where they are not readily at hand by 'appetitive behaviour'. The decisive difference is that the source of the sadistic passion lies in the character and not in a phylogenetically programmed neural area; *hence it is not common to all men, but only to those who share the same character.* We shall see later some examples of the sadistic and the destructive character and the conditions necessary for their formation.

Conditions for the Development of Character-Rooted Passions

The discussion of man's existential needs has shown that these can be satisfied in different ways. The need for an object of devotion can be answered by devotion to God, love, and truth – or by idolatry of destructive idols. The need for relatedness can be answered by love and kindness – or by dependence, sadism, masochism, destructiveness. The need for unity and rootedness can be answered by the passions for solidarity, brotherliness, love, and mystical experience – or by drunkenness, drug addiction, depersonalization. The need for effectiveness can be answered by love, productive work – or by sadism and destructiveness. The need for stimulation and excitation can be answered by productive interest in man, nature, art, ideas – or by a greedy pursuit of ever-changing pleasures.

What are the *conditions* for the development of character-rooted passions?

We must consider first that these passions do not appear as single units but as *syndromes*. Love, solidarity, justice, reason are interrelated; they are all manifestations of the same productive orientation that I shall call the 'life-furthering syndrome'. On the other hand, sadomasochism, destructiveness, greed, narcissism, incestuousness also belong together and are rooted in the same basic orientation: 'life-thwarting syndrome'. Where one element of the syndrome is to be found, the others also exist in various degrees, but this does not mean that someone is ruled either by the one *or* by the other syndrome. In fact, people in whom this is the case are the exceptions: the average person is a blend of both syndromes; what matters for the behaviour of the person and the possibility of change is precisely the respective strength of each syndrome.

Neurophysiological Conditions

As to the neurophysiological conditions for the development of the two respective kinds of passions, we must start out from the fact that man is unfinished and 'uncompleted'. (L. Eiseley, 1971.) Not only is his brain not fully developed at birth, but the state of disequilibrium in which he finds himself leaves him as an open-ended process to which there is no final solution.

But is he – being deprived of the help of instincts and equipped only with the 'weak reed' of reason by which he deceives himself so easily – left without any help from his neurophysiological equipment? It seems that this assumption would miss an important point. His brain, so superior to that of the primate not only in size but also in the quality and structure of its neurons, has the capacity to recognize what kinds of goals are conducive to man's health and growth, physically as well as psychically. It can set goals leading to the realization of man's real, rational needs, and man can organize his society in ways conducive to this realization. Man is not only unfinished, incomplete, burdened by contradictions; he can also be defined as a *being in active search of his optimal development*, even though this search must often fail because external conditions are too unfavourable.

The assumption that man is a being in active search of his optimal development is not without support from neuro-physiological data. No less an investigator than C. J. Herrick wrote:

Man's capacity for intelligently directed self-development confers upon him the ability to determine the pattern of his culture and so to shape the course of human evolution in directions of his own choice. This ability, which no other animals have, is man's most distinctive characteristic, and it is perhaps the most significant fact known to science. (C. J. Herrick, 1928)

Livingston makes some very pertinent remarks with regard to the same problem:

It is not established beyond peradventure of doubt that various levels of nervous system organization are interdependently inter-related with one another. Somehow, *by means that are still mysterious, purposive behaviour organized at each of these different levels of integrative function becomes expressed by a linked sequence of overall purposes representing some kind of final judicious reckoning* among contending functions. The purposes of the whole organism are clearly manifested and continuously served according to some integrated internal point of view. (R. B. Livingston, 1967a; italics added)

Discussing the problem of needs that transcend the primary physiological ones Livingston states:

Some goal-seeking systems at the molecular level can be identified by physical-chemical techniques. Other goal-seeking systems at the level of the brain circuitry can be identified by neuro-physiological techniques. At each level, parts of these systems are concerned with the appetites and satisfactions that govern behaviour. All of these goal-seeking systems originate in and are intrinsic to protoplasmic materials. Many such systems are peculiarly specialized and are located in particular nervous and endocrine systems. Evolutionarily elaborate organisms possess appetites and satisfactions, not only to fulfil vegetative needs; not simply for the obligate cooperations required for sexual union, the rearing of young, and the safeguarding of food, family and territory; not just for the adaptive behaviours essential to meet successfully the vicissitudes of environmental change; but also for *extra energies*, strivings, and outreachings – the *extravagances that go beyond mere survival*. (R. B. Livingston, 1967; italics added)

He goes on to say:

The brain is a product of evolution, just as are teeth and claws; but we can expect much more of the brain because of its capacities for constructive adaptation. Neuroscientists can take as their long-range objective the understanding of the fullest potentialities of mankind in order to help humanity become more fully self-aware and to illuminate man's nobler options. Above all, it is the human brain, with its capacities for memory, learning, communication, imagination, creativity, and the powers of self-awareness, that distinguishes humanity. (R. B. Livingston, 1967)

Livingston holds that cooperation, faith, mutual trust, and altruism are built into the fabric of the nervous system and propelled by internal satisfactions attached to them.[24] Internal satisfactions are by no means restricted to the appetites. According to Livingston:

Gratifications also relate to positive satisfactions springing from buoyant health, vigorous and rested; delight accompanying both genetically endowed and socially acquired values; joys, solitary and shared feelings of pleasant excitement, engendered by exposure to novelty and during the quest for novelty. Gratifications result from satisfaction of curiosity and the pleasure of inquiry, from the acquisition of widening degrees of individual and collective freedom. Positive features of satisfaction enable humans to sustain unbelievable privations and yet to cling to life and, beyond that, to attach importance to beliefs that may pass the values of life itself. (R. B. Livingston, 1967)

Livingston's crucial point, as well as that of the other authors to be cited in the following, is in fundamental opposition to older instinctivistic thinking. They do not

24. He adds that mammals and many other forms of life could not survive a single generation without built-in cooperative behaviour, thus confirming P. Kropotkin's findings in his famous book *Mutual Aid* (1955).

speculate on which *special* area of the brain 'generates' higher strivings, such as those for solidarity, altruism, mutual trust, and truth, but they look at *the brain system as a whole from the standpoint of evolution in the service of survival*.

One very interesting suggestion has been made by C. von Monakow. He proposed the existence of a *biological conscience* (syneidesis), whose function it is to secure optimal security satisfaction, adaptation, and strivings for perfection. Von Monakow argues that the functioning of the organism in a direction serving its development gives *Klisis* (joy, lust, happiness) – hence a desire to repeat this kind of behaviour; on the other hand, behaviour harmful to the optimal development of the organism results in *Ekklesis* (unpleasure, bad feeling) and drives a person to avoid the pain-producing behaviour (C. von Monakow, 1950).

H. von Foerster has argued that empathy and love are qualities inherent in the brain system. His starting point is the theory of cognition, and he raises the question of how it is possible for two people to communicate, since language presupposes shared experience. Since environment does not exist for man by itself but in its relationship to the human observer, von Foerster reasons, communication presupposes that we find

the like representation of environment in the two elements who are separated by their skins, but alike in their structure. When they realize and utilize this insight then A knows what A* knows, because A identifies himself with A* and we have the equality I-Thou ... Clearly, identification is the strongest coalition – and its most subtle manifestation is love. (H. von Foerster, 1963)[25]

All these speculations, however, seem to be contradicted by the hard fact that man in the forty thousand years since his final birth has failed to develop these 'higher' strivings

25. Shared experience is specifically the basis of all psychological understanding; the understanding of the unconscious of another person pre-supposes that we understand the other because we have access to our own unconscious and thus can share his experience. See E. Fromm, D. T. Suzuki, and R. de Martino (1960).

more fully but seems to have been governed principally by his greed and destructiveness. Why did the biologically built-in strivings not remain – or become – predominant?

Before entering into a discussion of this question, let us qualify it. While granting that we do not have much direct knowledge of man's psyche before the beginning of the Neolithic period, there are, as we have seen, good reasons to assume that the most primitive men, from the hunter-gatherers up to the early agriculturalists, were not characterized by destructiveness or sadism. In fact, the negative qualities that are commonly attributed to human nature became more powerful and widespread as civilization developed. Furthermore, it should be kept in mind that the version of the 'higher goals' was expressed early in history by great teachers who proclaimed the new goals in protest against the principles of their respective cultures; and these aims, in both religious and secular form, have had a profound appeal again and again to the hearts of men who were conditioned by their society to believe in the contrary. Indeed, man's striving for freedom, dignity, solidarity, and truth has been one of the strongest motivations to bring about historical change.

Even considering all these qualifications, however, the fact remains that built-in higher tendencies have thus far been largely defeated, and persons living today experience this with special anxiety.

Social Conditions

What are the reasons for this defeat?

The only satisfactory answer to this question seems to lie in the social circumstances under which man lives. Throughout most of his history these circumstances, while furthering man's intellectual and technical development, have been inimical to the full development of those built-in potentialities to which the authors cited above are referring.

The most elementary instances showing the influence of

environmental factors on personality are those of the *direct* influence of environment on the growth of the brain. It is by now a well-established fact that malnutrition can prevent the normal growth of the infant's brain. That not only food, but other factors, such as freedom of movement and play, can have a direct influence on the growth of the brain has also been shown by animal experiments. Investigators separated rats into two groups and placed them, respectively, in 'enriched' and 'restricted' environments. The former were raised in a large cage where they could move freely, play with various objects and with each other, whereas the 'restricted' animals were raised singly in small isolation cages. In other words, the 'enriched' animals had a much greater opportunity for stimulation and motor exercise than the 'restricted' animals. The investigators found that in the first group the cortical grey matter was thicker than in the 'restricted' group – although their body weight was lower (E. L. Bennett *et al.*, 1964).

In a similar study Altman 'obtained histological evidence of an increase in the area of the cortex in the enriched animals, and autoradiographic evidence of an enhanced rate of cellular proliferation in the mature enriched animals' (J. Altman and G. D. Das, 1964). Preliminary results from Altman's laboratory 'indicate that other behavioural variables, such as handling rats during infancy, can radically alter the development of the brain, in particular cell proliferation in such structures as the cerebellar cortex, the hippocampal dentate gyrus, and the neocortex' (J. Altman, 1967a).

Applying the results of these experiments to man would suggest that the growth of the brain depends not only on such outside factors as food, but also on the 'warmth' with which a baby is handled and held, on the degree of stimulation it receives, and on the degree of freedom it has to move, to play, and to express itself. But brain development does not stop in infancy, or even in puberty or adulthood. As R. B. Livingston has pointed out: 'There is no point beyond which development ceases, beyond which the capacities for reorganization following disease or injury disappear' (R. B. Livingston, 1967). It seems that throughout life such environmental factors as stimulation, encouragement, and affection may continue to have a subtle influence on brain process.

We know little as yet about the direct influence of the environment on the development of the brain. Fortunately we know a great deal more about the role of social factors on the development of character (although all affective processes have, of course, a substrate in brain processes). It would seem that at this point we have joined the main stream of thought in the social sciences – the thesis that man's character is formed by the society in which he lives, or, in behaviouristic terms, by the social conditioning to which he is exposed. However, there is a fundamental difference between this view and the one proposed here. The environmentalist view of the social sciences is essentially relativistic; according to it, man is a blank sheet of paper on which the culture writes its text. He is moulded by his society for, better or worse, 'better' or 'worse' being considered value judgements from an ethical or religious standpoint.[26] The position taken here assumes that man has an immanent goal, that man's biological constitution is the source of norms for living. He has the possibility for full development and growth, *provided the external conditions that are given are conducive to this aim.*

This means that there are specific environmental conditions conducive to the optimal growth of man and, if our previous assumptions are correct, to the development of the life-furthering syndrome. On the other hand, to the

26. The outstanding exception to the conventional environmentalist view is that of Marx, even though vulgar Marxism in its Stalinist or reformist version has done everything to obscure this. Marx proposed a concept of 'human nature in general' as distinct from 'human nature as modified in each historical epoch' (K. Marx, 1906). For him certain social conditions, such as capitalism, produce a 'crippled' man. Socialism, as he conceived it, will be conducive to the full self-realization of man.

extent these conditions are lacking, he will become a crippled, stunted man, characterized by the presence of the life-thwarting syndrome.

It is truly astonishing that this view should be considered 'idealistic' or 'unscientific' by so many who would not dream of questioning the relation between constitution and norms in regard to physical development and health. It is hardly necessary to belabour this point. There exists a wealth of data, particularly in the field of nutrition, to demonstrate that certain kinds of food are conducive to growth and the health of the body, while others are responsible for organic dysfunctioning, illness, and premature death. It is also well known that not only food can have such influence on health, but also other factors, such as exercise or stress. Man in this respect is not different from any other organism. As any farmer or horticulturalist knows, the seed, for its proper germination and for the growth of the plant, needs a certain degree of moisture, warmth, and type of soil. If these conditions are not met, the seed will rot and die in the soil; the plant will be stillborn. If the conditions are optimal, the fruit tree will grow to its optimal possibility and bear fruit that is as perfect as this particular tree can produce. If the conditions are less than optimal, the tree and its fruit will be defective or crippled.

The question, then, that confronts us is: Which are the environmental conditions that are conducive to the full development of man's potentialities?

Many thousands of books have been written about this question, and hundreds of different answers have been given. Surely I shall not attempt to give an answer within the context of this book.[27] Some general statements, however, can be made, even if briefly:

The historical record as well as the study of individuals indicate that the presence of freedom, activating stimuli, the absence of exploitative control, and the presence of

27. cf. E. Fromm (1955).

'man-centred' modes of production are favourable for the growth of man; and that the presence of the opposite conditions is unfavourable. Furthermore, an increasing number of people have become aware of the fact that it is not the presence of one or two conditions that have an impact, but a whole system of factors. This means that the general conditions conducive to the fullest growth of man – and, of course, each stage of individual development has its own specific conditions – can only be found in a social system in which various favourable conditions are combined to secure the right soil.

The reasons why social scientists have not considered the question of the optimal social conditions for man's growth a matter of primary concern can be easily discerned if one recognizes the sad fact that, with a few outstanding exceptions, social scientists are essentially apologists for and not critics of the existing social system. This can be so because, unlike the natural sciences, their results are of little value for the functioning of society. On the contrary, erroneous results and superficial treatment have a useful function as ideological 'cement', while the truth is, as always, a threat to the *status quo*.[28] In addition, the task of studying the problem adequately has been made more difficult by the assumption that 'what people desire is good for them'. One overlooked the fact that people's desires are often harmful for them, and that the desires themselves can be symptoms of dysfunctioning, or of suggestion, or of both. Everybody today knows, for instance, that drug addiction is not desirable, even if many people desire the use of drugs. Since our whole economic system rests on generating desires that the commodities can profitably satisfy, it is hardly to be expected that a critical analysis of the irrationality of desires would be popular.

But we cannot stop here. Why, we must ask, do not the majority of men use their reason to recognize their real interests as human beings? Is it only because they have been

28. cf. the brilliant critique of the social sciences by S. Andreski (1972).

brainwashed and forced to obey? Furthermore, why have not a greater number of leaders recognized that their own best interests as human beings were not served by the system they presided over? To explain everything in terms of their greed or their cunning, as the philosophers of the Enlightenment were prone to do, does not penetrate to the core of the problem.

As Marx has demonstrated in his theory of historical development, in the attempt to change and improve social conditions man is constantly limited by the material factors of his environment, such as ecological conditions, climate, technique, geographical situation, and cultural traditions. As we have seen, primitive hunter-gatherers and early agriculturalists lived in a relatively well-balanced environment that was conducive to generating constructive rather than destructive passions. But in the process of growth, man changes, and he changes his environment. He progresses intellectually and technologically; this progress, however, creates situations that are conducive to the development of the life-thwarting character syndrome. We have followed this development, however sketchily, in the description of the transformation of society from that of early hunter-gatherers to the 'urban revolution'. In order to create the necessary leisure to enable men to become philosophers and scholars, to build works of art like the Egyptian pyramids – briefly, in order to create culture – man had to have slaves, make war, and conquer territory. It was for this very growth in some respects, particularly intellectually, artistically, and scientifically, that man had to create circumstances that crippled him and prevented his growth in other respects, particularly affectively. This was so because the productive forces were not sufficiently developed to permit the coexistence of both technical and cultural progress *and* freedom, to permit uncrippled development for all. The material conditions have their own laws and the wish to change them is of itself not enough. Indeed, if the earth had been created as a paradise where man would not be bound by the stubbornness of material reality, his reason might have been sufficient condition to create the proper environment for his unimpeded growth, with enough for all to eat and, simultaneously, the possibility of freedom. But to speak in terms of the biblical myth, man was expelled from Paradise and cannot return. He was saddled with the curse of the conflict between himself and nature. The world was not made for man; he is thrown into it, and only by his own activity and reason can he create a world which is conducive to his full development, which is his human home. His rulers themselves were executors of historical necessity, even though they were often evil men who followed their whims and failed to execute their historical task. Irrationality and personal evil became decisive factors only in those periods when the external conditions were such that they would have permitted human progress and when this progress was impeded by the character deformation of the rulers – and the ruled.

Nevertheless, there have always been visionaries who clearly recognized the goals for man's social and individual evolution. But their 'Utopias' were not 'utopic' in the sense that they were unrealizable daydreams. They took place in the nowhere (u-topia). But nowhere is not 'at-no-time'. By this I mean to say, they were 'Utopian' because they did not exist at the moment at any given place – and perhaps could not exist; but Utopian does not mean that they cannot be realized in time – at another time. Marx's concept of socialism, until now unrealized anywhere in the world (and certainly not in the Socialist countries), was not considered a Utopia by him because he believed that at this point of historical evolution the material conditions for its realization were already present.[29]

29. This is the crucial point in which Sartre has never truly understood or integrated Marx's thought, trying to combine essentially voluntaristic theory with Marx's theory of history. cf. the excellent critique of Sartre by R. Dunayevskaya (1973).

On the Rationality of Instincts and Passions

It is a widely accepted notion that instincts are irrational because they defy logical thought. Is this correct? Furthermore, can the character-rooted passions be classified as either rational or irrational?

The terms 'reason' and 'rational' are conventionally applied only to thought processes; a 'rational' thought is supposed to obey the laws of logic and not to be distorted by emotional and often pathological factors. But 'rational' and 'irrational' are sometimes also applied to actions and feelings. Thus an economist may call irrational the introduction of expensive labour-saving machinery in a country that lacks skilled and abounds in unskilled workers. Or he may call the annual world expenditure of $180 billion for armaments (80 per cent of it by the superpowers) irrational because it serves the production of things that have no use value in times of peace. Or a psychiatrist may call a neurotic symptom, such as a wash compulsion or groundless anxieties, irrational because they are the outcome of a dysfunction of the mind and tend to further disturb its proper functioning.

I propose to call *rational any thought, feeling or act that promotes the adequate functioning and growth of the whole of which it is a part, and irrational that which tends to weaken or destroy the whole*. It is obvious that only the empirical analysis of a system can show what is to be considered rational or irrational, respectively.[30]

30. Although this use of rational is not customary philosophic terminology today, it has its basis in Western tradition. For Heraclitus *logos* (of which the Latin *ratio* is a translation) is an underlying organizational principle of the universe, related to the common meaning in his time of the logos as a 'proportion' (W. K. Guthrie, 1962). Also in Heraclitus, to follow the logos is 'to be awake'. Aristotle uses logos as reason in an ethical context (*Ethica Nicomachea*, V. 1134a) and frequently in the combination 'right reason'. Thomas Aquinas speaks of 'rational appetite' (*appetitus rationalis*) and distinguishes between reason concerned with action and deed, and reason concerned solely with knowledge. Spinoza speaks of rational and irrational affects, Pascal of

Applying this concept of rationality to instincts (organic drives), the unavoidable conclusion is that they are rational. From a Darwinian standpoint, it is precisely the function of instincts to sustain life adequately, to ensure the survival of the individual and the species. The animal behaves rationally because it is almost entirely determined by instinct, and man would behave rationally if he were mainly determined by instinct. His search for food, his defensive aggressiveness (or flight), and his sexual desires, as far as they are organically stimulated, are not conducive to irrational behaviour. Man's irrationality is caused by the fact that he lacks instincts, and not by their presence.

What about the rationality of his character-rooted passions? Following our criterion of rationality, they must be divided. The life-furthering passions must be considered rational because they further the growth and well-being of the organism; the life-strangling passions must be considered irrational because they interfere with growing and well-being. But a qualification is necessary. The destructive or cruel person has become so because he lacks the conditions for further growth. Under the given circumstances he cannot, as it were, do better. His passions are irrational in terms of the possibilities of man, yet they have their rationality in terms of the particular individual and social situation within which a person lives. The same applies to the historical process. The 'mega-machines' (L. Mumford, 1967) of antiquity were rational in this sense, even Fascism and Stalinism could be considered rational if they were the only historically possible next step under the circumstances. This, of course, is what their defenders claim. But they would have to prove that there were no

---

emotional reasoning. For Kant, practical reason (*Vernunft*) has the function of recognizing what *should be done*, while theoretical reason makes one recognize *what is*. Compare also Hegel's use of rationality in reference to emotions. Finally, I want to mention in this brief survey Whitehead's statement that 'the function of reason is to promote the art of life' (A. N. Whitehead, 1967).

other and historically more adequate options available, as I believe there were.[31]

It needs to be repeated that life-thwarting passions are as much an answer to man's existential needs as life-furthering passions: they are both profoundly human. The former necessarily develop when the realistic conditions for the realization of the latter are absent. Man the destroyer may be called vicious because destructiveness is a vice; but he is human. He has not 'regressed to animal existence' and is not motivated by animal instincts; he cannot change the structure of his brain. One might consider him an *existential failure*, a man who has failed to become what he could be according to the possibilities of his existence. In any case, for a man to be stunted in his growth and become vicious is as much a real possibility as to develop fully and to be productive; the one or the other outcome mainly depends on the presence – or absence – of social conditions conducive to growth.

It must at the same time be added that in speaking of social circumstances as being responsible for man's development, I do not imply that he is the helpless object of circumstances. Environmental factors further or hinder the development of certain traits and set the limits within which man acts. Nevertheless, man's reason and will are powerful factors in the process of his development, individually and socially. It is not history that makes man; man creates himself in the process of history. Only dogmatic thinking, the result of the laziness of mind and heart, tries to construct simplistic schemes of the either-or type that block any real understanding.[32]

31. This problem has been much obscured by the Freudian scheme of Id–Ego–Super-ego. This division has forced psychoanalytic theory to consider as belonging to the ego all that does not belong to the id or super-ego, and this simplistic (although often very sophisticated) approach has blocked the analysis of the problem of rationality.

32. Man is never so determined that a basic change, stimulated by a number of possible events and experiences, is not possible at some period of his life. His potential for life affirmation is never completely

Psychical Functions of the Passions

Man must satisfy his bodily needs in order to survive, and his instincts motivate him to act in favour of his survival. If his instincts determined most of his behaviour, he would have no special problems in living and would be 'a contented cow' provided he had ample food.[33] But for man the satisfaction of his organic drives alone does not make him happy, nor does it guarantee his sanity. Nor is his problem that of first satisfying his physical needs and then, as a kind of luxury, developing his character-rooted passions. The latter are present from the very beginning of his existence, and often have even greater strength than his organic drives.

When we look at individual and mass behaviour we find that the desire to satisfy hunger and sex constitutes only a minor part of human motivation. The major motivations of man are his rational and irrational passions: the strivings for love,[34] tenderness, solidarity, freedom, and truth, as well as the drive to control, to submit, to destroy; narcissism,

---

dead, and one can never predict that it will not emerge. This is the reason genuine conversion (repentance) can occur. To prove this thesis would require a book by itself. I shall refer here only to the ample material on profound changes that can occur in psychoanalytic therapy and the many changes that occur 'spontaneously'. The most impressive proof for the fact that environment inclines, but does not determine, is offered by the historical record. Even in the most vicious societies there are always outstanding personalities who embody the highest form of human existence. Some of them have been spokesmen for humanity, 'saviours', without whom man might have lost the vision of his goal; others remained unknown. They were the ones to whom the Jewish legend refers as the thirty-six just men in each generation, whose existence guarantees the survival of mankind.

33. This picture needs to be qualified even with regard to animals that have needs beyond their physiological survival – for instance, the need to play.

34. Of course animal infants need 'love', too, and its quality may differ little from that needed by human infants. But it differs from non-narcissistic human love which is referred to here.

greed, envy, ambition. These passions move him and excite him; they are the stuff from which not only dreams, but all religions, myths, drama, art are made – in short, all that makes life meaningful and worth living. People motivated by these passions risk their lives. They may commit suicide when they fail to attain the goal of their passion; but they do not commit suicide for the lack of sexual satisfaction, and not even because they are starving. But whether they are driven by hate or love, the power of the human passion is the same.

That this is so can hardly be doubted. The question why it is so is more difficult to answer. Yet some hypothetical speculations can be offered.

The first is a suggestion which only neurophysiologists could examine. Considering that the brain is in need of constant excitation, a fact we have already discussed, one could imagine that this need would require the existence of passionate strivings because they alone provide for constant excitation.

Another hypothesis lies in the realm already dealt with in this book – the uniqueness of human experience. As we have said, the fact that man is aware of himself, of his powerlessness and isolation, seems to make it intolerable for him to live as nothing but an object. All this, of course, was well-known to most thinkers, dramatists, and novelists throughout history. Can one really imagine that the core of the Oedipus drama is the frustration of Oedipus's sexual desires for his mother? Or that Shakespeare could have written a *Hamlet* centred around the sexual frustration of the play's principal character? Yet that is precisely what classic psychoanalysts seem to imagine, and with them, other contemporary reductionists.

Man's instinctual drives are necessary but trivial; man's passions that unify his energy in the search of their goal belong to the realm of the devotional or sacred. The system of the trivial is that of 'making a living'; the sphere of the 'sacred' is that of living beyond physical survival – it is the sphere in which man stakes his fate, often his life, the sphere in which his deepest motivations, those that make life worth living, are rooted.[35]

In his attempt to transcend the triviality of his life man is driven to seek adventure, to look beyond and even to cross the limiting frontier of human existence. This is what makes great virtues and great vices, creation as well as destruction, so exciting and attractive. The hero is the one who has the courage to go to the frontier without succumbing to fear and doubt. The average man is a hero even in his unsuccessful attempt to be a hero; he is motivated by the desire to make some sense of his life and by the passion to walk as far as *he* can to its frontiers.

This picture needs an important qualification. Individuals live in a society that provides them with ready-made patterns that pretend to give meaning to their lives. In our society, for instance, they are told that to be successful, to be a 'bread winner', to raise a family, to be a good citizen, to consume goods and pleasures gives meaning to life. But while for most people this suggestion works on the conscious level, they do not acquire a genuine sense of meaningfulness, they do not make up for the lacking centre within themselves. The suggested patterns wear thin and with increasing frequency fail. That this is happening today on a large scale is evidenced by the increase in drug addiction, by the lack of genuine interest in anything, in the decline of intellectual and artistic creativity, and in the increase of violence and destructiveness.

35. In order to appreciate this distinction properly one must remember that what a person *calls* sacred is not necessarily so. Today for instance, the concepts and symbols of Christianity are held to be sacred, although they no longer elicit a passionate involvement for most church-goers; on the other hand, the striving for the conquest of nature, for fame, power, and money, which are the real objects of devotion, are not called sacred because they have not been integrated into an explicit religious system. Only exceptionally, when one has spoken of 'sacred egoism' (in a national sense), or 'sacred revenge' has this been different in modern times.

11
Malignant Aggression: Cruelty and Destructiveness

Apparent Destructiveness

Very different from destructiveness are certain deeply buried archaic experiences that often appear to the modern observer as proofs for man's innate destructive acts. Yet a closer analysis can show that while they result in destructive acts, their motivation is not the passion to destroy.

One example is the passion to spill blood, often called 'blood lust'. For all practical purposes, to shed a person's blood means to kill him, and thus 'killing' and 'shedding blood' are synonyms. Yet the question arises whether there may not be an archaic pleasure in shedding blood that is different from the pleasure in killing.

At a deep, archaic level of experience, blood is a very peculiar substance. Quite generally, it has been equated with life and the life-force, and is one of the three sacred substances that emanate from the body. The other two are semen and milk. Semen expresses male, while milk expresses female and motherly creativity, and both were considered sacred in many cults and rituals. Blood transcends the difference between male and female. In the deepest layers of experience, one magically seizes upon the life-force itself by shedding blood.

The use of blood for religious purposes is well known. The priests of the Hebrew temple spread blood from the slaughtered animals as part of the service; the Aztec priests offered their gods the still-palpitating hearts of their victims. In many ritual customs brotherhood is confirmed symbolically by mixing together the blood of the persons involved.

Since blood is the 'juice of life', drinking blood is experienced in many instances as enhancing one's own life energy. In the orgies of Bacchus as well as in the rituals related to Ceres, one part of the mystery consisted of eating the raw flesh of the animal together with the blood. In the Dionysian festivals in Crete they used to tear the flesh off the living animal with their teeth. Such rituals are also to be found in relation to many chtonic gods and goddesses (J. Bryant, 1775). J. G. Bourke mentions that the Aryans who invaded India held the native Dasyu Indians in contempt because they ate uncooked human and animal flesh, and they expressed their natural disgust by calling them 'raw eaters'.[1] Very closely related to this drinking of blood and eating of raw meat are customs reported from still-existing primitive tribes. At certain religious ceremonies it is the duty of the Hamatsa Indians of north-west Canada to bite a piece of the arm, leg, or breast of a man.[2] That the drinking of blood is considered health-giving can even be seen in recent times. It was a Bulgarian custom to give a man who has been badly frightened the quivering heart of a dove slaughtered at that moment, to aid him in recovering from his fright (J. G. Bourke, 1913). Even in as highly developed a religion as Roman Catholicism we find the archaic practice of drinking wine after it has been consecrated as Christ's blood; and it would be a reductionist distortion to assume that this ritual is the expression of destructive impulses, rather than an affirmation of life and an expression of community.

To modern man the shedding of blood appears to be nothing but destructiveness. Certainly from a 'realistic'

1. How late this ritual of eating the flesh from a living animal must have existed can be seen from a Talmudic tradition which states that among the seven ethical norms accepted already by Noah (and through him by all mankind) was the prohibition to eat meat from a living animal.

2. Report on the North Western Indians of Canada, in *Proceedings of the British Association for the Advancement of Science*, meeting at Newcastle-upon-Tyne, 1889 (quoted by J. G. Bourke, 1913).

standpoint that is what it is, but if one considers not only the act itself but its meaning in the deepest and most archaic layers of experience, then one may arrive at a different conclusion. By shedding one's own blood or that of another, one is in touch with the life-force; this in itself can be an intoxicating experience on the archaic level, and when it is offered to the gods, it can be an act of the most sacred devotion; the wish to destroy need not be the motive.

Similar considerations apply also to the phenomenon of cannibalism. Those who argue in favour of man's innate destructiveness have often used cannibalism as a major argument to prove their theory. They point to the fact that in the Choukoutien caves skulls were found from which the brains had been extracted through the base. It was speculated that this was done in order to eat the brain, whose taste the killers allegedly liked. That is, of course, a possibility, although one that corresponds perhaps more to the view of the modern consumer. A more likely explanation is that the brain was used for magic-ritualistic purposes. As indicated earlier, this position has been taken by A. C. Blanc (1961), who found a strong similarity between the Peking Man skulls and those found in Monte Circeo dating almost half a million years later. If this interpretation is correct, the same holds true for ritualistic cannibalism and ritualistic drinking and shedding of blood.

To be sure, non-ritualistic cannibalism was a common practice among 'primitive' people in the last centuries. From all we know about the character of the hunter-food-gatherers still living today, or can assume about the prehistoric ones, they were not killers, and it is very unlikely that they were cannibals. As Mumford puts it succinctly: 'Just as primitive man was incapable of our own massive exhibitions of cruelty, torture and extermination, so he may have been quite innocent of manslaughter for food' (L. Mumford, 1967).

The foregoing remarks are meant as a warning against the

hasty interpretation of all destructive behaviour as the outcome of a destructive instinct, rather than to recognize the frequency of religious and non-destructive motivations behind such behaviour. They were not intended to minimize the outbursts of real cruelty and destructiveness to which we now turn.

Spontaneous Forms

Destructiveness[3] appears in two forms: spontaneous, and bound in the character structure. By the former I refer to the outburst of dormant (not necessarily repressed) destructive impulses that are activated by extraordinary circumstances, in contrast to the permanent, although not always expressed, presence of destructive traits in the character.

The Historical Record

The most ample – and horrifying – documentation for seemingly spontaneous forms of destructiveness are on the record of civilized history. The history of war is a report of ruthless and indiscriminate killing and torture, whose victims were men, women, and children. Many of these occurrences give the impression of orgies of destruction, in which neither conventional nor genuinely moral factors had any inhibitory effect. Killing was still the mildest manifestation of destructiveness. But the orgies did not stop here: men were castrated, women were disembowelled, prisoners were crucified or thrown before the lions. There is hardly a destructive act human imagination could think of that has not been acted out again and again. We have witnessed the same frenzied mutual killing of hundreds of

3. I use the term 'destructiveness' here to include both destructiveness proper ('necrophilia') and sadism, a distinction that will be made later.

thousands of Hindus and Moslems in India during the partition, and in Indonesia in the anti-Communist purge in 1965, where, according to varying sources, from four hundred thousand to a million real or alleged Communists, together with many Chinese were slaughtered (M. Caldwell, 1968). I need not go further in giving a more detailed description of the manifestations of human destructiveness: they are well known and, besides, often quoted by those who want to prove that destructiveness is innate, as for instance D. Freeman (1964).

As to the causes of destructiveness, they will be dealt with when we shall discuss sadism and necrophilia. I mentioned these outbursts here in order to give examples for destructiveness that is not bound in the character structure, as is the case with the sadistic and necrophilous character. But these destructive explosions are not spontaneous in the sense that they break out without any reason. In the first place, there are always external conditions that stimulate them, such as wars, religious or political conflicts, poverty, extreme boredom and insignificance of the individual. Secondly, there are subjective reasons: extreme group narcissism in national or religious terms, as in India, a certain proneness to a state of trance, as in parts of Indonesia. It is not human nature that makes a sudden appearance, but the destructive potential that is fostered by certain permanent conditions and mobilized by sudden traumatic events. Without these provoking factors, the destructive energies in these populations seem to be dormant, and not, as with the destructive *character*, a constantly flowing source of energy.

Vengeful Destructiveness

Vengeful destructiveness is a spontaneous reaction to intense and unjustified suffering inflicted upon a person or the members of the group with whom he is identified. It differs from normal defensive aggression in two ways: (1) it occurs *after* the damage has been done, and hence is not a defence against a *threatening* danger; (2) it is of much greater intensity, and is often cruel, lustful, and insatiable. Language itself expresses this particular quality of vengeance in the term 'thirst for vengeance'.

It hardly needs to be emphasized how widespread vengeful aggression is, both among individuals and groups. We find it in the form of blood revenge as an institution practically all over the world: east and north-east Africa, the Upper Congo, West Africa, among many frontier tribes in north-east India, Bengal, New Guinea, Polynesia, in Corsica (until recently), and it was widespread among the North American aborigines (M. R. Davie, 1929). Blood revenge is a sacred duty that falls upon the member of a family, clan, or tribe who has to kill a member of the corresponding unit if one of his people has been killed. In contrast to simple punishment, where the crime is expiated by the punishment of the murderer or those to whom he belongs, in the case of blood revenge the punishment of the aggressor does not end the sequence. The punitive killing represents a new killing which in turn obliges the members of the punished group to punish the punisher and so on *ad infinitum*. Theoretically, blood revenge is an endless chain, and in fact it sometimes leads to the extinction of families or larger groups. One even finds blood revenge – although as an exception – among very peaceful populations like the Greenlanders, who do not know the meaning of war, although as Davie writes: 'The practice is but slightly developed and the duty does not as a rule seem to weigh heavily upon the survivors' (M. R. Davie, 1929).

Not only blood revenge but all forms of punishment – from primitive to modern – are an expression of vengeance (K. A. Menninger, 1968). The classic example is the *lex talionis* of the Old Testament. The threat to punish a misdeed up to the third and fourth generation must also be considered an expression of revenge by a god whose commands have been disobeyed, even though it seems that the attempt was to weaken the traditional concept by adding 'keeping mercy for thousands, forgiving inequity, trans-gressions and sin'. The same idea can be found in many primitive societies – for instance, in the law of the Yakuts which says 'The blood of a man, if spilled, requires atone-ment.' Among the Yakuts the children of the murdered took vengeance on the children of the murderer to the ninth generation (M. R. Davie, 1929).

It cannot be denied that blood vengeance and criminal law, bad as they are, also have a certain social function in upholding social stability. The full power of the lust for vengeance can be seen in those instances where this function is lacking. Thus a large number of Germans were motivated by the wish for revenge because of the loss of the war in 1914–18, or more specifically because of the injustice of the Versailles peace treaty in its material conditions, and particularly in its demand that the German government should accept sole responsibility for the outbreak of the war. It is notorious that real or alleged atrocities can ignite the most intense rage and vengefulness. Hitler made the alleged mistreatment of the German minorities in Czechoslovakia the centre of the propaganda before he attacked the country; the wholesale massacre in Indonesia in 1965 was initially inflamed by the story of the mutilation of some generals who were opposed to Sukarno. One example of thirst for revenge that has lasted almost two thousand years is the reaction to the execution of Jesus allegedly by the Jews; the cry 'Christ-killers' has traditionally been one of the major sources of violent anti-Semitism.

Why is vengeance such a deep-seated and intense passion? I can only offer some speculations. Let us consider first the idea that vengeance is in some sense a magic act. By destroying the one who committed the atrocity his deed is magically undone. This is still expressed today by saying that through his punishment 'the criminal has paid his debt'; at least in theory, he is like someone who never committed a crime. Vengeance may be said to be a magic reparation; but even assuming that this is so, why is this desire for reparation so intense? Perhaps man is endowed with an elementary sense of justice; this may be because there is a deep-rooted sense of 'existential equality': we all are born from mothers, we were once powerless children, and we shall all die.[4] Although man can often not defend himself against the harm others inflict upon him, in his wish for revenge he tries to wipe the sheet clean by denying, magically, that the damage was ever done. (It seems that envy[5] has the same root. Cain could not stand the fact that he was rejected while his brother was accepted. The rejection was arbitrary, and it was not in his power to change it; this fundamental injustice aroused such envy that the score could only be evened out by killing Abel.) But there must be more to the cause of vengeance. Man seems to take justice into his own hands when God or secular authorities fail. It is as if in his passion for vengeance he elevates himself to the role of God and of the angels of vengeance. The act of vengeance may be his greatest hour just because of this self-elevation.

We can entertain some further speculations. Cruelties like physical mutilation, castration and torture violate the minimal demands of conscience common to all men. Is the passion for vengeance against those who commit such inhuman acts mobilized by this elementary conscience? Or could it be, in addition, a defence against the awareness of one's own destructiveness by the projective device: they – not I – are destructive and cruel?

Answers to these questions require further studies of the phenomenon of vengeance.

The considerations offered thus far, however, seem to support the view that the passion for vengeance is so deep-seated that one must think of it as being present in all men. Yet this assumption does not fit the facts. While it is indeed widespread, there are great differences in degree, up to the

4. Shylock in *The Merchant of Venice*, III, i, gives a beautiful and moving expression to this elementary sense of equality.

5. cf. G. M. Foster (1972).

point that certain cultures[6] and individuals seem to have only minimal traces of it. There must be factors that explain the difference. One such factor is that of scarcity versus abundance. The person – or group – who has confidence in life and enjoys it, whose material resources may not be ample but sufficient not to elicit stinginess, will be less eager for the reparation of damage than an anxious, hoarding person who is afraid that he can never make up for his losses.

This much can be stated with some degree of probability: the thirst for revenge can be plotted on a line at one end of which are people in whom nothing will arouse a wish for revenge; these are men who have reached a degree of development which in Buddhist or Christian terms is the ideal for all men. On the other end would be those who have an anxious, hoarding, or extremely narcissistic character, for whom even a slight damage will arouse an intense craving for revenge. This type would be exemplified by a man from whom a thief has stolen a few dollars and who wants him to be severely punished; or a professor who has been slighted by a student and therefore writes a negative report on him when he is asked to recommend the student for a good job; or a customer who has been treated 'wrongly' by a salesman and complains to the management, wanting the man to be fired. In these cases we are dealing with a character in which vengeance is a constantly present trait.

Ecstatic Destructiveness

Suffering from the awareness of his powerlessness and separateness, man can try to overcome his existential burden by achieving a trance-like state of ecstasy ('to be beside oneself') and thus to regain unity within himself and with nature. There are many ways to accomplish this. A very

6. For instance, the contrast between system A and system C cultures, discussed in Chapter 8.

transitory one is provided by nature in the sexual act. This experience may be said to be the natural prototype of complete concentration and momentary ecstasis; it may include the sexual partner but too often remains a narcissistic experience for each of the two, who perhaps share mutual gratitude for the pleasure they have given each other (conventionally felt as love).

We have already referred to other symbiotic, more lasting and intense ways to arrive at ecstasy. We find these in religious cults, such as ecstatic dance, the use of drugs, frenzied sexual orgies, or self-induced states of trance. An outstanding example of a self-induced state are the trance-producing ceremonies in Bali. They are particularly interesting in relation to the phenomenon of aggression because in one of the ceremonial dances[7] the participants use a *kris* (a special kind of dagger) with which they stab themselves (and occasionally each other) at the very height of the trance (J. Belav, 1960 and V. Monteil, 1970).

There are other forms of ecstasis in which hate and destructiveness are the centre of the experience. One example is the 'going berserk' to be found among the Teutonic tribes (berserk means 'bear shirt'). This was an initiation rite in which the male youth was induced into a state of identification with a bear. The initiated would attack people, trying to bite them, not speaking but simply making noises like a bear. To be in this trance-like state was the highest accomplishment of this ritual, and to have participated in it was the beginning of independent manhood. The expression *furor teutonicus* implies the sacred nature of this particular stage of rage. Several features in this ritual are worthy of note. First of all, it is rage for the sake of rage, not directed against an enemy or provoked by any damage or insult. It aimed at a trance-like state which in this case is organized around the all-pervasive feeling of rage. It may be that the induction of this state was helped by drugs (H. D. Fabing,

7. These dances are of high artistic value, and their function goes far beyond the one I have stressed here.

1956). The unifying force of absolute rage was required as a means to arrive at the experience of ecstasis. Secondly, it is a collective state based on tradition, the guidance of shamans, and the effect of group participation. Thirdly, it is an attempt to regress to animal existence, in this case that of the bear; the initiates behave like a predatory animal. Ultimately, it is a transitory and not a chronic state of rage.

Another example of a ritual that has survived until today and that shows the state of trance organized around rage and destructiveness can be seen in a small Spanish town. Every year on a certain date the men get together on the main square, each with a small or large drum. At exactly midday they begin to beat the drums and do not stop until twenty-four hours later. After a while they get into a state of frenzy that becomes a state of trance in the process of this continuous beating of the drums. After exactly twenty-four hours the ritual ends. The skin of many of the drums has been broken, the hands of the drummers are swollen and often bleeding. The most remarkable feature of this process is the faces of the participants: they are the faces of men in a trance and the expression they show is that of a frenzy of rage.[8] It is obvious that the beating of the drums gives expression to powerful destructive impulses. While the rhythm at the beginning of the ritual probably helped to stimulate the trance-like state, after a while each drummer is completely possessed by the passion to beat. This passion takes over completely, and only because of the strength of its intensity are the drummers capable of continuing for twenty-four hours in spite of their hurting hands and their increasingly exhausted bodies.

8. The name of the town is Calanda. I saw a film of this ritual and have never forgotten the extraordinary impression the orgy of hate made on me.

The Worship of Destructiveness

In many ways similar to ecstatic destructiveness is the chronic dedication of a person's whole life to hate and destructiveness. Not a momentary state as in ecstasis, it has nevertheless the function of taking hold of the whole person, of unifying him in the worship of one goal: to destroy. This state is a permanent idolatry of the god of destruction; his devotee has, as it were, given over his life to him.

Kern, von Salomon: A Clinical Case of Destruction Idolatry

An excellent example of this phenomenon can be found in the autobiographical novel by E. von Salomon (1930), one of the accessories to the murder in 1922 of W. Rathenau, the liberal and gifted German foreign minister.

Von Salomon was born in 1902, the son of a police officer, and was a military cadet when the German revolution broke out in 1918. He was filled with burning hate against the revolutionaries, but equally against the bourgeois middle class, which, he felt, was satisfied with the comforts of material existence and had lost the spirit of sacrifice and devotion to the nation. (He was at times in sympathy with the most radical wing of the left revolutionaries because they, too, wanted to destroy the existing order.) Von Salomon made friends with a like-minded fanatical group of ex-officers, among them Kern who later killed Rathenau. He was eventually apprehended and sentenced to five years in prison.[9] Like his hero Kern, von Salomon may be considered a prototype of the Nazis, but in contrast to most of the latter, von Salomon and his group were men without opportunism or desire for even the comforts of life.

In his autobiographical novel, von Salomon says of him-

9. I do not know whether or what kind of changes occurred in his personality in his later life. My analysis is strictly limited to what he says about himself and his friends at the time about which he writes, provided the novel is autobiographical.

self: 'I had always my special pleasure in destruction, thus I can feel in the midst of the daily pain an absorbing pleasure in seeing how the baggage of ideas and values has diminished, how the arsenal of idealisms has been ground piece by piece until nothing remained but a bundle of flesh with raw nerves; nerves that like taut strings rendered each tune vibrantly and doubly so in the thin air of isolation.'

Von Salomon had not always been as devoted to destruction as this sentence would make it appear. It seems that some of his friends, especially Kern who impressed him tremendously, had influenced him with their own more fanatical attitude. A very interesting discussion between von Salomon and Kern shows the latter's dedication to absolute destructiveness and hate.

Von Salomon begins the conversation by saying: 'I want power. I want an aim that fills my day, I want life totally with all the sweetness of this world, I want to know that the sacrifices are worth while.'

Kern answers him fiercely: 'Damn it, stop your questions. Tell me, if you know it, a greater happiness, if it is happiness that you are greedy for, than the one we experience only by the violence by which we perish like dogs.'

A few pages later, Kern says: 'I could not bear it if greatness could grow again out of the rubble of this time. We do not fight so that the nation is happy, we fight to force it into its line of fate. But if this man [Rathenau] gives the nation a face once more, if he can mobilize it once more to a will and to a form which died in the war, that I could not bear.'

In answering the question how he, as an imperial officer, survived the day of the revolution, he says:

I did not survive it; I have, as honour commanded, put a bullet in my head on the 19th November 1918; I am dead, what lives in me is not me. I have not known an 'I' since that day . . . I died for the nation. So everything lives in me only for the nation. How could I bear it if it were different! I do what I have to do, because I die every day. Since what I do is given only to one power everything I do is rooted in this power. *This power wants destruction and I destroy* . . . I know that I shall be ground to nothing, that I shall fall when this power releases me. [Italics added.]

We see in Kern's statements the intense masochism by which he makes himself a willing subject of a higher power, but what is most interesting in this context is the unifying force of hate and the wish for destruction that this man worships, and for which he is willing to give his life without hesitation.

Whether it was the influence of Kern's suicide before he could be arrested or the political failure of his ideas, it seems that in von Salomon the hope for power and its sweetness gave way to absolute hate and bitterness. In prison he felt so lonely that he could not bear it if the director tried to approach him 'with human concern'. He could not bear the questions of his fellow prisoners in the warmth of the first spring days. 'I crawled into my cell which was hostile to me – I hated the guard who opened the door and the man who brought me the soup and the dogs that played in front of the window. *I was afraid of joy*' (Italics added). He then describes how angry the tree in the courtyard made him when it began to flower. He reports about his response to the third Christmas in prison when the director tried to make the day pleasant for the prisoners in order to help them to forget:

But I, I do not want to forget. May I be damned if I forget. I want to visualize always every day and every hour of the past. This creates a potent hate. I do not want to forget any humiliation, any slighting, any arrogant gesture, I want to think of every meanness done to me, every word that caused me pain and was meant to cause pain. I want to remember every face and every experience and every enemy. I *want to load my whole life with the whole disgusting dirt, with this piled-up mass of disgusting memories.* I do not want to forget; *but the little good that happened to me, that I want to forget.* [Italics added.]

In a certain sense von Salomon, Kern, and their small circle might be considered revolutionaries; they wanted the total destruction of the existing social and political structure and its replacement by a nationalistic, militaristic order – of which they had hardly any concrete idea. But a revolutionary in a characterological sense is not characterized only by the wish to overthrow the old order; unless he is motivated by love of life and freedom, he is a destructive rebel. (This holds true also for those who participate in a genuine revolutionary movement, but are motivated by destructiveness.) If we analyse the psychic reality of these men, we find that they were destroyers and not revolutionaries. They hated not only their enemies, they hated life itself. This becomes very clear in Kern's statement and in von Salomon's description of his reaction to the men in prison, to trees, and to animals. He felt utterly unrelated and unresponsive to anybody or anything alive.

The peculiarity of this attitude is particularly striking if one thinks of the attitude of many genuine revolutionaries in their private lives, and particularly in prison. One is reminded of Rosa Luxemburg's famous letters from prison in which she describes with poetic tenderness the bird she can observe from her cell, letters in which no trace of bitterness is to be found. But one need not think only of an extraordinary person like Rosa Luxemburg. There were, and are, thousands upon thousands of revolutionaries in prison all over the world in whom the love of all that is alive never diminished during their years in prison.

In order to understand why persons like Kern and von Salomon sought fulfilment in hate and destruction we would have to know more about their life history; such knowledge is not available, and we must be satisfied in knowing about *one* condition for their worship of hate. The whole world had broken down, morally and socially. Their values of nationalism, their feudal concept of honour and obedience, these things had lost their foundation in the defeat of the monarchy. (Although in the last analysis it was not the military defeat by the Allies, but the victorious march of capitalism within Germany that destroyed their semi-feudal world.) What they had learned as officers was now useless, although fourteen years later their professional chances would have been excellent. Their thirst for revenge, the meaninglessness of their present existence, their social uprootedness, go far to explain their worship of hate. But we do not know to what extent their destructiveness was the expression of a character structure already formed many years before the First World War. This seems more likely to have been the case with Kern, while I assume that von Salomon's attitude was perhaps more transitional and strongly induced by Kern's impressive personality. It seems that Kern really belongs to the later discussion of the necrophilous character. I have included him here because he offers a good example of the idolatrous worship of hate.

One further observation may be relevant for these as well as for many other instances of destructiveness, especially among groups. I refer to the 'triggering' effect of destructive behaviour. A person may first react with defensive aggression against a threat; by this behaviour he has shed some of the conventional inhibitions to aggressive behaviour. This makes it easier for other kinds of aggressiveness, such as destruction and cruelty, to be unleashed. This may lead to a kind of chain reaction in which destructiveness becomes so intense that when a 'critical mass' is reached, the result is a state of ecstasis in a person, and particularly in a group.

The Destructive Character: Sadism

The phenomenon of spontaneous, transitory outbursts of destructiveness has so many facets that a great deal of further study is necessary in order to arrive at a more definite understanding than is offered in the tentative suggestions in the previous pages. On the other hand, the data on destructiveness in its character-bound forms are richer and more definite; this is not surprising if we consider that they were gained from prolonged observations of individuals in psychoanalysis and daily-life observations, and furthermore, that the conditions that generate these forms of character are relatively stable and of long duration.

There are two conventional concepts of the nature of sadism, sometimes used separately, sometimes in combination.

One concept is expressed in the term 'algolagnia' (*algos*, 'pain'; *lagneia*, 'lust') coined by von Schrenk-Notzing at the beginning of the century. He differentiated active algolagnia (sadism) from passive algolagnia (masochism). In this concept the essence of sadism is seen in the desire to inflict pain, regardless of any particular sexual involvement.[10]

The other concept sees sadism essentially as a sexual phenomenon – in Freud's terms, as a partial drive of the libido (in the first stage of his thinking) – and explains sadistic desires that have no overt connection with sexual strivings as being unconsciously motivated by them. A great deal of psychoanalytic ingenuity has been deployed to prove that the libido is the driving force of cruelty, even when the naked eye could not discover such sexual motivations.

This is not to deny that sexual sadism, together with masochism, is one of the most frequent and best-known sexual perversions. For men afflicted with this perversion it is a condition for sexual excitation and release. It ranges from the wish to cause physical pain to a woman – for instance, by beating her – to humiliating her, putting her in chains, or forcing her complete obedience in other ways. Sometimes the sadist needs to inflict intense pain and suffering in order to be sexually aroused: sometimes a small dose will have the desired effect. Many times a sadistic fantasy is sufficient to arouse sexual excitement, and there is no small number of men who have normal sexual intercourse with their wives, but unknown to their partner, need a sadistic fantasy to become sexually excited. In sexual

10. cf. J. P. de River (1956). The book contains a collection of interesting criminal case histories dealing with sadistic acts, but suffers from the indiscriminate use of the concept 'sadism' to cover various impulses to harm others.

masochism the procedure is reversed: the excitement lies in being beaten, abused, hurt. Both sadism and masochism as sexual perversions are to be found frequently among men. It would seem that sexual sadism is more frequent among men than among women, at least in our culture; whether masochism is more frequent among women is difficult to ascertain because of lack of reliable data on the subject.

Before starting the discussion of sadism, some comments seem appropriate on the question whether it is a perversion and, if so, in what sense.

It has become quite fashionable among some politically radical thinkers, such as Herbert Marcuse, to praise sadism as one of the expressions of human sexual freedom. Marquis de Sade's writings are reprinted by politically radical journals as manifestations of this 'freedom'. They accept de Sade's argument that sadism is a human desire, and that liberty requires that men have the right to satisfy their sadistic and masochistic desires, like all others, if this gives them pleasure.

The problem is quite complex. If one defines as perversion – as has been done – any sexual practice that does not lead to the procreation of children, i.e., which only serves sexual pleasure, then of course all those who are opposed to this traditional attitude will arise – and justly so – in the defence of 'perversions'. However, this is by no means the only definition of perversion, and in fact, it is a rather old-fashioned one.

Sexual desire, even when no love is present, is an expression of life and of mutual giving and sharing of pleasure. Sexual acts, however, that are characterized by the fact that one person becomes the object of the other's contempt, of his wish to hurt, his desire to control are the only true sexual perversions; not because they do not serve procreation, but because they pervert a life-serving impulse into a life-strangling one.

If one compares sadism with a form of sexual behaviour that has often been called perversion – i.e., all kinds of oral-genital contact – the difference becomes quite apparent. The latter behaviour is as little a perversion as kissing, because it does not imply control, or humiliation, of another person.

The argument that to follow one's desires is man's natural right and hence to be respected is very understandable from a rationalistic, pre-Freudian viewpoint, which assumed that man desires only what is good for him, and therefore that pleasure is a guide for desirable action. But after Freud this argument sounds rather stale. We know that many of man's desires are irrational, precisely because they harm him (if not others) and interfere with his development. The person who is motivated by the wish to destroy and who feels pleasure in the act of destruction could hardly present the excuse that he has the right to behave destructively because this is his desire and his source of pleasure. The defenders of the sadistic perversion may answer that they are not arguing in favour of the satisfaction of destructive, murderous wishes; that sadism is just one of the many manifestations of sexuality, 'a matter of taste', and no worse than any other form of sexual satisfaction.

This argument overlooks the most important point in the matter: the person who is sexually aroused by sadistic practices has a sadistic *character* – i.e., he *is* a sadist, a person with an intense desire to control, hurt, humiliate another person. The intensity of his sadistic desires affects his sexual impulses; this is not different from the fact that other non-sexual motivations, such as attraction to power, to wealth, or narcissism can arouse sexual desire. In fact, in no sphere of behaviour does the character of a person show more clearly than in the sexual act – precisely because it is the least 'learned' and patterned behaviour. A person's love, his tenderness, his sadism or masochism, his greed, his narcissism, his anxieties – indeed, his every character trait – is expressed in his sexual behaviour.

Sometimes the argument is presented that sadistic perversion is wholesome because it provides an innocent outlet for the sadistic tendencies inherent in all people. According to the logic of this argument Hitler's concentration camp guards would have been kind to the prisoners if they could have released their sadistic tendencies in their sexual relations.

Examples of Sexual Sadism-Masochism

The following examples of sexual sadism and masochism are from *The Story of O* by Pauline Réage (1965), a book that is somewhat less read than de Sade's classics.

> She rang. Pierre chained her hands above her head, to the chain of the bed. When she was thus bound, her lover kissed her again, standing beside her on the bed. Again he told her that he loved her, then he got off the bed and nodded for Pierre. He watched her struggle, so fruitlessly; he listened to her moans swell and become cries. When her tears flowed, he sent Pierre away. She still found the strength to tell him again that she loved him. Then he kissed her drenched face, her gasping mouth, and undid her bonds, laid her down, and left. (P. Réage, 1965)

O must have no will of her own; the lover and his friends must be in complete control of her; she finds her happiness in slavery and they in the role of absolute masters. The following extract gives a picture of this aspect of sado-masochistic performance. (It must be explained that one of the conditions of her lover's control is that she must submit to his friends as obediently as she does to him. One of them is Sir Stephen.)

> Finally she straightened up and, as though what she was going to say was stifling her, unfastened the top hooks of her tunic, until the cleavage of her breasts was visible. Then she stood up. Her hands and her knees were shaking.
> 'I'm yours,' she said at length to René. 'I'll be whatever you want me to be.'
> 'No,' he broke in, 'ours. Repeat after me: I belong to both of you. I shall be whatever both of you want me to be.'
> Sir Stephen's piercing grey eyes were fixed firmly upon her, as

were René's, and in them she was lost, slowly repeating after him the phrases he was dictating to her, but like a lesson of grammar, she was transposing them into the first person.

'To Sir Stephen and to me you grant the right . . .' The right to dispose of her body however they wished, in whatever place or manner they should choose, the right to keep her in chains, the right to whip her like a slave or prisoner for the slightest failing or infraction, or simply for their pleasure, the right to pay no heed to her pleas and cries, if they should make her cry out. (P. Réage, 1965)

Sadism (and masochism) as sexual perversions constitute only a fraction of the vast amount of sadism in which no sexual behaviour is involved. Non-sexual sadistic behaviour, aiming at the infliction of *physical* pain up to the extreme of death, has as its object a powerless being, whether man or animal. Prisoners of war, slaves, defeated enemies, children, sick people (especially the mentally sick), inmates of prisons, non-whites without weapons, dogs – they all have been the object of physical sadism, often including the most cruel torture. From the cruel spectacles in Rome to modern police units, torture has been used under the disguise of religious or political purposes, and sometimes plainly for the amusement of the impoverished masses. The Colosseum in Rome is indeed one of the greatest monuments to human sadism.

One of the most widespread manifestations of non-sexual sadism is the abuse of children. This form of sadism has become more widely known only in the last ten years by a number of investigations starting with the now classic work of C. H. Kempe *et al.* (1962). Since then a number of other papers have been published,[11] and further studies are under way on a national scale. They show that the abuse of children ranges from inflicting death by severe beating or intentional starvation to inflicting swellings and other non-fatal wounds. About the real incidence of such acts we really

11. cf. D. G. Gill (1970); in R. Helfner and C. H. Kempe, eds. (1968), cf. S. X. Radhill, also B. F. Steele and C. B. Pollock.

know next to nothing, since the available data come from public sources (police, for instance, called in by neighbours, and hospitals), but it is agreed that the number of reported cases is only a fraction of the whole. It seems that the most adequate data are those reported by Gill on the nationwide findings of a survey. I shall mention only one of these data: the ages at which children are mistreated can be divided into several periods: (1) from age one to age two; (2) the incidence doubles from age three to age nine; (3) from age nine to age fifteen the incidence decreases again to approximately the early level and gradually disappears after age sixteen (D. G. Gill, 1970). This means that sadism is most intense when the child is still helpless, but is beginning to have a will of its own and to react against the adult's wish to control him completely.

Mental cruelty, the wish to humiliate and to hurt another person's feelings, is probably even more widespread than physical sadism. This type of sadistic attack is much safer for the sadist; after all, no physical force but 'only' words have been used. On the other hand, the psychic pain can be as intense or even more so than the physical. I do not need to give examples for this mental sadism. Parents inflict it upon their children, professors on their students, superiors on their inferiors – in other words, it is employed in any situation where there is someone who cannot defend himself against the sadist. (If the teacher is helpless, the students often turn into sadists.) Mental sadism may be disguised in many seemingly harmless ways: a question, a smile, a confusing remark. Who does not know an 'artist' in this kind of sadism, the one who finds just the right word or the right gesture to embarrass or humiliate another in this innocent way? Naturally, this kind of sadism is often all the more effective if the humiliation is inflicted in front of others.[12]

12. The Talmud states that whoever humiliates someone in front of others is to be considered as one who has killed him.

Joseph Stalin: A Clinical Case of Non-sexual Sadism

One of the outstanding historical examples of both mental and physical sadism was Stalin. His behaviour is a textbook description of non-sexual, as de Sade's novels are of sexual sadism. It was he who was the first to order the torture of political prisoners since the beginning of the revolution, a measure that up to the time of his giving this order had been shunned by the Russian revolutionaries (R. A. Medvedev, 1971).[13] Under Stalin the methods of torture used by the NKVD surpassed in refinement and cruelty anything that the czarist police had thought of. Sometimes he personally gave orders about what kind of torture was to be used on a prisoner. He mainly practised mental sadism, of which I want to give a few illustrations. One particular form Stalin enjoyed was to assure people that they were safe, only to arrest them a day or two later. Of course, the arrest hit the victim all the more severely because he had felt especially safe; besides that, Stalin could enjoy the sadistic pleasure of knowing the man's real fate at the same time that he was assuring him of his favour. What greater superiority and control over another person is there?

Here are some specific examples reported by Medvedev:

Shortly before the arrest of the Civil War hero D. F. Serdich, Stalin toasted him at a reception, suggesting that they drink to 'Brüderschaft'. Just a few days before Bliukher's destruction, Stalin spoke of him warmly at a meeting. When an Armenian delegation came to him, Stalin asked about the poet Charents and said he should not be touched, but a few months later Charents was arrested and killed. The wife of Ordzhonikidze's Deputy Commissar, A. Serebrovskii, told about an unexpected phone call from Stalin one evening in 1937. 'I hear you are going about on foot,' Stalin said. 'That's no good. People might think what they shouldn't. I'll send you a car if yours is being repaired.' And the next morning a car from the Kremlin garage arrived for Mrs Serebrovskii's use. But two days later her husband was arrested, taken right from the hospital.

13. The quotations in this section are from the same work.

The famous historian and publicist I. Steklov, disturbed by all the arrests, phoned Stalin and asked for an appointment. 'Of course, come on over,' Stalin, said and reassured him when they met: 'What's the matter with you? The Party knows and trusts you; you have nothing to worry about.' Steklov returned home to his friends and family, and that very evening the N K V D came for him. Naturally the first thought of his friends and family was to appeal to Stalin, who seemed unaware of what was going on. It was much easier to believe in Stalin's ignorance than in subtle perfidy. In 1938 I. A. Akulov, one-time Procurator of the U S S R and later Secretary of the Central Executive Committee, fell while skating and suffered an almost fatal concussion. On Stalin's suggestion, outstanding surgeons were brought from abroad to save his life. After a long and difficult recovery, Akulov returned to work, whereupon he was arrested and shot.

A particularly refined form of sadism was Stalin's habit of arresting the wives – and sometimes children – of some of the highest Soviet or Party functionaries and keeping them in a labour camp, while their husbands had to do their jobs and bow and scrape before Stalin without daring even to ask for their release. Thus the wife of Kalinin, the Soviet Union's President, was arrested in 1937,[14] Molotov's wife, and the wife and son of Otto Kuusinen, one of the leading Komintern functionaries, all were in work camps. An unnamed witness states that Stalin in his presence asked Kuusinen why he did not try to get his son freed. 'Evidently there were serious reasons for his arrest,' Kuusinen answered. According to the witness, 'Stalin grinned and ordered the release of Kuusinen's son.' Kuusinen sent his wife parcels to her work camp, but did not even address them himself but had his housekeeper do it. Stalin had the wife of his private secretary arrested, while her husband remained in his position.

It does not require much imagination to visualize the

14. Medvedev reports that she was tortured by investigators until she signed statements compromising her husband; Stalin ignored them for the time being; he wanted them as a basis for the arrest of Kalinin and others whenever it would please him.

extreme humiliation of these high functionaries who could
not quit their positions, could not ask for the release of their
wives or sons, and had to agree with Stalin that the arrest
had been justified. Either such men had no feelings at all, or
they were morally broken and had lost all self-respect and
sense of dignity. A drastic example is the reaction of one of
the most powerful figures in the Soviet Union, Lazar
Kaganovich, to the arrest of his brother, Mikhail Moisee-
vich, who was Minister of the Aviation Industry before the
war:

He was a Stalinist, responsible for the repression of many people.
But after the war he fell out of Stalin's favour. As a result, some
arrested officials, who had allegedly set up an underground
'fascist centre', named Mikhail Kaganovich as an accomplice.
They made the obviously inspired (and utterly preposterous)
assertion that he (a Jew) was to be vice-president of the fascist
government if the Hitlerites took Moscow. When Stalin learned of
these depositions, which he obviously expected, he phoned Lazar
Kaganovich and said that his brother would have to be arrested
because he had connection with the fascists. 'Well, so what?'
said Lazar. 'If it's necessary, arrest him!' At a Politburo discussion of this subject, Stalin praised Lazar Kaganovich for his
'principles': he had agreed to his brother's arrest. But Stalin then
added that the arrest should not be made hastily. Mikhail Moise-
evich had been in the Party many years, Stalin said, and all the
depositions should be checked once more. So Mikoyan was
instructed to arrange a confrontation between M. M. and the
person who had testified against him. The confrontation was held
in Mikoyan's office. A man was brought in who repeated his
testimony in Kaganovich's presence, adding that some airplane
factories were deliberately built near the border before the war so
that the German's might capture them more easily. When Mikhail
Kaganovich had heard the testimony, he asked permission to go
to a little toilet adjoining Mikoyan's office. A few seconds later a
shot was heard there.

Still another form of Stalin's sadism was the unpredict-
ability of his behaviour. There are cases of people whom he
ordered to be arrested, but who after torture and severe

sentences were released after a few months or years and appointed to high offices, often without explanation. A telling example is Stalin's behaviour towards his old comrade, Sergei Ivanovich Kavtaradze,

who had once helped him hide from detectives in St Petersburg. In the twenties Kavtaradze joined the Trotskyite opposition, and left it only when the Trotskyite centre called on its supporters to stop oppositional activity. After Kirov's murder, Kavtaradze, exiled to Kazan as an ex-Trotskyite, wrote a letter to Stalin saying that he was not working against the Party. Stalin immediately brought Kavtaradze back from exile. Soon many central newspapers carried an article by Kavtaradze recounting an incident of his underground work with Stalin. Stalin liked the article, but Kavtaradze did not write any more on this subject. He did not even rejoin the Party, and lived by doing very modest editorial work. At the end of 1936 he and his wife were suddenly arrested and, after torture, were sentenced to be shot. He was accused of planning, together with Budu Mdivani, to murder Stalin. Soon after sentencing, Mdivani was shot. Kavtaradze, however, was kept in the death cell for a long time. Then he was suddenly taken to Beria's office, where he met his wife, who had aged beyond recognition. Both were released. First he lived in a hotel; then he got two rooms in a communal apartment and started to work. Stalin began to show him various signs of favour, inviting him to dinner and once even paying him a surprise visit along with Beria. (This visit caused great excitement in the communal apartment. One of Kavtaradze's neighbours fainted when, in her words, 'the portrait of Comrade Stalin' appeared on the threshold.) When he had Kavtaradze to dinner, Stalin himself would pour the soup, tell jokes, and reminisce. But during one of these dinners, Stalin suddenly went up to his guest and said, 'And still you wanted to kill me.'[15]

Stalin's behaviour in this case shows particularly clearly one element in his character – the wish to show people that he had absolute power and control over them. By his word he could kill them, have them tortured, have them rescued

15. Of course, Stalin knew quite well, says Medvedev, that Kavtaradze had not wanted to kill him.

again, have them rewarded; he had the power of God over life and death, the power of nature to make it grow and to destroy, to inflict pain and to heal. Life and death depended on his whim. This may also explain why he did not destroy some people like Litvinov (after the failure of his policy of understanding with the West), or Ehrenburg, who stood for everything Stalin hated, or Pasternak, who deviated in the opposite direction from Ehrenburg. Medvedev offers the explanation that in some cases he had to keep some old Bolsheviks alive to support the claim that he was continuing Lenin's work. But surely that could not have been said in Ehrenburg's case. I surmise that here, too, the motive was that Stalin enjoyed the sensation of control by whim and by mood, not restricted by any – even the most evil – principle.

The Nature of Sadism

I have given these examples of Stalin's sadism because they serve very well to introduce the central issue: *the nature of sadism*. Thus far we have dealt descriptively with various kinds of sadistic behaviour, sexual, physical, and mental. These different forms of sadism are not independent from each other; the problem is to find the common element, the essence of sadism. Orthodox psychoanalysis claimed that a particular aspect of sexuality was common to all these forms; in the second phase of Freud's theory it was asserted that sadism was a blending of Eros (sexuality) and the death instinct, directed outside oneself, while masochism is a blend of Eros and the death instinct, directed towards oneself.

Against this, I propose that the core of sadism, common to all its manifestations, is *the passion to have absolute and unrestricted control over a living being*, whether an animal, a child, a man, or a woman. To force someone to endure pain or humiliation without being able to defend himself is one of the manifestations of absolute control, but it is by no means the only one. The person who has complete control over another living being makes this being into his thing, his property, while he becomes the other being's god. Sometimes the control can even be helpful, and in that case we might speak of a benevolent sadism, such as one finds in instances where one person rules another for the other's own good, and in fact furthers him in many ways, except that he keeps him in bondage. But most sadism is malevolent. Complete control over another human being means crippling him, choking him, thwarting him. Such control can have all forms and all degrees.

Albert Camus's play, *Caligula*, provides an example of an extreme type of sadistic control which amounts to a desire for omnipotence. We see how Caligula, brought by circumstances to a position of unlimited power, gets ever more deeply involved in the craving for power. He sleeps with the wives of the senators and enjoys their humiliation when they have to act like admiring and fawning friends. He kills some of them, and those that remain still have to smile and joke. But even all this power does not satisfy him; he wants absolute power, he wants the impossible. As Camus has him say, 'I want the moon.'

It is easy enough to say that Caligula is mad, but his madness is a way of life; it is one solution of the problem of human existence, because it serves the illusion of omnipotence, of transcending the frontiers of human existence. In the process of trying to win absolute power Caligula lost all contact with men. He became an outcast by casting them out; he had to become mad because, when the bid for omnipotence failed, he was left a lonely, impotent individual.

The case of Caligula is of course exceptional. Few people ever have the chance to attain so much power that they can seduce themselves into the delusion that it might be absolute. But some have existed throughout history, up to our time; if they remain victorious, they are celebrated as great statesmen or generals; if they are defeated, they are considered madmen or criminals.

This extreme solution to the problem of human existence is barred to the average person. Yet in most social systems, including ours, even those on lower social levels can have control over somebody who is subject to their power. There are always children, wives, or dogs available; or there are helpless people, such as inmates of prisons, patients in hospitals, if they are not well-to-do (especially the mentally sick), pupils in schools, members of civilian bureaucracies. It depends on the social structure to what degree the factual power of superiors in each of these instances is controlled or restricted and, hence, how much possibility for sadistic satisfaction these situations offer. Aside from all these situations, religious and racial minorities, as far as they are powerless, offer a vast opportunity for sadistic satisfaction for even the poorest member of the majority.

Sadism is one of the answers to the problem of being born human when better ones are not attainable. The experience of absolute control over another being, of omnipotence as far as he, she, or it is concerned, creates the illusion of transcending the limitations of human existence, particularly for one whose real life is deprived of productivity and joy. Sadism has essentially no practical aim; it is not 'trivial' but 'devotional'. *It is transformation of impotence into the experience of omnipotence*; it is the religion of psychical cripples.

However, not every situation where a person or a group has uncontrolled power over another generates sadism. Many – perhaps most – parents, prison guards, school teachers, and bureaucrats are not sadistic. For any number of reasons, the character structure of many individuals is not conducive to the development of sadism even under circumstances that offer an opportunity for it. Persons who have a dominantly life-furthering character, will not easily be seduced by power. But it would be a dangerous over-simplification if I were to classify people into only two groups: the sadist devils and the non-sadistic saints. What matters is the intensity of the sadistic passion within the character structure of a given person. There are many in whose characters sadistic elements can be found, but balanced by such strong life-furthering trends that they cannot be classified as sadistic characters. Not rarely in such individuals the internal conflict between the two orientations results in an enhanced sensitivity towards sadism and in the reactive formation of allergic reactions against all its forms. (Traces of their sadistic tendencies may still show up in unimportant, marginal behaviour, slight enough to escape awareness.) There are others with a sadistic character in whom sadism is at least balanced by countervailing forces (not merely repressed), and while they may feel a certain amount of enjoyment in the control of helpless people, they would not participate in or get pleasure from actual torture and similar atrocities (except under extraordinary circumstances, such as mass frenzy). This can be demonstrated by the attitude of the Hitler régime towards the sadistic atrocities it ordered. It had to keep the extermination of Jews and of Polish and Russian civilians a close secret known only to a small group of the SS élite, but kept from the vast majority of the German population. In many speeches by Himmler and other executors of atrocities, it was stressed that the killings must be done in a 'humane' way, without sadistic excesses, since otherwise it would be too repugnant even to the SS men. In some instances orders were given that Russian and Polish civilians who were to be killed had to be put through a short, formal trial in order to give their executors the feeling that the shooting was 'legal'. While all this sounds absurd in its hypocrisy, it is nevertheless a proof that the Nazi leaders believed that large-scale sadistic acts would be revolting to most otherwise loyal adherents of the régime. A great deal of material has come to light since 1945, but a systematic investigation of the degree to which Germans were attracted by sadistic acts – even though they avoided knowing about them – has not yet been made.

Sadistic character traits can never be understood if one isolates them from the whole character structure. They are part of a syndrome that has to be understood as a whole. For the sadistic character everything living is to be controllable; living beings become things. Or, still more accurately, living beings are transformed into living, quivering, pulsating objects of control. Their responses are forced by the one who controls them. The sadist wants to become the master of life, and hence the quality of life should be maintained in his victim. This is, in fact, what distinguishes him from the destroying person. The destroyer wants to do away with a person, to eliminate him, to destroy life itself; the sadist wants the sensation of controlling and choking life.

Another trait of the sadist is that he is stimulated only by the helpless, never by those who are strong. It does not cause any sadistic pleasure, for instance, to inflict a wound on an enemy in a fight between equals, because in this situation the infliction of the wound is not an expression of control. For the sadistic character there is only one admirable quality, and that is power. He admires, loves, and submits to those who have power, and he despises and wants to control those who are powerless and cannot fight back.

The sadistic character is afraid of everything that is not certain and predictable, that offers surprises which would force him to spontaneous and original reactions. For this reason, he is afraid of life. Life frightens him precisely because it is by its very nature unpredictable and uncertain. It is structured but it is not orderly; there is only one certainty in life: that all men die. Love is equally uncertain. To be loved requires a capacity to be loving oneself, to arouse love, and it implies always a risk of rejection and failure. This is why the sadistic character can 'love' only when he controls, i.e., when he has power *over* the object of his love. The sadistic character is usually xenophobic and neophobic – one who is strange constitutes newness, and what is new arouses fear, suspicion, and dislike, because a spontaneous, alive, and not-routinized response would be required.

Another element in the syndrome is the submissiveness and cowardice of the sadist. It may sound like a contradiction that the sadist is a submissive person, and yet not only is it not a contradiction – it is, dynamically speaking, a necessity. He is sadistic because he feels impotent, unalive, and powerless. He tries to compensate for this lack by having power over others, by transforming the worm he feels himself to be into a god. But even the sadist who has power suffers from his human impotence. He may kill and torture, but he remains a loveless, isolated, frightened person in need of a higher power to whom he can submit. For those one step below Hitler, the Führer was his highest power; for Hitler himself, it was Fate, the laws of Evolution.

This need to submit is rooted in masochism. Sadism and masochism, which are invariably linked together, are opposites in behaviouristic terms, but they are actually two different facets of one fundamental situation: the sense of vital impotence. Both the sadist and the masochist need another being to 'complete' them, as it were. The sadist makes another being an extension of himself; the masochist makes himself the extension of another being. Both seek a symbiotic relationship because neither has his centre in himself. While it appears that the sadist is free of his victim, he needs the victim in a perverse way.

Because of the close connection between sadism and masochism it is more correct to speak of a sado-masochistic character, even though the one or the other aspect will be more dominant in a particular person. The sado-masochist has also been called the 'authoritarian character', translating the psychological aspect of his character structure into terms of a political attitude. This concept finds its justification in the fact that persons whose political attitude is generally described as authoritarian (active and passive) usually exhibit (in our society) the traits of the sado-masochistic character: control of those below and submission to those above.[16]

The sado-masochistic character cannot be fully understood without reference to Freud's concept of the 'anal character', enlarged by his disciples, especially by K. Abraham and Ernest Jones.

Freud (1908) believed that the anal character manifested itself in a *syndrome* of character traits: stubbornness, orderliness, and parsimony, to which punctuality and cleanliness were added later. He assumed that this syndrome was rooted in the 'anal libido' that has its source in the anal erogenous zone. The character traits of the syndrome were explained as reaction formations or sublimations of the aims of this anal libido.

In trying to substitute the *mode of relatedness* for the libido theory, I arrived at the hypothesis that the various traits of the syndrome are manifestations of the distance-keeping, controlling, rejecting, and hoarding mode of relatedness ('hoarding character') (E. Fromm, 1947). This does not imply that Freud's clinical observations with respect to the particular role of everything pertaining to faeces and bowel movement was not correct. On the contrary, in the psychoanalytic observation of individuals I have found Freud's observations fully confirmed. The difference lies, however, in the answer to the following: Is the anal libido the *source* of the preoccupation with faeces and, indirectly, of the anal

16. The authoritarian character was first analysed in the German study referred to in Chapter 2, n. 8 (p. 79). The analysis of the data showed that 78 per cent of the respondents had neither an authoritarian nor an anti-authoritarian character and hence would not, in the case of Hitler's victory, become ardent Nazis or ardent anti-Nazis. About 12 per cent had an anti-authoritarian character and would remain convinced enemies of Nazism, while about 10 per cent had an authoritarian character and would become ardent Nazis. These results correspond very roughly to what actually happened after 1933 (E. Fromm *et al.*, 1936). Later, the authoritarian character was studied by T. Adorno. However, in this study the authoritarian character is treated behaviouristically, not psychoanalytically in terms of the sado-masochistic character (T. Adorno *et al.*, 1950).

character syndrome, or is the syndrome the *manifestation* of a special mode of relatedness? In the latter case the anal interest has to be understood as another, but *symbolic* expression of the anal character, not as its *cause*. Faeces are, indeed, a very fitting symbol: they represent that which is eliminated from the human life process and which no longer serves man's life.[17]

The hoarding character is orderly with things, thoughts and feelings, but his orderliness is sterile and rigid. He cannot endure things to be out of place and has to put them in order; in this way he controls space; by irrational punctuality he controls time; by compulsive cleanliness he undoes the contact he had with the world which is considered dirty and hostile. (Sometimes, however, when no reaction-formation or sublimation has developed, he is not overclean but tends to be dirty.) The hoarding character experiences himself like a beleaguered fortress; he must prevent anything from going out and save what is inside the fortress. His stubbornness and obstinacy is a quasi-automatic defence against intrusion.

The hoarder tends to feel that he possesses only a fixed quantity of strength, energy, or mental capacity, and that this stock is diminished or exhausted by use and can never be replenished. He cannot understand the self-replenishing function of all living substance, and that activity and the use of our powers increase our strength while stagnation weakens it; to him, death and destruction have more reality than life and growth. The act of creation is a miracle of which he hears, but in which he does not believe. His highest values are order and security; his motto: 'There is nothing new under the sun.' In his relationship to others intimacy is a threat; either remoteness or possession of a person means security. The hoarder tends to be suspicious

17. Those wishing to speculate might consider that the fascination with faeces and smells constitutes a kind of neurophysiological regression to an evolutionary stage in which the animal was oriented more by smell than by sight.

and to have a special sense of justice that in essence says:
'Mine is mine and yours is yours.'

The anal-hoarding character has only one way to feel safe
in his relatedness to the world: by possessing and controlling
it, since he is incapable of relating himself by love and
productivity.

That the anal-hoarding character has the close relationship to sadism described by classic psychoanalysts is amply
borne out by the clinical data, and it makes little difference
whether one interprets this connection in terms of the libido
theory or in terms of the relatedness of man to the world.
It is also evidenced by the fact that social groups with an
anal-hoarding character tend to exhibit a marked degree
of sadism.[18]

Roughly equivalent to the sado-masochistic character, in
a social rather than a political sense, is the *bureaucratic
character*.[19] In the bureaucratic system every person controls
the one below him and is controlled by the one above. Both

18. cf. E. Fromm (1941), where I showed this connection in the
German lower middle class.

19. In speaking here of bureaucrats I refer to the old-fashioned, cold,
authoritarian bureaucrats as they are still found in many old-fashioned
schools, hospitals, prisons, railroads, and post offices. Big industry, which
is also a highly bureaucratic organization, has developed an entirely
different character-type – the friendly, smiling, 'understanding'
bureaucrat who has perhaps taken a course in 'human relations'. The
reasons for this change lie in the nature of modern industry, its need for
teamwork, for avoiding friction, for better labour relations, and a number
of other factors. It is not as if the new friendly bureaucrats were insincere, as if they were really sadists who smile instead of showing their
real faces; in fact, the old-fashioned sadist is not very suited to be a
modern bureaucrat, for the reasons just mentioned. The modern
bureaucrat is not a sadist turned friendly, but he is a thing to himself, and
his friendly treatment, while not false, is so superficial and thin as to
become false. But even this is not quite fair, because nobody really
expects it to be more than superficial and thin, except perhaps for the
short moment when they both smile and indulge in the delusion that this
is human contact. Two extended and thorough studies of the character
of the modern manager will confirm or correct these impressions.
(M. Maccoby; I. Millán, each forthcoming.)

sadistic and masochistic impulses can be fulfilled in such a system. Those below, the bureaucratic character will hold in contempt, those above, he will admire and fear. One only has to look at the facial expression and the voice of a certain type of bureaucrat criticizing his subordinate, or frowning when he is a minute late, or insisting on behaviour that at least symbolically expresses that during office hours he 'belongs' to the superior. Or one might think of the bureaucrat behind the post-office window and watch his hardly noticeable thin little smile as he shuts his window at 5.30 p.m. sharp, while the last two people who have already been waiting for half an hour have to leave and come back the next day. The point is not that he stops selling stamps at 5.30 sharp: the important aspect of his behaviour is the fact that he enjoys frustrating people, showing them that *he* controls them, a satisfaction that is expressed in his facial expression.[20]

Needless to say, not all old-fashioned bureacrats are sadistic. Only a depth psychological study could show what the incidence of sadism among this group is as compared with non-bureaucrats or modern bureaucrats. To mention only some outstanding examples, General Marshall and General Eisenhower, both among the highest ranking members of the military bureaucracy during the Second World War, were conspicuous for their lack of sadism and their genuine humane concern for the life of their soldiers. On the other hand a number of both German and French generals in the First World War were conspicuous for the ruthlessness and brutality with which they sacrificed the lives of their soldiers for no adequate tactical purpose.

In many cases the sadism is camouflaged by kindness and what looks like benevolence towards certain people in certain circumstances. But it would be erroneous to think that the kindness is simply intended to deceive, or even that it is only a gesture, not based on any genuine feeling. To understand

20. This is an example of the many behavioural data that elude the wide meshes of most psychological experiments and tests.

this phenomenon better, it is necessary to consider that most sane people wish to preserve a self-image that makes them out to be human in at least some respects. To be completely inhuman means to be completely isolated, to lose any sense of being part of humanity. Hence it is not surprising that there are many data which make one assume that the complete absence of any kindness, friendliness, or tenderness to any human being creates, in the long run, intolerable anxiety. There are reports[21] of cases of insanity and psychic disorders, for instance, among men who were in the Nazi special formations and who had to kill thousands of people. Under the Nazi régime a number of the functionaries who had to carry out the orders for the mass killings suffered nervous breakdowns that were called *Funktionärskrankheit* ('functionaries' disease').[22]

I have used the words 'control' and 'power' in reference to sadism, but one must be clearly aware of their ambiguity. Power can mean power *over* people, or it can mean power to do things. What the sadist is striving for is power *over* people, precisely because he lacks the power *to be*. Many writers, unfortunately, make use of this ambiguous meaning of the words 'power' and 'control', and in order to smuggle in the praise of 'power over' they identify it with 'power to'. Moreover, lack of control does not mean lack of any kind of organization, but only of those kinds in which the control is exploitative and the controlled cannot control the controllers. There are many examples from primitive societies and contemporary intentional communities in which there is rational authority based on real – not manipulated – consent of all, and where relations of 'power over' do not develop.

To be sure, the one who has no power to defend himself also suffers characterologically. He may become submissive and masochistic instead of sadistic. But his realistic power-

21. Indirectly admitted by Himmler in a speech, 6 October 1943. Koblenz, Nazi Archiv. NS 19, H.R. 10.

22. H. Brandt, personal communication.

lessness may also be conducive to the development of virtues like solidarity and compassion, as well as to creativity. Being powerless and hence in danger of being enslaved, or having power and hence being in danger of becoming dehumanized, are two evils. Which is to be shunned the most is a matter of religious and moral or political conviction. Buddhism, the Jewish tradition starting with the Prophets, and the Christian Gospels make a clear decision, contrary to contemporary thinking. It is quite legitimate to make subtle differences between power and non-power, but one danger is to be avoided: that of using the ambiguous meaning of certain words to recommend serving God and Caesar simultaneously, or still worse, to identify them.

Conditions That Generate Sadism

The problem of what factors are conducive to the development of sadism is too complicated to find an adequate answer in this book. One point, however, must be clear from the beginning: there is no simple relation between environment and character. This is because the individual character is determined by such individual factors as constitutionally given dispositions, idiosyncrasies of family life, exceptional events in a person's life. Not only do these individual factors play a role; environmental factors are also much more complex than is generally assumed. As I stressed before, a society is not *a* society. A society is a highly complex system; the old and the new lower middle classes, the middle classes, the upper classes, decaying élites, groups with or without religious or philosophical-moral traditions, small town and big cities – these are only some of the factors that have to be taken into account; no single isolated factor can account for the understanding of character structure as well as of the structure of the society. Therefore, if one wishes to correlate social structure and sadism, nothing short of a thorough empirical analysis of all factors will do. But at the same time it must be added that the power through which one group exploits and keeps down another tends to generate sadism in the controlling group, even though there will be many individual exceptions. Hence sadism will disappear (except as an individual sickness) only when exploitative control of any class, sex, or minority group has been done away with. With the exception of a few small societies this has not yet happened anywhere in history. Nevertheless, the establishment of an order based on law and preventing the most arbitrary use of power has been a step in this direction, even though this development has recently been arrested in many parts of the world where it once existed and is threatened even in the United States in the name of 'law and order'.

A society based on exploitative control also exhibits other predictable features. It tends to weaken the independence, integrity, critical thinking, and productivity of those submitted to it. This does not mean that it does not feed them with all sorts of amusements and stipulations, but only those that restrict the development of personality rather than further it. The Roman Caesars offered public spectacles, mainly of a sadistic nature. Contemporary society offers similar spectacles in the form of newspaper and television reports on crime, war, atrocities; where the contents are not gruesome, they are as unnourishing as the breakfast cereals that are promoted by the same mass media to the detriment of children's health. This cultural food does not offer activating stimuli, but promotes passivity and sloth. At best it offers fun and thrills, but almost no joy; for joy requires freedom, the loosening of the tight reins of control, which is precisely what is so difficult for the anal-sadistic type to do.

As to sadism in the individual, it corresponds to the social average, with individual deviations above and below. Individual factors enhancing sadism are all those conditions that tend to make the child or the grown-up feel empty and impotent (a non-sadistic child may become a sadistic adolescent or adult if new circumstances occur). Among such conditions are those that produce fright, such as terroristic punishment. By this I mean the kind of punishment that is not strictly limited in intensity, related to specific and stated misbehaviour, but that is arbitrary, fed by the punisher's sadism, and of fright-producing intensity. Depending on the temperament of the child, the fear of such punishment can become a dominant motive in his life, his sense of integrity may be slowly broken down, his self-respect lowered, and eventually he may have betrayed himself so often that he has no more sense of identity, that he is no longer 'he'.

The other condition for the generation of vital powerlessness is a situation of psychic scarcity. If there is no stimulation, nothing that awakens the faculties of a child, if there is an atmosphere of dullness and joylessness, the child freezes up; there is nothing upon which he can make a dent, nobody who responds or even listens, the child is left with a sense of powerlessness and impotence. Such a powerlessness does not necessarily result in the formation of the sadistic character; whether or not it does, depends on many other factors. Yet it is one of the main sources that contribute to the development of sadism, both individually and socially.

When the individual character deviates from the social character, the social group tends to reinforce all those character elements that correspond to it, while the opposite elements become dormant. If, for instance, a sadistic person lives within a group where the majority are non-sadistic and where sadistic behaviour is considered undesirable and unpleasant, the sadistic individual will not necessarily change his character, but he will not act upon it; his sadism will not disappear, but will 'dry up', as it were, for lack of being fed. Life in the kibbutzim and other intentional communities offers many examples of this, although there are also instances where the new atmosphere produces a real change of character.[23]

A person whose character is sadistic will be essentially

23. Dr Moshe Budmore, personal communication.

harmless in an anti-sadistic society; he will be considered to be suffering from an illness. He will never be popular and will have little, if any, access to positions in which he can have any social influence. If it is asked what makes the sadism of a person so intense, one must not think only of constitutional, biological factors (S. Freud, 1937), but of the psychic atmosphere that is largely responsible, not only for the generation of social sadism, but also for the vicissitudes of individually generated, idiosyncratic sadism. It is for this reason that the development of an individual can never be fully understood on the basis of his constitution and his family background alone. Unless we 'know the location of the person and his family within the social system, and the spirit of this system, we are barred from understanding why certain traits are so persistent and deep-seated.

Heinrich Himmler : A Clinical Case of Anal-Hoarding Sadism

Heinrich Himmler is an excellent example of a vicious, sadistic character who illustrates what has been said about the connection between sadism and the extreme forms of the anal-hoarding bureaucratic, authoritarian character.

The 'bloodhound of Europe', as he was called by many, Himmler was, together with Hitler, responsible for the slaughter of between fifteen and twenty million unarmed and powerless Russians, Poles, and Jews.

What kind of man was he ?[24]

24. The analysis of Himmler follows mainly the data given by B. F. Smith (1971) in his excellent biography. Smith used all available data on Himmler including: Himmler's six diaries (found in 1957) covering the years 1910–22, as well as a few loose diary pages from 1924; Himmler's list of the correspondence he received and sent between 1918 and 1926; Himmler's long, annotated list of his readings, comprising some two hundred seventy entries; numerous family documents, and Himmler's own collection of official papers and personal mementos. I have also used the study by J. Ackermann (1970), which contains a large number of excerpts from the Himmler diaries, and S. T. Angress and B. F. Smith (1959).

One may begin by considering a few descriptions of Himmler's character by various observers. Perhaps the most accurate, penetrating characterization of Himmler has been given by K. J. Burckhardt, at the time representative of the League of Nations in Danzig. Burckhardt writes: 'Himmler impressed one as of uncanny subalternity (*Subalternität*), narrow-minded conscientiousness, inhuman methodicalness, blended with an element of an automaton' (K. J. Burckhardt, 1960). This description contains most of the essential elements of the sadistic authoritarian character described above. It emphasizes Himmler's submissive subaltern attitude, his inhuman bureaucratic conscientiousness and methodicalness; it is not the description of a hater or of that of a monster as the latter is usually conceived, but of an extremely dehumanized bureaucrat.

Additional elements of Himmler's character structure are contributed by other observers. A leading Nazi, Dr Albert Krebs, who was excluded from the party in 1932, spent six hours of conversation with Himmler on a railroad train in 1929 – that is, when Himmler had little power – and noted his obvious insecurity and gaucheness. What made the trip almost intolerable for Krebs was the 'stupid and basically meaningless chatter with which he intruded upon me all the time'. His conversation was a peculiar mixture of martial braggadocio, *petit bourgeois* small talk (*Stammtischgeschwätz*) and zealous prophecy of a sectarian preacher (quoted by J. Ackermann, 1970). The intrusiveness with which Himmler forces another person to listen to his endless chatter, thus trying to dominate him, is typical of the sadistic character.

Interesting also is the characterization of Himmler by one of the most gifted German generals, Heinz Guderian:

The most opaque of all Hitler's followers was Heinrich Himmler. This insignificant man, with all signs of racial inferiority, behaved in a simple way. He tried to be courteous. His style of life was, in contrast to Goering's, almost Spartanly simple. But all the more unlimited [*ausschweifender*] were his fantasies . . . After 20 July

Himmler was plagued by military ambition. This drove him to get himself appointed Commander-in-Chief of the Reserve Army and even Commander-in-Chief of any army group. It was on the military level that Himmler failed first and completely. His judgement of our enemies must be called simply childish. I had occasion several times to observe his lack of self-confidence and of courage in Hitler's presence. (H. Guderian, 1951)

Another observer, a representative of the German banking élite, Emil Helfferich, wrote that Himmler was 'the type of a cruel educator of the old school, strict against himself but stricter against others ... The signs of compassion and especially friendly tone of his thank-you letters were all fake, as one often finds in clearly cold natures' (E. Helfferich, 1970).

A less negative picture is given by Himmler's aide-de-camp, K. Wolff: it mentions only his fanaticism and his lack of will, not his sadism: 'He could be a tender family father, a correct superior and a good comrade. At the same time he was an obsessed fanatic, an eccentric dreamer and ... a will-less instrument in Hitler's hands, to whom he was tied in an ever-increasing love/hate' (K. Wolff, 1961). Wolff describes two opposite personalities – apparently equally strong – the kind and the fanatic, and does not question the genuineness of the former. Himmler's older brother, Gebhard, describes Heinrich only in positive terms, although the younger brother had hurt and humiliated him long before he was politically powerful. Gebhard even praises the 'fatherly kindness and care with which he was concerned with the needs and worries of his subordinates'.[25]

These characterizations include Himmler's most significant character traits. His lifelessness, his banality, his wish to dominate, his insignificance, his submission to Hitler, his fanaticism. His friendly concern for others, mentioned by Wolff and by his older brother, was certainly a behaviour trait, but to what extent it was a character trait, i.e.,

25. Gebhard Himmler, from an unpublished sketch of Heinrich Himmler's personality.

Malignant Aggression: Cruelty and Destructiveness 401

genuine, is difficult to assess; considering Himmler's total personality, the genuine element in his kindliness must have been very small.

As the whole structure of Himmler's character becomes clearer, we shall find that he is indeed a textbook illustration for the anal (hoarding) sado-masochistic character, in which we have already noted *over-orderliness* and marked *pedantry* as outstanding traits. Since the age of fifteen, Himmler kept a record of his correspondence in which he noted every letter he received and wrote.

His enthusiasm for these operations and the pedantry and penchant for precise record keeping that he displayed while engaged in them revealed an important aspect of his personality. His book-keeper's mentality was most clearly shown in the way he handled the mail he received from Lu and Kaethe [close friends]. (The letters he received from his family have not been preserved.) On each item he wrote not only the date of receipt but even the precise hour and minute when the letter reached his hands. Since many of these items were birthday greetings and the like, his pedantry went beyond absurdity. (B. F. Smith, 1971)

Later on, when he was a chief of the SS, Himmler had a card index to record every object he had ever given to a person (B. F. Smith, 1971). At the suggestion of his father he also wrote a diary from the age of fourteen to twenty-four. Almost every day one finds meaningless entries to which rarely any deeper thought is added.

Himmler noted how long he had slept, when he went to dinner, where he had tea, or whether he smoked, whom he had met during the day, how long he had studied, to which church he had gone and when he had returned home in the evening. Furthermore he noted whom he visited, whether his hosts were nice to him, at what time he had taken the train to return to his parents, whether the train was late or on time. (B. F. Smith, 1971)

Here is an example of his diary entries in the weeks from 1 August to 16 August 1915 (B. F. Smith, 1971):

August   1. 15.   Sunday ... bathed (apparently in a lake, or the sea) a third time ... Daddy, Ernsti and I bathed after canoeing for the fourth time. Gebhard was too hot ...

2. 15.   Monday ... Evening for the fifth time bathed.

3.   Tuesday ... for the sixth time bathed ...

6.   Friday ... bathed a seventh time ... Bathed an eighth time.

7.   Saturday. Morning bathed for the ninth time ...

8.   ... bathed for the 10th time ...

9.   Morning bathed for the 11th time ... After that for the 12th time ...

12.   Played, then bathed for the 13th time ...

13. VIII   Played, then bathed for the 14th time ...

16. VIII   ... Then bathed for the 15th and last time ...

Another example is the following. On 23 August of the same year, Himmler noted that 8,000 Russians were taken prisoner at Gumbinnen; on 28 August, that there were already 30,000 Russian prisoners taken in East Prussia, and on 29 August, that the number of prisoners was not 30,000 but 60,000, and after a still more accurate count, 70,000. On 4 October he noted that the number of Russian prisoners had not been 70,000 but 90,000. He added: 'They multiply like vermin' (B. F. Smith, 1971).

On 26 August 1914 he made the following entry:

26 August. Played in the garden with Falk. 1,000 Russians captured by our troops east of the Weichsel. Advance of the Austrians. In the afternoon worked in the garden. Played piano. After coffee we visited the Kissenbarths. We were allowed to pick plums from the tree there. So frightfully many have fallen. We now have 42 cm. Cannons. (J. Ackermann, 1970.)

Ackermann comments that it remains obscure whether Himmler was concerned with the number of eatable plums or the number of killed men.

Perhaps some of Himmler's pedantry had been acquired

from his father, an extremely pedantic man, a high school teacher, later director whose main strength seems to have been his orderliness. He was a conservative, basically weak man, an old-fashioned, authoritarian father and teacher.

Another outstanding trait in Himmler's character structure is his *submissiveness*, his 'subalternity' as Burckhardt has called it. Even though he does not seem to have been excessively afraid of his father, he was most obedient. He belonged to those people who submit not because the authority is so frightening but because *they* are so frightened – not of the authority but of life – that they seek for an authority and want to submit to it. Their submission has, as it were, an opportunistic quality that is very apparent in Himmler's case. He used his father, his teachers, later his superiors in the army and in the Party, from Gregor Strasser to Hitler, to further his career and to defeat his competitors. Until the time that he found in Strasser and the Nazi leaders new and more powerful father figures, he had never rebelled. He wrote his diaries just as his father had told him to, and felt guilty when he missed a day's entry. He and his parents were Roman Catholics; they were regular church-goers, three to four times a week during the war, and he reassured his father that he need not worry about his reading immoral books like those of Zola. But there are no signs of religious fervour in the history of young Himmler; his and his family's attitude was a purely conventional one, characteristic of his class.

The change of allegiance from father to Strasser–Hitler, from Christianity to Aryan paganism, did not occur as a rebellion. It was smooth and cautious. No new step was taken before it was safe to take it. And at the end, when his idol, Hitler, was of no more use, he tried to betray him by attempting to work under new masters, the Allies, the arch-enemies of yesterday and the victors of today. In this respect lies perhaps the deepest character difference between Himmler and Hitler; the latter was a rebel (although not a revolutionary); the former lacked the rebellious element completely. For this reason there is also no basis for the speculation that Himmler's transformation into a Nazi was an act of rebellion against his father. The real motivation for this change seems to have been different. Himmler needed a strong, powerful guiding figure to compensate for his own weakness. His father was a weak man who, after the defeat of the imperial system and its values, had lost much of his former social prestige and pride. The young Nazi movement, while still not strong when Himmler joined it, was strong in the vehemence of its criticism not only of the left but also of the bourgeois system to which his father belonged. These young people played the role of heroes who own the future, and Himmler, the weak, submissive adolescent, found a more suitable image to submit to than his father was. Simultaneously, he could also look down on his father with some condescension, if not hidden contempt, which was as far as his rebellion went.

The most extreme example of his submission was that to Hitler, although one must suspect that his opportunism may have induced him to use a degree of flattery that was not entirely genuine. Hitler was for him the god-man to be compared to the significance of Christ in the Christian religion or of Krishna in the Bhagavad-Gita. He writes of him: 'He is destined by the Karma of the universal Germanness [*Germanentum*] to lead the fight against the east and to save the Germanness of the world; one of the very great figures of light has found its incarnation in him' (J. Ackermann, 1970). He submitted to the new Krishna–Christ–Hitler as he had to the old Christ-God, except much more fervently. It must be noted, however, that under the circumstances the new gods offered greater opportunities for fame and power.

Himmler's submission to a strong father-figure was accompanied by a deep and intense *dependence on his mother*, who loved him and doted on this son. Himmler certainly did not suffer from lack of love from his mother – a cliché to be found in a number of books and articles written about him.

One might say, however, that her love was primitive; it lacked insight or vision into what the growing boy needed; it was the love a mother has for an infant, and it did not change its quality as the boy grew up. Thus her love spoiled him and blocked his growth and made him dependent on her. Before I describe this dependency, I want to point out that in Himmler, as in so many others, the need for a strong father is generated by the person's helplessness, which in turn is generated by his remaining a little boy who longs for his mother (or a mother-figure) to love him, protect him, comfort him, and not to demand anything from him. Thus he feels not like a man but like a child: weak, helpless, without will or initiative. Hence he will often look for a strong leader to whom he can submit, who gives him a feeling of strength, and who – in an imitating relationship – becomes a substitute for the qualities he lacks.

There was a physical and mental flabbiness in Himmler that is frequently found in such 'mother's boys' and that he tried to overcome by 'practising his will-power' – but mainly by harshness and inhumanity. To him control and cruelty became the substitutes for strength; yet his attempt had to fail since no weakling becomes strong by being cruel; he only hides his weakness temporarily from himself and others, as long as he has the power to control them.

There is abundant evidence to show that Himmler was a typical 'mother's boy'. At the age of seventeen when he was in military training, away from his parents, he wrote in the first month

twenty-three letters home, and though he received ten or twelve in reply, he continually complained that the family did not write enough. The first sentence of his letter on 24 January is typical: 'Dear Mummy, Many thanks for your dear letter. Finally I received something from you.' Two days later, having received another note from home, he starts off in the same vein and adds, 'I have waited a painfully long time for it'. And two letters in three days did not stop him from lamenting on the 29th, 'again today I got nothing from you'.

His early letters combined pleas for mail with complaints about his living conditions: his room was barren and cold, and he suffered from the attentions of bedbugs; he found the food sparse and uninviting and pleaded for packages of food and enough money to allow him to eat at the canteen or the beer-hall restaurants in town. Trivial mishaps, such as the inadvertent picking up of the wrong clothes at the bath, assumed the dimensions of minor tragedies and were reported in detail to the family. In part these complaints and lamentations were appeals for help from Frau Himmler. In response, she dispatched a succession of money orders and of parcels containing food, extra bedding, insect powder, and clean laundry. Apparently much advice and many expressions of worry accompanied the provisions that arrived from Landshut. Under the impact of these messages Heinrich, aware that he must maintain his stance as a brave soldier, would sometimes try to retract the complaint that had set the whole operation in motion. But he always waited until he received the package before changing his tune, and his reserve never lasted long. In the matter of food he was completely unashamed and his letters are filled with appreciative remarks about his mother's cooking ('the *Apfelstrudel* which I ate after the training session was marvellous') and with requests for snacks such as apples and cookies. (B. F. Smith, 1971)

As time went by, his letters home became somewhat less frequent – although never falling below three a week – yet his requests for mail were as insistent as ever. Sometimes he could get quite unpleasant when his mother did not write him as much as he expected. 'Dear Mother,' he began a letter of 23 March 1917, 'Many thanks for your nice news (which I didn't get). It is really mean of you not to have written.'

This need to share everything with his parents, especially with his mother, remained the same when he worked as a *Praktikant* (a student of agriculture who does practical work on a farm). Then nineteen years old, he sent home at least eight letters and cards in the first three and a half weeks, although he often noted that he was too busy to write. When he fell sick with paratyphoid fever his mother was reduced almost to frenzy; on recovery, he spent a good deal of time in writing her all the details about his state of health, his temperature, bowel movements, aches and pains. At the same time he was clever enough not to want to give the impression that he was a cry-baby, interspersing his reports with reassurances that he was fine and chiding his mother for worrying. He even began his letters with three or four items of general interest and then added: 'Now as to how it goes with me I can see you, dear mother, fidgeting with impatience' (B. F. Smith, 1971). This may have been true, but the sentence is one example of a method Himmler used throughout his life – to project his desires and fears on others.

Thus far we have made the acquaintance of an obsessively orderly, hypochondriacal, opportunistic, narcissistic young man who felt like an infant and yearned for mother protection while simultaneously attempting to follow and imitate a father image.

Undoubtedly Himmler's dependent attitude, partly generated by his mother's over-indulgent attitude towards him, was increased by certain real weaknesses, both physical and mental. Physically, Himmler was not a very strong child and suffered from ill health from the age of three. At that time he contracted a serious respiratory infection that seems to have settled in his lungs and from which some children had died. His parents were frantic and brought the physician who had delivered the child all the way from Munich to Passau to treat him. To give the child the best care, Frau Himmler went with him to a place with a better climate, and the father visited when he could take time from his work. In 1904 the whole family moved back to Munich for the sake of the child's health. It is worth noting that the father approved of all these measures, which were costly and inconvenient for him, apparently without protesting.[26]

26. This is another factor that makes me assume that the father was not such a harsh and frightening disciplinarian as he is sometimes painted.

At the age of fifteen he began to have stomach trouble, which was to plague him for the rest of his life. From the whole picture of this illness it is likely that there was a strong psychogenic factor present. While he resented this stomach trouble as a symptom of weakness, it gave him the chance of being constantly occupied with himself and having people around him who listened to his complaints and fussed over him.[27]

Another illness of Himmler's was an alleged heart trouble that was supposed to have been the result of his work on the farm in 1919. The same Munich physician who had treated him for paratyphoid fever now made the diagnosis of a hypertrophied (enlarged) heart due to over-exertion during his military service. B. F. Smith comments that in those years the diagnosis of enlarged heart was frequently made and attributed to exertion in the war, and that today most physicians scoff at such diagnoses. Current medical opinion suggests that there was nothing wrong with Himmler's heart, and that aside from problems of insufficient nourishment and the aftermath of the paratyphoid fever, 'he was probably in reasonably good health' (B. F. Smith, 1971).

However this may be, the diagnosis must have increased Himmler's hypochondriac tendencies and his ties to his parents, who continued to be worried and concerned.

But Himmler's physical weakness went beyond those three groups of illnesses – lung, stomach, and heart. He had a soft and flabby appearance and was physically awkward and clumsy. For instance, when he got a bicycle and could accompany his brother Gebhard on his outings, 'Heinrich had a penchant for falling off his machine, tearing his clothes, and suffering other mishaps' (B. F. Smith, 1971). The same physical awkwardness showed in school and was probably even more humiliating.

27. When he was in power he found such a figure in Dr Kersten, who seems to have had some influence on him, which is not surprising, considering Kersten's function as a mother-figure.

We have an excellent report on Himmler during his school years by his co-student, G. W. F. Hallgarten, who later became an outstanding historian.[28] In his autobiography Hallgarten states that when he heard of Himmler's rise to power he could hardly imagine that this was the same person who had been his classmate.

Hallgarten describes Himmler as an extraordinarily milk-faced, plump boy who already wore glasses and often showed a 'half-embarrassed, half-vicious smile'. He was very popular with all teachers and was an exemplary pupil during all his school years, with the best qualifications in all essential subjects. In class he was considered to be over-ambitious (a *Streber*). There was only one subject in which Himmler was deficient, and that was gymnastics. Hallgarten describes in detail how humiliated Himmler was when he was not able to do relatively simple exercises, and was exposed not only to the ridicule of the teacher but also to that of his classmates, who were happy to see this ambitious boy in a position of inferiority (G. W. F. Hallgarten, 1969).

In spite of his orderliness, however, Himmler lacked discipline and initiative. He was a talker, and he knew it, berated himself for it and tried to overcome it. Most of all, he almost completely lacked strength of will; thus, not surprisingly, he praised a strong will and hardness as ideal virtues, but never acquired them. He compensated for his lack of will-power by his coercive power over others.

An illustration of his own awareness of his submissiveness and lack of will is an entry in his diary on 27 December 1919: 'God will bring everything to a good end but I shall not submit without will to fate, but steer it myself as best I can' (J. Ackermann, 1970). This sentence is rather tortuous and contradictory. He starts out acknowledging God's will (at that time he was still a practising Catholic); then he asserts that he 'will not submit', but qualifies it by adding 'without will' – thus solving the conflict between his actual

28. cf. G. W. F. Hallgarten (1963).

submissiveness and his ideal of having a strong will by the compromise that he will submit but with his will; then he promises himself to steer his own fate, but qualifies this 'declaration of independence' with the lame addition of 'as best I can'. Quite in contrast to Hitler, Himmler always was and remained a weakling, and he knew it. His life was a struggle against this awareness, an attempt to become strong. Himmler was much like an adolescent who wants to and yet cannot stop masturbating, who feels guilty and weak, accuses himself of his weakness, and is always trying to change and never succeeding. But the circumstances and his cleverness permitted him to gain a position of such power over others that he could live with the illusion of having become 'strong'.

Himmler felt not only weak and clumsy physically, but he also suffered from a sense of social inferiority. High school professors were on the lowest level of the monarchical system and were in awe of all the ranks above them. That was all the more acute in Himmler's family, since his father had been for a while the private tutor of Prince Heinrich of Bavaria and had later on kept up enough of a personal relationship so that he could ask the prince to be godfather of his second son, who thus acquired the name Heinrich. With this princely favour granted, the Himmler family had reached the height of their attainable ambitions; the connection would probably have had more favourable consequences had the prince not been killed in battle during the First World War (the only German prince to suffer such a fate). For young Himmler, one might assume, being so eager to hide his sense of worthlessness, the nobility must have seemed like a social heaven barred to him forever.

Yet Himmler's ambition achieved the impossible. From the timid, socially inferior adolescent who admired and envied the members of the nobility, he became the head of the SS, meant to be the new German nobility. No longer was there a Prince Heinrich above him, no longer any counts and barons and von's. He, the Reichsführer SS with his underlings, was the new nobleman; *he* was the Prince; at least this must have been his fantasy. Hallgarten's recollections of their school years points up this connection between the old nobility and the SS. There was a group of sons of noble families in Munich, who lived in a house of their own, but went to the same *Gymnasium* for instruction. Hallgarten remembers that they wore a uniform that was like the later SS uniform, with the exception that the colour was dark blue instead of the SS black. His suggestion that this uniform served as a model for the later SS uniform seems very plausible.

Himmler constantly preached courage and the sacrifice of self for the community. That this was a pretence becomes very apparent in the somewhat complicated history of his wish to join the army and go to the front in 1917. Like his older brother – and many other young men who had connections with the higher échelons of the establishment – Heinrich tried to enter a regiment for officers' training in order to become a cadet (*Fähnrich*, a commissioned officer's aspirant). This training had two advantages: the obvious one of achieving officer rank with the hope of continuing as a professional soldier later on, and the less obvious one that this training took a longer time than that of young men who were drafted or volunteered as common soldiers. One could expect that it would take eight or nine months before they could be sent to the front. Ordinary soldiers were usually sent to the front much faster at that period of the war.

Himmler's older brother Gebhard had already entered officers' training in 1916 and was eventually sent to the front. The fuss made by the family about the older brother and the departure of more and more young people headed for the front made Heinrich Himmler plead with his parents to be allowed to quit school and also enter officers' training. Himmler's father did everything he could to fulfil his son's wish by mobilizing his social connections. But in spite of a warm recommendation from the widow of Prince Heinrich, the regiment to which he was recommended already had sufficient candidates for officers' training and rejected him. The father, in his methodical way, applied to twenty-three regiments, after having jotted down the names of the top officers of each regiment and the names of important people who might have a connection with a regimental commander. In spite of this he got nothing but refusals. Even then Professor Himmler was not ready to admit defeat. Five days later he sent a twenty-fourth application to the 11th Infantry Regiment, which he had not yet approached. While his father was still fighting the battle of the applications, Heinrich temporarily lost hope, and apparently believed that he might be taken into the service as a common soldier. Using his father's connections, he applied to the city of Landshut for service in the *Hilfsdienst*, a kind of war work for those who had not been called up by the Army. He left school and entered this service, apparently with the hope that in this way he might be deferred for a while from the draft; but when the Bavarian School Ministry issued a special order that showed he was in no danger of being drafted, Heinrich re-entered school. Shortly afterwards, much to his and his father's surprise, the twenty-fourth application bore fruit, and he was ordered to report in a few days to the 11th Infantry Regiment in Regensburg.

At the end of the first week he heard a rumour that he was not going to be kept in officers' training, but was scheduled to be shipped to the front immediately. 'This tale reduced him to greater depths of gloom and washed away his ardour for combat' (B. F. Smith, 1971). While explaining to his parents that he was desperate only because he would not become an officer, he asked them to intervene with a second cousin who was a commissioned officer in this regiment and request his help in the matter. The parents, especially the mother, were almost as terrified as was the boy himself, and a month later Lieutenant Zahle, the cousin, was still assuring Heinrich that he was not going to be shipped to the front, urging him to calm down and go through with the programme.

As soon as his fear of being sent to the front was allayed, Heinrich assumed a position of self-confidence. He dared to smoke (although he had to beg his father for tobacco), and he judged the political situation by commenting on an erroneous report of Ludendorff's resignation that 'it did not please him'. He spent 1918 from the beginning of the year to early October in training and awaiting orders to go to the front. This time he seems to have been very eager to be sent and tried to win special favour with the officers to assure his own assignment in preference to that of his friend Kistler, who was also eager to go to the front, in case only one of them were to be assigned. But these efforts had no result, and so he resumed his social calls and theatre visits.

The obvious question here is why, at this point, he was eager to go to the front when several months earlier he had been so frightened. There are several answers to this seeming contradiction. His brother Gebhard had been promoted in battle to full cadet, and that must have made Heinrich very jealous and eager to show that he, too, was a hero. It may also be that the competition with Kistler was just enough of a stimulus to make him forget his anxieties through his wanting to beat Kistler in this little game. But it seems to me more likely that the main reason was something else. Just when Heinrich was making these efforts to be sent to the front he wrote: 'I see the political situation as very black, wholly black . . . I will never lose my resolve even if there is a revolution, which is not out of the question' (B. F. Smith, 1971). Himmler was shrewd enough to know, as almost everybody else knew in Germany in October 1918, that the war was over and lost. It was pretty safe to want to be sent to the front at that time, when the revolutionary wave was already being felt in Germany and three weeks later the revolution was to break out in full force. In fact, the rising opposition and revolutionary mood caused the military authorities not to send these young men to the front after all.

Another illustration for Himmler's lack of will and his indecisiveness was his professional life. His decision to study agriculture came as a complete surprise, and its motives are still not clear. With the classical education he had received, his family must have expected him to have a profession like his father. The most plausible explanation seems to be that he doubted his capacity for study in a more exacting, intellectual field, and that the study of agriculture seemed to be a way of attaining some academic rank. One must not forget that this choice of agriculture was the result of his disappointment in not reaching his first goal, to become a professional officer in the army. His agricultural career was interrupted by real or alleged heart disease, but this did not stop his intention to continue with it. One thing he did was to learn Russian, because he planned to emigrate to the east and become a farmer. He also seemed to think that eventually the *Freikorps* would conquer some territory in the east, and there would be a place for him. He wrote: 'At the moment I don't know why I am working. I work because it is my duty, because I find peace in work and for my German life's companion with whom one day in the east I'll live and fight through my life as a German, far from dear Germany' (B. F. Smith, 1971). And a month later: 'Today, inside myself, I have cut loose from everyone and now depend on myself alone. If I don't find a girl whose character suits mine and who loves me, I'll go to Russia alone' (B. F. Smith, 1971).

These statements are quite revealing. Himmler tries to deny his fears and loneliness and dependency by an assertion of his strong will. With or without a girl he will live far away from Germany, all by himself, and with this kind of talk he tries to convince himself that he is no longer 'mother's boy'. But actually he behaves like a boy of six who decides to run away from mother only to hide around the corner waiting for her to fetch him. Considering that he was at that time a young man of twenty, the whole plan, under the given circumstances, was one of those unrealistic, romantic fantasies to which Himmler was prone when he was not busy in the immediate pursuit of his interests.

When it turned out that there was no chance for settling in Russia, he began to learn Spanish with the idea of settling as a farmer in South America.[29] At different times he considered places like Peru, Georgia (USSR), and Turkey, but all these ideas were pure daydreaming. At this point of his life Himmler had nowhere to go. He could not become an officer. He did not even have the money to become a farmer in Germany – and much less in South America. He lacked not only the money but the imaginativeness, endurance and independence this would have required. He was in the same position as many others who became Nazis because they had nowhere to go socially or professionally, and yet were ambitious and had an ardent desire to rise.

The hopelessness with regard to achieving an aim, and probably the wish to be far away where nobody would know him, must have been greatly increased by the experience he had as a student in Munich. He became a member of a fraternity and did everything to make himself popular. He visited sick fraternity brothers and sought out members and alumni wherever he went. Yet he was troubled that he was not very popular with his fellow members, some of whom expressed their lack of confidence in him quite openly. His fixed ideas and his continuous organizing and gossiping increased his unpopularity, and he was rebuffed when he tried to be elected to an office in the fraternity. In his

29. His method is also characteristic of his pedantic, methodological orientation. He learns a language before having even the slightest idea of what the practical possibilities are for attaining the goal for which he is learning the language. But to learn a language does not do any harm; it does not require making a decision and lets him believe that he has a great plan, while he is actually doing nothing but drift. This is precisely his situation in the early 1920s.

relationship to girls he never got beyond his cautious and rigid position, and he put 'so much distance between himself and the opposite sex that there was soon little danger that his chastity would be threatened' (B. F. Smith, 1971).

The more desperate his own professional chances became, the more was Himmler attracted by radical right-wing ideas. He read anti-Semitic literature, and when German Foreign Minister Rathenau was murdered in 1922 he was pleased and called him a 'scoundrel'. He became a member of a somewhat mysterious extreme right-wing organization *der Freiweg*, and made the acquaintance of Ernest Röhm, an activist in the Hitler movement. In spite of all these new sympathies and connections with the radical Right, he was still cautious enough not to throw his lot completely in with them and remained in Munich and continued his customary life. 'For despite his politicking, and his torment about himself and his future, many of his habits and old ways, including church attendance, social calls, fraternity dances and shipments of dirty laundry to Ingolstadt [his mother], still held fast' (B. F. Smith, 1971). He was saved from his professional predicament by an offer of a job, made by the brother of one of his professors. It was that of technical assistant at a nitrogen fertilizer company, where he was assigned to work on the company's research on manure. But strangely enough, it was this very job that led him directly into the field of active politics. The plant in which he worked was in Schleissheim, north of Munich, and it so happened that one of the new para-military units, *Bund Blücher*, had its headquarters there. He would hardly avoid being drawn into this hum of activity, and after much hesitation he eventually joined Hitler's NSDAP,[30] one of the more active of competing right-wing groups. It would take too much space to describe the events in Germany and Bavaria at that time. Briefly, the Bavarian government

30. Nationalsozialistische Deutsche Arbeiterpartei ('National Socialist German Workers' Party').

toyed with the idea of turning against the Reich government in Berlin with the help of the right-wing groups, but finally failed to act. In the meantime Himmler left his job in Schleissheim and joined a military unit, a replacement company for a Reichswehr regiment. His company, however, was dissolved by the Reichswehr because there were too many who were willing to participate in an action against Berlin, and thus after only seven weeks Himmler's new military career was ended. But in the meantime he had made close connections with Röhm, and on the day of the Munich Putsch it was Himmler who carried the old imperial war flag, and marched at Röhm's side at the head of a column trying to seize the War Ministry. Röhm and his men surrounded the War Ministry, but were in turn surrounded by Bavarian police. Hitler's attempt to relieve Röhm had ended in his unsuccessful march against army troops at the *Feldherrnhalle*. The leaders of the Röhm group (*Reichskriegsflagge*) were taken into custody and Himmler and the rest of the men gave up their weapons, identified themselves to the police, and went home.

Himmler, although still impressed with himself for bearing the flag, was both frightened of being arrested and disappointed that the government was not interested in him. He did not dare to do anything that might lead to an arrest, like working with the forbidden organizations. (It should be realized that an arrest would not have had any frightful consequences. Most likely he would have been released, or acquitted, or have received a short sentence to be confined to a *Festung*, like Hitler – a comfortable place with all conveniences, except the right to leave.) Instead, he satisfied himself with rationalizations: 'As a friend, and especially as a soldier and devoted member of the *völkisch* movement, I will never run from danger, but we have a duty to each other and to the movement to hold ourselves in readiness for the struggle' (B. F. Smith, 1971). Accordingly, he worked in the *völkisch* movement, which was not forbidden, kept trying to get a job, and toyed with the idea of locating an attractive position in Turkey. He even wrote to the Soviet Embassy to inquire if there was any chance of going to the Ukraine – a strange step for this fanatical anti-Communist. In this period his anti-Semitism also became more vicious and was sexually tinged, probably because of his continued preoccupation with sex. He speculated about the morals of girls he met and seized upon erotic literature whenever it was available. While visiting old friends in 1924 he found in their library C. F. Schlichtegrolls' *Ein Sadist im Priesterrock* (A Sadist in Priestly Attire), which had been banned in Germany in 1904. He raced through it in one day. In general, he presented the picture one would expect as an inhibited and frightened young man who suffered from his inability to relate to women.

Eventually the problem of his future was solved. Gregor Strasser, a leader of the *Nationalsozialistische Freiheitsbewegung* and its *Gauleiter* for Lower Bavaria, offered him a job as his secretary and general assistant. He accepted immediately, went to Landshut and rose with Strasser in the party. Strasser represented quite different ideas from those of Hitler. He stressed the social revolutionary features in the Nazi programme and was a leader of this more radical wing, together with his brother Otto and Joseph Goebbels. They wanted to move Hitler away from his upper-class orientation and believed the Party should 'proclaim a message of social revolution with only a spice of anti-Semitism' (B. F. Smith, 1971). But Hitler did not change his course. Goebbels, knowing which side was stronger, gave up his own ideas and followed Hitler. Strasser left the party, and Röhm, the chief of the SA who also represented more radical revolutionary ideas, was murdered on Hitler's orders, in fact at the hands of Himmler's SS men. The death of Röhm and other leaders of the SA was the beginning and condition of Himmler's own rise to the top.

In 1925–6, however, the NSDAP was a small party, the Weimar Republic seemed to have become more stable, and Himmler apparently had some doubts. He had lost former friends, and 'even his parents made it clear that they not only disapproved of his party work but looked on him as the proverbial lost son' (B. F. Smith, 1971). His salary was small, and he often had to borrow money. Thus it is not surprising that again the old wish seized him to obtain a solid position as a farm administrator, and that he toyed once more with the notion of emigrating to Turkey. He remained, however, in his party post because all his attempts to find a job remained completely fruitless – not because his loyalty to the ideas of the party was so strong and unswerving. Shortly after, things brightened. Gregor Strasser became Reich propaganda leader for the party in 1929 and Himmler was made his deputy.

Only three years later Himmler commanded three hundred men of the *Schutz Staffeln*, which by 1933 had grown to an army of fifty thousand.

In his biography of Himmler, Smith comments: 'What disturbs us so profoundly is not the organization of the SS nor Himmler's ultimate position as Reich police chief, but the torture of millions of human beings and extermination of millions more. No direct answer to these questions is to be found in Himmler's childhood and youth' (B. F. Smith, 1971). I do not believe that he is right and shall attempt to show that Himmler's sadism was deeply rooted in his character structure long before he had the occasion to practise it on the scale that made his name enter history as a bloody monster.

We should keep in mind the broad definition of sadism, as the passion for absolute and unrestricted power over another human being; the infliction of physical pain is only one of the manifestations of this wish for omnipotence. We must also not forget that masochistic submissiveness is not the opposite of sadism, but part of the symbiotic system in which complete control and complete submission are manifestations of the same basic vital impotence.

One of the earliest indications of Himmler's pleasure in malignant denunciations of other people might be an incident during the war when Himmler was sixteen years old. Some well-to-do Saxons who spent a vacation in Bavaria had hoarded food there and sent it home, where such things were much more difficult to obtain. They were denounced in the newspaper, and Smith believes that the wealth of information Himmler had about the items they had brought 'certainly suggests that he played some part in its exposure' (B. F. Smith, 1971). A little poem Himmler wrote in 1919 also expresses his cruel streak (in B. F. Smith, 1971):

> Franzosen, Franzosen, O gebt nur recht Acht
> Für euch wird kein Pardon gemacht.
> Uns're Kugeln pfeifen und sausen
> Und verbreiten euch Schrecken und Grauen
> Wenn wir da so unheimlich hausen.
>
> (Frenchmen, Frenchmen, oh pay close attention
> For there will be no pardon for you.
> Our bullets will whistle and pass
> Spreading fright and horror among you
> As we so uncannily do as we wish.)

From the age of twenty-one when he felt somewhat more independent because he had begun to find new friends and father-figures, he began to be slightly condescending towards his father, although he always couched his preaching in appropriate forms, while the condescending preaching to his older brother Gebhard became increasingly vicious.

It is necessary, in order to trace the development of Himmler's sadism, to understand the significance of his relationship to Gebhard.[31] Gebhard was actually the opposite of Heinrich; he was easy-going, popular, unafraid, and attractive to girls. When the two were younger, Heinrich seems to have admired Gebhard, but this admiration changed to bitter envy when Gebhard succeeded in the various things in which Heinrich failed. He went into the war, was promoted on the battlefield, and received the

31. My source for the following discussion of Heinrich's relationship with Gebhard is the description in B. F. Smith (1971).

Iron Cross 1st class. He fell in love with an attractive girl and became engaged to her while his younger brother, possessing neither glory nor love, was awkward, weak, and unpopular. Heinrich shifted his loyalty from Gebhard to his second cousin Ludwig, who had reasons to feel jealous of Gebhard. At first he only criticized his brother caustically for his lack of discipline and purpose, for not being sufficiently heroic, and for being careless – as usual, criticizing others for the very vices he himself had. But the future Minister of Police appears fully fledged in his relationship to Gebhard after the latter successfully courted a distant and apparently attractive cousin of theirs named Paula. The girl did not fit Heinrich's idea of a shy, retiring, and chaste fiancée, and, unfortunately, there was some trouble between Paula and Gebhard because of an alleged earlier 'indiscretion' on her side. Gebhard wrote Heinrich imploring him to go to Paula's home and help them to settle the question. This unusual request shows to what extent Heinrich had already succeeded in subduing his older brother, probably by intriguing with his parents. Heinrich went to see Paula, but it is not known what happened. The letter he drafted to her a few weeks later, however, after she had apparently made four pledges of fidelity, shows us something of his coercive character:

I will gladly believe that you will uphold these four things, especially as long as Gebhard works directly on you through his personal presence. But that is not enough. A man must have certainty from his bride, even if he is not present for years, and doesn't see her and they don't hear anything from each other for a long time (which in the coming terrible war years only too easily could be the case), that she herself with no word, no glance, no kiss, no gesture and no thought will be untrue to him ... You have a test which you should and *must* [underlined in the original] be able to withstand, and have in a shameful manner not withstood ... If your union is to be a happy one for you two and for the health of *das Volk* – which must be built on sound, moral families – you must control yourself with *barbaric* [underlined in the original] strength. Since you do not handle yourself strongly and firmly, and only control yourself to a small degree, and since your future husband, as I have already said, is too good for you, and possesses too little understanding of people and can't learn it since this age won't let it be learned, someone else must do it. Since you both approached me on this affair and drew me in, I feel myself obligated to do it.

For the next seven months Heinrich avoided outright meddling, until in February 1924 he got some kind of information that convinced him, rightly or wrongly, that Paula had again committed an 'indiscretion'. This time he did not even tell his brother, but told the story immediately to his parents and tried to convince them that the family honour demanded an end to the engagement. His mother capitulated and agreed in tears, and eventually he persuaded his father as well; only then did he confront Gebhard directly. 'When Gebhard agreed to go along and allowed the engagement to end, Heinrich was triumphant and at the same time scornful of his brother's lack of resistance. It was, he said, "as if he [Gebhard] had absolutely no soul".' This twenty-four-year-old young man had succeeded in breaking down his father, his mother, and his older brother, and in making himself the virtual dictator of the family.

The termination of the engagement was especially distasteful to the Himmlers, all the more so because Paula's family was distantly related to them. 'Yet whenever his parents or Gebhard showed any reluctance about going through with the break, Heinrich was ready to apply more pressure. He visited mutual friends to explain why the engagement must end and in the process tore the girl's reputation to shreds. When a letter arrived from Paula, his response was to stress the need "to stand firm and not let oneself be deterred by doubts".' At this point the wish to control his brother and parents assumed features of pure sadistic viciousness. He wanted to destroy the girl's reputation, and in order to humiliate the parents, Gebhard, and the girl's family even more, insisted that all presents that had been exchanged must be returned. The father's wish that they end the engagement by mutual consent was turned down by Heinrich, whose hard line triumphed and who eventually rejected all compromise. Himmler had won a total victory and made everybody thoroughly unhappy.

In most cases, the story would have ended here, but not so for Heinrich Himmler. He engaged a private detective to watch Paula's conduct and asked him to collect stories 'that you have heard and which you can prove!' The private detective sent him a collection of stories that might have been compromising. Himmler used the occasion to humiliate Paula's family still more by returning some more gifts he had received from the family which he had allegedly forgotten to return before, just adding his visiting card.

His final onslaught came two months later in a letter to mutual friends. He asks them to tell Paula to stop saying nasty things about the Himmlers and adds the warning that, although he is a nice fellow, '*I will be completely different if anyone forces me to it. Then, I will not be stopped by any false sense of pity until the opponent is socially and morally ousted from the ranks of society.*' [Italics added.]

This was the height of vicious control that Himmler could exert under the circumstances. When by his cunning he was able to use the new political circumstances for his own purposes, he had the possibility to act out his sadism on a historical scale. Yet the Reichsführer SS spoke in terms that were not essentially different from those used by the youthful Himmler in his threat to Paula. This is illustrated by Himmler's speech about twenty years later (1943) about the ethics of the black order:

One principle must have absolute validity for the SS man, to be honest, decent, loyal, and to be a good comrade to members of our own blood and to nobody else. What happens to the Russians or to the Czechs is a matter of complete indifference to me. What of good blood other peoples have we will take from them by robbing them of their children if necessary, and bringing them up among ourselves. Whether other nations live in prosperity, or whether they perish from hunger, that interests me only inasmuch as we need slaves for our culture; otherwise it does not interest me. Whether in the construction of ditches for Panzers 10,000 Russian women fall down or not, interests me only inasmuch as the ditch is ready for Germany. *We shall never be cruel and heartless where it does not have to be.* (J. Ackermann, 1970; italics added)

In this statement the sadist is free to express himself fully. He will rob other people's children if their blood is good. He will take the older ones as 'slaves for our culture', and whether they live or die is of no interest to him. The closing of the speech is typical Himmler and Nazi double-talk. He protests his moral kindness by assuring his listeners and himself that he is cruel and heartless only if necessary. This is the same rationalization he used already in his threat to Paula: I shall be pitiless 'if anyone forces me to it'.

Himmler was a frightened man and always needed rationalizations to embellish his sadism. He may also have needed to protect himself from being confronted with the evidence of his cruelty. Karl Wolff reports that Himmler witnessed a mass execution in Minsk in the late summer of 1941 and was rather shaken by it. But he said, 'Nevertheless, I think it is right that we look at this. Who is to decide over life and death must know what dying is like and what he asks the execution commanders to do' (K. Wolff, 1961). Many of his S S men became sick after these mass executions; some committed suicide, became psychotic, or suffered from other severe mental damage.[32]

One cannot speak of Himmler's sadistic character without discussing what has often been described as his kindness. I have already mentioned that he tried to make himself popular by visiting sick fraternity brothers, but he did similar things also on other occasions. He gave an old woman cake and rolls and recorded in his diary: 'If I could

32. cf. R. Höss, commandant in Auschwitz (quoted by J. Ackermann, 1970). See also Himmler's October 1943 speech, to the highest S S leaders, on 'nervous breakdowns' as one possible consequence of his extermination campaign (Koblenz, Nazi Archiv. N S 19, H.R. 10).

only do more, but we are ourselves poor devils' (not true, because his family was a well-to-do-middle-class family and far from being poor devils). He organized a benefit with his friends and gave the proceeds to Viennese children, and he behaved in a 'fatherly' way to his SS men, as many have commented. From the whole picture of Himmler's character, however, I get the impression that most of these friendly acts were not expressions of genuine friendliness. He had a need to compensate for his own lack of feeling and cold indifference, and to convince himself and others that he was not what he was, or, to put it differently, that he felt what he did not feel. He had to deny his cruelty and coldness by a show of kindness and concern. Even his aversion to hunting animals, which he described as cowardly, could not have been very serious since he proposed in one of his letters that the hunting of big animals should be facilitated for the SS men as a reward for good conduct. He was friendly to children and animals, but even here scepticism must be permitted, because there is almost nothing this man did that did not have the purpose of furthering his own career. Of course, even a sadist like Himmler can have some positive human traits, like kindness to some people in some situations; one would expect him to have such traits. What makes it so difficult to believe in them in Himmler is his complete coldness and the exclusive pursuit of his selfish goals.

There is also a benevolent type of sadism in which control over the other person does not have the aim of harming him, but is meant to work for his own good.[33] It may be that Himmler had some of this benevolent sadism, which often gives the impression of kindness. (In his letters to his parents his condescending preaching has perhaps a benevolent aspect, as has his relationship to his SS men.) An example is Himmler's 16 September 1938 letter to a high SS officer, Count Kottulinsky: 'Dear Kottulinsky, You were very sick and had much trouble with your heart. In the interests of

33. cf. the discussion of 'benevolent' sadism in E. Fromm (1941).

your health, I forbid you any smoking for the next two years. After these two years, you will send me a medical report on your health; after that I shall decide whether the prohibition of smoking will be lifted or will be continued. Heil Hitler' (quoted by H. Heiber, 1958). We find the same tone of the schoolmaster in a letter (30 September 1942) to the chief physician of the S S, Grawitz, who had written him an unsatisfactory report on medical experiments on the concentration camp inmates.

This letter should not be the cause of your asking yourself for hours whether I shall fire you as Chief Physician, it has only the intention to make you give up now after many years your main defect, your vanity, and yet seriously and really to approach all your tasks also the most disagreeable ones with courage and eventually to give up the drive and the opinion that one can get things in order by much talk and chatter. If you learn this and work on yourself, then everything is in order and I shall then be satisfied again with you and your work. (Quoted by H. Heiber, 1958)

Himmler's letter to Grawitz is interesting not only for its schoolmasterish tone but also because Himmler admonishes the doctor to give up the very defects which were so clearly his own – vanity, lack of courage, and talkativeness. The collection is full of similar letters in which he plays the role of a strict and wise father. Many of the officers to whom they were written were members of the feudal class, and one may not go far astray if one assumes that it gave Himmler a particular satisfaction to show them his superiority and to treat them like schoolboys. (This is no longer benevolent.)

Himmler's end was as much in line with his character as his life had been. When it was clear that Germany had lost the war, he was preparing negotiations with the Western powers, through Swedish intermediaries, which would leave him in a leading role, and offered concessions with regard to the fate of the Jews. In these negotiations he surrendered one by one the political dogmas to which he had clung so tenaciously. Of course, simply by initiating them, *der treue*

Heinrich (loyal Heinrich), as he was called, committed the last act of treachery to his idol, Hitler. That he thought the Allies would accept him as the new German 'Führer' was a sign of his mediocre intelligence and lack of political judgement, as well as of his narcissistic grandiosity, which made him think that he was the most important man even in a defeated Germany. He declined the suggestion of General Ohlendorf to surrender to the Allies and to take responsibility for the S S. The man who had preached loyalty and responsibility now showed, true to character, complete disloyalty and irresponsibility. He fled with a black patch over his eye and without his moustache, with false papers, and in the uniform of a corporal. When he was arrested and brought into a prisoner-of-war camp, his narcissism apparently could not tolerate being treated like thousands of unknown soldiers. He asked to see the commander of the camp and told him, 'I am Heinrich Himmler.' Sometime later he bit the cyanide capsule he carried in a hollow tooth. Only a few years earlier, in 1938, he had said in a speech to his officers, 'I have no understanding of a person who throws away his life like a dirty shirt because he believes in this way he will evade difficulties. Such a person must be interred like an animal' (J. Ackermann, 1970).

Thus the circle of his life closed. He had to attain absolute power in order to overcome his own experience of weakness and vital impotence. After he had achieved this aim, he tried to cling to this power by betraying his idol. When he was in a prison camp, as an ordinary soldier, one among hundreds of thousands, he could not bear his reduction to complete powerlessness. He preferred to die, rather than to be thrown back to the role of the powerless man that was for him that of the weakling.

To Sum Up

Himmler is an example of the typical anal-hoarding, sadistic, authoritarian character. He was weak (and did not only *feel* weak); he found a certain sense of security in his orderliness and pedantry, by submitting to strong father images, and eventually he developed a passion for unlimited control over others as the one way to overcome his sense of vital impotence, shyness, uneasiness. He was extremely envious of others whom life had endowed with more strength and self-esteem. His vital impotence and the resulting envy led to the malicious wish to humiliate and destroy them, whether it was his brother Gebhard's fiancée or the Jews. He was utterly cold and without mercy, which made him feel more isolated and more frightened.

Himmler was also an absolute opportunist. His sadistic passion was always governed by what he thought was advantageous for him; he was disloyal and an inveterate liar – not only towards others, but equally towards himself. Every one of the virtues he eternally preached was conspicuous by its absence within himself. He coined the SS motto, 'Loyalty is our Honour', and betrayed Hitler. He preached strength, firmness, and courage, yet he was weak, flabby, and cowardly. The '*treue Heinrich*' was a living lie. Perhaps the only true thing he ever said about himself was a sentence he wrote to his father while he was in military training: 'Have no fears on my account because I am sly as a fox' (B. F. Smith 1971).[34]

34. Himmler is a good example of the contradiction between image and reality among many political leaders: he is the ruthless sadist and coward who builds up the image of a kind, loyal, courageous man. Hitler, the 'saviour' of Germany, who 'loved' his country beyond anything else, was a ruthless destroyer not only of his enemies but of Germany herself. Stalin, the 'kind father of his country', almost destroyed it and morally poisoned it. Another outstanding example of fakery was Mussolini: he, who played the role of the aggressive, courageous male whose motto was 'to live dangerously', was of an exceptional personal cowardice. Angelica Balabanof, who was co-editor of *Avanti* in

A behaviourist might still ask whether Himmler was not a normal man until circumstances made it advantageous for him to act sadistically.

I believe our analysis has already answered this question. We have seen that all the conditions for a sadistic development were given in his earlier development. We have followed the development of his early insecurity, unmanliness, cowardice, sense of impotence, and these attributes alone would indicate the probability of sadistic compensations. Moreover, we have seen the development of his over-orderly, pedantic, typically anal-hoarding, authoritarian character. Eventually we have seen his overt pernicious sadism in dealing with his brother's fiancée, long before he had any power. We must come to the conclusion that the *Reichsführer* SS was a sadistic character before he was a *Reichsführer*; his position gave him the power to act out his sadism on the historical stage; but the sadism was there before.

This question leads to another that has often been raised: What would have become of Himmler had he not been born at the time of the Nazi power, yet endowed with the same character he had at the time of his intervention with his brother's engagement? The answer is not too difficult to find. Since he was of average intelligence and very orderly, he probably would have found a place in a bureaucratic system, say as a school teacher, postal clerk, or employee in a large business enterprise. Since he ruthlessly sought his

---

Milan when Mussolini was still a Socialist, told me that the physician who took blood from him for a test said he had rarely seen a man who behaved as cowardly in this situation as Mussolini. Furthermore, Mussolini waited for her every afternoon to leave the office, so that he could walk home with her. He said 'I am afraid of every shadow and every tree.' (At that time there was no danger whatsoever to his safety.) There are many other examples of his cowardliness; one from his later years is when his son-in-law, Count Ciano, was condemned to death and he, Mussolini – the only one who could have commuted the sentence – could not be reached during the twenty-four hours in which a stay of execution could have been ordered.

advantage, by cleverly flattering his superiors and intriguing against his colleagues he might have risen to quite
a high position; probably not to a top position because he
lacked any constructive imagination or good judgement.
He would have been thoroughly disliked by his colleagues
and perhaps would have become the favourite of a powerful
superior. He would have made a good agent for Ford, in
Henry Ford's anti-union days, but hardly a good personnel
chief in a modern corporation, because his coldness would
have made him too unpopular. At his funeral his boss and
the minister would have eulogized him as a kind father and
husband, a responsible citizen whose selfless services as a
church warden would always remain an example and an
inspiration.

There are thousands of Himmlers living among us.
Socially speaking, they do only minor harm in normal life,
although one must not underestimate the number of people
whom they damage and make thoroughly unhappy. But
when forces of destruction and hate threaten to engulf the
whole body politic, such people become extremely dangerous; they are the ones who yearn to serve the government
as its agents for terror, for torture and killing. Many people
commit the severe error of believing that one can easily
recognize a potential Himmler from far away. One of the
purposes of characterological studies is to show that the
potential Himmler looks like anybody else, except to those
who have learned to read character and who do not have to
wait until circumstances permit the 'monster' to show his
colours.

What are the factors that made Himmler a merciless
sadist? A simple answer could be found by referring to our
previous discussion of the factors that tend to produce the
hoarding character. But this would not be a satisfactory
answer because Himmler's character presented an extreme
and very malignant form of the hoarding character, which
is much less frequent than the only slightly sadistic hoarder.

If we try to look for the factors responsible for the character development of 'the bloodhound of Europe' we first run across his relationship to his parents. He was bound to his mother who encouraged his dependency, and he had an authoritarian, rather weak father. But are there not millions who have the same antecedents and who do not become Himmlers? Indeed, one or two isolated factors can never explain a person's specific character; only a whole system of interrelated factors can more or less fully account for character development. In Himmler we have seen some other factors: his physical weakness and awkwardness, perhaps generated by a number of physical illnesses and an impaired constitution; his sense of social inferiority based on his social fringe position, increased by his father's submissive and worshipful attitude towards the aristocracy; his timidity towards women, which may have had its cause in his fixation to his mother that made him feel helpless and unmanly; his extreme narcissism and jealousy of his older brother, who had all the qualities Himmler lacked. There are numerous other factors we have not touched upon, partly because of lack of information, that would give us a fuller picture. We must also consider that there may be genetically determined factors that, while not the source of sadism, are responsible for a disposition towards it. But perhaps more than of any other factor we must think of the pathogenic influence of the dry, banal, pedantic, dishonest, unalive atmosphere in which the Himmler family lived. There were no values except the insincere profession of patriotism and honesty, there was no hope except that of managing to hold on to their precarious position on the social ladder. There was no fresh air, spiritually or mentally, that could have encouraged the weak little boy to branch out and develop. And there was not only this family. The Himmlers were part of a social class on the lowest fringe of the imperial system that suffered from resentment, im-potence, and joylessness. This was the soil on which

Himmler grew – and he became increasingly more vicious as the revolution defeated his social status and values, and as it became clearer to him that he had no future in professional terms.

12

Malignant Aggression: Necrophilia

The Traditional Concept

The term 'necrophilia', love of the dead,[1] has been applied generally only to two kinds of phenomena: (1) sexual necrophilia, a man's desire to have sexual intercourse or any other kind of sexual contact with a female corpse, and (2) non-sexual necrophilia, the desire to handle, to be near to, and to gaze at corpses, and particularly the desire to dismember them. But the term has generally not been applied to a *character-rooted passion*, the soil in which its more overt and cruder manifestation grows. A look at some examples of necrophilia in the traditional sense will make it easier to identify the less obvious *necrophilous character*.

Reports on cases of necrophilia can be found in a number of works, especially those on sexual perversions and criminology. The most complete selection is given by H. von Hentig, one of the foremost German criminologists, in a work dealing exclusively with this subject. (In German as well as in the criminal law of other countries, necrophilia constitutes a crime.) He cites as examples of necrophilia:

1. The Greek *nekros* means 'corpse', the dead, the inhabitants of the underworld. In Latin, *nex, necis* means violent death, murder. Quite clearly *nekros* does not refer to death but to the dead, the corpse and the murdered (whose death was apparently distinguished from natural death). 'To die', 'death', has a different meaning; it does not refer to the corpse but to the act of dying. In Greek it is *thanatos*, in Latin *mors, mori*. The words 'die' and 'death' go back to the Indo-germanic root *dheu, dhou*. (I am indebted to Dr Ivan Illich for giving me extended material on the etymology of these concepts, from which I have quoted only the most important data.)

(1) acts of sexual contact with a female corpse (intercourse, manipulation of sexual organs), (2) sexual excitement produced by the sight of a woman's corpse, (3) attractions to corpses and graves and to objects connected with the grave, such as flowers or pictures,[2] (4) acts of dismemberment of a corpse, and (5) the craving to touch or to smell the odour of corpses or anything putrid (H. von Hentig, 1964).

Von Hentig shares the opinion of other authors – such as T. Spoerri (1959), whom he quotes – that necrophilia is much more frequent than is generally assumed. For practical reasons, however, this perversion meets with very limited possibilities for satisfaction. The only people who have easy access to corpses and the opportunity to act out such a perversion are grave-diggers and morgue attendants. Thus it is not surprising to find that most examples given deal with this group of people. Of course, it is also possible that these occupations may in themselves tend to attract necrophilous persons. Murderers, of course, also have the opportunity to practise necrophilia, but considering that murder used to be relatively rare, we cannot expect to find many instances in this category, except in some of these cases classified as 'lust murder'. However, von Hentig quotes a number of examples in which outsiders have dug up corpses, abducted them, and used them sexually to satisfy their necrophilous craving. The conclusion is unavoidable that since necrophilia is relatively frequent among those who have an easy opportunity, it must also be present, at least in fantasies or acted out in other, less obvious ways, in many others who lack this opportunity.

This is a case history of a twenty-one-year-old morgue attendant reported by J. P. de River. At the age of eighteen he fell in love with a girl with whom he had sexual intercourse just once, because she was in poor health (pulmonary tuberculosis). He states: 'I have never gotten over the death of my sweetheart, and whenever I commit the act of

2. In some countries it is customary to exhibit a portrait of the deceased on the grave.

masturbation, I visualize having sexual intercourse with my dead sweetheart.' De River's report continues:

Upon the death of his sweetheart, he was so emotionally upset at seeing her laid out in a white shroud that he had a crying spell, and he allowed himself to be removed from the side of the casket with great reluctance. At this time he felt an urge to jump into the casket with her, and he actually wanted to be buried alive with his sweetheart. He created quite a scene at the burial, and at the time everyone, including his family thought this was the result of his great grief at seeing her laid away; but he now comes to realize that it was a fit of passion and that he was overcome with a great sexual urge at the sight of the deceased. At that time, he had just completed his last year in high school, and he tried to prevail upon his mother to allow him to enter medical school, but because of lack of funds he was unable to do so. However, at his suggestion, she allowed him to enter a school of undertaking and embalming, because the course was much cheaper and shorter.

D. W. studied very hard at this school, realizing at last that he had found a profession in which he would be most happy. He was always intensely interested in the female bodies in the embalming room, and on numerous occasions he had a great desire to have an act of sexual intercourse with a female cadaver. He realized that this was wrong and fought the desire off on numerous occasions until one day, near the completion of his studies, when he was alone in the room with the body of a young girl, the urge to commit an act of sexual intercourse upon the body of the deceased victim was so great and the circumstances so ideal he let himself go. He took advantage of this opportunity and exposed his privates, touching his penis to her thigh, at which time he became greatly excited. Losing control of himself, he leaped upon the body and copulated his mouth to the private parts of the cadaver. He states that this caused him such sexual stimulation that he had a seminal emission. He was then seized with great remorse and fear – the fear of being detected and found out by his fellow students. Shortly after the commission of this act, he graduated from the school, and secured a position as morgue attendant in a mid-western city. As he was the junior member of the staff of morgue attendants, he was frequently called upon to remain alone in the morgue at night. D. W. states, 'I was glad of the opportunity of being alone, as I had come to realize that I was different from other men, in that I longed to be alone with the dead, and this would give me ample opportunity to attempt an act of coitus with a corpse – a feeling that I came to realize existed ever since the death of my sweetheart.'

He violated scores of female corpses in the two years that he remained attached to the morgue, by practising various perversions on them, ranging in age from infants to elderly women. He usually began by sucking their breasts and copulating his mouth to their privates, after which acts he would become so excited that he would crawl upon their bodies, and with superhuman effort he would perform the act of coitus. He has had as many as four or five acts a week of this nature, depending upon the number of female corpses in the morgue.

. . . On one occasion, he was so impressed with the corpse of a young girl fifteen years of age that when alone with her the first night after death, he drank some of her blood. This made him so sexually excited that he put a rubber tube up into the urethra and with his mouth sucked the urine from her bladder. On this occasion he felt more and more of an urge to go further and felt that if he could only devour her – eat her up – even chew part of her body, it would give him great satisfaction. He was unable to resist this desire, and turning the body upon its face, he bit into the flesh of the buttocks near the rectum. He then crawled upon the cadaver and performed an act of sodomy on the corpse. (J. P. de River, 1956)

This case history is particularly interesting for several reasons. First and most obviously, because it combines necrophilia with necrophagia and anal eroticism. The other, less obvious point lies in the beginning of the perversion. If one knew the story only up to the death of his sweetheart, one might be prone to interpret his behaviour as an expression of the intensity of his love. But the rest of the story throws a very different light on the beginning: one could hardly explain his indiscriminate necrophilous and necrophagous desires as being caused by the love for his sweetheart. One is forced to assume that his 'mourning' behaviour was not the expression of love, but the first symptom of his necrophilous desires. It would then also appear that the fact that he had sexual intercourse with his sweet-heart only once is poorly rationalized by her illness. It is more likely that because of his necrophilous tendencies he had little desire for sexual intercourse with a live woman.

De River gives another, less complex case history of a necrophilous morgue attendant. The subject is an un-married man, aged forty-three, who states:

At the age of eleven, while a grave-digger in Milan, Italy, I began masturbating, and when alone would do so while touching the bodies of the dead, young, good-looking women. Later I began inserting my penis into the dead girls. I came to America and left the east coast after a short stay, and came to the west coast where I secured a job washing bodies at a mortuary. Here I resumed my practice of having intercourse with dead girls, sometimes in the caskets or on the tables where the bodies are washed.

The report continues:

He admits using his mouth on the private parts, and sucking the breasts of young girl corpses. When asked how many women he has had, he states: 'Maybe hundreds, as it has been going on since I was eleven years old' (J. P. de River, 1956).

The literature quoted by von Hentig reports many similar cases.

A great attenuated form of necrophilia is to be found in individuals who become sexually excited by the sight of corpses and sometimes masturbate in front of them. The number of such persons can hardly be estimated because they are rarely discovered.

The second form of necrophilia appears unalloyed with sex, in acts of the pure passion to destroy. Often this urge to destroy is already manifest in childhood; sometimes it shows itself only at a later age. Von Hentig writes very sensitively that the aim of necrophilous destructiveness is the passion 'to tear apart living structures' (*lebendige Zusammenhänge*). This desire to tear apart what is alive finds its clearest ex-pression in a craving to dismember bodies. A typical case reported by Spoerri is that of a man going to the cemetery at night with all the necessary instruments, digging up the coffin, opening it, and taking the corpse with him to a place where he could hide it; he would then cut off the legs and the head and cut open the stomach (T. Spoerri, 1959). Sometimes the object of dismemberment is not a human being but an animal. Von Hentig tells about a man who stabbed thirty-six cows and mares to death and then cut off various parts of their bodies. But we hardly need the literature; there are enough newspaper reports about murders where the victim has been dismembered or mutilated. These cases are usually subsumed under the classification of murder, but they are committed by necrophilous murderers who are different from most murderers, whose motive is gain, jealousy, or revenge. The real aim of necrophilous murderers is not the death of the victim – which is, of course, a necessary condition – but the act of dismemberment. In my own clinical experience I have seen sufficient evidence that the desire for dismemberment is highly characteristic of the necrophilous character. For example, I have seen (directly or through supervision) several persons who expressed the desire for dismemberment in a very attenuated form; they would draw the figure of a nude woman, then cut out the arms, legs, head, etc., and play with these parts of the dismembered drawing. This 'play' was in fact, however, the satisfaction of an intense craving for dismemberment acted out in a safe and harmless way.

In many other necrophilous people I have observed that they had many dreams in which they saw parts of dismembered bodies floating or lying around, sometimes in blood, often in dirty water, together with faeces. The desire to dismember bodies, if it appears frequently in fantasies and dreams, is one of the most reliable factors for the diagnosis of the necrophilous character.

There are other, less drastic forms of overt necrophilia. One of them is the craving to be near corpses, cemeteries, or any object in decomposition. H. J. Rauch tells of a girl who

suffered from an urge to be close to corpses, in whose presence she would become rigid and unable to tear herself
away (H. J. Rauch, 1947).[3] Stekel tells of a woman who
stated: 'I often think of cemeteries and of the manner in
which corpses decay in the grave' (quoted by H. von
Hentig, 1964).

This interest in decay is frequently expressed in the craving to smell the odour of something that is decaying. This is
very apparent in the following case of a thirty-two-year-old,
highly educated man who was almost totally blind. He was
frightened of noise, 'but liked to hear women's cries of pain
and loved the smell of decaying flesh. He had a craving for
the corpses of tall, fat women and wanted to crawl into
them.' He asked his grandmother whether he could have her
corpse later. 'He would like to drown in the decay of her
remnants' (T. Spoerri, 1959). Von Hentig speaks of
'sniffers' (*Schnüffler*), for whom the smell of human excrements or of anything putrid is exciting, and he considers this
trait a manifestation of necrophilia. With the addition of
cases of necrophilous fetishism – the objects of which are
connected with graves, such as grass, flowers, pictures – we
can end this brief survey of necrophilous practices reported
in the literature.

The Necrophilous Character[4]

The term 'necrophilous', to denote a character trait rather
than a perverse act in the traditional sense, was used by the

3. An unauthenticated story about Hitler describes a similar scene of
his not being able to tear himself away from the sight of a decayed
corpse of a soldier.

4. In order to avoid misunderstandings I want to stress at the outset of
this discussion that describing here the full-grown 'necrophilous character' does not imply that people are either necrophilous – or not. The
necrophilous character is an extreme form in which necrophilia is the
dominant trait. In reality, most people are a blend of necrophilous and
biophilous tendencies, and the conflict between the two is often the
source of a productive development.

Spanish philosopher Miguel de Unamuno in 1936[5] on the occasion of a speech by the nationalist general Millán Astray at the University of Salamanca, where Unamuno was rector at the beginning of the Spanish Civil War. The general's favourite motto was *Viva la Muerte!* ('Long live death!') and one of his followers shouted it from the back of the hall. When the general had finished his speech, Unamuno rose and said:

Just now I heard a *necrophilous* and senseless cry: 'Long live death!' And I, who have spent my life shaping paradoxes which have aroused the uncomprehending anger of others, I must tell you, as an expert authority, that this outlandish paradox is repellent to me. General Millán Astray is a cripple. Let it be said without any slighting undertone. He is a war invalid. So was Cervantes. Unfortunately there are too many cripples in Spain just now. And soon there will be even more of them if God does not come to our aid. It pains me to think that General Millán Astray should dictate the pattern of mass psychology. A cripple who lacks the spiritual greatness of a Cervantes is wont to seek ominous relief in causing mutilation around him. (M. de Unamuno, 1936)

At this Millán Astray was unable to restrain himself any longer. '*Abajo la inteligencia!*' ('Down with intelligence!') he shouted. 'Long live death!' There was a clamour of support for this remark from the Falangists.

But Unamuno went on:

This is the temple of the intellect. And I am its high priest. It is you who profane its sacred precincts. You will win, because you have more than enough brute force. But you will not convince. For to convince you need to persuade. And in order to persuade you would need what you lack: Reason and Right in the struggle I consider it futile to exhort you to think of Spain. I have done. (M. de Unamuno, 1936)[6]

5. According to R. A. Medvedev (*Let History Judge*, New York: A.A. Knopf, 1971) Lenin seems to have been the first to use the term 'necrophilia' (*trupolozhestvo*) in this psychological sense (V. I. Lenin, *Sochineniia*).

6. Unamuno remained under house arrest until his death a few months later (H. Thomas, 1961).

I adopted the use of the term from Unamuno and have been studying the phenomenon of character-rooted necrophilia since about 1961.[7] My theoretical concepts were gained mainly by observations of persons in analysis.[8] The study of certain historical personalities – Hitler, for example – and the observation of individuals and of the character and behaviour of social classes offered additional data for the analysis of the necrophilic character. But as much as my clinical observations influenced me, I believe the decisive impulse came from Freud's theory of the life and the death instincts. I had been deeply impressed by his concept that the striving for life and the striving for destruction were the two most fundamental forces within man; but I could not reconcile myself to Freud's theoretical explanation. Yet Freud's idea guided me to see clinical data in a new light and to re-formulate – and thus to preserve – Freud's concept on a different theoretical basis and based on clinical data which, as I shall show later, link up with Freud's earlier findings on the anal character.

Necrophilia in the characterological sense can be described as *the passionate attraction to all that is dead, decayed, putrid, sickly; it is the passion to transform that which is alive into something unalive; to destroy for the sake of destruction; the exclusive interest in all that is purely mechanical. It is the passion to tear apart living structures.*

Necrophilic Dreams

The attraction to what is dead and putrid can be observed most clearly in the dreams of necrophilous persons.

Dream 1. 'I find myself sitting on the toilet; I have diarrhoea and defecate with an explosive force which sounds as if a bomb had exploded and the house might collapse. I

7. A preliminary report of my findings appears in E. Fromm (1964).
8. On the basis of reviewing older case histories of people I had analysed and case histories presented by younger psychoanalysts in seminars, or by those whose work I have supervised.

want to take a bath, but when I try to turn on the water I discover that the tub is already filled with dirty water: I see faeces together with a cut-off leg and arm floating in the water.'

The dreamer was an intensely necrophilous person who had had a number of similar dreams. When the analyst asked the dreamer what his feelings were in the dream about what was going on, he reported that he did not feel the situation to be frightening, but that it embarrassed him to tell the dream to the analyst.

This dream shows several elements characteristic of necrophilia, among which the theme of dismembered parts of the body is the most obvious. In addition, there is the close connection between necrophilia and anality (to be discussed later) and the theme of destruction; if we translate from symbolic to clear language, the dreamer feels that he wants to destroy the whole building by the force of his elimination.

Dream 2. 'I am going to visit a friend; I walk in the direction of his house, which is well-known to me. Suddenly the scene shifts. I am in a kind of dry, desert-like scenery; no plants or trees. I still seem to be trying to find my friend's house, but the only house in sight is a peculiar building which does not have any windows. I enter through a small door; when I close it I hear a peculiar noise, as if the door had been locked, not just shut. I try the door-knob and cannot open it. With great anxiety I walk through a very narrow corridor – in fact it is so low that I have to crawl – and find myself in a large, oval, darkened room. It looks like a big vault. When I get accustomed to the dark I see a number of skeletons lying on the ground and I know that this is my grave. I wake up with a feeling of panic.'

This dream hardly requires any interpretation. The 'vault' is a tomb and simultaneously symbolizes the womb. The 'house of the friend' is a symbol of life. Instead of walking towards life, to visit a friend, the dreamer walks towards a place of the dead. The desert-like scenery and the tomb are symbols of the dead. By itself, such a dream is not necessarily indicative of necrophilia; it might be nothing but the symbolic expression of the fear of dying. But it is different if, as was the case with this dreamer, he has many dreams in which he sees tombs, mummies, skeletons; in other words, when the imagination of his dream life is mainly occupied with visions from the world of the dead.

Dream 3. This is a short dream of a woman suffering from a severe depression: 'I am defecating; it goes on and on, until the excrement goes beyond the toilet seat, begins to fill the bathroom, rises higher and higher – I am drowning in it[9] – at this moment I wake up with unspeakable horror.' For this person the whole of life has been transformed into dirt; she can produce nothing but dirt; her world becomes dirt, and her death is the final union with dirt. We find the same theme in the myth of Midas; everything he touches is transformed into gold – symbolically, as Freud has shown, dirt or faeces.[10]

Dream 4. The following is a dream of Albert Speer (12 September 1962) during the years of his life in the Spandau prison.

'Hitler is to come for an inspection. I, at the time still a Minister of State, take a broom in my hands to help sweep up the dirt in the factory. After the inspection I find myself in his car, trying vainly to put my arm into the sleeve of my jacket which I had taken off while sweeping. My hand lands again and again in the pocket. Our drive ends at a large square surrounded by government buildings. On one side is a war memorial. Hitler approaches it and lays down a wreath. We enter the marble vestibule of one of the government buildings. Hitler says to his adjutant: "Where are the wreaths?" The adjutant to an officer: "As you know, he now lays wreaths everywhere." The officer is wearing a light-coloured, almost white uniform made of some sort of glove-leather; over the jacket he wears, as though he were

9. cf. the earlier example of a man's conscious wish to drown in the decay of his grandmother.
10. cf. the rich material on dirt and faeces in J. G. Bourke (1913).

an altar-boy, a loose garment decorated with lace and embroidery. The wreath arrives. Hitler steps towards the right of the hall where there is another memorial with many wreaths already at its base. He kneels, and begins to intone a plaintive melody in the style of a Gregorian chant, in which is repeated again and again a long-drawn-out "Jesus Maria". Numerous other memorial plaques line the walls of this long, high-ceilinged, marble hall. Hitler, in an ever-faster sequence, lays wreath after wreath, which are handed to him by the busy adjutants. His plaintive tones become more and more monotonous, the row of memorial plaques seems to be endless.'[11]

This dream is interesting for many reasons. It is one of those in which the dreamer expresses his insight into another person rather than his own feelings and desires.[12] These insights are sometimes more precise than the dreamer's conscious impression of another person. In this case Speer clearly expresses in a Chaplinesque style his view of Hitler's necrophilous character. He sees him as a man who devotes all his time to paying homage to death, but in a very peculiar way his actions are entirely mechanical, leaving no room for feelings. The wreath-laying becomes an organizational ritual to the point of absurdity. In juxtaposition, the same Hitler, having returned to the religious belief of his childhood, is completely immersed in the intonation of plaintive tones. The dream ends by stressing the monotony and the mechanized manner of his grief ritual.

In the beginning of the dream, the dreamer brings to life a situation out of reality, from the time when he is still a Minister of State and a very active man who does things himself. Perhaps the dirt he is sweeping is a symbolic expression of the dirt of the Nazi régime, his inability to put his arm into the jacket sleeve is most likely a symbolic expression of his feeling that he cannot participate further in this system; this forms the transition to the main part of the

11. Albert Speer, personal communication.
12. I have quoted such dreams in *The Forgotten Language* (1951).

dream in which he recognizes that all that is left are the dead and the necrophilous, mechanical, boring Hitler.

Dream 5. 'I have made a great invention, the "super-destroyer". It is a machine which, if one secret button is pushed that I alone know, can destroy all life in North America within the first hour, and within the next hour all life on earth. I alone, knowing the formula of the chemical substance, can protect myself. (Next scene.) I have pushed the button: I notice no more life, I am alone, I feel exuberant.'

This dream is an expression of pure destructiveness in an extremely narcissistic person, unrelated to others and with no need of anyone. This was a recurrent dream with this person, together with other necrophilous dreams. He was suffering from severe mental sickness.

Dream 6. 'I am invited to a party with many young men and women. We are all dancing. But something strange is going on; the rhythm becomes slower and slower, and it seems that soon nobody will move any more. At this moment an oversized couple enter the room; it seems they have a great deal of equipment in two big cartons. They approach the first dancing couple; the man takes a big knife and cuts the boy in his back; strangely no blood flows and the boy does not seem to feel any pain; the tall man then takes something I cannot see, like a little box, and puts it into the boy's back; it is very small. He then puts a kind of small key, or perhaps a button, into the little box (but in such a way that the boy can touch it) and makes a movement as if he were winding a watch. While the tall man was doing this with the boy, his partner performed the same operation on the girl. When they have finished the young couple continue dancing, but fast and energetically. The tall couple perform the same operation on the other nine couples present, and after they leave everybody seems to be in an excited and happy mood.'

The meaning of the dream is rather clear when we translate it from symbolic into plain language. The dreamer feels that life is slowly ebbing, that its energy is spent. But a gadget can become a substitute. Persons, like clocks, can be wound up, and they will then appear to be intensely 'alive' although in fact they will have become automatons.

The dreamer is a young man of nineteen, studying engineering and completely absorbed in all that is technical. Had he only had this one dream, it might be thought an expression of his technical interests. He had, however, many dreams in which the other aspects of necrophilia are present. The dream was not essentially a reflection of his professional interests; his professional interests are, rather, a reflection of his necrophilous orientation.

Dream 7. This dream of a successful professional is particularly interesting because it illustrates a point concerning the necrophilous character of modern technique that will be discussed further on.

'I am slowly approaching the entrance of a cavern and can already see something in it that impresses me greatly; inside are two humanized swine manipulating a small old wagon of the kind used in mines; they place it on the rails that go into the interior of the cavern. Inside the little wagon I see normal human beings; they seem to be dead, but I know that they are asleep.

'I do not know whether this is another dream or the continuation of the previous one – I believe I woke up, but am not sure. The beginning is the same. I am once more approaching the entrance to a cavern; I leave the sun and the blue sky behind. I go in deeper and see a very intense glow at the end; when I arrive there I marvel at the sight of an extraordinarily modern city; everything is full of light which I now know is artificial – by electricity. The city is made completely of steel and glass – the future. I continue walking and suddenly realize that I have seen no one – no animal or person. I now find myself before a large machine, a sort of enormous, very modern electric transformer, connected to numerous thick cables, like high-tension cables; they look like black hoses. The thought comes to me that these cables are conducting blood; I feel very excited, and find an object in my trouser pocket which I immediately recognize; it is a small pocket-knife my father gave me when I was about twelve years old. I approach the machine and make a cut in one of the cables with my little knife; suddenly something spurts out, and I get soaked by it. It is blood. I awaken in great anxiety and am sweating.'

After having related his dream, the dreamer added: 'I do not understand the machine and the blood very well, but here blood substitutes electricity, both being energy. I do not know why I think of it like this; perhaps I think that the machine takes blood out of men.'

This, as is the case of Speer's dream, is not the dream of a necrophilous, but of a biophilous person who recognizes the necrophilous character of the contemporary world. The cavern, as so often, is a symbol of the dead, like a tomb. The cavern is a mine, and the people working there are swine, or dead. (The 'knowledge' that they are not really dead is a correction out of an awareness of reality that sometimes enters into dream imagery.) The meaning is: this is a place of degraded and corpse-like men. This scene of the first act of the dream plays in an older stage of industrial development. The second act plays in the fully developed cybernetic age of the future. The beautiful modern city is dead; there are no animals, no persons. A powerful technique sucks the life (blood) out of man and transforms it into electricity. When the dreamer tries to cut the electric cables (perhaps to destroy them), he is soaked by the blood spurting out – as if he were committing a murder. In his sleep the dreamer has a vision of the deadness of totally technicized society with a clarity and artistic sense that we might find in Blake or in a surrealist painting. Yet when he is awake he knows little of what he 'knows' when he is not exposed to the noise of common *non*sense.

'Unintended' Necrophilic Actions

Dreams are one of the most explicit expressions of the necrophilous strivings, but by no means the only one. Sometimes
necrophilic trends can be expressed in marginal, unintended
'insignificant' actions, the 'psychopathology of everyday
life', which Freud interpreted as an expression of repressed
strivings. Here is an example taken from a very complex
personality, that of Winston Churchill. The incident was the
following: Field Marshal Sir Alan F. Brooke, Chief of the
Imperial Staff, and Churchill were having lunch together in
North Africa during the Second World War; it was a hot
day and there were many flies. Churchill killed as many as
he could, as most people would probably have done. But
then he did something bizarre. (Sir Alan reports a feeling
of being shocked.) Towards the end of the lunch he collected
all the dead flies and lined them up in a row on the table-
cloth, acting like an aristocratic hunter whose men line up
all the animals taken, for his gratification (Viscount
Alanbrooke, 1957).[13]

If one were to 'explain' Churchill's behaviour as just a
'habit', the question would remain: What does this rather
unusual habit *mean*? Although it seems to express a necrophilous trend, this does not necessarily imply that Churchill
had a necrophilous character, but he might well have had a
strong necrophilous streak. (Churchill's character is much
too complex to be discussed in a few pages.)

I have mentioned this behaviour of Churchill because it
is well authenticated and because his personality is well-
known. Similar marginal behavioural details can be observed in many people. One of the most frequent is the
habit of some persons to break and mutilate small things like
matches or flowers; some hurt themselves by picking at
wounds. The tendency is expressed more drastically when

13. The fact that Churchill's physician, Lord Moran, mentions the
same incident in his diaries (Lord Moran, 1966) makes one assume that
Churchill must have done this rather frequently.

people injure something beautiful like a building, a piece of furniture – and in extreme cases slash a painting in a museum, or inflict wounds on themselves.

Another illustration of necrophilous behaviour can be found in people – especially medical students and physicians – who are especially attracted by skeletons. Such an attraction is usually explained by their professional interests, but the following report from psychoanalytic data shows that this is not always so. A medical student who had a skeleton in his bedroom told the analyst after some time and with great embarrassment that he often took the skeleton into his bed, embraced it, and sometimes kissed it. This same person showed a number of other necrophilous traits.

Another manifestation of the necrophilous character is the conviction that the only way to solve a problem or a conflict is by force and violence. The question involved is not whether force should be used under certain circumstances; what is characteristic for the necrophile is that force – as Simone Weil said, 'the power to transform a man into a corpse' – is the first and last solution for everything; that the Gordian knot must always be cut and never dissolved patiently. Basically, these persons' answer to life's problems is destruction, never sympathetic effort, construction, or example. Theirs is the queen's answer in *Alice in Wonderland*: 'off with their heads!' Motivated by this impulse they usually fail to see other options that require no destruction, nor do they recognize how futile has force often proved to be in the long run. We find the classic expression for this attitude in King Solomon's judgement in the case of the two women who both claimed a child as her own. When the king proposes to divide the child, the true mother prefers to allow the other woman to have it; the women who pretends to be the mother chooses to divide. Her solution is the typical decision of a necrophilous, property-obsessed person.

A somewhat less drastic expression of necrophilia is a marked interest in sickness in all its forms, as well as in death. An example is the mother who is always interested in her child's sicknesses, his failures, and makes dark prognoses for the future; at the same time she is unimpressed by a favourable change, she does not respond to the child's joy or enthusiasm, and she will not notice anything new that is growing within him. She does not harm the child in any obvious way, yet she may slowly strangle his joy of life, his faith in growth, and eventually she will infect him with her own necrophilous orientation.

Anyone who has occasion to listen to conversations of people of all social classes from middle age onward will be impressed by the extent of their talk about the sicknesses and death of other people. To be sure, there are a number of factors responsible for this. For many people, especially those with no outside interests, sickness and death are the only dramatic elements in their lives; it is one of the few subjects about which they can talk, aside from events in the family. But granting all this, there are many persons for whom these explanations do not suffice. They can usually be recognized by the animation and excitement that comes over them when they talk about sicknesses or other sad events like death, financial troubles, and so forth. The necrophilous person's particular interest in the dead is often shown not only in his conversation but in the way he reads the newspapers. He is most interested – and hence reads *first* – the death notices and obituaries; he also likes to talk about death from various aspects: what people died of, under what conditions, who died recently, who is likely to die, and so on. He likes to go to funeral parlours and cemeteries and usually does not miss an occasion to do so when it is socially opportune. It is easy to see that this affinity for burials and cemeteries is only a somewhat attenuated form of the more gross manifest interest in morgues and graves described earlier.

A somewhat less easily identifiable trait of the necrophilous person is the particular kind of lifelessness in his conversation. This is not a matter of what the conversation is about. A very intelligent, erudite necrophilous person may talk about things that would be very interesting were it not for the way in which he presents his ideas. He remains stiff, cold, aloof; his presentation of the subject is pedantic and lifeless. On the other hand the opposite character type, the life-loving person, may talk of an experience that in itself is not particularly interesting, but there is life in the way he presents it; he is stimulating; that is why one listens with interest and pleasure. The necrophilous person is a wet blanket and a joy killer in a group; he is boring rather than animating; he deadens everything and makes people feel tired, in contrast to the biophilous person who makes people feel more alive.

Still another dimension of necrophilous reactions is the attitude towards the past and property. For the necrophilous character only the past is experienced as quite real, not the present or the future. What has been, i.e., what is dead, rules his life: institutions, laws, property, traditions, and possessions. Briefly, *things rule man; having* rules *being; the dead* rule *the living*. In the necrophile's thinking – personal, philosophical, and political – the past is sacred, nothing new is valuable, drastic change is a crime against the 'natural' order.[14]

Another aspect of necrophilia is the relation to colour. The necrophilous person generally has a predilection for dark, light-absorbing colours, such as black or brown, and a dislike for bright, radiant colours.[15] One can observe this preference in their dress or in the colours they choose if they paint. Of course, in cases when dark clothes are worn out of

14. For Marx, capital and labour were not merely two economic categories. Capital for him was the manifestation of the past, of labour transformed and amassed into things; labour was the manifestation of *life*, of human energy applied to nature in the process of transforming it. The choice between capitalism and socialism (as he understood it) amounted to this: Who (what) was to rule over what (whom)? What is dead over what is alive, or what is alive over what is dead? (cf. E. Fromm, 1961, 1968).

15. This colour preference is similar to the one often found in depressed persons.

tradition, the colour has no significance in relation to character.

As we have already seen in the clinical material above, the necrophilous person is characterized by a special affinity to bad odours – originally the odour of decaying or putrid flesh. This is indeed the case with many such persons, and it manifests itself in two forms: (1) the frank enjoyment of bad odours; such people are attracted by the smell of faeces, urine, or decay, and they tend to frequent smelly toilets; (2) – the more frequent form – the repression of the desire to enjoy bad odours; this form leads to the reaction formation of wanting to get rid of a bad odour that in reality does not exist. (This is similar to the over-cleanliness of the anal character.) Whether of the one form or the other the necrophilic persons are concerned with bad odours. As noted earlier, their fascination with bad odours frequently gives such persons the appearance of being 'sniffers' (H. von Hentig, 1964). Not infrequently this sniffing tendency even shows in their facial expression. Many necrophilous individuals give the impression of constantly smelling a bad odour. Anybody who studies the many pictures of Hitler, for instance, can easily discover this sniffing expression in his face. This expression is not always present in necrophiles, but when it is, it is one of the most reliable criteria of such a passion. Another characteristic element in the facial expression is the necrophile's incapacity to laugh. His laughter is actually a kind of smirk; it is unalive and lacks the liberating and joyous quality of normal laughter. In fact it is not only the absence of the capacity for 'free' laughter that is characteristic of the necrophile, but the general immobility and lack of expression in his face. While watching television one can sometimes observe a speaker whose face remains completely unmoved while he is speaking; he grins only at the beginning or the end of his speech when, according to American custom, he knows that he is expected to smile. Such persons cannot talk and smile at the same time, because they can direct their attention only

to the one or the other activity; their smile is not spontaneous but planned, like the unspontaneous gesture of a
poor actor. The skin is often indicative of necrophiles: it
gives the impression of being lifeless, 'dry', sallow; when
we sense sometimes that a person has a 'dirty' face, we are
not claiming that the face is unwashed, but are responding
to the particular quality of a necrophilous expression.

The Necrophilic's Language

The language of the necrophilous person is characterized by
the predominant use of words referring to destruction and to
faeces and toilets. While the use of the word 'shit' has become very widespread today, it is nevertheless not difficult
to discern people whose favourite word it is, far beyond its
current frequency. An example is a twenty-two-year-old
man for whom everything was 'shitty': life, people, ideas,
and nature. The same young man said proudly of himself:
'I am an artist of destruction.' We found many examples of
necrophilous language while analysing the answers to the
questionnaire addressed to German workers and employees
mentioned earlier (in Chapter 2, footnote 8, and Chapter 8,
footnote 16). The answers to one question: 'What is your
opinion about women's using lipstick and make-up?'[16]
provides an illustration. Many respondents answered: 'It is
bourgeois', or 'unnatural', or 'not hygienic'. They simply
answered in terms of the prevalent ideology. But a minority
gave such answers as 'It is poisonous', or 'It makes women
look like whores.' The use of these realistically unwarranted
terms was highly indicative of their character structure;
almost invariably, the respondents who used these words
showed a destructive trend in most other answers.

In order to test the validity of the hypothesis about necrophilia, Michael Maccoby and I designed an interpretative

16. In the early thirties this was a controversial point among this
sector of the population, since many considered the use of make-up a
bourgeois, unnatural habit.

questionnaire basically on the lines of the one used in the Frankfurt study, but with fixed, rather than open-ended questions, twelve in all; some referred to attitudes typical of the anal-hoarding character, while others referred to the necrophilous characteristics I have described thus far. Maccoby applied the questionnaire to samples of people in six very different populations (as to class, race, and education). Space does not permit going into the details of the method or of the results obtained. Suffice it to say that analysis established (1) the presence of a necrophilous syndrome, confirming the theoretical model; (2) that life-loving and necrophilous tendencies could be measured; (3) that these tendencies were, in fact, significantly correlated with socio-political concerns. On the basis of an interpretative analysis of the questionnaires, we judge that about 10 to 15 per cent of the samples interviewed would be dominantly necrophilous ... Interviewers noted a sterility about many such people and their houses. They live in a deadened, joyless atmosphere ... (M. Maccoby, 1972).

The study asked the respondents a number of questions that permitted correlating their political opinions to their character. I refer the reader to the great many data in Maccoby's paper; I shall mention here only the following:

In all of the samples, we found that anti-life tendencies were significantly correlated to political positions that supported increased military power and favoured repression against dissenters. The following priorities were considered most important by individuals who have dominant anti-life tendencies: tighter control of rioters, tighter enforcement of anti-drug laws, winning the war in Vietnam, controlling subversive groups, strengthening the police, and fighting Communism throughout the world. (M. Maccoby, 1972)

The Connection Between Necrophilia and the Worship of Technique

Lewis Mumford has shown the connection between destructiveness and power-centred 'mega-machines' as they existed in Mesopotamia and Egypt some five thousand years ago, societies that have, as he has pointed out, much in common with the mega-machines of Europe and North America today. He writes:

Conceptually the instruments of mechanization five thousand years ago were already detached from other human functions and purposes than the constant increase of order, power, predictability, and above all, control. With this proto-scientific ideology went a corresponding regimentation and degradation of once-autonomous human activities: 'mass culture' and 'mass control' made their first appearance. With mordant symbolism, the ultimate products of the mega-machine in Egypt were colossal tombs, inhabited by mummified corpses; while later in Assyria, as repeatedly in every other expanding empire, the chief testimony to its technical efficiency was a waste of destroyed villages and cities, and poisoned soils: the prototype of smilar 'civilized' atrocities today. (L. Mumford, 1967)

Let us begin with the consideration of the simplest and most obvious characteristics of contemporary industrial man: the stifling of his focal interest in people, nature, and living structures, together with the increasing attraction of mechanical, non-alive artifacts. Examples abound. All over the industrialized world there are men who feel more tender towards, and are more interested in, their automobiles than their wives. They are proud of their car; they cherish it; they wash it (even many of those who could pay to have this job done), and in some countries many give it a loving nick-name; they observe it and are concerned at the slightest symptom of a dysfunction. To be sure a car is not a sexual object – but it is an object of love; life without a car seems to some more intolerable than life without a woman. Is this attachment to automobiles not somewhat peculiar, or even perverse?

Or another example, taking pictures. Anyone who has the occasion to observe tourists – or maybe to observe himself – can discover that taking pictures has become a substitute for seeing. Of course, you have to look in order to direct your lens to the desired object; then you push the button, the film is processed and taken home. But *looking* is not *seeing*. Seeing is a human function, one of the greatest gifts with which man is endowed; it requires activity, inner openness, interest, patience, concentration. Taking a *snapshot* (the aggressive expression is significant) means essentially to transform the act of seeing into an object – the picture to be shown later to friends as a proof that 'you have been there'. The same is the case with those music lovers for whom listening to music is only the pretext for experimenting with the technical qualities of their record players or high-fidelity sets and the particular technical improvements they have added. Listening to music has been transformed for them into studying the product of high technical performance.

Another example is the gadgeteer, the person who is intent on replacing every application of human effort with a 'handy', 'work-saving' contraption. Among such people may be numbered the sales personnel who make even the simplest addition by machine, as well as people who refuse to walk even a block, but will automatically take the car. And many of us probably know of home-workshop gadget-makers who construct mechanically operated devices that by the mere press of a button or flick of a switch can start a fountain, or swing open a door, or set off even more impractical, often absurd, Rube Goldberg contrivances.

It should be clear that in speaking of this kind of behaviour I do not imply that using an automobile, or taking pictures, or using gadgets is in itself a manifestation of necrophilous tendencies. But it assumes this quality when it becomes a *substitute* for interest in life and for exercising the rich functions with which the human being is endowed. I also do not imply that the engineer who is passionately interested in the construction of machines of all kinds shows, for this reason, a necrophilous tendency. He may be a very productive person with great love of life that he expresses in his attitude towards people, towards nature, towards art, and in his constructive technical ideas. I am referring, rather, to those individuals whose interest in artifacts has *replaced* their interest in what is alive and who deal with technical matters in a pedantic and unalive way.

The necrophilous quality of these phenomena becomes more clearly visible if we examine the more direct evidence of the fusion of technique and destructiveness of which our epoch offers so many examples. The overt connection between destruction and the worship of technique found its first explicit and eloquent expression in F. T. Marinetti, the founder and leader of Italian Futurism and a lifelong Fascist. His first *Futurist Manifesto* (1909) proclaims the ideals that were to find their full realization in National Socialism and in the methods used in warfare beginning with the Second World War.[17] His remarkable sensitivity as an artist enabled him to give expression to a powerful trend that was hardly visible at the time:

1. We intend to sing the love of danger, the habit of energy and fearlessness.

2. Courage, audacity, and revolt will be essential elements of our poetry.

3. Up to now literature has exalted a pensive immobility, ecstacy, and sleep. We intend to exalt aggressive action, a feverish insomnia, the racer's stride, the moral leap, the punch and the slap.

4. We say that the world's magnificence has been enriched by a new beauty; the beauty of speed. *A racing car whose hood is adorned with great pipes, like serpents of explosive breath – a roaring car that seems to ride on grapeshot – is more beautiful than the 'Victory of Samothrace'.*

5. We shall sing a hymn to the man at the wheel, who hurls the lance of his spirit across the Earth, along the circle of its orbit.

6. The poet must spend himself with ardour, splendour, and generosity, to swell the enthusiastic fervour of the primordial elements.

7. *Except in struggle, there is no more beauty. No work without an*

17. R. W. Flint (1971), the editor of Marinetti's work, tries to de-emphasize Marinetti's Fascist allegiance, but in my opinion his arguments are not convincing.

aggressive character can be a masterpiece. Poetry must be conceived as a violent attack on unknown forces, to reduce and prostrate them before man.

8. We stand on the last promontory of the centuries! – Why should we look back, when what we want is to break down the mysterious doors of the Impossible? Time and Space died yesterday. We already live in the absolute, because we have created eternal, omnipresent speed.

9. *We will glorify war – the world's only hygiene – militarism, patriotism, the destructive gesture of freedom bringers, beautiful ideas worth dying for, and scorn for woman.*

10. *We will destroy the museums, libraries, academies of every kind, will fight moralism, feminism, every opportunistic or utilitarian cowardice.*

11. We will sing of great crowds excited by work, by pleasure, and by riot; we will sing of the multi-coloured, polyphonic tides of revolution in the modern capitals; we will sing of the vibrant nightly fervour of arsenals and shipyards blazing with violent electric moons; greedy railway stations that devour smoke-plumed serpents; factories hung on clouds by the crooked lines of their smoke; bridges that stride the rivers like giant gymnasts, flashing in the sun, with a glitter of knives; adventurous steamers that sniff the horizon; deep-chested locomotives whose wheels paw the tracks like the hooves of enormous steel horses bridled by tubing; and the sleek flight of planes whose propellers chatter in the wind like banners and seem to cheer like an enthusiastic crowd. (R. W. Flint, 1971; italics added)

Here we see the essential elements of necrophilia: worship of speed and the machine; poetry as a means of attack; glorification of war; destruction of culture; hate against women; locomotives and aeroplanes as living forces.

The second *Futurist Manifesto* (1916) develops the idea of the new religion of speed:

Speed, having as its essence the intuitive synthesis of every force in movement, is naturally *pure*. Slowness, having as its essence the rational analysis of every exhaustion in repose, is naturally *unclean*. After the destruction of the antique good and the antique evil, we create a new good, speed, and a new evil, slowness.

Speed=synthesis of every courage in action. *Aggressive and warlike*.

Slowness=analysis of every stagnant prudence. Passive and pacifistic ...

If prayer means communication with the divinity, *running at high speed is a prayer. Holiness of wheels and rails. One must kneel on the tracks to pray to the divine velocity. One must kneel before the whirling speed of a gyroscope compass:* 20,000 revolutions per minute, the highest mechanical speed reached by man.

The intoxication of great speeds in cars is nothing but the joy of feeling oneself fused with the only divinity. Sportsmen are the first catechumens of this religion. *Forthcoming destruction of houses and cities, to make way for great meeting places for cars and planes.* (R. W. Flint, 1971; italics added)

It has been said that Marinetti was a revolutionary, that he broke with the past, that he opened the doors to a vision of a new world of Nietzschean supermen, that together with Picasso and Apollinaire, he was one of the most important forces in modern art. Let me answer that his revolutionary ideas place him close to Mussolini, and still closer to Hitler. It is precisely this blending of rhetorical professions of a revolutionary spirit, the worship of technique, and the aims of destruction that characterize Nazism. Mussolini and Hitler were, perhaps, rebels (Hitler more than Mussolini), but they were not revolutionaries. They had no genuinely creative ideas, nor did they accomplish any significant changes that benefited man. They lacked the essential criterion of the revolutionary spirit; love of life, the desire to serve its unfolding and growth, and a passion for independence.[18]

The fusion of technique and destructiveness was not yet visible in the First World War. There was little destruction by planes, and the tank was only a further evolution of traditional weapons. The Second World War brought about

18. This is not the place to analyse certain phenomena in modern art and literature in order to determine whether they exhibit necrophilous elements. In the area of painting, it is a problem outside my competence; as far as literature is concerned, it is too complex to be dealt with briefly; I plan to deal with this topic in a later book.

a decisive change: the use of the aeroplane for mass killing.[19] The men dropping the bombs were hardly aware that they were killing or burning to death thousands of human beings in a few minutes. The aircrews were a team; one man piloted the plane, another navigated it, another dropped the bombs. They were not concerned with killing and were hardly aware of an enemy. They were concerned with the proper handling of their complicated machine along the lines laid down in meticulously organized plans. That as the result of their acts many thousands, and sometimes over a hundred thousand people, would be killed, burnt, and maimed was of course known to them cerebrally, but hardly comprehended affectively; it was, paradoxical as this may sound, none of their concern. It is probably for this reason that they – or at least most of them – did not feel guilty for acts that belong to the most horrible a human being can perform.

Modern aerial warfare destruction follows the principle of modern technical production,[20] in which both the worker and the engineer are completely alienated from the product of their work. They perform technical tasks in accordance with the general plan of management, but often do not even see the finished product; even if they do, it is none of their concern or responsibility. They are not supposed to ask themselves whether it is a useful or a harmful product – this is a matter for management to decide; as far as the latter is concerned, however, 'useful' simply means 'profitable' and has no reference to the real use of the product. In war

19. The Battle of Britain at the beginning of the war was still fought in the old-fashioned style; the British fighter pilots engaged their German adversaries; their plane was their individual vehicle; they were motivated by the passion to save their country from German invasion. It was their personal skill, courage, and determination that decided the outcome; in principle, their fighting was not different from that of the heroes of the Trojan war.

20. Lewis Mumford has pointed to the two poles of civilization, 'mechanically organized work and mechanically organized destruction' (L. Mumford, 1967).

'profitable' means all that serves the defeat of the enemy, and often the decision as to what is profitable in this sense is based on data as vague as those that led to the construction of Ford's Edsel. For the engineer as well as for the pilot it is enough to know the decisions of management, and he is not supposed to question them, nor is he interested in doing so. Whether it is a matter of killing one hundred thousand people in Dresden or Hiroshima or of devastating the land and people of Vietnam, it is not up to him to worry about the military or moral justification of the orders; his only task is to serve his machine properly.

One might object to this interpretation by stressing the fact that soldiers have always owed unquestioning obedience to orders. This is true enough, but the objection ignores the important difference between the ground soldiers and the bomber pilot. The former is close to the destruction caused by his weapons, and he does not, by a single act, cause the destruction of large masses of human beings whom he has never seen. The most one could say is that traditional army discipline and feelings of patriotic duty will also, in the case of pilots increase the readiness for unquestioning execution of orders; but this does not seem to be the main point, as it undoubtedly is for the average soldier who fights on the ground. These pilots are highly trained, technically minded people who hardly need this additional motivation to do their job properly and without hesitation.

Even the mass murder of the Jews by the Nazis was organized like a production process, although the mass killing in the gas chambers did not require a high degree of technical sophistication. At one end of the process the victims were selected in accordance with the criterion of their capability for doing useful work. Those who did not fall into this category were led into the chambers and told that it was for a hygienic purpose; the gas was let in; clothes and other useful objects such as hair, gold teeth, were removed from the bodies, sorted out and 'recycled', and the corpses were burned. The victims were 'processed' methodically, efficiently; the executioners did not have to see the agony; they participated in the economic-political programme of the Führer, but were one step removed from direct and immediate killing with their own hands.[21] No doubt, to harden one's heart against being touched by the fate of human beings whom one has seen and selected, and who are to be murdered only a few hundred yards away within the hour requires a much more thorough hardening than is the case with the aircrews who drop bombs. But in spite of this difference the fact remains that the two situations have a very important element in common: the technicalization of destruction, and with it the removal of the full affective recognition of what one is doing. Once this process has been fully established there is no limit to destructiveness because nobody *destroys*: one only serves the machine for programmed – hence, apparently rational – purposes.

If these considerations regarding the technical-bureaucratic nature of modern large-scale destructiveness are correct, do they not lead to the repudiation of my central hypothesis concerning the necrophilous nature of the spirit of total technique? Do we not have to admit that contemporary technical man is not motivated by a passion for destruction, but would be more properly described as a totally alienated man whose dominant orientation is cerebral, who feels little love but also little desire to destroy, who has become, in a characterological sense, an automaton, but not a destroyer?

This is not an easy question to answer. To be sure, in Marinetti, in Hitler, in thousands of members of the Nazi

21. I should like to remind those who may say that this 'one step' was too little to matter, that millions of otherwise decent people show no reaction when cruelties are committed many steps removed from them by their state or party. How many steps removed were the men who profited from the atrocities committed against the blacks in Africa by the Belgian administration at the beginning of this century? To be sure, one step is less than five, but it is only a quantitative difference.

and Stalinist secret police, guards in concentration camps, members of execution commandos the passion to destroy is the dominant motivation. But were they not perhaps 'old-fashioned' types? Are we justified in interpreting the spirit of the 'technotronic' society as necrophilous?

In order to answer these questions some other problems need to be clarified which I have left out of this presentation thus far. The first is the connection between the anal-hoarding character and necrophilia.

The clinical data and the examples of the dreams of nec-rophiles have illustrated the marked presence of anal character traits. The concern with the process of elimination and with faeces is, as we saw, the symbolic expression of the interest in all that is decayed or putrid, all that is not alive. However, while the 'normal' anal-hoarding character is lacking in aliveness, he is not necrophilous. Freud and his co-workers went a step further; they discovered that sadism was often a by-product of the anal character. This is not always the case, but it occurs in those people who are most hostile and more narcissistic than the average hoarding character. But even the sadists are still *with* others; they want to control, but not to destroy them. Those in whom even this perverse kind of relatedness is lacking, who are still more narcissistic and more hostile, are the necrophiles. Their aim is to transform all that is alive into dead matter; they want to destroy everything and everybody, often even themselves; their enemy is life itself.

This hypothesis suggests that the development: normal anal character ⟶ sadistic character ⟶ necrophilous character is determined by the increase of narcissism, un-relatedness, and destructiveness (in this continuum there are innumerable shadings between the two poles) and that necrophilia can be described as *the malignant form of the anal character*.

If this notion of the close connection between the anal character and necrophilia were as simple as I have described it in this schematic presentation, it would be neat enough to be theoretically satisfying. But the connections are by no means so neat. The anal character that was typical of the nineteenth-century middle class is becoming increasingly less frequent among the sector of the population that is fully integrated into the economically most advanced forms of production.[22] While statistically speaking the phenomenon of total alienation probably does not yet exist in the majority of the American population, it is characteristic of the sector that is most indicative of the direction in which the whole society is moving. In fact, the character of the new type of man does not seem to fit into any of the older categories, such as the oral, anal, or genital characters. I have tried to understand this new type as a 'marketing character' (E. Fromm, 1947).

For the marketing character everything is transformed into a commodity – not only things, but the person himself, his physical energy, his skills, his knowledge, his opinions, his feelings, even his smiles. This character type is a historically new phenomenon because it is the product of a fully developed capitalism that is centred around the market the commodity market, the labour market, and the perso ality market – and whose principle it is to make a profit ! favourable exchange.[23]

The anal character, like the oral or genital, belongs to a period before total alienation has fully developed. These character types are possible as long as there is real sensuous experience of one's body, its functions, and its products. Cybernetic man is so alienated that he experiences his body

22. The studies undertaken by M. Maccoby on the character of managers in the United States (in the Harvard Project on Technology, Work, and Character; forthcoming) and by I. Millán on Mexican managers, *Carácter Social y Desarrollo* [*Social character and development*], (National Autonomous University of Mexico; forthcoming) will doubtless help a great deal to confirm or question my hypothesis.

23. This market is by no means entirely free in contemporary capitalism. The labour market is determined to a large extent by social and political factors, and the commodity market is highly manipulated.

only as an *instrument* for success. His body must look youthful and healthy; it is experienced narcissistically as a most precious asset on the personality market.

At this point we return to the question that led to this detour. Is necrophilia really characteristic for man in the second half of the twentieth century in the United States and in other equally highly developed capitalist or state capitalist societies?

This new type of man, after all, is not interested in faeces or corpses; in fact, he is so phobic towards corpses that he makes them look more alive than the person was when living. (This does not seem to be a reaction formation, but rather a part of the whole orientation that denies natural, not man-made reality.) But he does something much more drastic. He turns his interest away from life, persons, nature, ideas – in short from everything that is alive; he transforms all life into things, including himself and the manifestations of his human faculties of reason, seeing, hearing, tasting, loving. Sexuality becomes a technical skill (the 'love machine'), feelings are flattened and sometimes substituted for by sentimentality; joy, the expression of intense aliveness, is replaced by 'fun' or excitement; and whatever love and tenderness man has is directed towards machines and gadgets. The world becomes a sum of lifeless artifacts; from synthetic food to synthetic organs, the whole man becomes part of the total machinery that he controls and is simultaneously controlled by. He has no plan, no goal for life, except doing what the logic of technique determines him to do. He aspires to make robots as one of the greatest achievements of his technical mind, and some specialists assure us that the robot will hardly be distinguished from living men. This achievement will not seem so astonishing when man himself is hardly distinguishable from a robot.

The world of life has become a world of 'no-life'; persons have become 'non-persons', a world of death. Death is no longer symbolically expressed by unpleasant-smelling faeces or corpses. Its symbols are now clean, shining machines;

men are not attracted to smelly toilets, but to structures of aluminium and glass.[24] But the reality behind this anti-septic façade becomes increasingly visible. Man, in the name of progress, is transforming the world into a stinking and poisonous place (and this is not symbolic). He pollutes the air, the water, the soil, the animals – and himself. He is doing this to a degree that has made it doubtful whether the earth will still be livable within a hundred years from now. He knows the facts, but in spite of many protesters, those in charge go on in the pursuit of technical 'progress' and are willing to sacrifice all life in the worship of their idol. In earlier times men also sacrificed their children or war prisoners, but never before in history has man been willing to sacrifice all life to the Moloch – his own and that of all his descendants. It makes little difference whether he does it intentionally or not. If he had no knowledge of the possible danger, he might be acquitted from responsibility. But it is the necrophilous element in his character that prevents him from making use of the knowledge he has.

The same is true for the preparation of nuclear war. The two super-powers are constantly increasing their capacities to destroy each other, and at least large parts of the human race with them. Yet they have not done anything serious to eliminate the danger – and the only serious thing would be the destruction of all nuclear weapons. In fact, those in charge were already close to using nuclear weapons several times – and gambled with the danger. Strategic reasoning – for instance, Herman Kahn's *On Thermonuclear War* (1960) – calmly raises the question whether fifty million dead would still be 'acceptable'. That this is the spirit of necrophilia can hardly be questioned.

The phenomena about which there is so much indigna-tion – drug addiction, crime, the cultural and spiritual decay, contempt for genuine ethical values – are all related to the growing attraction to death and dirt. How can one expect

24. cf. 'Dream 7' earlier in this chapter.

that the young, the poor, and those without hope would not be attracted to decay when it is promoted by those who direct the course of modern society?

We must conclude that the lifeless world of total technicalization is only another form of the world of death and decay. This fact is not conscious to most, but to use an expression of Freud's, the repressed often returns, and the fascination with death and decay becomes as visible as in the malignant anal character.

Thus far we have considered the connection: mechanical – lifeless – anal. But another connection can hardly fail to come to mind as we consider the character of the totally alienated, cybernetic man: his *schizoid* or *schizophrenic* qualities. Perhaps the most striking trait in him is the split between thought–affect–will. (It was this split that had prompted E. Bleuler to choose the name 'schizophrenia' – from Greek *schizo*, to split; *phren*, psyche – for this type of illness.) In the description of the cybernetic man we have already seen some illustrations of this split, for instance in the bomber pilot's absence of affect, combined with the clear knowledge that he is killing a hundred thousand people by pushing a button. But we do not have to go to such extremes to observe this phenomenon. We have already described it in its more general manifestations. The cybernetic man is almost exclusively cerebrally oriented: he is a *monocerebral man*. His approach to the whole world around him – and to himself – is intellectual; he wants to know what things are, how they function, and how they can be constructed or manipulated. This approach was fostered by science, and it has become dominant since the end of the Middle Ages. It is the very essence of modern progress, the basis of the technical domination of the world and of mass consumption.

Is there anything ominous about this orientation? Indeed it might seem that this aspect of 'progress' is not ominous, were it not for some worrisome facts. In the first place this 'monocerebral' orientation is by no means only to be found in those who are engaged in scientific work; it is common to a vast part of the population: clerical workers, salesmen, engineers, physicians, managers, and especially many intellectuals and artists[25] – in fact, one may surmise, to most of the urban population. They all approach the world as a conglomerate of things to be understood in order to be used effectively. Second, and not less important, this cerebral-intellectual approach goes together with the absence of an affective response. One might say feelings have withered, rather than that they are repressed; inasmuch as they are alive they are not cultivated, and are relatively crude; they take the form of passions, such as the passion to win, to prove superior to others, to destroy, or the excitement in sex, speed, and noise. One further factor must be added. The monocerebral man is characterized by another very significant feature: a special kind of narcissism that has as its object himself – his body and his skill – in brief, himself as an instrument of success. The monocerebral man is so much part of the machinery that he has built, that his machines are just as much the object of his narcissism as he is himself; in fact, between the two exists a kind of symbiotic relationship: 'the union of one individual self with another self (or any other power outside of the own self) in such a way as to make each lose the integrity of its own self and to make them dependent on each other' (E. Fromm. 1941).[26] In a symbolic sense it is not nature any

25. It is a remarkable fact that the most creative contemporary scientists, men such as Einstein, Born, Heisenberg, Schrodinger, have been among the least alienated and monocerebral individuals. Their scientific concern has had none of the schizoid quality of the majority. It is characteristic of them that their philosophical, moral, and spiritual concerns have pervaded their whole personality. They have demonstrated that the scientific approach as such does not have to lead to alienation; it is rather the social climate that deforms the scientific approach into a schizoid approach.

26. Margaret S. Mahler has applied the term 'symbiosis' in her outstanding study of the symbiotic relationship between mother and child (M. S. Mahler, 1968).

more that is man's mother but the 'second nature' he has built, the machines that nourish and protect him.

Another feature of the cybernetic man – his tendency to behave in a routinized, stereotyped, and unspontaneous manner – is to be found in a more drastic form in many schizophrenic obsessional stereotypes. The similarities between schizophrenic patients and monocerebral man are striking; perhaps still more striking is the picture offered by another category not identical with yet related to schizophrenia, that of 'autistic children', first described by L. Kanner (1944) and later elaborated by M. S. Mahler (1968). (See also L. Bender's discussion of schizophrenic children [1942].) Following Mahler's description of the autistic syndrome, these traits are most important: (1) 'a loss of that primordial differentiation between living and lifeless matter, that von Monakow called *protodiakrisis*' (M. S. Mahler, 1968); (2) an attachment to lifeless objects, such as a chair or a toy, combined with the inability to relate to a living person, particularly their mothers, who often report that they 'cannot reach their children'; (3) an obsessive drive for the observation of sameness described by Kanner as a classical feature of infantile autism; (4) the intense desire to be left alone – 'the most striking feature in the autistic child is his spectacular struggle against any demand of human, of social contact' (M. S. Mahler, 1968); (5) the use of language (if they speak) for manipulative purposes, but not as a means of interpersonal communication – 'these autistic children, with signals and gestures, command the adult to serve as an executive extension of a semi-animate or inanimate mechanical kind, like a switch or a layer of a machine' (M. S. Mahler, 1968); (6) Mahler mentions one further trait that is of special interest in view of my foregoing comments on the decreased significance of the 'anal' complex in the monocerebral man: 'Most autistic children have a relatively low cathexis of their body surface, which accounts for their grossly deficient pain sensitivity. Along with this cathectic deficiency of the sensorium goes a lack of hierarchic stratification, of zonal libidinization and sequence' (M. S. Mahler, 1968).[27]

I refer especially to the lack of differentiation between living and lifeless matter, the unrelatedness to other people, the use of language for manipulation rather than for communication, the preponderant interest in the mechanical rather than the living. Striking as these similarities are, only extended studies could establish whether there is a form of mental pathology in adults which would correspond to that of the autistic child. It is perhaps less speculative to think about a connection of the functioning of cybernetic man and schizophrenic processes. But this constitutes an extremely difficult problem, for several reasons:

1. The definitions of schizophrenia differ tremendously among various psychiatric schools. They range from the traditional definition of schizophrenia as an organically caused illness, to the various definitions to some extent common to the school of Adolf Meyer (Sullivan, Lidz), to Fromm–Reichmann, and to the more radical school of Laing, who do not define schizophrenia as an illness, but as a psychological process to be understood in terms of a response to the subtle and complex interpersonal relations operating since early childhood. As much as somatic changes can be discovered, Laing would explain them as results, not as causes of the interpersonal processes.

2. Schizophrenia is not one phenomenon, but the term comprises a number of different forms of disturbances so that, from E. Bleuler on, one speaks of schizophrenias, rather than of schizophrenia as one disease entity.

3. The dynamic investigation of schizophrenia is of a relatively recent date, and until more investigative work has been done our knowledge of the schizophrenias will remain very inadequate.

27. I am particularly indebted to David S. Schechter and Gertrud Hunziker-Fromm, among others; their sharing their clinical experiences and views on autistic children with me was especially valuable for me because I have not worked with autistic children myself.

One aspect of the problem which, I believe, is particularly in need of further elucidation is the connection between schizophrenia and other types of psychotic processes, especially those usually called endogenous depressions. To be sure, even an investigator as enlightened and advanced as Eugen Bleuler made a clear distinction between psychotic depression and schizophrenia, and it seems undeniable that the two processes by and large manifest themselves in two different forms (even though the need for many mixed labels – combining schizophrenic, depressive, and paranoid features – seems to make the distinction questionable). The question arises whether the two mental illnesses are not different forms of the same fundamental process, and on the other hand whether the differences among various kinds of schizophrenias are not sometimes greater than the difference between certain manifestations of the depressive and the schizophrenic processes, respectively. If that were so, we would also not have to be too much worried about an obvious contradiction between the assumption of schizophrenic elements in modern man and the diagnosis of chronic depression made earlier in connection with the analysis of boredom. We might hypothesize that neither label is fully adequate – or that we may just forget about the labels.[28]

It would indeed be surprising if the monocerebral cybernetic man did *not* offer a picture of low-grade chronic

28. On the basis of such considerations, the Meyerian psychiatrists and Laing decline to use these nosological labels at all. This change has largely resulted from the new approach to the mentally ill. As long as one could approach the patient psychotherapeutically, the main point of interest was the diagnostic label, useful for the decision of whether or not to put him in an institution for the mentally ill. Since one began to help the patient by psychoanalytically oriented therapy, the labels became unimportant, because the psychiatrist's interest was focused on understanding the processes going on in the patient, experiencing him as a human being who is not basically different from the 'participant observer'. This new attitude towards the psychotic patient may be considered an expression of a radical humanism, which is developing in our time in spite of the process of dehumanization that is predominant.

schizophrenic – to use the term for simplicity's sake – process. He lives in an atmosphere that is only quantitatively less than that shown by Laing and others in their presentation of schizogenetic (schizophrenia-producing) families.

I believe that it is legitimate to speak of an 'insane society' and of the problem of what happens to the sane man in such a society (E. Fromm, 1955). If a society produced a majority of members who suffer from severe schizophrenia, it would undermine its own existence. The full-fledged schizophrenic person is characterized by the fact that he has cut off all relations with the world outside; he has withdrawn into his own private world, and the main reason he is considered severely sick is a social one: he does not function socially; he cannot take care of himself properly; he needs in some way or other the help of others. (This is not entirely true, either, as experience has shown in all those places where chronic schizophrenics worked or took care of themselves, although with the help of certain people who arranged favourable conditions and at least some material contributions from the state.) A society, not to speak of a large and complex one, could not be run by schizophrenic persons. Yet it can be very well managed by persons suffering from low-grade schizophrenia, who are perfectly capable of managing the things to be managed if a society is to function. Such people have not lost the capacity to look at the world 'realistically', provided we mean by this to conceive of things intellectually as they need to be conceived of in order to deal with them effectively. They may have lost entirely the capacity to experience things personally, i.e., subjectively, and with their hearts. The fully developed person can, for instance, see a rose and experience it as warming or even fiery (if he puts this experience into words we call him a poet), but he also knows that the rose – in the realm of physical reality – does not warm as fire does. Modern man experiences the world *only* in terms of practical ends. But his defect is not smaller than that of the so-called sick person who *cannot* experience the world 'objectively', but who has retained the other human faculty of personal, subjective, symbolic experience.

Spinoza, in his *Ethics*, was, I believe, the first one to express the concept of 'normal' insanity:

> Many people are seized by one and the same affect with great consistency. All his senses are so strongly affected by one object that he believes this object to be present even if it is not. If this happens while the person is awake, the person is believed to be insane ... But if the *greedy* person thinks only of money and possessions, the *ambitious* one only of fame, one does not think of them as being insane, but only as annoying; generally one has contempt for them. But *factually* greediness, ambition, and so forth are forms of insanity, although usually one does not think of them as 'illness'. (B. de Spinoza, 1927)

The change from the seventeenth century to our time becomes apparent in the fact that an attitude which Spinoza says one 'generally ... has contempt for' is considered today not contemptuous but laudable.

We must take one more step. The 'pathology of normalcy' (E. Fromm, 1955) rarely deteriorates to graver forms of mental illness because society produces the antidote against such deterioration. When pathological processes become socially patterned, they lose their individual character. On the contrary, the sick individual finds himself at home with all other similarly sick individuals. The whole culture is geared to this kind of pathology and arranges the means to give satisfactions which fit the pathology. The result is that the average individual does not experience the separateness and isolation the fully schizophrenic person feels. He feels at ease among those who suffer from the same deformation; in fact, it is the fully sane person who feels isolated in the insane society – and he may suffer so much from the incapacity to communicate that it is he who may become psychotic.

In the context of this study the crucial question is whether the hypothesis of a quasi-autistic or of low-grade schizophrenic disturbance would help us to explain some of the violence spreading today. We are here at the point of almost pure speculation, and further investigations and new data are needed. To be sure, in autism there is a good deal of destructiveness to be found, but we do not know yet where this category applies here. As far as schizophrenic processes are concerned, fifty years ago the answer would have seemed to be clear. It was generally assumed that schizophrenic patients are violent, and that for this reason they needed to be put in institutions from which they could not escape. The experiences with chronic schizophrenics working on farms or under their own management (as Laing arranged it in London) have demonstrated that the schizophrenic person is rarely violent, when he is left in peace.[29]

But the 'normal' low-grade schizophrenic person is *not* left alone. He is pushed, interfered with, his extreme sensibilities are hurt, many times every day, so that indeed we could understand that this pathology of normalcy would engender destructiveness in many individuals. Least of all, of course, among those who are best adapted to the social system and most of all with those who are neither socially rewarded nor have their place in a social structure meaningful to them: the poor, the black, the young, the unemployed.

All these speculations on the connection between low-grade schizophrenic (and autistic) processes and destructiveness must be left unresolved at this point. Eventually the

29. The picture of autistic children is somewhat different. With them, intense destructiveness seems to be more frequent. To account for the difference it might be helpful to consider that the schizophrenic patient has cut off his ties with social reality, hence does not feel threatened, and in consequence prone to violence, if he is left alone. The autistic child, on the other hand, is not left alone. The parents try to make him play the game of normal life and intrude in his private world. In addition, by the age factor, the child is forced to keep his ties with his family and cannot yet afford, as it were, to withdraw completely. This situation may produce intense hate and destructiveness and account for the relatively greater frequency of violent tendencies among autistic children than among adult schizophrenic individuals if left alone. These speculations are of course very hypothetical and will need to be confirmed or rejected by specialists in this field.

discussion will lead to the question whether there is any connection between certain kinds of schizophrenic processes and necrophilia. But on the basis of my knowledge and experience I cannot go further than to raise the question in the hope that it might stimulate others to further studies. We must be satisfied with stating that the atmospheres of family life which have proved to be schizogenic resemble very closely the social atmosphere which engenders necrophilia. One word, however, must be added. A mono-cerebral orientation is incapable of visualizing aims which further the growth of a society's members and its own survival. To formulate these aims *reason* is required, and reason is more than mere intelligence; it develops only when the brain and the heart are united, when feeling and thinking are integrated, and when both are rational (in the sense proposed earlier). The loss of the ability to think in terms of constructive visions is in itself a severe threat to survival.

If we stopped here, the picture would be incomplete and undialectical. Simultaneously with the increasing necrophilous development, the opposite trend, that of love of life, is also developing. It manifests itself in many forms: in the protest against the deadening of life, a protest by people among all social strata and age groups, but particularly by the young. There is hope in the rising protest against pollution and war; in the growing concern for the *quality* of life; in the attitude of many young professionals who prefer meaningful and interesting work to high income and prestige; in the widespread search for spiritual values – misguided and naïve though it often is. This protest is also to be understood in the attraction to drugs among the young, despite their mistaken attempt to attain greater aliveness by using the methods of the consumer society. The anti-necrophilous tendencies have also manifested themselves in the many politico-human conversions that have taken place in connection with the Vietnam war. Such cases show that although the love for life can be deeply repressed, what is *repressed* is not *dead*. Love of life is so much a biologically given quality in man that one should assume that, aside from a small minority, it can always come to the fore, although usually only under special personal and historical circumstances. (It can happen in the psychoanalytic process, too.) Indeed, the presence and even the increase of anti-necrophilous tendencies is the one hope we have that the great experiment, *Homo sapiens*, will not fail. There is, I believe, no country where the chances for such reassertion of life are greater than in the technically most developed country, the United States, where the hope that more 'progress' will bring happiness has been proved to be an illusion for most of those who have already had a chance to get a taste of the new 'paradise'. Whether such a fundamental change will happen, nobody knows. The forces working against it are formidable and there is no reason for optimism. But I believe there is reason for hope.

Hypothesis on Incest and the Oedipus Complex

As to the conditions that contribute to the development of necrophilia, our knowledge is still very limited and only further research will throw more light on this problem. We may safely assume that a very unalive, necrophilous family environment will often be a contributing factor in the formation of necrophilia. Lack of enlivening stimulation, the absence of hope, and a destructive spirit of the society as a whole are certainly of real significance for fostering necrophilia. That genetic factors play a role in the formation of necrophilia is, in my opinion, very likely.

In the following I want to present a hypothesis concerning what I believe may be the earliest roots of necrophilia, a hypothesis that is speculative even though it is based on the observation of a number of cases and supported by ample material from the fields of myth and religion. I believe it to be of sufficient importance to be worthy of presentation, providing its tentative character is kept in mind.

This hypothesis leads us to a phenomenon that seems, at first glance at least, to have little connection with necrophilia: the phenomenon of *incest* that has become so familiar through Freud's concept of the Oedipus complex. First we must take a brief look at the Freudian concept in order to lay the foundation for what follows.

According to the classic concept a little boy at the age of five or six chooses his mother as the first object of his sexual (phallic) desires ('phallic stage'). Given the family situation, this makes of his father a hated rival. (Orthodox psychoanalysts have greatly overrated the little boy's hatred of the father. Statements like: 'When father dies I will marry mother', attributed to little boys and often quoted as proof of their death wishes, are not to be taken literally, because at this age death is not yet fully experienced as a reality, but rather as an equivalent of 'being away'. Furthermore, although some rivalry with father exists, the main source of deep antagonism lies in the rebellion of the boy against patriarchal, oppressive authority [E. Fromm, 1951]. The contribution of 'Oedipal hate' to destructiveness, is, in my opinion, relatively small.) Since he cannot do away with his father he becomes afraid of him – fearing, specifically, that father will castrate him, his little rival. This 'castration fear' makes the boy give up his sexual desires for mother.

In normal development the son is capable of shifting his interest to other women, particularly after he has reached full sexual–genital development – about the time of puberty. He overcomes his rivalry with his father by identifying with him and particularly with his commands and prohibitions. The father's norms are internalized and become the superego of the son. In cases of pathological development the conflict is not resolved in this way. The son does not give up his sexual attachment to mother and in his later life is attracted by women who fulfil the function mother did. As a result he is incapable of falling in love with a woman of his own age and remains afraid of the threatening father or the

father substitutes. He usually expects from the mother substitutes the same qualities mother once showed him:
unconditional love, protection, admiration, security.

This type of mother-fixated men are well-known; they are
usually quite affectionate and in a qualified sense 'loving',
but they are also quite narcissistic. The feeling that they are
more important to mother than father makes them feel that
they are 'wonderful', and since they are already grown up
and need not do anything in reality to establish their greatness; they are great because – and as long as – mother (or
her substitute) loves them exclusively and unconditionally.
As a result they tend to be extremely jealous – they
must keep their unique position – and they are simultaneously insecure and anxious whenever they have to perform
a real task; while they might not fail, their actual performance can never really equal their narcissistic conviction of
superiority over any man (while having at the same time a
nagging, unconscious feeling of inferiority to all). The type
I have just described is the more extreme case. There are
many mother-fixated men whose tie to mother is less
intense, and in whom the narcissistic illusion of achievement
is blended with realistic achievements.

Freud assumed that the essence of the tie to mother was
the little boy's sexual attraction to her, and that hate of the
father was a logical consequence. My observations, through
many years, have tended to confirm my conviction that the
sexual attachment to mother is generally not the cause of an
intense affective bond. While limitation of space does not
permit a full discussion of the reasons for this conviction, the
following remarks may help to clarify at least one of its
aspects.

At birth, and still for some time afterward, the infant's
attachment to mother occurs in a mainly narcissistic frame
of reference (although soon after birth the child already
begins to show some interest in and response to objects outside himself). While physiologically the infant has his own
independent existence, psychologically he continues an

'intra-uterine' life in some respects and to some degree. He still lives through mother: she feeds him, cares for him, stimulates him, and gives him the warmth – bodily and emotional – that is a condition for his healthy development. In the process of further development the infant's attachment to mother becomes warmer, more personal as it were; she changes from being a quasi intra-uterine home into a *person* for whom the child feels warm affection. In this process the little boy breaks through the narcissistic shell; he loves mother, even though this love is still characterized by lack of equality and reciprocity and coloured by inherent dependency. At a period when the little boy begins to react sexually (in Freud's 'phallic phase') the affectionate feeling for mother results also in erotic and sexual desire for her. However, the sexual attraction to mother is usually not exclusive. As Freud himself reports, for instance in the case history of Little Hans (S. Freud, 1909), sexual attraction to their mothers can be observed in little boys around the age of five, but at the same time they are equally attracted to girls their own age. This is not surprising; it is a well-established fact that the sexual drive as such is not closely bound to one object, but is rather fickle; what can make the relationship to *one* person so intense and lasting is its affective function. In those cases in which the fixation to mother remains strong after puberty and throughout life, the reason lies in the strength of the affective tie to her.

Indeed, the fixation to mother is not only a developmental problem of the child. To be sure the child is forced into an intense, symbiotic dependency on mother for obvious biological reasons. But the adult, while physically capable of shifting for himself, finds himself also in a helpless and powerless situation rooted, as we have shown earlier, in the conditions of human existence. We only understand the power of the passion to cling to mother if we see its roots not solely in childhood dependence but in 'the human situation'. The effective tie to mother is so intense because it represents one of the basic answers to man's existential situation: the desire to return to 'paradise' where the existential dichotomies had not yet developed – where man can live without self-awareness, without work, without suffering, in harmony with nature, himself and his mate. With the new dimension of awareness (the Tree of Knowledge of Good and Evil), conflict comes into existence and man – male and female – is cursed. Man is driven from paradise and not permitted to return. Is it not astonishing that he never loses his desire to return, even though he 'knows' that he cannot do so since he is burdened with the fact of being man?

The sexual aspect of the attraction to mother is itself a positive sign. It shows that mother has become a person, a woman, and that the boy is already a little man. The particular intensity of the sexual attraction to be found in some instances may be considered a defence against a more infantile passive dependency. In those situations in which the incestuous tie to mother is not resolved around the time of puberty[30] and lasts throughout life, we deal with a neurotic development; the male will remain dependent on mother or her substitutes, afraid of women, and more of a child than any adult should be for his own good. Such a development is often caused by a mother who for any number of reasons – such as lack of love for her husband, or narcissistic pride in or possessiveness of *her* son – is over-attracted to her little boy and in many different ways (pampering, over-protectiveness, over-admiration, etc.) seduces him to become over-attracted to her.[31]

30. Initiation rites have the function of breaking this tie and marking the transition into adult life.

31. Freud, in his respect for the conventions of bourgeois life, systematically exculpated the parents of his child patients from having done anything to harm the child. Everything, including incestuous desires, was supposed to be part of the infant's unprovoked fantasy, cf. E. Fromm (1970b). This paper is based on a discussion held at the Mexican Institute of Psychoanalysis by a group consisting, aside from the author, of Drs F. Narváez Manzano, Victor F. Saavedra Mancera, L. Santarelli Carmelo, J. Silva García, and E. Zajur Dip.

This warm, erotically and often sexually tinged tie to mother is what Freud had in mind when he described the Oedipus complex. While this type of incestuous fixation is most frequent, there is another, much less frequent kind of incestuous fixation that has very different qualities and may be called malignant. It is this type of incestuous fixation that, in my hypothesis, is related to necrophilia – in fact it may be considered one of its earliest roots.

I am speaking of children in whom no affective bonds towards mother emerge to break through the shell of autistic self-sufficiency. We are familiar with extreme forms of such self-sufficiency in the case of *autistic* children.[32] These children never break out of the shell of their narcissism: they never experience the mother as a love object; they never form any affective attachment to others, but, rather, look through them as if they were inanimate objects, and they often show a particular interest in mechanical things.

Autistic children seem to form the one pole of a continuum – at the other pole of which we can locate children whose affection for mother and others is most fully developed. It seems a legitimate assumption that we find children on this continuum who are not autistic, but close to it, and who show the traits of autistic children in a less drastic way. The question arises: What happens to the incestuous fixation to mother in such autistic or near autistic infants?

It would seem that such infants never develop warm, erotic, and later, sexual feelings towards mother, or that they ever have a desire to be near her. Nor do they later fall in love with mother substitutes. For them mother is a symbol: a phantom rather than a real person. She is a symbol of earth, of home, of blood, of race, of nation, of the deepest ground from which life emerges and to which it returns. But she is also the symbol of chaos and death; she is not the

32. cf. E. Bleuler (1951); H. S. Sullivan (1953); M. S. Mahler and B. J. Gosliner (1955); L. Bender (1927); M. R. Green and D. E. Schecter (1957).

life-giving mother, but the death-giving mother; her embrace is death, her womb is a tomb. The attraction to the death-mother could not be affection or love; it is not an attraction in the common psychological sense denoting something pleasant and warm, but in the sense in which one would speak of magnetic attraction, or the attraction of gravity. The person tied to mother by malignant incestuous bonds remains narcissistic, cold, unresponsive; he is drawn to her as iron is drawn to a magnet; she is the ocean in which he wants to drown,[33] the ground in which he wants to be buried. The reason for this development seems to be that the state of unmitigated narcissistic aloneness is intolerable; if there is no way of being related to mother or her substitute by warm, enjoyable bonds, the relatedness to her and to the whole world must become one of final union in death.

The double role of mother as goddess of creation and goddess of destruction is well documented in many myths and in religious ideas. The same earth from which man is made, the womb from which all trees and grasses are born, is the place to which the body is returned; the womb of mother earth becomes the tomb. A classic example for the double-faced mother goddess is the Indian goddess Kali, the giver of life and the destroyer. There are also the Neolithic period goddesses with the same two faces. It would take too much space to cite the many other examples of the double role of the mother goddesses. One more datum presenting the same double function of mother should be mentioned however: the double face of the mother image in dreams. While mother may often appear in dreams as the benevolent, all-loving figure, in the dreams of many persons she is symbolized as a dangerous snake, a quick-striking, dangerous animal, such as a lion, a tiger, or a hyena. I have found clinically that the fear of the destructive mother is by far more intense than of the punishing, castrating father. It seems that one can ward off the danger coming

33. I have seen a number of this type of incestuous patients with a longing to be drowned in the ocean, a frequent mother symbol.

from father by obedience; but there is no defence against mother's destructiveness; her love cannot be earned, since it is unconditional; her hate cannot be averted, since there are no 'reasons' for it, either. Her love is grace, her hate is curse, and neither is subject to the influence of their recipient.

In conclusion it can be stated that *benign incestuousness is in itself a normal, transitory stage of development, while malignant incestuousness is a pathological phenomenon that occurs when certain conditions inhibit the development of benign incestuous bonds.* It is the latter that I consider, hypothetically, one of the earliest roots, if not *the* root, of necrophilia.

This incestuous attraction to death, where it exists, is a passion in conflict with all other impulses fighting for the preservation of life. Hence it works in the dark and is usually entirely unconscious. The person with this malignant incestuousness will attempt to relate to people by less destructive bonds, such as sadistic control of others or the satisfaction of narcissism by gaining boundless admiration. If his life provides such relatively satisfactory solutions as success in work, prestige, etc., the destructiveness may never be expressed overtly in any major ways. If, on the other hand, he experiences failures, the malignant tendencies will come to the fore and the craving for destruction – of himself and others – will rule supreme.

While we know a great deal about the factors causing benign incestuousness, we know little about the conditions responsible for infantile autism and, hence, malignant incestuousness. We can only speculate in different directions. We can hardly avoid the assumption that genetic factors must be involved; of course I do not refer to genes responsible for this type of incestuousness, but to the child's genetically given disposition for coldness that would in turn be responsible for his failure to develop a warm attachment to mother. We would expect to find a second condition in the character of the mother. If she herself is a cold, rejecting, necrophilous person, she would make it difficult for the infant to develop a warm, affectionate relationship to her. We must consider, however, that we cannot look at the mother and the child except in the process of their inter- action. An infant with a strong disposition for warmth may either effect a change in mother's attitude or become warmly attached to a mother substitute: a grandmother or a grand- father, an older sibling, or whoever else may be available. On the other hand, a cold child may be influenced and changed to some degree by a mother of more than average warmth and concern. It is sometimes also difficult to discern the fundamental coldness of the mother towards the child when it is overlaid by the conventional features of a sweet and loving mother.

A third possibility is traumatic experiences in the first years of the child's life that created active hate and resent- ment to such a degree that the child 'froze up', and thus malignant incestuousness developed. One must always be alert to such possibilities. But in searching for traumatic experiences it should be very clear that these must be rather exceptional. In the literature quoted above, a number of very valuable hypotheses as to the causes for the develop- ment of autism and early schizophrenia have been presented that stress particularly the defensive function of autism against an intrusive mother.

This hypothesis regarding malignant incestuousness and its role as an early root of necrophilia needs further study.[34] In the following chapter, the analysis of Hitler will offer an example of an incestuous fixation to mother, the peculiar- ities of which can best be explained on the basis of this hypothesis.

34. I intend to publish a longer, more documented version of what has been but briefly sketched here.

The Relation of Freud's Life and Death Instincts to Biophilia and Necrophilia

To conclude this discussion of necrophilia and its opposite biophilia (love of life), it may be helpful to present a brief sketch of the relation of this concept to Freud's concept of the death instinct and the life instinct (Eros). It is the effort of Eros to combine organic substances into ever larger unities, whereas the death instinct tries to separate and to disintegrate living structure. The relation of the death instinct with necrophilia hardly needs any further explanation. In order to elucidate the relation between life instinct and biophilia, however, a short explanation of the latter is necessary.

Biophilia is the passionate love of life and of all that is alive; it is the wish to further growth, whether in a person, a plant, an idea, or a social group. The biophilous person prefers to construct rather than to retain. He wants to be more rather than to have more. He is capable of wondering, and he prefers to see something new rather than to find confirmation of the old. He loves the adventure of living more than he does certainty. He sees the whole rather than only the parts, structures rather than summations. He wants to mould and to influence by love, reason, and example; not by force, by cutting things apart, by the bureaucratic manner of administering people as if they were things. Because he enjoys life and all its manifestations he is not a passionate consumer of newly packaged 'excitement'.

Biophilic ethics have their own principle of good and evil. Good is all that serves life; evil is all that serves death. Good is reverence for life,[35] all that enhances life, growth, unfolding. Evil is all that stifles life, narrows it down, cuts it into pieces.

The difference between Freud's concept and the one

35. This is the main thesis of Albert Schweitzer, one of the great representatives of the love of life – both in his writings and in his person.

486 The Varieties of Aggression and Destructiveness

presented here does not lie in their substance but in the fact
that in Freud's concept both tendencies have equal rank, as
it were, both being biologically given. Biophilia, on the
other hand, is understood to refer to a biologically normal
impulse, while necrophilia is understood as a *psychopathological* phenomenon. The latter necessarily emerges as the
result of stunted growth, of psychical 'crippledness'. It is the
outcome of unlived life, of the failure to arrive at a certain
stage beyond narcissism and indifference. *Destructiveness is
not parallel to, but the alternative to biophilia. Love of life or love
of the dead is the fundamental alternative that confronts every human
being. Necrophilia grows as the development of biophilia is stunted.
Man is biologically endowed with the capacity for biophilia, but
psychologically he has the potential for necrophilia as an alternative
solution.*

The psychical necessity for the development of necrophilia as a result of crippledness must be understood in
reference to man's existential situation, as I discussed
earlier. If man cannot create anything or move anybody, if
he cannot break out of the prison of his total narcissism and
isolation, he can escape the unbearable sense of vital impotence and nothingness only by affirming himself in the
act of destruction of the life that he is unable to create.
Great effort, patience, and care are not required; for
destruction, all that is necessary is strong arms, or a knife,
or a gun.[36]

36. As shown in great detail in my discussion of Freud's theory of
aggression in the Appendix, in his change from the older concepts to
the new polarity, Eros – death instinct, Freud actually changed his whole
concept of instinct. In the older version, sexuality was a physiological,
mechanistic concept aroused by excitation of various erogenous zones,
and its satisfaction consisted in the reduction of the tension produced
by the increasing excitation. The death and life instincts, on the contrary, are not attached to any particular bodily zone; they lack the
rhythmic character of tension —> de-tension —> tension; they are
conceived in biological, vitalistic terms. Freud never tried to bridge the
gap between these two concepts; their unity was preserved semantically
by the equation: life = eros = sexuality (libido). In the hypothesis
proposed here, the older and the later phase of Freud's theory would

Clinical/Methodological Principles

I will close this discussion of necrophilia with some general clinical and methodological remarks.

1. The presence of one or two traits is insufficient for the diagnosis of a necrophilous character. This is so for various reasons. Sometimes a particular behaviour that would seem to indicate necrophilia may not be a character trait but be due to cultural tradition or other similar factors.

2. On the other hand it is not necessary to find all characteristically necrophilous features together in order to make the diagnosis. There are many factors, personal and cultural, that are responsible for this unevenness; in addition, some necrophilous traits may not be discovered in people who hide them successfully.

3. It is of particular importance to understand that only a relatively small minority are *completely* necrophilous; one might consider them as severely pathological cases and look for a genetic disposition for this illness. As is to be expected on biological grounds, the vast majority are not entirely without some, even if weak, biophilous tendencies. Among them will be a certain percentage of people whose necrophilia is so predominant that we are justified in calling them necrophilous persons. By far the larger number are those in whom necrophilous trends are to be found together with biophilous trends strong enough to create an internal conflict that is often very productive. The outcome of this conflict for the motivation of a person depends on many variables. First of all, on the respective intensity of each trend; second, on the presence of social conditions that

---

be linked through the assumption that necrophilia is the malignant form of the anal character and biophilia is the fully developed form of the 'genital' character. Of course, one must not forget that in my use of the terms 'anal' (hoarding) and 'genital' (productive) character, I have kept Freud's clinical description, but have given up the notion of the physiological roots of these passions.

would strengthen one of the two respective orientations; furthermore, on particular events in the life of the person that can incline him in the one or the other direction. Then come the people who are so predominantly biophilous that their necrophilous impulses are easily curbed or repressed, or serve to build up a particular sensitivity *against* the necrophilous tendencies in themselves and others. Eventually there is the group of people – again only a small minority – in whom there is no trace of necrophilia, who are pure biophiles motivated by the most intense and pure love for all that is alive. Albert Schweitzer, Albert Einstein, and Pope John XXIII are among the well-known recent examples of this minority.

Consequently there is no fixed border between the necrophilous and the biophilous orientation. As with most other character traits, there are as many combinations as there are individuals. For all practical purposes, however, it is quite possible to distinguish between predominantly necrophilous and predominantly biophilous persons.

4. Since most of the methods that can be used for discovering the necrophilous character have already been mentioned, I can be very brief in summing them up. They are: (a) minute observation of a person's behaviour, especially what is unintended, including facial expression, choice of words, but also their general philosophy, and the most important decisions the person has made in his life; (b) study of dreams, jokes, fantasies; (c) evaluation of a person's treatment of others, the effect on them, and what kind of people are liked or disliked; (d) the use of projective tests like the Rorschach inkblot test. (M. Maccoby has used the test for the diagnosis of necrophilia with satisfactory results.)

5. It is hardly necessary to stress that severely necrophilous persons are very dangerous. They are the haters, the racists, those in favour of war, bloodshed, and destruction. They are dangerous not only if they are political leaders, but also as the potential cohorts for a dictatorial leader.

They become the executioners, terrorists, torturers; without them no terror system could be set up. But the less intense necrophiles are also politically important; while they may not be among its first adherents, they are necessary for the existence of a terror régime because they form a solid basis, although not necessarily a majority, for it to gain and hold power.

6. Considering these facts, would it not be of great social and political significance to know what percentage of the population can be considered to be predominantly necrophilous or predominantly biophilous? To know not only the respective incidence of each group but also how they are related to age, sex, education, class, occupation, and geographical location? We study political opinions, value judgements, etc., and get satisfactory results for the whole American population by the use of adequate sampling techniques. But the results tell us only what *opinions* people have, not what their *character* is – in other words what the *effective* convictions are that motivate them. If we were to study an equally adequate sample, but with a different method that would permit us to recognize the driving and largely unconscious forces behind manifest behaviour and opinions, we would, indeed, know a great deal more about the intensity and direction of human energy in the United States. We might even protect ourselves from some of the surprises that, once they have happened, are declared to be unexplainable. Or is it that we are interested only in the energy that is needed for material production and not in the forms of *human* energy that is in itself a decisive factor in the social process?

13

Malignant Aggression: Adolf Hitler, A Clinical Case of Necrophilia

Preliminary Remarks

An analytic psychobiographical study aims at answering
two questions: (1) What are the driving forces that motivate
a person, the passions that impel or incline him to behave as
he does? (2) What are the conditions – internal and external – responsible for the development of these specific
passions (character traits)? The following analysis of Hitler
has these aims, but it differs from the classic Freudian
method in certain significant respects.

In the following analysis of Hitler's character I have
focused on Hitler's necrophilia and have only briefly
touched upon other aspects such as his exploitative character and of Germany as a symbolic representation of the
mother figure.

One difference that has already been discussed and hence
needs to be mentioned here only briefly lies in the notion
that these passions are not mainly of an instinctive or, more
specifically, of a sexual nature. Another difference lies in the
assumption that even if we know nothing of a person's
childhood, the analysis of dreams, unintended behaviour,
gestures, language, and behaviour that is rationally not
fully explainable permits one to form a picture of the
essential and mostly unconscious passions ('X-ray approach'). The interpretation of such data requires the
particular training and skill of psychoanalysis.

The most important difference is the following: classic
analysts assume that character development is finished
around the age of five or six years, and that no essential

changes occur afterwards other than by the intervention of therapy. My experience has led me to the conviction that this concept is untenable; it is mechanistic and does not take into account the whole process of living and of character as a developing system.

When an individual is born he is by no means faceless. Not only is he born with genetically determined temperamental and other inherited dispositions that have greater affinity to certain character traits rather than to others, but prenatal events and birth itself form additional dispositions. All this makes up, as it were, the face of the individual at birth. Then he comes in contact with a particular kind of environment – parents and other significant people around him – to which he responds and which tends to influence the further development of his character. At the age of eighteen months the infant's character is much more definitely formed and determined than it was at birth. Yet it is not finished, and its development could go in several directions, depending on the influences that operate on it. By the age of six, let us say, the character is still more determined and fixed, but not without the capacity for change, provided new, significant circumstances occur that may provoke such change. Speaking more generally, the formation and fixity of the character has to be understood in terms of a sliding scale; the individual begins life with certain qualities that dispose him to go in certain directions, but his personality is still malleable enough to allow the character to develop in many different directions within the given framework. Every step in life narrows down the number of possible future outcomes. The more the character is fixed, the greater must be the impact of new factors if they are to produce fundamental changes in the direction of the further evolution of the system. Eventually, the freedom to change becomes so minimal that only a miracle would seem capable of effecting a change.

This does not imply that influences of early childhood are not as a rule more effective than later events. But although they *incline more*, they do not *determine* a person completely. In order to make up for the greater degree of impressionability of early age, later events have to be more intense and more dramatic. The impression that the character never changes is largely based on the fact that the life of most people is so prefabricated and unspontaneous that nothing new ever really happens, and later events only confirm the earlier ones.

The number of real possibilities for the character to develop in different directions is in inverse proportion to the fixity the character system has assumed. But in principle the character system is never so completely fixed that new developments could not occur as the result of extraordinary experiences, although such occurrences are, statistically speaking, not probable.

The practical aspect of these theoretical considerations is that one cannot expect to find the character as it is, say, at the age of twenty to be a repetition of the character as it was at the age of five; more specifically, taking Hitler as an example, one could not expect to find a fully developed necrophilous character system in his childhood, but one could expect to find certain necrophilous roots that are conducive to development of a full-fledged necrophilous character as one of several real possibilities. But only after a great number of internal and external events have accrued will the character system have developed in such a way that necrophilia becomes the (almost) unchangeable outcome, and then we can discover it in various overt and covert forms. I shall try to show these early roots in the analysis of Hitler's character and how the conditions for the development of necrophilia increased at various stages of his development, until finally, there was hardly any other possibility left.

Hitler's Parentage and Early Years[1]

Klara Hitler

The most important influence on a child is the character of its parents, rather than this or that single event. For those who believe in the simplistic formula that the bad development of a child is roughly proportionate to the 'badness' of the parents, the study of the character of Hitler's parents, as far as the known data show, offers a surprise: both father and mother seem to have been stable, well-intentioned people, and not destructive.

Hitler's mother, Klara, seems to have been a well-adjusted and sympathetic woman. She was an uneducated, simple country girl who had worked as a maid in the house of Alois Hitler, who was her uncle and future husband. Klara became Alois's mistress and was pregnant by him at the time his wife died. She married the widowed Alois on 7 January 1885; she was twenty-four years old and he was forty-seven.

She was hardworking and responsible; in spite of a marriage that was not too happy, she never complained. She fulfilled her obligations humanely and conscientiously.

Her life was centred on the tasks of maintaining her home and caring for her husband and the children of the family. She was a model housekeeper, who maintained a spotless home and performed her duties with precision. Nothing could distract her from her round of household toil, not even the prospect of a little gossip.

1. In the descriptions of Hitler's parents and his infancy, childhood, and youth I follow mainly the two most important works dealing with his early years, the excellent books by B. F. Smith (1967) and W. Maser (1971). I have also used A. Kubizek (1954) and A. Hitler (1943). Hitler's book largely serves propaganda purposes and contains many untruths; Kubizek, the friend of Hitler's youth who admired him in their youth as well as when Hitler was in power, is to be used with some caution. Maser, though a historian, is often unreliable in the use of his sources. Smith is by far the most objective and reliable source for Hitler's youth.

Her home and the furthering of the family interest were all-important; by careful management she was able to increase the family possessions, much to her joy. Even more important to her than the house were the children. Everyone who knew her agreed that it was in her love and devotion for the children that Klara's life centred. The only serious charge ever raised against her is that because of this love and devotion she was over-indulgent and thus encouraged a sense of uniqueness in her son – a somewhat strange charge to be brought against a mother. The children did not share this view. Her stepchildren and her own offspring who survived infancy loved and respected their mother. (B. F. Smith, 1967)

The accusation that she was over-indulgent to her son and encouraged a sense of uniqueness (read *narcissism*) in him is not as strange as Smith thinks – and furthermore it is probably true. But this period of over-indulgence lasted only up to the time when Hitler ended the period of his infancy and entered school. This change in her attitude was probably brought about, or at least facilitated, by her giving birth to another son at the time Hitler was five years old. But her whole attitude during the rest of her life proves that the birth of the new child was not as traumatic an event as some psychoanalysts like to think; she probably stopped spoiling Adolf, but she did not suddenly ignore him. She was increasingly aware of the necessity for him to grow up, adjust himself to reality, and as we shall see, she did everything she could to further this process.

This picture of a responsible and loving mother raises some serious questions in view of the hypothesis of Hitler's quasi autistic childhood and his 'malignant incestuousness'. How could Hitler's early development be explained under these circumstances? We can think of several possibilities: (1) that Hitler was *constitutionally* so cold and withdrawn that his near-autistic orientation existed in spite of a warm and loving mother. (2) It is possible that her over-attachment to this son, of which we have evidence, was felt by the already shy child as a strong intrusion to which he reacted

by a more drastic withdrawal.[2] We do not know enough of
Klara's personality to be sure which of these conditions
prevailed, but they are compatible with the picture of
Klara's behaviour as we can construe it from the data we
do have.

Another possibility is that she was a sad person, who was
motivated by a sense of duty but conveyed little warmth or
joy to her son. After all she did not have a happy life. As was
usual in the German-Austrian middle class she was
expected to bear children, take care of the household, and
subordinate herself to her authoritarian husband. Her age,
her lack of education, his elevated social position, and his
selfish – though not vicious – disposition, tended to intensify
this traditional position. Thus she may have become a sad,
disappointed, depressed woman perhaps as a result of
circumstances rather than on the basis of her character.
Finally it is possible that underneath her caring attitude
was a deep-seated schizoid and withdrawn attitude. But
this is the least likely of the possibilities. At any rate, we do
not have enough concrete details about her personality
to decide which of these hypotheses is most likely to be
correct.

Alois Hitler

Alois Hitler was a much less sympathetic figure. Born as an
illegitimate child, using his mother's name, Schicklgruber
(changed much later to that of Hitler), starting with poor
financial resources, he was a real self-made man. Through
hard work and discipline he succeeded in rising from being a
low official in the Austro-Hungarian customs service to a
relatively high position – 'higher collector of customs' – that
clearly gave him the status of a respected member of the
middle class. He was economical and succeeded in saving
enough money to own a house, a farm, and to leave his

2. As indicated before, intrusion as a condition for autism was found by
students of the autistic child.

family an estate which, together with his pension, provided for a financially comfortable existence. He was undoubtedly a selfish man who showed little concern for his wife's feelings, but apparently he was not too different in this from the average member of his class.

Alois Hitler was a man who loved life, particularly in the form of women and wine. Not that he was a woman chaser, but he was not bound by the moral restrictions of the Austrian middle class. In addition he enjoyed his glass of wine and may sometimes have had a glass too many, but he was by no means a drunkard as has been indicated in various articles. The most outstanding manifestation of his life-loving nature, however, was his deep and lasting interest in bees and bee-keeping. He would with great pleasure spend most of his free time with his beehives, the only serious, active interest he had outside of his work. His life's dream was to own a farm where he could keep bees on a larger scale. He did eventually realize this dream; although it turned out that the farm he first bought was too big, towards the end of his life he owned just the right acreage and enjoyed it immensely.

Alois Hitler has sometimes been described as a brutal tyrant – I assume because that would fit better into a simplistic explanation of his son's character. He was not a tyrant, but an authoritarian who believed in duty and responsibility and thought he had to determine his son's life as long as the latter was not yet of age. According to the evidence we have, he never beat his son; he scolded him, argued with him, tried to make him see what was good for him, but he was not a frightening figure who struck terror in his son. As we shall see further on, his son's growing irresponsibility and avoidance of reality made it all the more imperative for the father to try to lecture and correct him. There are many data to show that Alois was not inconsiderate or arrogant to people, by no means a fanatic, and, on the whole, rather tolerant. His political attitude corresponds to this description: he was anti-clerical and

liberal, with much interest in politics. His last words just
before he died of a heart attack while reading the newspaper were an angry expression against 'those blacks' as the
reactionary clericals were called.

How can we explain that these two well-meaning, stable,
very normal, and certainly not destructive people gave birth
to the future 'monster', Adolf Hitler?[3]

3. There are two psychoanalytic attempts to account for Hitler's evilness: (1) the conventional orthodox analysis by W. C. Langer (1972),
which was originally written in 1943 as a report for the Office of Strategic
Services and classified as 'Secret'; (2) the study by J. Brosse (1972).
Langer's analysis, especially at a time when the data on Hitler's life was
scarce, has some good points, although it is greatly hampered by his
theoretical frame of reference. Langer stresses that Hitler's early attachment to his mother led to the formation of a particularly intense Oedipus
complex (i.e., the wish to rid himself of the father), and furthermore,
that Hitler must have observed his parents during sexual intercourse and
that he must have become indignant both against his father, for his
'brutality', and against his mother for her 'betrayal'. Since all boys are
supposed to have an Oedipus complex and to have witnessed their
parents' intercourse (particularly in those classes with less living space
than the middle class), it is hard to see why a condition that is practically
universal should explain a specific character, not to speak of such an
abnormal one as Hitler's.

The psychoanalytic study of Hitler by J. Brosse has more material and
is very sensitive; Brosse recognized clearly Hitler's hatred of life and in
this respect comes to conclusions similar to those in this book. The only
element that mars Brosse's book is his need to couch his findings in terms
of the libido theory. He goes one step beyond the conventional theory
of the Oedipus complex and of the 'primal scene'. The deepest, driving,
unconscious force in Hitler 'consisted in the murder of the phallic mother,
i.e., not only of the father but also of the mother – of father and mother
united in the sexual act ... What he wants to reduce to nothing is not
so much his birth but his conception, that is, in other words, the "primal
scene", the original scene, the intercourse of his parents; and not the
scene the child could have witnessed, but that which took place absolutely before him ... at which he was present in imagination and
retrospectively, at which he was in a certain degree even potentially
present, since it had to do with his own conception ... Hate against life
is nothing but this: hate against the act by which the parents have
given him life ...' (J. Brosse, 1972; this, as well as further quotations
from Brosse, are my translation). As a symbolic, surrealistic description
of the total hate against life, this imagery has its merits. But as a factual

From Infancy to Age Six (1889–95)

The little boy, it seems, was the apple of his mother's eye. She pampered him, never scolded him, admired him; he could do no wrong. All her interest and affection were concentrated on him. Her attitude very probably built up his narcissism and his passivity. He was wonderful without having to make any effort, since mother admired him anyway; he did not have to make an effort because mother took care of all his wishes. He in turn, dominated her and threw tantrums when he felt frustrated. But, as we stated before, her over-attachment may have been felt by him as an intrusion towards which he acted with increased withdrawal, thus laying the basis for his semi-autistic early attitude. This constellation was accentuated by the fact that his father, due to the particularities of his working conditions, did not spend much time at home. Whatever good the balancing influence of a male authority would have been, it was absent. The little boy's passivity and dependence may have been increased by a certain sickliness that, in turn, tended to increase the attention paid him by his mother.

This phase came to a close when Hitler was six. Several facts marked its end.

The most obvious, especially from the classic psychoanalytic standpoint, was the birth of a brother when Adolf was five, which removed Adolf from his position of mother's chief object of devotion. Actually, such an event often has a wholesome, rather than a traumatic influence; it tends to decrease the reasons for dependency on mother and the

analysis of the cause for Hitler's hate against life it borders on the absurd.

I attempted a short analysis of Hitler's character based on the concept of the authoritarian-sadomasochistic character without, however, dealing with Hitler's childhood history (E. Fromm, 1941). I believe that what I wrote then is still valid, but that Hitler's sadism is secondary in comparison with his necrophilia, which is dealt with in the following analysis.

consequent passivity. Contrary to the cliché, the evidence shows that instead of suffering pangs of jealousy, young Hitler fully enjoyed the year after his brother's birth.[4] Largely responsible for this was the fact that his father took up a new post in Linz, while the family, apparently fearing to move the baby, stayed behind in Passau for a full year.

For one whole year, Adolf lived in a five-year-old's paradise playing games and roughhousing with the children of the neighbourhood. Miniature wars and fights between cowboys and Indians appear to have been his favourites, and they were to continue as his major diversions for many years. Since Passau was in Germany – on the German side of the Austro-German border, where the Austrian customs inspection took place – war games would have pitted French against German in the spirit of 1870, yet there was no particular importance in the nationality of the victims. Europe was full of heroic little boys who massacred all national and ethnic groups impartially. This year of childhood combat was important in Hitler's life not because it was spent on German soil and added a Bavarian touch to his speech, but because it was a year of escape into almost complete freedom. At home he began to assert himself more and probably displayed the first signs of consuming anger when he did not get his way. Outside play, without limit to action or imagination, reigned supreme. (B. F. Smith, 1967)

This paradisal life was abruptly ended when the father resigned from the customs service and the family moved to Hafeld, near Lambach, and his six-year-old son had to enter school. Adolf 'found his life suddenly confined in a narrow circle of activities demanding responsibility and discipline. For the first time he was steadily and systematically forced to conform' (B. F. Smith, 1967).

4. It can be argued, of course, that the evidence does not show us his *unconscious* disappointment and resentment. But since one cannot discover any signs of it, such an argument is without value. Its only basis is the dogmatic assumption that the birth of a sibling must have such an effect. This results in a circuituous reasoning in which one takes as a fact what the theory requires, and then claims that the theory is confirmed by the facts.

What can we say about the child's character development by the end of this first period of his life?

This is the period in which, according to Freudian theory, both aspects of the Oedipus complex are fully developed: sexual attraction to mother and hostility to father. The data *seem* to confirm the Freudian assumption: young Hitler was deeply attached to mother and antagonistic to his father; but he failed to solve the Oedipus complex by identifying himself with father through the formation of the super-ego and overcoming his attachment to mother; feeling betrayed by her by the birth of a rival he withdrew from her.

Serious questions arise, however, concerning the Freudian interpretation. If the birth of his brother when Adolf was five had been so traumatic, leading to the breaking of the tie to mother and replacing 'love' for her by resentment and hate, why should the year after this event have been such a happy one – in fact probably the happiest period of his childhood? Can we really explain his hate of his father as a result of his Oedipal rivalry if we consider the fact that his mother's relationship to her husband seems to have been one of little intensity and warmth? Is it not rather to be understood as the antagonism to a father who demanded discipline and responsibility?

These questions would seem to find an answer in the hypothesis on malignant incestuousness discussed earlier. This hypothesis would lead to the assumption that Hitler's fixation to his mother was not a warm and affectionate one; that he remained cold and did not break through his narcissistic shell; that she did not assume the role of a real person for him, but that of a symbol for the impersonal power of earth, blood, fate – and death. However, in spite of his coldness, he was symbiotically attached to the mother figure and her symbolizations, the last aim of which is the union with mother in death. If this was so, one could understand why the birth of a brother would not have been the cause for his withdrawal from mother. In fact, one could not even say that he withdrew from her, if it is true that affectively he had never felt close to her. Most importantly, one could understand that the beginning of Hitler's later manifest necrophilous development is to be found in the malignant incestuousness that characterizes his early relationship to his mother. This hypothesis would also explain why Hitler later never fell in love with motherly figures, why the tie to his real mother as a person was expressed by that to blood, soil, the race, and eventually to chaos and death. Germany became the central symbol for mother. His fixation to mother-Germany was the basis for his hate against the poison (syphilis and Jews) from which he had to save her, but, on a deeper level, of his long-repressed desire to destroy mother-Germany; his end seems to bear out the hypothesis of the malignant incestuousness.

Hitler's relationship to his mother and to mother figures was quite different from what we find in most other 'mother-fixated' men. In these men the tie to mother is much warmer, more intense, one might say more real; such people have a strong desire to be near mother, to tell her everything; they are really 'in love' with her (if 'love' is properly qualified by its infantile nature). Later on in life they tend to fall in love with mother figures, that is to say, they are intensely attracted to them to the point of having love affairs with or marrying them. (Whether the root of this attraction is sexual or whether the sexual attraction is a secondary manifestation of the primary affective attraction is of no consequence at this point.) But Hitler was never attracted to his mother in this way, at least not after the age of five, and probably not even before; as a child he took pleasure exclusively in leaving the house to play soldiers or Indians with other boys. He had little interest in her, and did not care.

His mother was aware of this. Kubizek reports that she told him her son was irresponsible and wasting his small inheritance; that she had many responsibilities for her small daughter, 'but Adolf does not think of this; he goes his way as if he were alone in the world'. This lack of considerateness and concern for his mother characterized also his re-action to her illness. In spite of the cancer diagnosed and operated on in January 1907 and from which she died in December of the same year, he left for Vienna that September. His mother tried, out of concern for him, to understate how bad she felt, and he accepted this, making no attempt to find out how she really was by visiting her in Linz – a trip that offered no problem as far as time or money was concerned – and he hardly wrote to her from Vienna to let her know how he was, thus causing her a good deal of worry. According to Smith he came home only after being notified of her death. According to Kubizek's report, when her illness had disabled her completely, she asked him to come and take care of her because there was nobody else available. He came at the end of November and took care of her for about three weeks until her death. Kubizek remarks on how surprised he was to see his friend cleaning the floor and cooking for his mother. Hitler even went so far in his interest in his eleven-year-old sister's welfare as to make her promise her mother that she would work diligently in school. Kubizek describes Hitler's attitude towards his mother in very sentimental terms, trying to show how deeply he loved her. But his testimony in this respect is not too credible: Hitler, as always, would have tried to make the most of this occasion to make a good impression; he could hardly have refused his mother's appeal, and three weeks was not a long time to perform the role of loving son. The description of this kindness and considerateness is in contrast to the whole of Hitler's behaviour towards his mother, so that Kubizek's description is not very con-vincing.[5]

5. Since Kubizek admired Hitler when they were young as well as later, when Hitler was in power, it is impossible to say whether the facts he reports are true, except when they are corroborated by other sources; his own 'impressions' are highly biased in Hitler's favour. Maser gives an even more glowing description of Hitler's loving kindness to his mother and of his despair at her death. Maser's description is based on a memor-andum that the Jewish physician, Dr E. Bloch, who treated Hitler's

It seems that Hitler's mother never became to him a person to whom he was lovingly or tenderly attached. She was a symbol of a protecting and admiring goddess, but also of the goddess of death and chaos. At the same time she was an object for his sadistic control, arousing a deep fury in him when she was not fully obliging.

Childhood. Ages Six to Eleven (1895–1900)

The change from early to late childhood was abrupt. Alois Hitler had retired from the customs service and hence had all the time he wanted to devote himself to his family and especially the education of his son. He purchased a house with nine acres in Hafeld, near Lambach. Young Hitler had to enter the small country school at Fischlam near Hafeld, where he did very well. He conformed with his father's demands, at least outwardly, but as Smith writes: 'There were reservations. He was still able to manipulate his mother to a degree, and his temper could explode at any time against anyone.' This kind of life must have felt unsatisfactory to the little boy, in spite of the fact that there were no violent clashes with his father. But Adolf found for himself one area in life where he could forget all the regimentation and what he felt was *a lack of freedom*. This area was his continuing interest in playing Indians and soldiers with other boys. Already at this early age, 'freedom' meant, for Hitler, irresponsibility, lack of constraint, and most importantly, 'freedom from reality'; it meant also to control gangs. If one examines the meaning and function of these games for

mother, wrote thirty-one years later in 1938 for the Nazi authorities. With all due respect to the memory of Dr Bloch, a statement written by a Jew, in Germany, in 1938, for the Nazis can hardly be considered unbiased, but motivated rather by an attempt to curry favour; this is humanly understandable, but deprives the document of any value as a historical source. That the historian Maser does not even question the validity of Bloch's statement is one example for many other severe defects in his method of using sources, some of which I shall have occasion to mention further on.

Hitler, one discovers that they were the first expression of the traits that were to develop increasingly in him as he grew older: the need to control, and a defective realism. Descriptively, these games appear to be very harmless and normal at this age; that they were not, we shall see later when we see that he remained addicted to them until an age when normal boys have outgrown this youthful pastime.

Some changes occurred in the family in the following years. Alois's eldest son left home at the age of fourteen, to his father's great annoyance, so that Adolf now had to assume the role of eldest son. Alois sold the farm and moved to the town of Lambach. Adolf continued his schooling in the relatively modern elementary school in Lambach, and there, too, he did very well and avoided any major confrontations with his often angry and disgruntled father.

In 1898 the family moved again, this time to a house in Leonding on the outskirts of Linz, and Adolf entered his third elementary school, in Linz. Alois Hitler seems to have felt more contented at the new place than ever before. He could take care of his bees on the half acre of land and talk politics in the tavern. Yet he remained a strict authoritarian and left no doubts about who was in control. Josef Mayerhofer, his best friend in Leonding, later said of him:

'He was strict with his family, no kid gloves as far as they were concerned; his wife had nothing to smile about.' Mayerhofer emphasized, though, that the rough exterior was partly bluff and that the children were not physically abused. 'He never touched him [Adolf]. I don't believe that [he beat him], but he often scolded and bawled at him. "That miserable urchin!" he used to say, "I'll bash him yet!" But his bark was worse than his bite. The boy stood in awe of him, though.' (B. F. Smith, 1967)

This is not the picture of a brutal tyrant, but of an authoritarian, somewhat unapproachable father of whom the son was afraid; this fear may have been one of the sources of Hitler's submissiveness, of which we shall hear more later. But one must not take this awe-inspiring quality of the father out of context; a son who had not insisted so much on being left alone and on being irresponsible might have arrived at a friendlier relationship with this type of father who, after all, meant well and who was by no means a destructive man. The cliché about 'hate against the authoritarian father' is sometimes as much overworked as that about the Oedipus complex.

Altogether the five years of elementary school went by much better than one might have expected. This was due to the factors already mentioned and to the realistic circumstances in school. He was most likely above the average intelligence of the other boys, was well treated by the teachers because of his superior family background, and got top grades without having to make much of an effort. Thus school work was really no challenge and did not seriously disturb his finely balanced system of compromise between rebelliousness and adaptation.

At the end of this period no conspicuous deterioration is visible as compared with its beginning, yet there were alarming features: he had not succeeded in overcoming his early narcissism; he had not moved closer to reality; he had not developed any active interests and instead had built for himself a magic realm of freedom and power. The first years in school did not help him to grow beyond where he had been when he entered school. But still, there was little open conflict, and on the surface he seemed to have adjusted himself well enough.

Pre-adolescence and Adolescence: Ages Eleven to Seventeen (1900–1906)

Hitler's entry into secondary school (*Realschule*) and the years that followed until his father's death brought about a decisive turn for the worse and reinforced the conditions for his malignant development.

The decisive events in the next three years, until his father's death in 1903 are: (1) his failure in high school, (2) the conflict with his father who insisted that he become a civil servant, and (3) his losing himself increasingly more in the fantasy world of his games.

Hitler himself, in *Mein Kampf*, offers a plausible and self-serving picture of these events: he, the free and independent human being, could not stand to be a bureaucrat, but wanted to become an artist; he rebelled against school, and did poor work in order to get his father to give him permission to become an artist.

If we examine the known data carefully, the picture that emerges is the reverse: (1) He did poorly in school for a number of reasons to be discussed presently. (2) His idea of becoming an artist was essentially a rationalization for his incapacity for any kind of disciplined work and effort. (3) His conflict with his father was not simply centred around his refusal to become a civil servant, but was due to his rejection of all demands of reality.

About the failure there can be no doubt, since it was rather drastic. Already in the first year he did so poorly that he had to repeat the whole year. In the following years he had to take extra examinations in some subjects in order to be allowed to go to the next class, and even at the end of the third year, he passed in Linz only under the condition that he would leave the school. As a result he entered high school in Steyr, but at the end of the fourth year, in Steyr, he decided not to continue his school career for one more year until graduation from *Realschule*. An incident at the end of his last school year is rather symbolic for his high school career. After receiving his certificate he went with his classmates to drink wine and, when he got home, discovered he had lost his certificate. He was still wondering what excuse he could make, when he was called to see the director of the school; the certificate had been found in a street; he had used it as toilet paper! Even granting that he was probably more or less drunk, this behaviour expresses symbolically much of his hate and contempt for school.

Some of the reasons for Hitler's failure in high school are more obvious than others. The most obvious is that in elementary school he had been in a superior position. Being above average in intelligence and talent and a good talker, he did not have to make a great effort to be superior to his classmates and to get excellent grades. In high school the situation was different. There the average intelligence was higher than in elementary school. His teachers were much better educated and demanded more; they were also not impressed by his social background, since it was not outstanding in the social composition of the high school students. Briefly, in order to succeed in high school one had to really work; the amount of work required was not backbreaking, but it was a good deal more than young Hitler was accustomed to, was willing to do, or was capable of doing. For this extremely narcissistic boy who in elementary school was able to 'succeed without trying', the new situation must have been shocking. It challenged his narcissistic manner of behaving and demonstrated that reality could not be handled as before.

This situation of failing in high school after successful years in elementary school is not rare; it often stimulates a child to change his behaviour, to overcome – at least to some extent – his infantile attitude and to learn to make an effort. In Hitler's case the situation had no such effect. On the contrary, instead of taking a step towards reality he withdrew more into his fantasy world and away from closer contact with people.

Had his failure in high school been caused by the fact that most of the subjects dealt with in school were of no interest to him, he would have worked hard in those that did interest him; that this was not the case is evidenced by the fact that he did not even make a sufficient effort to get an outstanding grade in German history, a subject that roused his enthusiasm and excited him greatly. (The only good marks he got were in drawing – but since he had talent in art, he did not need to exert much effort.) This hypothesis is confirmed most clearly by the fact that in later life he was unable to make a sustained effort even in a field that was perhaps the only one that really interested him – architecture. The theme of Hitler's incapacity for systematic work, except under the influence of most pressing needs or when driven by his passions, will be dealt with later. It is mentioned here only to stress that his failure in high school cannot be explained by his 'artistic' interests.

During these years in high school Hitler withdrew increasingly from reality. He had no real interest in anybody – his mother, father, or siblings. He dealt with them as his interest in being left alone made it opportune, but they were remote from him affectively. His only strong and passionate interest was in his war games with other boys, in which he was the leader and organizer. While these games had been quite appropriate for a boy of nine, ten, or eleven, they were peculiar for a boy in high school. Characteristic is a scene at his confirmation at the age of fifteen. A relative had kindly arranged a little party in honour of the confirmand, but Hitler was grouchy and unfriendly, and as soon as he could he ran off to play war with other boys.

These games had several functions. They gave him the satisfaction of being the leader and confirmed his conviction that by his persuasive power he could make others follow him; they increased his narcissism, and, most importantly, they put the centre of his life in fantasy, thus furthering the process of his withdrawal from reality, from real persons, real accomplishment, and real knowledge. Another expression of this attraction to fantasy was his ardent interest in the novels of Karl May. May was a German writer who wrote many fascinating stories about the North American Indians that had the colour of reality, although the author had never seen any Indians. Virtually all boys in Germany and Austria read May's stories; they were as popular as James Fenimore Cooper's were in the United States. Hitler's enthusiasm for May's writings was quite normal for someone in the last years of elementary school, but, writes Smith:

It took on more serious overtones in later years. For Hitler never gave up Karl May. He read him in adolescence and as a young man in his twenties. Even as Reich Chancellor, he continued to be fascinated by him, re-reading the whole series on the American West. Furthermore, he never attempted to disguise or hide his enjoyment of, and admiration for May's books. In the *Table Talk* [H. Picker, 1963] he extolls May and describes how he enjoyed his work. He talked about him with nearly everyone – his press chief, his secretary, his servant and his old party comrades. (B. F. Smith, 1967)

My interpretation of this fact, however, differs from Smith's. Smith believes that since Hitler's childhood infatuation with May's novels was such a happy experience it was 'a satisfying and necessary carry-over into a period when his early adjustments failed to solve the challenges of adolescence'. While this may be true to some extent, I believe that it does not touch the main point. May's novels have to be connected with Hitler's war games and are an expression of his fantasy life. Although adequate enough at a certain age, that they continued to fascinate him suggest that they represent a flight from reality, a manifestation of a narcissistic attitude centred around one theme: Hitler, the leader, fighter, and victor. To be sure, the evidence of this is not sufficient to be convincing. But if one connects Hitler's behaviour in these youthful years with the data from his later life, a pattern emerges: that of a highly narcissistic, withdrawn person for whom fantasy is more real than reality. When we see the young Hitler at sixteen already so much given to fantasy life, the question that arises is: How could this withdrawn dreamer succeed in making himself the master of Europe – even though only for a while? The answer to this question must wait until we have progressed further in the analysis of Hitler's subsequent development.

Whatever the reason for his failure in the *Realschule* were, there can be little doubt about its emotional consequences for young Hitler. Here is a boy, admired by his mother, successful in elementary school, the leader of the boys' gangs, for whom all these unearned successes had been a confirmation of his narcissistic conviction of having outstanding gifts. With hardly any transition he finds himself in a situation of failure; he had no way of hiding his failure from his father and mother; his narcissism must have been badly wounded, his pride hurt. If he could have recognized that his failure had been caused by his incapacity to work hard, he might have overcome its consequences, since there is no doubt that he was more than sufficiently gifted to be successful in high school,[6] but his untouchable narcissism made such insight impossible. As a consequence, not being able to change reality, he had to falsify and reject it. He falsified it by accusing his teachers and his father of being the cause of his failure and by claiming that his failure was the expression of his passion for freedom and independence. He rejected it by creating the symbol of the 'artist'; the dream of becoming a great artist was for him reality, and yet the fact that he did not work seriously to achieve his aim showed the fantasy character of this idea. Failure in school was Hitler's first defeat and humiliation, followed by a number of others; it is safe to assume that it must have greatly reinforced his contempt for and resentment of anybody who was a cause or a witness of his defeat; and this resentment could very well have constituted the beginning of his necrophilia had we no reasons to believe that its roots are to be found already in his malignant incestuousness.

The death of his father when Hitler was fourteen years old did not have an appreciable effect on him. If it were true, as

6. His teacher, E. Huemer, said this about his former pupil when he was a witness for Hitler after the unsuccessful putsch in Munich: 'Hitler was decidedly talented, even though one-sidely, but had little self-control; at the very least he was also considered stubborn, wilful, argumentative and short-tempered, and it was certainly difficult for him to adapt to the framework of a school organization. He was also not very industrious; otherwise he would have been much more successful, considering his undeniable talents' (W. Masters, 1971).

Hitler himself wrote later, that his failure in school originated in the conflict with his father, once the brutal tyrant
and rival had died, the hour of liberation should have been
at hand. He would now have felt free, made realistic plans
for his future, worked hard for their realization – and perhaps turned his affection once more towards his mother.
But nothing of the kind happened. He continued to live in
the same fashion as before; he was, as Smith puts it, 'little
more than a composite of pleasurable games and dreams',
and could not find a way out of this state of mind.

We must now take another look at Adolf's conflict with
his father since his entry into the *Realschule*. Alois Hitler had
decided that his son should attend high school; while Hitler
showed little interest in this plan, he accepted it. The real
conflict, according to his report in *Mein Kampf*, arose when
his father insisted that he should become a civil servant.
This wish was in itself quite natural, since the father was
impressed by his own success in this field and felt that it
would also be the best career for his son. When Hitler
brought forward a counterproposal, that of wanting to
become an artist, a painter, the father, according to Hitler,
said, 'No, never as long as I live.' Hitler then threatened
to quit studying altogether, and when the father did not
yield, 'I silently transformed my threat into reality'
(A. Hitler, 1943). This is Hitler's explanation for his failure
in school, but it is too convenient to be true.

It coincides exactly with Hitler's picture of himself as a hard
and determined man who had managed to rise a long way by
1924 (when *Mein Kampf* was written) and would go on to final
victory. At the same time, it is the basis for the picture of the
frustrated artist who went into politics with the resolve to save
Germany. Most important, it explains away his poor grades in
Realschule and his slow maturation, while at the same time it
makes his adolescence appear heroic – a difficult task for any
politically conscious autobiographer. In fact, the story served
the later Führer's purpose so well that one may well ask whether
or not he invented the whole episode. (B. F. Smith, 1967)

That the father wished his son to become a civil servant may very well have been true; on the other hand the father took no drastic measures to force his son. Nor did Hitler do what his older brother had done at the age of fifteen – show his independence and defy his father by taking the drastic step of leaving home. On the contrary, he adjusted himself to the situation and just withdrew more into himself.

In order to understand the conflict we must appreciate the father's position. He must have observed, as the mother did, that his son had no sense of responsibility, did not want to work, and showed no interest. Being an intelligent and well-intentioned man, his concern must have been not so much for his son to become a civil servant, but for him to become *somebody*. He must have sensed that the plan to become an artist was an excuse for further drifting and lack of seriousness. If his son had made a counter-proposal – for instance, that he would like to study architecture – and proved his seriousness by getting good marks in school, the father's response might have been quite different. But Hitler did not make any proposal that would have shown his father that he was serious. He did not even ask to be allowed to take drawing lessons if he did well in school. That it was not defiance against father which made him do so poorly in school is clearly evidenced by his response to his mother's attempt to bring him back to reality. After his father's death, and having left the *Realschule*, he decided to stay at home

reading, drawing and dreaming. Comfortably established in the flat on the Humboldtstrasse [where his mother had now moved], he could afford to indulge himself. He tolerated the presence of young Paula [his five-years-younger sister] and his mother in his sanctuary because he could not get away from them without making the nauseating decision to leave home and go to work. However, they were not allowed to interfere, though his mother paid the bills and his sister cleaned up after him. (B. F. Smith 1967)

Klara was clearly worried about him and admonished him to be more serious. She did not insist on a civil service career, but tried to help him establish a serious interest in something. She sent him to an art school in Munich. He stayed there for a few months, but that was all. Hitler liked to dress elegantly, and his mother 'paid for the clothes which turned him into something of a dandy, perhaps in the hope that this would serve as a bridge to wider social horizons. If this was her plan, it failed completely. The clothes merely served as symbols of independence and self-sufficient isolation' (B. F. Smith, 1967).

Klara made another attempt to revive Hitler's interest. She gave him the money to visit Vienna for four weeks. He sent her some postcards raving about 'the mighty majesty', 'dignity', and 'grandeur' of the buildings. His spelling and punctuation, however, were well below the standard one would expect of a seventeen-year-old who had completed four years in high school. His mother permitted him to take music lessons (his father had suggested some years before that he take singing lessons), which Hitler did – for about four months, ending them at the beginning of 1907. He quit because he disliked practising scales, although the lessons might have stopped anyway because the onset of his mother's serious illness forced the family to reduce expenses.

His response to his mother's by no means authoritarian – and almost psychotherapeutic – attempts to awaken his interest in something real shows that his negative reaction to his father had not only been defiance against the demand that he become a civil servant, but the reaction of a withdrawn, drifting boy against a man who represented reality and responsibility. This was the core of the conflict – it was not simply dislike for the civil service, and even less was it an Oedipal rivalry.

Hitler's tendency to loaf and to avoid hard – or even not so hard – work requires an explanation. It will help us if we keep in mind the well-established observation that this kind of behaviour is frequently to be found among mother-bound children. It is their often unconscious expectation that mother will do everything for them, just as she did when they were infants. They feel that they do not have to make an active effort, that they do not have to keep order: they can let their things lie around expecting mother to clean up after them. They live in a kind of 'paradise' where nothing is expected of them and everything is provided for. I believe this explanation holds true in Hitler's case, too. In my judgement it does not contradict the hypothesis regarding the cold and impersonal character of his tie to mother. She fulfils this function *qua* mother, even though she is not loved or cared for in a personal way.

The description of Hitler's laziness in school, his incapacity for serious work, and his refusal to continue his studies will suggest a question to quite a few readers: What is so remarkable about it? There are a large number of high school drop-outs today, many of whom complain about the pedantic and sterile nature of school work, who have plans for a free life not hobbled by fatherly and other authorities. Yet they are not necrophilous individuals; on the contrary, many represent a genuine life-loving, independent, frank type of personality. Some readers may even question whether my description of Hitler's failure is not written in a very conservative spirit.

To such objections I would like to answer: (1) There are, of course, many kinds of drop-outs, and no general statement can be made about them; rather each different type of drop-out can only be dealt with in specific terms. (2) In contrast to today, drop-outs were extremely rare when Hitler was an adolescent; hence, there was no pattern to follow that might make it easy for an individual to become a drop-out. (3) Much more decisive than the foregoing reasons is one that applies to Hitler specifically: he was not only not interested in his school subjects; he was also uninterested in *everything*. He did not work hard at anything – either then or later. (We shall see this in his lack of effort in the study of architecture.) That he was lazy was not because he was a person who was satisfied with enjoying life without being specially concerned with achieving a goal. On the contrary he was filled with a burning ambition for power; endowed with extraordinary vital energy, he was tense and almost incapable of any quiet enjoyment. This does not fit the picture presented by most drop-outs; and those drop-outs who fit Hitler's picture, if they simultaneously show an ardent wish for power and complete lack of affection for anyone, constitute a very serious problem – in fact, a serious danger.

As for possible objection that I am being 'conservative' in my attitudes when I insist that lack of capacity to work and lack of responsibility are negative qualities, this brings us to consideration of a crucial point in present-day youthful radicalism. It is one thing for a person to be uninterested in certain subjects or to prefer certain others or to reject school altogether. But to avoid responsibility and serious effort constitutes certain failure in the process of growth, a fact that is not changed by putting the blame on society. And anyone who thinks that loafing qualifies one as a revolutionary is thoroughly mistaken. Effort, devotion, concentration are of the essence in a fully developed person, including the revolutionary; young people who think differently might do well to think about the personalities of Marx, Engels, Lenin, Rosa Luxemburg, Mao Tse-tung – each of whom shares with the other two vital qualities: a capacity for hard work and a sense of responsibility.

Vienna (1907–1913)

At the beginning of 1907 Hitler's mother made it financially possible for him to move to Vienna to study painting at the Academy of Arts. With this move Hitler was finally independent; free from the pressure of his father; he could plan and act as he liked. He did not even have to cope with financial problems, since the inheritance from his father and the pension the state paid orphans of deceased officials allowed him to live comfortably for some time.[7] He stayed in Vienna from 1907 to 1913, from late adolescence to early manhood.

What did he make of himself in this decisive period?

To begin with he made the situation in Vienna easier for himself by persuading his companion of the last years in Linz, A. Kubizek, to join him there. Kubizek himself was most eager to go; but to win over Kubizek's father, who was dead set against his son's artistic plans, was no small feat, and it was one of the earlier demonstrations of Hitler's persuasive powers. Kubizek was, like Hitler, an ardent admirer of Wagner's music, and because of this shared enthusiasm they had met at the Linz opera house and become fast friends. Kubizek worked as an apprentice in his father's upholstery shop, but he, too, had great dreams: he also wanted to become an artist, a musician. He was more responsible and industrious than Hitler, but a less weighty personality. Thus, he soon came under Hitler's dominant influence. Hitler practised on him his power to influence people; he received the complete admiration of his friend and thus a constant affirmation of his narcissism. In many respects his friendship provided Hitler with a substitute for the satisfaction the games with boys' gangs had given him: to be the leader and to be admired.

Shortly after his arrival in Vienna Hitler went to the Academy of Arts and registered for the yearly examination. He apparently had no doubt that he would be accepted. However, he failed; he was rejected in the second part of the examination, after having passed the first part (W. Maser, 1971). As Hitler wrote in *Mein Kampf*: 'When I received my rejection it struck me as a bolt from the blue.' He reported that one of the professors at the Academy of Arts told him that he seemed to be more gifted for architecture than for painting. But even if this report is true, Hitler did not follow it up. He could have been admitted to the school of archi-

7. Hitler's own statement in *Mein Kampf* about his poverty are essentially untrue.

tecture if he had gone to *Realschule* for one more year; but there is no evidence that he ever seriously thought about it. Hitler's own report in *Mein Kampf* is insincere. He wrote that since he had no high school diploma the fulfilment of his wish to become an architect was 'physically impossible'. Then he went on to boast: 'I wanted to become an architect but obstacles do not exist to be surrendered to but only to be defeated. I was determined to overcome these obstacles . . .' The facts are precisely the opposite:

His personality and way of life prevented him from acknowledging his errors and accepting his rejection as a sign of the need for any change. His escapism was reinforced by his social affectations and his scorn for work which seemed dirty, degrading, or tiring. He was a confused and snobbish young man who had indulged himself for so long that he would neither work at an unpleasant task nor consider anyone except himself and the manner of life he enjoyed. His solution to rejection by the Academy was to go back to the Stumpergasse and settle down as if nothing had happened. In this sanctuary, he resumed what he grandly called his 'studies', doodling and reading, with excursions around town or to the opera. (B. F. Smith, 1967)

He pretended to everybody that he was enrolled as an art student at the academy, and even lied about this to Kubizek after the latter arrived in Vienna. When Kubizek eventually became suspicious because he could not understand how his friend could sleep late in the mornings and yet be a student, Hitler told him the truth in a violent outburst of rage against the professors at the art academy. He promised that he would show them, and study architecture by himself. His method of 'studying' was to walk the streets, look at the monumental buildings, come home, and make endless sketches of the façades. The belief that in this way he was preparing himself to become an architect was a symptom of his lack of realism. He talked with Kubizek about his plans for the reconstruction of all Vienna or for writing an opera; he went to Parliament to listen to the debates of the Reichsrat; he applied a second time for acceptance at the

Academy of Arts, this time he was not even admitted to the first test.

He had spent over a year in Vienna, doing no serious work, failing twice in the examination, still pretending that he was on the way to becoming a great artist. But in spite of the pretence, he must have felt that this year had brought him defeat. This defeat was much more severe than that in high school which he could explain by the idea that he intended to be an artist. When he failed as an artist no such explanation was available. He had been rejected in the very field in which he was sure that he would be great; nothing was left for him but to blame the art professors, society, the whole world. His resentment against life must have grown. His narcissism – even more than at the time of his first failure – must have driven him into a still further withdrawal from reality in order to protect it from being shattered.[8]

At this point a process of almost complete withdrawal from people began that found its main expression in the fact that he drastically broke up the only close relationship he had: that with Kubizek. He left the room they shared, to which Kubizek was supposed to return after a visit at home, without leaving his new address. Kubizek remained out of touch with him until the time Hitler was already Reichschancellor.

8. In his attempt to make the most of Hitler's seriousness in regard to studying art, Maser reports that Hitler took lessons from a sculptor, the high school professor, Panholzer. But the only evidence he offers for this statement is a letter written by the mother of Hitler's landlady to the professor of stage design, Roller, asking him to see Hitler and to advise him. Maser quotes no evidence to show what the result of this visit was – provided it took place at all. He only mentions that thirty years later Hitler named Panholzer (according to the grammatical construction of Maser's sentence it should read Roller) as his teacher. This is one of the many instances where Maser uses a statement made by Hitler about himself as sufficient evidence. But how Maser could know that Hitler had to work 'in a disciplined and orderly fashion' at Panholzer's atelier remains a mystery, as well as why the budding painter and architect should have wanted to take instructions from a sculptor (W. Maser, 1971).

The pleasant period of loafing, talking, walking, and sketching had gradually come to an end. Hitler had money left for less than one year, provided he would economize. Having no audience to talk to, he began to read more. Austria at that time had many political and ideological groupings centred around German nationalism, racism, 'national socialism' (in Bohemia), and anti-Semitism. Each of these groups published its own pamphlets, preached its own ideology that was specific, and offered *the* solution. Hitler read these pamphlets avidly and acquired the raw material from which he later constructed his own brand of racism, anti-Semitism, and 'socialism'. Thus, while in this period in Vienna he did not prepare for the career of an artist, he did lay the foundations for his real future profession, political leader.

By the autumn of 1909 his money had given out and he skipped his lodging without paying the rent he owed. The worst period began at this point. He slept on benches, sometimes in flop-houses, and in December 1909 he joined the ranks of the real tramps, spending the nights in a place for destitute men that was sustained by a philanthropic society. The young man who had come to Vienna two and a half years before with the conviction that he would become a great artist had been reduced to the status of a homeless tramp, eager to get a bowl of hot soup, with no prospects of any kind and making no effort to support himself. Indeed, as Smith writes, his entry into the home for the homeless 'was a declaration of utter defeat'.

This defeat was one not only for Hitler the artist, but also for Hitler the proud and well-dressed bourgeois who had nothing but contempt for the lower classes. He had now become a bum, an outcast; he belonged to the dregs of society. This would have been an intense humiliation even for a less narcissistic member of the middle class. Since he was stable enough not to go to pieces, this situation must have strengthened him. The worst had happened, and he emerged toughened, his narcissism unbroken; everything depended now on wiping out the humiliation by taking revenge on all his 'enemies' and devoting his life to the goal of proving that his narcissistic self-image had not been a fantasy but was reality.

This process can be better understood if we recall the clinical observations made earlier regarding the fate of extremely narcissistic persons who are defeated. Usually they do not recover. Since their inner, subjective, and the outer, objective reality are completely torn apart, they may become psychotic or suffer from other severe mental disturbances; if they are lucky they may find some niche in reality – a minor job for instance, that permits them to hold on to their narcissistic fantasy while they blame the world and muddle through their lives without a major catastrophe. But there is another outcome open only to those who have special gifts; they can try to change reality in such a way that their grandiose fantasies are proved to be real. This requires not only talent but also historical circumstances that make it possible. Most frequently this solution is open to political leaders in periods of social crisis; if they have the talent to appeal to large masses and are shrewd enough to know how to organize them, they can make reality conform to their dream. Frequently the demagogue on this side of the borderline to a psychosis saves his sanity by making ideas that seemed 'crazy' before appear to be 'sane' now. In his political fight he is driven not only by the passion for power, but also by the need to save his sanity.

We must now return to where we left Hitler at the most desperate and miserable point in his life. This period did not last very long – perhaps two months – and at no time did he do any manual work, as he claims in *Mein Kampf*. His circumstances shortly began to improve, when an older tramp, Hanisch, befriended him; Hanisch was a sordid character, with a political outlook similar to Hitler's and an interest in painting.[9] Most importantly, he had a practical

9. The following text is based mainly on B. F. Smith (1967).

idea of how they could both avoid destitution: if Hitler would ask his family for a small sum to buy painting materials, he could paint postcards and Hanisch would sell them. Hitler followed his advice; with the fifty kronen he received he bought the material and a very much needed overcoat and moved with Hanisch to the Männerheim, a well-run men's hostel where he could use the larger common-room to paint in. Everything went well. He painted postcards and Hanisch peddled them; then came larger water colours and oils, which Hanisch sold to frame makers and art dealers. There was only one problem: Hitler did not work too diligently; as soon as he had a little money he would stop painting and begin to spend his time talking politics with the other inmates of the home. Nevertheless he had a steady though small income. Eventually there was a quarrel with Hanisch whom Hitler accused of having sold a painting without giving him his share (50 per cent) of the price. He denounced Hanisch to the police for theft, and Hanisch was arrested. Hitler then continued the business on his own, painting and selling his own work (especially to two Jewish art dealers). This time he seems to have worked more systematically; he had become a small businessman; he lived economically and even saved a little money. One can hardly say that he had become a 'painter' or an 'artist' since what he did was mainly to copy from photographs and repeat those pictures which proved to have a demand on the market. He stayed on at the Männerheim; his position in the 'Heim', however, had changed. He was now a *permanent* lodger, and this meant that he belonged to the small group of 'permanents' who looked down on the 'transients' as inferior to themselves, and who formed a respected élite within the system of the home.

There were probably several reasons for his decision to stay in the home. The least likely is that, as Maser stresses, it was cheaper. For the fifteen kronen per month he paid in the home he could have found an adequate private room. But a number of psychological reasons suggest themselves.

Hitler, like many unrelated persons, was afraid of being alone. He needed to compensate for his inner aloneness by superficial contact with others. More than this, he needed an audience that he could impress; this was well provided by the Männerheim, most of whose tenants were marginal types, loners, who had somehow failed to achieve a more normal life. Hitler was clearly superior to them in intelligence and vitality. They had the same function as the boys' gangs and Kubizek had had. They permitted him to practise his capacity to impress and influence other people and, hence, to confirm his own sense of power. While he sat and painted he would interrupt himself and start to make violent political speeches, very much in the style for which he was later well known. The Männerheim became for him a training school for the career of political demagogue.

A crucial question arises when we consider Hitler's existence at this time: Had he not acquired the capacity for steady work, changing from a lazy drifter to a somewhat prosperous small businessman? Had he not found himself and achieved a healthy mental balance?

On the surface it may look as if this was so. Perhaps it was a case of late maturation, but can one call it normality? If it had been, the detailed analysis of his emotional development would have been quite unnecessary. It would have been sufficient to state that after certain characterological difficulties in his youth Hitler had become, at the age of twenty-three or twenty-four, a well-adjusted and mentally healthy man.

However if one examines the situation more thoroughly this interpretation is hardly tenable.

Here is a man with extraordinary vitality, a burning passion for greatness and power, with the firm belief that he would become a greater painter or architect. What was the reality?

He had completely failed in this aim; he had become a small businessman; his power consisted in impressing a small group of loners whom he constantly harangued, without even succeeding in finding followers among them. Maybe if Hitler had been a smaller man with less vitality and less grandiosity, this solution would have pleased him, and he would have been satisfied in having achieved the permanent petty bourgeois existence of a commercial artist. But to imagine that of Hitler would be almost absurd. There had been only one change: the months of intense poverty had taught him to work – mediocre as his work was. But otherwise his character had not been changed – except, perhaps, in the sense of becoming more deeply engraved. He remained an extremely narcissistic man without any interest in anybody or anything, living in an atmosphere of half-fantasy and half-truth, with a burning wish to conquer, and filled with hate and resentment; he remained a man without any realistic goal, plan, or concept about how to realize his ambitions.

Munich

This aimlessness became evident in his sudden decision to break up his existence in the Männerheim and to move to Munich and enroll there in the Academy of Arts. He had almost no knowledge about the situation in Munich; least of all did he inquire whether there was a market for his paintings as there was in Vienna. He just moved there, having a little money saved to help him over the first months. The decision proved to be a mistake. His dream of being admitted to the art academy in Munich failed to materialize. There was a smaller market for his paintings and, according to Smith, he was forced to hawk his pictures in beer halls and to sell them from door to door. According to Maser, Hitler's income tax declaration shows that he was earning about one hundred marks per month, which would have been comparable to his Viennese income. But the fact remains that in Munich he also remained a commercial artist who mainly did copy work. Hitler's dream of becoming a great painter had definitely failed, and with his small talent and lack of training there was no connection between even the best prospects in his painting career and his great hopes.

Is it surprising that the outbreak of the First World War was a godsend to him and that he thanked heaven for this event which at one stroke wiped out the necessity to decide what he wanted to do with his life? The war broke out just at the point when he could hardly avoid any longer the full realization of his failure as an artist, and it replaced his sense of humiliation with a feeling of pride in being a 'hero'. Hitler was a dutiful soldier, and though not promoted (except in a minor way), he was decorated for bravery and respected by his superiors. He was no longer an outcast; he was a hero fighting for Germany, for its existence and glory, and for the values of nationalism. He could indulge in his strivings for destruction and victory – but now the war was real, no longer the fantasy war of little boys; and perhaps he himself was more real during these four years than at any other time. He was responsible, disciplined, and quite a different man from the loafer of the days in Vienna. The war ended with what seemed to him to be his own latest failure: defeat and revolution. The defeat might still have been bearable, but the revolution was not. The revolutionaries attacked everything that was sacred to Hitler's reactionary nationalism, and they won; they were the masters of the day, particularly in Munich, where they created a short-lived 'Räte Republik'.

The victory of the revolutionaries gave Hitler's destructiveness its final and ineradicable form. The revolution was an attack on him, on his values, on his hopes, on his grandiosity in which he and Germany were one. His humiliation was all the greater since some of the revolutionary leaders were Jews, whom he had considered his arch-enemies for many years, and who made him be the hapless spectator of the destruction of his nationalist, *petit bourgeois* ideals. This final humiliation could only be wiped out by the destruction of all whom he held responsible for it. His hate, his thirst for revenge were also directed against the victorious Allied powers who forced Germany to accept the Treaty of Versailles, but to a lesser degree than against the revolutionaries, and particularly the Jews.

Hitler's failures had grown by stages: as a high school student, a drop-out from the middle class in Vienna, an art academy reject. Each failure caused a graver wound to his narcissism and a deeper humiliation than the previous one; in the same degree as his failures, grew also his indulgence in fantasy, his resentment, his wish for revenge, and his necrophilia that probably had its earliest roots in his malignant incestuousness. The start of the war had seemed to end the period of his failures, but it ended in a new humiliation: the defeat of the German armies and the victory of the revolutionaries. This time Hitler had the opportunity to transform his personal defeat and humiliation into a national and social defeat and humiliation, which thus enabled him to forget his personal failures. This time not *he* had failed and been humiliated, but Germany; by avenging and saving Germany he would avenge himself, and by wiping out Germany's shame he would wipe out his own. His aim now was to become a great demagogue, no longer a great artist; he had found the area for which he had a real gift and, hence, a real chance of success.

We do not have sufficiently detailed material up to this period to demonstrate the presence of strong manifest necrophilous trends in his behaviour. We have only seen the characterological ground that *favoured* the growth of such tendencies: his malignant incestuousness, narcissism, coldness, lack of interest, self-indulgence, lack of realism, which necessarily resulted in failures and humiliations. From 1918 on, since there is ample material available about Hitler's life, we can recognize the manifestations of his necrophilia with increasing clarity.

A Comment on Methodology

Some readers may object and ask: Do we need to *prove* Hitler's necrophilia? Is his destructiveness not a fact that is beyond question?

To be sure, we do not have to prove the reality of Hitler's extraordinarily destructive *actions*. But destructive actions are not necessarily manifestations of a destructive, necrophilous character. Was Napoleon a necrophile because he never hesitated to sacrifice his soldiers' lives for his personal ambition and vanity? Were the many political and military leaders throughout history who ordered large-scale destruction all necrophiles? To be sure anyone who orders or condones destruction betrays that he has hardened his heart. Yet, depending on the motivations and circumstances, even a not-necrophilous general or political leader can order severe destruction. The question raised in this book is not concerned with *behaviour*, but with *character*. To be more specific: the question is not whether Hitler *behaved* destructively, but whether he was motivated by an intense passion to destroy, a passion for destruction that was part of his *character*. This has to be proved, not taken for granted. A psychological study must make every effort to be objective, particularly so in the case of a person like Adolf Hitler. Even if Hitler had died in 1933, at a time before he had actually committed many overt acts of large-scale destruction, he could very probably have been diagnosed as a necrophilous character on the basis of a detailed analysis of his whole personality. The crescendo of destruction that grew starting with the conquest of Poland up to his orders to destroy most of Germany and its population would only be the final confirmation of the earlier characterological diagnosis. On the other hand, even if we knew nothing about his past up to 1933, many details of his later behaviour justify the diagnosis of severe necrophilia, rather than only indicate that he was, in behaviouristic terms,

a man who caused much destruction. From a behaviourist
standpoint this distinction between behaviour and motivating forces is of course meaningless; if one wants to understand the dynamics of the whole person, however, and
particularly his unconscious sector, it is essential. In Hitler's
case the use of the psychoanalytic method is all the more
important because he repressed the awareness of his
necrophilous passion to an extraordinary degree and in
many different ways.

Hitler's Destructiveness[10]

Hitler's objects of destruction were cities and people. The
great builder, the enthusiastic planner of a new Vienna,
Linz, Munich, and Berlin, was the same man who wanted to
destroy Paris, level Leningrad, and eventually demolish all
of Germany. These intentions are well authenticated.
Speer reports that at the height of his success, after he visited
the recently conquered Paris, Hitler remarked to him,
'Wasn't Paris beautiful? . . . In the past I often considered
whether we would not have to destroy Paris. But when we
are finished in Berlin, Paris will only be a shadow. So why
should we destroy it?' (A. Speer, 1970). In the end, of

10. Of the voluminous literature on Hitler and his period from 1914 to
1946 I have used mainly A. Speer (1970) and W. Maser (1971), the
latter, however, with some caution, as already noted in connection with
his references to Hitler's youth. I owe a great deal of information and insight, also, to numerous personal communications from Albert Speer.
(Speer has genuinely repented his participation in the Nazi régime, and I
believe his statement that he has become an entirely different man.) Additional valuable sources are: P. E. Schramm (1965) and H. Krausnick
et al. (1968), important because both quote many important sources, and
Hitler's *Table Talks* (H. Picker, 1965) with an Introduction by Schramm,
an excellent source. I have also used E. Hanfstaengl (1970), but with
great caution. Hitler's *Mein Kampf* (1943) served little as a historical
source. Many other books were consulted, and some of these, too, were
quoted in the text.

course, Hitler ordered Paris destroyed – an order that was not executed by the German commander of Paris.

The most extreme expression of his mania for destroying buildings and cities was his 'scorched-earth' decree for Germany in September 1944, in which he ordered that before the enemy should occupy German territory

everything, simply everything essential to the maintenance of life would be destroyed: the ration card records, the files of marriage and resident registries, the records of bank accounts. In addition, food supplies were to be destroyed, farms burned down and cattle killed. Not even those works of art that the bombs had spared were to be preserved. Monuments, palaces, castles and churches, theatres and opera houses were also to be levelled. (A. Speer, 1970)

This also meant, of course, that there would be no water, no electricity, no sanitary facilities – i.e., there would be epidemics, illness, and death for millions who could not escape. For Speer, not a necrophilous destroyer but a biophilous builder, this order opened up an abyss between himself and Hitler. Seeking the cooperation of a number of generals and party officials who were not driven by Hitler's lust for destruction, Speer risked his life to sabotage Hitler's orders. Due to his efforts and those of a number of other people as well as to a number of other circumstances, Hitler's scorched-earth policy was never carried out.

Hitler's passion to destroy buildings and cities deserves particular attention because of its connection with his passion for building. One might even go so far as to say that his plans to rebuild cities were an excuse for first destroying them. But I believe it would be erroneous to explain his interest in architecture as *nothing but* a cover for his wish to destroy. His interest in architecture was probably genuine, and as we shall see later on, the only thing in life – apart from power, victory, and destruction – that genuinely interested him.

Hitler's destructiveness is also to be seen in his plans for the future of the Poles after his victory over them. They were to be culturally castrated; teaching was to be restricted to knowledge of traffic signals, some German, and, as to geography, the fact that Berlin is the capital of Germany; arithmetic was entirely superfluous. There was to be no medical care; low living standards; all they were good for was as cheap labour and obedient slaves (H. Picker, 1965).

Among the first *human* objects to be killed were *defective* people. Hitler had already written in *Mein Kampf*: 'Defective people [must] be prevented from propagating equally defective offspring ... For if necessary, the incurably sick will be pitilessly segregated – a barbaric measure for the unfortunate who is struck by it, but a blessing for his fellowmen and posterity' (A. Hitler, 1943). He translated these ideas into action by killing defective people rather than just isolating them. Another early manifestation of his destructiveness is the treacherous murder of Ernst Röhm (with whom he was seen chatting amiably only a few days before Röhm's death) and other SA leaders merely for reasons of political expediency (to reassure the industrialists and generals by exterminating the leaders of the 'anti-capitalist' wing of the movement).

Another expression of Hitler's indulgence in fantasies of unlimited destruction are his remarks on measures he would take if there were a mutiny, such as the one in 1918. He would immediately kill all leaders of opposing political currents, also those of political catholicism, and all inmates of concentration camps. He figured that in this way he would kill several hundred thousand people (H. Picker, 1965).

The main victims of physical destruction would be the Jews, Poles, and Russians. Let us deal only with the destruction of the Jews; the facts are too well-known to need elaboration here. It must be noted, however, that their systematic slaughter began only with the outbreak of the Second World War. There is no convincing evidence that

Hitler contemplated the annihilation of Jewry until shortly before then, although he may have kept his ideas secret; until that time it was the policy to promote the emigration of all Jews from Germany, and the Nazi government even made efforts to facilitate this emigration. But on 30 January 1939 he told Czechslovakian Foreign Minister Chvalkovsky quite frankly: 'We are going to destroy the Jews. They are not going to get away with what they did on 9 November 1918. The day of reckoning has come' (H. Krausnick *et al.*, 1968).[11] He made a less explicit statement before the Reichstag on the same day: 'If the Jewish international financiers inside and outside Europe succeeded in involving the nations in another war, the result will not be world bolshevism and therefore a victory for Judaism; it will be the end of the Jews in Europe.'[12]

The statement to Chvalkovsky is particularly interesting from a psychological standpoint. Here Hitler does not give any rationalizing explanation, such as that the Jews are a danger to Germany, but reveals one of his real motives: revenge for the 'crime' of being revolutionaries committed by a small number of Jews twenty years earlier. The sadistic quality of his hate against the Jews was revealed by 'certain remarks that he made about the Jews to his closest colleagues after the Party rally: "Out with them from all the professions and into the ghetto with them; fence them in somewhere where they can perish as they deserve while the German people look on, the way people stare at wild animals"' (H. Krausnick *et al.*, 1968).

11. This, as well as other quotes from German and French sources, are my translation.

12. Handwritten notes by Hitler's former senior officer and later adjutant, Consul General Fritz Wiedeman (retired). Hitler's utterances were made on almost the same day on which Goering ordered a 'Reich Central Office' for the emigration of the Jews to be headed by Eichmann. Eichmann had already worked out a method earlier to expel the Jews. H. Krausnick *et al.* (1968) suggest that Hitler may have disliked this less extreme solution, but agreed to it 'because for the time it was the only practical way'.

Hitler felt that the Jews were poisoning the Aryan blood and the Aryan soul. In order to understand how this feeling is related to the whole necrophilous complex we must deal with a seemingly completely different concern of Hitler's: syphilis. In *Mein Kampf* he spoke of syphilis as being among 'the most important vital questions of the nation'. He wrote:

> Running parallel to the political, ethical, and moral contamination of the people, there had been for many years a no less terrible poisoning of the health of the national body. Especially in the big cities, syphilis was beginning to spread more and more, while tuberculosis steadily reaped its harvest of death throughout nearly the whole country. (A. Hitler, 1943)

This was not true; neither tuberculosis nor syphilis constituted a major threat of the proportions Hitler attributes to them. But it is a typical fantasy for a necrophile: the fear of dirt and of poison and of the danger of being contaminated by them. It is an expression of, and simultaneously a defence against, the necrophilous attitude that experiences the outside world as dirty and poisonous. Most likely his hate against the Jews was rooted in this complex: Jews are foreigners; foreigners are poisonous (like syphilis); hence foreigners have to be eradicated. That the Jews were poisoning not only the blood but also the soul is only a further extension of the original notion.[13]

The more he sensed that victory was doubtful, the more Hitler the destroyer came fully into his own: for every step towards defeat many hecatombs had to die. Eventually it became time for the Germans themselves to be destroyed. Already on 27 January 1942, over a year before Stalingrad, Hitler said, 'If the German people are not ready to fight for their survival (*Selbstbehauptung*), well, then they have to disappear (*dann soll es verschwinden*)' (H. Picker, 1965). When defeat was unavoidable, he ordered this threatened destruction of Germany to begin – of her soil, buildings,

13. cf. the discussion of Germany as a mother symbol, p. 501.

factories, works of art. When the Russians were about to take Hitler's bunker, the moment for the *grand finale* of destruction had come. His dog had to die with him, and his mistress Eva Braun, who had come to the shelter against his orders in order to die with him, would die there, too. Hitler, so touched by Fraulein Braun's act of loyalty, rewarded her by contracting a legal marriage; the readiness to die for him was apparently the only act by which a woman could prove that she loved him. Goebbels also remained faithful to the man to whom he had sold his soul; he ordered his wife and their six small children to die with him. Like any normal mother, Goebbels' wife would never have killed her children, and least of all for the flimsy propaganda reasons her husband gave her, but she had no choice; when Speer visited her for the last time, Goebbels made it impossible for her to talk alone with him, even for a minute. All she could say was that she was happy that her eldest son (from a previous marriage) was not there also.[14] Hitler's defeat and death had to be accompanied by the death of those near him, by the death of the Germans, by the destruction of the world if he could have had his way. Total destruction was to be the background for his own destruction.

Let us return to the question whether one can explain Hitler's acts as justified by traditional reasons of state: whether he was humanly different from any other statesman or general who starts a war and gives orders by which millions of persons are killed. In some respects Hitler was like many 'normal' leaders of big powers, and it is rather hypocritical to declare his war policy unique, in the face of what leaders of other powerful nations are on record as having done. What is special in Hitler's case is the disproportionality between the destruction he ordered and the realistic reasons for it. His actions, from the killing of many millions of Jews, Russians, and Poles to the final order for the destruction of all Germans, cannot be explained as

14. A. Speer, personal communication.

strategically motivated, but are the product of the passion of a deeply necrophilous man. This fact is sometimes obscured by putting the whole emphasis on Hitler's destruction of the Jews, an emphasis that overlooks the fact that the Jews were only one of the many victims Hitler wanted to destroy. To be sure, it is correct to say that Hitler was a Jew-hater, but it is equally correct to say that he was a German-hater. He was a hater of mankind, a hater of life itself. This will become even clearer when we look at Hitler in terms of other necrophilic manifestations that were dealt with in general terms in the earlier discussion of necrophilia.

Let us look first at certain spontaneous expressions of his necrophilous orientation. Speer reports Hitler's reaction to the final scene of a newsreel about the bombing of Warsaw:

Clouds of smoke darkened the sky: dive bombers tilted and hurtled towards their goal; we could watch the flight of the released bombs, the pull-out of the planes and the cloud from the explosions expanding gigantically. The effect was enhanced by running the film in slow motion. Hitler was fascinated. The film ended with a montage showing a plane diving towards the outlines of the British Isles. A burst of flames followed, and the island flew into the air in tatters. Hitler's enthusiasm was unbounded. 'That is what will happen to them!' he cried out, carried away. 'That is how we will annihilate them!' (A. Speer, 1970)

Hanfstaengl reports a conversation held in the middle of the twenties in which he tried to persuade Hitler to visit England; he told Hitler of the interesting sights there and mentioned Henry VIII. Hitler responded: 'Six wives – hm, six wives – not bad, and two of them he eliminated on the scaffold. We should really visit England and go to the Tower to look at the place where they were executed. This would be worth while' (E. Hanfstaengl, 1970). Indeed, this place of execution interested him more than the rest of England.

Characteristic, also, is Hitler's reaction to a film *Fredericus*

Rex in 1923. In this movie Frederick's father wants to execute both his son and his friend for an attempt to flee the country. While still in the theatre and again on the way home, Hitler repeated, 'He [the son] is also to be killed – magnificent. This means: off with the head of anybody who sins against the state, even if he is one's own son!' He went on to say that this method must be applied in the case of the French (who at the time had occupied the valuable Ruhr area) and concluded: 'What does it matter if a dozen of our cities on the Rhine and Ruhr are consumed by fire and if a few hundred thousand people lose their lives!' (E. Hanfstaengl, 1970).

Characteristic of his necrophilous orientation are certain often repeated *jokes*. While Hitler kept to a vegetarian diet, his guests were served a regular dinner. 'If there was a meat broth,' reports Speer, 'I could depend on his speaking of "corpse tea"; in connection with crayfish he brought out his story of a deceased grandmother whose relations had thrown her body into the brook to lure the crustaceans; for eels, that they were best fattened and caught by using dead cats' (A. Speer, 1970).

Hitler's *face* also betrayed the sniffing expression mentioned in the discussion of necrophilia, as if he were constantly smelling a bad odour; this is quite apparent from a large number of photographs. His laugh was never free, but was a kind of smirk, as one can also recognize from photographs. This trait is particularly noticeable at the peak of his career, after the surrender of France in the railroad car in Compiègne. As depicted in a newsreel at the time, after he left the car he performed a little 'dance', struck his thighs and belly with his hands, and made an ugly smirk, as if he had just swallowed France.[15]

Another of Hitler's necrophilous traits was *boredom*. His conversations at table are the most drastic manifestation of this form of lifelessness. At Obersalzberg, after the afternoon

15. This is a telling manifestation of his 'oral-sadistic', exploitative character.

dinner he and his company would walk to the teahouse where tea and coffee with cakes and other sweets were served. 'Here, at the coffee table, Hitler was particularly fond of drifting into endless monologues. The subjects were mostly familiar to the company, who therefore listened absently, though pretending attention. Occasionally Hitler himself fell asleep over one of his monologues. The company then continued chatting in whispers, hoping that he would awaken in time for the evening meal' (A. Speer, 1970). Afterwards they all returned to the house and two hours later supper was served. After supper two movies were shown, and were occasionally followed by some trivial talk about them.

From one o'clock on, some members of the company, in spite of all their efforts to control themselves, could no longer repress their yawns. But the social occasion dragged on in monotonous, wearing emptiness for another hour or more, until at last Eva Braun had a few words with Hitler and was permitted to go upstairs.[16] Hitler would stand up about a quarter of an hour later, to bid his company good night. Those who remained, liberated, often followed those numbing hours with a gay party over champagne and cognac. (A. Speer, 1970)[17]

Hitler's destructiveness can be recognized through its main manifestations, some of which I have mentioned, but it was not recognized by millions of Germans or by statesmen and politicians all over the world. On the contrary, he was considered a great patriot, motivated by love for his

16. Speer reports that the conversations during meals in Berlin were not less trivial and boring, and that Hitler 'did not even try to cover up the frequent repetitions which were so embarrassing to his listeners.' (A. Speer, 1970.)

17. In the *Table Talks* with the generals at his headquarters in 1941–42 Hitler obviously made a greater effort and tried to impress his guests with his erudition and knowledge. These talks consisted of endless monologues ranging over all possible subjects. It was the same Hitler, who had lectured the loners in the Männerheim. But now his audience consisted of the leaders of the German army; his self-confidence had been greatly increased and his range (though not depth) of knowledge had been broadened by years of further reading. Yet in the last analysis the change is only superficial.

country; the saviour who would liberate Germany from the Versailles treaty and from acute economic disaster; the great constructor who would build a new, prosperous Germany. How could the Germans and the world not have seen the great destroyer behind the mask of the builder?

There are many reasons. Hitler was a consummate liar and actor. He proclaimed his desire for peace and insisted after every new success that this was the last demand he would make; he conveyed this convincingly both by his words and his highly controlled voice. But it was only his future enemies that he deceived. For example, in one of his talks to his generals, he proclaimed: 'Man has a sense for the discovery of beauty. How rich is the world for one who makes use of this sense ... Beauty must have power over men ... [After the end of the war] I want to devote myself to my thoughts for five to ten years, and to writing them down. Wars come and go. What remains are only the values of culture ...' He wants to create a new era of tolerance and accuses the Jews of having introduced intolerance through Christianity (H. Picker, 1965).

Repression of Destructiveness

Hitler was probably not even consciously lying when he spoke thus; he was simply assuming the old role of 'artist' and 'writer', never having admitted his failure in both those fields. Utterances of this kind, however, had a much more important function, one that is related to the core of Hitler's character structure: the repression of the awareness of his destructiveness. First in *rationalizations*: any destruction he ordered he rationalized as being only for the sake of the survival, growth, splendour of the German nation: it was in defence against enemies who wanted to destroy Germany (Jews, Russians, eventually England and America); he was acting in the name of the biological law of survival ('If I am to believe in a divine command, it can only be the one to preserve the species' [H. Picker, 1965].) In other words, when Hitler gave his orders for destruction he was only aware of his 'duty' and of his noble intentions; these required destructive acts, but he repressed the *awareness* of his *craving* for destruction. Thus he avoided confronting himself with his true motivations.

A still more efficient form of repression are *reaction formations*. This is a clinically well-established form of dealing with repressed strivings; a person denies their existence by developing traits that are exactly the opposite. One example of these reaction formations was his vegetarianism. Not that all vegetarianism has this function, but that it did in Hitler's case is indicated by the fact that he stopped eating meat after the suicide of his half-niece Geli Raubal, who had been his mistress. His whole behaviour at this time shows that he felt an intense guilt for her suicide. Even if we discard as unproven the suspicion found in the literature that he actually killed her in a fit of rage over her infatuation with a Jewish artist, he could be blamed for her suicide. He held her like a prisoner, was extremely jealous, and had started a lively flirtation with Eva Braun. After Geli's death he fell into a state of depression, started a kind of mourning cult (her room remained undisturbed as long as he lived in Munich, and he visited it every Christmas). His abstinence from meat was an atonement for his guilt and the proof of his incapacity to kill. His antipathy for hunting probably had the same function.

The most distinct manifestations of this reaction formation can be seen in the following facts cited by W. Maser (1971). Hitler did not get involved in any of the fighting with political opponents in the years before his seizure of power. Only once did he touch a political opponent. He was never present at a murder or an execution. (When Röhm asked before he was killed that the Führer himself should come and shoot him, he knew what he was talking about.) When some of his comrades were killed in the attempted coup in Munich (9 November 1923), he fought with ideas of suicide and began to suffer twitching of his left arm, a condition which returned after the defeat in Stalingrad. It was impossible for his generals to persuade him to visit the front. 'Not a few military and other persons were firmly convinced that he evaded such visits because he could not tolerate the view of dead and wounded soldiers' (W. Maser, 1971).[18] The reason for this behaviour was not lack of physical courage, amply demonstrated in the First World War, or his tender feelings for the German soldiers, for whom he felt as little as for anybody else (W. Maser, 1971).[19] In my opinion this phobic reaction to seeing corpses is a defence reaction against the awareness of his own destructiveness. As long as he only gave and signed orders, he had only spoken and written. In other words, 'he' has not shed blood as long as he avoided *seeing* the corpses in reality and protected himself from the affective awareness of his passion for destruction. This phobic defence reaction is basically the same mechanism as that at the bottom of Hitler's somewhat compulsive over-cleanliness, mentioned by Speer.[20] This symptom in the mild form it had in Hitler, as well as in the severe form of a full-grown washing compulsion, usually has one function: that of washing off the dirt, the blood which symbolically adheres to one's hands (or the whole body); the awareness of the blood and dirt is repressed; what is conscious is only the need to be 'clean'. The refusal to see corpses is similar to this compulsion; both serve the denial of destructiveness.

Towards the end of his life, when he sensed the approach of his final defeat, Hitler was no longer able to continue repressing his destructiveness. A drastic example is his reaction to the sight of the dead bodies of the leaders of the aborted revolt of the generals in 1944. The man who had not been able to see corpses now gave orders to be shown

18. Maser's statement is also confirmed by Speer in a personal communication.

19. Maser's statement is based on General W. Warlimont's authority (1964).

20. A. Speer, personal communication.

the film taken of the torture and execution of the generals and of the corpses in their prison garb hanging from meat hooks. He put a photograph of this scene on his desk.[20] His previous threat to destroy Germany in case of defeat was now to be translated into reality; it was not due to Hitler that Germany was spared.

Other Aspects of Hitler's Personality

We cannot understand Hitler or anyone else by seeing only one of his passions, even if it is the most fundamental of them. To comprehend how this man, driven by destructiveness, succeeded in becoming the most powerful man in Europe, admired by many Germans (and not a few other people), we must try to grasp his *whole* character structure, his special talents and gifts, and the social situation within which he functioned.

In addition to necrophilia Hitler also presents the picture of sadism, although this is overshadowed by the intensity of his lust for plain destruction. Since I analysed Hitler's sado-masochistic, authoritarian character in an earlier work (E. Fromm, 1941), I can be very brief here. Both in his writing and his speeches, Hitler expressed the craving for power over weaker people. He explained the advantage of having mass meetings in the evening thus:

It seems that in the morning and even during the day men's will power revolts with highest energy against an attempt at being forced under another's will and another's opinion. In the evening, however, they succumb more easily to the dominating force of a stronger will. For truly every such meeting presents a wrestling match between two opposed forces. The superior oratorical talent of a domineering apostolic nature will now succeed more easily in winning for the new will people who themselves have in turn experienced a weakening of their force of resistance in the most natural way, than people who still have full command of the energy of their minds and their will power. (A. Hitler, 1943)

20. A. Speer, personal communication.

At the same time his submissive attitude made him feel that he was acting in the name of a higher power, 'Providence', or biological law. In one sentence Hitler gave expression both to his sadistic and his necrophilous aspects: 'What they [the masses] want is the victory of the stronger and the annihilation or the unconditional surrender of the weaker' (A. Hitler, 1943). The sadist would demand *surrender*; only the necrophile demands *annihilation*. The word 'or' connects the sadistic and the necrophilous sides of Hitler's character; but we know from the record that the wish for annihilation was stronger in him than that for mere surrender.

Three other character traits closely related to each other were his narcissism, his withdrawn attitude, and his lack of any feeling of love, warmth, or compassion.

His *narcissism*[21] is the most easily recognizable trait in the picture. He shows all the typical symptoms of an extremely narcissistic person: he is interested only in himself, *his* desires, *his* thought, *his* wishes; he talked endlessly about his ideas, his past, his plans; the world is real only as far as it is the object of his schemes and desires; other people matter only as far as they serve him or can be used; he always knows everything better than anyone else. This certainty in one's own ideas and schemes is a typical characteristic of intense narcissism.

Hitler came to his conclusions mainly on an emotional basis, not as a result of examining *knowledge*. For him, political, economic, and social *facts* were replaced by *ideology*. Once he believed in an ideology because it appealed to his emotions, he believed the facts that the ideology proclaimed as true. This does not mean he neglected facts entirely; to some extent he was a shrewd observer and evaluated certain facts better than many less narcissistic people. But this capacity, which I shall discuss further on, does not exclude his lack of realism in essential matters concerning which his beliefs and decisions are made largely on a narcissistic basis.

21. cf. the discussion on narcissism in Chapter 9.

Hanfstaengl reports a telling illustration of Hitler's narcissism: Goebbels had ordered a tape recording made of some of Hitler's speeches. Whenever Hitler visited him, Goebbels would play these recordings; Hitler would 'throw himself in a big overstuffed chair and enjoy his voice in a trance-like state (*in einer Art von Vollnarkose*) like the Greek youth who was tragically in love with himself and found his death in the water while admiring his own image on its smooth surface' (E. Hanfstaengl, 1970). P. E. Schramm speaks of Hitler's 'cult of the ego. He was dominated, according to [General] Alfred Jodl by an "almost mystical conviction of his infallibility as leader of the nation and of the war"' (H. Picker, 1965). Speer writes about Hitler's 'megalomania' as shown in his building plans. His own palace in Berlin was to be the biggest residence ever built, one hundred and fifty times the size of the chancellor's residence at the time of Bismarck (A. Speer, 1970).

Related to his narcissism is Hitler's utter *lack of interest in anybody or anything*, except what was of service to him, and his cold remoteness from everybody. To his absolute narcissism corresponded an almost absolute lack of love, tenderness, or empathy for anybody. In his whole history one can not find a single person who could be called his friend; Kubizek and Speer come closer to this description than anyone else, yet they could by no means be called 'friends'. Kubizek, being of the same age, served him as audience, admirer, and companion; but Hitler was never frank with him. The relationship with Speer was different; Speer probably represented for Hitler the image of himself as an architect; *he*, Hitler, would be a great builder through the medium of Speer. He seems even to have had some genuine affection for Speer – the only instance where we find this, perhaps with the exception of Kubizek – and I surmise that one reason for this rare phenomenon may have been that architecture was the only field in which Hitler had a real interest in something outside of himself, the only area in which he was alive. Nevertheless, Speer was not his friend;

as Speer put it succinctly at the Nuremberg trial: 'If Hitler had had any friends, I would have been his friend.' The fact was that Hitler had no friends; he was always a secretive loner, whether as a painter of postcards in Vienna or as the Führer of the Reich. Speer remarks on his 'inability to make human contacts'. Hitler himself was aware of his complete loneliness. Speer reports Hitler's telling him that after his (Hitler's) eventual retirement he would be soon forgotten:

> People would turn to his successor quickly enough once it became evident that power was now in those hands ... Everyone would forsake him. Playing with this idea, with a good measure of self-pity, he continued: 'Perhaps one of my former associates will visit me occasionally. But I don't count on it. Aside from Fräulein Braun, I'll take no one with me. Fräulein Braun and my dog. I'll be lonely. For why should anyone voluntarily stay with me for any length of time? Nobody will take notice of me any more. They'll all go running after my successor. Perhaps once a year they'll show up for my birthday.' (A. Speer, 1970)

In these sentiments Hitler not only expresses the notion that nobody has any affection for him, but also the conviction that the only reason for attachment to him is his power; his friends were his dog and the woman whom he neither loved nor respected, but completely controlled.

Hitler was cold and pitiless. This was noticed by such sensitive people as H. Rauschning (1940) and Speer. The latter gives a telling example; he as well as Goebbels tried to persuade Hitler, for propaganda purposes, to visit the bombed cities. 'But Hitler regularly brushed away any such suggestion. During his drives from Stettin Station to the Chancellery, or to his apartment in Prinzregentenstrasse in Munich, he now ordered his chauffeur to take the shortest route, whereas he formerly loved long detours. Since I accompanied him several times on such drives, I saw with what absence of emotion he noted the new areas of rubble through which his car would pass' (A. Speer, 1970). The only living creature 'who aroused any flicker of human feeling in Hitler' was his dog (A. Speer, 1970).

Many other, less sensitive people were deceived; what they believed to be *warmth* was in fact *excitation*, which emerged when Hitler spoke about his favourite topics or was in a vengeful and destructive mood. In the whole literature about Hitler I was unable to find any instance in which he showed compassion for anybody; of course, not for his enemies, but neither for the fighting soldiers and eventually for the German civilians. Never were his tactical decisions in the war – mainly his insistence on not retreating (for instance in the battle for Stalingrad) influenced by concern about the number of soldiers who would be sacrificed; they were only so many 'guns'.

Summarizing, Speer states: 'Hitler lacked all the more gentle virtues of man: tenderness, love, poetry, were alien to his nature. On the surface he showed courtesy, charm, tranquility, correctness, amiability, self-control. This outer skin obviously had the function to cover up the really dominant traits with a complete although thin layer' (Afterword by A. Speer, in J. Brosse, 1972).

Relations to Women

Hitler's relations to women show the same lack of love and tenderness or compassion as do his relations to men. This statement would seem to contradict that Hitler was very attached to his mother; but if we assume that Hitler's incestuousness was of the malignant type, i.e., that he was tied to mother, but that this tie was cold and impersonal, we will be prepared to find that his relations to women in his later life were also cold and impersonal.

Among the women in whom Hitler was interested we can distinguish essentially two categories, characterized mainly by their respective social positions: (1) the 'respectable' women, distinguished by their wealth, social status, or by being successful actresses, and (2) the women who were socially 'beneath' him, like his half-niece, Geli Raubal, and his mistress of many years, Eva Braun. His behaviour and feelings towards the first group were quite different from those towards the second group.

Among the women in the first group were a number of elderly and wealthy society ladies in Munich who befriended him and made considerable gifts to him personally and to the party. More importantly, they introduced him to upper-class life and manners. He accepted their gifts and adoration graciously, but never fell in love with or was erotically attracted to these mother figures.

With other socially superior women he was always somewhat shy and timid. His youthful infatuation with Stephanie, a young and pretty upper-class girl in Linz, is a prototype for this attitude; he was smitten by her, and if we follow Kubizek's report, he would walk by her house and try to see her on walks, yet he never dared to address her or make any attempt, through a third person, to be introduced. Eventually he wrote her a letter expressing his wish to marry her later on, after he had become somebody, but did not sign it. This whole behaviour, bearing the stamp of a lack of realism, may be attributed to his youth, but according to many other reports, such as those by Hanfstaengl and Speer, he showed the same timidity towards women in later years. It seems that his attitude towards desirable women whom he admired remained one of distant admiration. In Munich he liked to look at good-looking women; when he came to power he liked to surround himself with beautiful women, especially film actresses, but there is no evidence that he ever fell in love with any of them. Towards these women 'Hitler behaved rather like the graduate of the dancing class at the final dance. He displayed a shy eagerness to do nothing wrong, to offer a sufficient number of compliments, and to welcome them and bid them good-bye with the Austrian kissing of the hand' (A. Speer, 1970).

There were also the women he did not admire or respect, such as Geli Raubal and Eva Braun, but who submitted to him. It was with this type of woman that he seems mainly to have had sexual relations.

Hitler's sexual life has been the subject of much speculation. It has often been claimed that he was a homosexual, but there is no evidence of it, nor does it seem likely to have been the case.[22] On the other hand, there is no evidence that his sexual relations were normal, or even that he was sexually potent. Most of the data in regard to Hitler's sexual life come from Hanfstaengl, who had plenty of occasions to observe him in Munich and Berlin in the twenties and early thirties.[23]

Hanfstaengl reports a statement made by Geli Raubal to a friend: 'My uncle is a monster. Nobody can imagine what he demands from me!' This statement is somewhat corroborated by another story reported by Hanfstaengl, told him by F. Schwartz, the treasurer of the Party in the twenties. According to the latter, Hitler was blackmailed by a man who had gotten possession of pornographic sketches Hitler had made of Geli, showing her in positions 'which any professional model would decline to assume'. Hitler gave orders to pay off the man, but he did not permit the sketches to be destroyed; they had to be preserved in his safe in the Brown House. Nobody knows what these sketches portrayed, but it is safe to assume that they were not just sketches of Geli in the nude, since in the Munich of the

22. cf. W. Maser (1971). J. Brosse (1972), although he admits there is no direct evidence for it, bases his claim that Hitler had strong latent homosexual tendencies on the tortuous argument that this is likely because Hitler had paranoid tendencies, his reasoning being based on the Freudian assumption of the close relationship between paranoia and unconscious homosexuality.

23. Unfortunately, Hanfstaengl is not a reliable witness. His autobiography is largely self-serving; in it he attempts to present himself as a man who tried to exercise a good influence on Hitler, and who, after his break with Hitler, became an 'adviser' to President Roosevelt – a rather exaggerated claim. Nevertheless, in his description of Hitler's relations with women we can grant him a basic credibility, since this topic did not serve to enhance his own political stature.

twenties that could hardly have been compromising enough to blackmail Hitler. It is probable that the sketches portrayed some perverse pose or position, and that Hitler's sexual desires were somewhat abnormal; whether he was totally incapable of performing the normal sexual act, as Hanfstaengl claims, is beyond our knowing. But it is likely that the sexual interests of a cold, timid, sadistic, and destructive man like Hitler were mainly of a perverse nature. Since we have no data, it is not very helpful to try to construct a detailed picture of his sexual tastes. The most one can guess, I believe, is that his sexual desires were largely voyeuristic, anal-sadistic with the inferior type of women, and masochistic with admired women.

We have no evidence concerning his sexual relations with Eva Braun, either, but we do know a great deal more about his affective relationship to her. It is clear that he treated her with complete lack of consideration. His birthday gifts to her are only one example; he would tell an adjutant to buy her some cheap costume jewellery and the obligatory flowers.[24] 'In general Hitler showed little consideration for her feelings. In her presence he would enlarge on his attitude towards women as though she were not present: "a highly intelligent man should take a primitive and stupid woman"' (A. Speer, 1970).

We get a further insight into Hitler's attitude towards Eva Braun from the latter's diary. Her writing is difficult to decipher in part, but probably reads as follows:

11th March, 1935. I wish only for one thing – to be severely ill and not to know anything about him for at least a week. Why does nothing happen to me? Why must I go through all this? If I had only never met him. I am desperate. Now I am again buying sleeping powders, then I get into a dreamlike state and do not think about it so much any more.

Why doesn't the devil get me? I am sure it would be more pleasant with him than here.

For three hours I waited in front of the Carlton and had to

watch while he brought flowers . . . and took her to dinner. [Remark added later, on March 16:] crazy imagination.

He uses me only for certain purposes, it is not possible otherwise. [Added later:] nonsense!

When he says he is fond of me [*er hat mich lieb*] he means it only at a moment, exactly like his promises which he never keeps.

April 1, 1935. Last night we were invited by him to the Vier Jahreszeiten [a Munich restaurant]. I had to sit beside him for three hours and could not say a single word to him. On parting he gave me, as once before, an envelope with money. How lovely it would have been if he had written me a greeting or a kind word with it: it would have given me so much pleasure. But he does not think of such things.

May 28, 1935. I have just sent him a letter that for me is decisive, whether he . . . [indecipherable].

Well, we shall see. If I do not have an answer by tonight at 10, I will simply take my twenty-five pills and shall softly . . . sleep.

Is that his . . . love as he has assured me so often, if he has no kind word for me in three months? . . .

Good Lord, I am afraid that he will not answer me today. If only somebody would help me, everything is so terrible and hopeless. Perhaps my letter reached him at an inappropriate moment. Perhaps I should not have written him at all? Whatever it may be, the uncertainty is more terrible to bear than a sudden end.

I have decided on thirty-five pieces [sleeping pills]; this time it is really to be a 'dead sure' matter. If he would at least have somebody phone me. (Eva Braun, 1935)[25]

In the same diary she complains that on the occasion of her birthday he did not give her any of the things she had wanted so much (a small dog and clothes), but only had someone bring her flowers; she bought herself some jewellery for about twelve dollars, hoping that at least he would like to see it on her.

There are some data on Hitler's masochistic behaviour towards women whom he admired. Hanfstaengl reports about such an incident in connection with Hitler's attitude towards his (Hanfstaengl's) wife. At a visit to Hanfstaengl's home, while the latter had left for a few minutes, Hitler fell on his knees before Mrs Hanfstaengl, called himself her slave, and deplored the fate that had given him, too late, the bittersweet experience of meeting her. The essential point of this report, Hitler's masochistic behaviour, is corroborated by a document W. C. Langer (1972) was able to dig out. Renée Muller, a film actress, confided to her director, A. Zeissler, what happened during the evening she spent at the Chancellery:

> She had been sure that he was going to have intercourse with her; that they had both undressed and were apparently getting ready for bed when Hitler fell on the floor and begged her to kick him. She demurred, but he pleaded with her and condemned himself as unworthy, heaped all kinds of accusations on his own head, and just grovelled in an agonizing manner. The scene became intolerable to her, and she finally acceded to his wishes and kicked him. This excited him greatly, and he begged for more and more, always saying that it was even better than he deserved and that he was not worthy to be in the same room with her. As she continued to kick him he became more and more excited. (A. Zeissler, 1943)

Renée Muller committed suicide shortly afterwards.

There were a number of other women of the upper class who are said to have been in love with Hitler; but there is not enough evidence to prove that he had sexual relations with them. It is remarkable that quite a few women who had been close to Hitler committed – or tried to commit – suicide: Geli Raubal, Eva Braun (twice), Renée Muller, Unity Mitford, and a few, more doubtful cases quoted by Maser. One can hardly help speculating that Hitler's destructiveness was not without effect on them.

Whatever the nature of Hitler's perversion, the details hardly matter, nor does his sexual life explain anything more about him than what we know already. In fact, the credibility of the scarce data we have on his sexual life rests mainly on our knowledge of his character.

Gifts and Talents

The characterological analysis of Hitler has shown us a withdrawn, extremely narcissistic, unrelated, undisciplined, sado-masochistic, and necrophilous person. Surely these qualities would not explain his success, unless he was a man of considerable gifts and talents.

What were they?

The greatest of Hitler's talents was his capacity to influence, impress, and persuade people. We have seen that he had this ability even as a child. He recognized and practised it in his role as leader of the boys' gangs in the war games; later in his relation to Kubizek, his first real follower; then with the inmates of the Männerheim in Vienna. Shortly after the revolution, in 1919, he was sent out by his military superiors with the mission to convert the soldiers to right-wing ideas and to arouse their hate against the revolutionaries. He met with the small and insignificant group of the Socialist Workers' Party (fifty members) and succeeded within a year in becoming the Party's undisputed leader, renaming it the National Socialist German Worker's Party, changing its constitution, and being accepted as one of the most popular speakers in Munich.

The reasons for this capacity to influence people – which is, of course, the essential talent of all demagogues – are manifold.

One must first think of what has often been called his *magnetism*, which, according to most observers, originated in his eyes (H. Picker, 1965; W. Maser, 1971; A. Speer, 1970). There are a number of reports showing that even people who are biased against him suddenly become converted when he looked straight at them. Professor A. von Müller, who gave a course on history to the soldiers training for intelligence work in Munich, gives the following picture of his first meeting with Hitler:

At the end of my lecture I noticed a small group that made me stop. They stood as if mesmerized by a man in their midst who spoke to them in a strange guttural voice without stopping, and with increasing excitation; I had the peculiar feeling that their own excitation was caused by his, and simultaneously that theirs gave his voice its energy. I saw a pallid, thin face ... with a short clipped moustache and conspicuously large, pale blue, fanatically cold, shining eyes. (W. Maser, 1971)

There are many reports mentioning the magnetic qualities of Hitler's eyes. Since I never saw him except in pictures, which give only a most inadequate impression of this peculiar quality, I can only speculate on what it was. Such speculation is facilitated, however, by a frequently made observation that extremely narcissistic people – especially fanatics – often show a particular glitter in their eyes that gives them an appearance of great intensity, otherworldliness, and devotion. In fact, it is sometimes not easy to distinguish between the expression in the eyes of an extremely devoted, almost saintly man and those of a highly narcissistic, sometimes even half-crazy man. The only distinguishing quality is the presence – or absence – of warmth, and all reports agree that Hitler had cold eyes, that his whole facial expression was cold, that there was an absence of any warmth or compassion. While this trait could have a negative effect – as in fact it did on many – it often enhances magnetic power. Cold ruthlessness and the lack of humanity in a face produces fear; one prefers to admire rather than be afraid. The word 'awe' best characterizes this blend of feelings; awe means something terrible (as in 'awful') as well as something admirable (as in to be in awe of somebody).[26]

Another factor in Hitler's impressiveness was his narcissism and the unshakeable *certainty* that, like so many narcissists, he felt about his ideas. In order to understand this phenomenon we must consider that, as far as our knowledge is concerned, nothing is certain except death.

26. In Hebrew the word *norah* has the same double meaning; it is used as an attribute for God and represents an archaic attitude in which God is simultaneously horrible and sublime.

But to say that nothing is certain does not imply that everything is a matter of guesswork. From an educated guess, to a hypothesis, to a theory, an ever increasing approximation of certainty exists mediated by reason, realistic observation, critical thought, and imagination. For the one who has these capacities, relative uncertainty is very acceptable because it is the result of the active use of his faculties, while certainty is boring because it is dead. But for those without these faculties, especially at a time of as much social and political uncertainty as there was in Germany in the twenties, the fanatic who pretends to be certain becomes a most attractive figure, somebody akin to a saviour.

A related factor that facilitated Hitler's influence was his gift for oversimplification. His speeches were not restrained by intellectual or moral scruples. He picked out the facts that served his thesis, connected the pieces, and made up a plausible argument, plausible at least for uncritical minds. He was also a consummate actor, showing a remarkable capacity for mimicking the speech and gestures of the most diverse people.[27] He had complete control over his voice, consciously playing on it in order to achieve the desired effect. When he spoke to students, he could be calm and reasonable. He also knew the right tone for speaking to his tough and uneducated old Munich cronies, or to a German prince, or to his generals. He could make an angry scene when he wanted to break down the Czechoslovakian or Polish ministers in order to make them surrender, and he could be the perfect and amiable host to Neville Chamberlain.

One cannot speak about Hitler's talent for impressing others without mentioning his *attacks of anger*. Those occasional outbursts have largely contributed to the cliché about Hitler, especially widespread outside of Germany, presenting him as someone constantly angry, shouting, incapable of self-control. Such a picture is by no means correct. Hitler was generally courteous, polite, and

27. A. Speer, personal communication.

controlled; his spells of anger, even though they were not rare, were the exception, but they could be of the greatest intensity. These angry outbursts occurred on two kinds of occasions. First, in his speeches, especially towards the conclusion. This anger was quite authentic because it was fed by his very genuine passion of hate and destruction, to which he gave full and uninhibited expression at a certain point in his speeches. It was the very authenticity of his hate that made it so impressive and infectious. Genuine as these oratorical expressions of hate were, they were not, however, uncontrolled. Hitler knew very well when the time had arrived to let go and to whip up the audience's emotions, and only then did he open the floodgates of his hate.

His angry outbursts in conversations seem to have been of another nature, not unlike those he had had as a child, when he felt frustrated.[28] Speer has compared them with the tantrums of a six-year-old, which was in many aspects Hitler's 'emotional age'. He used these outbursts to intimidate people, but he could also control them when he felt it was expedient to do so.

A good illustration is provided by a scene described by one of the most outstanding German military leaders, General Heinz Guderian:

'With an angry red face, raised fists, the trembling man [Hitler] stood before me, beside himself with rage and having lost all composure (*fassungslos*) ... He shouted more and more loudly, his face was distorted.' When Guderian was not impressed by this spectacle and insisted on his original opinion that had so infuriated him, Hitler suddenly changed, smiled very amiably and told Guderian: 'Please go on with your report; today the General Staff has won a battle.' (A. Bullock, 1965)

Speer's appraisal of Hitler's outbursts is corroborated by many other reports in the literature:

28. We must leave the question open whether Hitler's explosions of temper were the result of organic neurophysiologic factors or whether such factors at least lowered his threshold for anger.

After dramatic negotiations Hitler was apt to deride his opposites. Once he described Schuschnigg's visit to Obersalzberg on 12 February 1939. By a pretended fit of passion he had made the Austrian Chancellor realize the gravity of the situation, he said, and finally forced him to yield. Many of those hysterical scenes that have been reported were probably carefully staged. In general, self-control was one of Hitler's most striking characteristics. In those early days he lost control of himself only a very few times, at least in my presence. (A. Speer, 1970)

Another of Hitler's remarkable gifts was his extraordinary *memory*. P. E. Schramm gives a vivid description:

One capacity that astounded everybody again and again – including those who were not under his spell, was his stupendous memory; a memory that could exactly retain even unimportant details, like the characters in Karl May's novels, the authors of books he had once read, even the make of the bicycle he had ridden in 1915. He remembered exactly the dates in his political career, the inns he had been to, the streets he had driven on. (H. Picker, 1965)

A number of reports show Hitler's faculty for remembering figures and technical details – the exact calibre and range of any type of gun, the number of submarines at sea and at home ports, and many other details of military importance. No wonder that his generals were often deeply impressed by the thoroughness of his knowledge, which in fact was mainly a feat of memory.

This brings us to a very important question, that of Hitler's *erudition* and *knowledge*, a question that is of special importance today when there is an increasing tendency to restore the image of Hitler, and an undiluted admiration of Hitler's greatness is expressed in a number of recent books by former Nazis.[29]

Maser takes a somewhat contradictory position. He

29. cf. H. S. Ziegler (1965); also H. S. Ziegler, ed. (1970). According to various reports we can expect quite a number of books and articles to appear in Germany, England, and the United States in the near future that will try to present a refurbished picture of Hitler, the great leader.

cautions the reader that many statements made by Hitler about his own erudition are of doubtful value in the absence of objective evidence. (For instance, Hitler claimed that he read one serious book every night, and that since he was twenty-two he had seriously studied world history; the history of art, of culture, of architecture, and political science.) In spite of this initial warning Maser asserts, without citing sources, that according to 'well-authenticated' reports of witnesses, Hitler had begun in his later school years to study advanced works in science and art, but was most at home in those branches of history that he himself claimed to have mastered. How uncritical such an evaluation of Hitler's knowledge is can be seen from one drastic example: Maser writes that Hitler's remarks in the *Zwiegespräche* confirm only 'what Hitler had convincingly proved before, both publicly and in private conversations: his remarkable knowledge of the Bible and of the Talmud' (W. Maser, 1971). The Talmud is a large and difficult work and only someone who has devoted years to its study could have a 'remarkable knowledge' of it. The facts are simple: the anti-Semitic literature with which Hitler was quite familiar, cites a number of sentences from the Talmud, sometimes distorted or taken out of context, in order to prove the sinister nature of the Jews. Hitler remembered these phrases and bluffed his listeners into believing that he had mastered a whole literature. That he should thus bluff his listeners is understandable; that he could still bluff a historian thirty years later is regrettable.

Hitler could, indeed, talk glibly and with a claim to knowledge about almost everything under the sun, as anyone who reads the *Table Talks* (H. Picker, 1965) can easily convince himself. He held forth on palaeontology, anthropology, and every aspect of history, philosophy, religion, psychology of women, and biology.

What does a critical examination of Hitler's erudition and knowledge show?

In school he was never capable of making an effort to do

serious reading, even in subjects like history that had captured his interest. In his Viennese years he spent most of his
time walking the streets, looking at buildings, sketching, and
talking. The capacity for sustained study and serious, pain-
staking reading could have emerged after the war, but there
is no evidence for it except Hitler's own claims. (He is supposed to have carried a volume of Schopenhauer with him
during the war. How much he read of it we do not know.)
On the other hand, an examination of the *Table Talks*,
of his speeches, and of *Mein Kampf* suggests that he must
indeed have been a greedy, voracious reader with a
tremendous capacity for gleaning and retaining facts,
and then using them whenever possible to underscore his
biases.

Read with some objectivity, *Mein Kampf* emerges as
hardly the work of a man with any solid knowledge, but as a
cleverly – and dishonestly – constructed propaganda pam-
phlet. As for his speeches, while tremendously effective,
they were those of a rabble-rousing demagogue, not of an
educated (self or otherwise) man. The *Table Talks* show
him at his highest conversational level. But they also reveal
him as a very gifted, half-educated man with no sound
foundation in anything, who rambled from one field of
knowledge to another, yet, helped by his prodigious memory, managed to combine into a more or less coherent whole
all the bits of information he had picked up in the kind of
informational reading he did do. Sometimes he made severe
blunders that showed his lack of basic knowledge, but by
and large he seems to have impressed his listeners, although
most likely not all of them.

(In trying to determine the effect of the *Table Talks* on
Hitler's guests, one should remember that while the men
who listened to him were well-educated and intelligent,
some of them were fascinated by him and were therefore
prone to overlook the lack of foundation in his ramblings.
They may also have been impressed by the extremely
wide range of subjects on which Hitler talked with such

self-assurance; brought up in the tradition of intellectual honesty, it would have been difficult for them to believe that here sat a man who was largely bluffing.)

The evidence indicates that, with rare exceptions, Hitler read nothing that challenged biased fanatical premises or that required critical and objective thought. In accordance with his character his motive for reading was not knowledge but ammunition for his passion for persuading others – and himself. He wanted to be excited by everything he read; he looked for an immediate emotional satisfaction through confirmation of his biases. Just as he was not interested in music by Bach or Mozart, but only in Wagner's operas, he was not interested in books that required participation and patience and had the beauty of truth. He devoured printed pages, but in a completely receptive and greedy way. Few serious books in any field can be read in this way; the proper material for this kind of reading are political pamphlets and pseudo-scientific books, such as those on race by Gobineau or Chamberlain as well as popularized books on Darwinism, and others not too difficult to understand from which Hitler could pick out what suited him. He may also have read books on subjects that genuinely interested him, such as architecture and military history, but we do not know to what extent. By and large, it can be assumed that Hitler read popular literature (including pamphlets), in which he found many quotations from more serious sources; these he retained and quoted in his turn as if he had read the originals. The real problem is not how many books Hitler read, but whether he had acquired the basic quality of an educated man – i.e., the capacity for objectivity and reason in the assimilation of knowledge. It has often been said that Hitler was an auto-didact, but this term is misleading: Hitler was not a *self-taught* man but a *half-taught* man, and the half that was missing was the knowledge of what knowledge is.

Hitler's basic lack of education manifests itself in still

another way. He had, of course, the possibility of inviting German scholars in any field in order to learn from them and increase his knowledge. But according to the reports by Schramm as well as by Speer, he almost totally avoided doing this.[30] He felt uneasy with people who were his equals – or his superiors – in any respect, as is frequently the case with narcissistic and authoritarian characters. He had to be in a position where he could play the role of the infallible one; if this was not possible, such a discussion threatened the whole edifice of his inflated knowledge, just as a serious book would have done.

The only exception to Hitler's avoidance of specialists is found in his relation to architects, in particular, to Professor P. L. Troost. Troost was not subservient to Hitler; for instance, when Hitler came to Troost's apartment, Troost never went to meet him at the stairs, nor did he ever accompany Hitler downstairs when he left. Nevertheless, Hitler's admiration for Troost was unmitigated. He was never arrogant or argumentative, but behaved towards Troost like a student (A. Speer, 1970). Even in a photograph published in Speer's book one can recognize Hitler's almost timid attitude towards the professor. I suggest that Hitler behaved as he did towards Troost because of his interest in architecture, which I have already stressed.

Hitler's taste in music and painting, like that in history and philosophy, was determined almost exclusively by his passions. Each evening after supper in Obersalzberg he saw two films; his favourites were operettas and musicals; no travelogues, films on nature, or educational films (A. Speer, 1970). I have already mentioned that such films as *Fredericus Rex* delighted him. In music he was interested almost exclusively in operettas and Wagnerian music, whose

30. On one occasion he rationalized this unwillingness by telling Speer that most German scholars would probably not want to see him. This was, regrettably perhaps, not true, and Hitler must have known it (A. Speer, 1970).

emotionalism was a kind of tonic to him. Hanfstaengl often played a few minutes of Wagner for him, especially when he felt low or depressed, and Hitler would respond as to an energizing drug.

There is no evidence that the one-time painter had any serious interest in painting. He preferred to look at the outside of a museum, its architecture, rather than to go inside and look at the paintings. Hanfstaengl gives a vivid description of a visit to the Kaiser Friedrich Museum in Berlin in the early twenties. The first painting before which Hitler stopped was Rembrandt's *Man with the Golden Helmet.* 'Is this not unique?' he said to the young son of a Party member whom he had taken on this visit. 'His heroic soldierly expression. A fight through and through. Here one can see that Rembrandt was, after all, Aryan and Germanic, even though he occasionally took his models from the Jewish quarter in Amsterdam.'

Hitler, the 'painter', mostly copied postcards and old etchings; the subjects were largely the façades of buildings ('architectural drawing'), but also landscapes and portraits and illustrations for advertisements. The principle that guided him was exclusively that of easy saleability, and he would, as we have seen, repeat certain sketches and water-colours when they found a demand. His drawings and paintings show the quality one would expect from a man who paints thus. They were pleasant, but unalive and lacking in personal expression. The best of his work seems to be his architectural sketches. But even when he did not copy, as during the war, they had a precise, patient, and pedantic style; no personal impulse can be felt in them, although they were 'well executed' (A. Speer, 1970). Even Hitler himself admitted later that his motive for painting was simply to make a living, and that he was only a 'small painter' (*ein kleiner Maler*). He said to his crony Hoffmann, the photographer, in 1944, 'I do not want to become a painter. I painted only to be able to live and to study' (W. Maser, 1971). One may conclude that he was a commercial artist, a copyist with talent for drawing; he did not have the talent to become a great painter.[31]

This impression of Hitler's lack of originality is reinforced when one looks at the more than one hundred sketches Speer has in his possession. Even though I am not competent as a judge of art, I believe no psychologically sensitive person can fail to note the extremely pedantic and lifeless character of these sketches. There is, for instance, one small detail of a sketch for the interior of a theatre that Hitler repeated many times, virtually without any change; there are similar repetitions of a sketch of an obelisk. Sometimes one can see the aggression in the intense pencil strokes, while other pictures lack any personal expression. It is very interesting to find that interspersed with these sketches (done between 1925 and 1940) are artless drawings of submarines, tanks, and other military equipment.[32]

The fact that Hitler had little interest in painting should not make us assume that his interest in architecture was not genuine. This is of great importance for the understanding of Hitler's personality, because it would seem to be the only genuine interest in his life. By this I mean one that was not

31. Maser, in order to make the most of Hitler's talent as a painter, explains Hitler's method of copying thus: 'Hitler copied not because he lacked talent . . . but because he was too lazy to go out and paint' (W. Maser, 1971). This statement is an example of Maser's tendency to elevate Hitler's stature, especially since it is so obviously wrong – in one respect at least: the one activity Hitler *did* like was to *go out*, albeit to walk the streets. Another example of Maser's bias in favour of Hitler's painting talent is his statement that Dr Bloch (the Jewish physician who treated Hitler's mother), in keeping some watercolours that Hitler had given him, 'certainly did not keep [them] until after 1938 because Adolf and Klara Hitler had been patients until 1907'. Maser thus implies that the fact that the doctor kept the paintings indicates that the paintings had artistic value. But why should the doctor not have kept them just because the Hitlers had once been his patients? He would not have been the first physician to keep mementos expressing the gratitude of his patients – and after 1933 any Hitler memento was certainly a great asset for a man in Bloch's situation.

32. I am indebted to Mr Speer for showing me these sketches; they offer a key to the nature of Hitler's pedantic, lifeless character.

primarily narcissistic, that was not a manifestation of destructiveness, that was not faked. It is, of course, not easy to judge how authentic are the interests of a man who is so accustomed to lie about himself. Yet I believe there are sufficient data to demonstrate the genuineness of his architectural interests. The most important fact in this regard is Hitler's unending enthusiasm for discussing architectural plans, reported so vividly by Speer; one can see that here he was motivated by a real interest in something other than himself. He was not lecturing but asking questions and engaging in a real discussion. I believe that in his interest in architecture the power-driven, feelingless, destructive man for once came to life, even though every time, the total impact of his character left Speer exhausted. I do not mean to say that Hitler was a changed man when he talked about architecture, but that it was the one situation when the 'monster' was closest to being human.

These considerations do not imply that Hitler was right in his claim that external circumstances forced him to give up his plan to become an architect. We have seen that he would have had to do relatively little to achieve this aim, but did not make the effort because he was more driven by his craving for omnipotence and destruction than stimulated by his love for architecture. The assumption of the genuineness of his architectural interest does not negate the megalomanic quality of his concern or his poor taste. As Speer remarks, his preference was for the neo-baroque of the eighties and nineties, and reverted to its decadent forms made popular by Kaiser Wilhelm II. That his taste was as poor in architecture as in other fields is not surprising. Taste cannot be separated from character; a brutal, primitive, unfeeling person like Hitler, blind to everything except what could be of use to him, can hardly fail to have poor taste. Yet I think it is important to note that Hitler's interest in architecture was the one constructive element in his character – perhaps the one bridge that linked him with life.

Veneer

The understanding of Hitler's personality requires the recognition that the veneer covering the substance of this restlessly driven man was that of an amiable, courteous, controlled, almost shy man. He was especially courteous to women, never failing to bring or send them flowers on the proper occasions; he offered them cookies and tea; he would not sit until his secretaries had taken a chair. Schramm, in his introduction to the *Table Talks*, gives a vivid picture of the effect Hitler had on his environment: 'The circle of intimates was under the impression that the "boss" was much concerned with the wellbeing of those around him, participating in their joys and woes. Thus, for instance, that he pondered before their birthdays what gift would cause special pleasure . . .' Dr H. Picker, the young man who until he joined the group at Hitler's table

had experienced Hitler only from afar as the 'statesman', was strongly impressed by the humanness that Hitler radiated within his narrow circle, the benevolence he showed to the younger ones, his readiness to laugh . . . Yes, in his circle Hitler, the man without family or friends, was a good 'comrade' – and he had learned what comradeship means in the First World War, retaining this knowledge in later life. The people around Hitler also knew how intensely he reacted to beautiful and well-dressed women. They knew his fondness for children; they observed how attached he was to his dogs and how relaxed he became when he could study the behaviour of these animals. (H. Picker, 1965)

Hitler could play this role of the friendly, amiable, kind, considerate man very well; not only because he was an excellent actor but also because he liked the role. It was valuable for him to deceive his closest circle about the depth of his own destructiveness and, most of all, to deceive himself.[33]

Who can know whether there was any genuine element of

33. Schramm notes that Hitler made no mention during the *Table Talks* of any of the horrible orders he gave during the period in which these table conversations took place.

kindness or goodwill in Hitler's behaviour? We should assume there was, because there are few people in whom all traces of kindness and affection are missing. But the rest of what we have seen of his character makes us assume that most of this kindness was only a veneer. Hitler's concern for birthdays, for instance, contrasted with his behaviour towards Eva Braun, whom he did not intend to impress as a gentleman. As for Hitler's laughter – apparently Picker was not sensitive enough to notice its particular quality. Regarding Hitler's comradely attitude in the war, as recorded by Picker – Hanfstaengl quotes a report written by Hitler's superior officer stating that, although Hitler was an eager and dutiful soldier, 'He has been excluded from further promotion because of his arrogant attitude towards his comrades and because of his spit-licking subservience towards his superiors' (E. Hanfstaengl, 1970). As for his love for children – a trait sported by most politicians – Speer doubts whether it was genuine.[34] Concerning his affection for dogs – Schramm reveals the nature of this affection: he writes that Hitler had ordered the construction of an obstacle track in his headquarters, similar to those used for the training of the infantry, in which the dogs had to prove their courage as well as intelligence. Schramm was shown by the non-commissioned officer who took care of the dogs how fast they could follow the alternating commands of 'up' and 'down'. Schramm comments: 'I had the impression that I was observing a machine and not a dog, and wondered whether Hitler, in training the dogs, was not dominated by the intention to extinguish the will in this animal' (H. Picker, 1965).

Schramm writes that Hitler had two faces: the friendly one, and the horrifying one – and that both were genuine. Often the same idea is expressed when people speak of a Jekyll-and-Hyde personality, implying that both are genuine. But this view is psychologically untenable, especially since Freud. The real division is between the unconscious

34. A. Speer, personal communication.

core of the character structure and the role a person plays, including rationalizations, compensations, and other defences that cover up the underlying reality. Even apart from Freud, this view is often dangerously naïve. Who has not met people who not only deceive with words – which is minor – but with their whole behaviour, their manner, their tone of voice, and their gestures? Many individuals are skilful enough to give a reasonably good performance of the character they pretend to be; they are so skilful in playing a role that they sometimes deceive even people who are by no means psychologically naïve. Lacking any centre within himself, any genuine principles, values, or convictions, Hitler could 'play' the kindly gentleman and not be aware himself at the moment that it was a role.

Hitler liked this role, not only in order to deceive; his liking for it was related to his social background. I do not refer so much to the fact that his father was an illegitimate child and that his mother was uneducated, but to his family's peculiar social situation. Partly because of his job, partly for personal reasons, his father lived with his family at various times in five different towns. Besides this, his role as an imperial customs official separated him somewhat from the local middle class socially, although in terms of income and social position he was their equal. Thus the Hitler family was never fully integrated into the middle class society in the various places where they lived. Besides, even though they were well off, they were culturally on the lower level of bourgeois life. The father came from a low social background, was interested only in politics and bees, and spent much of his free time at the tavern; his mother was uneducated and only interested in her family. As an ambitious, vain young man, Hitler must have felt socially insecure, and wanted to be counted among the more prosperous and affluent levels of the middle class. Even in Linz he had a yearning for elegant clothes, and on his walks he was meticulously clothed and carried a cane. Maser reports that in Munich Hitler had a dress suit (white tie) and that his suits were always neat and never frayed. Later, the uniform took care of the problem of clothes, but his manners were meant to be those of a member of a well-brought-up bourgeois. The flowers, his taste in the decoration of his house, and his general demeanour revealed the somewhat forced attempt to prove that he had 'arrived'. Hitler was the true *bourgeois-gentilhomme*; the *nouveau riche*, eager to show that he is a gentleman.[35] He hated the lower classes because he had to prove that he did not belong to them. Hitler was an up-rooted man; not so much because he was an Austrian posing as a German, but because he was not rooted in any social class. He did not belong to the working class; neither did he belong to the bourgeoisie. He was a loner socially, not only psychologically. The only roots he could experience were the most archaic – those of race and blood.

Hitler's admiration for the upper classes was by no means a rare phenomenon; we find the same attitude – usually deeply repressed – among such socialist leaders of the same period as Ramsay MacDonald, for example. Such men came from the lower middle class, and their deep craving was to be 'received' by the upper class, the industrialists, and the generals. Hitler was less humble; he wanted to force those who wielded real power to share it with him, and in a more formal sense even, that they should obey him. Hitler, the rebel, the leader of a *workers'* party was enamoured with the rich and their style of life, in spite of his many utterances against them before he came to power. Hitler, the kind considerate man, was a role; his wish to 'belong' and to be a 'gentleman' was real. Hitler was in a way a grotesque figure: a man driven by the passion to destroy, a man without compassion, a volcano of archaic passions – trying to appear a well-bred, considerate, even harmless gentleman. No wonder that he could deceive many who for any number of reasons did not mind being deceived.

35. Chaplin's Monsieur Verdoux, the kind, middle class, husband who makes a living by murdering wealthy women, offers a certain parallel.

A grotesque symbol of the blend between the correct bourgeois and the murderer is his marriage to Eva Braun in the bunker, shortly before their deaths. Formal marriage was the highest distinction Hitler, the *petit bourgeois* could confer upon his mistress and the highest achievement for her, whose values were entirely the traditional, bourgeois norms. Everything was very correct; the proper civil servant authorized to perform a marriage ceremony had to be found; this took many hours, because it was difficult to locate a justice of the peace in that small part of Berlin not yet occupied by the Soviet troops. But the Supreme Leader did not feel he could change the rules of this bureaucratic procedure by appointing somebody among those present a justice of the peace. It was necessary to wait for hours until the proper official arrived. The marriage ceremony was properly performed, champagne was served. Hitler the 'gentleman' had acted correctly – making it clear, however, that only imminent death could move him to legitimize his relationship to his mistress. (With a modicum of consideration, not to speak of affection, he could have made this gesture some weeks earlier.) Hitler and the killer functioned as before. Even his marriage to Eva did not hinder him from having her brother-in-law executed for alleged disloyalty. Shortly before, he had his physician, Dr Karl Brandt, loyal to him since 1934, sentenced to death by a court martial that consisted of Goebbels, SS General Berger, and the Youth Leader, Axmann, with Hitler acting as both 'prosecutor' and supreme authority. The reason for the death sentence, on which Hitler insisted, was that Brandt had left his family in Thuringia to be 'rolled over by the Americans' rather than bring them to Obersalzberg; the suspicion was that Brandt was using his wife as a courier to the Americans. (Brandt's life was saved by Himmler who at that time was trying to ingratiate himself with the Americans.)

Regardless of the personal and social reasons for Hitler's veneer it was also an important asset. It helped him to deceive those industrial, military, and nationalist political leaders of Germany, as well as many politicians of foreign countries who might have been repelled by his brutality and destructiveness. To be sure, many saw through his façade, but many more did not, and thus a favourable climate was created that permitted Hitler to follow his path of destruction.

Defects of Will and Realism

Hitler himself considered his greatest asset to be his unbending will. Whether he was right depends on what one means by 'will'. Looking at his career, a first glance would seem to indicate that he was, indeed, a man of extraordinary willpower. It was his aim to be great, and despite that he started out as a nobody, within only twenty years he had realized his aims beyond anything even he could have dreamed of. Does it not require an extraordinary will to achieve such an aim?

This notion becomes questionable, however, if we recall how little will-power Hitler showed as a child and as a youth. We have seen that he was a loafer, undisciplined, and unwilling to make any effort. This is not what we would expect to find in a person equipped with strong willpower. The fact is that what Hitler called his 'will' were his passions which fired him on and relentlessly drove him to seek their realization. His will was as boundless and raw as that of a six-year-old child, as Speer said. A six-year-old who makes no compromise and throws a tantrum when he is frustrated may be said to have a strong 'will', but it would be more correct to say that he is driven by his impulses and is incapable of accepting frustration. When Hitler saw no opportunity to achieve his aim, he merely marked time, loafed and did just enough to make a living. In the years until the First World War he had not the slightest idea, nor any semblance of a plan to achieve his aim. Had it not been for the political situation after the war, he would probably have continued to drift, maybe getting minor jobs, although it would have been very difficult for him due to his lack of discipline. His best occupational chance might have been as a salesman of a commodity of questionable value whose success depends mainly on forceful persuasion. But his waiting was rewarded; his fantastic desires and his great talent for persuasion became linked with social and political reality. The reactionary army officers hired him not only to spy on other soldiers, but to convert them to reactionary, militaristic ideas. From these small beginnings Hitler became the super-salesman of a commodity for which there was much demand on the part of disappointed and frustrated 'little men' and in whose sale first the army and then other powerful groups were vitally interested – a nationalist, anti-Communist, militarist ideology. When he had proved his success in this job, considerable sectors among German bankers and industrialists supported him financially to such an extent that he was able to seize power.

The weakness of Hitler's will shows in his hesitancy and doubt when he had to make a decision, a fact on which many observers have commented. He had the tendency, to be found among many people who lack a strong will, to let events come to a point where he is spared the need to make a decision because the decision is forced upon him; but it does not do this by itself. Hitler stoked the fire, closed more and more avenues of retreat, brought the whole situation to a boiling point where he would *have* to act as he did. With his self-deceptive technique he spared himself the difficulty of having to decide. His 'decision' was actually submission to an inescapable *fait accompli*, but one of his own doing. Just to give one example: it seems doubtful that he originally wanted to conquer Poland, for whose reactionary leader, Colonel Beck, he had great sympathy. But when Beck rejected Hitler's relatively mild demands, the latter got angry and heated up the situation with Poland to a point that left no other outcome but war.

Once Hitler had decided on a course, he pursued it with unwavering determination and with what one *might* call an

'iron will' to win. In order to understand this seeming contradiction we must examine, however briefly, the concept
of will. First, it is useful to distinguish between 'rational
will' and 'irrational will'. By rational will I understand the
energetic effort to reach a rationally desirable aim; this requires realism, discipline, patience, and the overcoming of
self-indulgence. By irrational will I mean a passionate striving, fed by the energy of irrational passions that lacks the
qualities needed for rational will.[36] Irrational will is like a
river bursting a dam; it is powerful, but man is not the
master of this will; he is driven by it, forced by it, its slave.
Hitler's will was, indeed, strong, if we understand it as irrational will. But his rational will was weak.

In addition to the weakness of his will, another quality
tended to undo what Hitler's other gifts had helped him to
achieve: his defective sense of reality. Hitler's poor contact
with reality, as we have seen, as already evident in his
absorption in boys' war games up to the age of sixteen. This
fantasy world was much more real to him than the real
world. His plan to be an artist had little connection with
reality – it was mainly a daydream – and his activity as a
commercial artist in no way corresponded to his vision.
People were not fully real to him, either; they were all
instruments; he remained without contact even though he
was often a shrewd judge.[37] Yet while Hitler did not fully
perceive reality, neither did he live exclusively in a world of
fantasy. His was a world with a particular blend between

36. cf. the discussion on rational and irrational passions in Chapter 10.
37. Speer expresses Hitler's lack of contact with reality in a slightly different, very intuitive formulation: 'There was actually something insub-
stantial about him. But this was perhaps a permanent quality he had. In
retrospect I sometimes ask myself whether this intangibility, this insub-
stantiality, had not characterized him from early youth up to the moment of his suicide. It sometimes seems to me that his seizures of violence
could come upon him all the more strongly because there were no human
emotions in him to oppose them. He simply could not let anyone approach his inner being because that core was lifeless, empty' (A. Speer,
1970).

reality and fantasy in which nothing was entirely real and nothing was entirely unreal. In some instances, particularly in his insights into the motivations of his opponents, he had a remarkable appreciation of reality. He was not impressed by what people *said*, but by what he recognized as their real – implicit or not even fully conscious – motivations. A good example is his estimate of British-French political beha- viour. It can be said that in a certain sense Hitler's victory began with the unwillingness of Great Britain to follow the decision of the League of Nations in regard to an effective blockade of Italy after Mussolini began his attack against Ethiopia, 1935–6. Under all kinds of subterfuges Italy con- tinued to receive oil, which was vitally necessary for con- ducting the war, while Ethiopia had the greatest difficulty even in obtaining arms from abroad. The next event that emboldened Hitler was the handling of the Spanish Civil War, 1936–9. Great Britain prevented the constitutional government of Spain from importing arms for its defence, and the French government, under the Socialist, Blum, did not dare to act without Great Britain's approval. However, the committee of democratic powers that was charged with enforcing non-intervention in Spain did nothing to prevent Hitler or Mussolini from continuing their military interven- tion in favour of Franco.[38] The next event was the failure of the French and the British to resist Hitler's occupation of the demilitarized Rhineland in 1936, at a time when the German army was completely unprepared for war. (Hitler remarked in the *Table Talks* [H. Picker, 1965] that if France had had a real statesman at the time, the French would have resisted his occupation of the Rhineland.) The last step, Chamberlain's visit to beg Hitler for moderation, was

38. Sir A. Cadogan, Permanent Under-Secretary in the British Foreign Office, a Conservative who helped to shape British policy at that time, gives an excellent and detailed picture of the handling of the Spanish Civil War that was largely motivated by the Conservatives' sympathy with Mussolini and Hitler, their inclination to permit Hitler to attack the Soviet Union, and their own incapacity to appreciate Hitler's inten- tions (Sir A. Cadogan, 1972).

hardly necessary to confirm Hitler's conviction that Great Britain and France were unwilling to act upon their words. In this instance Hitler showed the realistic insight into human behaviour of a shrewd horse trader who recognizes when the other party is bluffing. What Hitler did not see was the wider *political* and economic reality. He failed to appreciate Great Britain's traditional interest in the balance of power on the Continent; he did not recognize that Chamberlain and his circle did not represent the political interests of all the Conservatives, much less public opinion among the entire British population. He relied on the opinion of Joachim von Ribbentrop, a man with a facile, but very superficial intelligence, completely unprepared to understand the political, economic, and social intricacies of the British system.

The same failure of realistic judgement is shown in his lack of any real knowledge about the United States and in his failure to attempt to inform himself. All relevant reports agree that he was content with superficial ideas, such as that the Americans were too soft to be good soldiers, that America was run by the Jews, that the American government would not dare to enter the war because the country was so full of conflicts that a revolution might break out.

Hitler's strategy shows an equal lack of full appreciation of reality and objectivity. In his richly documented and penetrating analysis, P. E. Schramm (1965) points out this defect in Hitler's strategic approach. Schramm does not try to minimize Hitler's merits as a strategist, and he mentions three instances (according to General A. Jodl) of bold and imaginative plans. But from 1942 onward, Hitler's judgement in military matters was very defective. He did the same as he had done with his reading material; he picked out those data in military reports that fitted in with his plans and paid no attention to those that would have made him question them. His orders not to retreat which led to the catastrophe of Stalingrad and heavy losses of soldiers at many other parts of the front, is characterized by

Schramm as 'increasingly senseless'. His plans for the last
offensive attack in the Ardennes neglected to take into
account important factors in the actual tactical situation.
Schramm notes that Hitler's strategy was a 'prestige' and
'propaganda' strategy. Lack of realism made him fail to
fully recognize that warfare and propaganda are determined by different laws and principals. Hitler's estrange-
ment from reality becomes grotesquely manifest when, on
24 April 1945, two days before his suicide, after he had
already planned his end, he issued an order that 'fundamental decisions have to be brought to the attention of the
Führer thirty-six hours before [their execution]' (P. E.
Schramm, 1965).

The blending of Hitler's defective will with his defective
sense of reality leads to the question whether he really had
the will to win or whether unconsciously, and in spite of all
apparent efforts to the contrary, his course was set towards
catastrophe. Several very sensitive observers have expressed
the strong suspicion that the latter might have been the case.
C. Burckhardt, one of the keenest observers of Hitler, writes:
'It is not altogether far-fetched to assume that the insatiable
hater operating within him [Hitler] was connected in
unconscious parts of his being with the veiled but always
present certainty that the end would be marked by the most
horrible failure and by personal extinction, as, in fact,
happened in the Reichschancellery on 30 April 1945'
(C. Burckhardt, 1965). Speer reports that in the years
before the war when Hitler discussed his architectural plans
with such enthusiasm, he dimly sensed that Hitler did not
really believe in their realization; this was not a clear
conviction, but a kind of intuitive feeling he had.[39] J. Brosse
expresses the same idea; he raises the question whether
Hitler ever believed in final victory, or even really desired it
(J. Brosse, 1972). On the basis of my analysis of Hitler I have
arrived at a similar conclusion. I question whether a man
with such intense and all-absorbing destructiveness could

39. A. Speer, personal communication.

in the depth of his being really have wanted the constructive work that victory would have implied. Of course, Burckhardt, Speer, Brosse, and I are not describing the conscious part of Hitler's mind. The assumption that he neither believed in nor wanted to realize his artistic and political dreams refers to what one would have to consider as being entirely unconscious; without the concept of unconscious motivations the statement that Hitler might not have wanted to win sounds absurd.[40]

Hitler was a gambler; he gambled with the lives of all Germans as well as with his own life. When the game was up and he had lost, there was not even too much reason for regret. He had had what he had always wanted: power and the satisfaction of his hate and of his lust for destruction. His defeat could not take this satisfaction from him. The megalomaniac and destroyer had not really lost. Those who lost were the millions of human beings – Germans, members of other nations and of racial minorities – for whom death in battle was the mildest form of suffering. Since Hitler was entirely without compassion for anyone, their suffering caused him no pain or remorse.

In analysing Hitler we have found a number of severely pathological traits: we hypothesized the presence of a semi-autistic streak in the child; we found extreme narcissism, lack of contact with others, flaws in his perception of reality, intense necrophilia. One can legitimately assume the presence of a psychotic, perhaps schizophrenic streak in him. But does this mean that Hitler was a 'madman', that he suffered from a psychosis or from paranoia, as it has been sometimes said? The answer, I believe, is in the negative. In spite of the mad streak in Hitler he was sane enough to pursue his aims purposefully and – for a while – successfully. With all the errors in judgement he made due to his

40. There is a great deal of clinical material that demonstrates that people can strive for their own destruction, although their conscious aim is exactly the opposite. Not only psychoanalysis but also great drama offer such material.

narcissism and his destructiveness, it cannot be denied that he was a demagogue and a politician of outstanding skill who at no point showed frankly psychotic reactions. Even in his last days, when he was a physically and mentally broken man, he remained controlled. As to his paranoid tendencies, his suspiciousness was realistically sufficiently well founded – as various plots against him have demonstrated – that one can hardly call it a manifestation of paranoia. Certainly, had Hitler been a defendant in a court of justice, even in a most impartial one, a plea of insanity would have had no chance. Yet although in conventional terms Hitler was not a psychotic man, in dynamic, interpersonal terms he was a very sick man. The whole question whether Hitler can be considered insane is beset by the difficulty that has been discussed earlier about the questionable value of psychiatric labels; statements about the difference between a psychotic streak and a full-fledged psychosis may have their value in a court of justice for deciding whether a person should be sent to prison or to a mental hospital, but in the last analysis what we are dealing with are interpersonal processes that defy such labels. But clinical analysis must not be used to obscure the *moral* problem of evil. Just as there are evil and benign 'sane' men, there are evil madmen and benign madmen. Evilness must be seen for what it is, and moral judgement is not suspended by clinical diagnosis. But even the most evil man is human and calls for our compassion.

Concluding this analysis of Hitler's character a few words may be useful to indicate the purpose of incorporating this lengthy material, as well as that about Himmler, in this study. Aside from the obvious theoretical aim of clarifying the concept of sadism and necrophilia by presenting clinical illustrations, I had still another aim: that of pointing to the main fallacy which prevents people from recognizing potential Hitlers before they have shown their true faces. This fallacy lies in the belief that a thoroughly destructive and evil man must be a devil – and look his part; that he must be devoid of any positive quality; that he must bear the sign of Cain so visibly that everyone can recognize his destructiveness from afar. Such devils exist, but they are rare. As I indicated earlier, much more often the intensely destructive person will show a front of kindliness; courtesy; love of family, of children, of animals; he will speak of his ideals and good intentions. But not only this. There is hardly a man who is utterly devoid of any kindness, of any good intention. If he were, he would be on the verge of insanity, except congenital 'moral idiots'. *Hence, as long as one believes that the evil man wears horns, one will not discover an evil man.*

The naïve assumption that an evil man is easily recognizable results in a great danger: one fails to recognize evil men before they have begun their work of destruction. I believe that the majority of people do not have the intensely destructive character of a Hitler. But even if one would estimate that such persons formed 10 per cent of our population, there are enough of them to be very dangerous if they attain influence and power. To be sure, not every destroyer would become a Hitler, because he would lack Hitler's talents; he might only become an efficient member of the SS. But on the other hand, Hitler was no genius, and his talents were not unique. What was unique was the socio-political situation in which he could rise; there are probably hundreds of Hitlers among us who would come forth if their historical hour arrived.

To analyse a figure like Hitler with objectivity and without passion is not only dictated by scientific conscience but also because it is the condition of learning an important lesson for the present and the future. Any analysis that would distort Hitler's picture by depriving him of his humanity would only intensify the tendency to be blind to the potential Hitlers unless they wear horns.

Epilogue:
On the Ambiguity of Hope

In this study I have tried to demonstrate that prehistorical man, living in bands as hunter and food gatherer, was characterized by a minimum of destructiveness and an optimum of cooperation and sharing, and that only with the increasing productivity and division of labour, the formation of a large surplus, and the building of states with hierarchies and élites, large-scale destructiveness and cruelty came into existence and grew as civilization and the role of power grew.

Has this study contributed valid arguments in favour of the thesis that aggression and destructiveness can once again assume a minimal role in the fabric of human motivations? I believe it has, and I hope that many of my readers do too.

As far as aggression is *biologically* given in man's genes, it is not spontaneous, but a defence against threats to man's vital interests, that of his growth and his and the species' survival. This defensive aggression was relatively small under certain primitive conditions – when no man was much of a threat to another. Man has gone through an extraordinary development since then. It is legitimate to imagine that man will complete the full circle and construct a society in which no one is threatened: not the child by the parent; not the parent by the superior; no social class by another; no nation by a super-power. To achieve this aim is tremendously difficult for economic, political, cultural and psychological reasons – and the added difficulty that the nations of the world worship idols – and different idols – and thus do not understand each other, even though they understand each other's languages. To ignore these difficulties is folly; but the empirical study of all data shows that a real possibility exists to build such a world in a foreseeable future if the political and psychological road-blocks are removed.

The *malignant* forms of aggression, on the other hand – sadism and necrophilia – are *not* innate; hence, they can be substantially reduced when the socio-economic conditions are replaced by conditions that are favourable to the full development of man's genuine needs and capacities; to the development of human self-activity and man's creative power as its own end. Exploitation and manipulation produce boredom and triviality; they cripple man, and all factors that make man into a psychic cripple turn him also into a sadist or a destroyer.

This position will be characterized by some as 'over-optimistic', 'utopian', or 'unrealistic'. In order to appreciate the merits of such criticism a discussion of the concept of the ambiguity of hope and of the nature of optimism and pessimism seems called for.

Assume that I am planning a week-end trip to the country and it is doubtful that the weather will be fine. I may say 'I'm optimistic' as far as the weather is concerned. But if my child is gravely sick and his life hangs in the balance, to say 'I'm optimistic' would seem strange to sensitive ears, because in this context the expression sounds detached and distant. Yet I could not very well say, 'I am *convinced* my child will live,' because, under the circumstances, I have no realistic basis for being convinced.

What, then, could I say?

The most adequate words would perhaps be: 'I have faith my child will live.' But 'faith', because of its theological implications, is not a word for today. Yet it is the best we have, because faith implies an extremely important element: my ardent, intense wish for my child to live, hence my doing everything possible to bring about his recovery. I am not just an observer, separate from my child, as I am in the case of being 'optimistic'. I am part of the situation that I observe; I am *engaged*; my child about whom I, the 'subject', make a prognostic statement is not an 'object'; my faith is rooted in my relatedness to my child; it is a blend of knowledge and of participation. This is true, of course, only if by faith is meant 'rational faith' (E. Fromm, 1947), which is based on the clear awareness of all relevant data, and not, like 'irrational faith', an illusion based on our desires.

Optimism is an alienated form of faith, pessimism an alienated form of despair. If one truly responds to man and his future, i.e., concernedly and 'responsibly', one can respond only by faith or by despair. Rational faith as well as rational despair are based on the most thorough, critical knowledge of all the factors that are relevant for the survival of man. The basis of rational faith in man is the presence of a real possibility for his salvation; the basis for rational despair would be the knowledge that no such possibility can be seen.

One point needs to be emphasized in this context. Most people are quite ready to denounce faith in man's improvement as unrealistic; but they do not recognize that despair is often just as unrealistic. It is easy to say: 'Man has always been a killer.' But the statement nevertheless is not correct, for it neglects to take into account the intricacies of the history of destructiveness. It is equally easy to say, 'The desire to exploit others is just human nature'; but again, the statement neglects (or distorts) the facts. In brief, the statement, 'Human nature is evil,' is not a bit more realistic than the statement, 'Human nature is good.' But the first statement is much easier to make; anyone who wants to prove man's evilness finds followers most readily, for he offers everybody an alibi for his own sins – and seemingly risks nothing. Yet the spreading of irrational despair is in itself destructive, as all untruth is; it discourages and confuses. Preaching irrational faith or announcing false Messiahs is hardly less destructive – it seduces and then paralyses.

The attitude of the majority is neither that of faith nor

that of despair, but, unfortunately, that of complete indifference to the future of man. With those who are not entirely indifferent, the attitude is that of 'optimism' or of 'pessimism'. The optimists are the believers in the dogma of the continuous march of 'progress'. They are accustomed to identifying human achievement with technical achievement, human freedom with freedom *from* direct coercion and the consumer's freedom *to* choose between many allegedly different commodities. The dignity, cooperativeness, kindness of the primitive do not impress them; technical achievement, wealth, toughness do. Centuries of rule over technically backward people of different colour have left their stamp on the optimists' minds. How could a 'savage' be human and equal, not to speak of superior, to the men who can fly to the moon – or by pushing a button, destroy millions of living beings?

The optimists live well enough, at least for the moment, and they can afford to be 'optimists'. Or at least that is what they think because they are so alienated that even the threat to the future of their grandchildren does not genuinely affect them.

The 'pessimists' are really not very different from the optimists. They live just as comfortably and are just as little engaged. The fate of humanity is as little their concern as it is the optimists'. They do not feel despair; if they did, they would not, and could not, live as contentedly as they do. And while their pessimism functions largely to protect the pessimists from any inner demand to do something, by projecting the idea that *nothing can be done*, the optimists defend themselves against the same inner demand by persuading themselves that everything is moving in the right direction anyway, so *nothing needs to be done*.

The position taken in this book is one of rational faith in man's capacity to extricate himself from what seems the fatal web of circumstances that he has created. It is the position of those who are neither 'optimists' nor 'pessimists', but radicals who have rational faith in man's capacity to avoid the ultimate catastrophe. This humanist radicalism goes to the roots, and thus to the causes; it seeks to liberate man from the chains of illusions; it postulates that fundamental changes are necessary, not only in our economic and political structure but also in our values, in our concept of man's aims, and in our personal conduct.

To have faith means to dare, to think the unthinkable, yet to act within the limits of the realistically possible; it is the paradoxical hope to expect the Messiah every day, yet not to lose heart when he has not come at the appointed hour. This hope is not passive and it is not patient; on the contrary, it is impatient and active, looking for every possibility of action within the realm of real possibilities. Least of all is it passive as far as the growth and the liberation of one's own person are concerned. To be sure, there are severe limitations to personal development determined by the social structure. But those alleged radicals who counsel that no personal change is possible or even desirable within present-day society use their revolutionary ideology as an excuse for their personal resistance to inner change.

The situation of mankind today is too serious to permit us to listen to the demagogues – least of all demagogues who are attracted to destruction – or even to the leaders who use only their brains and whose hearts have hardened. Critical and radical thought will only bear fruit when it is blended with the most precious quality man is endowed with – the love of life.

freedom to avoid ... ultimate sanctions. This means the
individuals ... to take ... and ties to the community, and
to behave ... in the social ... If permitted
their fundamental changes are necessary, ... unit. In our
... and political science ... in only various ...
... open ... in ... and personal conduct.

... Thus, to present conform ... the traditional, yet
... to act within the limits of the socially possible, is the
... provident hope to ... our ... the repressive
... has frozen not ... but some of ... and them. This
... hope is ... and ... is ... to the ... in its
... and new ... is ... for any ... readiness of action
within the ... of ... possible ... I use all its positive
... to act ... and the ... of one's own powers
are released. To be sure, these are ... solutions, to
... the depressant demanded ... for the ... structure,
therefore, all policies ... who cannot find ... problem,
... a problem on even ... while specifically
observing their ... ideological ... to excuse further
... reluctance to those changes.

The demand ... with ... reduce ... to the two
to ... to the ... consists of all of those ... who
are ... forced to ... whatever given to the ... who are
... themselves, and who are ... being ... unified
and reacted to right with only been ... with a ... is blended
with the inner product ... with ... freedom ... with ... the
... result ...

Appendix:
Freud's Theory of Aggressiveness
and Destructiveness

1

The Evolution of Freud's Concept of Aggressiveness and Destructiveness

Perhaps the most remarkable element in Freud's study of aggression is that until 1920 he paid hardly any attention to human aggressivity and destructiveness. He himself expressed his bewilderment over this fact many years later in *Civilization and Its Discontents* (1930): 'But I can no longer understand how we can have overlooked the ubiquity of non-erotic aggressivity and destructiveness and can have failed to give it its due place in our interpretation of life' (S. Freud, 1930).

In order to understand this peculiar blind spot, it will be helpful to put ourselves into the mood of the European middle classes at the time before the First World War. There had been no major war since 1871. The bourgeoisie was progressing steadily, both politically and socially, and the sharp antagonism between the classes was becoming smaller, due to the steady improvements in the situation of the working class. The world seemed peaceful and becoming ever more civilized, especially when one did not pay much attention to the greater part of the human race living in Asia, Africa, and South America under conditions of utter poverty and degradation. Human destructiveness seemed to be a factor that had played a role in the Dark Ages and during many earlier centuries, but had now been replaced by reason and goodwill. The psychological problems that were being uncovered were those arising from the over-strict moral code of the middle class, and Freud was so impressed with evidence of the damaging results of sexual repression that he simply failed to attach importance to the problem of aggressiveness, until it could not be overlooked any longer due to the First World War. This war constitutes the dividing line within the development of Freud's theory of aggressivity.

In the *Three Essays on the Theory of Sexuality* (1905) Freud considered aggressiveness to be one of the 'component instincts' of the sexual instinct. He wrote: 'Thus sadism would correspond to an aggressive component of the sexual instinct which has become independent and exaggerated and, by displacement, has usurped the leading position' (S. Freud, 1905).[1]

However, as so often with Freud, quite in contrast to the main line of his theory, he had a thought that was to remain dormant until much later. In Section 4 of the *Three Essays* he wrote: 'It may be assumed that the impulses of cruelty arise from sources which are in fact *independent of sexuality*, but may become united with it at an early stage' (S. Freud, 1905; italics added).

But in spite of this remark, four years later Freud stated very explicitly in the story of Little Hans in his *Analysis of a Phobia in a Five-Year-Old Boy*: 'I cannot bring myself to assume the existence of a special aggressive instinct alongside of the familiar instincts of self-preservation and of sex, and on an equal footing with them' (S. Freud, 1909). One can recognize in this formulation a certain hesitancy in Freud's statement. 'I cannot bring myself to assume' is not quite as strong as a simple and complete negation would be, and the additional qualification 'on an equal footing' seems to leave the possibility that there could be an independent aggressiveness if it were not on an equal footing.

In *Instincts and Their Vicissitudes* (1915) Freud continued

1. For the evolution of Freud's theory of aggression, cf. also J. Strachey's summary in the editor's Introduction to *Civilization and Its Discontents* (Freud, 1930).

both lines of thought – that of destructiveness as a component of the sexual instinct, and as a force independent of sexuality:

Preliminary stages of love emerge as provisional sexual aims while the sexual instincts are passing through their complicated development. As the first of these aims we recognize the phase of incorporating or devouring – a type of love which is consistent with abolishing the object's separate existence and which may therefore be described as ambivalent. At the higher stage of the pregenital sadistic-anal organization, the striving for the object appears in the form of an urge for mastery, to which injury or annihilation of the object is a matter of indifference. Love in this form and at this preliminary stage is hardly to be distinguished from hate in its attitude towards the object. Not until the gential organization is established does love become the opposite of hate. (S. Freud, 1915)

But in this same paper Freud also takes up the other position that he had expressed in the *Three Essays* – although altered in 1915 – namely, that of an aggressiveness *independent* from the sexual instinct. This alternative hypothesis assumes that the ego instincts are the source of aggressiveness. Freud wrote:

Hate, as a relation to objects, is older than love. *It derives from the narcissistic ego's primordial repudiation of the external world*[2] with its outpouring of stimuli. As an expression of the reaction of unpleasure evoked by objects, *it always remains in an intimate relation with the self-preservative instincts*; so that sexual and ego-instincts can readily develop an antithesis which repeats that of love and hate. When the ego-instincts dominate the sexual function, as is the case at the stage of the sadistic-anal organization, they impart the qualities of hate to the instinctual aim as well. (S. Freud, 1915; italics added)

Here Freud assumes that hate is older than love and that it is rooted in the ego instincts, or instincts of self-preserva-

2. In this statement we find an expression of Freud's general axiom of tension reduction as the fundamental law of nervous functioning. See also the detailed discussion of this axiom at the end of this Appendix.

tion, which first of all repudiate the 'stream of stimuli' flowing from the outside world and are the antithesis to the sexual impulses. It should be mentioned in passing how important this position is for Freud's whole model of man. The infant is seen as primarily repudiating stimuli and hating the world for its intrusion. This position is contrary to the one supported by a good deal of clinical evidence as it has emerged recently, showing that man, and even an infant a few days after birth, is eager for stimuli, needs them, does not always hate the world for its intrusion.

Freud even goes a step further in his formulation about hate in the same paper:

> The ego hates, abhors and pursues with intent to destroy all objects which are a source of unpleasurable feeling for it, without taking into account whether they mean a frustration of sexual satisfaction or of the satisfaction of self-preservative needs. Indeed it may be asserted that *the true prototypes of the relation of hate are derived not from sexual life, but from the ego's struggle to preserve and maintain itself.* (S. Freud, 1915; italics added)

With the paper on *Instincts and Their Vicissitudes* (1915) the first phase of Freud's thinking about destructiveness ends. We saw that he followed two concepts simultaneously: aggressiveness as a part of the sexual drive (oral and anal sadism), and aggressiveness as being independent from the sexual instinct, as a quality of the ego instincts which oppose and hate the intrusion of outside stimuli and obstacles to the satisfaction of sexual needs and those for self-preservation.

In 1920, with *Beyond the Pleasure Principle* Freud begins a fundamental revision of his whole theory of instincts. In this work Freud attributed to the 'compulsion to repeat' the characteristics of an instinct; here, too, he postulated for the first time the new dichotomy of Eros and the death instinct, the nature of which he discussed in greater detail in *The Ego and the Id* (1923) and in his further writings. This new dichotomy of life (Eros) and death instinct(s)[3] takes the

3. In the further development of this concept Freud tends to speak more of *a* life instinct (Eros) and *a* death instinct.

place of the original dichotomy between ego and sexual instincts. Though Freud attempts to identify Eros with libido, the new polarity constitutes an entirely different concept of drive from the old one.[4]

Freud himself gives a succinct description of the development of his new theory in *Civilization and Its Discontents* (1930). He wrote,

> To begin with, ego-instincts and object-instincts confronted each other. It was to denote the energy of the latter and only the latter instincts that I introduced the term 'libido'.[5] Thus the antithesis between the ego-instincts and the 'libidinal' instincts of love (in its widest sense) which were directed to an object[6] ... But these discrepancies [with regard to sadism] were got over; after all, sadism was clearly a part of sexual life, in the activities of which affection could be replaced by cruelty ... The decisive step forward was the introduction of the concept of narcissism – that is to say, the discovery that the ego itself is cathected with libido, that the ego, indeed, is the libido's original home, and remains to some extent its headquarters[7] ... My next step was taken in *Beyond the Pleasure Principle* (1920), when the compulsion to repeat and the conservative character of instinctual life first attracted my attention. Starting from speculations on the beginning of life and from biological parallels, I drew the conclusion that, *besides the instinct to preserve living substance and to join it into ever larger units, there must exist another, contrary instinct seeking to dissolve*

4. To go into the details of Freud's attempt to identify Eros and sexuality would require a whole chapter by itself and be interesting probably only to the specialized student of Freud's theory.

5. Freud's reference here is to Section II of his first paper on anxiety neurosis (Freud, 1895).

6. In this formulation the basic conflict in man seems to be that between egotism and altruism. In Freud's theory of Id and Ego (pleasure principle and reality principle) both sides of the polarity are egotistic: satisfaction of one's own libidinal needs and satisfaction of one's need for self-preservation.

7. In fact, Freud alternated between this view and the one that the id was the seat, or 'reservoir' of the libido. J. Strachey, the editor of the standard edition has given a detailed history of these vacillations throughout the whole of Freud's work. See Appendix B to *The Ego and the Id* (Freud, 1923).

those units and to bring them back to their primaeval, inorganic state.
That is to say, as well as Eros there was an instinct of death.
(S. Freud, 1930; italics added)

When Freud wrote *Beyond the Pleasure Principle* he was by
no means convinced that the new hypothesis was valid. 'It
may be asked', he wrote, 'whether and how far I am myself
convinced of the truth of the hypotheses that have been set
out in these pages. My answer would be that I am not
convinced myself and that I do not seek to persuade other
people to believe in them. Or, more precisely, that I do not
know how far I believe in them' (S. Freud, 1920). After
having tried to construct a new theoretical edifice, one which
threatened the validity of many former concepts, and after
having done this with a tremendous intellectual effort, this
sincerity of Freud's, which runs so shiningly through his
whole work, is particularly impressive. He spent the next
eighteen years working on the new theory, and acquired
increasingly the sense of conviction he did not yet have in the
beginning. Not that he added entirely new aspects to the
hypothesis; what he did was, rather, an intellectual 'working
through' that left him convinced, and must have made it all
the more disappointing that not many of his own adherents
really understood and shared his views.

The new theory found its first full elaboration in *The Ego
and the Id* (1923). Of particular importance is the assumption about the

special physiological process (of anabolism or catabolism) [which]
would be associated with each of the two classes of instincts;
both kinds of instinct would be active in every particle of living
substance, though in unequal proportions, so that some one
substance might be the principal representative of Eros. This
hypothesis throws no light whatsoever upon the manner in which
the two classes of instincts are fused, blended, and alloyed with each
other; but that this takes place regularly and very extensively
is an assumption indispensable to our conception. It appears that,
as a result of the combination of unicellular organisms into multi-
cellular forms of life, *the death instinct of the single cell* can successfully

be neutralized and the *destructive impulses be diverted* on to the external world through the instrumentality of a special organ. This special organ would seem to be the muscular apparatus; and the death instinct would thus seem to express itself – though probably only in part – as an instinct of destruction directed against the external world and other organisms. (S. Freud, 1923; italics added)

In these formulations Freud reveals the new direction of his thinking more explicitly than in *Beyond the Pleasure Principle*. Instead of the mechanistic physiologic approach of the older theory, which was built on the model of chemically produced tension and the need to reduce this tension to its normal threshold (pleasure principle), the approach of the new theory is a biological one in which each living cell is supposed to be endowed with the two basic qualities of living matter, Eros, and the striving for death; however, the principle of tension reduction is preserved in a more radical form: the reduction of excitation to zero (nirvana principle).

A year later (1924), in *Economic Problem of Masochism* Freud takes one further step in clarifying the relation between the two instincts. He wrote:

The libido has the task of making the destroying instinct innocuous, and it fulfils the task by diverting that instinct to a great extent outwards – soon with the help of a special organic system, the muscular apparatus – towards objects in the external world. The instinct is then called the destructive instinct, the instinct for mastery, or the will to power.[8] A portion of the instinct is placed directly in the service of the sexual function, where it has an important part to play. This is sadism proper. Another portion does not share in this transposition outwards; it remains inside the organism and, with the help of the accompanying sexual excitation

8. Freud combines here three very difficult tendencies. The instinct to destroy is basically different from the will for power: in the first case I want to destroy the object; in the second, I want to keep and control it, and both are entirely different from the drive for mastery, whose aim it is to create and produce, which in fact is the precise opposite of the will to destroy.

described above, becomes libidinally bound there. It is in this portion that we have to recognize the original, erotogenic masochism. (S. Freud, 1924)

In the *New Introductory Lectures* (1933) the position taken earlier is maintained: Freud speaks of 'the erotic instincts, which seek to combine more and more living substance into ever greater unities, and the death instincts, which oppose this effort and lead what is living back into an inorganic state' (S. Freud, 1933). In the same lectures Freud wrote about the original destructive instinct:

We can only perceive it under two conditions: if it is combined with erotic instincts into masochism or if – with a greater or lesser erotic addition – it is directed against the external world as aggressiveness. And now we are struck by the significance of the possibility that the aggressiveness may not be able to find satisfaction in the external world because it comes up against real obstacles. If this happens, it will perhaps retreat and increase the amount of self-destructiveness holding sway in the interior. We shall hear how this is in fact what occurs and how important a process this is. Impeded aggressiveness seems to involve a grave injury. *It really seems as though it is necessary for us to destroy some other thing or person in order not to destroy ourselves, in order to guard against the impulsion to self-destruction. A sad disclosure indeed for the moralist!* (S. Freud, 1933; italics added)

In his last two papers, written one and two years before his death, Freud did not make any important alterations in the concepts as he had developed them in the foregoing years. In *Analysis Terminable and Interminable* (1937) he emphasizes even more the power of the death instinct. As Strachey writes in his editorial notes: 'But the most powerful impeding factor of all' he wrote, '*and one totally beyond any possibility of control . . . is the death instinct*' (S. Freud, 1937; italics added). In *An Outline of Psychoanalysis* (written in 1938; published in 1940) Freud reaffirms in a systematic way his earlier assumptions without making any relevant changes.

2

Analysis of the Vicissitudes and a Critique of Freud's
Theories of the Death Instinct and Eros

The foregoing brief description of Freud's new theories, that
of Eros and of the death instinct, could not show sufficiently
how radical the change was from the old to the new theory,
or that Freud did not see the radical nature of this change
and as a consequence was stuck in many theoretical inconsistencies and immanent contradictions. In the following
pages I shall attempt to describe the significance of the
changes and to analyse the conflict between the old and the
new theory.

Freud, after the First World War, had two new visions.
The first was that of the power and intensity of aggressive-
destructive strivings in man, independent from sexuality.
Saying that this was a *new* vision is not entirely correct.
As I have already shown, he had not been entirely unaware
of the existence of aggressive impulses independent from
sexuality. But this insight was expressed only sporadically,
and it never changed the main hypothesis about the basic
polarity between sexual instincts and ego instincts, even
though this theory was later modified by the introduction
of the concept of narcissism. In the theory of the death
instinct the awareness of human destructiveness burst forth
in full strength, and destructiveness became the one pole
of existence which, fighting with the other pole, Eros, forms
the very essence of life. Destructiveness becomes a *primary*
phenomenon of life.

The second vision that marks Freud's new theory is not
only without antecedents in his former theory, but in full
contradiction to it. It is the vision that Eros, present in every
cell of living substance, has as its aim the unification and
integration of all cells, and beyond that, the service of
civilization, the integration of smaller units into the unity
of mankind (S. Freud, 1930). Freud discovers non-sexual

love. He calls the life instinct also 'love instinct'; love is identified with life and growth, and – fighting with the death instinct – it determines human existence. In Freud's older theory man was looked upon as an isolated system, driven by two impulses: one to survive (ego instinct) and one to have pleasure by overcoming the tensions that in turn were chemically produced within the body and localized in the 'erogenous zones' of which the genitals were one. In this picture man was primarily isolated, but entered into relations with members of the other sex in order to satisfy his striving for pleasure. The relationship between the two sexes was conceived in a way that resembles human relations on the market-place. Each is only concerned with the satisfaction of his needs, but it is precisely for the sake of his satisfaction that he has to enter into relations with others who offer what he needs, and need what he offers.

In the Eros theory this is entirely different. Man is no longer conceived as primarily isolated and egotistical, as *l'homme machine*, but as being primarily related to others, impelled by the life instincts which make him need union with others. Life, love, and growth are one and the same, more deeply rooted and fundamental than sexuality and 'pleasure'.

The change in Freud's new vision shows clearly in his new evaluation of the biblical commandment: Thou shalt love thy neighbour as thyself. In *Why War?* (1933a) he wrote:

Anything that encourages the growth of emotional ties between men must operate against war. These ties may be of two kinds. In the first place they may be relations resembling those towards a loved object, though *without having a sexual aim*. There is no need for psychoanalysis to be ashamed to speak of love in this connection, for religion itself uses the same words: 'Thou shalt love thy neighbour as thyself.' This, however, is more easily said than done. The second kind of emotional tie is by means of identification. Whatever leads men to share important interests produces this community of feeling, these identifications. And the structure of human society is to a large extent based on them. (Freud, 1933a; italics added)

These lines are written by the same man who only three years earlier had ended a comment on this same biblical commandment by saying: 'What is the point of a precept enunciated with so much solemnity if its fulfilment *cannot be recommended as reasonable*?' (S. Freud, 1930).⁹

9. Freud arrived at this conclusion on the basis of the following argument: 'The clue may be supplied by one of the ideal demands, as we have called them, of civilized society. It runs: "Thou shalt love thy neighbour as thyself." It is known throughout the world and is undoubtedly older than Christianity, which puts it forward as its proudest claim. Yet it is certainly not very old; even in historical times it was still strange to mankind. Let us adopt a naïve attitude towards it, as though we were hearing it for the first time; we shall be unable then to suppress a feeling of surprise and bewilderment. Why should we do it? What good will it do us? But, above all, how shall we achieve it? How can it be possible? My love is something valuable to me which I ought not to throw away without reflection. It imposes duties on me for whose fulfilment I must be ready to make sacrifices. If I love someone, he must deserve it in some way. (I leave out of account the use he may be to me, and also his possible significance for me as a sexual object, for neither of these two kinds of relationships comes into question where the precept to love my neighbour is concerned.) He deserves it if he is so like me in important ways that I can love myself in him; and he deserves it if he is so much more perfect than myself that I can love my ideal of my own self in him. Again, I have to love him if he is my friend's son, since the pain my friend would feel if any harm came to him would be my pain too – I should have to share it. But if he is a stranger to me and if he cannot attract me by any worth of his own or any significance that he may already have acquired for my emotional life, it will be hard for me to love him. Indeed, I should be wrong to do so, for my love is valued by all my own people as a sign of my preferring them, and it is an injustice to them if I put a stranger on a par with them. But if I am to love him (with this universal love) merely because he, too, is an inhabitant of this earth, like an insect, an earthworm or a grass-snake, then I fear that only a small modicum of my love will fall to his share – not by any possibility as much as, by the judgement of my reason, I am entitled to retain for myself' (S. Freud, 1930). It is interesting to note how Freud conceived of love en-

Nothing short of a radical change of viewpoint had occurred. Freud, the enemy of religion, which he had called an illusion preventing man from reaching maturity and independence, now quotes one of the most fundamental commandments to be found in all great humanistic religions, as a support for his psychological assumption. He emphasizes that there is 'no need for psychoanalysis to be ashamed to speak of love in this connection' (Freud, 1933a),[10] but, indeed, he needs this assertion to overcome the embarrassment he must have felt in making this drastic change with regard to the concept of brotherly love.

Was Freud aware how drastic the change in his approach was? Was he conscious of the profound and irreconcilable contradiction between the old and the new theories? Quite obviously he was not. In *The Ego and the Id* (1923) he identified Eros (life instinct or love instinct) with the sexual instincts (plus the instinct for self preservation):

According to this view we have to distinguish two classes of instincts, one of which, *the sexual instincts or Eros*, is by far the more conspicuous and accessible to study. It comprises not merely the uninhibited sexual instinct proper and the instinctual impulses of an aim-inhibited or sublimated nature derived from it, but also the self-preservative instinct, which must be assigned to the ego and which at the beginning of our analytic work we had good

---

tirely in the frame of reference of bourgeois ethics, specifically the social character of the middle class of the nineteenth century. The first question is: 'What good will it do us?' – the principle of profit. The next premise is that love must be 'deserved' (the patriarchal principle in contrast to the matriarchal principle of unconditional and undeserved love and, furthermore, on the narcissistic principle that the other 'deserves' my love only inasmuch as he is like me in important ways; even loving one's friend's son is explained in egoistic terms, because if harm came to him and thus indirectly to my friend his pain would be my pain. Eventually love is conceived as a certain quantitatively fixed amount, love for all my fellow creatures could only leave a very small amount of love for each one.

10. cf. also S. Freud (1908a).

reason for contrasting with the sexual object-instincts. (S. Freud, 1923; italics added)

It is precisely because of his unawareness of the contradiction that he made the attempt to reconcile the old and the new theories in such a way that they seemed to form a continuity without a sharp break. This attempt had to lead to many immanent contradictions and inconsistencies in the new theory which Freud again and again tried to bridge, smooth over, or deny, yet without ever succeeding in doing so. In the following pages I shall attempt to describe the vicissitudes of the new theory produced by Freud's failure to recognize that the new wine – and in this case, I believe, the better wine – could not be filled into the old bottles.

Before we start this analysis still another change must be mentioned which, also going unrecognized, complicated matters still more. Freud had built his older theory on a scientific model that is easy to recognize: the mechanistic-materialistic model that had been the scientific ideal of his teacher, von Brucke, and the entire circle of mechanistic-materialists like Helmholtz, Buchner, von Brucke, and others.[11] They looked on man as a machine driven by chemical processes; feelings, affects, and emotions were explained as being caused by specific and identifiable physiological processes. Most of hormonology and of the neurophysiological findings of the last decades were unknown to these men, yet with daring and ingenuity they

11. The dependence of Freud's theory formation on the thinking of his teachers has been described by Peter Ammacher (1962). Robert R. Holt summarizes approvingly the main thesis of this work in·the following: 'Many of the most puzzling and seemingly arbitrary turns of psychoanalytic theory, involving propositions that are false to the extent that they are testable at all, are either hidden biological assumptions or result directly from such assumptions, which Freud learned from his teachers in medical school. They became a basic part of his intellectual equipment, as unquestioned as the assumption of the universal determinism, were probably not always recognized by him as biological, and thus were retained as necessary ingredients when he attempted to turn away from neurologizing to the construction of an abstract, psychological model' (R. R. Holt, 1965).

insisted on the correctness of their approach. Needs and interests for which no somatic sources could be found were ignored, and the understanding of those processes which were not neglected followed the principles of mechanistic thinking. The model of von Brucke's physiology and Freud's model of man could be repeated today in a properly programmed computer. 'He' develops a certain amount of tension which at a certain threshold has to be relieved and reduced, while this realization is checked by another part, the ego, which observes reality and inhibits relief when it conflicts with the needs for survival. This Freudian robot would be similar to Isaac Asimov's science-fiction robot, but the programming would be different. Its first law would not be not to hurt human beings, but to avoid self-damage or self-destruction.

The new theory does not follow this mechanistic 'physiologizing' model. It is centred around a biological orientation in which the fundamental forces of life (and its opposite: death) become the primal forces motivating man. The nature of the cell, that is, of all living substance, becomes the theoretical basis for a theory of motivation, not a physiological process that goes on in certain organs of the body. The new theory was perhaps closer to a vitalistic philosophy[12] than to the concept of the German mechanistic materialists. But, as I already said, Freud was not clearly aware of this change; hence he tries again and again to apply his physiologizing method to the new theory and necessarily has to fail in this attempt to square the circle. However, in one important regard both theories have a common premise which has been the unchanged axiom of Freud's thinking: the concept that the governing law of the psychic apparatus is the tendency to reduce tension (or excitation) to a constant low level (the constancy principle – upon which the pleasure principle rests), or to the zero level (the nirvana principle, upon which the death instinct is based).

12. cf. J. Pratt (1958).

We must now return to a more detailed analysis of Freud's two new visions, that of the death instinct and of the life instinct as the primal determining forces of human existence.[13]

What reasons motivated Freud to postulate the death instinct?

One reason which I have already mentioned was probably the impact of the First World War. He, like many other men of his time and age, had shared the optimistic vision so characteristic of the European middle class, and saw himself suddenly confronted with a fury of hate and destruction hardly believable before 1 August 1914.

One might speculate that to this historical factor a personal factor could be added. As we know from Ernest Jones's biography (E. Jones, 1957), Freud was a man preoccupied with death. He thought of dying every day, after he was forty; he had attacks of *Todesangst* ('fear of death'), and sometimes he would add to his 'good-bye': 'You might never see me again.' One might surmise that Freud's severe illness would have impressed him as a confirmation of his fear of death, and thus contributed to the formulation of the death instinct. This speculation, however, is untenable in this simplified form since the first signs of his illness did not appear until February 1923, several years after his conception of the death instinct (E. Jones, 1957). But it may be not too far-fetched to assume that his earlier preoccupation with death grew in intensity as he became sick and led him to a concept in which the conflict between life and death was at the centre of human experience, rather than the conflict between the two life-affirmative drives, sexual desire and ego drives. To assume that man needs to die because death is the hidden goal of his life might be con-

13. Freud's terminology is not always consistent. He speaks sometimes of life and death instincts, sometimes of a life and death instinct (singular). The death instinct(s) is also called destructive instinct(s). The word *thanatos* (parallel to Eros), as equivalent to death instinct was not used by Freud, but introduced into the discussion by P. Federn.

sidered a kind of comfort destined to alleviate his fear of death.

While these historical and personal factors constitute one set of motivations for the construction of the death instinct, there is another set of factors which must have inclined him to conceive of the theory of the death instinct. Freud always thought in dualistic terms. He saw opposite forces battling each other and the life process as the outcome of this battle. Sex and the drive for self-preservation was the original form assumed by the dualistic theory. But with the concept of narcissism which put the self-preservative instinct in the camp of the libido, the old dualism seemed to be threatened. Did the theory of narcissism not impose a monistic theory that all instincts were libidinous? And even worse, would that not justify one of the main heresies of Jung, the concept of libido as denoting *all psychic energy*? Indeed, Freud had to extricate himself from this intolerable dilemma, intolerable because it would have amounted to agreeing with Jung's concept of libido. He had to find a new instinct, opposed to the libido, as the basis for a new dualistic approach. The death instinct fulfilled this requirement. Instead of the old dualism, a new one had been found, and existence could be viewed again dualistically as the battlefield of opposing instincts, Eros and the death instincts.

In the case of the new dualism Freud followed a pattern of thinking about which more will be said later, namely he constructed two broad concepts into which every phenomenon had to fit. He had done that with the concept of sexuality by enlarging it, so that everything that was not ego instinct belonged to the sexual instinct. He followed the same method again with the death instinct. He made it so broad that as a result every striving which was not subsumed under Eros belonged to the death instinct, and vice versa. In this way aggressiveness, destructiveness, sadism, the drive for control and mastery were, in spite of their qualitative differences, manifestations of the same force — the death instinct.

Still in another aspect did Freud follow the same pattern of thinking that had had such a strong hold over him in the earlier phase of his theoretical system. About the death instinct he says that it is originally all inside; then part of it is sent outwards and acts as aggressiveness, while part of it remains in the interior as primary masochism. But when the part that was sent outwards meets with obstacles too great to overcome, the death instinct is redirected inwards and manifests itself as secondary masochism. This pattern of reasoning is exactly the same as that employed by Freud in his discussion of narcissism. At first all libido is in the ego (primary narcissism) then it is extended outwards to objects (object libido), but it is often redirected again to the interior and then forms the so-called secondary narcissism.

Many times 'death instinct' is used synonymously with 'instinct of destruction' and 'aggressive instincts'.[14] But at the same time, Freud makes fine distinctions between these different terms. By and large, as James Strachey has pointed out in his introduction to *Civilization and Its Discontents* (S. Freud, 1930), in Freud's later writings (for instance *Civilization and Its Discontents*, 1930; *The Ego and the Id*, 1923; *New Introductory Lectures*, 1933; *An Outline of Psychoanalysis*, 1938) the aggressive instinct is something secondary, derived from the primary self-destruction.

In the following paragraph I quote some examples of this relation between death instinct and aggressiveness. In *Civilization and Its Discontents* Freud speaks of the death instinct being 'diverted towards the external world and comes to light as an instinct of aggressiveness and destructiveness'. In the *New Introductory Lectures* he speaks of 'self-destructiveness *as an expression* of a "death instinct" which cannot fail to be present in every vital process' (italics added). In the same work Freud makes this thought still more explicit: 'We are led to the view that masochism is older than sadism, and that sadism is the destructive instinct directed outwards, thus acquiring the characteristic of

14. cf., for instance, S. Freud (1930).

aggressiveness' (S. Freud, 1933). The amount of destructive instinct which remains in the interior either combines 'with erotic instincts into masochism or – with a greater or lesser erotic addition – it is directed against the external world as aggressiveness' (S. Freud, 1933). But, so, continues Freud, if the aggressiveness directed outwards meets with too strong obstacles, it returns and increases the amount of self-destructiveness holding sway in the interior. The end of this theoretical and somewhat contradictory development is reached in Freud's last two papers. In the *Outline* he says that within the id 'the organic *instincts* operate which are themselves compounded of fusions of *two primal forces* (Eros and Destructiveness) in varying proportions . . .' (S. Freud, 1938; italics added). In *Analysis Terminable and Interminable* Freud speaks also of death instinct and Eros as of two 'primal instincts' (S. Freud, 1937).

It is amazing and impressive how firmly Freud stuck to his concept of the death instinct, in spite of great theoretical difficulties that he tried hard – and in my opinion, vainly – to overcome.

The main difficulty perhaps lies in the assumption of the identity of two tendencies, that of the body's tendency to return to the original, inorganic state (as an outcome of the principle of repetition compulsion) and that of the instinct to destroy, either oneself or others. For the first tendency the term *thanatos* (first used by P. Federn) referring to death, may be adequate, or even 'nirvana principle', indicating the tendency to the reduction of *tension*, of energy to the point of the end of all energetic strivings.[15] But is this slow decrease of life-force the same as destructiveness? Of course, logically it could be argued – and Freud implicitly

15. The use of 'nirvana' principle is unfortunate inasmuch as it mis-interprets the Buddhist nirvana. Nirvana is precisely not a state of life-lessness brought about by nature (which, according to Buddhism has the opposite tendency), but by the spiritual effort of man who finds salvation and the completion of life if he has succeeded in overcoming all greed and egoism and is filled with compassion for all sentient beings. In the state of nirvana the Buddha experienced supreme joy.

does so – that if a tendency towards dying is inherent in the organism, there must be an active force that tends to destroy. (This is really the same kind of thinking that we find among the instinctivists who postulate a special instinct behind every kind of behaviour.) But if we go beyond such circular reasoning, is there any evidence or even reason for this identity of the tendency to cessation of all excitation and the impulse to destroy? It hardly seems so. If we assume, following Freud's reasoning on the basis of the repetition compulsion, that life has an inherent tendency for slowing down and eventually to die, such a biological innate tendency would be quite different from the active impulse to destroy. If we add that this same tendency to die is also supposed to be the source of the passion for power and the instinct for mastery, and – when mixed with sexuality the source of sadism[16] and masochism, the theoretical *tour de force* must end in failure. The 'nirvana principle' and the passion for destruction are two disparate entities that cannot be brought under the same category of death instinct(s).

A further difficulty lies in the fact that the death 'instinct' does not fit Freud's general concept of instincts. First of all it does not have, as do the instincts in Freud's earlier theory, a special zone in the body from which it originates, but it is a biological force inherent in all living substance. This point has been made convincingly by Otto Fenichel:

Dissimulation in the cells ... – that is to say an objective destruction – cannot be the source of a destructive instinct in the same sense that a chemically determined sensitization of the central organ through stimulation of the erotogenic zones is the source of the sexual instinct. For according to the definition, instinct aims at *eliminating* the somatic change which we designate as the source of the instinct; but the death instinct does not aim at eliminating

16. Freud does not pay attention to the fact that the destructive instinct aims at the destruction of the object, while sadism wants to keep it in order to control, humiliate or hurt it. See the discussion of sadism in Chapter 11.

dissimulation. For this reason it does not seem to me possible to set up the 'death instinct' as one species of instinct over against another species. (O. Fenichel, 1953)

Fenichel points here to one of the theoretical difficulties Freud created for himself, even though, as we may say, he repressed the awareness of it. This difficulty is all the more serious since Freud, as I shall show later, had to come to the result that Eros does not fulfil the theoretical conditions of an instinct either. Certainly, had Freud not had strong personal motivations, he would not have used the term 'instinct' in a completely different sense from the original one without pointing out this difference himself. (This difficulty makes itself felt even in the terminology. Eros cannot be used together with 'instinct', and logically Freud never talked about an 'Eros instinct'. But he made a place for the term 'instinct' by using 'life instinct' alternatively with Eros.)

Actually, the death instinct has no connection with Freud's earlier theory, except in the general axiom of drive reduction. As we have seen, in the earlier theory aggression was either a component drive of pregenital sexuality or an ego drive directed against stimuli from the outside. In the theory of the death instinct no connection is made with the former sources of aggression, except that the death instinct is now used to explain sadism (as a mixture with sexuality) (S. Freud, 1933).[17]

To sum up, the concept of the death instinct was determined by two main requisites: first, by the need to accommodate Freud's new conviction of the power of human aggression; second, by the need to stick to a dualistic concept of instincts. After the ego instincts had also been considered to be libidinous, Freud had to find a new dichotomy and the one between Eros and the death instinct offered itself as the most convenient one. But while convenient

17. Later on I shall try to show that there is, indeed, a possible connection between the libido theory and the theory of the death instinct through the link of the theory of anal libido.

from the standpoint of the immediate solution of a difficulty, it was very inconvenient from the standpoint of the development of Freud's whole theory of instinctual motivation. The death instinct became a 'catch-all' concept, by the use of which one tried without success to resolve incompatible contradictions. Freud, perhaps due to his age and illness, did not approach the problem frontally and thus patched up the contradictions. Most of the other psychoanalysts who did not accept his concept of Eros and death instinct found an easy solution; they transformed the death instinct into a 'destructive instinct' opposite to the old sexual instinct. They thus combined their loyalty to Freud with their inability to go beyond the old-fashioned instinct theory. Even considering the difficulties of the new theory it constituted a considerable achievement: it recognized as the basic conflict of human existence the choice between life and death, and it relinquished the old physiological concept of drives for a more profound biological speculation. Freud did not have the satisfaction of finding a solution, and he had to leave his instinct theory as a torso. The further development of Freud's theory must face the problem and deal squarely with the difficulties, hoping to find new solutions.

In discussing the theory of the *life instinct* and of Eros, we find that the theoretical difficulties are, if anything, even more serious than those connected with the concept of the death instinct. The reason for the difficulties is rather obvious. In the libido theory the excitation was due to the chemically determined sensitization, through the stimulation of the various erotogenic zones. In the case of the life instinct we are dealing with a tendency, characteristic of all living substance, for which there is no specific physiological source or specific organ. How could the old sexual instinct and the new life instinct – how could sexuality and Eros be the same?

Yet, although Freud wrote in the *New Introductory Lectures* that the new theory had 'replaced' the libido theory, he affirms in the same lectures and elsewhere that the sexual instincts and Eros are identical. He wrote: 'Our hypothesis is that there are two essentially different classes of instincts: the sexual instincts, understood in the widest sense – Eros, if you prefer that name – and the aggressive instincts, whose aim is destruction' (S. Freud, 1933). Or, in *An Outline of Psychoanalysis*: 'The total available energy of Eros ... henceforth we shall speak of as "libido"' ... (S. Freud, 1938). Sometimes he identifies Eros with the sexual instinct *and* the instinct for self-preservation (S. Freud, 1923) which was only logical after he had revised the original theory and classified both the original enemies, the self-preservative and the sexual instincts, as being libidinous. But while Freud sometimes equates Eros and libido, he expresses a slightly different viewpoint in his last work, *An Outline of Psychoanalysis*. Here he writes: 'The greater part of what we know about Eros – that is to say, about its exponent, the libido – has been gained from a study of the sexual function, which, indeed, on the prevailing view, *even if not according to our theory*, coincides with Eros' (S. Freud, 1938; italics added). According to this statement, and in contradiction to those quoted before, Eros and sexuality do *not* coincide. It seems that what Freud has in mind here is that Eros is a 'primal instinct' (aside from the death instinct), of which the sexual instinct is *one exponent*. In fact, he returns here to a view expressed already in *Beyond the Pleasure Principle* where he says in a footnote that the sexual instinct 'was transformed for us into Eros, which seeks to force together and hold together the portions of living substance. What are commonly called the sexual instincts are looked upon by us as the part of Eros which is directed towards objects' (S. Freud, 1920).

One time Freud even makes the attempt to indicate that his original concept of sexuality 'was by no means identical with the impulsion towards a union of the two sexes or towards producing a pleasurable sensation in the genitals; it had far more resemblance to the all-inclusive and all preserving Eros of Plato's *Symposium*' (S. Freud, 1925). The truth of the first part of this statement is obvious. Freud had always defined sexuality as broader than genital sexuality. But it is difficult to see on what basis he maintains that his older concept of sexuality resembled that of the Platonic Eros.

The older sexual theory was precisely the opposite of the Platonic theory. The libido was, according to Freud, male, and there was no corresponding female libido. The woman was, in line with Freud's extreme patriarchal bias, not man's equal but a crippled, castrated male. The very essence of the Platonic myth is that male and female were once one and were then divided into halves, which implies, of course, that the two halves are equals, that they form a polarity endowed with the tendency to unite again.

The only reason for Freud's attempt to interpret the old libido theory in the light of Plato's Eros must have been the wish to deny the discontinuity of the two phases, even at the expense of an obvious distortion of his older theory.

As in the case of the death instinct, Freud ran into a difficulty with regard to the instinctual nature of the life instinct. As Fenichel has pointed out, the death instinct cannot be called an 'instinct' in terms of Freud's *new* concept of instinct, developed first in *Beyond the Pleasure Principle* and continued throughout his later work, including the *Outline of Psychoanalysis* (O. Fenichel, 1953). Freud wrote: 'Though they [the instincts] are the ultimate cause of all activity, they are of a conservative nature; the state, whatever it may be, which an organism has reached, gives rise to a tendency to re-establish that state as soon as it has been abandoned' (S. Freud, 1938).

Have Eros and the life instinct this conservative quality of all instincts, and thus can they be properly called an instinct? Freud was trying hard to find a solution that would save the conservative character of the life instincts.

In speaking of the germ cells that 'work against the death of the living substance and succeed in winning for it what we can only regard as potential immortality' he stated:

> The instincts which watch over the destinies of these elementary organisms that survive the whole individual, which provide them with a safe shelter while they are defenceless against the stimuli of the external world, which bring about their meeting with other germ cells, and so on – these constitute the group of the sexual instincts. They are conservative in the same sense as the other instincts in that they bring back earlier states of living substance; but they are conservative to a higher degree in that they are peculiarly resistant to external influences; and they are conservative too in another sense in that they preserve life itself for a comparatively long period. They are the true life instincts. They operate against the purpose of the other instincts, which leads, by reason of their function, to death; and this fact indicates that there is an opposition between them and the other instincts, an opposition whose importance was long ago recognized by the theory of the neuroses. It is as though the life of the organism moved with a vacillating rhythm. One group of instincts rushes forward so as to reach the final aim of life as swiftly as possible; but when a particular stage in the advance has been reached, the other group jerks back to a certain point to make a fresh start and so prolong the journey. And even though it is certain that sexuality *and the distinction between the sexes did not exist when life began*, the possibility remains that the instincts which were later to be described as sexual may have been in operation from the very first, and it may not be true that it was only at a later time that they started upon their work of opposing the activities of the 'ego instincts'. (S. Freud, 1920; italics added)

What is most interesting in this passage, and also the reason I quote it at length, is how almost desperately Freud tried to save the conservative concept of all instincts and hence also of the life instinct. He had to take refuge in a new formulation of the sexual instinct as one that watches over the destinies of the germ cell, a definition different from his whole concept of instinct in his previous work.

A few years later, in *The Ego and the Id*, Freud makes the same attempt to give Eros the status of a true instinct, by ascribing to it a conservative nature. He wrote:

On the basis of theoretical considerations, supported by biology, we put forward the hypothesis of a death instinct, the task of which is to lead organic life back into the inanimate state; on the other hand, we supposed that Eros, by bringing about a more and more far-reaching combination of the particles into which living substance is dispersed, aims at complicating life and at the same time, of course, at preserving it. Acting in this way, both the instincts would be conservative in the strictest sense of the word, since both would be endeavouring to re-establish a state of things that was disturbed by the emergence of life. The emergence of life would thus be the cause of the continuance of life and also at the same time of the striving towards death; and life itself would be a conflict and compromise between these two trends. The problem of the origin of life would remain a cosmological one; and the problem of the goal and purpose of life would be answered dualistically. (S. Freud, 1923)

Eros aims at complicating life and preserving it, and hence it is also conservative, because with the emergence of life an instinct is born which is to preserve it. But, we must ask, if it is the nature of the instinct to re-establish the earliest state of existence, inorganic matter, how can it at the same time tend to re-establish a later form of existence, namely life?

After these futile attempts to save the conservative character of the life instinct, Freud, in the *Outline*, finally arrives at a negative solution: 'In the case of Eros (and the love instinct) we can*not* apply this formula [of the conservative character of the instincts]. To do so would presuppose that living substance was once a unity which had later been torn apart and was now striving towards re-union' (S. Freud, 1938; italics added). Freud adds here a significant footnote: 'Certain writers have imagined something of the sort, but nothing like it is known to us from the actual history of living substance' (S. Freud, 1938). Quite obviously Freud refers here to Plato's Eros myth, yet he objects to it as a product of poetic imagination. This rejection is truly puzzling. The Platonic answer would indeed satisfy the theoretical requirement of the conservative nature of Eros. If male and female were unified in the beginning, then separated, and were driven by the wish for reunion, what could be more fitting to accommodate the formula that the instinct tends to restore an earlier situation? Why did Freud not accept this way out and thus rid himself of the theoretical embarrassment that Eros was not a true instinct?

Perhaps some more light is thrown on this question if we compare this footnote in the *Outline* with a much more detailed and earlier statement in *Beyond the Pleasure Principle*. Here he quoted Plato's report in the *Symposium* concerning the original unity of man who was then divided by Zeus into two halves, and after this division, each desiring his other half, they came together and threw their arms about one another eager to grow into one. He wrote:

> Shall we follow the hint given us by the poet-philosopher, and venture upon the hypothesis that living substance at the time of its coming to life was torn apart into small particles, which have ever since endeavoured to reunite through the sexual instincts? That these instincts, in which the chemical affinity of inanimate matter persisted, gradually succeeded, as they developed through the kingdom of the protista, in overcoming the difficulties put in the way of that endeavour by an environment charged with dangerous stimuli – stimuli which compelled them to form a protective cortical layer? That these splintered fragments of living substance in this way attained a multicellular condition and finally transferred the instinct for reuniting in the most highly concentrated form, to the germ cells? – But here, I think, the moment has come for breaking off. (Freud, 1920)[18]

We easily see the difference between the two statements: in the earlier formulation (*Beyond the Pleasure Principle*) Freud leaves the answer open, while in the later statement (*An Outline of Psychoanalysis*) the answer is definitely negative.

But much more important is the particular formulation that is common to both statements. Both times he speaks of 'living substance' having been torn apart. The Platonic

18. In a footnote Freud quotes a similar idea from the Brihadâramyaka *upanishad*.

myth, however, does not speak of 'living substance' having been torn apart, but of *male* and *female* having been torn apart and striving to be reunited. Why did Freud insist on 'living substance' as the crucial point?

I believe the answer may lie in a subjective factor. Freud was deeply imbued with the patriarchal feeling that men were superior to women, and not their equals. Hence the theory of a male–female polarity – which like all polarity implies difference *and* equality – was unacceptable to him. This emotional male bias had, at a much earlier period, led him to the theory that women are crippled men, governed by the castration complex and penis envy, inferior to men also by the fact that their super-ego is weaker, their narcissism, however, stronger than that of men. While one can admire the brilliance of his construction, it is hard to deny that the assumption that one half of the human race is a crippled version of the other half is nothing short of an absurdity, only explainable by the depth of sex prejudice (not too different from racial prejudice and/or religious prejudice). Is it surprising, then, that Freud was blocked here, too, when by following Plato's myth he would have been forced into an assumption of male–female equality? Indeed, Freud could not take this step; thus he changed male–female union to union of 'living substance' and rejected the logical way out of the difficulty that Eros did not partake in the conservative nature of instincts.

I have dwelt so long on this point for several reasons. First of all, because it helps to understand the immanent contradictions in Freud's theory if we know the motivations that compelled him to arrive at these contradictory solutions. Second, because the problem discussed here is interesting beyond the special problem of the vicissitudes of Freud's instinct theory. We try here to understand Freud's conscious thought as a compromise between the new vision and older thought habits, rooted in his 'patriarchal complex', which prevented him from expressing his new vision in a clear and unambiguous way. In other words, Freud was the prisoner of the feelings and thought habits of his society, which he was unable to transcend.[19] When a new vision struck him, only part of it – or its consequences – became conscious, while another part remained unconscious because it was incompatible with his 'complex' and previous conscious thought. His conscious thinking had to try to deny the contradictions and inconsistencies by making constructions that were sufficiently plausible to satisfy conscious thought processes.[20]

Freud did not and – as I have tried to show – could not choose the solution of making Eros fit his own definition of instincts, that is, their conservative nature. Was there another theoretical option open to him? I believe there was.

19. As, for instance, John Stuart Mill, J. J. Bachofen, Karl Marx, Friedrich Engels, and quite a few others had done.

20. This process occurs in many great creative thinkers. Spinoza is a striking example. The problem, for instance, whether Spinoza was a theist or not cannot be fully understood unless one takes into account the difference between his conscious thought habits (in theistic terms), the new vision (non-theistic), and the resulting compromise of a definition of God that is, in fact, a denial of God. This method of examining an author's writings is psychoanalytic in some important respects. One reads between the lines of the written text as a psychoanalyst reads between the lines of a patient's free associations or dreams. The starting point is the fact that we find contradictions in the thought of an eminent thinker. Since he would have noticed these contradictions himself, and probably would have solved them were it a matter of theoretical talent, we must assume that the immanent contradictions are caused by the conflict between two structures. The old one, which still occupies most of the conscious territory, and a radically new one, which does not succeed in expressing itself fully in conscious thought; that is to say, part of which remains unconscious. The immanent contradiction can be treated like a symptom or a dream, as a compromise between an older structure of affectively rooted conscious thought and a new structure of a theoretical vision that cannot be expressed fully because of the strength of old ideas and feelings. The author, even if he is a genius, may be entirely unaware of the existence or nature of these contradictions, while an outsider – not caught in the same premises – may see them very easily. Kant was, perhaps, referring to this when he noted: 'Sometimes we understand the author better than the author understands himself.'

He could have found another solution to accommodate his new vision, the dominant role of love and of destructiveness, within his old traditional libido theory. He could have set up a polarity between *pregenital sexuality* (oral and anal sadism) as the source of destructiveness and genital sexuality as the source of love.[21] But of course this solution was difficult for Freud to accept for a reason mentioned before in another context. It would have come dangerously close to a monistic view, because both destructiveness *and* love would have been libidinous. Yet, Freud had already built the basis for connecting destructiveness with pregenital sexuality by arriving at the conclusion that the destructive part of the anal-sadistic libido is the death instinct (S. Freud, 1923, 1920). If that is so, it seems fair to speculate that the anal libido itself must have a deep affinity to the death instinct; in fact the further conclusion might seem warranted that it is of the essence of the anal libido to aim for destruction.

But Freud does not come to this conclusion, and it is interesting to speculate why he did not.

The first reason lies in too narrow an interpretation of the anal libido. For Freud and his pupils the essential aspect of anality lies in the tendency to control and possess (aside from a friendly aspect of retaining). Now, controlling and possessing are certainly tendencies opposite of loving, furthering, liberating, which form a syndrome among themselves. But 'possession' and 'control' do not contain the very essence of destructiveness, the wish to destroy, and hostility to life. No doubt, the anal character has a deep interest in and affinity to faeces as part of their general affinity to all that is not alive. Faeces are the product finally eliminated by the body, being of no further use to it. The anal character is attracted by faeces as he is attracted by everything that is useless for life, such as dirt, death, decay.[22] We can say that

21. Ernst Simmel has suggested precisely such a solution (E. Simmel, 1944).

22. The affinity between anality and necrophilia is discussed in Chapter 12. I mention there that the typical necrophilic dream is full

the tendency to control and possess is only one aspect of the anal character, but milder and less malignant than hate against life. I believe that had Freud seen this direct connection between faeces and death he might have arrived at the conclusion that the main polarity is that between the genital and the anal orientations, two clinically well-studied entities that are the equivalent of Eros and of the death instinct. Had he done so, Eros and the death instinct would not have appeared as two biologically given and equally strong tendencies, but Eros would have been looked upon as the biologically normal aim of development, while the death instinct would have been looked upon as based on a failure of normal development and in this sense as a pathological, though deeply rooted striving. If one wants to entertain a biological speculation one might relate anality to the fact that orientation by smell is characteristic of all four-legged mammals, and that the erect posture implies the change from orientation by smell to orientation by sight. The change in function of the old olfactory brain would correspond to the same transformation of orientation. In view of this, one might consider that the anal character constitutes a regressive phase of biological development for which there might even be a constitutional-genetic basis. The anality of the infant could be considered as representing an evolutionary repetition of a biologically earlier phase in the process of transition to fully developed human functioning. (In Freud's terms, anality–destructiveness would have the conservative nature of an instinct, i.e., the return from genitality-love-sight orientation to anality-destruction-smell orientation.)

The relationship between death instinct and life instinct would have been essentially the same as that between pregenital and genital libido in Freud's developmental scheme. The libido fixation on the anal level would have been a

of symbols like faeces, corpses – whole or dismembered – tombs, ruins, etc., and include examples of such necrophilous dreams.

pathological phenomenon, but one with deep roots in the psychosexual constitution, while the genital level would be characteristic for the healthy individual. In this speculation, then, the anal level would have two rather different aspects: one, the drive to control; the other, the drive to destroy. As I have attempted to show, this would be the difference between sadism and necrophilia.

But Freud did not make this connection, and perhaps could not make it for the reasons that have been discussed earlier in connection with the difficulties in the theory of Eros.

3
The Power and Limitations of the Death Instinct

In the previous pages I have pointed to the immanent contradictions into which Freud was forced when he changed from the libido theory to the Eros–death-instinct theory. There is another conflict of a different kind in the latter theory which must attract our attention: the conflict between Freud the theoretician and Freud the humanist. The theoretician arrives at the conclusion that man has only the alternative between destroying himself (slowly, by illness) or destroying others; or – putting it in other words – between causing suffering either to himself or to others. The humanist rebels against the idea of this tragic alternative that would make war a rational solution of this aspect of human existence.

Not that Freud was averse to tragic alternatives. On the contrary, in his earlier theory he had constructed such a tragic alternative: repression of instinctual demands (especially pregenital ones) was supposed to be the basis of the development of civilization; the repressed instinctual drive was 'sublimated' into valuable cultural channels, but still at the expense of full human happiness. On the other hand, repression led not only to increasing civilization, but also to the development of neurosis among the many in whom the repressive process did not work successfully. Lack of civilization combined with full happiness, or civilization combined with neurosis and diminished happiness seemed to be the alternative.[23]

The contradiction between the death instinct and Eros confronts man with a real and truly tragic alternative. A real alternative because he can decide to attack and wage war, to be aggressive, and to express his hostility because he prefers to do this rather than to be sick. That this alternative is a tragic one hardly needs to be proved, at least not as far as Freud or any other humanist is concerned.

Freud makes no attempt to befog the issue by blurring the sharpness of the conflict. As quoted earlier, in the *New Introductory Lectures* he wrote:

And now we are struck by the significance of the possibility that the aggressiveness may not be able to find satisfaction in the external world because it comes up against real obstacles. If this happens, it will perhaps retreat and increase the amount of self-destructiveness holding sway in the interior. We shall hear how this is in fact what occurs and how important a process this is. (S. Freud, 1933)

23. cf., for instance, *Civilized Sexual Morality and Modern Nervous Illness* where Freud wrote: 'We may justly hold our civilization responsible for the threat of neurasthenia' (S. Freud, 1908a).
Herbert Marcuse makes the point that Freud said that full happiness requires the full expression of all sexual instincts (which in Freud's sense would mean particularly the pregenital components) (H. Marcuse, 1955). Regardless of whether Freud is right in his opinion, Marcuse overlooks the fact that Freud's main point was that of the tragic alternatives. Hence, it is not at all a Freudian view that the goal should be the unlimited expression of all components of the sexual instinct. On the contrary, Freud – being on the side of civilization against barbarism – prefers repression to its opposite. Besides, Freud always spoke of the repressive influence of *civilization* on the instincts, and the idea that this happens only in capitalism and need not happen in socialism is completely contrary to his thinking. Marcuse's ideas on this subject suffer from insufficient knowledge of the details of Freud's theory.

In *An Outline of Psychoanalysis* he wrote: 'Holding back aggressiveness is in general unhealthy and leads to illness' (S. Freud, 1938). After having thus drawn the lines sharply, how does Freud respond to the impulse not to leave human affairs in such a hopeless view, and to avoid siding with those who recommend war as the best medicine for the human race?

Indeed, Freud made several theoretical attempts to find a way out of the dilemma between the theoretician and the humanist. One attempt lies in the idea that the destructive instinct can be transformed into conscience. In *Civilization and Its Discontents* Freud asks: 'What happens to him [the aggressor] to render his desire for aggression innocuous?' Freud answers thus:

Something very remarkable, which we should never have guessed and which is nevertheless quite obvious. His aggressiveness is introjected, internalized; it is in point of fact sent back to where it came from – that is, it is directed towards his own ego. There it is taken over by a portion of the ego, which sets itself over against the rest of the ego as super-ego, and which now, in the form of 'conscience', is ready to put into action against the ego the same harsh aggressiveness that the ego would have liked to satisfy upon other, extraneous individuals. The tension between the harsh super-ego and the ego that is subjected to it, is called by us the sense of guilt; it expresses itself as a need for punishment. Civilization, therefore, obtains mastery over the individual's dangerous desire for aggression by weakening and disarming it and by setting up an agency within him to watch over it, like a garrison in a conquered city. (S. Freud, 1930)[24]

The transformation of destructiveness into a self-punishing conscience does not seem to be as much of an advantage as Freud implies. According to his theory conscience would have to be as cruel as the death instinct, since it is charged

24. Freud's concept of conscience as essentially punishing is surely a very narrow one, in the tradition of certain religious ideas; it is that of an 'authoritarian' not a 'humanistic' conscience; cf. E. Fromm (1947).

with its energies, and no reason is given why the death instinct should be 'weakened' and 'disarmed'. It would
rather seem that the following analogy would express the
real consequences of Freud's thought more logically: a city
that has been ruled by a cruel enemy defeats him with the
help of a dictator who then sets up a system that is just as
cruel as that of the defeated enemy; and thus, what is
gained?

However, this theory of the strict conscience as a manifestation of the death instinct is not the only attempt Freud
makes to mitigate his concept of a tragic alternative.
Another less tragic explanation is expressed in the following:
'The instinct of destruction, moderated and tamed, and, as
it were, inhibited in its aim, must, when it is directed towards objects, provide the ego with the satisfaction of its
vital needs and with control over nature' (S. Freud, 1930).
This seems to be a good example of 'sublimation';[25] the
aim of the instinct is not weakened, but it is directed towards
other socially valuable aims, in this case the 'domination
over nature'.

This sounds, indeed, like a perfect solution. Man is freed
from the tragic choice between destroying either others or
himself, because the energy of the destructive instinct is
used for the control over nature. But, we must ask, can this
really be so? Can it be true that destructiveness becomes
transformed into constructiveness? What can 'control over
nature' mean? Taming and breeding animals, gathering

25. Freud did not use in general the term 'sublimation' in connection
with the death instinct, but it seems to me that the concept with which
the following paragraph deals is the same as that which Freud calls
sublimation in relation to the libido. The concept of 'sublimation'
however is questionable even when Freud applied it to sexual, and especially to pregenital instincts. In terms of the older theory, the example
was popular that a surgeon uses the sublimated energy of his sadism.
But is this really true? After all, the surgeon does not only cut: he also
mends, and it is more likely that the best surgeons are not motivated
by sublimated sadism, but by many other factors, such as having
manual dexterity, the wish to heal through immediate action, the
capacity for making quick decisions, etc.

and cultivating plants, weaving cloth, building huts, manu-facturing pottery, and many more activities including the construction of machines, railroads, aeroplanes, skyscrapers. All these are acts of constructing, building, unifying, syn-thesizing, and, indeed, if one wanted to attribute them to one of the two basic instincts, they might be considered as being motivated by Eros rather than by the death instinct. With the possible exception of killing animals for their con-sumption and killing men in war, both of which could be considered as rooted in destructiveness, material production is not destructive but constructive.

Freud makes one other attempt to soften the harshness of his alternative in his answer to Albert Einstein's letter on the topic *Why War?* Not even on this occasion, when confronted with the question of the psychological causes of war by one of the greatest scientists and humanists of the century, did Freud try to hide or mitigate the harsh-ness of his previous alternatives. With the fullest clarity he wrote:

As a result of a little speculation, we have come to suppose that this instinct is at work in every living creature and is striving to bring it to ruin and to reduce life to its original condition of inanimate matter. Thus it quite seriously deserves to be called a death instinct, while the erotic instincts represent the effort to live. The death instinct turns into the destructive instinct when, with the help of special organs, it is directed outwards, on to objects. The organism preserves its own life, so to say, by destroying an extraneous one. Some portion of the death instinct, however, remains operative *within* the organism, and we have sought to trace quite a number of normal and pathological phenomena to this internalization of the destructive instinct. We have even been guilty of the heresy of attributing the origin of conscience to this diversion inwards of aggressiveness. You will notice that it is by no means a trivial matter if this process is carried too far; it is posit-ively unhealthy. On the other hand if these forces are turned to destruction in the external world, the organism will be relieved and the effect must be beneficial. *This would serve as a biological justification for all the ugly and dangerous impulses against which we are struggling. It must be admitted that they stand nearer to Nature than does our resistance to them for which an explanation also needs to be found.* (S. Freud, 1933a; italics added)

After having made this very clear and uncompromising statement summing up his previously expressed views about the death instinct, and after having stated that he could hardly believe the stories about those happy regions where there are races 'who know neither coercion nor aggression', Freud tried towards the end of the letter to arrive at a less pessimistic solution than the beginning seemed to foreshadow. His hope is founded on several possibilities: 'If willingness to engage in war,' he wrote, 'is an effect of the destructive instinct, the most obvious plan will be to bring Eros, its antagonist, into play against it. Anything that encourages the growth of emotional ties between men must operate against war' (S. Freud, 1933a).

It is remarkable and moving how Freud the humanist and, as he calls himself, 'pacifist', tries here almost frantically to evade the logical consequences of his own premises. If the death instinct is as powerful and fundamental as Freud claims throughout, how can it be considerably reduced by bringing Eros into play, considering that they are both contained in every cell and that they constitute an irreducible quality of living matter?

Freud's second argument in favour of peace is even more fundamental. At the end of his letter to Einstein he writes:

Now war is in the crassest opposition to the psychical attitude imposed on us by the process of civilization, and for that reason we are bound to rebel against it; we simply cannot any longer put up with it. This is not merely an intellectual and emotional repudiation; we pacifists have a *constitutional* intolerance of war, an idiosyncrasy magnified, as it were, to the highest degree. It seems, indeed, as though the lowering of aesthetic standards in war plays a scarcely smaller part in our rebellion than do its cruelties. And how long shall we have to wait before the rest of mankind become pacifists too? There is no telling. (S. Freud, 1933a)

And at the end of this letter Freud touches upon a thought found occasionally in his work,[26] that of *the process of civilization as a factor leading to a lasting, as it were, a 'constitutional', 'organic' repression of instincts*.

Freud had already expressed this view much earlier, in the *Three Essays*, when he spoke of the sharp conflict between instinct and civilization: 'One gets an impression from civilized children that the construction of these dams is a product of education, and no doubt, education has much to do with it. But in reality *this development is organically determined* and fixed by heredity, and it can occasionally occur without any help at all from education' (S. Freud, 1905; italics added).

In *Civilization and Its Discontents* Freud continued this line of thinking by speaking of an 'organic repression', for instance in the case of the taboo related to menstruation or anal erotism, thus paving the way to civilization. We find, even as early as 1897, Freud expressed himself in a letter to Fliess (14 November 1897; Letter 75) that 'something organic played a part in repression' (S. Freud, 1897).[27]

The various statements quoted here show that Freud's reliance on a 'constitutional' intolerance to war was not only an attempt to transcend the tragic perspective of his death instinct concept produced *ad hoc*, as it were, by his discussion with Einstein, but was in accord with a line of thinking that, although never dominant, had been in the background of his thoughts since 1897.

26. cf. S. Freud (1930), as well as sources quoted in the editor's Introduction to that paper.

27. I gratefully acknowledge the very helpful summary of all Freud's views on 'organic repression' by the editor of the standard edition, James Strachey, in his Introduction to *Civilization and Its Discontents* (Freud, 1930). This acknowledgement is also extended to all his other introductions, which enable the reader, even if well acquainted with Freud's work, to locate more quickly a quotation he is searching for, and beyond that, to recall out-of-the-way quotations he has forgotten. Needless to say that for the student less familiar with Freud's work, they are also a most helpful guide.

If Freud's assumptions were right, that civilization produces 'constitutional' and hereditary repressions, that is, that in the process of civilization certain instinctual needs are in fact weakened, then indeed he would have found a way out of the dilemma. Then civilized man would not be prompted by certain instinctual demands contrary to civilization to the same degree as primitive man. The impulse to destroy would not have the same intensity and power in civilized man that it would have in primitive man. This line of thinking would also lead to the speculation that certain inhibitions against killing might have been built up during the process of civilization and become hereditarily fixed. However, even if one could discover such hereditary factors in general, it would be exceedingly difficult to assume their existence in the case of the death instinct.

According to Freud's concept the death instinct is a tendency inherent in all living substance; it seems to be a theoretically difficult proposition to assume that this fundamental biological force could be weakened in the course of civilization. With the same logic one could assume that Eros could be constitutionally weakened and such assumptions would lead to the more general assumption that the very nature of living substance could be altered by the process of civilization, by means of an 'organic' repression.[28]

However this may be, today it would seem to be one of the most important subjects for research to try to establish the facts with regard to this point. Is there sufficient evidence to show that there has been a constitutional, organic repression of certain instinctual demands in the course of civilization? Is this repression one that is different from repression in Freud's usual sense, inasmuch as it weakens the instinctual demand, rather than removing it from consciousness or diverting it to other aims? And more specifically, in the course of history have man's destructive impulses become weaker, or have inhibitory impulses

28. What speaks most against Freud's assumption was that prehistoric man was not more but less aggressive than civilized man.

developed that are now hereditarily fixed? To answer this question would require extended studies, especially in anthropology, socio-psychology, and genetics.

Looking back at the various attempts Freud made to mitigate the sharpness of his fundamental alternative – destruction of others or of oneself – one can only admire his persistence in trying to find a way out of the dilemma and, at the same time, his honesty in having refrained from believing that he had found a satisfactory solution. Thus, in the *Outline* he no longer makes reference to the factors limiting the power of destructiveness (except the role of the super-ego) and concludes this topic by saying: 'This is one of the dangers to health by which human beings are faced on their path to cultural development. Holding back aggressiveness is in general unhealthy and leads to illness (to mortification)' (S. Freud, 1938).[29]

4
Critique of the Substance of the Theory

We must proceed now from the immanent critique of Freud's theory of the death and life instincts to a critique of the substance of his argument. Since a great deal has been written about this I need not enter into a discussion of all the points of such a critique. I shall mention only those of particular interest from my own point of view, or which have not been adequately dealt with by other writers.

Perhaps the greatest weakness of Freud's assumption lies both here and with regard to some other problems in the fact that the theoretician and system builder in him ran ahead of the clinical observer. Furthermore Freud was

29. I want to point out once more the change in Freud's view concerning the relationship between instinct and civilization. In terms of the libido theory, civilization results in the repression of *sexual* strivings and may cause *neurosis*. In the new theory, civilization leads to the holding back of *aggressiveness* and results in *physical illness*.

guided onesidedly by *intellectual* imagination rather than by *experimental* imagination; had this not been so, he would have sensed that sadism, aggressiveness, destructiveness, mastery, and will for power are qualitatively entirely different phenomena, even though the borderline may not always be clearly demarcated. But Freud thought in abstract theoretical terms which implied that all that was not love was death instinct, since every tendency had to be subsumed under the new duality. The result of putting different and partly contradictory psychical tendencies into one category leads necessarily to the result that one understands none of them; one is forced to speak in an alienated language about phenomena of which one can speak meaningfully only if one's words refer to different, specific forms of experience.

Yet it is a testimony to Freud's capacity to transcend at times his commitment to a dualistic instinct theory that we find that he did see some essential differences in quality between various forms of aggressiveness, even though he did not differentiate them by different terms. Here are the three main forms he saw:

1. Impulses of cruelty, independent of sexuality, based on the self-preservative instincts; their aim is to realize realistic dangers and to defend themselves against attack (Freud, 1905). The function of this aggression is survival, i.e., defence against threats to vital interests. This type would correspond roughly with what I have called 'defensive aggression'.

2. In his concept of sadism Freud saw one form of destructiveness for which the act of destroying, forcing, torturing, is lustful (although he explained the particular quality of this form of destructiveness as an alloy of sexual lust and non-sexual death instinct). This type would correspond to 'sadism'.

3. Eventually, Freud recognized a third type of destructiveness that he described as follows: 'But even where it emerges without any sexual purpose, in the blindest fury of

destructiveness, we cannot fail to recognize that the satisfaction of the instinct is accompanied by an extraordinarily high degree of narcissistic enjoyment, owing to its presenting the ego with a fulfilment of the latter's old wishes for omnipotence.'

It is not easy to say which phenomenon Freud refers to here. Pure destructiveness of the necrophilous person, or the extreme form of the power-drunk, sadistic member of a lynching or raping mob. Perhaps the difficulty lies in the general problem of differentiating between extreme forms of sadistic, omnipotent rage and pure necrophilia, a difficulty I have commented on in the text. But whatever the answer is, the fact remains that Freud recognized different phenomena, yet gave up this differentiation when he had to make the clinical facts fit his theoretical requirements.

Where are we left after this analysis of Freud's theory of the death instinct? Is it essentially different from the construct of a 'destructive instinct' that many psychoanalysts make, or from Freud's earlier construct, that of the libido? We have in the course of this discussion pointed out subtle changes and contradictions in Freud's development of the theory of aggression. We have seen, in the answer to Einstein, that Freud for a moment indulged in speculations that tended to make his position less harsh and less apt to be used as a justification of war. But when we look over Freud's theoretical edifice once more, it becomes clear that in spite of all this, the basic character of the death instinct follows in a certain way the logic of the hydraulic model that Freud had originally applied to the sexual instinct. A striving for death is constantly generated in all living substance, leaving only one alternative: either to do the silent work of man's destruction from within, or to turn towards the outside as 'destructiveness' and to save man from self-destruction by the destruction of others. As Freud put it: 'Holding back aggressiveness is in general unhealthy and leads to illness (to mortification)' (S. Freud, 1938).

Summing up his examination of Freud's theory of life and

death instinct, it is hard to avoid the conclusion that Freud, since 1920, got entangled in two basically different concepts and in two distinct approaches to the problem of human motivation. The first, the conflict between self-preservation and sexuality, was the traditional concept, reason versus passion, duty versus natural inclination, or hunger versus love, as the driving forces in man. The later theory, based on the conflict between the inclination to live and the one to die, between integration and disintegration, between love and hate, was entirely different. While one may say that it was based on the popular concept of love and hate as the two forces driving man, it was in fact more profound and original; it followed the Platonic tradition of Eros and considered love as the energy that binds all living substance together and is the guarantor of life. More specifically even, it seems to follow Empedocles' idea that the world of living creatures can exist only as long as the struggle between the contrary forces of Strife and Aphrodite, or love, the power of attraction and repulsion are active together.[30]

5
The Principle of Excitation Reduction: the Basis for the Pleasure Principle and Death Instinct

The differences between Freud's old and new theories, however, must not make one forget that there was one axiom, deeply fixed in Freud's mind since he studied with von Brucke, that is common to both theories. This axiom is the 'principle of tension reduction' underlying Freud's thinking from 1888 to his last discussion of the death instinct.

30. The similarities between Empedocles' and Freud's concepts are perhaps not as real as they appear at first glance. For Empedocles, Love is attraction between dissimilars; Strife is attraction of like to like. A serious comparison requires the examination of Empedocles' whole system (cf. W. K. C. Guthrie, 1965).

Already at the very beginning of his work in 1888 Freud spoke of a 'stable amount of excitation' (S. Freud, 1888). He formulated the principle more explicitly in 1892 when he wrote: '*The nervous system endeavours to keep constant something in its functional relations that we may describe as the "sum of excitation". It puts this precondition of health into effect by disposing associatively of every sensible accretion of excitation* (Eregungszuwachs) *or by discharging it by an appropriate motor reaction*' (S. Freud, 1892; italics added).

Correspondingly Freud defined a psychical trauma, as he employed it in his theory of hysteria, as: '*Any impression which the nervous system has difficulty in disposing of by means of associative or motor reaction becomes a psychical trauma*' (S. Freud, 1892; italics added).

In the *Project for a Scientific Psychology* (1895a) Freud spoke of the 'principle of neuronic inertia' that asserts that 'neurons tend to divest themselves of Q. On this basis the structure and development as well as the functions (of neurons) are to be understood' (Freud, 1895a). What Freud means by Q is not entirely clear. He defines it in this paper as 'what distinguishes activity from rest' (Freud, 1895a),[31] meaning nervous energy.[32] At any rate, one is on safe

31. For a detailed discussion of the meaning of 'Q' cf. J. Strachey, *Standard Edition*, vol. 3, Appendix C.

32. cf. J. Strachey's explanatory notes to vol. 3 of the *Standard Edition*. Strachey stresses the fact that the concept of psychical energy is nowhere to be found in the Project, while it is in common use in *The Interpretation of Dreams*. Furthermore, Strachey calls attention to the fact that traces of the old neurological background are to be found in Freud's writings long after he had accepted the concept of a psychical – as distinguished from the physical – energy; even as late as 1915, in the paper on *The Unconscious* Freud speaks of 'nervous' rather than of psychical energy. Strachey states that, in fact, 'many major characteristics of Q survived in a transmogrified shape to the very end of Freud's writings' (vol. 1, p. 345). Freud himself came to the conclusion that we did not know the answer to what Q is. He wrote in *Beyond the Pleasure Principle*: 'The indefiniteness of all our discussions on what we describe as metapsychology is of course due to the fact that we know nothing of the nature of the excitatory process that takes place in the elements of the psychical systems, and that we do not feel justified in framing any

ground in saying that in those early years lies the beginning of what Freud later called the principle of 'constancy', or implying the reduction of all nervous activity to a minimal level. Twenty-five years later, in *Beyond the Pleasure Principle*, Freud stated the principle in psychological terms as follows: 'The mental apparatus endeavours to keep the quantity of excitation present in it *as low as possible or at least to keep it constant*' (S. Freud, 1920; italics added). Freud here speaks of the same principle – 'constancy' or 'inertia' – as having two versions: one of keeping excitation constant, the other of reducing it to the lowest possible level. Freud sometimes used either of the two terms denoting one or the other version of the basic principle.[33]

The pleasure principle is based on the constancy principle. Chemically produced libidinous excitation needs to be reduced to its normal level; this principle of keeping tension constant governs the functioning of the nervous apparatus. Tension that has risen above its regular level is felt as 'unpleasure', its reduction to the constant level as 'pleasure'. 'The facts which have caused us to believe in the dominance of the pleasure principle also find expression in the hypothesis that the mental apparatus endeavours to keep the quantity of excitation present in it as low as possible, or, at least to keep it constant ... *The pleasure principle follows from the principle of constancy*' (S. Freud, 1920; italics added). Unless one understands Freud's axiom of tension reduction, one will never understand his position, which was not centred around the concept of a hedonistic striving for pleasure, but rather on the assumption of the physiological necessity to reduce tension and with it – psychically –

hypothesis on the subject. We are consequently operating all the time with a large unknown factor, which we are obliged to carry over into every new formula' (S. Freud, 1920).

33. J. Bowlby, in his excellent discussion of this problem, states that originally Freud considered the principle of inertia as primary and that of constancy as secondary. The reading of the relevant passages leads me to a different assumption that seems also to correspond to J. Strachey's interpretation (cf. J. Bowlby, 1969).

unpleasure. The pleasure principle is based on keeping excitation at a certain constant level. But the principle of constancy implies *also* the tendency to keep excitation on a *minimal* level; in this version it becomes the basis for the death instinct. As Freud stated it:

> The dominating tendency of mental life, and perhaps of nervous life in general, is the effort to reduce, to keep constant, or to remove internal tension due to stimuli (the nirvana principle, to borrow a term from Barbara Law) – a tendency which finds expression in the pleasure principle; and our recognition of that fact is one of our strongest reasons for believing in the existence of death instincts. (S. Freud, 1920)

Freud arrives at this point at an almost untenable position; the principles of constancy, inertia, nirvana, are identical; the principle of tension reduction governs the sexual instinct (in terms of the pleasure principle) and is at the same time the essence of the death instinct. Considering that Freud ascribes to the death instinct not only self-destruction but also destruction against others, he would arrive at the paradox that the pleasure principle and the destructive instinct owe their existence to the same principle. Freud, quite naturally, could not be satisfied with such an idea, especially since it would correspond to a monistic rather than the dualistic model of conflicting forces which Freud never gave up. Four years later Freud wrote in the *Economic Problem of Masochism*:

> But we have unhesitatingly identified the pleasure-unpleasure principle with this nirvana principle ... The nirvana principle (and the pleasure principle which is supposedly identical with it) would be entirely in the service of the death instincts, whose aim is to conduct the restlessness of life into the stability of the inorganic state, and it would have the function of giving warnings against the demands of the life instincts – the libido – which try to disturb the intended course of life. *But such a view cannot be correct.* (S. Freud, 1924; italics added)

In order to prove the incorrectness of this view Freud takes a step that ordinary expedience would have recommended from the very beginning. He wrote:

> It seems that in the series of feelings of tension we have a direct sense of the increase and decrease of amounts of stimulus, and it cannot be doubted that there are pleasurable tensions and unpleasurable relaxations of tension. The state of sexual excitation is the most striking example of a pleasurable increase of stimulus of this sort, but it is certainly not the only one.
>
> Pleasure and unpleasure, therefore, cannot be referred to an increase or decrease of a quantity (which we describe as 'tension due to stimulus'), although they obviously have a great deal to do with that factor. It appears that they depend, not on this quantitative factor, but on some characteristic of it which we can only describe as a qualitative one. It we were able to say what this qualitative characteristic is, we should be much further advanced in psychology. Perhaps it is the rhythm, the temporal sequence of changes, rises and falls in the quality of stimulus. We do not know. (S. Freud, 1924)

However, Freud did not pursue this thought any further, although he seemed not to be satisfied with this explanation. Instead he offered another one that is meant to overcome the danger of the identification of pleasure with destruction. He continued:

> However this may be, we must recognize that the nirvana principle, belonging as it does to the death instinct, has undergone a modification in living organisms through which it has become the pleasure principle; and we shall henceforward avoid regarding the two principles as one ... The *nirvana* principle expresses the trend of the death instinct; the *pleasure* principle represents the demands of the libido; and the modification of the latter principle, the *reality* principle represents the influence of the external world. (S. Freud, 1924)

It seems that this explanation is a theoretical fiat rather than an explanation for the assertion that the pleasure principle and the death instinct are not identical.

While Freud's attempt to extricate himself from a paradoxical position is, in my opinion, unsuccessful, although most brilliant, the important problem at this point is not whether he succeeded or not. It is, rather, that Freud's whole psychological thinking from the very beginning to the end was dominated by the axiom that the principle of reduction of excitation was the governing principle of all psychic and nervous life.

We know the origins of this axiom. Freud himself quoted G. T. Fechner (1873) as the father of this idea. He wrote:

> We cannot, however, remain indifferent to the discovery that an investigator of such penetration as G. T. Fechner held a view on the subject of pleasure and unpleasure which coincides in all essentials with the one that has been forced upon us by psycho-analytic work. Fechner's statement is to be found contained in a small work, *Einige Ideen zur Schöpfungs – und Entwicklungsgeschichte der Organismen*, 1873 (Part XI, Supplement, 94) and reads as follows: 'In so far as conscious impulses always have some relation to pleasure or unpleasure, pleasure and unpleasure too can be regarded as having a psycho-physical relation to conditions of stability and instability. This provides a basis for a hypothesis into which I propose to enter in greater detail elsewhere. According to this hypothesis, every psycho-physical motion rising above the threshold of consciousness is attended by pleasure in proportion as, beyond a certain limit, it approximates to complete stability, and is attended by unpleasure in proportion as, beyond a certain limit, it deviates from complete stability; while between the two limits, which may be described as qualitative thresholds of pleasure and unpleasure, there is a certain margin of aesthetic indifference . . .'[34]

> The facts which have caused us to believe in the dominance of the pleasure principle in mental life also find expression in the hypothesis that the mental apparatus endeavours to keep the quantity of excitation present in it as low as possible or at least to keep it constant. This later hypothesis is only another way of stating the pleasure principle; for if the work of the mental apparatus is directed towards keeping the quantity of excitation low,

---

34. Freud stated in *The Ego and the Id*: 'If it is true that Fechner's principle of constancy governs life, which thus consists of a continuous descent towards death . . .' (S. Freud, 1923). This 'descent towards death' is not to be found in Fechner's statement; it is Freud's special version of an enlargement of Fechner's principle.

then anything that is calculated to increase that quantity is bound to be felt as adverse to the functioning of the apparatus, that is as unpleasurable. The pleasure principle follows from the principle of constancy; actually the latter principle was inferred from the facts which forced us to adopt the pleasure principle. Moreover, a more detailed discussion will show that the tendency which we thus attribute to the mental apparatus is subsumed as a special case under Fechner's principle of the 'tendency towards stability', to which he has brought the feelings of pleasure and unpleasure into relation. (S. Freud, 1920)

But Fechner was by no means the only representative of the principle of tension reduction. Stimulated by the energy concept of physics, the concept of energy and energy conservation became popular among physiologists. If Freud was influenced by these physical theories, they would have seemed to imply that the death instinct was only one particular instance of the general physical law. But the fallacy of such a conclusion becomes apparent if we consider the difference between inorganic and organic matter. René Dubos has expressed this point very succinctly. He wrote:

According to one of the most fundamental laws of physics, the universal tendency in the world of matter is for everything to run downhill, to fall to the lowest possible level of tension, with constant loss of potential energy and of organization. In contrast, life constantly creates and maintains order out of the randomness of matter. To apprehend the deep significance of this fact one need only think what happens to any living organism – the very smallest as well as the largest and most evolved – when finally it dies. (R. Dubos, 1962)

Two English writers, R. Kapp (1931) and L. S. Penrose (1931) have criticized the attempts of some authors to connect physical theory with the death instinct so convincingly that one 'must finally dispose of the idea that there could be any relationship between entropy and the death instinct'.[35]

35. E. Jones (1957); cf. the literature quoted by Jones, especially S. Bernfield and S. Feitelberg (1930); cf. also K. H. Pribram (1962).

Whether or not Freud had in mind the connection between entropy and the death instinct does not matter too much. Even if he did not, the whole principle of excitation and energy reduction to the lowest minimal level rests upon the basic error that Dubos points to in the above quotation; the error of ignoring the fundamental difference between life and non-life, between 'organisms' and 'things'.

In order to get away from laws valid only for organic matter, in later years another analogy has been preferred to that of entropy, namely the concept of 'homeostasis' as developed by Walter B. Cannon (1963). But Jones and others who see in this concept an analogy to Freud's Nirvana principle confuse the two principles. Freud speaks of the tendency to abolish – or reduce – excitation. Cannon, on the other hand, and many later investigators, speak of the necessity of keeping a relatively stable inner environment. This stability implies that the inner environment tends to remain stable, but not that it tends to reduce energy to the minimal point. The confusion apparently arises because of the ambiguity of the words 'stability' and 'constancy'. A simple example can demonstrate the fallacy. If the temperature of a room is to be kept at a stable or constant level via a thermostat, it means it should neither go above nor below a certain level; if, however, the tendency were that the temperature should be on a minimal level, it would be an entirely different matter; in fact, the homeostatic principle of stability contradicts the Nirvana principle of total or relative energy reduction.

There seems to be little doubt that Freud's basis axiom of tension reduction, which is father both of the pleasure principle and of the death instinct, owes its existence to the thinking characteristic of German mechanistic materialism. It was not clinical experience that suggested this concept to Freud; Freud's deep attachment to the physiological theories of his teachers saddled him and later psychoanalysis with the 'axiom'. It forced clinical observation and the resulting formulation of theory into the narrow framework of tension reduction, which could hardly be squared with the wealth of data showing that man, at all ages, seeks excitation, stimulation, relations of love and friendship, is eager to increase his relatedness to the world; in short, man seems to be motivated just as much by the principle of tension increase as by that of tension reduction. But although many psychoanalysts were impressed by the limited validity of tension reduction, they did not change their fundamental position and tried to muddle along with a peculiar mixture of Freud's metapsychological concepts and the logic of their clinical data.

Perhaps the puzzle of Freud's self-deception about the validity of the concept of the death instinct requires still another element for its solution. Every careful reader of Freud's work must also be aware how tentatively and cautiously he treated his new theoretical constructions when presenting them for the first time. He made no claim for their validity and sometimes even spoke deprecatingly of their value. But the more time passed, the more hypothetical constructs turned into theories upon which new constructions and theories were built. Freud the theorist was very well aware of the doubtful validity of many of his constructs. Why did he forget these original doubts? It is hard to answer this question; one possible answer may be found in his role as the leader of the psychoanalytic movement.[36] Those of his students who dared to criticize fundamental aspects of his theories left him or were squeezed out in one way or another. Those who built the movement were mostly pedestrian men, from the standpoint of their theoretical capacity, and it would have been difficult for them to follow Freud through basic theoretical changes. They needed a dogma in which they believed and around which they could organize the movement.[37] Thus Freud the

36. cf. E. Fromm (1959).

37. This is borne out by the reaction of the majority of Freudians to the death instinct. They could not follow this new and profound specula-

scientist became to some extent the prisoner of Freud the leader of the movement; or to put it differently, Freud the teacher became the prisoner of his faithful, but uncreative disciples.

---

tion and found a way out by formulating Freud's ideas about aggression in terms of the old instinct theory.

Bibliography

For reasons of space this bibliography does not list all materials consulted, but, with a few exceptions, only those books and papers specifically noted in the text or footnotes.

ABRAMOVA, Z. A. (1967). *Palaeolithic Art in the U.S.S.R.*, trans. Catherine Page. Arctic Anthropology, vol. 4. Moscow-Leningrad: Akademiia Nauk SSSR. (Quoted in A. Marschack, ed., 1972, q.v.)

ACKERMANN, J. (1970). *Heinrich Himmler als Ideologe*. Göttingen: Musterschmidt.

ACKERT, K. (1967). (Quoted in B. Kaada, 1967, q.v.)

ADORNO, T. W., FRENKEL-BRUNSWIK, E., LEVINSON, D. F., and SANFORD, R. N. (1950). *The Authoritarian Personality*. New York: Harper & Bros.

ALANBROOKE, Viscount [ALAN FRANCIS BROOKE]. (1957). *The Turning of the Tide*. London: Collins.

ALEE, W. C., NISSEN, H. W., and NIMKOFF, M. F. (1953). A Reexamination of the Concept of Instinct. *Psych. Rev.* 60 (5): 287–97.

ALEXANDER, F. (1921). Metapsychologische Betrachtungen. *Intern. Ztsch. f. Psychoanalyse.* 6: 270–85. (Quoted in E. Jones, 1957, q.v.)

ALTMAN, J. (1967). Effects of Early Experience on Brain Morphology. In *Malnutrition, Learning, and Behavior*, ed. N. S. Scrimshaw and J. E. Gordon. Cambridge: M.I.T. Press, 1972. (Quoted in G. C. Quarton, T. O. Melnechuk, and F. O. Schmitt, 1967, q.v.)

ALTMAN, J. (1967a). Postnatal Growth and Differentiation of the Mammalian Brain, with Implications for a Morphological Theory of Memory. In *The Neurosciences: A Study Program*, ed. G. C. Quarton, T. O. Melnechuk, and F. O. Schmitt. New York: Rockefeller Univ. Press, 1967.

ALTMAN, J., and DAS, C. D. (1964). Autobiographic Examination of the Effects of Enriched Environment on the Rate of Glial Multiplication in the Adult Rat Brain. *Nature.* 204: 1161–3. (Quoted by J. Altman, in G. C. Quarton, T. O. Melnechuk, and F. O. Schmitt, 1967, q.v.)

ALTMAN, S. A. (1960). A Field Study of the Sociobiology of Rhesus Monkeys, *Macaca mulata.* Thesis, Harvard Univ. Unpublished.

AMES, O. (1939). *Economic Annuals and Human Cultures.* Cambridge: Botanical Museum of Harvard Univ.

AMMACHER, P. (1962). On the Significance of Freud's Neurological Background. In *Psychological Issues.* Seattle: Univ. of Washington Press.

ANDERSON, E. (1967). *Plants, Man and Life.* Rev. ed. Berkeley: Univ. of California Press. (1st ed. Boston: Little, Brown, 1952.)

ANDRESKI, S. (1964). Origins of War. In *The Natural History of Aggression,* ed. J. D. Carthy and F. J. Ebling. New York: Academic.

ANDRESKI, S. (1972). *Social Science as Sorcery.* London: A. Deutsch.

ANGRESS, W. T., and SMITH, B. F. (1959). Diaries of Heinrich Himmler's Early Years. *Journal of Modern History.* 51 (Sept.)

ARAMONI, A. (1965). *Psicoánalisis de la Dinámica de un Pueblo* (*México, Tierra de Hombres*) [Psychoanalysis of the dynamics of a people (Mexico, land of men)]. Mexico: B. Costa-Amic, Editorial.

ARDREY, R. (1961). *African Genesis.* New York: Atheneum. London: Collins.

ARDREY, R. (1966). *The Territorial Imperative: A Personal Inquiry into the Animal Origins of Property and Nations.* New York: Atheneum. London: Collins.

AVIS, V. See Washburn, S. L. (1958), joint author.

BACHOFEN, J. J. (1967). *Myth, Religion and the Mother Right: Selected Writings of Johann Jakob Bachofen,* ed. J. Campbell; trans. R. Manheim. Princeton: Princeton Univ. Press. (Original ed. *Das Mutterrecht,* 1861.)

BANKS, C. See Haney, C. In press, joint author.

BARNETT, S. A. (1958). An Analysis of Social Behavior in Wild Rats. *Proc. Zool. Soc. Lond.* 130: 107–52.

BARNETT, S. A. (1958a). Experiments on 'Neophobia' in Wild and Laboratory Rats. *Brit. Jour. Med. Psychol.* 49: 195–201.

BARNETT, S. A., and SPENCER, M. M. (1951). Feeding, Social Behaviour and Interspecific Competition in Wild Rats. *Behaviour*. 3: 229–42.

BARTELL, G. T. (1971). *Group Sex*. New York: Peter H. Wyden.

BEACH, F. A. (1945). Bisexual Mating Behavior in the Male Rat: Effects of Castration and Hormone Administration. *Physiol. Zool.* 18: 390.

BEACH, F. A. (1955). The Descent of Instinct. *Psych. Rev.* 62 (6): 401–10.

BEEMAN, E. A. (1947). The Effect of Male Hormone on Aggressive Behavior in Mice. *Physiol. Zool.* 20: 373.

BEG, M. A. See Southwick, C. H. (1965), joint author.

BELAV, J. (1960). *Trance in Bali*. New York: Columbia Univ. Press.

BENDER, L. (1942). Childhood Schizophrenia. *Nerv. Child*. 1: 138–40.

BENEDICT, R. (1934). *Patterns of Culture*. New York: New American Library, Mentor. London: Routledge.

BENEDICT, R. (1959). The Natural History of War. In *An American Anthropologist at Work*, ed. M. Mead. Boston: Houghton Mifflin.

BENJAMIN, W. (1968). The Work of Art in the Age of Mechanical Reproduction. In *Illuminations* by W. Benjamin. New York: Harcourt Brace Jovanovich. London: Cape.

BENNETT, E. L., DIAMOND, M. C., KRECH, D., and ROSENZWEIG, M. R. (1964). Chemical and Anatomical Plasticity of the Brain. *Science*. 146: 610–19. (Quoted by J. Altman in G. C. Quarton, T. O. Melnechuk, and F. O. Schmitt, 1967, q.v.)

BERGOUNIOUX, F. M. (1964). Notes on the Mentality of Primitive Man. In *Social Life of Early Man*, ed. S. L. Washburn. Chicago: Aldine.

BERKOWITZ, L. (1962). The Frustration-Aggression Theory Revisited. In *Aggression: A Social Psychological Analysis* by L. Berkowitz. New York: McGraw-Hill.

BERKOWITZ, L. (1967). Readiness or Necessity? *Cont. Psychol.* 12: 580–83

BERKOWITZ, L (1969). The Frustration-Aggression Hypothesis Revisited. In *The Roots of Aggression: A Re-examination of the Frustration-Aggression Hypothesis*, ed. L. Berkowitz. New York: Atherton.

BERNFELD, S. (1934). Ueber die Einteilung der Triebe. *Imago*. 21.

BERNFELD, S. and FEITELBERG, S. (1930). Der Entropiesatz und der Todestrieb [Principles of Entropy and the death instinct]. *Imago.* 17: 137–206. (Quoted in E. Jones, 1957, q.v. See also R. Kapp, 1931.)

BERTALANFFY, L. von (1956). Comments on Aggression. Paper presented at the 1956 Winter Meeting of the American Psychoanalytic Association, New York City.

BERTALANFFY, L. von (1968). *General System Theory.* New York: G. Braziller. London: Allen Lane; Penguin Books.

BETTELHEIM, B. (1960). *The Informed Heart: Autonomy in a Mass Age.* New York: Macmillan Free Press.

BEXTON, W. H., HERON, W., and SCOTT, T. H. (1954). Effect of Decreased Variation in the Sensory Environment. *Can. Jour. of Psych.* 8 (2): 10–76.

BINGHAM, H. C. (1932). *Gorillas in Native Habitat.* Publication No. 426. Washington, D.C.: Carnegie Inst. of Washington.

BIRD, H. G. See Clark, G. (1946), joint author.

BLANC, A. C. (1961). Some Evidence for the Ideologies of Early Man. In *Social Life of Early Man*, ed. S. L. Washburn. Chicago: Aldine.

BLEULER, E. (1951). *Autistic Thinking. Organization and Pathology of Thought.* New York: Columbia Univ. Press.

BLEULER, E. (1969). *Lehrbuch der Psychiatrie.* 11th ed. Heidelberg: Springer-Verlag.

BLISS, E. L., ed. (1968). *Roots of Behavior.* New York: Hafner.

BOULDING, K. E. (1967). Review in *Peace and War Report.* (Mar.): 15–17.

BOURKE, J. G. (1913). *Der Unrat in Sitte, Brauch, Blauben und Gewohnheitrecht der Völker* [Scatalogical rites of all nations] with an Introduction by S. Freud. Leipzig: Ethnologischer Verlag.

BOWLBY, J. (1958). The Nature of the Child's Tie to His Mother. *Int. Journ. of Psychoan.* 39: 350–73.

BOWLBY, J. (1969). *Attachment and Love.* International Psychoanalytic Library. London: Hogarth.

BOWLBY, J. See Durbin, E. F. M. (1939), joint author.

BRANDT, H. (1970). *The Search for a Third Way.* Garden City: Doubleday.

BRAUN, E. (1935). *Diaries.* Alexandria: Archives.

BROSSE, J. (1972). *Hitler avant Hitler.* Paris: Fayard.

BRYANT, J. (1775). *Mythology.* Vol. 2. London. (quoted in J. G. Bourke, 1913, q.v.)

BUCKE, R. M. (1946). *Cosmic Consciousness*, ed. G. M. Acklom. Rev. ed. New York: Dutton.

BULLOCK, A. (1965). *A Study in Tyranny.* (Quoted in W. Maser, 1971, q.v.)

BULLOCK, T. H. (1961). The Origins of Patterned Nervous Discharge. *Behaviour.* 17: 48–59.

BURCKHARDT, C. (1965) (Quoted in P. E. Schramm. 1965, q.v.)

BURCKHARDT, K. J. (1960). *Meine Danziger Mission, 1937–39.* (Quoted in J. Ackermann, 1970, q.v.)

BURTON, A. (1967). The Meaning of Psychotherapy. *Jour. of Existentialism.* 29.

BUSS, A. H. (1961). *The Psychology of Aggression.* New York: Wiley.

CABOT, C. (Quoted in C. and W. M. S. Russell, 1968 q.v.)

CADOGAN, Sir A. (1972). *The Diaries of Sir Alexander Cadogan 1938–1945,* ed. David Dilks. New York: Putnam. London: Cassell.

CALDWELL, M. (1968). *Indonesia.* New York: Oxford Univ. Press.

CALHOUN, J. B. (1948). Mortality and Movement of Brown Rats (*Rattus norvegicus*) in Artificially Supersaturated Populations. *Jour. of Wildlife Management.* 12: 167–72.

CAMPBELL, B. G. (1966). *Human Evolution.* Chicago: Aldine. London: Heinemann.

CANNON, W. B. (1963). *Wisdom of the Body.* Rev. ed. New York: Norton.

CARPENTER, C. R. (1934). A Field Study of the Behavior and Social Relations of Howling Monkeys. *Comp. Psych. Monog.* 10 (48).

CARRIGHAR, S. (1968). War Is Not in Our Genes. In *Man and Aggression,* ed. M. F. A. Montagu, New York: Oxford Univ. Press.

CARTHY, J. D., and EBLING, F. J., eds. (1964). *The Natural History of Aggression.* New York: Academic.

CHILDE, V. G. (1936). *Man Makes Himself.* London: Watts.

CHOMSKY, N. (1959). Review of *Verbal Behavior* by B. F. Skinner. *Language.* 35: 26–58.

CHOMSKY, N. (1971). The Case Against B. F. Skinner. *The New York Review of Books.* (30 Dec.)

CHURCHMAN, C. W. (1968). *The System Approach.* New York: Dell, Delta Books.

CLARK, G., and BIRD, H. G. (1946). Hormonal Modification of Social Behavior. *Psychosom. Med. Jour.* 8: 320–31. (Quoted in J. P. Scott, 1958, q.v.)

CLARKE, G. (1969). *World Prehistory.* New York: Cambridge Univ. Press.

CLAUSEWITZ, K. von (1961). *On War*, ed. F. N. Maude; trans. J. J. Graham. Rev. ed. New York: Barnes & Noble. London: Routledge. (1st ed. *Vom Kriege*, 1833) Chapter 2, section 17.

COBLINER, G. See Spitz, R. (1965), joint author.

COLE, S. (1967). *The Neolithic Revolution.* 7th ed. London: Trustees of the British Museum.

COLLIAS, N. (Quoted in C. and W. M. S. Russell, 1968, q.v.)

DARWIN, C. (1946). *The Descent of Man.* London: Watts. (1st ed., 1872.) *The Origin of Species and the Descent of Man.* New York: Modern Library, 1936.

DAS, G. O. See Altman, J. (1964), joint author.

DAVIE, M. R. (1929). *The Evolution of War.* Port Washington, N.Y.: Kennikat.

DEETZ, J. (1968). Discussion remarks. In *Man, the Hunter*, ed. R. B. Lee and I. DeVore. Chicago: Aldine.

DELGADO, J. M. R. (1967). Aggression and Defense Under Cerebral Radio Control. In *Aggression and Defense: Neural Mechanisms and Social Patterns.* Brain Function, vol. 5, ed. C. D. Clemente and D. B. Lindsley. Berkeley: Univ. of California Press.

DELGADO, J. M. R. (1969). *Physical Control of the Mind.* World Perspective Series, ed. R. N. Anshen. New York: Harper & Row.

DEMENT, W. (1960). The Effect of Dream Deprivation. *Science.* 131: 1705–7.

DE RIVER, J. P. (1956). *The Sexual Criminal: A Psychoanalytic Study.* 2nd ed. Springfield, Ill.: C. C. Thomas. (Quoted in H. von Hentig, 1964, q.v.)

DEVORE, I., ed. (1965). *Primate Behavior: Field Studies of Primates and Apes.* New York: Holt, Rinehart & Winston.

DEVORE, I. (1970). (Quoted in D. Ploog and T. O. Melnechuk, 1970, q.v.)

DEVORE, I. See Hall, K. R. L. (1965), joint author.

DEVORE, I. See Lee, R. B. (1968), joint author.

DEVORE, I. See Washburn, S. L. (1971), joint author.

DOANE, B. K., MAHATOO, W., HERON, W., and SCOTT, T. H.

(1959). Changes in Perceptual Function after Isolation. *Can. Jour. of Psych.* 13 (3): 210–19.

DOBZHANSKY, T. (1962). *Mankind Evolving: The Evolution of the Human Species.* New Haven: Yale Univ. Press.

DOLLARD, J., MILLER, N. E., MOWRER, O. H., SEARS, G. H., and SEARS, R. R. (1939). *Frustration and Aggression.* New Haven: Yale Univ. Press.

DUBOS, R. (1962). *The Torch of Life.* Credo Series, ed. R. N. Anshen. New York: Simon & Schuster.

DUNAYEVSKAYA, R. (1973). *Philosophy and Revolution.* New York: Dell.

DURBIN, E. F. M., and BOWLBY, J. (1939). *Personal Aggressiveness in War.* New York: Columbia Univ. Press.

DURKHEIM, E. (1897). *Le Suicide.* Paris: Librarie Félix Alcan.

DUYVENDAK, J. J. L. (1928). Introduction. In *The Book of Lord Shang,* trans. J. J. L. Duyvendak. London. (Quoted in S. Andreski, 1964, q.v.)

EBLING, F. J. See Carthy, J. D. (1964), joint author.

EGGAN, D. (1943). The General Problem of Hopi Adjustment. *Amer. Anthropologist.* 45: 357–73.

EGGER, M. D., and FLYNN, J. P. (1963). Effects of Electrical Stimulation of the Amygdala on Hypothalamically Elicited Attack Behavior in Cats. *Jour. Neuro. Physiol.* 26: 705–20. (Quoted in B. Kaada, 1967, q.v.)

EIBL-EIBESFELDT, I. (1972). *On Love and Hate: The Natural History of Behavior Patterns,* trans. G. Strachan, New York: Holt, Rinehart & Winston.

EISELEY, L. (1971). The Uncompleted Man. In *In the Name of Life,* ed. B. Landis and E. S. Tauber. New York: Holt, Rinehart & Winston.

EISENBERG, L. (1972). The Human Nature of Human Nature. *Science.* 179 (14 Apr.)

ENGELS, F. (1891). *The Origin of Family, Private Property and the State, in the Light of the Researches of Lewis H. Morgan.* New York: Int. Univs. Press, 1942.

ENGELS, F. See Marx, K., joint author.

ERIKSON, E. H. (1964). *Childhood and Society.* Rev. ed. New York: Norton. London: Hogarth Press, Harmondsworth: Penguin Books.

ERVIN, F. R. See Mark, V. H. (1970), joint author.

FABING, H. D. (1956). On Going Berserk: A Neurochemical Enquiry. *Science Monthly.* 83: 232–7.

FANTZ, R. L. (1958). Pattern Vision in Young Infants. *Psych. Rec.* 8: 43–7. (Quoted in D. E. Schecter, 1973, q.v.)

FECHNER, G. T. (1873). *Einige Ideen zur Schopfungs – und Entwicklungsgeschichte der Organismen.* Pt 11, supp. 94.

FENICHEL, O. (1953). A Critique of the Death Instinct. In *Collected Papers.* 1st series. New York: Norton.

FISCHER, F. (1967). *Germany's Aims in the First World War.* New York: Norton. London: Chatto & Windus. (1st ed. *Der Griff nach der Weltmacht.* Düsseldorf: Droste Verlag, 1961.)

FLAUBERT, G. (1964). *The Legend of St. Julian the Hospitaler.* New York: New American Library.

FLETCHER, R. (1968). *Instinct in Man.* New York: Int. Univs. Press. London: Allen & Unwin. (1st ed. 1957.)

FLINT, R. W., ed. (1971). *Selected Writings of F. T. Marinetti.* New York: Farrar, Strauss & Giroux.

FLYNN, J. P. See Egger, M. D. (1963), joint author.

FOERSTER, H. von (1963). Logical Structure of Environment and Its Internal Representation. In *Internal Design Conference, Aspen, 1962,* ed. A. E. Eckerstrom. Zeeland, Mich.: Miller. Inc.

FOERSTER, H. von (1970). Molecular Ethnology. In *Molecular Mechanisms in Memory and Learning.* New York: Plenum.

FOERSTER, H. von (1971). Perception of the Future and the Future of Perception. Address at the 24th Conference on World Affairs. Boulder: Univ. of Colorado. 29 Mar.

FOSTER, G. M. (1972). The Anatomy of Envy. *Current Anthropology.* 13 (2): 165–202.

FREEMAN, D. (1964). Human Aggression in Anthropological Perspective. In *Natural History of Aggression,* ed. J. D. Carthy and F. J. Ebling. New York: Academic, 1964.

FREUCHEN, P. (1961). *Book of the Eskimos.* New York: World. (Quoted in E. R. Service, 1966, q.v.)

FREUD, S. (1888). *Hysteria.* S.E., vol. 1.*

FREUD, S. (1892). Sketches for the 'Preliminary Communication of 1893'. S. E., vol. 1.

*Except for Letter 75, to Fliess (1897), the source for the works of S. Freud noted throughout this book is the *Standard Edition of the Complete Psychological Works of Sigmund Freud* (shortened in this bibliography to S. E.), 23 vols., ed. J. Strachey. London: Hogarth Press, 1886-1939.

Bibliography 641

FREUD, S. (1895). 'The Clinical Symptomatology of Anxiety Neurosis.' In *On the Grounds for Detaching a Particular Syndrome from Neurasthenia under the Description of 'Anxiety Neurosis'*. S.E., vol. 3.

FREUD, S. (1895a). *Project for a Scientific Psychology*. S.E., vol. 1.

FREUD, S. (1897). Letter 75, to Fliess. *Letters 1873–1939*. London: Hogarth, 1961.

FREUD, S. (1898). *Sexuality in the Development of Neurosis*. S.E., vol. 3.

FREUD, S. (1900). *The Interpretation of Dreams*. S.E., vol. 3.

FREUD, S. (1905). *Three Essays on the Theory of Sexuality*. S.E., vol. 7.

FREUD, S. (1908). *Character and Anal Eroticism*. S.E., vol. 9.

FREUD, S. (1908a). *Civilized Sexual Morality and Modern Nervous Illness*. S.E., vol. 9.

FREUD, S. (1909). *Analysis of a Phobia in a Five-Year-Old Boy*. S.E., vol. 10.

FREUD, S. (1913). *Totem and Tabu*. S.E., vol. 13.

FREUD, S. (1914). *On Narcissism*. S.E., vol. 14.

FRUED, S. (1915). *Instincts and Their Vicissitudes*. S.E., vol. 14.

FREUD, S. (1915a). *The Unconscious*. S.E., vol. 14.

FREUD, S. (1915–16). *Introductory Lectures on Psychoanalysis*. S.E., vol. 15.

FREUD, S. (1916–17). *Introductory Lectures on Psychoanalysis*. S.E., vol. 16.

FREUD, S. (1920). *Beyond the Pleasure Principle*. S.E., vol. 18.

FREUD, S. (1923). *The Ego and the Id*. S.E., vol. 19.

FREUD, S. (1924). *Economic Problem of Masochism*, S.E., vol. 19.

FREUD, S. (1925). *The Resistance to Psychoanalysis*. S.E., vol. 19.

FREUD, S. (1927). *The Future of an Illusion*. S.E., vol. 21.

FREUD, S. (1930). *Civilization and Its Discontents*. S.E., vol. 21.

FREUD, S. (1931). *Female Sexuality*. S.E., vol. 21.

FREUD, S. (1933). *New Introductory Lectures*. S.E., vol. 22.

FREUD, S. (1933a). *Why War?* S.E., vol. 22.

FREUD, S. (1937). *Analysis Terminable and Interminable*. S.E., vol. 23.

FREUD, S. (1938; pub. 1940). *An Outline of Psychoanalysis*. S.E., vol. 23.

FROMM, E. (1932). Die psychoanalytische Charakterologie und ihre Bedeutung für Sozialforschung. *Ztsch. f. Sozialforschung*. 1: 253–77. Psychoanalytic Characterology and Its Relevance for Social Psychology. In *The Crisis of Psychoanalysis* by E. Fromm, New York: Holt, Rinehart & Winston, 1970. London: Cape, 1971.

FROMM, E. (1934). Die Sozialpsychologische Bedeutung der Mutterrechtstheorie. *Ztsch. f. Sozialforschung.* 3: 196–277. The Theory of Mother Right and Its Relevance for Social Psychology. In *The Crisis of Psychoanalysis* by E. Fromm. New York: Holt, Rinehart & Winston, 1970. London: Cape, 1971.

FROMM, E. (1941). *Escape from Freedom.* New York: Holt, Rinehart & Winston.

FROMM, E. (1947). *Man for Himself: An Inquiry into the Psychology of Ethics.* New York: Holt, Rinehart & Winston. London: Routledge, 1956.

FROMM, E. (1950). *Psychoanalysis and Religion.* New Haven: Yale Univ. Press.

FROMM, E. (1951). *The Forgotten Language: An Introduction to the Understanding of Dreams, Fairytales, and Myths.* New York: Holt, Rinehart & Winston.

FROMM, E. (1955). *The Sane Society.* New York: Holt, Rinehart & Winston. London: Routledge, 1971.

FROMM, E. (1959). *Sigmund Freud's Mission.* New York: Harper & Bros.

FROMM, E. (1961). *Marx's Concept of Man.* New York: Frederick Ungar.

FROMM, E. (1963). *The Dogma of Christ and Other Essays on Religion, Psychology and Culture.* New York: Holt, Rinehart & Winston. (1st ed. in German, 1931.)

FROMM, E. (1964). *The Heart of Man.* New York: Harper & Row. London: Routledge, 1965.

FROMM, E. (1968). Marx's Contribution to the Knowledge of Man. *Social Science Information.* 7 (3): 7–17. (Reprinted in E. Fromm, 1970, q.v.)

FROMM, E. (1968a). *The Revolution of Hope.* New York: Harper & Row.

FROMM, E. (1970). *The Crisis of Psychoanalysis: Essays on Freud, Marx, and Social Psychology.* New York: Holt, Rinehart & Winston. London: Cape, 1971.

FROMM, E. (1970a) Freud's Model of Man and Its Social Determinants. In *The Crisis of Psychoanalysis* by E. Fromm. New York: Holt, Rinehart & Winston. London: Cape, 1971.

FROMM, E. (1970b). The Oedipus Complex: Comments on the

Case of Little Hans. In *The Crisis of Psychoanalysis* by E. Fromm. New York: Holt, Rinehart & Winston. London: Cape, 1971.

FROMM, E., and MACCOBY, M. (1970). *Social Character in a Mexican Village*. Englewood Cliffs, N.J.: Prentice-Hall.

FROMM, E., with the collaboration of E. Schachtel, A. Hartoch-Schachtel, P. Lazarsfeld, *et al.* 1936. The Authoritarian Character Structure of German Workers and Employees Before Hitler. Unpublished.

FROMM, E., SUZUKI, D. T., and MARTINO, R. de (1960). *Zen Buddhism and Psychoanalysis*. New York: Harper & Bros.

FROMM, E., and XIRAU, R., eds. (1968). *The Nature of Man*. New York: Macmillan.

GARATTINI, S., and SIGG, E. B. (1969). Relationship of Aggressive Behavior to Adrenal and Gonadal Function in Male Mice. In *Aggressive Behavior*, ed. S. Garattini and E. B. Sigg, Amsterdam: Excerpta Medica Foundation.

GILL, D. G. (1970). *Violence Against Children*. Cambridge: Harvard Univ. Press.

GINSBERG, M. See Glover, E. (1934), joint author.

GLICKMAN, S. E., and SROGES, R. W. (1966). Curiosity in Zoo Animals. *Behaviour*. 26: 151–88.

GLOVER, E., and GINSBERG, M. (1934). A Symposium on the Psychology of Peace and War. *Brit. Jour. Med. Psych.* 14: 274–93.

GOODALL, J. (1965). Chimpanzees of the Gombe Stream Reserve. In *Primate Behavior: Field Studies of Primates and Apes*, ed. I. DeVore. New York: Holt, Rinehart & Winston.

GOODALL, J. See also Van Lawick-Goodall, J.

GOSLINER, B. J. See Mahler, H. S. (1955), joint author.

GOWER, G. (1968). Man Has No Killer Instinct. In *Man and Aggression*, ed. M. F. A. Montagu. New York: Oxford Univ. Press.

GREEN, M. R., and SCHECTER, D. E. (1957). Autistic and Symbiotic Disorders in Three Blind Children. *Psychiat. Quar.* 31: 628–48.

GROOS, K. (1901). *The Play of Man*. New York: D. L. Appleton.

GUDERIAN, H. (1951). *Erinnerungen eines Soldaten*. Heidelberg. (Quoted in J. Ackermann, 1970, q.v.)

GUNTRIP, H. (1971). The Promise of Psychoanalysis. In *In the Name of Life*, ed. B. Landis and E. S. Tauber. New York: Holt, Rinehart & Winston.

GUTHRIE, W. K. (1962). *Earlier Presocratics and the Pythagoreans.* A History of Greek Philosophy, vol. 1. New York and London: Cambridge Univ. Press.

GUTHRIE, W. K. (1965). *Presocratic Traditions from Parmenides to Democritus.* A History of Greek Philosophy, vol. 2. New York and London: Cambridge Univ. Press.

GUTTINGER, R. C. (Quoted in C. and W. M. S. Russell, 1968, q.v.)

HALL, K. R. L. (1960). The Social Vigilance Behaviour of the Chacma Baboon, *Papio ursinus. Behaviour.* 16: 261–94.

HALL, K. R. L. (1964). Aggression in Monkey and Ape Societies. In *The Natural History of Aggression,* ed. J. D. Carthy and F. J. Ebling. New York: Academic.

HALL, K. R. L., and DeVORE, I (1965). Baboon Social Behavior. In *Primate Behavior: Field Studies of Primates and Apes,* ed. I. DeVore. New York: Holt, Rinehart & Winston.

HALL, T. E. (1963). Proxemics – A Study of Man's Spatial Relationships. In *Man's Image in Medicine and Anthropology,* ed. I. Galdston. New York: Int. Univs. Press.

HALL, T. E. (1966). *The Hidden Dimension.* Garden City: Doubleday.

HALLGARTEN, G. W. F. (1963). *Imperialism vor 1914.* Munich. C. H. Becksche Verlagsbuchhandlung.

HALLGARTEN, G. W. F. (1969). *Als die Schattenfielen, Memoiren 1900–1968.* Ullstein Vlg.

HANEY, C., BANKS, C., and ZIMBARDO, P. In press. Interpersonal Dynamics in a Simulated Prison. *Int. Jour. of Criminology and Penology.* 1.

HANFSTAENGL, E. (1970). *Zwischen Weissem und Braunem Haus* [Between the white and the brown house]. Munich: R. Piper.

HARLOW, H. F. (1969). William James and Instinct Theory. In *William James, Unfinished Business,* ed. B. Macleod. Washington, D.C.: Amer. Psychol. Assoc.

HARLOW, H. F., McGAUGH, J. L., and THOMPSON, R. F. (1971). *Psychology.* San Francisco: Albion.

HART, C. W. M., and PILLING, A. R. (1960). *The Tiwi of North Australia* (Case Histories in Cultural Anthropology). New York: Holt, Rinehart & Winston.

HARTMANN, H., KRIS, E., and LOEWENSTEIN, R. M. (1949).

The Psychoanalytic Study of the Child. Vols. 3, 4. New York: Int. Univs. Press.

HARTOCH-SCHACHTEL, A. See Fromm, E. (1936).

HAYES, C. (1951). *The Ape in Our House.* New York: Harper & Bros.

HAYES, C. See Hayes, K. J. (1951), joint author.

HAYES, K. J., and HAYES, C. (1951). The Intellectual Development of a Home-Raised Chimpanzee. *Proc. Amer. Phil. Soc.* 95: 105–9.

HEATH, R. G. (1962). Brain Centers and Control of Behavior. In *Psychosomatic Medicine*, ed. R. G. Heath. Philadelphia: Lea & Fabiger.

HEATH, R. G., ed. (1964). *The Role of Pleasure in Behavior.* New York: Harper & Row.

HEDIGER, H. (1942). *Wildtiere in Gefangenschaft.* Basel: Bruno Schwab. Translated as *Wild Animals in Captivity*, New York and London, Dover, 1965.

HEIBER, H., ed. (1958). *Reichsfuhrer: Letters to and from Himmler.* Deutschverlagsanstalt.

HEIDEL, A. (1942). *The Babylonian Genesis: Enuma Elish.* Chicago: Univ. of Chicago Press.

HEISENBERG, W. (1958). The Representation of Nature in Contemporary Physics. *Daedalus.* 87(3): 95–108.

HELFFERICH, E. (Quoted in J. Ackermann, 1970, q.v.)

HELFNER, R., and KEMPE, C. H., eds. (1968). *The Battered Child.* Chicago: Univ. of Chicago Press.

HELMUTH, H. (1967). Zum Verhalten des Menschen: die Aggression. *Ztsch. f. Ethnologie.* 92: 265–73.

HENTIG, H. von (1964). *Der Nekrotope Mensch.* Stuttgart: F. Enke Verlag.

HERON, W. (1957). The Pathology of Boredom. *Sci. Amer.* (Jan.)

HERON, W., DOANE, B. K., and SCOTT, T. H. (1956). *Can. Jour. of Psych.* 10 (1): 13–18.

HERRICK, C. J. (1928). *Brains of Rats and Man.* Chicago: Univ. of Chicago Press. (Quoted by R. B. Livingston, 1967a, q.v.)

HERRIGEL, E. (1953). *Zen in the Art of Archery.* New York: Pantheon. London: Routledge.

HESS, W. R. (1954). *Diencephalon Automatic and Extrapyramidal Structures.* New York: Grune & Stratton.

HINDE, R. A. (1960). Energy Models of Motivation. In *Readings in Animal Behavior*, ed. T. E. McGill. New York: Holt, Rinehart & Winston.

HINDE, R. A. (1967). *New Society.* 9: 302.

HITLER, A. (1943). *Mein Kampf*, trans. R. Manhein. Boston: Houghton Mifflin. London: Hutchinson.

HOEBEL, E. A. (1954). *The Law of Primitive Man.* Cambridge: Harvard Univ. Press. (Quoted in E. R. Service, 1966, q.v.)

HOEBEL, E. A. (1958). *Man in the Primitive World.* New York: McGraw-Hill.

HOLBACH, P. H. D. (1822). *Systeme Social.* Paris. (Quoted in *Die Heilige Familie* by K. Marx, 1844.)

HOLT, R. R. (1965). A Review of Some of Freud's Biological Assumptions and Their Influence on His Theories. In *Psychoanalysis and Current Biological Thought*, ed. N. S. Greenfield and W. C. Lewis. Madison: Univ. of Wisconsin Press.

HORKHEIMER, M., ed. (1936). *Autoritat und Familie.* Paris: Librarie Félix Alcan.

HOWELL, F. C. See Washburn, S. L. (1960), joint author.

JACOBS, P. A., BRUNTON, M., MELVILLE, M. M., BRITAIN, R. P., and McCLEMONT, W. F. (1965). Aggressive Behavior: Mental Subnormality and the XYY Male. *Nature.* 208: 1351–2.

JAMES, W. (1890). *Principles of Psychology.* New York: Holt, Rinehart & Winston.

JAMES, W. (1911). The Moral Equivalents of War. In *Memories and Studies* by W. James. New York: Longman's Green.

JAMES, W. (1923). *Outline of Psychology.* New York: Scribner's.

JAY, M. (1973). *The Dialectical Imagination.* Boston: Little, Brown. London: Heinemann.

JAY, P. See Washburn, S. L., and Jay, P. (1968), joint editors.

JONES, E. (1957). *The Life and Work of Sigmund Freud.* Vol. 3. New York: Basic Books. London: Hogarth Press.

KAADA, B. (1967). *Aggression and Defense: Neural Mechanisms and Social Patterns.* Brain Function, vol. 5, ed. C. D. Clemente and D. B. Lindsley. Los Angeles: Univ. of Californa Press.

KAHN, H. (1960). *On Thermonuclear War.* Princeton: Princeton Univ. Press.

KANNER, L. (1944). Early Infantile Autism. *Jour. Pediat.* 25: 211–17.

KAPP, R. (1931). Comments on Bernfeld and Feitelberg's 'Principles of Entropy and the Death Instinct'. *Int. Jour. Psychoan.* 12: 82–6.

KEMPE, C. H. *et al.* (1962). The Battered Child Syndrome. *Jour. A.M.A.* 181 (1): 17–24.

KEMPE, C. H. See Helfner, R. (1968), joint author.

KEMPNER, R. M. W. (1969). *Das Dritte Reich am Kreuzverhör.* Munich: Bechtle Verlag.

KLÜVER, H., and BUCY, P. C. (1934). Preliminary Analysis of Functions of the Temporal Lobes in Monkeys. *Arch. Neurol. Psych.* 42: 929.

KOFFLER, F. See Tauber, E. W. (1966), joint author.

KORTLANDT, A. (1962). Chimpanzees in the Wild. *Sci. Amer.* 206 (5): 128–38.

KRAUSNICK, H., BUCHHEIM, H., BROSZAT, M., and JACOBSEN, H. A. (1968). *Anatomy of the SS State.* New York: Walker. London: Paladin.

KREBS, A. (Quoted in J. Ackermann, 1970, q.v.)

KROPOTKIN, P. (1955). *Mutual Aid.* Boston: Porter Sargent. London: Allen Lane.

KUBIZEK, A. (1953). *Adolf Hitler, Mein Jugenfreund* [Adolf Hitler, the friend of my youth]. Graz: L. Stocker Verlag.

KUMMER, H. (1951). Soziales Verhalten einer Mantelpavian-gruppe. *Beiheft z. Schweizerischen Ztsch. f. Psychologie und ihre Anwendungen* 33: 1–91. (Quoted in C. and W. M. S. Russell, 1968, q.v.)

LAGERSPETZ, K. M. J. (1969). Aggression and Aggressiveness in Laboratory Mice. In *Aggressive Behavior,* ed. S. Garattini and E. B. Sigg. Amsterdam: Excerpta Medica Foundation.

LANCASTER, C. S. See Washburn, S. L., and Lancaster, C. S. (1968), joint authors.

LANGER, W. C. (1972). *The Mind of Adolf Hitler,* New York: Basic Books. London: Pan Books.

LAUGHLIN, W. S. (1968). Hunting: An Integrating Biobehavior System and Its Evolutionary Importance. In *Man, the Hunter,* ed. R. B. Lee and I. DeVore. Chicago: Aldine.

LAZARSFELD, P. See Fromm, E. (1936).

LEE, R. B. (1968). What Hunters Do for a Living: Or How to Make Out on Scarce Resources. In *Man, the Hunter,* ed. R. B. Lee and I. DeVore. Chicago: Aldine.

LEE, R. B., and DEVORE, I. (1968). *Man, the Hunter*. Chicago: Aldine.

LEHRMAN, D. S. (1953). Problems Raised by Instinct Theory: A Critique of Konrad Lorenz's Theory of Instinctive Behavior. *Quar. Rev. Biol.* 28 (4): 337–64.

LENIN, V. I. *Sochineniia*. 4th ed. Vol. 35. (Quoted in R. A. Medvedev, 1971, q.v.)

LEYHAUSEN, P. (1956). Verhaltensstudien an Katzen. *Beih. z. Ztsch. f. Tierpsychologie*. (Quoted in C. and W. M. S. Russell, 1968, q.v.)

LEYHAUSEN, P. (1965). The Communal Organization of Solitary Mammals. *Symposia Zool. Soc. Lond.* No. 14: 249–63.

LEYHAUSEN, P. See Lorenz, K., (1968), joint author.

LINDSLEY, D. B. (1964). The Ontogeny of Pleasure: Neural and Behavioral Development. In *The Role of Pleasure in Behavior*, ed. R. G. Heath. New York: Harper & Row.

LIVINGSTON, R. B. (1962). How Man Looks at His Own Brain: An Adventure Shared by Psychology and Neurology. In *Biologically Oriented Fields*. Psychology: A Study of a Science, ed. S. Koch. New York: McGraw-Hill.

LIVINGSTON, R. B. (1967). Brain Circuitry Relating to Complex Behavior. In *The Neurosciences: A Study Program*, ed. G. C. Quarton, T. O. Melnechuk, and F. O. Schmitt. New York: Rockefeller Univ. Press.

LIVINGSTON, R. B. (1967a). Reinforcement. In *The Neurosciences: A Study Program*, ed. G. C. Quarton, T. O. Melnechuk, and F. O. Schmitt. New York: Rockefeller Univ. Press.

LORENZ, K. (1937). Über die Bildung des Instinktbegriffes. In *Über tierisches und menschliches Verhalten*. Munich: R. Piper, 1965.

LORENZ, K. (1940). Durch Domestikation verursachte Störungen arteigenen Verhaltens. *Ztsch. z. angew. Psychol. Charakterkunde.* 59: 75.

LORENZ, K. (1950). The Comparative Method in Studying Innate Behavior Patterns. *Symp. Soc. Exp. Biol.* (Animal Behavior). 4: 221–68.

LORENZ, K. (1952). *King Solomon's Ring*. New York: Crowell. London: Methuen.

LORENZ, K. (1955). Über das Toten von Artgenossen. *Jahrb. d. Max-Planck-Ges.* 105–140. (Quoted by K. Lorenz, 1966, q.v.)

LORENZ, K. (1964). Ritualized Aggression. In *The Natural History of Aggression*, ed. J. D. Carthy and F. J. Ebling. New York: Academic.

LORENZ, K. (1965). *Evolution and Modification of Behavior*. Chicago: Univ. of Chicago Press.

LORENZ, K. (1966). *On Aggression*. New York: Harcourt Brace Jovanovich. London: Methuen. (1st ed. *Das Sogenannte Böse, Zur Naturgeschichte der Aggression*. [The so-called evil, natural history of aggression]. Vienna: Borotha-Schoeler Verlag, 1963.)

LORENZ, K. (1970). The Establishment of the Instinct Concept, trans. R. Martin, from the German papers pub. 1931–42. In *Studies in Animal and Human Behavior*. Cambridge: Harvard Univ. Press. London: Methuen.

LORENZ, K., and LEYHAUSEN, P. (1968). *Antriebe tierischen und menschlichen Verhaltens*. Munich: R. Piper.

MACCOBY, M. (1972). Emotional Attitudes and Political Choices. *Politics and Society* (Winter): 209–39.

MACCOBY, M. (1972a). *Technology, Work and Character*. Program on Technology and Society (a final review). Cambridge: Harvard Univ.

MACCOBY, M. (Forthcoming). *Social Character, Work, and Technology* (working title).

MACCOBY, M. See Fromm, E. (1970), joint author.

MACCORQUODALE, K. (1970). On Chomsky's Review of *Verbal Behavior* by B. F. Skinner. *Jour. of the Exp. Anal. of Behavior*. 13 (1): 83–99.

McDERMOTT, J. J., ed. (1967). *The Writings of William James: A Comprehensive Edition*. New York: Random House.

McDOUGALL, W. (1913). The Sources and Direction of Psycho-Physical Energy. *Amer. Jour. of Insanity*. 69.

McDOUGALL, W. (1923). *An Introduction to Social Psychology*. 7th ed. Boston: John W. Luce. London: Methuen.

McDOUGALL, W. (1923a). *An Outline of Psychology*. London: Methuen.

McDOUGALL, W. (1932). *The Energies of Men: A Study of the Fundamentals of Dynamic Psychology*. New York: Scribner's.

McDOUGALL, W. (1948). *The Energies of Men*. 7th ed. London: Methuen.

McGAUGH, J. L. See Harlow, H. F. (1971), joint author.

MacLEAN, P. D. (1958). The Limbic System with Respect to

Self-Preservation and the Preservation of the Species. *Jour. Nerv. Ment. Dis.* 127: 1–11.

MAHLER, M. S. (1968). *On Human Symbiosis and the Vicissitudes of Individuation.* Vol. 1. New York: Int. Univs. Press.

MAHLER, M. S., and GOSLINER, B. J. (1955). On Symbiotic Child Psychosis. In *Psychoanalytic Study of the Child.* New York: Int. Univs. Press.

MAHRINGER, J. (1952). *Vorgeschichtliche Kultur.* Benziger Verlag.

MAIER, N. R. F., and SCHNEIRLA, T. C. (1964). *Principles of Animal Psychology.* New York: Dover.

MARCUSE, H. (1955). *Eros and Civilization.* Boston: Beacon. London: Sphere.

MARCUSE, H. (1964). *One Dimensional Man.* Boston: Beacon. London: Routledge; Sphere.

MARINETTI, F. T. (1909). *Futurist Manifesto.* See Flint, R. W., ed. (1971).

MARINETTI, F. T. (1916). *Futurist Manifesto.* See Flint, R. W., ed. (1971).

MARK, V. H., and ERVIN, F. R. (1970). *Violence and the Brain.* New York: Harper & Row.

MARSHACK, A. (1972). *The Roots of Civilization.* New York: McGraw-Hill. London: Weidenfeld & Nicolson.

MARX, K. (1906). *Capital.* Vol. 1. Charles S. Kerr. New York: Int. Univs. Press. London: Dent; Laurence & Wishart.

MARX, K. and ENGELS, F. *Gesamtausgabe* (MEGA) [Complete works of Marx and Engels]. Vol. 5. Moscow.

MASER, W. (1971). *Adolph Hitler, Legende, Mythos, Wirklichkeit.* Munich: Bechtle Verlag.

MASLOW, A. (1954). *Motivation and Personality.* New York: Harper & Bros.

MASON, W. A. (1970). Chimpanzee Social Behavior. In *The Chimpanzee,* ed. G. H. Bourne. Vol. 2. Baltimore: Univ. Park.

MATTHEWS, L. H. (1963). *Symposium on Aggression.* Institute of Biology.

MATURANA, H. R., and VARELA, F. G. (Forthcoming.) *Autopoietic Systems.*

MAYO, E. (1933). *The Human Problems of an Industrial Civilization.* New York: Macmillan.

MEAD, M. (1961). *Cooperation and Competition Among Primitive Peoples.* Rev. ed. Boston: Beacon. (1st ed. New York: McGraw-Hill, 1937.)

MEDVEDEV, R. A. (1971). *Let History Judge.* New York: Knopf. London: Macmillan.

MAGARGEE, E. I. (1969). The Psychology of Violence: A Critical Review of Theories of Violence. Prepared for the U.S. National Commission on the Causes and Prevention of Violence, Task Force III: Individual Acts of Violence.

MEGGITT, M. J. (1960). *Desert People.* Chicago: Univ. of Chicago Press. (Quoted in E. R. Service, 1966, q.v.)

MEGGITT, M. J. (1964). *Aboriginal Food-Gatherers of Tropical Australia.* Morges, Switzerland: Int. Union for Conservation of Nature and Natural Resources. (Quoted in E. R. Service, 1966, q.v.)

MELLAART, J. (1967). *Çatal Hüyük: A Neolithic Town in Anatolia.* London: Thames & Hudson. New York: McGraw-Hill.

MELNECHUK, T. O. See Ploog, D. (1970), joint author.

MENNINGER, K. A. (1968). *The Crime of Punishment.* New York: Viking.

MILGRAM, S. (1963). Behavioral Study of Obedience. *Jour. Abn.* [Social & Socl. Psychol. 67: 371–8.

MILLÁN, I. (Forthcoming (1974)). *Caracter Social y Desarrollo* Social character and development].

MILLER, N. E. (1941). Frustration-Aggression Hypothesis. *Psych. Rev.* 48: 337–342.

MILNER, P. See Olds, J. (1954), joint author.

MONAKOW, C. von (1950). *Gehirn und Gewissen* [Brain and conscience]. Zurich: Morgarten.

MONTAGU, M. F. A. (1967). *The Human Revolution.* New York: Bantam.

MONTAGU, M. F. A. (1968). Chromosomes and Crime. *Psychology Today.* 2 (5): 42–4, 46–9.

MONTAGU, M. F. A. (1968a). The New Litany of Innate Depravity: Or Original Sin Revisited. In *Man and Aggression,* ed. M. F. A. Montagu. New York: Oxford Univ. Press.

MONTEIL, V. (1970). *Indonésie.* Paris: Horizons de France.

MORAN, Lord (1966). *Churchill: Taken from the Diaries of Lord Moran.* Boston: Houghton Mifflin. London: Constable.

MORGAN, L. H. (1870). *Systems of Sanguinity and Affinity of the Human Family.* Publication 218. Washington, D.C.: Smithsonian Inst.

MORGAN, L. H. (1877). *Ancient Society: Or Researches in the Lines of*

Human Progress from Savagery Through Barbarism to Civilization.
New York: H. Holt.

MORRIS, D. (1967). *The Naked Ape.* New York: McGraw-Hill.
London: Cape; Corgi.

MOYER, K. E. (1968). Kinds of Aggression and Their Physiological Basis. In *Communication in Behavioral Biology.* Pt A, vol. 2.
New York: Academic.

MUMFORD, L. (1961). *The City in History.* New York: Harcourt
Brace Jovanovich. Harmondsworth: Penguin Books, 1966.

MUMFORD, L. (1967). *The Myth of the Machine: Techniques in
Human Development.* New York: Harcourt Brace Jovanovich.
London: Secker & Warburg.

MURDOCK, G. P. (1934). *Our Primitive Contemporaries.* New York:
Macmillan.

MURDOCK, G. P. (1968). Discussion remarks. In *Man, the Hunter,*
ed. R. B. Lee and I. DeVore. Chicago: Aldine.

NAPIER, J. (1970). *The Roots of Mankind.* Washington, D.C.:
Smithsonian Inst. London: Allen & Unwin.

NARR, K. J. (1961). *Urgeschichte der Kultur.* Stuttgart: Kröner
Verlag.

NIELSEN, J. (1968). Y Chromosomes in Male Psychiatric Patients
above 180 cms. Tall. *Brit. Jour. Psychiat.* 114: 1589–90.

NISSEN, H. W. (1931). A Field Study of the Chimpanzee. *Comp.
Psych. Monog.* 8 (36).

NISSEN, H. W. See Alee, W. C. (1953), joint author.

NIMKOFF, M. F. See Alee, W. C. (1953), joint author.

OKLADNIKOV, A. P. (1972). (Quoted in A. Marshack, 1972, q.v.)

OLDS, J., and MILNER, J. (1954). Positive Reinforcement
Produced by Electrical Stimulation of the Septal Area and
Other Regions of the Rat Brain. *Jour. Comp. Physiol.* 47: 419–28.

OPPENHEIMER, J. R. (1955). Address at the 63rd Annual Meeting of the American Psych. Assoc. 4 Sept.

OZBEKHAN, H. (1966). The Triumph of Technology: 'Can'
Implies 'Ought'. In *Planning for Diversity and Choice: Possible
Futures and Their Relations to the Non-Controlled Environment,* ed.
S. Anderson. Cambridge: M.I.T. Press, 1968.

PALMER, S. (1955). Crime, Law. *Criminology and Political Science.*
66: 323–4.

PASTORE, N. (1949). *The Nature-Nurture Controversy.* New York: Columbia Univ. Press, King's Crown.

PENFIELD, W. (1960). Introduction. In *Neurophysiological Basis of the Higher Functions of the Nervous System.* Handbook of Physiology. 12 vols., ed. J. Field. Sec. 1, vol. 3, ed. H. W. Magoun *et al.* Washington, D.C.: American Physiological Soc.

PENROSE, L. S. (1931). Freud's Theory of Instinct and Other Psycho-Biological Theories. *Inter. Jour. of Psychoan.* 12: 92.

PERRY, W. J. (1917). An Ethnological Study of Warfare. In *Manchester Memoirs.* Vol. 61. Manchester: Manchester Literary and Philosophical Society.

PERRY, W. J. (1923). *The Children of the Sun.* London.

PERRY, W. J. (1923a). *The Growth of Civilization.* New York.

PIAGET, J. (1952). *The Origins of Intelligence in Children.* New York: Int. Univs. Press. London: Routledge.

PICKER, H. (1965). *Hitler's Tischgespräche im Führerhauptquartier,* [Hitler's table talk in the Führer's headquarters], ed, and with an Introduction by P. E. Schramm. Stuttgart: Seewald Verlag.

PIGGOTT, S. (1960). Theory and Prehistory. In *The Evolution of Man: Mind, Culture and Society.* 'Evolution after Darwin', vol. 2, ed. S. Tax. Chicago: Univ. of Chicago Press.

PILBEAM, D. (1970). *The Evolution of Man.* London: Thames & Hudson.

PILBEAM, D., and SIMONS, E. L. (1965). Some Problems of Hominid Classification. *Amer. Sci.* 53: 237–59.

PILLING, A. R. See Hart, C. W. M. (1960), joint author.

PLOOG, D. (1970). Social Communication Among Animals. In *Neurosciences: Second Study Program,* ed. F. O. Schmitt. New York: Rockefeller Univ. Press.

PLOOG, D., and MELNECHUK, T. O. (1970). Primate Communication. In *Neurosciences Research Symposium Summaries.* Vol. 4, ed. F. O. Schmitt, T. O. Melnechuk, G. C. Quarton, and G. Adelman. Cambridge: M.I.T. Press.

POLLOCK, C. B. See Steele, B. F. (1968), joint author.

PORTMANN, A. (1965). *Vom Ursprung des Menschen.* Basel: F. Rein Lardt.

PRATT, J. (1958). Epilegomena to the Study of Freudian Instinct Theory. *Int. Jour. of Psychoan.* 39: 17.

PRIBRAM, K. (1962). The Neurophysiology of Sigmund Freud. In *Experimental Foundation of Clinical Psychology,* ed. A. J. Bachrach. New York: Basic Books.

QUARTON, G. C., MELNECHUK, T. O., and SCHMITT, F. O., eds. (1967). *The Neurosciences: A Study Program*. New York: Rockefeller Univ. Press.

RADHILL, S. X. (1968). A History of Child Abuse and Infanticide. In *The Battered Child*, ed. R. Helfner and C. H. Kempe. Chicago: Univ. of Chicago Press.

RAPAPORT, D. C. (1971). Foreword. In *Primitive War* by H. H. Turney-High. 2nd ed. Columbia: Univ. of South Carolina Press, 1971.

RAUCH, H. J. (1947). *Arch f. Psychiatrie und Nervenkrankheiten*. Berlin. (Quoted in H. von Hentig, 1964, q.v.)

RAUSCHNING, H. (1940). *The Voice of Destruction*. New York: Putnam.

RÉAGE, P. (1965). *The Story of O*. New York: Grove Press. London: Corgi.

RENSCH, B., ed. (1965). *Homo Sapiens*. Göttingen: Vanderhoek & Ruprecht.

REYNOLDS, V. (1961). The Social Life of a Colony of Rhesus Monkeys (*Macaca mulata*). Ph.D. thesis, Univ. of London. (Quoted in C. and W. M. S. Russell, 1968, q.v.)

REYNOLDS, V., and REYNOLDS, F. (1965). The Chimpanzees of the Bodongo Forest. In *Primate Behavior: Field Studies of Primates and Apes*, ed. I. DeVore. New York: Holt, Rinehart & Winston.

ROE, A., and SIMPSON, G. C., eds. (1967). *Behavior and Evolution*. Rev. ed. New Haven: Yale Univ. Press. (1st ed. 1958.)

ROGERS, C. R., and SKINNER, B. F. (1956). Some Issues Concerning the Control of Human Behavior: A Symposium. *Science*. 124: 1057–66.

ROWELL, T. E. (1966). Hierarchy in the Organization of the Captive Baboon Group. *Animal Behavior*. 14 (4): 430–43.

RUSSELL, C., and RUSSELL, W. M. S. (1968). *Violence, Monkeys and Man*. London: Macmillan.

RUSSELL, C., and RUSSELL, W. M. S. (1968a). Violence: What Are Its Roots? *New Society*. (24 Oct.): 595–600.

SAHLINS, M. D. (1960). The Origin of Society. *Sci. Amer.* 203 (3).

SAHLINS, M. D. (1968). Notes on the Original Affluent Society. In *Man, the Hunter*, ed. R. B. Lee and I. DeVore. Chicago: Aldine.

SALOMON, E. von (1930). *Die Geächteten*. Rowohlt, Taschenbuch Ausgabe. *The Outlaws*, London: Jonathan Cape, 1962.

SAUER, C. O. (1952). *Agricultural Origins and Dispersals*. New York: American Geographic Soc.

SCHACHTEL, E. See Fromm, E. (1936).

SCHALLER, G. B. (1963). *The Mountain Gorilla*. Chicago: Univ. of Chicago Press.

SCHALLER, G. B. (1965). The Behavior of the Mountain Gorilla. In *Primate Behavior: Field Studies of Primates and Apes*, ed. I. DeVore. New York: Holt, Rinehart & Winston.

SCHECTER, D. E. (1968). The Oedipus Complex: Considerations of Ego Development and Parental Interaction. *Cont. Psychoan.* 4 (2): 117.

SCHECTER, D. E. (1973). On the Emergence of Human Relatedness. In *Interpersonal Explorations in Psychoanalysis*, ed. E. G. Witenberg. New York: Basic Books.

SCHECTER, D. E. See Green, M. R. (1957), joint author.

SCHNEIRLA, T. C. (1966). *Quar. Rev. Biol.* 41: 283.

SCHNEIRLA, T. C. See Maier, N. R. F. (1964), joint author.

SCHRAMM, P. E. (1965). *Hitler als militärischer Führer*. 2nd ed. Frankfurt: Athenäum Verlag.

SCHRAMM, P. E. See Picker, H. (1965).

SCHWIDETZKI, I. (1971). *Das Menschenbild der Biologie*. Stuttgart: G. Fischer Verlag.

SCOTT, J. P. (1958). *Aggression*. Chicago: Univ. of Chicago Press.

SCOTT, J. P. (1968). Hostility and Aggression in Animals. In *Roots of Behavior*, ed. E. L. Bliss. New York: Hafner.

SCOTT, J. P. (1968a). That Old-Time Aggression. In *Man and Aggression*, ed. M. F. A. Montagu. New York: Oxford Univ. Press.

SCOTT, J. P., BEXTON, W. H., HERON, W., and DOANE, B. K. (1959). Cognitive Effects of Perceptual Isolation. *Can. Jour. of Psych.* 13 (3): 200–209.

SECHENOV, I. M. (1863). *Reflexes of the Brain*. Cambridge: M.I.T. Press. (Quoted in D. B. Lindsley, 1964, q.v.)

SERVICE, E. R. (1966). *The Hunters*. Englewood Cliffs, N.J.: Prentice-Hall.

SHAH, S. A. (1970). Report on XYY Chromosomal Abnormality. *National Institute of Mental Health Conference Report*, Washington, D.C.: U.S. Govt. Printing Office.

SIDDIQI, M. R. See Southwick, C. H. (1965), joint author.

SIGG, E. B. See Garattini, S. (1969), joint author.

SIMMEL, E. (1944). Self-Preservation and the Death Instinct. *Psychoan. Quar.* 13: 160.

SIMONS, E. L. See Pilbeam, D. R. (1965), joint author.

SIMPSON, G. G. (1944). *Tempo and Mode in Evolution.* New York: Columbia Univ. Press.

SIMPSON, G. G. (1949). *The Meaning of Evolution.* New Haven: Yale Univ. Press.

SIMPSON, G. G. (1953). *The Major Features of Evolution.* New York: Columbia Univ. Press.

SIMPSON, G. G. (1964). *Biology and Man.* New York: Harcourt Brace Jovanovich.

SIMPSON, G. G. See Roe, A. (1967), joint eds.

SKINNER, B. F. (1953). *Science and Human Behavior.* New York: Macmillan.

SKINNER, B. F. (1961). The Design of Cultures. *Daedalus.* 534–46.

SKINNER, B. F. (1963). Behaviorism at Fifty. *Science.* 134: 566–602. In *Behaviorism and Phenomenology,* ed. T. W. Wann, Chicago: Univ. of Chicago Press, 1964.

SKINNER, B. F. (1971). *Beyond Freedom and Dignity.* New York: Knopf.

SKINNER, B. F. See Rogers, C. R., (1956) joint author.

SMITH, B. F. (1967). *Adolf Hitler: His Family, Childhood and Youth.* Stanford: Hoover Inst., Stanford Univ.

SMITH, B. F. (1971). *Heinrich Himmler: A Nazi in the Making, 1900–1926.* Stanford: Hoover Inst., Stanford Univ.

SMITH, B. F. See Angress, S. J. (1959), joint author.

SMITH, G. E. (1924). *Essays on the Evolution of Man.* London: Humphrey Milford.

SMITH, G. E. (1924a). *The Evolution of Man.* New York: Oxford Univ. Press.

SMOLLA, G. (1967). *Studium Universale: Epochen der Menschlichen Frühzeit.* Munich: Karl Alber Freiburg.

SOUTHWICK, C. H. (1964). An Experimental Study of Intragroup Agnostic Behavior in Rhesus Monkeys (*Macaca mulata*). *Behavior.* 28: 182–209.

SOUTHWICK, C. H., BEG, M. A., and SIDDIQI, M. R. (1965). Rhesus Monkeys in North India. In *Primate Behavior: Field Studies of Primates and Apes,* ed. I. DeVore. New York: Holt, Rinehart & Winston.

SPEER, A. (1970). *Inside the Third Reich: Memoirs of Albert Speer*, trans. R. and C. Winston; Introduction by E. Davidson. London: Weidenfeld & Nicolson. New York: Macmillan.

SPEER, A. (1972). Afterword. In *Hitler avant Hitler* by J. Brosse. Paris: Fayard.

SPENCER, M. M. See Barnett, S. A. (1951), joint author.

SPINOZA, BENEDICTUS DE (1927). *Ethics*. New York: Oxford Univ. Press. London: Dent.

SPITZ, R., and COBLINER, G. (1965). *The First Year of Life: A Psychoanalytic Study of Normal and Deviant Development of Object Relations*. New York: Int. Univs. Press.

SPOERRI, T. (1959). *Ueber Nikrophile*. Basel. (Quoted in H. von Hentig, 1964, q.v.)

SROGES, R. W. See Glickman, S. E. 1966, joint author.

STEELE, B. F., and POLLOCK, C. B. (1968). A Psychiatric Study of Parents Who Abuse Infants and Small Children. In *The Battered Child*, ed. R. Helfner and C. H. Kempe. Chicago: Univ. of Chicago Press.

STEINER, J. M. In preparation. Study based on interviews with former Nazi concentration camp guards.

STEWART, U. H. (1968). Casual Factors and Processes in the Evolution of Prefarming Societies. In *Man, the Hunter*, ed. R. B. Lee and I. DeVore. Chicago: Aldine.

STRACHEY, A. (1957). *The Unconscious Motives of War*. London: Allen & Unwin.

STRACHEY, J., ed. (1886–1939). *Standard Edition of the Complete Psychological Works of Sigmund Freud*. 23 vols. London: Hogarth.

STRACHEY, J. (1961). Editor's Introduction. In *Civilization and Its Discontents* by S. Freud, S.E., vol. 21.

SULLIVAN, H. S. (1953). *Interpersonal Theory of Psychiatry*. New York: Norton.

TAUBER, E., and KOFFLER, F. (1966). Optomotor Response in Human Infants to Apparent Motion: Evidence of Inactiveness. *Science*. 152: 382–3.

TAX, S., ed. (1960). *The Evolution of Man: Mind, Culture and Society*. 'Evolution After Darwin', vol. 2. Chicago: Univ. of Chicago Press.

THOMAS, H. (1961). *The Spanish Civil War*. New York: Harper & Bros. Harmondsworth: Penguin Books, 1965.

THOMPSON, R. F. See Harlow, H. F. (1971), joint author.

658   *Bibliography*

THUCYDIDES, (1959). *Peloponnesian War: The Thomas Hobbes Translation*, ed. David Grene. 2 vols. Ann Arbor: Univ. of Michigan Press.

TINBERGEN, N. (1948). Physiologische Instinktforschung. *Experientia.* 4: 121–33.

TINBERGEN, N. (1953). *Social Behavior in Animals.* New York: Wiley. London: Chapman & Hale.

TINBERGEN, N. (1968). Of War and Peace in Animals and Men. *Science.* 160: 1411–18.

TÖNNIES, F. (1926). *Gesellschaft und Gemeinschaft.* Berlin: Curtius. *Fundamental Concepts of Society*, trans. and with a Supplement by C. H. P. Loomis. New York: American Book, 1940.

TURNBULL, C. M. (1965). *Wayward Servants, or the Two Worlds of the African Pygmies.* London: Eyre & Spottiswoode.

TURNEY-HIGH, H. H. (1971). *Primitive War.* 2nd ed. Columbia: Univ. of South Carolina Press. (1st ed. New York: Columbia Univ. Press, 1949.)

UNAMUNO, M. de (1936). (Quoted in H. Thomas, 1961, q.v.)

UNDERHILL, R. (1953). *Here Come the Navaho.* Washington, D.C.: Bur. of Indian Affairs, U.S. Dept. of the Interior.

VALENSTEIN, E. (1968). Biology of Drives. *Neurosciences Research Program Bulletin.* 6: 1. Cambridge: M.I.T. Press.

VAN LAWICK-GOODALL, J. (1968). The Behavior of Free-Living Chimpanzees in the Gombe Stream Reserve. *Animal Behavior Monographs*, ed. J. M. Cullen and C. G. Beer. Vol. I, pt. 3. London: Balliere, Tindall & Castle.

VAN LAWICK-GOODALL, J. (1971). *In the Shadow of Man.* Boston: Houghton Mifflin. London: Collins.

VAN LAWICK-GOODALL, J. See also Goodall, J.

VARELA, F. C. See Maturana, H. R. (Forthcoming), joint author.

VOLLHARD, E. (Quoted in A. C. Blanc, 1961, q.v.)

WAELDER, R. (1956). Critical Discussion of the Concept of an Instinct of Destruction. *Bul. Phil. Assoc.* 97–109.

WARLIMONT, W. (1964). *Im Hauptquartier der Deutschen Wehrmacht 1939–1945.* Frankfurt M.-Bonn.

WASHBURN, S. L. (1957). Australopithecines, the Hunters or the Hunted? *Amer. Anthropologist.* 59.

WASHBURN, S. L. (1959). Speculations on the Interrelations of the History of Tools and Biological Evolution. In *The Evolution of Man's Capacity for Culture*. ed. J. N. Spuhler. Detroit: Wayne State Univ. Press.

WASHBURN, S. L., ed. (1961). *Social Life of Early Man*. Chicago: Aldine.

WASHBURN, S. L., and AVIS, V. (1958). Evolution of Human Behavior. In *Behavior and Evolution*, ed. A. Roe and G. G. Simpson. Rev. ed. New Haven: Yale Univ. Press, 1967.

WASHBURN, S. L., and DEVORE, I. (1961). The Social Life of Baboons. *Sci. Amer.* 31 (June): 353–9.

WASHBURN, S. L., and HOWELL, F. C. (1960). Human Evolution and Culture. In *The Evolution of Man*, ed. S. Tax. Chicago: Univ. of Chicago Press.

WASHBURN, S. L., and JAY, P., eds. (1968). *Perspectives of Human Evolution*. New York: Holt, Rinehart & Winston.

WASHBURN, S. L., and LANCASTER, C. S. (1968). The Evolution of Hunting. In *Man, the Hunter*, ed. R. B. Lee and I. DeVore. Chicago: Aldine.

WATSON, J. B. (1914). *Behavior: An Introduction to Comparative Psychology*. New York: H. Holt.

WATSON, J. B. (1958). *Behaviorism*. Chicago: Univ. of Chicago Press.

WEISS, P. (1925). Tierisches Verhalten als 'Systemreaktion'. Die Orientierung der Ruhestellungen von Schmetterlingen (Vanessa) gegen Licht und Schwerkraft. *Biologia Generalis*. 1: 168–248.

WEISS, P. (1967). $1 + 1 \neq 2$ [When one plus one does not equal two.] In *The Neurosciences: A Study Program*, ed. G. C. Quarton, T. O. Melnechuk, and F. O. Schmitt. New York: Rockefeller Univ. Press.

WEISS, P. (1970). The Living System. In *Beyond Reductionism*, ed. A. Koestler and L. Smithies. New York: Macmillan.

WHITE, B. L. See Wolff, P. (1965), joint author.

WHITE, R. W. (1959). Motivation Reconsidered: The Concept of Competence. *Psych. Rev.* 66: 297–323.

WHITEHEAD, A. N. (1967). *The Function of Reason*. Rev. ed. Boston: Beacon.

WICKER, T. (1971). 'Op-Ed' section. *The New York Times*. (18 Sept.)

WIESEL, E. (1972). *Souls on Fire*. New York: Random House. London: Weidenfeld & Nicolson.

660 *Bibliography*

WOLFF, K. (1961). Eichmann's Chief, Heinrich Himmler. *Neue Illustrierte.* 17 (16): 20. (Quoted in J. Ackermann, 1970, q.v.)

WOLFF, P., and WHITE, B. L. (1965). Visual Pursuit and Attention in Young Infants. *Jour. Child Psychiat.* 4. (Quoted in D. E. Schecter, 1973, q.v.)

WORDEN, F. G. (Forthcoming). *Scientific Concepts and the Nature of Conscious Experience.* American Handbook of Psychiatry, vol. 6. New York: Basic Books.

WRIGHT, Q. (1965). *A Study of War.* 2nd ed. Chicago: Univ. of Chicago Press.

YERKES, R. M., and YERKES, A. V. (1929). *The Great Apes: A Study of Anthropoid Life.* New Haven: Yale Univ. Press.

YOUNG, J. (1971). *An Introduction to the Study of Man.* New York: Oxford Univ. Press, Clarendon.

ZEISSLER, A. (1943). Interview, June 24. (Quoted in W. C. Langer, 1972, q.v.)

ZIEGLER, H. S. (1965). *Adolf Hitler.* 3rd ed. Göttingen: K. W. Schutz Verlag.

ZIEGLER, H. S., ed. (1970). *Wer War Hitler?* Beiträge zur Hitlerforschung, herausgegeben in Verbindung mit dem Institut für Deutsch Nachriegsgeschichte, Verlag der *Deutschen Hochschullehrzeitung* [Who was Hitler? Contributions to the research on Hitler, undertaken in conjunction with the Institute for Postwar History, publishing house of the German high school teachers' journal]. Göttingen: Grabert Verlag.

ZIMBARDO, P. (1972). Pathology of Imprisonment. *Trans-Action.* 9 (Apr.): 4–8.

ZIMBARDO, P. See Haney, C. In press, joint author.

ZING YANG KUO (1960). Studies on the Basic Factors in Animal Fighting: VII, Inter-species Co-existence in Mammals. *Jour. Gen. Psychol.* 97: 211–25.

ZUCKERMAN, S. (1932). *The Social Life of Monkeys and Apes.* London: K. Paul, Trench, Trubner.

Index

More about Penguins
and Pelicans

Psychology in Pelicans

Pelicans have achieved an enviable reputation for publishing first-class books on psychology for the general reader. Among the titles available are:

The Divided Self

R. D. LAING

'It is a study that makes all other I have read on schizophrenia seem fragmentary ... the author brings through his vision and perception, that particular touch of genius which causes one to say "Yes, I have always thought that, why have I never thought of it before?"' – *Journal of Analytical Psychology*

Suicide and Attempted Suicide

E. STENGEL

The author draws on a wealth of international research into the incidence, methods and social and personal dynamics of suicidal acts, producing a book of authority and real importance.

New Horizons in Psychology, Volume One

ED. BRIAN M. FOSS

Genetics, motivation, drugs, operant conditioning, programmed learning and behaviour therapy are some of the new developments in psychology affecting scientific thinking and influencing our lives today. This expert volume is both a progress report and an indication of future directions.

Psychology in Pelicans

The Psychology of Human Ageing

D. B. BROMLEY

Infant and adolescent psychology have been very thoroughly explored, but the study of ageing lags behind. This new introduction to human ageing and its mental effects is written by the Scientific Advisor in Gerontology to the Medical Research Council, and is of importance to both the student of psychology and the layman.

The Psychology of Learning

R. BORGER AND A. E. M. SEABORNE

Only a small part of learning takes place in schools. In this book two psychologists discuss the laws which seem to govern the process of learning in its widest sense. They also provide a thorough survey of programmed learning techniques and the newer developments in the formal teaching of schools and universities.

The Psychology of Study

C. A. MACE

An explanation of the mental processes by which we all 'read, mark, learn and inwardly digest' information of all kinds. There are chapters on perception, memory, original thinking, concentration and preparation for exams.

The Psychology of Thinking

R. THOMSON

The achievements and limitations of recent studies into 'thinking' are discussed and evaluated. The direct experimental investigation of adult thought processes, and the intelligent behaviour of animals, are also dealt with.

A Peregrine Book

Power, Violence, Decision

W. J. M. MACKENZIE

Power, Violence, Decision, writes the author, 'has three guiding
principles. The first is that politics is both necessary and
dangerous. The second is that politics is an autonomous
form of human action; to be understood, not to be
explained away. The third is that political words are an
integral part of political action; they are action, not merely
understanding or explanation.'

Politics is about decision-making and one of its motive
forces is violence or fear of violence. Using source material
which ranges from Marx to Kurt Vonnegut, Professor
Mackenzie attempts an unprecedented synthesis of the motive
forces behind decision-making.

The ambiguous myth of Prometheus, most recently used by
Robert Lowell to express America's situation in the 1960s,
is taken as an underlying theme. And, against a background
of myth and poetry, the author skilfully points out the
metaphors to which the social sciences have recourse in
their attempts to tame these concepts of power, violence
and decision.

Collected Essays, Journalism and Letters of George Orwell

Edited by Sonia Orwell and Ian Angus

1: An Age Like This, 1920–1940

This first volume is drawn from the years when George Orwell began to explore the life of the poor and was struggling to establish himself as a novelist and factual reporter. Disillusioned with Communism in Spain, rejected for service in the war against Hitler, already ill, he faced hostilities in a mood of frustration.

2: My Country Right or Left, 1940–1943

The second volume principally covers the two years when George Orwell worked as a Talks Assistant, and later Producer, in the Indian section of the B.B.C. At the same time he was writing for *Horizon*, *Tribune*, the *New Statesman*, and other periodicals. His war-time diaries are included here.

3: As I Please, 1943–1945

For some eighteen months during the war Orwell was employed as literary editor of *Tribune*. The new freedom he experienced was expressed in the title and style of the regular feature he contributed – 'As I Please'. *Animal Farm*, the book most likely to immortalize his name, was written during the period covered by this volume . . . and refused by three leading publishers. Briefly after the Second Front, he was a war correspondent.

4: In Front of Your Nose, 1945–1950

This last volume contains the letters, reviews and other pieces which Orwell wrote during the last five years of his life: they include 'Such, such were the joys', a reminiscence of his preparatory school. *Animal Farm* had eventually relieved him of financial worry, but during the drafting and writing of *Nineteen Eighty-Four* he was increasingly handicapped by the illness of which he died early in 1950.

George Orwell

Animal Farm

In this searing satire upon dictatorship George Orwell, who
has been compared to Swift, tells the story of a revolution
that went wrong. The animals on a farm, led by the pigs,
drive out their master and take over the farm. But the
purity of their original doctrine is soon perverted.

Nineteen Eighty-Four

1984. Throughout Oceania 'The Party' rules through the
agency of all-powerful ministries. The authorities use every
device to keep a check on the people's thoughts, words, and
deeds. Against this nightmare background is played out the
drama of Winston Smith, who rebels.

Down and Out in Paris and London

Orwell's lively and factual record of his experiences among
the poor of two capital cities. Few writers have possessed a
greater gift for spotting the personality behind the rags,
or described the reality of poverty with so little pretence.

Homage to Catalonia

Told with all the honesty and bitterness of a fighting man
only a few months after the events, this book not
unnaturally offended the Left. The same naïve enthusiasm
and reluctant disillusionment of a Republican volunteer
during the Spanish Civil War foreshadow Orwell's
masterpiece of satire, *Animal Farm*.

Also published:
Burmese Days
A Clergyman's Daughter
Keep the Aspidistra Flying
The Decline of the English Murder and other essays

Human Aggression

ANTHONY STORR

In this monograph the author of *Sexual Deviation* and *The Integrity of the Personality* writes both as a psychotherapist and as a human being living in an age when 'The End is Nigh' could well be the truth. But the coin of aggression, as he shows, bears two faces. As a positive and natural drive he discusses its normal role in the social structure of both animals and men and its function in childhood, adult life, and sexual relations: in its negative aspect he considers hostility in relation to depressive, schizoid, paranoid, and psychopathic personalities. He closes with a plea – modest, humane, and never Utopian – for attitudes and policies which in the long run might reduce hostility between men and nations.

'The sound common sense underlying the whole book makes it intelligible to everybody; ... The book is a real synthesis of psychoanalytical and ethological thought' – Konrad Lorenz

'Can do nothing but good. It is sensible, imaginative and well-informed' – Cyril Connolly in the *Sunday Times*